Perspectives from the Past

PRIMARY SOURCES IN WESTERN CIVILIZATIONS

Fifth Edition

VOLUME 2

From the Age of Exploration
through Contemporary Times

JAMES M. BROPHY • JOSHUA COLE • JOHN ROBERTSON

THOMAS MAX SAFLEY • CAROL SYMES

W • W • NORTON & COMPANY NEW YORK • LONDON

W. W. Norton & Company has been independent since its founding in 1923, when William Warder Norton and Mary D. Herter Norton first published lectures delivered at the People's Institute, the adult education division of New York City's Cooper Union. The firm soon expanded its program beyond the Institute, publishing books by celebrated academics from America and abroad. By mid-century, the two major pillars of Norton's publishing program—trade books and college texts—were firmly established. In the 1950s, the Norton family transferred control of the company to its employees, and today—with a staff of four hundred and a comparable number of trade, college, and professional titles published each year—W. W. Norton & Company stands as the largest and oldest publishing house owned wholly by its employees.

Editor: Jon Durbin
Editorial Assistant: Justin Cahill
Project Editor: Kate Feighery
Composition: DBS, Inc.
Manufacturing: Maple-Vail
Book design: Jack Meserole
Production manager: Eric Pier-Hocking

Acknowledgments and copyrights continue on page 599, which serves as a continuation of the copyright page.

Library of Congress Cataloging-in-Publication Data

Perspectives from the past : primary sources in Western civilizations /
James M. Brophy . . . [et al.]. —5th ed.
   v. cm.
  Includes bibliographical references.
  Contents: v. 1. From the ancient Near East through the age of absolutism —v. 2.
From the age of exploration through contemporary times.
  ISBN 978-0-393-91294-4 (v. 1 : pbk.)—**ISBN 978-0-393-91295-1** (v. 2 : pbk.)
  1. Civilization, Western--History--Sources.
  I. Brophy, James M.
  CB245.P45 2012
  909'.09821--dc23

2011043354

W. W. Norton & Company, Inc., 500 Fifth Avenue, New York, N.Y. 10110-0017
www.wwnorton.com

W. W. Norton & Company Ltd., Castle House,
75/76 Wells Street, London W1T 3QT

2 3 4 5 6 7 8 9 0

ABOUT THE AUTHORS

JAMES M. BROPHY is professor of modern European history at the University of Delaware, where he has taught since 1992. He received his B.A. from Vassar College and did his graduate training at Universität Tübingen and Indiana University, where he specialized in the social and political history of nineteenth-century Europe. He is the author of *Capitalism, Politics, and Railroads in Prussia, 1830–1870* (1998), *Popular Culture and the Public Sphere in the Rhineland, 1800–1850* (2007), and numerous articles on nineteenth-century German history. He further serves on the board of editors for the journal, *Central European History*. He regularly teaches the Western civilization survey as well as courses and seminars on historiography, nationalism, modern European history, modern German history, and the Holocaust.

JOSHUA COLE is associate professor of history at the University of Michigan. He received his B.A. from Brown University and his M.A. and Ph.D. from the University of California, Berkeley. The author of *The Power of Large Numbers: Population, Politics, and Gender in Nineteenth-Century France* (2000), he has also published articles on French and German social and cultural history in the modern period. His current research is on the legacy of colonial violence in France, Algeria, and Madagascar, with a focus on the problems created by this history of violence in the postcolonial world. He has enjoyed teaching European history in a global context since 1993.

JOHN ROBERTSON received both his M.A. (1976) and his Ph.D. (1981) in ancient history from the University of Pennsylvania. A specialist in the social and economic history of the ancient Near East, he has published several articles in major scholarly journals and contributed articles to such major reference works as the *Anchor Bible Dictionary, Civilizations of the Ancient Near East,* and the *Blackwell Companion to the Ancient Near East.* He has also participated in archaeological excavations in Syria and Greece as well as the American Southwest. Since 1982, he has been a member of the faculty of the department of history at Central Michigan University, where he has taught the history of Western civilization for both the department of history and the university honors program, as well as more specialized courses in the history of the ancient Near East and the Islamic and modern Middle East.

THOMAS MAX SAFLEY teaches the history of early modern Europe at the University of Pennsylvania. A specialist in economic and social history, he has particular research interests in the history of marriage and the family, of poverty and charity, and of labor and business. In addition to numerous articles and reviews, he is the author of *Let No Man Put Asunder: The Control of Marriage in the German Southwest, 1550–1620* (1984), *Charity and Economy in the Orphanages of Early Modern Augsburg* (1996), *Matheus Miller's Memoir: A Merchant's Life in the Seventeenth Century* (2000), and

The Children of the Laboring Poor: Expectation and Experience among the Orphans of Early Modern Augsburg (2004). He is co-editor of *The Workplace before the Factory: Artisans and Proletarians, 1500–1800* (1993) and *The Reformation of Charity: The Secular and the Sacred in Early Modern Poor Relief* (2003). He also serves on the editorial board of the *Sixteenth Century Journal.* At the University of Pennsylvania, he regularly teaches the introductory survey of European history and advanced lecture courses on the early modern period. He also offers a broad array of undergraduate and graduate seminars.

CAROL SYMES is Associate Professor of History and Director of Undergraduate Studies in the History Department at the University of Illinois, Urbana-Champaign, where she has won the top teaching award in the College of Liberal Arts and Sciences. Her main areas of study include medieval Europe, especially France and England; cultural history; history of information media and communication technologies; and history of theatre. She is the author of *A Common Stage: Theater and Public Life in Medieval Arras.*

CONTENTS

CHAPTER 11 ⌇ CONQUEST, COMMERCE, AND COLONIZATION, 1300–1600   2

CHAPTER 12 ⌇ RENAISSANCE IDEALS AND REALITIES, c. 1350–1550   31

CHAPTER 13   THE AGE OF DISSENT AND DIVISION, 1500–1600   63

CHAPTER 14   RELIGION, WARFARE, AND SOVEREIGNTY: 1540–1660   99

CHAPTER 15 ⤳ ABSOLUTISM AND EMPIRE, 1660–1789   130

CHAPTER 16 ⤳ THE NEW SCIENCE OF THE SEVENTEENTH CENTURY   182

CHAPTER **17**   THE ENLIGHTENMENT   216

CHAPTER **18**   THE FRENCH REVOLUTION   272

CHAPTER 19 ❧ THE INDUSTRIAL REVOLUTION AND NINETEENTH-CENTURY SOCIETY   301

CHAPTER 20 ❧ FROM RESTORATION TO REVOLUTION, 1815–1848   337

CHAPTER 21 ✎ WHAT IS A NATION? TERRITORIES, STATES, AND CITIZENS, 1848–1871   372

CHAPTER 22 ✎ IMPERIALISM AND COLONIALISM, 1870–1914   395

CHAPTER 23   MODERN INDUSTRY AND MASS POLITICS, 1870–1914   421

CHAPTER 24   THE FIRST WORLD WAR   468

CHAPTER 27 ∽ THE COLD WAR WORLD: GLOBAL POLITICS, ECONOMIC RECOVERY, AND CULTURAL CHANGE   554

CHAPTER 28 ∽ A WORLD WITHOUT WALLS: GLOBALIZATION AND THE WEST   578

PREFACE FOR INSTRUCTORS

The authors of this text are very pleased to have been afforded the opportunity to design and compile this reader, which is the outgrowth of approximately nine decades of combined experience teaching the history of Western civilization. In the course of acquiring that experience, the authors were frustrated by what we perceived as serious shortcomings in most of the available supplementary readers. Among the more notable deficiencies are a frequent over-emphasis on political and intellectual history at the expense of social and economic history and on elite culture at the expense of sources relating to the experiences of people of lesser socioeconomic station and, especially, of women. There is also an underrepresentation of sources relating the experiences and perspectives of European societies east of what is today Germany and a focus on Western civilization that often has neglected to address the West's important interactions with, and development of attitudes toward, non-Western peoples and civilizations. Some texts, in a laudable attempt to be more inclusive, incorporate more selections to serve up a veritable smorgasbord of thematically unlinked snippets, many of them so abbreviated or cited so dis-jointedly that the student can hardly gain a proper appreciation of their context or of the nature and structure of the documents from which they are derived. For ancient and medieval sources, this problem is all too often com-pounded by the use of translations that are either obsolete (from the stand-point of recent advances in philology) or rendered in an antiquated idiom that is hardly conducive to engaging students' interest. Finally, many readers are compiled by only one editor, who, whatever his or her experience and scholarly credentials, may understandably be hard pressed to command adequately the range and variety of primary sources available for examining the diverse as-pects of Western civilization.

We by no means have the hubris to believe that what we have assembled will satisfy all the desiderata of every instructor. Nonetheless, to address the concerns noted above, and others, we have endeavored to produce a text that incorporates, as much as possible, the following features:

- Selections that consist of complete texts or lengthy excerpts of primary-source documents, ranging from one to eight pages in length and rendered in authoritative and eloquent, yet idiomatic, translations.

- Recognition that visual artifacts are also meaningful primary sources. Each chapter of this edition contains two visual features (photographs, paintings, posters, cartoons, sculptures, etc.) intended to help students learn how to analyze and interpret visual sources.

• An appropriate balance of primary sources from the Western canon, works that are illustrative of the origins and development of Western political institutions, intellectual life, and high culture or that illustrate aspects of social and economic history as well as more mundane aspects of life in Western societies. In other words, we have strived to provide selections pertinent to the lives, roles, achievements, and contributions of elite and commoner, ruler and ruled, master and servant, man and woman.

• Selections that reflect the experiences and perspectives of women and the dynamics of gender relations, including family and household structure.

• Selections that attempt to place a focus on the western European experience within a broader, even global perspective, by including selections relating to eastern Europe, the ancient and Islamic Middle East, Africa, Asia, and the Western Hemisphere. Thus, interspersed among the works of Western authors are excerpts from ancient Egyptian and Babylonian literature and private letters, the Qur'an, and works of such figures as Ali ibn al-Athir, Ibn Battuta, Edward Morel, Mohandas Gandhi, Frantz Fanon, Tadataka Kuribayashi, and Achille Mbembe. Readings such as these are intended to help students trace the evolution of the concept of the West and its relations with the non-West—matters of immense significance as an increasingly global society stands at the beginning of the twenty-first century.

• The incorporation of several unifying questions and issues to link documents both within and among chapters in a coherent, pedagogically useful internal framework. The documents in this reader have been chosen with an overarching purpose of interweaving a number of thematic threads that compose vital elements in the colorful fabrics of Western civilization: What are the status, responsibilities, and rights of the individual within the local community and broader society, and how have they changed over time? How have people defined their own communities, and how have they viewed outsiders? Who should have power within and over the community and society, and why? How have people responded to changes in the material world around them? Who or what controls the cosmos, and how have humankind's perceptions of its appropriate role and function within the cosmos changed?

The pedagogical and critical apparatus provided in this reader has been designed to guide the student to an appreciation of the sources but without imparting too much in the way of historical interpretation. For each chapter we have supplied an introduction that provides a historical context for the readings and alerts the student to the thematic threads that link them. Each reading in turn has an introduction that supplies an even more specific context and alerts the student to issues of interpretation or biased perspective. Finally, each selection is accompanied by several questions intended to stimulate analysis and discussion. The placement of these questions after each selection is quite intentional, as it is our hope that students will engage each document without a preconceived or predetermined sense of why it may be important and will instead learn to trust their own critical capacities and discern the significance of a reading on their own.

While the Fifth Edition remains a wonderful collection of primary sources organized around the aforementioned features, it has also been made more affordable and compact to meet the changing needs of instructors and students. Nearly 100 instructors participated in our online survey to identify the most essential and highly teachable primary sources to include in the new edition. As a result, the Fifth Edition is more streamlined and compact. At the table of contents level, we have also brought it in closer alignment with our best-selling survey texts, *Western Civilizations*, Seventeenth Edition and *Western Civilizations*, Brief Third Edition by Cole, Symes, Coffin, and Stacey. Finally, as a result of the streamlining efforts, we were able to drop the standalone price of the text by 40%, and we can package each volume for $10 net with Norton's fine survey texts. Undoubtedly, students will be more inclined to buy our reader, and, we hope, to spend time reading it as well.

Obviously, to organize a project as complex as a reader of this kind and to bring it to a successful and timely fruition require the skills, support, inspiration, and dedication of many people other than the authors. We wish to express our admiration and profound gratitude to the editorial and marketing staff of W. W. Norton, especially to Kate Feighery, Jason Spears, Justin Cahill, who did a fantastic job researching sources and pulling the manuscript together in good order, Bethany Salminen for her work in securing permissions, and, most especially, to Jon Durbin, who assembled the team, helped us to define and refine our work, organized the project, offered useful insight and judicious criticism, and kept all of us on task and on time. The credit for this reader is surely as much theirs as ours.

For this edition we have included the following new documents:

- from The Religious Peace of Augsburg
- Catherine the Great, from *Proposals for a New Code of Law*
- Daniel Defoe, from *The Complete English Tradesman*
- from The Charter of the Dutch West India Company
- Mark Mazower, from *Dark Continent: Europe's Twentieth Century*
- Nicolas Sarkozy, from Speech at the University of Cheikh Anta Diop, Senegal, July 26, 2007
- Achille Mbembe, from "Nicolas Sarkozy's Africa"
- Olivier Roy, from *Globalized Islam: The Search for a New Ummah*

In addition, we would like to thank the following faculty for their valuable input as we developed the Fifth Edition:

- David Aliano, College of Mount Saint Vincent
- James Allen, Ramapo College of New Jersey

- Ken Bartlett, University of Toronto
- Benita Blessing, University of Massachusetts, Amherst
- Richard Brabander, Bridgewater State University
- Kathren Brown, Utah Valley University
- Jodi Campbell, Texas Christian University
- Peter Catapano, New York City College of Technology
- Tamara Chaplin, University of Illinois at Urbana-Champaign
- Frederick Corney, The College of William & Mary
- Jason Coy, College of Charleston
- Sarah Davis-Secord, University of Texas at Arlington
- Rene M Descartes, SUNY Cobleskill
- John Eastby, Hampden-Sydney College
- Benjamin Ehlers, University of Georgia
- Kathleen Fichtel, West Virginia University
- Deanna Forsman, North Hennepin Community College
- David Gallo, College of Mount Saint Vincent
- Steven Garfinkle, Western Washington University
- Norman Goda, University of Florida
- Peter Goddard, University of Guelph
- Andrew Goldman, Gonzaga University
- Rita V. Gomez, Anne Arundel Community College
- Robert Grasso, Monmouth University
- Madonna Hettinger, The College of Wooster
- Warren Johnston, Algoma University
- Philip Kaplan, University of North Florida
- Michael Kinney, Calhoun Community College
- Christine Kooi, Louisiana State University
- Glenn Kranking, Gustavus Adolphus College
- Chris Laney, Berkshire Community College
- Elizabeth Lehfeldt, Cleveland State University
- Janice Liedl, Laurentian University
- Kate Martin, Cape Cod Community College
- Martin Menke, Rivier College
- Jeffrey Lee Meriwether, Roger Williams University

- Lynn Mollenauer, University of North Carolina at Wilmington
- Rachel Nunez, Hollins University
- Bill Olejniczak, College of Charleston
- Daniel Opler, College of Mount Saint Vincent
- Christopher Otter, Ohio State University
- Matthew Pehl, Augustana College
- Samuel Pierce, College of Charleston
- Robert Policelli, University of North Carolina at Chapel Hill
- Peter Pozefsky, College of Wooster
- Sandra Pryor, Old Dominion University
- Matthew Ruane, Florida Institute of Technology
- David A. Serafini, Western Kentucky University
- David Shearer, University of Delaware
- Robert Simmons, Calhoun Community College
- Philip H. Slaby, Guilford College
- Susan L. Smith, Orange Coast College
- David Snyder, University of South Carolina
- Peter Utgaard, Cuyamaca College
- James Vanstone, John Abbott College
- Rachelle Wadsworth, Florida State College at Jacksonville
- Philip Whalen, Coastal Carolina University
- Aaron Wilson, Creighton University
- Matthew D. Zarzeczny, Ashland University

PREFACE FOR STUDENTS

Good Tips for Learning How to Analyze Primary Sources

The purpose of this collection of illustrations and documents is to provide the student with the raw materials of history, the sources, in the form of the objects and written words that survive from the past. Your textbook relies on such documents, known as primary sources, as well as on the works of many past and present historians who have analyzed and interpreted these sources—the secondary literature. In some cases the historians were themselves sources, eyewitnesses to the events they recorded. Authors of textbooks select which facts and interpretations they think you should know, and so the textbook filters what you think about the human past by limiting the information available to you. Textbooks are useful because they provide a coherent historical narrative for students of history, but it is important to remember that they are only an introduction to the rich complexity of human experience over time.

A collection of historical documents and artifacts provides a vital supplement to the textbook, but it also has problems. First, the sources, mostly not intended for us to read and study, exist for the reasons that prompted some people to create them and others to preserve them. These reasons may include a measure of lies, self-deception, or ignorance about what was really happening and being recorded. So we must ask the following questions about any document or object—a treaty, contract, painting, photograph, poem, newspaper article, or sculpture: Why does it exist? What specific purpose did it serve when it was done? Who is its author? What motives prompted the creator to produce this material in this form?

The second major problem is that we, the editors of this collection, have selected, from millions of possible choices, these particular documents and objects, and not others. Even in this process, because of the limitations of space and our own personal experiences, we present a necessarily partial and highly selective view of Western civilization (also because of space limitations, it has been necessary to delete portions from some of the longer sections).* Our purpose is not to repeat what you can find in the textbook but to give you the opportunity to see and discuss how historians, now including you, make history out of documents and objects, and their understanding of why people behave the way they do.

The illustrations in this collection provide a glimpse at the millions of material objects that survive from the past. These churches, buildings, paintings, mosaics, sculptures, photographs, and other items make up an important set of sources for the historian to consider about the past. It is certainly difficult to appreciate an immense building or a small manuscript painting from a photograph. Nevertheless, the editors of this collection include illustrations in the Fifth Edition to make clear the full range of sources that historians utilize. Also, the illustrations in many cases complement the written documents and in every case provide opportunities for a broader discussion of historical questions and the variety of sources that can help answer them.

Before exploring in more detail what documents are, we should be clear about what history is. Simply put, history is what we can say about the human past, in this case about the vast area of Western civilization from its remote origins to the most recent past. We can say, or write, things about the past because people left us their words, in the form of documents, and we can, like detectives, question these sources and then try to understand what happened. Before the written word, there is no history in the strictest sense; instead there are preliterate societies and the tens of thousands of years for which we know only what the anthropologists and archaeologists can tell us from the physical remains of bodies and objects made by human hands. And yet during this time profoundly important human institutions like language, the family, and religion first appeared. History begins with writing because that is when the documentation starts. These accomplishments of our remote ancestors occurred over tens of thousands of years, broken into ages of stone, copper, and bronze. Objects and images, but no words, reveal advances in weapons, art, farming, and other activities.

Although history cannot exist without written documents, we must remember that this evidence is complex and ambiguous. In the first place, it first appears in ancient languages, and the majority of documents in this book were not originally in English. The act of translating the documents into modern English raises another barrier or filter, and we must use our imaginations to

---

We indicate omissions, no matter how brief, with three spaced asterisks (* *), running them in when the opening, middle, or closing of a paragraph has been deleted and centering them between lines when a full paragraph is dropped. Why asterisks, when ellipsis dots are the standard? Because authors use ellipsis dots, and we want to distinguish our deletions from theirs.

recreate the past worlds in which modern words like *liberty, race,* or *sin* had different meanings. One job of the historian is to understand the language of the documents in their widest possible contexts. All the authors intended their documents to communicate something, but as time passes, languages and contexts change, and so it becomes more difficult for us to figure out what a document meant then and may mean now. Language is an imperfect way to communicate, but we must make the best of what we have. If we recollect how difficult it is sometimes to understand the events we see and experience, then we can perhaps understand how careful we must be when we interpret someone else's report about an event in the past, especially when that past is far removed in space and time from our experience.

The documents give us the language, or testimony, of witnesses, observers, or people with some point to make. Some documents claim to reveal religious truths and interpreting these claims requires historians to inquire respectfully and sincerely. Historical evidence, like any other, must be examined for flaws, contradictions, lies, and what it tells us that the writer did not necessarily intend to reveal. Like a patient detective, we must question our witnesses with a full awareness of their limited and often-biased perception, piecing together our knowledge of their history with the aid of multiple testimonies and a broad context. Consider the document, whatever it is, as testimony and a piece of a bigger puzzle, many of the remaining pieces of which are missing or broken. It is useful at the beginning to be clear about the simple issues—What type of document is this evidence? Who wrote it? Where and when was it written? Why does it exist? Try to understand the context of the document by relating it to the wider world—how do words by Plato or about the Nazi Party fit with what you already know about ancient Greece or twentieth-century Germany?

When the document, or witness, has been correctly identified and placed in some context, we may then interrogate it further by asking questions about the words before us. Not all documents suggest the same questions, but there are some general questions that apply to nearly every document. One place to begin is to ask, Who or what is left out? Once you see the main point, it is interesting to ask what the documents tell us about people and subjects often left out of the records—women, children, or religious or ethnic minorities, for example. Or, if the document is about a religious minority, we can ask what it tells us about the majority. Take the document and try to turn it inside out by determining the basic assumptions or biases of its author, and then explore what has been intentionally or unintentionally left out. look for anomalies— pieces of evidence that appear out of place or simply weird; they are often clues to understanding the distances between us and the sources. Another way to ask a fresh question of an old witness is to look beneath the surface and see what else is there. For example, if the document in question seems mainly to offer evidence on religion, ask what it tells us about the economy or contemporary eating habits or whatever else might occur to you. Documents frequently reveal excellent information on topics far from their ostensible subjects, if we remember to ask.

Every document in this collection is some kind of story, either long or short. The stories are almost all nonfiction, at least in theory, but they all have characters; a plot, or story line; and above all a point to the story, the meaning. We have suggested some possible meanings in the sample questions at the end of each document, but these questions are just there to help your thinking or get a discussion going, about the many possible meanings of the documents. You can ask what the meaning was in the document's own time, as well as what we might now see as a meaning that makes sense to us of some pieces of the past. The point of the story in a document may often concern a central issue in history, the process of change. If history is what we can say about the human past, then the most important words describe how change occurs, for example, rapidly, as in revolutions and wars, or more slowly, as in marriage customs or family life. Every document casts some light on human change, and the meaning of the story often relates to why something changed.

History is often at its dullest when a document simply describes a static situation, for example, a law or farming. However, even a good description reveals choices and emphasis. If you ask, Why this law now? Why farm in this way? How did these activities influence human behavior? you can see that the real subject of nearly all documents is human change, on some level. You will find that people can and will strongly disagree about the meaning of a story: they can and will use the same evidence from a document to draw radically different meanings. This is one of the challenges of history and what makes it fun, for some explanations and meanings make more sense than others in the broader context of what you know about an episode or period of history. Argue about meaning, and you will learn something about not only your own biases and values but also the process of sifting facts for good arguments and answers. These skills have a value well beyond the study of history.

The documents and objects in this collection, even the most general works of philosophy or social analysis, reveal the particular and contingent aspects of history. Even the most abstract of these documents and objects comes from a specific time, place, and person and sheds some light on a unique set of circumstances. When history is like the other social sciences (anthropology, economics, sociology, political science, and others), it tries to deal with typical or average people, societies, or behavior. When history is like the other humanities (literature, philosophy, religion, art, and others), it stresses individual people, their quirks and uniqueness. The documents and objects also illustrate the contingent aspect of history, which unlike the social or natural sciences but like the humanities, appears to lack rules or laws. History depends on what people did, subject to the restrictions of their natures, resources, climate, and other natural factors—people with histories of their own! Rerunning this history is not like a movie, and it would never turn out the same way twice, for it is specific and contingent to the way it turned out this time. The documents and objects do not tell a story of an orderly progression from simple to complex societies or from bad to good ones. Instead, history continues, and people cope, or not, with the issues of religious faith, family life, making a living, and creating artifacts and documents. These documents and objects collectively provide perspectives on how experiments in living succeeded or failed. We invite you to use them to learn more about the people of the past than the textbooks can say and to use your imaginations to get these witnesses to answer your questions about the process and meaning of human change.

WHERE TO BEGIN?

A Primary Source Checklist

This checklist is a series of questions that can be used to analyze most of the documents and objects in this reader.

✔ What type of document or object is this evidence?

✔ Why does the document or object exist? What motives prompted the author to create the material in this form?

✔ Who created this work?

✔ Who or what is left out—women, children, minorities, members of the majority?

✔ In addition to the main subject, what other kinds of information can be obtained?

✔ How do the subjects of the document or object relate to what we know about broader society?

✔ What was the meaning of the document or object in its own time? What is its meaning for the audience?

✔ What does the document or object tell us about change or stability in society?

Perspectives from the Past

PRIMARY SOURCES IN WESTERN

CIVILIZATIONS

Fifth Edition

11 ⌘ CONQUEST, COMMERCE, AND COLONIZATION, 1300–1600

The commercial revolution of the Middle Ages fostered a desire by Europeans to extend trading networks. Trade was not the only motive for travel. Religious pilgrimages and missions, the Crusades, and greed also motivated some people to venture beyond the frontiers of Europe. Successful trade depended on reliable knowledge about the world. Better maps and accounts of travels made it possible for people to find their way over the vast stretches of Asia to China or across the Atlantic. The most adventurous travel was by sea, and better ships, sails, ropes, compasses, and astrolabes made it easier to sail long distances out of sight of land. The great inland sea, the Mediterranean, whose waters touched Africa, Asia, and Europe, witnessed the first advances in sailing techniques, and also the first experiments in European colonization on islands like Crete and Cyprus. Muslim merchants continued to dominate the trading networks in the Indian Ocean.

Beginning in the mid-thirteenth century, missionaries such as William of Rubruck and intrepid merchants such as the Polos of Venice followed the Silk Road across central Asia to China, "the east beyond the east." A small trade continued along this route to Europe until the mid-fourteenth century, when plague and changes in the Mongol Empire made travel across Asia more difficult. Accounts of the East and its immense riches in spices, precious gems and gold, and silk continued to intrigue Europeans. Muslim travelers such as Ibn Battuta displayed a similar curiosity about Muslim states across Asia. In the fifteenth century, Chinese explorers made it all the way to Madagascar off the coast of southern Africa. The impulse to explore so far from home waned when the emperors stopped supporting these trading voyages. If Europeans wanted regular trade with China, they needed to find new, safe routes not controlled by the emerging Islamic Ottoman and Mamluk Empires in the East.

The Portuguese, facing the Atlantic, the Ocean Sea, began to explore the west coast of Africa in search of gold. In the fourteenth century, Portuguese and Italian sailors found the islands—the Azores and Madeira, both uninhabited, and the Canaries, peopled by the Canarians. Spanish and French traders and explorers also took an interest in the opportunities for trade and settlement, but only the Portuguese sailed farther south beyond the Saharan coast. Merchants and sailors from Lisbon hoped to confirm ancient speculations that it was possible to circumnavigate Africa and find a way to the Indian Ocean. Explorations of the West African coast opened up a lucrative trade in gold and slaves that made tiny Portugal a world power. The patronage of Prince Henry the Navigator (1394–1460) established a seafaring tradition that enabled Bartolomeu Dias to round the Cape of Good Hope in 1488. Vasco de Gama sailed for India in 1497 and eventually rewarded his investors with fabulous profits in spices.

Only after reaching the "new worlds" of Asia and Africa did Europeans "discover" the Americas. The Italian-born Christopher Columbus (c. 1450–1506) convinced Isabella of Castile and Ferdinand of Aragon to gamble on a sea route across the perilous Atlantic to the East. Until his dying day, Columbus remained convinced that the people he called Indians lived off the coast of Asia. His search for wealth was frustrated, moreover, but he laid the foundations for trading in slaves and the exploitation of indigenous peoples that reached its bloody culmination with Hernando Cortéz, in Mexico in 1519, and the Pizarros in Peru, in 1533.

At the same time, a demographic catastrophe occurred in the Americas, as European diseases, such as smallpox, wiped out a high percentage (in some places perhaps as much as 90 percent) of the population. Colonists planning to make money in the mines or the newly established sugar plantations thus relied increasingly on African slaves for labor. Supplying slaves to the new world thus became an increasingly lucrative trade and the first global economy.

WILLIAM OF RUBRUCK

FROM *On the Mongols*

William of Rubruck, a Franciscan monk from Flanders, was sent in 1253 to the Mongols by Louis IX of France, then on crusade in the East. The Mongol Empire, established by Chingis, or Genghis, Khan (1167–1227) and extended by successors such as Mangu (1251–1259), had sent scouting parties as far west as Poland and Hungary. In the first section of this account, William describes Mongol culture to the French king. In the second section, he is at the Mongol capital of Caracorum in Mongolia, seeking another audience with Mangu.

From *The Journey of William of Rubruck to the Eastern Parts of the World, 1253–55: As Narrated by Himself*, translated and edited by William Woodville Rockhill (London: Hakluyt Society, 1900), pp. 56–66, 68–83, 235–239.

Commerce and Conquest

The matrons make for themselves most beautiful (luggage) carts, which I would not know how to describe to you unless by a drawing, and I would depict them all to you if I knew how to paint. A single rich Moal or Tartar has quite c or cc such carts with coffers. Baatu has xxvi wives, each of whom has a large dwelling, exclusive of the other little ones which they set up after the big one, and which are like closets, in which the sewing girls live, and to each of these (large) dwellings are attached quite cc carts. And when they set up their houses, the first wife places her dwelling on the extreme west side, and after her the others according to their rank, so that the last wife will be in the extreme east; and there will be the distance of a stone's throw between the *iurt* of one wife and that of another. The *ordu* of a rich Moal seems like a large town, though there will be very few men in it. One girl will lead xx or xxx carts, for the country is flat, and they tie the ox or camel carts the one after the other, and a girl will sit on the front one driving the ox, and all the others follow after with the same gait. Should it happen that they come to some bad piece of road, they untie them, and take them across one by one. So they go along slowly, as a sheep or an ox might walk.

When they have fixed their dwelling, the door turned to the south, they set up the couch of the master on the north side. The side for the women is always the east side, that is to say, on the left of the house of the master, he sitting on his couch with his face turned to the south. The side for the men is the west side, that is, on the right. Men coming into the house would never hang up their bows on the side of the women

And over the head of the master is always an image of felt, like a doll or statuette, which they call the brother of the master; another similar one is above the head of the mistress, which they call the brother of the mistress, and they are attached to the wall; and higher up between the two of them is a little lank one (*macilenta*), who is, as it were, the guardian of the whole dwelling. The mistress places in her house on her right side, in a conspicuous place at the foot of her couch, a goat-skin full of wool or other stuff, and beside it a very little statuette looking in the direction of the attendants and women. Beside the entry on the women's side is yet another image, with a cow's tit for the women, who milk the cows; for it is part of the duty of the women to milk the cows. On the other side of the entry, toward the men, is another statue with a mare's tit for the men who milk the mares.

And when they have come together to drink, they first sprinkle with liquor this image which is over the master's head, then the other images in order. Then an attendant goes out of the dwelling with a cup and liquor, and sprinkles three times to the south, each time bending the knee, and that to do reverence to the fire; then to the east, and that to do reverence to the air; then to the west to do reverence to the water; to the north they sprinkle for the dead. When the master takes the cup in hand and is about to drink, he first pours a portion on the ground. If he were to drink seated on a horse, he first before he drinks pours a little on the neck or the mane of the horse. Then when the attendant has sprinkled toward the four quarters of the world he goes back into the house, where two attendants are ready with two cups and platters to carry drink to the master and the wife seated near him upon the couch. And when he hath several wives, she with whom he hath slept that night sits beside him in the day, and it becometh all the others to come to her dwelling that day to drink, and court is held there that day, and the gifts which are brought that day are placed in the treasury of that lady. A bench with a skin of milk, or some other drink, and with cups, stands in the entry.

In winter they make a capital drink of rice, of millet, and of honey; it is clear as wine: and wine is carried to them from remote parts. In summer they care only for *cosmos*. There is always *cosmos* near the house, before the entry door, and beside it stands a guitar-player with his guitar. Lutes and vielles such as we have I did not see there, but many other instruments which are unknown among us. And when the master begins to drink, then one of the attendants cries with a loud voice, "Ha!" and the guitarist strikes his guitar, and when they have a great feast they all clap their hands, and also dance about to the sound of the guitar, the and she who has the least nose is held the most beautiful. They disfigure themselves horribly by painting their faces. They never lie down in bed when having their children.

The Duties of the Women and Their Work

It is the duty of the women to drive the carts, get the dwellings on and off them, milk the cows, make butter and *gruit*, and to dress and sew skins, which they do with a thread made of tendons. They divide the tendons into fine shreds, and then twist them into one long thread. They also sew the boots, the socks and the clothing. They never wash clothes, for they say that God would be angered thereat, and that it would thunder if they hung them up to dry. They will even beat those they find washing them. Thunder they fear extraordinarily; and when it thunders they will turn out of their dwellings all strangers, wrap themselves in black felt, and thus hide themselves till it has passed away. Furthermore, they never wash their bowls, but when the meat is cooked they rinse out the dish in which they are about to put it with some of the boiling broth from the kettle, which they pour back into it. They also make the felt and cover the houses.

The men make bows and arrows, manufacture stirrups and bits, make saddles, do the carpentering on (the framework of) their dwellings and the carts; they take care of the horses, milk the mares, churn the *cosmos* or mare's milk, make the skins in which it is put; they also look after the camels and load them. Both sexes look after the sheep and goats, sometimes the men, othertimes the women, milking them.

They dress skins with a thick mixture of sour ewe's milk and salt. When they want to wash their hands or head, they fill their mouths with water, which they let trickle on to their hands, and in this way they also wet their hair and wash their heads.

As to their marriages, you must know that no one among them has a wife unless he buys her; so it sometimes happens that girls are well past marriageable age before they marry, for their parents always keep them until they sell them. They observe the first and second degrees of consanguinity, but no degree of affinity; thus (one person) will have at the same time or successively two sisters. Among them no widow marries, for the following reason: they believe that all who serve them in this life shall serve them in the next, so as regards a widow they believe that she will always return to her first husband after death. Hence this shameful custom prevails among them, that sometimes a son takes to wife all his father's wives, except his own mother; for the *orda* of the father and mother always belongs to the youngest son, so it is he who must provide for all his father's wives who come to him with the paternal household, and if he wishes it he uses them as wives, for he esteems not himself injured if they return to his father after death. When then anyone has made a bargain with another to take his daughter, the father of the girl gives a feast, and the girl flees to her relatives and hides there. Then the father says: "Here, my daughter is yours; take her wheresoever you find her." Then he searches for her with his friends till he finds her, and he must take her by force and carry her off with a semblance of violence to his house.

Of Their Justice and Judgments, Death and Burial

As to their justice you must know that when two men fight together no one dares interfere, even a father dare not aid a son; but he who has the worse of it may appeal to the court of the lord, and if anyone touches him after the appeal, he is put to death. But action must be taken at once without any delay, and the injured one must lead him (who has offended) as a captive. They inflict capital punishment on no one unless he be taken in the act or confesses. When one is accused by a number of persons, they torture him so that he confesses. They punish homicide with capital punishment, and also cohabiting with a woman not one's own. By not one's own, I mean not his wife or bondwoman, for with one's slaves one may do as one pleases. They also punish with death grand larceny, but as for petty thefts, such as that of a sheep, so long as one has not repeatedly been taken in the act, they beat him cruelly, and if they administer an hundred blows they must use an hundred sticks: I speak of the case of those beaten under order of authority. In like manner false envoys, that is to say persons who pass themselves off as ambassadors but who are not, are put to death. Likewise sorcerers, of whom I shall however tell you more, for such they consider to be witches.

When anyone dies, they lament with loud wailing, then they are free, for they pay no taxes for the year. And if anyone is present at the death of an adult, he may not enter the dwelling even of Mangu Chan for the year. If it be a child who dies, he may not enter it for a month. Beside the tomb of the dead they always leave a tent if he be one of the nobles, that is of the family of Chingis, who was their first father and lord. Of him who is dead the burying place is not known. And always around these places where they bury their nobles there is a camp with men watching the tombs. I did not understand that they bury treasure with their dead. The Comans raise a great tumulus over the dead, and set up a statue to him, its face to the east, and holding a cup in its hand at the height of the navel. They make also pyramids to the rich, that is to say, little pointed structures, and in some places I saw great tiled covered towers, and in others stone houses, though there were no stones thereabout. Over a person recently dead I saw hung on long poles the skins of xvi horses, four facing each quarter of the world; and they had placed also *cosmos* for him to drink, and meat for him to eat, and for all that they said of him that he had been baptised. Farther east I saw other tombs in shape like great yards covered with big flat stones, some round, some square, and four high vertical stones at the corners facing the four quarters of the world. When anyone sickens he lies on his couch, and places a sign over his dwelling that there is a sick person therein, and that no one shall enter. So no one visits a sick person, save him who serves him. And when anyone from the great *ordu* is ill, they place guards all round the *ordu*, who permit no one

to pass those bounds. For they fear lest an evil spirit or some wind should come with those who enter. They call, however, their priests, who are these same soothsayers.

∗   ∗   ∗

Friar William's Last Audience with Mangu

On Pentecost day (31st May) Mangu Chan called me before him, and also the Tuin with whom I had discussed; but before I went in, the interpreter, master William's son, said to me that we should have to go back to our country, and that I must not raise any objection, for he understood that it was a settled matter. When I came before the Chan, I had to bend the knees, and so did the Tuin beside me, with his interpreter. Then (the Chan) said to me: "Tell me the truth, whether you said the other day, when I sent my secretaries to you, that I was a Tuin." I replied: "My lord, I did not say that; I will tell you what I said, if it pleases you." Then I repeated to him what I had said, and he replied: "I thought full well that you did not say it, for you should not have said it; but your interpreter translated badly." And he held out toward me the staff on which he leaned, saying: "Fear not." And I, smiling, said in an undertone: "If I had been afraid, I should not have come here." He asked the interpreter what I had said, and he repeated it to him. After that he began confiding to me his creed: "We Moal," he said, "believe that there is only one God, by whom we live and by whom we die, and for whom we have an upright heart." Then I said: "May it be so, for without His grace this cannot be." He asked what I had said; the interpreter told him. Then he added: "But as God gives us the different fingers of the hand, so he gives to men divers ways. God gives you the Scriptures, and you Christians keep them not. You do not find (in them, for example) that one should find fault with another, do you?" "No, my lord," I said; "but I told you from the first that I did not want to wrangle with anyone." "I do not intend to say it," he said, "for you. Likewise you do not find that a man should depart from justice for money." "No, my lord," I said. "And truly I came not to these parts to obtain money; on the contrary I have refused what has been offered me." And there was a secretary present, who bore witness that I had refused an *iascot* and silken cloths. "I do not say it," he said, "for you. God gave you therefore the Scriptures, and you do not keep them; He gave us diviners, we do what they tell us, and we live in peace."

He drank four times, I believe, before he finished saying all this. And I was listening attentively for him to say something else of his creed, when he began talking of my return journey, saying: "You have stayed here a long while; I wish you to go back. You have said that you would not dare take my ambassadors with you; will you take my words, or my letters?" And from that time I never found the opportunity nor the time when I could show him the Catholic Faith. For no one can speak in his presence but so much as he wishes, unless he be an ambassador; for an ambassador can say whatever he chooses, and they always ask if he wishes to say something more. As for me, it was not allowed me to speak more; I had only to listen to him, and reply to his questions. So I answered him that he should make me understand his words, and have them put down in writing, for I would willingly take them as best I could. Then he asked me if I wanted gold or silver or costly clothing. I said: "We take no such things; but we have no travelling money, and without your assistance we cannot get out of your country." He said: "I will have you given all you require while in my possessions; do you want anything more?" I replied: "That suffices us." Then he asked: "How far do you wish to be taken?" I said: "Our power extends to the country of the king of Hermenia; if we were (escorted) that far, it would suffice me." He answered: "I will have you taken that far; after that look out for yourself." And he added: "There are two eyes in the head; but though they be two, they have but one sight, and when one turns its glance there goes the other. You came from Baatu, and so you must go back by way of him." When he had said this, I asked permission of him to speak. "Speak," he said. Then I said: "My lord, we are not men of war. We wish that

those should have dominion over the world who rule it most justly, in accordance with the will of God. Our office is to teach men to live after the will of God. For that we have come here, and willingly would we remain here if it pleased you. Since it pleases you that we go back, that must then be. I will go back, and I will carry your letters as well as I can, as you have ordered. I would ask of your majesty that since I shall carry your letters, I may also come back to you with your consent; principally because you have poor slaves at Bolat, who are of our tongue, and who have no priest to teach them and their sons their religion, and willingly would I remain with them." Then he replied: "If your masters should send you back to me (you will be welcome)." I said: "My lord, I know not the will of my masters; but I have their permission to go wherever I wish, where it is needful to preach the word of God; and it seems to me that it is very needful in these parts; so whether he sends back envoys by us or not, if it pleases you I will come back."

Then he remained silent and sat for a long time as if thinking, and the interpreter told me to speak no more. So I waited anxiously for what he would reply. Finally he said: "You have a long way to go, comfort yourself with food, so that you may reach your country in good health." And he had me given to drink, and then I went out from before him, and after that I went not back again. If I had had the power to work by signs and wonders like Moses, perhaps he would have humbled himself.

*   *   *

REVIEW QUESTIONS

1. What valuable insights does William offer about Mongol culture?
2. According to William, how does the role of women in Mongol society compare with that of European women?
3. What ideas about religion determine the outlooks of Mangu and William?

IBN BATTUTA

FROM *The Travels*

Ibn Battuta (1304–c. 1377), from Tangier in Morocco, was an extraordinary traveler whose journeys took him as far as China and India. He wrote extensive accounts of his travels; here he describes Muslim Cairo at its zenith, before the Black Death.

From *The Travels of Ibn Battuta*, A.D. 1325–1354, edited by H. A. R. Gibb (London: Hakluyt Society, 1958), pp. 41–53.

*   *   *

Commerce

I arrived at length at the city of Miṣr, mother of cities and seat of Pharaoh the tyrant, mistress of broad provinces and fruitful lands, boundless in multitude of buildings, peerless in beauty and splendour, the meeting-place of comer and goer, the stopping-place of feeble and strong. Therein is what you will of learned and simple, grave and gay, prudent and foolish, base and noble, of high estate and low estate, unknown and famous; she surges as the waves of the sea with her throngs of folk and can scarce contain them for all the capacity of her situation and sustaining power. Her youth is ever new in spite of length of days, and the star of her horoscope does not move from the mansion of fortune; her conquering capital (*al-Qāhira*) has subdued the nations, and her kings have grasped the forelocks of both Arab and non-Arab. She has as her peculiar possession the majestic Nile, which dispenses her district from the need of entreating the distillation [of the rain]; her territory is a month's journey for a hastening traveller, of generous soil, and extending a friendly welcome to strangers.

Ibn Juzayy remarks: Of Cairo the poet says—

No common town is Cairo, by thy life! Nay, she
Is heaven on earth for those with eyes to see;

Her youth those boys and maids with lustrous eyes,
Kawthar her Nile, her Rawḍa Paradise.

*   *   *

It is said that in Cairo there are twelve thousand water-carriers who transport water on camels, and thirty thousand hirers of mules and donkeys, and that on its Nile there are thirty-six thousand vessels belonging to the Sultan and his subjects, which sail upstream to Upper Egypt and downstream to Alexandria and Damietta, laden with goods and commodities of all kinds. On the bank of the Nile opposite Cairo is the place known as al-Rawḍa ['the Garden'], which is a pleasure park and promenade, containing many beautiful gardens. The people of Cairo are fond of pleasure and amusement. I once witnessed a fête there which was held for al-Malik al-Nāṣir's recovery from a fracture which he had suffered in his hand. All the merchants decorated their bazaars and had rich stuffs, ornaments, and silken fabrics hung up in their shops for several days.

The Mosque of 'Amr b. al-'Āṣ, and the Colleges, Hospital, and Convents

The Mosque of 'Amr b. al-'Āṣ is a noble mosque, highly venerated and widely celebrated. The Friday service is held in it, and the road runs right through it from east to west. To the west of it is the cell where the Imām Abū 'Abdallāh al-Shāfi'ī used to teach. As for the madrasas in Cairo, they are too many for anyone to count; and as for the Māristān, which is "between the two castles" near the mausoleum of al-Malik al-Manṣūr Qalā'ūn, no description is adequate to its beauties. It is equipped with innumerable conveniences and medicaments, and its revenue is reported to be a thousand dinars a day. The convents too are numerous. The people there call them *khawāniq,* the singular being *khānqa,* and the amīrs in Cairo vie with one another in building them.

Each convent in Cairo is affected to the use of a separate congregation of poor brethren, most of whom are Persians, men of good education and adepts in the "way" of Sufism. Each has a shaikh and a warden, and the organization of their affairs is admirable. It is one of their customs in the matter of their food that the steward of the house comes in the morning to the faqīrs, each of whom then specifies what food he desires. When they assemble for meals, each person is given his bread and soup in a separate dish, none sharing with another. They eat twice a day. They receive winter clothing and summer clothing and a monthly allowance varying from twenty to thirty dirhams each. Every Thursday night they are given sugar cakes, soap to wash their clothes, the price of admission to the bath-house, and oil to feed their lamps. These men are celibate; the married men have separate convents. Amongst the stipulations required of them are attendance at the five daily prayers, spending the night in the convent, and assembly in mass in a chapel within the convent. Another of their customs is that each one of them sits upon a prayer-carpet reserved for his exclusive use. When they pray the dawn prayer they recite the chapters of *Victory,* of *the Kingdom,* and of *'Amma.* After this copies of the Holy Qur'ān are brought, divided into sections, and each faqīr takes a section. After 'sealing' the Qur'ān and reciting a *dhikr,* the Qur'ān-readers give a recital according to the custom of the Easterners. They hold a similar service following the mid-afternoon prayer.

They have a regular ritual for the admission of newcomers. The applicant comes to the gate of the convent and takes up his stand there, with his waist girt, a prayer mat on his shoulder, the staff in his right hand and the jug in his left. The gate-keeper informs the steward of the convent that he is there. The steward then comes out to him and asks him from what country he has come, what convents he has stayed in on his way, and who was his spiritual director (*shaikh*). When he has ascertained the truth of his answers, he admits him into the convent, spreads his prayer-mat for him in a place befitting his station, and shows him the lavatory. The newcomer renews his ablutions and, returning to his mat, ungirds his waist, and prays two prostrations, then he clasps the hand of the shaikh and those of the others present, and takes his seat amongst them. Another custom of theirs is that on Fridays the servant collects all their prayer-mats and takes them to the mosque, where he spreads them in readiness for their coming. The faqīrs come out in a body, accompanied by their shaikh, proceed to the mosque, and pray each on his own mat. When they have finished the prayer they recite the Qur'ān according to their custom, and thereafter return in a body to the convent, accompanied by their shaikh.

The Qarāfa of Cairo and Its Sanctuaries

At [Old] Cairo too is [the cemetery called] al-Qarāfa, a place of vast repute for blessed power, whose special virtue is affirmed in a tradition related by al-Qurṭubī amongst others, for it is a part of the amount al-Muqaṭṭam, of which God has promised that it shall be one of the gardens of Paradise. These people build in the Qarāfa beautiful domed chapels and surround them by walls, so that they look like houses, and they construct chambers in them and hire the services of Qur'ān-readers, who recite night and day in beautiful voices. There are some of them who build a religious house or a madrasa by the side of the mausoleum. They go out every Thursday evening to spend the night there with their children and womenfolk and make a circuit of the famous sanctuaries. They go out also to spend the night there on the night of mid-Sha'bān, and the market-people take out all kinds of eatables.

Among the celebrated sanctuaries is the imposing holy shrine where rests the head of al-Ḥusain b. 'Alī * * *. Beside it is a vast convent, of wonderful workmanship, on the doors of which there are silver rings, and plates also on them of the same metal. This shrine is paid its full meed of respect and veneration.

Amongst the monuments is the tomb of the Lady (*Sayyida*) Nafīsa, daughter of Zaid b. 'Alī b. al-Ḥusain b. 'Alī (upon them be peace). She was a woman answered in prayer and zealous in her devotions. This mausoleum is of elegant construction and resplendent brightness, and beside it is a convent which is visited by a great concourse during the days of the feast dedicated to her. Another is the tomb of the Imām Abū 'Abdallāh Muḥammad b. Idrīs al-Shāfi'ī, close by which is a large convent. The mausoleum enjoys an immense revenue and is surmounted by the famous dome, of admirable workmanship and marvellous construction, an exceedingly fine piece of architecture and exceptionally lofty, the diameter of which exceeds thirty cubits. The Qarāfa of Cairo contains also an incalculable number of graves of men eminent for learning and religion, and in it lie a goodly number of the Companions and of the leading figures of both earlier and later generations (God be pleased with them). * * *

*   *   *

The Egyptian Nile

The Egyptian Nile surpasses all rivers of the earth in sweetness of taste, breadth of channel and magnitude of utility. Cities and villages succeed one another along its banks without interruption and have no equal in the inhabited world, nor is any river known whose basin is so intensively cultivated as that of the Nile. There is no river on earth but it which is called a sea; God Most High has said "If thou fearest for him, cast him into the *yamm,*" thus calling it *yamm,* which means "sea" (*bahr*). It is related in an unimpeachable Tradition that the Prophet of God (God's blessing and peace upon him) reached on the night of his Ascension the Lote-Tree of the Extremity, and lo, at its base were four streams, two outer streams and two inner streams. He asked Gabriel (peace be upon him) what streams these were, and he replied 'The two inner streams flow through Paradise, and as for the two outer streams they are the Nile and Euphrates'. It is also related in the Traditions of the Prophet that the Nile, Euphrates, Saiḥān and Jaiḥān are, each one, rivers of Paradise. The course of the Nile is from south to north, contrary to all the great rivers. One extraordinary thing about it is that it begins to rise in the extreme hot weather, at the time when rivers generally diminish and dry up, and begins to subside at the time when rivers increase in volume and overflow. The river of Sind [Indus] resembles it in this respect, and will be mentioned later. The first beginning of the Nile flood is in Ḥazīrān, that is June; and when its rise amounts to sixteen cubits, the land-tax due to the Sultan is payable in full. If it rises another cubit, there is plenty in that year, and complete well-being. But if it reaches eighteen cubits it does damage to the cultivated lands and causes an outbreak of plague. If it falls short of sixteen by a cubit, the Sultan's land-tax is diminished, and if it is two cubits short the people make solemn prayers for rain and there is the greatest misery.

The Nile is one of the five great rivers of the world, which are the Nile, Euphrates, Tigris, Saiḥūn [Syr Darya] and Jaiḥūn [Amu Darya]; five other rivers rival these, the river of Sind, which is called Panj Āb [i.e. Five Rivers], the river of Hindustān which is called the Kank [or Gang, i.e. Ganges]—to it the Hindus go on pilgrimage, and when they burn their dead they throw the ashes of them into it, and they say that it comes from Paradise—the river Jūn, also in Hindustān, the river Itil [Volga] in the Qifjaq [Kipchak] steppe, on the shore of which is the city of al-Sarā, and the river Sarū in the land of al-Khiṭā [Cathay], on the banks of which is the city of Khān-Bāliq [Peking], whence it descends to the city of al-Khansā [Hang-chow] and from there to the city of al-Zaitūn [Zayton] in the land of China. We shall speak of all these in their proper places, if God will. Some distance below Cairo the Nile divides into three sections, and none of these streams can be crossed except by boat, winter or summer. The inhabitants of every township have canals led off the Nile; when it is in flood it fills these and they inundate the cultivated fields.

The Pyramids and Berbās

These are among the marvels which have been celebrated through the course of ages, and there is much talk and theorizing amongst men about them, their significance and the origin of their construction. They aver that all branches of knowledge which came into existence before the Deluge were derived from Hermes the Ancient, who lived in the remotest part of the Sa'īd [Upper Egypt]; he is also called by the name of Khanūkh [Enoch] that is Idrīs (on him be peace). It is said that he was the first to speculate on the movements of the spheres and the celestial bodies, and the first to construct temples and glorify God in them; and that he warned men of the coming of the Deluge, and fearing for the disappearance of knowledge and destruction of the practical arts built the pyramids and berbas, in which he depicted all the practical arts and their tools, and made diagrams of the sciences, in order that they might remain immortalized. It is said also that the seat of learning and kingship in Egypt was the city of Manūf [Memphis], which is one *barīd* from al-Fusṭāṭ. When Alexandria was built, the people removed to it, and it became the seat of learning and kingship until the coming of Islām, when 'Amr b. al-'Āṣ (God be pleased with him) laid out the city of al-Fusṭāṭ, which remains the capital of Egypt to this day.

The pyramids is an edifice of solid hewn stone, of immense height and circular plan, broad at the base and narrow at the top, like the figure of a cone. They have no doorways and the manner of their erection is unknown. One of the tales related about them is that a certain king of Egypt before the Flood dreamed a dream which filled him with terror and determined him to build these pyramids on the western side of the Nile, as a depository for the sciences and for the bodies of the kings. He asked the astrologers whether they would be opened in the future at any spot, and they told him that an opening would be made on the north side, and informed him of the exact spot where the opening would begin, and of the sum of money which would be expended in making the opening. He then ordered to be deposited in that place the sum of money which they had told him would be spent in breaching it. By pressing forward its construction, he completed it in sixty years, and wrote this inscription upon them: "We erected these pyramids in the space of sixty years; let him who will, pull them down in the space of six hundred years; yet to pull down is easier than to build." Now when the Caliphate devolved upon the Commander of the Faithful al-Ma'mūn, he proposed to pull them down, and although one of the Egyptian shaikhs advised him not to do so he persisted in his design and ordered that they should be breached from the north side. So they set about lighting fires up against them and then sprinkling them with vinegar and battering them with a mangonel, until the breach which is still to be seen in them was opened up. There they found, facing the hole, a sum of money which the Commander of the Faithful ordered to be weighted. He then calculated what had been spent on making the breach, and finding the two sums equal, was greatly astonished. At the same time they found the breadth of the wall to be twenty cubits.

The Sultan of Egypt

The Sultan of Egypt at the time of my entry was al-Malik al-Nāṣir Abu'l-Fatḥ Muḥammad, son of al-Malik al-Manṣūr Saif al-Dīn Qalā'ūn al-Ṣāliḥī. Qalā'ūn was known as al-Alfī ['the Thousand-man'] because al-Malik al-Ṣāliḥ bought him for a thousand dinars of gold. He came originally from Qifjaq [Kipchak]. Al-Malik al-Nāṣir (God's mercy upon him) was a man of generous character and great virtues, and sufficient proof of his nobility is furnished by his devotion to the service of the two holy sanctuaries of Mecca and Madīna and the works of beneficence which he does every year to assist the pilgrims, in furnishing camels loaded with provisions and water for those without means and the helpless, and for carrying those who cannot keep up with the caravan or are too weak to walk on foot, both on the Egyptian pilgrim-road and on that from Damascus. He also built a great convent at Siryāquṣ, in the outskirts of Cairo. But the convent built by our lord the Commander of the Faithful and Defender of the Faith, the refuge of the poor and needy, Caliph of God upon earth, whose zeal in the Holy War transcends its obligations, Abū 'Inān (God be his strength and aid, and grant him the signal victory, and prosper him), in the outskirts of his sublime residence, the luminous city (God guard it), has no equal to it in the inhabited world for perfection of architecture, beauty of construction, and plaster carving such as none of the Easterners can accomplish. We shall speak in due course of the schools, hospitals, and convents which he (God be his strength) has founded in his land (God guard it and preserve it by the prolongation of his reign).

*   *   *

REVIEW QUESTIONS

1. Based on this description, how does old Cairo compare with a contemporary European city?
2. According to Ibn Battuta, what are the most important features of a city?
3. How much does the author seem to know about the pyramids and the Nile?

DOUKAS

FROM *Decline and Fall of Byzantium to the Ottoman Turks*

Doukas (or Ducas), a fifteenth-century Byzantine historian, was descended from a noble Greek family. For a time he worked for the Genoese colonial administration at New Phocaea in Asia Minor. Doukas wrote his history to illustrate what he hoped were temporary Ottoman triumphs over the Greek world. The historian was present at the Ottoman siege of Lesbos in 1462, after which he disappears from the historical record, probably through death or enslavement. This section of Doukas's history concerns the conquest of Constantinople in 1453.

From *Decline and Fall of Byzantium to the Ottoman Turks*, by Doukas, translated by Harry J. Magoulias (Detroit: Wayne State University Press, 1975), pp. 220–27, 240–41.

*   *   *

When all preparations had been completed according to plan, Mehmed sent an envoy to the emperor inside the City with the following message, "The preparations for the assault have been concluded. It is now time to consummate what we planned long ago. Let us leave the outcome of this undertaking to God. What say you? Do you wish to quit the City and go wherever you like together with your officials and their possessions, leaving behind the populace unharmed by us and by you? Or do you choose to resist and to lose your life and belongings, and to have the Turks take the populace captive and scatter them throughout the earth?" The emperor and the senate answered, "If you so wish, as your fathers did before you, you too, by the grace of God, can live peacefully with us. They regarded my parents as their fathers, and as such honored them, and they looked upon this City as their fatherland. In time of difficulty, they entered within her walls and were saved. No one who resisted her lived long. Keep the fortresses and the lands which have been unjustly seized from us as justly yours. Extract as much tribute annually as we are able to pay you, and depart in peace. Can you be certain that victory instead of defeat awaits you? The right to surrender the City to you belongs neither to me nor to anyone who dwells therein. Rather than to have our lives spared, it is our common resolve willingly to die."

When the tyrant heard this reply, he despaired of a peaceful surrender of the City. He therefore instructed the heralds to announce to the entire army the day on which the assault would be launched. He also affirmed on oath that he desired for himself no gain other than the buildings and walls of the City. As for the treasures and captives to be taken, he declared, "Let those be your reward." The troops shouted their approval.

As night fell, he sent heralds around the camp with instructions that large torches and fires should be lighted at every tent. And once the torches were burning, they were all to chant and shout in their foul and impious tongue. This strange spectacle was indeed incredible. As the torches poured their light over land and sea, brighter than the sun, they illuminated the entire City, Galata, all the islands, ships and boats as far as Skutari. The entire surface of the water flashed so brightly that it was like lightning. Would that it had been lightning, the lightning which not only produces light but also burns and utterly consumes everything! The Romans thought that fire had fallen on the camp and ran up to the breach in the wall. When they saw the Turks dancing and heard their joyous shouts, they foresaw the future. With a contrite heart they prayed to God, "Spare us, O Lord, from Thy just wrath and deliver us from the hands of the enemy." The spectacle and din affected the citizens so much that they appeared to be half-dead, unable to breathe either in or out.

Giovanni labored throughout the night. He ordered all the brushwood in the City gathered and placed at the breach. He also constructed a second fosse within for protection where the walls had been destroyed. The Romans realized that their movements were conspicuous and that they could not pass through the gate to oppose the Turks at the outer fortifications because the fallen walls exposed them. There were, however, some old men who knew of an underground sallyport located at the lower end of the palace that, many years before, had been sealed shut. When the emperor was informed of its existence, he commanded that it be opened. The soldiers could now sally through because it was screened by solid walls, and they gave battle to the Turks in the enclosure. The name of this hidden door was Kerkoporta.

On Sunday, the tyrant began to engage in full scale warfare. Right into the evening and through the night he gave no rest to the Romans. That Sunday was the Feast of All Saints, the twenty-seventh day of May.

From daybreak he engaged in light skirmishes until the ninth hour [3 p.m.], and after the ninth hour he arrayed the army from the palace to the Golden Gate. He also deployed the eighty ships from the Xyloporta Gate to the Plataea Gate. The remaining ships, which were stationed at the Double Columns, began an encircling maneuver, starting from the Horaia Gate and continuing past the Acropolis of Demetrios the Great and the small postern located at the Hodegetria monastery. Sailing past the Great Palace and crossing the harbor, they completed the encirclement as far as Vlangas. In addition to all kinds of equipment, each vessel carried a scaling ladder equal to the height of the walls.

Just as the sun set, the call to battle rang out. The battle array was most formidable indeed! The tyrant himself was on horseback on Monday evening. Exactly opposite the fallen walls he gave battle with his faithful slaves, young and all-powerful, fighting like lions, more than ten thousand of them. To the rear and on both flanks there were more than one hundred thousand fighting cavalrymen. To the south of these and as far as the harbor of the Golden Gate there were another hundred thousand troops and more. From the spot where the ruler was standing to the extremities of the palace there were another fifty thousand soldiers. The troops on the ships and at the bridge were beyond number.

The City's defenders were deployed in the following manner: The emperor and Giovanni Giustiniani were stationed at the fallen walls, outside the stockade in the enclosure, with about three thousand Latins and Romans. The grand duke was posted at the Imperial Gate with about five hundred troops. At the sea walls and along the battlements from the Xyloporta Gate to the Horaia Gate, more than five hundred crossbowmen and archers were arrayed. Making the complete circuit from the Horaia Gate to the Golden Gate there was stationed in each bastion a single archer, crossbowman, or gunner. They spent the entire night on watch with no sleep at all.

The Turks with Mehmed rushed to the walls, carrying a great number of scaling ladders which had been constructed beforehand. Behind the lines, the tyrant, brandishing an iron mace, forced his archers to the walls by using both flattery and threats. The City's defenders fought back bravely with all the strength they could muster. Giovanni and his men, supported by the emperor in arms, together with all his troops, fought back courageously.

But just as Fortune's feats of arms were about to snatch victory from Turkish hands, from the very middle of the embattled Roman troops, God removed their general, a mighty warrior of gigantic stature. He was wounded just before dawn by lead shot which went through the back of his arm, penetrating his iron breastplate which had been forged in the manner of Achilles' weapons. Unable to relieve the pain of the wound, he cried out to the emperor, "Stand your ground bravely, and I will retire to the ship to attend to my wound. Then I will quickly return." It was in that hour that the words spoken by Jeremias to the Jews were fulfilled, "Thus shall ye say to Sedekias: Thus saith the Lord God of Israel. Behold, I will turn back the weapons of war *which are in your hands,*

wherewith ye fight against the king of Babylon and the Chaldeans that have besieged you from outside the wall; and I will gather them into the midst of this city. And I will fight against you with an outstretched hand *or* with an *uplifted* arm with wrath and anger and *great irritation*. And I will smite the dwellers in this city, both men and cattle with grievous death, and they shall die. I will not spare them, and I will not have compassion upon them!"[1] When the emperor beheld Giovanni in retreat, he lost heart and so did his companions. Yet they continued the fight with all their strength.

The Turks gradually made their way to the walls, and, using their shields for cover, threw up their scaling ladders. Thwarted, however, by stone-throwers from above, they achieved nothing. Their assault, therefore, was repulsed. All the Romans with the emperor held their ground against the enemy, and all their strength and purpose were exerted to prevent the Turks from entering through the fallen walls. Unbeknown to them, however, God willed that the Turks would be brought in by another way. When they saw the sallyport, to which we referred above, open, some fifty of the tyrant's renowned slaves leaped inside. They climbed to the top of the walls and zealously slew anyone they met and struck down the sentinels who discharged missiles from above. It was a sight filled with horror! Some of the Romans and Latins who were preventing the Turks from attaching scaling ladders to the walls were cut to pieces, while others, closing their eyes, jumped from the wall and ended their lives horribly by smashing their bodies. Unimpeded, the Turks threw up the scaling ladders and ascended like soaring eagles.

The Romans and the emperor did not know what had happened because the entry of the Turks took place at a distance; indeed, their paramount concern was the enemy before them. The fierce Turkish warriors outnumbered the Romans twenty to one. The Romans, moreover, were not as experienced in warfare as the ordinary Turks. Their attention and concern, therefore, were focused on the Turkish ground attack. Then sud-

---

[1] Jeremiah 21: 3–6. Doukas's additions are in italics.

denly arrows fell from above, slaughtering many Romans. When they looked up and saw the Turks, they fled behind the walls. Unable to enter through the Gate of Charisios because of the press of the multitude, only those got through who were stronger and able to trample down the weaker. When the tyrant's troops witnessed the rout of the Romans, they shouted with one voice and pursued them inside, trampling upon the wretches and slaughtering them. When they reached the gate, they were unable to get through because it was blocked by the bodies of the dead and the dying. The majority entered through the breaches in the walls and they cut down all those they met.

The emperor, despairing and hopeless, stood with sword and shield in hand and poignantly cried out, "Is there no one among the Christians who will take my head from me?" He was abandoned and alone. Then one of the Turks wounded him by striking him flush, and he, in turn, gave the Turk a blow. A second Turk delivered a mortal blow from behind and the emperor fell to the earth. They slew him as a common soldier and left him, because they did not know he was the emperor.

Only three Turks perished and all the rest made their way inside. It was the first hour of the day [6 a.m.], and the sun had not yet risen. As they entered the City and spread out from the Gate of Charisios to the palace, they slew those who resisted and those who fled. Some two thousand fighting men were slaughtered. The Turks were apprehensive because they had estimated that within the City there must be at least fifty thousand soldiers. Consequently, they slew the two thousand. Had they known that the total number of armed troops did not exceed eight thousand men, they would not have killed any of them. This nation is a lover of money and if a patricide fell into their hands, they would release him for gold. How much truer this would be for him who had done no wrong but had instead been wronged by them. After the conflict I met many Turks who related the following to me, "Fearful of those ahead of us, we slew as many as we met. Had we known that there was such a dearth of men in the City, we would have sold them all like sheep."

Some of the Azabs, that is, the tyrant's retinue who are also called Janissaries, overran the palace. Others swarmed over the Monastery of the Great Forerunner called Petra and the Monastery of Chora in which was found the icon of my Immaculate Mother of God. O tongue and lips, how can I relate what happened there to the icon because of your sins? While the apostates were anxious to go elsewhere for more plunder, one of the infidels, extending his befouled hands, hacked the icon into four pieces with an axe. Casting lots, each received his equal share and its accompanying ornament. After they seized the monastery's precious vessels, they rode off.

Breaking into the protostrator's home, they broke open the coffers full of treasures amassed long ago. In so doing, they aroused the noblewomen from their sleep. It was the twenty-ninth day of May, and the morning sleep of the youths and maidens was sweet indeed; they slept unafraid and carefree as they had done yesterday and the day before.

Then a great horde of mounted infidels charged down the street leading to the Great Church. The actions of both Turks and Romans made quite a spectacle! In the early dawn, as the Turks poured into the City and the citizens took flight, some of the fleeing Romans managed to reach their homes and rescue their children and wives. As they moved, bloodstained, across the Forum of the Bull and passed the Column of the Cross [Forum of Constantine], their wives asked, "What is to become of us?" When they heard the fearful cry, "The Turks are slaughtering Romans within the City's walls," they did not believe it at first. They cursed and reviled the ill-omened messenger instead. But behind him came a second, and then a third, and all were covered with blood, and they knew that the cup of the Lord's wrath had touched their lips. Monks and nuns, therefore, and men and women, carrying their infants in their arms and abandoning their homes to anyone who wished to break in, ran to the Great Church. The thoroughfare, overflowing with people, was a sight to behold!

Why were they all seeking refuge in the Great Church? Many years before they had heard from some false prophets that the City was fated to be surrendered to the Turks who would enter with great force, and that the Romans would be cut down by them as far as the Column of Constantine the Great. Afterwards, however, an angel, descending and holding a sword, would deliver the empire and the sword to an unknown man, extremely plain and poor, standing at the Column. "Take this sword," the angel would say, "and avenge the people of the Lord." Then the Turks would take flight and the Romans would follow hard upon them, cutting them down. They would drive them from the City and from the West, and from the East as far as the borders of Persia, to a place called Monodendrion. Because they fully expected these prophecies to be realized, some ran and advised others to run also. This was the conviction of the Romans who long ago had contemplated what their present action would be, contending, "If we leave the Column of the Cross behind us, we will avoid future wrath." This was the cause then of the flight into the Great Church. In one hour's time that enormous temple was filled with men and women. There was a throng too many to count, above and below, in the courtyards and everywhere. They bolted the doors and waited, hoping to be rescued by the anonymous savior.

O miserable Romans! O wretches! The temple which only yesterday you called a cave and altar of heretics, and not one of you would enter so as not to be defiled because the liturgy was offered by clerics who had embraced Church Union, and now, because of the impending wrath you push your way inside, seeking to be saved. But not even the impending just wrath could move your hearts to peace. And even if, in such a calamity, an angel were to descend from heaven and say to you, "If you will accept the Union and a state of peace in the Church, I will expel the enemy from the City," even then you would not assent. And if you did assent, it would only be a lie! They who but a few days before had said, "It would be better to fall into the hands of the Turks than into the clutches of the Franks," knew this was true.

Pillaging, slaughtering, and taking captives on the way, the Turks reached the temple before the termination of the first hour. The gates were barred, but they broke them with axes. They en-

tered with swords flashing and, beholding the myriad populace, each Turk caught and bound his own captive. There was no one who resisted or who did not surrender himself like a sheep. Who can recount the calamity of that time and place? Who can describe the wailing and the cries of the babes, the mothers' tearful screams and the fathers' lamentations? The commonest Turk sought the most tender maiden. The lovely nun, who heretofore belonged only to the one God, was now seized and bound by another master. The rapine caused the tugging and pulling of braids of hair, the exposure of bosoms and breasts, and outstretched arms. The female slave was bound with her mistress, the master with his slave, the archimandrite with the doorkeeper, tender youths with virgins, who had never been exposed to the sun and hardly ever seen by their own fathers, were dragged about, forcibly pushed together and flogged. The despoiler led them to a certain spot, and placing them in safekeeping, returned to take a second and even a third prize. The abductors, the avengers of God, were in a great hurry. Within one hour they had bound everyone, the male captives with cords and the women with their own veils. The infinite chains of captives who like herds of kine and flocks of sheep poured out of the temple and the temple sanctuary made an extraordinary spectacle! They wept and wailed and there was none to show them mercy.

What became of the temple treasures? What shall I say and how shall I say it? My tongue is stuck fast in my larynx. I am unable to draw breath through my sealed mouth. In that same hour the dogs hacked the holy icons to pieces, removing the ornaments. As for the chains, candelabra, holy altar coverings, and lamps, some they destroyed and the rest they seized. All the precious and sacred vessels of the holy sacristy, fashioned from gold and silver and other valuable materials, they collected in an instant, leaving the temple desolate and naked; absolutely nothing was left behind.

*   *   *

Three days after the Fall, Mehmed released the ships so that they might sail to their own province and city. They carried so much cargo that they almost sank from the weight. What cargo did they carry? Costly apparel, silver, gold, copper and tin vessels, and books beyond number. They were filled to capacity with captives—priests and laymen, nuns and monks. The tents at the fosse were also teeming with captives and with the multifarious articles enumerated above. It was indeed spectacular to see a barbarian wearing an episcopal *sakkos*,[2] and another girded about with a golden stole and leading around dogs that were arrayed in fabrics embroidered with golden lambs instead of in coarse blankets. Others were sitting and feasting, eating a variety of fruits from the sacred patens in front of them, and drinking unwatered wine from the sacred chalices. Innumerable books were loaded onto the wagons and hauled in all directions; they were dispersed throughout East and West. For a single gold coin, ten books were sold—the works of Aristotle and Plato, books of theological content and on every subject. Gold and silver were pulled from the Evangelistaries which were adorned with many different jewels; some were sold and the rest were thrown away. All the icons were thrown to the flames and the meats they ate were roasted by the fire that was kindled.

On the fifth day Mehmed visited Galata. Ordering a census taken of all the inhabitants, he found that many of the homes had been bolted because the Latins had fled in the ships. He ordered the homes opened and an inventory taken of their belongings. He stipulated that should the owners return within a period of three months, they would be allowed to repossess their possessions, but if they failed to return, all would then be confiscated by the ruler. Afterwards, he commanded the entire army with the assistance of the outlying villages to demolish and raze the walls of Galata. Once this was accomplished they would be dismissed. His orders were executed. The land walls were overthrown but the walls along the harbor were allowed to stand.

In order to prepare enough lime to rebuild the fallen walls of the City, Mehmed ordered the lime-slakers to work the whole month of August. After five thousand families were registered from both the eastern and western provinces, Mehmed instructed them and their entire households to take up residence in the City by September on penalty of death. He next appointed his slave Sulayman *eparch*. He converted the Great Church into an altar for his God and Muhammad, but left the other churches desolate. He returned triumphant to Adrianople with innumerable captives and booty.

He departed from the City on the eighteenth day of June, taking with him in wagons and on horseback all the noblewomen and their daughters. The wife of the grand duke died en route near the village of Mesene and she was buried there. She was renowned for her charity and compassion for the indigent and for being a prudent woman who exercised restraint over the many passions of the spirit.

Mehmed's majestic triumphal entry into Adrianople was followed—and what a spectacle it was—by all the noblewomen and Christian governors and rulers streaming in and greeting him with "Hail!" With what heart and intent did their lips and mouths say this? Afraid that they might suffer the same fate as the City, they involuntarily made their submission with gifts. The tyrant was sitting on his throne, haughty and proud, boasting about the fall of the City. The Christian rulers stood there trembling and wondering what the future held in store for them.

First, he demanded of the Serb ambassador the annual payment of twelve thousand gold coins to the Turkish throne. The despots of the Peloponnesos were instructed to appear in person annually with gifts to make their obeisance and to submit the payment of ten thousand gold coins. The lord of Chios was to make an annual payment of six thousand gold coins and the lord of Mitylene three thousand gold coins annually. The emperor of Trebizond and all those who resided along the Black Sea were to come annually with gifts to make obeisance and to pay the tribute.

*   *   *

---

[2] An episcopal garment.

REVIEW QUESTIONS

1. How does Doukas explain the reason for the fall of Constantinople?
2. What signs of bias appear in Doukas's account of the Turks and Sultan Mehmed?
3. What difference did the end of the Byzantine state make to the history of the eastern Mediterranean? How does Doukas describe the immediate aftermath of Turkish occupation?

ALVISE DA MOSTO

Voyage to Africa

Alvise da Mosto (died 1483), also known as Cadamosto, was a member of a prominent family in the Venetian nobility. Alvise passed his early years as a merchant, visiting Flanders and Portugal. In 1454, he accompanied a Portuguese expedition engaged in trade and exploration south of the Sahara. The account of this voyage and another one the following year constitutes one of the earliest European descriptions of central Africa. This excerpt contains Alvise's first impressions of the empire of Mali (here called Melli), inhabited by the people he called the Azanegi (Tuaregs) and the Wolof people, a large tribe south of the Senegal River.

From *The Voyages of Cadamosto*, translated and edited by G. R. Crone (London: Hakluyt Society, 1937), pp. 20–33.

*   *   *

You should know that these people have no knowledge of any Christians except the Portuguese, against whom they have waged war for [thirteen or] fourteen years, many of them having been taken prisoners, as I have already said, and sold into slavery. It is asserted that when for the first time they saw sails, that is, ships, on the sea (which neither they nor their forefathers had ever seen before), they believed that they were great sea-birds with white wings, which were flying, and had come from some strange place: when the sails were lowered for the landing, some of them, watching from far off, thought that the ships were fishes. Others again said that they were phantoms that went by night, at which they were greatly terrified. The reason for this belief was because these caravels within a short space of time appeared at many places, where attacks were delivered, especially at night, by their crews. Thus one such assault might be separated from the next by a hundred or more miles, according to the plans of the sailors, or as the winds, blowing hither and thither, served them. Perceiving this, they said amongst themselves, "If these be human creatures, how can they travel so great a distance in one night, a distance which we could not go in three days?" Thus, as they did not understand the art of navigation, they all thought that the ships were phantoms. This I know is testified to by many Portuguese who at that time were trading in caravels on this coast, and also by those who were captured on these raids. And from this it may be judged how strange many of our ways appeared to them, if such an opinion could prevail.

Beyond the said mart of Edon [Oden], six days journey further inland, there is a place called

Tagaza, that is to say in our tongue "cargador," where a very great quantity of rock-salt is mined. Every year large caravans of camels belonging to the above mentioned Arabs and Azanaghi, leaving in many parties, carry it to Tanbutu [Timbuktu]; thence they go to Melli, the empire of the Blacks, where, so rapidly is it sold, within eight days of its arrival all is disposed of at a price of two to three hundred *mitigalli* a load, according to the quantity [a *mitigallo* is worth about a ducat]: then with the gold they return to their homes.

In this empire of Melli it is very hot, and the pasturage is very unsuitable for fourfooted animals: so that of the majority which come with the caravans no more than twenty-five out of a hundred return. There are no quadrupeds in this country, because they all die, and many also of the Arabs and Azanaghi sicken in this place and die, on account of the great heat. It is said that on horseback it is about forty days from Tagaza to Tanbutu, and thirty from Tanbutu to Melli.

I enquired of them what the merchants of Melli did with this salt, and was told that a small quantity is consumed in their country. Since it is below the meridional and on the equinoctial, where the day is constantly about as long as the night, it is extremely hot at certain seasons of the year: this causes the blood to putrefy, so that were it not for this salt, they would die. The remedy they employ is as follows: they take a small piece of the salt, mix it in a jar with a little water, and drink it every day. They say that this saves them. The remainder of this salt they carry away on a long journey in pieces as large as a man can, with a certain knack, bear on his head.

You must know that when this salt is carried to Melli by camel it goes in large pieces [as it is dug out from the mines], of a size most easily carried on camels, two pieces on each animal. Then at Melli, these Blacks break it in smaller pieces, in order to carry it on their heads, so that each man carries one piece, and thus they form a great army of men on foot, who transport it a great distance. Those who carry it have two forked sticks, one in each hand: when they are tired, they plant them in the ground, and rest their load upon them. In this way they carry it until they reach certain waters: I could not learn from them whether it is fresh or sea water, so that I do not know if it is a river or the sea, though they consider it to be the sea. [I think however it must be a river, for if it were the sea, in such a hot country there would be no lack of salt.] These Blacks are obliged to carry it in this way, because they have no camels or other beasts of burden, as these cannot live in the great heat. It may be imagined how many men are required to carry it on foot, and how many are those who consume it every year. Having reached these waters with the salt, they proceed in this fashion: all those who have the salt pile it in rows, each marking his own. Having made these piles, the whole caravan retires half a day's journey. Then there come another race of Blacks who do not wish to be seen or to speak. They arrive in large boats, from which it appears that they come from islands, and disembark. Seeing the salt, they place a quantity of gold opposite each pile, and then turn back, leaving salt and gold. When they have gone, the negroes who own the salt return: if they are satisfied with the quantity of gold, they leave the salt and retire with the gold. Then the Blacks of the gold return, and remove those piles which are without gold. By the other piles of salt they place more gold, if it pleases them, or else they leave the salt. In this way, by long and ancient custom, they carry on their trade without seeing or speaking to each other. Although it is difficult to believe this, I can testify that I have had this information from many merchants, Arab as well as Azanaghi, and also from persons in whom faith can be placed.

How the Emperor Sought to Take One of These Traders Prisoner

Reflecting upon this, I asked the merchants how it came to be that the Emperor of Melli, who, they said, was so great a lord, had not wished so to proceed as to find out by love or by other means what people these were who did not wish to speak or to be seen. They replied that, not many years previously, an Emperor of Melli determined at all costs to get one of them in his power, and having taken counsel about it, ordered some of his men to leave a few days before the salt caravan, and proceed to the place where it was customary to pile the salt, to dig trenches near by, in which to conceal themselves. When the Blacks returned to set the gold by the salt, they were to attack them and to take two or three, whom they were to convey under close guard to Melli. To be brief, this was done. They seized four, the others taking to flight: of the four they released three, surmising that one would satisfy the desires of the lord, and not wishing to anger these Blacks more. They spoke to this man in several Negro languages, but he would not reply, or speak at all, neither would he eat. He lived four days and then died. For this reason these Blacks of Melli are of the opinion, after the experience they had with him who would not speak, that they are dumb. Others think that they behave thus from disdain [of doing what their ancestors had never done]. This death vexed all the Blacks of Melli, for on account of it their lord could not achieve his intention. On returning to him they related the incident in due order.

Then the lord was very displeased with them, and asked what the Blacks looked like. They replied they were very black in colour, with well-formed bodies, a span higher than they themselves. The lower lip, more than a span in width, hung down, huge and red, over the breast, displaying the inner part glistening like blood.[1] The upper lip was as small as their own. This form of the lips displayed the gums and teeth, the latter, they said, being bigger than their own: they had two large teeth on each side, and large black eyes. Their appearance is terrifying, and the gums exude blood, as do the lips.

Because of this incident, none of the emperor's men have since been willing to embroil themselves in similar affairs, since, as a result of the capture and death of this one Negro, it was three years before the others would resume the customary exchange of gold for salt. It was thought that their lips became putrid, being in a warmer country than ours: so that these Blacks, having borne much sickness and death [for this space of time], and having no other way of obtaining the salt to cure themselves, resumed the accustomed trade. On

this account, it is our opinion, being unable to live without salt, they set off their plight against our action, just as the Emperor did not care whether these Blacks spoke or not, so long as he had the profit of the gold. This is what I understood from this incident, and since it is related by so many we can accept it. Because I have seen and understood such things in the world, I am one of those who are willing to believe this and other matters to be possible.

The gold thus brought to Melli is divided in three parts: one portion goes with the caravan which takes the road from Melli to a place that is called Cochia. This is the route which runs towards Soria [and il Cairo]: the second and third portions go with a caravan from Melli to Tanbutu. There they are separated: one portion goes to Atoet, whence it is carried to Tunis in Barbary through all the coast beyond: the other part goes to the above mentioned Hoden, whence it spreads towards Orā and Hona, towns in Barbary within the Strecto de Zibelterra, Afezes, Amarochos, Arzib, Azafi, and Amessa, towns in Barbary beyond the Straits. In these places it is bought by us Italians and other Christians from the Moors with the various merchandize we give them.

To return to my first subject, this is the best thing that is brought from the said land and country of the Azanaghi, that is, the brown men. Of that portion of the gold which is brought every year to Hoden, as described already, some quantity is carried to the sea coast, and sold to the Spaniards who are continuously stationed on the said island of Argin for the trade of merchandize, in exchange for other things.

In this land of the brown men, no money is coined, and they have never used it. Nor, formerly, was money to be found in any of their towns. Their sole method is to barter article for article, or two articles for one, and by such means they live. It is true that I understand that inland these Azanaghi, and also the Arabs in some of their districts, are wont to employ white cowries, of those small kinds which are brought to Venice from the Levant. They give certain numbers of these according to the things they have to buy. I should explain that the gold they sell they give by the

---

[1] This suggests the use of the labret, which is still worn by the Lobi women.

weight of a *mitigallo;* according to the practice in Barbary, this *mitigallo* is of the value of a ducat, more or less.

*   *   *

The Rio de Senega, Which Divides the Desert from the Fertile Land

When we had passed in sight of this Cauo Bianco, we sailed on our journey to the river called the Rio de Senega, the first river of the Land of the Blacks, which debouches on this coast. This river separates the Blacks from the brown people called Azanaghi, and also the dry and arid land, that is, the above mentioned desert, from the fertile country of the Blacks. The river is large; its mouth being over a mile wide, and quite deep. There is another mouth a little distance beyond, with an island between. Thus it enters the sea by two mouths, and before each of them about a mile out to sea are shoals and broad sand-banks. In this place the water increases and decreases every six hours, that is, with the rise and fall of the tide. The tide ascends the river more than sixty miles, according to the information I have had from Portuguese who have been [many miles] up it [in caravels]. He who wishes to enter this river must go in with the tide, on account of the shoals and banks at the mouth. From Cauo Bianco it is 380 miles to the river: all the coast is sandy to within about twenty miles of the mouth. It is called Costa de Antte rotte, and is of the Azanaghi, or brown men.

It appears to me a very marvellous thing that beyond the river all men are very black, tall and big, their bodies well formed; and the whole country green, full of trees, and fertile: while on this side, the men are brownish, small, lean, ill-nourished, and small in stature: the country sterile and arid. This river is said to be a branch of the river Nile, of the four royal rivers: it flows through all Ethiopia, watering the country as in Egypt: passing through "lo caiero," it waters all the land of Egypt. This river has many other very large branches, in addition to that of Senega, and they are great rivers on this coast of Ethiopia, of which more will be related later.

The Lords Who Rule on the Coast of Capo Verde

The country of these first Blacks of the Kingdom of Senega is at the beginning of the first Kingdom of Ethiopia. It is all low-lying country, and many people live on the banks of this river. They are called Zilofi. For a great distance beyond, it is low country, and beyond the river likewise, except for Cauo Verde, which is the highest land on all this coast, for 400 miles beyond this Cauo Verde, and for 900 miles on this side of the said cape, the whole coast is flat. [And the people who dwell along its banks are called Gilofi. And all this coast and the known country behind is all lowland as far as the river, and also beyond this river to Capo Verde. This Cape is the highest land on the whole coast, that is for four hundred miles beyond the said Cape.]

The King of Senega in my time was called Zu-chalin [Zucolin—a youth of twenty-two years. This Kingdom does not descend by inheritance] but in this land there are divers lesser lords, who [three or four of whom] through jealousy, at times agree among themselves, and set up a King of their own, if he is in truth of noble parentage. This King rules as long as is pleasing to the said lords [that is, according to the treatment they receive from him]. Frequently [they banish him by force: and as frequently] the King makes himself so powerful that he can defend himself against them. Thus his position is not stable and firm, as is that of the Soldan of Babilonia: but he is always in dread of deposition [death or exile].

You must know that this King is lord of a very poor people, and has no city in his country, but villages with huts of straw only. [They do not know how to build houses with walls:] they have no lime with which to build walls, and there is great lack of stones. This Kingdom, also, is very small; it extends no more than two hundred miles along the coast, and, from the information I had, about the same distance inland or a little more. The king lives thus: he has no fixed income [from taxes]: save that each year the lords of the country, in order to stand well with him, present him with horses, which are much esteemed owing to their scarcity, forage, beasts such as cows and goats, vegetables, millet, and the like. The King supports himself by raids, which result in many slaves from his own as well as neighbouring countries. He employs these slaves [in many ways, mainly] in cultivating the land allotted to him: but he also sells many to the Azanaghi [and Arab] merchants in return for horses and other goods, and also to Christians, since they have begun to trade with these Blacks.

The King is permitted to have as many wives as he wishes, as also are all the chiefs and men of this country, that is, as many as they can support. Thus this King has always thirty of them, though he favours one more than another, according to those from whom they are descended. This is his manner of living with his wives: he has certain villages and places, in some of which he keeps eight or ten of them. Each has a house of her own, with young servants to attend her, and slaves to cultivate the possessions and lands assigned by the lord, [with the fruits of which they are able to support themselves]. They have also a certain number of beasts, such as cows and goats, for their use; in this way his wives have the land sown and the beasts tended, and so gain a living. When the King arrives at one of these villages, he goes to the house of one of his wives, for they are obliged to provide, out of this produce, for him and those accompanying him. Every morning, at sunrise, each prepares three or four dishes of various foods, either meat, fish, or other Moorish foods according to their practice. These are sent by their slaves to be put at the disposal of their lord, so that within an hour forty or fifty dishes are assembled; when the time at which the lord wishes to eat has arrived, he picks out whatever tempts him, and gives the remainder to those in his train. But he never gives his people abundance to eat, so that they are always hungry. In this fashion he journeys from place to place without giving any thought to his victuals, and lodges sometimes with one wife, sometimes with another, so that he begets numerous sons, for when one is pregnant he leaves her alone. All the other chiefs of this country live in this same fashion.

The Customs of the Blacks, and Their Beliefs

The faith of these first Blacks is Muhammadanism: they are not however, as are the white Moors, very resolute in this faith, especially the common people. The chiefs adhere to the tenets of the Muhammadans because they have around them priests of the Azanaghi or Arabs, [who have reached this country]. These give them some instruction in the laws of Muhammad, enlarging upon the great disgrace of being rulers and yet living without any divine law, and behaving as do their people and lowly men, who live without laws; and since they have converse with none but these Azanaghi and Arab priests, they are converted to the law of Muhammad. But since they have had converse with Christians, they believe less in it, for our customs please them, and they also realise our wealth and ingenuity in everything as compared with theirs. They say that the God, who has bestowed so many benefits, has shown his great love for us, which could only be if his law were good—but that, none the less, theirs is still the law of God, through which they will find salvation, as we through ours.

These people dress thus: almost all constantly go naked, except for a goatskin fashioned in the form of drawers, with which they hide their shame. But the chiefs and those of standing wear a cotton garment—for cotton grows in these lands. Their women spin it into cloth of a span in width. They are unable to make wider cloth because they do not understand how to card it for weaving. When they wish to make a larger piece, they sew four or five of these strips together. These garments are made to reach half way down the thigh, with wide sleeves to the elbow. They also wear breeches of this cotton, which are tied across, and reach to the ankles, and are otherwise so large as to be from thirty to thirty-five, or even forty *palmi* round the top; when they are girded round the waist, they are much crumpled and form a sack in front, and the hinder part reaches to the ground, and waggles like a tail—the most comical thing to be seen in the world. They would come in these wide petticoats with these tails and ask us if we had ever seen a more beautiful dress or fashion: for they hold it for certain that they are the most beautiful garments in the world. Their women, both married and single, all go covered with girdles, below which they wear a sheet of these cotton strips bound across, half way down their legs. Men and women always go barefoot. They wear nothing on their heads: the hair of both sexes is fashioned into neat tresses arranged in various styles, though their hair by nature is no longer than a span. You must know also that the men of these lands perform many women's tasks, such as spinning, washing clothes and such things. It is always very hot there, and the further one goes inland, the greater the heat: by comparison, it is no colder in these parts in January than it is in April in our country of Italy.

Men Clean in Their Persons and Filthy in Eating

The men and women are clean in their persons, since they wash themselves all over four or five times a day: but in eating they are filthy, and ill-mannered. In matters of which they have no experience they are credulous and awkward, but in those to which they are accustomed they are the equal of our skilled men. They are talkative, and never at a loss for something to say: in general they are great liars and cheats: but on the other hand, charitable, receiving strangers willingly, and providing a night's lodging and one or two meals without any charge.

*   *   *

REVIEW QUESTIONS

1. What does da Mosto's account reveal about the earliest phases of the African slave trade?
2. His description of the silent trade is the first extended account we have of this remarkable type of barter. How plausible is this account, and what might it teach the economic historian about markets?
3. Alvise da Mosto was the first European ethnographer of the Wolof. What perspective frames his view of the Wolof? What contrasts are there in the way he described them, compared to the way William of Rubruck described the Mongols (pp. 3–9)? How do you account for these differences?

CHRISTOPHER COLUMBUS

Letter on His First Voyage

Christopher Columbus (c. 1450–1506) was born somewhere around Genoa and made his living as a sailor from an early age. Columbus saw much of the Mediterranean and Atlantic world and acquired real skill as a mapmaker and navigator. Self-taught in geography, Columbus developed an erroneous theory of the globe's size that made sailing across the Atlantic to China and Japan a daring but plausible adventure. After he had spent years looking for a patron among the rulers of Europe, Isabella of Castile took the lead (along with her husband Ferdinand of Aragon) in sponsoring Columbus's first voyage. This letter is one of his earliest accounts of this trip in 1492.

From *Selected Documents Illustrating the Four Voyages of Christopher Columbus*, translated and edited by Cecil Jane (London: Hakluyt Society, 1930), pp. 3–18.

Sir, As I know that you will be pleased at the great victory with which Our Lord has crowned my voyage, I write this to you, from which you will learn how in thirty-three days, I passed from the Canary Islands to the Indies with the fleet which the most illustrious king and queen, our sovereigns, gave to me. And there I found very many islands filled with people innumerable, and of them all I have taken possession for their highnesses, by proclamation made and with the royal standard unfurled, and no opposition was offered to me. To the first island which I found, I gave the name *San Salvador,* in emembrance of the Divine Majesty, Who has marvellously bestowed all this; the Indians call it "Guanahani." To the second, I gave the name *Isla de Santa María de Concepción;* to the third, *Fernandina;* to the fourth, *Isabella;* to the fifth, *Isla Juana,* and so to each one I gave a new name.

When I reached Juana, I followed its coast to the westward, and I found it to be so extensive that I thought that it must be the mainland, the province of Catayo. And since there were neither towns nor villages on the seashore, but only small hamlets, with the people of which I could not have speech, because they all fled immediately, I went forward on the same course, thinking that I should not fail to find great cities and towns. And, at the end of many leagues, seeing that there was no change and that the coast was bearing me northwards, which I wished to avoid, since winter was already beginning and I proposed to make from it to the south, and as moreover the wind was carrying me forward, I determined not to wait for a change in the weather and retraced my path as far as a certain harbour known to me. And from that point, I sent two men inland to learn if there were a king or great cities. They travelled three days' journey and found an infinity of small hamlets and people without number, but nothing of importance. For this reason, they returned.

I understood sufficiently from other Indians, whom I had already taken, that this land was nothing but an island. And therefore I followed its coast eastwards for one hundred and seven leagues to the point where it ended. And from that cape, I saw another island, distant eighteen leagues from the former, to the east, to which I at once gave the name "Española." And I went there and followed its northern coast, as I had in the case of Juana, to the eastward for one hundred and eighty-eight great leagues in a straight line. This island and all the others are very fertile to a limitless degree, and this island is extremely so. In it there are many harbours on the coast of the sea, beyond comparison with others which I know in Christendom, and many rivers, good and large, which is marvellous. Its lands are high, and there are in it very many sierras and very lofty mountains, beyond comparison with the island of Teneriffe. All are most beautiful, of a thousand shapes, and all are accessible and filled with trees of a thousand kinds and tall, and they seem to touch the sky. And I am told that they never lose their foliage, as I can understand, for I saw them as green and as lovely as they are in Spain in May, and some of them were flowering, some bearing fruit, and some in another stage, according to their nature. And the nightingale was singing and other birds of a thousand kinds in the month of November there where I went. There are six or eight kinds of palm, which are a wonder to behold on account of their beautiful variety, but so are the other trees and fruits and plants. In it are marvellous pine groves, and there are very large tracts of cultivatable lands, and there is honey, and there are birds of many kinds and fruits in great diversity. In the interior are mines of metals, and the population is without number. Española is a marvel.

The sierras and mountains, the plains and arable lands and pastures, are so lovely and rich for planting and sowing, for breeding cattle of every kind, for building towns and villages. The harbours of the sea here are such as cannot be believed to exist unless they have been seen, and so with the rivers, many and great, and good waters, the majority of which contain gold. In the trees and fruits and plants, there is a great difference from those of Juana. In this island, there are many spices and great mines of gold and of other metals.

The people of this island, and of all the other islands which I have found and of which I have information, all go naked, men and women, as their mothers bore them, although some women cover a single place with the leaf of a plant or with a net of cotton which they make for the purpose. They have no iron or steel or weapons, nor are they fitted to use them, not because they are not well built men and of handsome stature, but because they are very marvellously timorous. They have no other arms than weapons made of canes, cut in seeding time, to the ends of which they fix a small sharpened stick. And they do not dare to make use of these, for many times it has happened that I have sent ashore two or three men to some town to have speech, and countless people have come out to them, and as soon as they have seen my men approaching they have fled, even a father not waiting for his son. And this, not because ill has been done to anyone; on the contrary, at every point where I have been and have been able to have speech, I have given to them of all that I had, such as cloth and many other things, without receiving anything for it; but so they are, incurably timid. It is true that, after they have been reassured and have lost their fear, they are so guileless and so generous with all they possess, that no one would believe it who has not seen it. They never refuse anything which they possess, if it be asked of them; on the contrary, they invite anyone to share it, and display as much love as if they would give their hearts, and whether the thing be of value or whether it be of small price, at once with whatever trifle of whatever kind it may be that is given to them, with that they are content. I forbade that they should be given things so worthless as fragments of broken crockery and scraps of broken glass, and ends of straps, although when they were able to get them, they fancied that they possessed the best jewel in the world. So it was found that a sailor for a strap received gold to the weight of two and a half *castellanos,* and others much more for other things which were worth much less. As for new *blancas,* for them they would give everything which they had, although it might be two or three *castellanos'* weight of gold or an *arroba* or two of spun cotton. . . . They took even the pieces of the broken hoops of the wine barrels and, like savages, gave what they had, so that it seemed to me to be wrong and I forbade it. And I gave a thousand handsome good things, which I had brought, in

order that they might conceive affection, and more than that, might become Christians and be inclined to the love and service of their highnesses and of the whole Castilian nation, and strive to aid us and to give us of the things which they have in abundance and which are necessary to us. And they do not know any creed and are not idolaters; only they all believe that power and good are in the heavens, and they are very firmly convinced that I, with these ships and men, came from the heavens, and in this belief they everywhere received me, after they had overcome their fear. And this does not come because they are ignorant; on the contrary, they are of a very acute intelligence and are men who navigate all those seas, so that it is amazing how good an account they give of everything, but it is because they have never seen people clothed or ships of such a kind.

And as soon as I arrived in the Indies, in the first island which I found, I took by force some of them, in order that they might learn and give me information of that which there is in those parts, and so it was that they soon understood us, and we them, either by speech or signs, and they have been very serviceable. I still take them with me, and they are always assured that I come from Heaven, for all the intercourse which they have had with me; and they were the first to announce this wherever I went, and the others went running from house to house and to the neighbouring towns, with loud cries of, 'Come! Come to see the people from Heaven!' So all, men and women alike, when their minds were set at rest concerning us, came, so that not one, great or small, remained behind, and all brought something to eat and drink, which they gave with extraordinary affection. In all the island, they have very many canoes, like rowing *fustas,* some larger, some smaller, and some are larger than a *fusta* of eighteen benches. They are not so broad, because they are made of a single log of wood, but a *fusta* would not keep up with them in rowing, since their speed is a thing incredible. And in these they navigate among all those islands, which are innumerable, and carry their goods. One of these canoes I have seen with seventy and eighty men in her, and each one with his oar.

In all these islands, I saw no great diversity in the appearance of the people or in their manners and language. On the contrary, they all understand one another, which is a very curious thing, on account of which I hope that their highnesses will determine upon their conversion to our holy faith, towards which they are very inclined.

I have already said how I have gone one hundred and seven leagues in a straight line from west to east along the seashore of the island Juana, and as a result of that voyage, I can say that this island is larger than England and Scotland together, for, beyond these one hundred and seven leagues, there remain to the westward two provinces to which I have not gone. One of these provinces they call "Avan," and there the people are born with tails; and these provinces cannot have a length of less than fifty or sixty leagues, as I could understand from those Indians whom I have and who know all the islands.

The other, Española, has a circumference greater than all Spain, from Colibre, by the seacoast, to Fuenterabia in Vizcaya, since I voyaged along one side one hundred and eighty-eight great leagues in a straight line from west to east. It is a land to be desired and, seen, it is never to be left. And in it, although of all I have taken possession for their highnesses and all are more richly endowed than I know how, or am able, to say, and I hold them all for their highnesses, so that they may dispose of them as, and as absolutely as, of the kingdoms of Castile, in this Española, in the situation most convenient and in the best position for the mines of gold and for all intercourse as well with the mainland here as with that there, belonging to the Grand Khan, where will be great trade and gain, I have taken possession of a large town, to which I gave the name *Villa de Navidad,* and in it I have made fortifications and a fort, which now will by this time be entirely finished, and I have left in it sufficient men for such a purpose with arms and artillery and provisions for more than a year, and a *fusta,* and one, a master of all sea-craft, to build others, and great friendship with the king of that land, so much so, that he was proud to call me, and to treat me as, a

brother. And even if he were to change his attitude to one of hostility towards these men, he and his do not know what arms are and they go naked, as I have already said, and are the most timorous people that there are in the world, so that the men whom I have left there alone would suffice to destroy all that land, and the island is without danger for their persons, if they know how to govern themselves.

In all these islands, it seems to me that all men are content with one woman, and to their chief or king they give as many as twenty. It appears to me that the women work more than the men. And I have not been able to learn if they hold private property; what seemed to me to appear was that, in that which one had, all took a share, especially of eatable things.

In these islands I have so far found no human monstrosities, as many expected, but on the contrary the whole population is very well-formed, nor are they Negroes as in Guinea, but their hair is flowing, and they are not born where there is intense force in the rays of the sun; it is true that the sun has there great power, although it is distant from the equinoctial line twenty-six degrees. In these islands, where there are high mountains, the cold was severe this winter, but they endure it, being used to it and with the help of meats which they eat with many and extremely hot spices. As I have found no monsters, so I have had no report of any, except in an island "Quaris," the second at the coming into the Indies, which is inhabited by a people who are regarded in all the islands as very fierce and who eat human flesh. They have many canoes with which they range through all the islands of India and pillage and take as much as they can. They are no more malformed than the others, except that they have the custom of wearing their hair long like women, and they use bows and arrows of the same cane stems, with a small piece of wood at the end, owing to lack of iron which they do not possess. They are ferocious among these other people who are cowardly to an excessive degree, but I make no more account of them than of the rest. These are those who have intercourse with the women of "Matinino," which is the first island met on the way from Spain to the Indies, in which there is not a man. These women engage in no feminine occupation, but use bows and arrows of cane, like those already mentioned, and they arm and protect themselves with plates of copper, of which they have much.

In another island, which they assure me is larger than Española, the people have no hair. In it, there is gold incalculable, and from it and from the other islands, I bring with me Indians as evidence.

In conclusion, to speak only of that which has been accomplished on this voyage, which was so hasty, their highnesses can see that I will give them as much gold as they may need, if their highnesses will render me very slight assistance; moreover, spice and cotton, as much as their highnesses shall command; and mastic, as much as they shall order to be shipped and which, up to now, has been found only in Greece, in the island of Chios, and the Seignory sells it for what it pleases; and aloe wood, as much as they shall order to be shipped, and slaves, as many as they shall order to be shipped and who will be from the idolaters. And I believe that I have found rhubarb and cinamon, and I shall find a thousand other things of value, which the people whom I have left there will have discovered, for I have not delayed at any point, so far as the wind allowed me to sail, except in the town of Navidad, in order to leave it secured and well established, and in truth, I should have done much more, if the ships had served me, as reason demanded.

This is enough . . . and the eternal God, our Lord, Who gives to all those who walk in His way triumph over things which appear to be impossible, and this was notably one; for, although men have talked or have written of these lands, all was conjectural, without suggestion of ocular evidence, but amounted only to this, that those who heard for the most part listened and judged it to be rather a fable than as having any vestige of truth. So that, since Our Redeemer has given this victory to our most illustrious king and queen, and to

their renowned kingdoms, in so great a matter, for this all Christendom ought to feel delight and make great feasts and give solemn thanks to the Holy Trinity with many solemn prayers for the great exaltation which they shall have, in the turning of so many peoples to our holy faith, and afterwards for temporal benefits, for not only Spain but all Christians will have hence refreshment and gain.

This, in accordance with that which has been accomplished, thus briefly.

Done in the caravel, off the Canary Islands, on the fifteenth of February, in the year one thousand four hundred and ninety-three.

At your orders.   El Almirante.

After having written this, and being in the sea of Castile, there came on me so great a south-south-west wind, that I was obliged to lighten ship. But I ran here to-day into this port of Lisbon, which was the greatest marvel in the world, whence I decided to write to their highnesses. In all the Indies, I have always found weather like May; where I went in thirty-three days and I had returned in twenty-eight, save for these storms which have detained me for fourteen days, beating about in this sea. Here all the sailors say that never has there been so bad a winter nor so many ships lost.

Done on the fourth day of March.

REVIEW QUESTIONS

1. What can we learn about Columbus's personality and motives from this letter?
2. Columbus provides here the first Western account of the people he called Indians. What do we learn about his interests and abilities as an ethnographer?
3. Compare this account to those of William of Rubruck (pp. 3–9) and Alvise da Mosto (pp. 20–25). What can you conclude from their similiarities and differences?

CONQUEST OF MEXICO, FLORENTINE CODEX (C. 1555)

The Franciscan friar Bernardino de Sahagún (d. 1590) directed the team of Nahua artists who produced the Florentine Codex. This book is an account of Cortéz's expedition of 1519, which resulted in the destruction of the Aztec Empire. The story is told in Nahuatl, and is accompanied by over 100 illustrations. Scholars have debated the extent to which the text and pictures allowed the Nahua to express their own views of these events. Sahagún began collecting information in the 1540s, and this chapter may have been composed around 1555. These six pictures show characteristic battle scenes; in the last one, the native Mexicans have captured a Spanish cannon. Guns and steel certainly played a role in the Spanish conquest of Mexico. What evidence do these pictures provide of this? Perhaps even more striking were the roles of horses. What advantages did these animals provide the Spaniards? Why would indigenous artists have been involved in a project like this? What are the advantages and shortcomings of this historical source?

12   RENAISSANCE IDEALS AND REALITIES, c. 1350–1550

The Renaissance began as an Italian phenomenon, occurring between c. 1350 and 1520, that spread to the rest of Europe over the course of the 1500s and early 1600s. Its principal manifestations were the revival of classicism and naturalism in arts and literature, the rise of the modern dynastic state as the dominant political structure, and an economic crisis fueled by industrial change and economic contraction.

Until recently, scholars have traditionally viewed the Renaissance as a period of great change. Contemporaries used the term rinascita *to express their sense of a rebirth, a perfection in the arts. Some modern scholars view the period as one of fundamental change, an abrupt departure from the past, and have identified the following several characteristics that set the Renaissance apart as a discrete period of history. Scholars and artists revived classical antiquity as a subject of study and emulation. The state emerged as a work of art, that is, as a calculated design by persons in pursuit of power. The universal man, well rounded in physical and intellectual endeavors, became the political and pedagogical ideal of the age. The social mobility born of a rapidly changing economy led to an aristocracy of merit, a fusion of nobility and bourgeoisie in which achievement mattered more than lineage.*

All of these characteristics have been criticized and reviewed by latter-day historians of the Renaissance, most of whom would emphasize its continuity with the Middle Ages. Few, however, would disagree that the age was unusually self-conscious—aware of its achievements, intrigued by its potential, and impatient of its limits. The following selections capture something of this mentality.

LEON BATTISTA ALBERTI

FROM *I Libri della Famiglia*

Leon Battista Alberti (1404–1474) embodied the Renaissance universal man. Born the illegitimate son of a Florentine merchant, he was an athlete, polymath, and artist. He earned a degree in canon law at the University of Bologna in 1428 and migrated to Rome, where he entered papal service. It was there, in 1438, that he began to write On the Family. *Written in the form of a dialogue among the members of the Alberti family, gathered at the deathbed of Leon Battista's father in 1421, it examines the ideal family as a unit for the begetting and rearing of children, for the amassing and maintaining of fortunes, and for the accumulation and exercise of power. It was also a sly exercise in satire, insofar as it indirectly criticizes his brothers and uncles for violating his father's dying wish that Leon Battista be treated as a legitimate member of the family.*

From *I Libri della Famiglia*, translated by Renee New Watkins (Columbia: University of South Carolina Press, 1969).

*   *   *

XIII

Lionardo: If I had children, you may be sure I should think about them, but my thoughts would be untroubled. My first consideration would only be to make my children grow up with good character and virtue. Whatever activities suited their taste would suit me. Any activity which is not dishonest is not displeasing to an honorable mind. The activities which lead to honor and praise belong to honorable and wellborn men. Certainly I will admit that every son cannot achieve all that his father might wish. If he does something he is able to do, however, I like that better than to have him strike out in a direction where he cannot follow through. I also think it is more praiseworthy for a man, even if he does not altogether succeed, to do his best in some field rather than sit inactive, inert, and idle. There is an old saying which our ancestors often repeated: "Idleness is the mother of vice." It is an ugly and hateful thing to see a man keep himself forever useless, like that idle fellow who when they asked him why he spent all day as if condemned to sit or lie on public benches, answered "I am waiting to get fat." The man who heard him was disgusted, and asked him rather to try to fatten up a pig, since at least something useful might come of it. Thus quite correctly he showed him what an idle fellow amounts to, which is less than a pig.

I'll go further, Adovardo. However rich and noble a father may be, he should try to have his son learn, besides the noble skills, some occupation which is not degrading. By means of this occupation in case of misfortune he can live honestly by his own labor and the work of his hands. Are the vicissitudes of this world so little or so infrequent that we can ignore the possibility of adverse circumstances? Was not the son of Perseus, king of Macedonia, seen sweating and soiled in a Roman factory, employed in making his living with heavy and painful labor? If the instability of things could thus transport the son of a famous and powerful king to such depths of poverty and need, it is right for us private citizens as well as for men of higher station to provide against every misfortune. If none in our house ever had to devote himself to such laboring occupations, thank fortune for it, and let us make sure that none will have to in the future. A wise and foresightful pilot, to be able to survive in adverse storms, carries more rope, anchors, and sheets than he needs for good weather. So let the father see that his sons enjoy some praiseworthy and useful activity. In this matter let him consider first of all the honesty of the work, and then adapt his course to what he knows his son can actually accomplish, and finally try to choose a field in which, by applying himself, the young man can hope to earn a reputation.

*   *   *

Battista: Whatever you think. The only question we have is what are the things that make a family fortunate. Go on with what you have to say and we shall listen.

*   *   *

Lionardo: In our discussion we may establish four general precepts as sound and firm foundation for all the other points to be developed or added. I shall name them. In the family the number of men must not diminish but augment; possessions must not grow less, but more; all forms of disgrace are to be shunned—a good name and fine reputation is precious and worth pursuing; hatreds, enmities, rancor must be carefully avoided, while good will, numerous acquaintances, and friendships are something to look for, augment, and cultivate.

*   *   *

If a family is not to fall for these reasons into what we have described as the most unfortunate condition of decline, but is to grow, instead, in fame and in the prosperous multitude of its youth, we must persuade our young men to take wives. We must use every argument for this purpose, offer incentive, promise reward, employ all our wit, persistence, and cunning. A most appropriate reason for taking a wife may be found in what we

were saying before, about the evil of sensual indulgence, for the condemnation of such things may lead young men to desire honorable satisfactions. As other incentives, we may also speak to them of the delights of this primary and natural companionship of marriage. Children act as pledges and securities of marital love and kindness. At the same time they offer a focus for all a man's hopes and desires. Sad, indeed, is the man who has labored to get wealth and power and lands, and then has no true heir and perpetuator of his memory. No one can be more suited than a man's true and legitimate sons to gain advantages by virtue of his character, position, and authority, and to enjoy the fruits and rewards of his labor. If a man leaves such heirs, furthermore, he need not consider himself wholly dead and gone. His children keep his own position and his true image in the family. Dido, the Phoenician, when Aeneas left her, his mistress, cried out with tears, among her great sorrows no desire above this one: "Ah, had I but a small Aeneas now, to play beside me." As you were first poisoned, wretched and abandoned woman, by that man whose fatal and consuming love you did embrace, so another little Aeneas might by his similar face and gestures have offered you some consolation in your grief and anguish.

*   *   *

When, by the urging and counsel of their elders and of the whole family, young men have arrived at the point of marriage, their mothers and other female relatives and friends, who have known the virgins of the neighborhood from earliest childhood and know the way their upbringing has formed them, should select all the well-born and well-brought-up girls and present that list to the new groom-to-be. He can then choose the one who suits him best. The elders of the house and all of the family shall reject no daughter-in-law unless she is tainted with the breath of scandal or bad reputation. Aside from that, let the man who will have to satisfy her satisfy himself. He should act as do wise heads of families before they acquire some property—they like to look it over several times before they actually sign a contract. It is good in the case of any purchase and contract to inform oneself fully and to take counsel. One should consult a good number of persons and be very careful in order to avoid belated regrets. The man who has decided to marry must be still more cautious. I recommend that he examine and anticipate in every way, and consider for many days, what sort of person it is he is to live with for all his years as husband and companion. Let him be minded to marry for two purposes: first to perpetuate himself in his children, and second to have a steady and constant companion all his life. A woman is needed, therefore, who is likely to bear children and who is desirable as a perpetual mate.

* * *

To sum up this whole subject in a few words, for I want above all to be brief on this point, let a man get himself new kinsmen of better than plebeian blood, of a fortune more than diminutive, of a decent occupation, and of modest and respectable habits. Let them not be too far above himself, lest their greatness overshadow his own honor and position. Too high a family may disturb his own and his family's peace and tranquillity, and also, if one of them falls, you cannot help to support him without collapsing or wearing yourself out as you stagger under a weight too great for your arms and your strength. I also do not want the new relatives to rank too low, for while the first error puts you in a position of servitude, the second causes expense. Let them be equals, then, and, to repeat, modest and respectable people.

* * *

We have, as I said, made the house numerous and full of young people. It is essential to give them something to do now, and not let them grow lazy. Idleness is not only useless and generally despised in young men, but a positive burden and danger to the family. I do not need to teach you to shun idleness, when I know you are hard workers and active. I do encourage you to continue as

you are doing in every sort of activity and hard discipline that you may attain excellence and deserve fame. Only think this matter over and consider whether any man, even if he is not necessarily ambitious of gaining glory but merely a little shy of falling into disgrace, can ever be, in actuality or even if we merely try to imagine him, a man not heartily opposed to idleness and to mere sitting. Who has ever dreamed he might reach any grace or dignity without hard work in the noblest arts, without assiduous efforts, without plenty of sweat poured out in manly and strenuous exertions? Certainly a man who would wish for the favor of praise and fame must avoid and resist idleness and inertia just as he would do major and hateful enemies. There is nothing that leads more quickly to dishonor and disgrace than idleness. The lap of the idler has always been the nest and lair of vice. Nothing is so harmful and pestilent in public and private life as the lazy and passive citizen. From idleness springs lasciviousness; from lasciviousness comes a contempt for the law; from disobedience to law comes ruin and the destruction of the country itself. To the extent that men tolerate the first resistance of men's will to the customs and ways of the country, their spirits soon turn to arrogance, pride, and the harmful power of avarice and greed. Thieves, murderers, adulterers, and all sorts of criminals and evil men run wild.

* * *

To this I might add that man ought to give some reward to God, to satisfy him with good works in return for the wonderful gifts which He gave to the spirit of man exalting and magnifying it beyond that of all other earthly beings. Nature, that is, God, made man a composite of two parts, one celestial and divine, the other most beautiful and noble among mortal things. He provided him with a form and a body suited to every sort of movement, so as to enable him to perceive and to flee from that which threatened to harm and oppose him. He gave him speech and judgment so that he would be able to seek after and to find what he needed and could use. He gave him movement and sentiment, desire and the power of excitement, so that he might clearly appreciate and pursue useful things and shun those harmful and dangerous to him. He gave him intelligence, teachability, memory and reason, qualities divine in themselves and which enable man to investigate, to distinguish, to know what to avoid and what to desire in order best to preserve himself. To these great gifts, admirable beyond measure, God added still another power of the spirit and mind of man, namely moderation. As a curb on greed and on excessive lusts, he gave him modesty and the desire for honor. Further, God established in the human mind a strong tie to bind together human beings in society, namely justice, equity, liberality, and love. These are the means by which a man can gain the favor and praise of other men, as well as the mercy and grace of the creator. Beyond this, God filled the manly breast with powers that make man able to bear fatigue, adversity, and the hard blows of fortune. He is able to undertake what is difficult, to overcome sorrow, not even to fear death—such are his qualities of strength, of endurance and fortitude, such can be his contempt for transitory things. These are qualities which enable us to honor and serve God as fully as we should, with piety, with moderation, and with every other perfect and honorable deed. Let us agree, then, that man was not born to languish in idleness but to labor and create magnificent and great works, first for the pleasure and glory of God, and second for his own enjoyment of that life of perfect virtue and its fruit, which is happiness.

*   *   *

Let men seek their own happiness first, and they will obtain the happiness of their family also. As I have said, happiness cannot be gained without good works and just and righteous deeds. Works are just and good which not only do no harm to anyone, but which benefit many. Works are righteous if they are without a trace of the dishonorable or any element of dishonesty. The best works are those which benefit many people. Those are most virtuous, perhaps, which cannot

be pursued without strength and nobility. We must give ourselves to manly effort, then, and follow the noblest pursuits.

It seems to me, before we dedicate ourselves to any particular activity, it would be wise to think over and examine the question of what is our easiest way to reach or come near to happiness. Not every man easily attains happiness. Nature did not make all men of the same humor, or of the same intelligence or will, or equally endowed with skill and power. Rather nature planned that where I might be weak, you would make good the deficiency, and in some other way you would lack the virtue found in another. Why this? So that I should have need of you, and you of him, he of another, and some other of me. In this way one man's need for another serves as the cause and means to keep us all united in general friendship and alliance. This may, indeed, have been the source and beginning of republics. Laws may have begun thus rather than as I was saying before; fire and water alone may not have been the cause of so great a union among men as society gives them. Society is a union sustained by laws, by reason, and by custom.

Let us not digress. To decide which is the most suitable career for himself, a man must take two things into account: the first is his own intelligence, his mind and his body, everything about himself; and the second, the question requiring close consideration, is that of outside supports, the help and resources which are necessary or useful and to which he must have early access, welcome, and free right of use if he is to enter the field for which he seems more suited than for any other. Take an example: if a man wished to perform great feats of arms while he knew he was himself but a weak fellow, not very robust, incapable of bearing up through dust and storm and sun, this would not be the right profession for him to pursue. If I, being poor, longed to devote my life to letters, though I had not the money to pay the considerable expenses attached to such a career, again this would be a poor choice of career. If you are equipped with numerous relatives, plenty of friends, abundant wealth, and if you possess within yourself intelligence, eloquence, and such tact as to keep you out of any rough or awkward situations, and you decide to dedicate yourself to civic affairs, you might do extremely well.

*   *   *

We should also consider at this point how much reward and profit, how much honor and fame, you can gain from any work or achievement you undertake to perform. The only condition is that you surpass everyone else in the field. In every craft the most skilled master, as you know, gains most riches and has the best position and the greatest stature among his companions. Think how even in so humble a profession as shoemaking men search out the best among the cobblers. If it is true of the humblest occupations that the most skilled practitioners are ever most in demand and so become most famous, consider whether in the highest professions the opposite suddenly holds true. In fact you will find it still more to the point to be the best in these, or at least one of the best. If you succeed in these fields, you know that you have been given a greater portion of happiness than other men. If you are learned, you realize the misfortune of the ignorant. You know, in addition, that the unhappiest lot falls to those who, being ignorant, desire still to appear learned.

*   *   *

Consider in your own mind what a boon to know more than others and to put the knowledge to good use at the right time and place. If you think it over, I am sure you will realize that in every field a man who would appear to be valuable must be valuable in fact. Now we have stated this much: that youth should not be wasted but should be directed to some honorable kind of work, that a man should do his utmost in that work, and that he should choose the field which will be most helpful to his family and bring him most fame. A career should suit our own nature and the state of our fortunes, and should be pursued in such a way that we may never, by our own fault at least, fall short of the first rank.

Riches, however, are for nearly everyone the primary reason for working at all. They are also most useful in making it possible to persevere in our undertakings until we win approval and attain public favor, position, and fame. This is the time, therefore, to explain how wealth is acquired and how it is kept. It was also one of the four things which we said were necessary to bring about and to preserve contentment in a family. Now, then, let us begin to accumulate wealth. Perhaps the present moment, as the evening grows dark, is just right for this subject, for no occupation seems less attractive to a man of large and liberal spirit than the kind of labor by which wealth is in fact gathered. If you will count over in your imagination the actual careers that bring great profits, you will see that all basically concern themselves with buying and selling or with lending and collecting the returns. Having neither petty nor vulgar minds, I imagine you probably find these activities, which are solely directed to making a profit, somewhat below you. They seem entirely to lack honor and distinction.

*   *   *

Those who thus dismiss all mercenary activities are wrong, I believe. If the pursuit of wealth is not as glorious as are other great pursuits, yet a man is not contemptible if, being unsuited by nature to achieve anything much in other finer fields of work, he devotes himself to this kind of activity. Here, it may be, he knows he is not inadequately equipped to do well. Here everyone admits he is very useful to the republic and still more to his own family. Wealth, if it is used to help the needy, can gain a man esteem and praise. With wealth, if it is used to do great and noble things and to show a fine magnanimity and splendor, fame and dignity can be attained. In emergencies and times of need we see every day how useful is the wealth of private citizens to the country itself. From public funds alone it is not always possible to pay the wages of those whose arms and blood defend the country's liberty and dignity. Nor can republics increase their glory and their might without enormous expenditure.

*   *   *

Why have I gone on at length on these topics? Only to show you that, among occupations, there are quite a few, both honorable and highly esteemed, by means of which wealth in no small measure may be gained. One of these occupations, as you know, is that of merchant. You can easily call to mind other similar careers which are both honorable and highly profitable. You want to know, then, what they are. Let us run through them. We shall spread out all the occupations before us and choose the best among them, then we shall try to define how they make us wealthy and prosperous. Occupations that do not bring profit and gain will never make you rich. Those that bring frequent and large profits are the ones that make you rich. The only system for becoming rich, by our own industry and by the means that luck, friends, or anyone's favor can give us, is to make profits. And how do men grow poor? Ill fortune certainly plays a part, this I admit, but excluding fortune, let us speak here of industry. If riches come through profits, and these through labor, diligence, and hard work, then poverty, which is the reverse of profit, will follow from the reverse of these virtues, namely from neglect, laziness, and sloth. These are the fault neither of fortune nor of others, but of oneself. One grows poor, also, by spending too much. Prodigality dissipates wealth and throws it away. The opposite of prodigality, the opposite of neglect, are carefulness and conscientiousness, in short, good management. Good management is the means to preserve wealth. Thus we have found out that to become rich one must make profits, keep what one has gained, and exercise rational good management.

*   *   *

REVIEW QUESTIONS

1. What, according to Alberti, is the role and nature of a father?
2. How is a father's authority different from other kinds of authority?
3. What is the role of education in the formation of human nature?
4. How does this view differ from that of other authors?
5. What is Alberti's definition of honor?
6. What is its relationship to the family? Why is it so important to Alberti?
7. How might Alberti define the family?

LEONARDO DA VINCI

FROM *The Notebooks*

Leonardo da Vinci (1452–1519) was born in the countryside of Florence, the illegitimate son of a notary in the town of Vinci. He was self-taught and could read Latin only poorly. He was left-handed, a condition viewed by contemporaries as a deformity. Sometime around 1481, he moved to Milan, where his patrons were the dukes Gian Galeazzo (1476–94) and Ludovico Sforza (1494–1500). During the French invasion of 1499, Leonardo fled Milan and led a peripatetic existence until 1508, when he returned to the city. In 1513, he was taken to France, where he lived the remainder of his days. He is widely acclaimed as a genius, the designer of futuristic machines of many sorts. Among these was a device for grinding concave mirrors and lenses that made possible the invention of the telescope in 1509. He was a great artist in many media as well as a keen observer of nature. His interests ranged from aerodynamics to physics to biology to anatomy to optics. His writings on perspective are drawn from his notebooks, which he wrote backward, in a mirror hand, and in no particular order, and which were never published in his lifetime.

From *Leonardo da Vinci's Notebooks*, translated by Edward MacCurdy (London: Duckworth & Co., 1906).

*   *   *

Principle of Perspective

All things transmit their image to the eye by means of pyramids; the nearer to the eye these are intersected the smaller the image of their cause will appear.

If you should ask how you can demonstrate these points to me from experience, I should tell you, as regards the vanishing point which moves with you, to notice as you go along by lands ploughed in straight furrows, the ends of which start from the path where you are walking, you will see that continually each pair of furrows seem to approach each other and to join at their ends.

As regards the point that comes to the eye, it may be comprehended with greater ease; for if you look in the eye of anyone you will see your own image there; consequently if you suppose two lines to start from your ears and proceed to the ears of the image which you see of yourself in the eye of the other person, you will clearly recognise that these lines contract so much that when they have continued only a little way beyond your image as mirrored in the said eye they will touch one another in a point.

The thing that is nearer to the eye always appears larger than another of the same size which is more remote.

Perspective is of such a nature that it makes what is flat appear in relief, and what is in relief appear flat.

The perspective by means of which a thing is represented will be better understood when it is seen from the view-point at which it was drawn.

If you wish to represent a thing near, which should produce the effect of natural things, it is impossible for your perspective not to appear false, by reason of all the illusory appearances and errors in proportion of which the existence may be assumed in a mediocre work, unless whoever is looking at this perspective finds himself surveying it from the exact distance, elevation, angle of vision or point at which you were situated to make this perspective. Therefore it would be necessary to make a window of the size of your face or in truth a hole through which you would look at the said work. And if you should do this, then without any doubt your work will produce the effect of nature if the light and shade are correctly rendered, and you will hardly be able to convince yourself that these things are painted. Otherwise do not trouble yourself about representing anything, unless you take your view-point at a distance of at least twenty times the maximum width and height of the thing that you represent; and this will satisfy every beholder who places himself in front of the work at any angle whatever.

If you wish to see a proof of this quickly, take a piece of a staff like a small column eight times as high as its width without plinth or capital, then measure off on a flat wall forty equal spaces which are in conformity with the spaces; they will make between them forty columns similar to your small column. Then let there be set up in front of the middle of these spaces, at a distance of four braccia from the wall, a thin band of iron, in the centre of which there is a small round hole of the size of a large pearl; place a light beside this hole so as to touch it, then go and place your column above each mark of the wall and draw the outline of the shadow, then shade it and observe it through the hole in the iron.

In Vitolone there are eight hundred and five conclusions about perspective.

Perspective

No visible body can be comprehended and well judged by human eyes, except by the difference of the background where the extremities of this body terminate and are bounded, and so far as its contour lines are concerned no object will seem to be separated from this background. The moon, although far distant from the body of the sun, when by reason of eclipses it finds itself between our eyes and the sun, having the sun for its background will seem to human eyes to be joined and attached to it.

Perspective comes to aid us where judgment fails in things that diminish.

It is possible to bring about that the eye does not see distant objects as much diminished as they are in natural perspective, where they are diminished by reason of the convexity of the eye, which is obliged to intersect upon its surface the pyramids of every kind of image that approach the eye at a right angle. But the method that I show here in the margin cuts these pyramids at right angles near the surface of the pupil. But whereas the convex pupil of the eye can take in the whole of our hemisphere, this will show only a single star; but

where many small stars transmit their images to the surface of the pupil these stars are very small; here only one will be visible but it will be large; and so the moon will be greater in size and its spots more distinct. You should place close to the eye a glass filled with the water mentioned in chapter four of book 113 'Concerning Natural Things', water which causes things congealed in balls of crystalline glass to appear as though they were without glass.

Of the eye. Of bodies less than the pupil of the eye that which is nearest to it will be least discerned by this pupil—and from this experience it follows that the power of sight is not reduced to a point.

But the images of objects which meet in the pupil of the eye are spread over this pupil in the same way as they are spread about in the air; and the proof of this is pointed out to us when we look at the starry heavens without fixing our gaze more upon one star than upon another, for then the sky shows itself to us strewn with stars, and they bear to the eye the same proportions as in the sky, and the spaces between them also are the same.

Natural perspective acts in the opposite way, for the greater the distance the smaller does the thing seen appear, and the less the distance the larger it appears. But this invention constrains the beholder to stand with his eye at a small hole, and then with this small hole it will be seen well. But since many eyes come together to see at the same time one and the same work produced by this art, only one of them will have a good view of the function of this perspective and all the others will only see it confusedly. It is well therefore to shun this compound perspective, and to keep to the simple which does not purport to view planes foreshortened but as far as possible in exact form.

And of this simple perspective in which the plane intersects the pyramid that conveys the images to the eye that are at an equal distance from the visual faculty, an example is afforded us by the curve of the pupil of the eye upon which these pyramids intersect at an equal distance from the visual faculty.

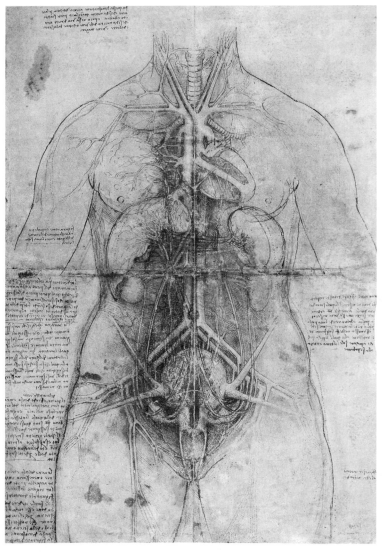

DRAWING OF A WOMAN'S TORSO   LEONARDO DA VINCI

During his period of service to the Duke of Milan, 1482–1499, Leonardo da Vinci began a wide range of scientific studies, in addition to his artistic creativity. These included reflections on geometry, mechanics and architecture, sketches for public works, advanced weapons, and fanciful inventions. He also undertook a series of anatomical studies based on the dissection of human cadavers, an illegal and immoral activity in his day. The "Drawing of a Woman's Torso" is one of the results. What does this sketch reveal about the importance of naturalism in Renaissance art? How might such studies have influenced later developments in the science of human anatomy? What new perspectives does this image cast on the so-called glorification of man during the Renaissance?

Of Equal Things the More Remote Appears Smaller

The practice of perspective is divided into two parts, of which the first treats of all the things seen by the eye at whatsoever distance, and this in itself shows all these things diminished as the eye beholds them, without the man being obliged to stand in one place rather than in another, provided that the wall does not foreshorten it a second time.

But the second practice is a combination of perspective made partly by art and partly by nature, and the work done according to its rules has no part that is not influenced by natural and accidental perspective. Natural perspective I understand has to do with the flat surface on which this perspective is represented; which surface, although it is parallel to it in length and height, is constrained to diminish the distant parts more than its near ones. And this is proved by the first of what has been said above, and its diminution is natural.

Accidental perspective, that is that which is created by art, acts in the contrary way; because it causes bodies equal in themselves to increase on the foreshortened plane, in proportion as the eye is more natural and nearer to the plane, and as the part of this plane where it is represented is more remote from the eye.

*   *   *

REVIEW QUESTIONS

1. According to Leonardo, what is the relationship between perspective in nature and perspective in the human eye?
2. What is the relationship between perspective and mathematical principles?
3. Is perspective a constant or contingent?
4. What implications does this have for painting?
5. How might it shape the enterprise of reading?

BALDESAR CASTIGLIONE

FROM *The Book of the Courtier*

Baldesar Castiglione (1478–1529) was born near Mantua and educated in Milan. He entered the service of the duke of Milan in 1496. After the duke was carried to France as a prisoner, Castiglione returned to Mantua. In 1504, he entered the court of Guidobaldo of Montefeltro, duke of Urbino, where he remained until 1524; this is the setting of The Book of the Courtier. *Although he wrote elegant verse in Latin and Italian, this reflection on courtly life was Castiglione's claim to fame. Fashioned as a discourse among courtiers and ladies of the court, it described the ideal courtier and presented the Renaissance man.*

From *The Book of the Courtier*, by Count Baldesar Castiglione, translated by Leonard Eckstein Opdycke (New York: Charles Scribner's Sons, 1903), pp. 22–23, 25–26, 59, 175–77, 247.

*   *   *

"I wish, then, that this Courtier of ours should be nobly born and of gentle race; because it is far less unseemly for one of ignoble birth to fail in worthy deeds, than for one of noble birth, who, if he strays from the path of his predecessors, stains his family name, and not only fails to achieve but loses what has been achieved already; for noble birth is like a bright lamp that manifests and makes visible good and evil deeds, and kindles and stimulates to virtue both by fear of shame and by hope of praise. And since this splendour of nobility does not illumine the deeds of the humbly born, they lack that stimulus and fear of shame, nor do they feel any obligation to advance beyond what their predecessors have done; while to the nobly born it seems a reproach not to reach at least the goal set them by their ancestors. And thus it nearly always happens that both in the profession of arms and in other worthy pursuits the most famous men have been of noble birth, because nature has implanted in everything that hidden seed which gives a certain force and quality of its own essence to all things that are derived from it, and makes them like itself: as we see not only in the breeds of horses and of other animals, but also in trees, the shoots of which nearly always resemble the trunk; and if they sometimes degenerate, it arises from poor cultivation. And so it is with men, who if rightly trained are nearly always like those from whom they spring, and often better; but if there be no one to give them proper care, they become like savages and never reach perfection.

*   *   *

"But to return to our subject: I say that there is a middle state between perfect grace on the one hand and senseless folly on the other; and those who are not thus perfectly endowed by nature, with study and toil can in great part polish and amend their natural defects. Besides his noble birth, then, I would have the Courtier favoured in this regard also, and endowed by nature not only with talent and beauty of person and feature, but with a certain grace and (as we say) air that shall make him at first sight pleasing and agreeable to all who see him; and I would have this an ornament that should dispose and unite all his actions, and in his outward aspect give promise of whatever is worthy the society and favour of every great lord." * * *

—"But to come to some details, I am of opinion that the principal and true profession of the Courtier ought to be that of arms; which I would have him follow actively above all else, and be known among others as bold and strong, and loyal to whomsoever he serves. And he will win a reputation for these good qualities by exercising them at all times and in all places, since one may never fail in this without severest censure. And just as among women, their fair fame once sullied never recovers its first lustre, so the reputation of a gentleman who bears arms, if once it be in the least tarnished with cowardice or other disgrace, remains forever infamous before the world and full of ignominy. Therefore the more our Courtier excels in this art, the more he will be worthy of praise; and yet I do not deem essential in him that perfect knowledge of things and those other qualities that befit a commander; since this would be too wide a sea, let us be content, as we have said, with perfect loyalty and unconquered courage, and that he be always seen to possess them. For the courageous are often recognized even more in small things than in great; and frequently in perils of importance and where there are many spectators, some men are to be found, who, although their hearts be dead within them, yet, moved by shame or by the presence of others, press forward almost with their eyes shut, and do their duty God knows how. While on occasions of little moment, when they think they can avoid putting themselves in danger without being detected, they are glad to keep safe. But those who, even when they do not expect to be observed or seen or recognized by anyone, show their ardour and neglect nothing, however paltry, that may be laid to their charge,— they have that strength of mind which we seek in our Courtier.

"Not that we would have him look so fierce, or go about blustering, or say that he has taken his cuirass to wife, or threaten with those grim scowls that we have often seen in Berto; because to such men as this, one might justly say that which a brave lady jestingly said in gentle company to one whom I will not name at present; who, being invited by her out of compliment to dance, refused not only that, but to listen to the music, and many other entertainments proposed to him,—saying always that such silly trifles were not his business; so that at last the lady said, 'What is your business, then?' He replied with a sour look, 'To fight.' Then the lady at once said, 'Now that you are in no war and out of fighting trim, I should think it were a good thing to have yourself well oiled, and to stow yourself with all your battle harness in a closet until you be needed, lest you grow more rusty than you are;' and so, amid much laughter from the bystanders, she left the discomfited fellow to his silly presumption.

"Therefore let the man we are seeking, be very bold, stern, and always among the first, where the enemy are to be seen; and in every other place, gentle, modest, reserved, above all things avoiding ostentation and that impudent self-praise by which men ever excite hatred and disgust in all who hear them."

*   *   *

"I would have him more than passably accomplished in letters, at least in those studies that are called the humanities, and conversant not only with the Latin language but with the Greek, for the sake of the many different things that have been admirably written therein. Let him be well versed in the poets, and not less in the orators and historians, and also proficient in writing verse and prose, especially in this vulgar tongue of ours; for besides the enjoyment he will find in it, he will by this means never lack agreeable entertainment with ladies, who are usually fond of such things. And if other occupations or want of study prevent his reaching such perfection as to render his writings worthy of great praise, let him be careful to suppress them so that others may not laugh at him, and let him show them only to a friend whom he can trust: because they will at least be of this service to him, that the exercise will enable him to judge the work of others. For it very rarely happens that a man who is not accustomed to write, however learned he may be, can ever quite appreciate the toil and industry of writers, or taste the sweetness and excellence of style, and those latent niceties that are often found in the ancients.

"Moreover these studies will also make him fluent, and as Aristippus said to the tyrant, confident and assured in speaking with everyone. Hence I would have our Courtier keep one precept fixed in mind; which is that in this and everything else he should be always on his guard, and diffident rather than forward, and that he should keep from falsely persuading himself that he knows that which he does not know. * * *

Then my lady Duchess said:

"Do not wander from your subject, my lord Magnifico, but hold to the order given you and describe the Court Lady, to the end that so noble a Lady as this may have someone competent to serve her worthily."

The Magnifico continued:

"Then, my Lady, to show that your commands have power to induce me to essay even that which I know not how to do, I will speak of this excellent Lady as I would have her; and when I have fashioned her to my liking, not being able then to have another such, like Pygmalion I will take her for my own.

"And although my lord Gaspar has said that the same rules which are set the Courtier, serve also for the Lady, I am of another mind; for while some qualities are common to both and as necessary to man as to woman, there are nevertheless some others that befit woman more than man, and some are befitting man to which she ought to be wholly a stranger. The same I say of bodily exercises; but above all, methinks that in her ways, manners, words, gestures and bearing, a woman ought to be very unlike a man; for just as it befits him to show a certain stout and sturdy manliness, so it is becoming in a woman to have a soft and dainty tenderness with an air of womanly sweetness in her every movement, which, in her going or staying or saying what you will, shall always make her seem the woman, without any likeness of a man.

"Now, if this precept be added to the rules that these gentlemen have taught the Courtier, I certainly think she ought to be able to profit by many of them, and to adorn herself with admirable accomplishments, as my lord Gaspar says. For I believe that many faculties of the mind are as necessary to woman as to man; likewise gentle birth, to avoid affectation, to be naturally graceful in all her doings, to be mannerly, clever, prudent, not arrogant, not envious, not slanderous, not vain, not quarrelsome, not silly, to know how to win and keep the favour of her mistress and of all others, to practise well and gracefully the exercises that befit women. I am quite of the opinion, too, that beauty is more necessary to her than to the Courtier, for in truth that woman lacks much who lacks beauty. Then, too, she ought to be more circumspect and take greater care not to give occasion for evil being said of her, and so to act that she may not only escape a stain of guilt but even of suspicion, for a woman has not so many ways of defending herself against false imputations as has a man.

"But as Count Ludovico has explained very minutely the chief profession of the Courtier, and has insisted it be that of arms, methinks it is also fitting to tell what in my judgment is that of the Court Lady: and when I have done this, I shall think myself quit of the greater part of my duty.

"Laying aside, then, those faculties of the mind that she ought to have in common with the Courtier (such as prudence, magnanimity, continence, and many others), and likewise those qualities that befit all women (such as kindness, discretion, ability to manage her husband's property and her house and children if she be married, and all those capacities that are requisite in a good housewife), I say that in a lady who lives at court methinks above all else a certain pleasant affability is befitting, whereby she may be able to entertain politely every sort of man with agreeable and seemly converse, suited to the time and place, and to the rank of the person with whom she may speak, uniting with calm and modest manners, and with that seemliness which should ever dispose all her actions, a quick vivacity of spirit whereby she

may show herself alien to all indelicacy; but with such a kindly manner as shall make us think her no less chaste, prudent and benign, than agreeable, witty and discreet; and so she must preserve a certain mean (difficult and composed almost of contraries), and must barely touch certain limits but not pass them.

"Thus, in her wish to be thought good and pure, the Lady ought not to be so coy and seem so to abhor company and talk that are a little free, as to take her leave as soon as she finds herself therein; for it might easily be thought that she was pretending to be thus austere in order to hide something about herself which she feared others might come to know; and such prudish manners are always odious. Nor ought she, on the other hand, for the sake of showing herself free and agreeable, to utter unseemly words or practise a certain wild and unbridled familiarity and ways likely to make that believed of her which perhaps is not true; but when she is present at such talk, she ought to listen with a little blush and shame.

"Likewise she ought to avoid an errour into which I have seen many women fall, which is that of saying and of willingly listening to evil about other women. For those women who, on hearing the unseemly ways of other women described, grow angry thereat and seem to disbelieve it and to regard it almost monstrous that a woman should be immodest,—they, by accounting the offence so heinous, give reason to think that they do not commit it. But those who go about continually prying into other women's intrigues, and narrate them so minutely and with such zest, seem to be envious of them and to wish that everyone may know it, to the end that like matters may not be reckoned as a fault in their own case; and thus they fall into certain laughs and ways that show they then feel greatest pleasure. And hence it comes that men, while seeming to listen gladly, usually hold such women in small respect and have very little regard for them, and think these ways of theirs are an invitation to advance farther, and thus often go such lengths with them as bring them deserved reproach, and finally esteem them so lightly as to despise their company and even find them tedious.

"And on the other hand, there is no man so shameless and insolent as not to have reverence for those women who are esteemed good and virtuous; because this gravity (tempered with wisdom and goodness) is as it were a shield against the insolence and coarseness of the presumptuous. Thus we see that a word or laugh or act of kindness (however small it be) from a virtuous woman is more prized by everyone, than all the endearments and caresses of those who show their lack of shame so openly; and if they are not immodest, by their unseemly laughter, their loquacity, insolence and like scurrile manners, they give sign of being so. ⋆ ⋆ ⋆

"I think then that the aim of the perfect Courtier, which has not been spoken of till now, is so to win for himself, by means of the accomplishments ascribed to him by these gentlemen, the favour and mind of the prince whom he serves, that he may be able to say, and always shall say, the truth about everything which it is fitting for the prince to know, without fear or risk of giving offence thereby; and that when he sees his prince's mind inclined to do something wrong, he may be quick to oppose, and gently to make use of the favour acquired by his good accomplishments, so as to banish every bad intent and lead his prince into the path of virtue. And thus, possessing the goodness which these gentlemen have described, together with readiness of wit and pleasantness, and shrewdness and knowledge of letters and many other things,—the Courtier will in every case be able deftly to show the prince how much honour and profit accrue to him and his from justice, liberality, magnanimity, gentleness, and the other virtues that become a good prince; and on the other hand how much infamy and loss proceed from the vices opposed to them. Therefore I think that just as music, festivals, games, and the other pleasant accomplishments are as it were the flower, in like manner to lead or help one's prince towards right, and to frighten him from wrong, are the true fruit of Courtiership.

"And since the merit of well-doing lies chiefly in two things, one of which is the choice of an end for our intentions that shall be truly good, and the other ability to find means suitable and fitting to conduce to that good end marked out,—certain it is that that man's mind tends to the best end, who purposes to see to it that his prince shall be deceived by no one, shall hearken not to flatterers or to slanderers and liars, and shall distinguish good and evil, and love the one and hate the other.

⋆   ⋆   ⋆

REVIEW QUESTIONS

1. What does Castiglione mean by "grace"? How is it created?
2. To what extent is grace the product of birth or nature?
3. How is grace gendered?
4. What does a courtier's conduct tell others about his status?
5. If status was once thought to reside in one's birth and lineage, how does the courtier alter that notion?
6. How does Castiglione's courtier differ from a medieval monk or knight?
7. Is the courtier's virtue the expression of his nature, cultivation, or education?

PORTRAIT OF POPE LEO X AND TWO CARDINALS (1518)   RAPHAEL

This intriguing portrait of Pope Leo X and two of his cardinals, relatives elevated through acts of nepotism, reveals the full sophistication of Raphael's artistry. He created an attractive painting of his patron in full papal regalia. At the same time, he subtly included less attractive hints about the subject's office and character. What might this portrait tell us of Leo's character? What does the portrait tell us about Renaissance values? Is Raphael exercising a subtle criticism of the church through his portrait of its head? If so, what elements of his criticism are explicit in the painting?

GIOVANNI PICO DELLA MIRANDOLA

FROM "Oration on the Dignity of Man"

Giovanni Pico della Mirandola (1463–1494) is a singular figure in the history of Renaissance humanism. Although the corpus of his published works remained small as a result of his early death, the breadth of his learning won him the admiration of scholars past and present. He received a thorough classical education in Greek and Latin, and studied the scholastic tradition of the Middle Ages as well as Jewish and Arabic philosophy. His conception of the dignity of man and harmony among philosophers found expression in his "Oration on the Dignity of Man." In 1486, Pico published his 900 theses, inviting all scholars to a public debate in January 1487. Before it could take place, however, Pope Innocent VIII appointed a commission to examine the theses, some of which were found to be heretical. An attempt to defend the incriminated points plunged Pico into a conflict with ecclesiastical authorities that lasted several years. The oration, never published in its author's lifetime, was written as an introductory speech for the disputation.

From *Reflections on the Philosophy of the History of Mankind*, by J. G. Herder and F. E. Manuel (Chicago: University of Chicago Press, 1968).

I have read in the records of the Arabians, reverend Fathers, that Abdala the Saracen, when questioned as to what on this stage of the world, as it were, could be seen most worthy of wonder, replied: "There is nothing to be seen more wonderful than man." In agreement with this opinion is the saying of Hermes Trismegistus: "A great miracle, Asclepius, is man." But when I weighed the reason for these maxims, the many grounds for the excellence of human nature reported by many men failed to satisfy me—that man is the intermediary between creatures, the intimate of the gods, the king of the lower beings, by the acuteness of his senses, by the discernment of his reason, and by the light of his intelligence the interpreter of nature, the interval between fixed eternity and fleeting time, and (as the Persians say) the bond, nay, rather, the marriage song of the world, on David's testimony but little lower than the angels. Admittedly great though these reasons be, they are not the principal grounds, that is, those which may rightfully claim for themselves the privilege of the highest admiration. For why should we not admire more the angels themselves and the blessed choirs of heaven? At last it seems to me I have come to understand why man is the most fortunate of creatures and consequently worthy of all admiration and what precisely is that rank which is his lot in the universal chain of Being—a rank to be envied not only by brutes but even by the stars and by minds beyond this world. It is a matter past faith and a wondrous one. Why should it not be? For it is on this very account that man is rightly called and judged a great miracle and a wonderful creature indeed.

But hear, Fathers, exactly what this rank is and, as friendly auditors, conformably to your kindness, do me this favor. God the Father, the supreme Architect, had already built this cosmic home we behold, the most sacred temple of His godhead, by the laws of His mysterious wisdom. The region above the heavens He had adorned with

Intelligences, the heavenly spheres He had quickened with eternal souls, and the excrementary and filthy parts of the lower world He had filled with a multitude of animals of every kind. But, when the work was finished, the Craftsman kept wishing that there were someone to ponder the plan of so great a work, to love its beauty, and to wonder at its vastness. Therefore, when everything was done (as Moses and Timaeus bear witness), He finally took thought concerning the creation of man. But there was not among His archetypes that from which He could fashion a new offspring, nor was there in His treasure-houses anything which He might bestow on His new son as an inheritance, nor was there in the seats of all the world a place where the latter might sit to contemplate the universe. All was now complete; all things had been assigned to the highest, the middle, and the lowest orders. But in its final creation it was not the part of the Father's power to fail as though exhausted. It was not the part of His wisdom to waver in a needful matter through poverty of counsel. It was not the part of His kindly love that he who was to praise God's divine generosity in regard to others should be compelled to condemn it in regard to himself.

At last the best of artisans ordained that that creature to whom He had been able to give nothing proper to himself should have joint possession of whatever had been peculiar to each of the different kinds of being. He therefore took man as a creature of indeterminate nature and, assigning him a place in the middle of the world, addressed him thus: "Neither a fixed abode nor a form that is thine alone nor any function peculiar to thyself have we given thee, Adam, to the end that according to thy longing and according to thy judgment thou mayest have and possess what abode, what form, and what functions thou thyself shalt desire. The nature of all other beings is limited and constrained within the bounds of laws prescribed by Us. Thou, constrained by no limits, in accordance with thine own free will, in whose hand We have placed thee, shalt ordain for thyself the limits of thy nature. We have set thee at the world's center that thou mayest from thence more easily observe whatever is in the world. We have made thee neither of heaven nor of earth, neither mortal nor immortal, so that with freedom of choice and with honor, as though the maker and molder of thyself, thou mayest fashion thyself in whatever shape thou shalt prefer. Thou shalt have the power to degenerate into the lower forms of life, which are brutish. Thou shalt have the power, out of thy soul's judgment, to be reborn into the higher forms, which are divine."

O supreme generosity of God the Father, O highest and most marvelous felicity of man! To him it is granted to have whatever he chooses, to be whatever he wills. Beasts as soon as they are born (so says Lucilius) bring with them from their mother's womb all they will ever possess. Spiritual beings, either from the beginning or soon thereafter, become what they are to be for ever and ever. On man when he came into life the Father conferred the seeds of all kinds and the germs of every way of life. Whatever seeds each man cultivates will grow to maturity and bear in him their own fruit. If they be vegetative, he will be like a plant. If sensitive, he will become brutish. If rational, he will grow into a heavenly being. If intellectual, he will be an angel and the son of God. And if, happy in the lot of no created thing, he withdraws into the center of his own unity, his spirit, made one with God, in the solitary darkness of God, who is set above all things, shall surpass them all. Who would not admire this our chameleon? Or who could more greatly admire aught else whatever? It is man who Asclepius of Athens, arguing from his mutability of character and from his self-transforming nature, on just grounds says was symbolized by Proteus in the mysteries. Hence those metamorphoses renowned among the Hebrews and the Pythagoreans.

*   *   *

REVIEW QUESTIONS

1. How does Pico reorder the hierarchy of creation?

2. What does he claim for human nature that sets it apart?
3. How does Pico conceive of human will?
4. What implications does that conception have?

5. What is Pico's understanding of the relationship of humankind to God?
6. What are its implications?

NICCOLÒ MACHIAVELLI

FROM *The Prince*

Niccolò Machiavelli (1469–1527) was the son of a Florentine lawyer. Little is known of him until 1498, when he entered the service of the Florentine Republic of Pier Soderini as secretary to the second chancery, a minor bureaucratic post he held for fourteen years. From this position, Machiavelli observed the political process of his day. A staunch republican, he lost his position in government in 1512, when Soderini's republic was toppled and the Medici of Florence were restored to power by a papal army. He spent the rest of his days in retirement, possibly trying to restore himself to the graces of the Medici and the pope, but certainly engaged in the scholarly and literary pursuits that would establish his reputation as a political analyst. Among the fruits of these labors was The Prince, *written in 1513. Of the many observations and ideas expressed in this short work, two at least became fundamental truths of modern politics. One was the necessity of national unity based on a common language, culture, and economy. The other was the preservation of national unity through the concentration and exercise of power by the state. As controversial as they were prescient in Machiavelli's day, these ideas encouraged later scholars to number him among the first modern students of politics.*

From *The Prince*, by Niccolò Machiavelli, translated by Robert M. Adams, A Norton Critical Edition, 2d ed. (New York: Norton, 1977), pp. 31–32, 44–50.

How to Measure the Strength of Any Prince's State

There is one other consideration to bear in mind regarding these civil principates; that is, whether a prince is strong enough to stand on his own feet in case of need, or whether he is in constant need of help from others. And to make the matter clearer, let me say that in my opinion princes control their own destiny when they command enough money or men to assemble an adequate army and make a stand against anyone who attacks them. I think princes who need outside protection are those who can't take the field against their foes, but have to hide behind their walls and defend themselves there. I've already mentioned the first class, and will save whatever else I have to say about them till later. As for the others, all I can say is that they should keep their cities well fortified and well supplied, and pay no heed to the surrounding countryside. Whenever a man has fortified his city strongly, and has dealt with his subjects as I described above and will describe further below, people will be slow to attack him; men are always wary of tasks that seem hard, and it can't seem easy to attack a prince whose city is in fine fettle, and whose people do not hate him.

*   *   *

Thus a prince who has a strong city and does not earn his people's hatred cannot be attacked, or if he were, that attacker would be driven off to his own disgrace; because the way things keep changing in this world, it's almost impossible for a prince with his armies to devote an entire year to a siege while doing nothing else. Maybe someone will object: when the people see their possessions outside the walls being burnt up, they will get impatient; a long siege and their own self-interest will make them forget the prince. But to this I answer that a brave, strong prince will overcome all these problems, giving his subjects hope at one minute that the storm will soon pass, stirring them up at another moment to fear the enemy's cruelty, and on still other occasions restraining those who seem too rash. Besides, the enemy will generally do his burning and ravishing of the countryside as soon as he begins the siege, when men's minds are still passionate and earnest for the defense; thus the prince has less reason to worry, because, after a few days, when tempers have cooled, the harm will already have been done, the losses inflicted, and there will clearly be no cure. At that point, the people will rally even more strongly behind their prince, because they will feel he owes them something, since their houses were burnt and their fields ravaged in defense of his cause. Indeed, men are so constructed that they feel themselves committed as much by the benefits they grant as by those they receive. Hence, all things considered, it should not be hard for a prudent prince to keep his subjects in good

spirits throughout a siege, as long as he does not run short of food or weapons.

*   *   *

On the Reasons Why Men Are Praised or Blamed—Especially Princes

It remains now to be seen what style and principles a prince ought to adopt in dealing with his subjects and friends. I know the subject has been treated frequently before, and I'm afraid people will think me rash for trying to do so again, especially since I intend to differ in this discussion from what others have said. But since I intend to write something useful to an understanding reader, it seemed better to go after the real truth of the matter than to repeat what people have imagined. A great many men have imagined states and princedoms such as nobody ever saw or knew in the real world, for there's such a difference between the way we really live and the way we ought to live that the man who neglects the real to study the ideal will learn how to accomplish his ruin, not his salvation. Any man who tries to be good all the time is bound to come to ruin among the great number who are not good. Hence a prince who wants to keep his post must learn how not to be good, and use that knowledge, or refrain from using it, as necessity requires.

Putting aside, then, all the imaginary things that are said about princes, and getting down to the truth, let me say that whenever men are discussed (and especially princes because they are prominent), there are certain qualities that bring them either praise or blame. Thus some are considered generous, others stingy (I use a Tuscan term, since "greedy" in our speech means a man who wants to take other people's goods; we call a man "stingy" who clings to his own); some are givers, others grabbers; some cruel, others merciful; one man is treacherous, another faithful; one is feeble and effeminate, another fierce and spirited; one humane, another proud; one lustful, another chaste; one straightforward, another sly; one harsh, another gentle; one serious, another playful; one religious, another skeptical, and so on. I know everyone will agree that among these many qualities a prince certainly ought to have all those that are considered good. But since it is impossible to have and exercise them all, because the conditions of human life simply do not allow it, a prince must be shrewd enough to avoid the public disgrace of those vices that would lose him his state. If he possibly can, he should also guard against vices that will not lose him his state; but if he cannot prevent them, he should not be too worried about indulging them. And furthermore, he should not be too worried about incurring blame for any vice without which he would find it hard to save his state. For if you look at matters carefully, you will see that something resembling virtue, if you follow it, may be your ruin, while something else resembling vice will lead, if you follow it, to your security and well-being.

On Liberality and Stinginess

Let me begin, then, with the first of the qualities mentioned above, by saying that a reputation for liberality is doubtless very fine; but the generosity that earns you that reputation can do you great harm. For if you exercise your generosity in a really virtuous way, as you should, nobody will know of it, and you cannot escape the odium of the opposite vice. Hence if you wish to be widely known as a generous man, you must seize every opportunity to make a big display of your giving. A prince of this character is bound to use up his entire revenue in works of ostentation. Thus, in the end, if he wants to keep a name for generosity, he will have to load his people with exorbitant taxes and squeeze money out of them in every way he can. This is the first step in making him odious to his subjects; for when he is poor, nobody will respect him. Then, when his generosity has angered many and brought rewards to a few, the slightest difficulty will trouble him, and at the first approach of danger, down he goes. If by chance he foresees this, and tries to change his ways, he will immediately be labelled a miser.

Since a prince cannot use this virtue [*virtù*] of liberality in such a way as to become known for it unless he harms his own security, he won't mind, if he judges prudently of things, being known as a miser. In due course he will be thought the more liberal man, when people see that his parsimony enables him to live on his income, to defend himself against his enemies, and to undertake major projects without burdening his people with taxes. Thus he will be acting liberally toward all those people from whom he takes nothing (and there are an immense number of them), and in a stingy way toward those people on whom he bestows nothing (and they are very few). In our times, we have seen great things being accomplished only by men who have had the name of misers; all the others have gone under. Pope Julius II, though he used his reputation as a generous man to gain the papacy, sacrificed it in order to be able to make war; the present king of France has waged many wars without levying a single extra tax on his people, simply because he could take care of the extra expenses out of the savings from his long parsimony. If the present king of Spain had a reputation for generosity, he would never have been able to undertake so many campaigns, or win so many of them.

*   *   *

On Cruelty and Clemency: Whether It Is Better to Be Loved or Feared

Continuing now with our list of qualities, let me say that every prince should prefer to be considered merciful rather than cruel, yet he should be careful not to mismanage this clemency of his. People thought Cesare Borgia was cruel, but that cruelty of his reorganized the Romagna, united it, and established it in peace and loyalty. Anyone who views the matter realistically will see that this prince was much more merciful than the people of Florence, who, to avoid the reputation of cruelty, allowed Pistoia to be destroyed. Thus, no prince should mind being called cruel for what he does to keep his subjects united and loyal; he may make examples of a very few, but he will be more merciful in reality than those who, in their tenderheartedness, allow disorders to occur, with their attendant murders and lootings. Such turbulence brings harm to an entire community, while the executions ordered by a prince affect only one individual at a time. A new prince, above all others, cannot possibly avoid a name for cruelty, since new states are always in danger. And Virgil, speaking through the mouth of Dido, says:

> Res dura et regni novitas me talia cogunt
> Moliri, et late fines custode tueri.[1]

Yet a prince should be slow to believe rumors and to commit himself to action on the basis of them. He should not be afraid of his own thoughts; he ought to proceed cautiously, moderating his conduct with prudence and humanity, allowing neither overconfidence to make him careless, nor overtimidity to make him intolerable.

Here the question arises: is it better to be loved than feared, or vice versa? I don't doubt that every prince would like to be both; but since it is hard to accommodate these qualities, if you have to make a choice, to be feared is much safer than to be loved. For it is a good general rule about men, that they are ungrateful, fickle, liars and deceivers, fearful of danger and greedy for gain. While you serve their welfare, they are all yours, offering their blood, their belongings, their lives, and their children's lives, as we noted above—so long as the danger is remote. But when the danger is close at hand, they turn against you. Then, any prince who has relied on their words and has made no other preparations will come to grief; because friendships that are bought at a price, and not with greatness and nobility of soul, may be paid for but they are not acquired, and they cannot be used in time of need. People are less concerned with offending a man who makes himself loved than one

who makes himself feared: the reason is that love is a link of obligation which men, because they are rotten, will break any time they think doing so serves their advantage; but fear involves dread of punishment, from which they can never escape.

Still, a prince should make himself feared in such a way that, even if he gets no love, he gets no hate either; because it is perfectly possible to be feared and not hated, and this will be the result if only the prince will keep his hands off the property of his subjects or citizens, and off their women. When he does have to shed blood, he should be sure to have a strong justification and manifest cause; but above all, he should not confiscate people's property, because men are quicker to forget the death of a father than the loss of a patrimony. Besides, pretexts for confiscation are always plentiful; it never fails that a prince who starts living by plunder can find reasons to rob someone else. Excuses for proceeding against someone's life are much rarer and more quickly exhausted.

*   *   *

Returning to the question of being feared or loved, I conclude that since men love at their own inclination but can be made to fear at the inclination of the prince, a shrewd prince will lay his foundations on what is under his own control, not on what is controlled by others. He should simply take pains not to be hated, as I said.

The Way Princes Should Keep Their Word

How praiseworthy it is for a prince to keep his word and live with integrity rather than by craftiness, everyone understands; yet we see from recent experience that those princes have accomplished most who paid little heed to keeping their promises, but who knew how craftily to manipulate the minds of men. In the end, they won out over those who tried to act honestly.

You should consider then, that there are two

---

[1] "Severe pressures and the newness of the regime compel me to these measures. I must maintain the borders against foreign enemies."

ways of fighting, one with laws and the other with force. The first is properly a human method, the second belongs to beasts. But as the first method does not always suffice, you sometimes have to turn to the second. Thus a prince must know how to make good use of both the beast and the man. Ancient writers made subtle note of this fact when they wrote that Achilles and many other princes of antiquity were sent to be reared by Chiron the centaur, who trained them in his discipline. Having a teacher who is half man and half beast can only mean that a prince must know how to use both these two natures, and that one without the other has no lasting effect.

Since a prince must know how to use the character of beasts, he should pick for imitation the fox and the lion. As the lion cannot protect himself from traps, and the fox cannot defend himself from wolves, you have to be a fox in order to be wary of traps, and a lion to overawe the wolves. Those who try to live by the lion alone are badly mistaken. Thus a prudent prince cannot and should not keep his word when to do so would go against his interest, or when the reasons that made him pledge it no longer apply. Doubtless if all men were good, this rule would be bad; but since they are a sad lot, and keep no faith with you, you in your turn are under no obligation to keep it with them.

*   *   *

REVIEW QUESTIONS

1. What, according to Machiavelli, is the basis of political authority?
2. How does his theory differ from others of his day?
3. When he claims that a prince must assume many guises, what is Machiavelli saying about his understanding of human nature?
4. What is the role of artifice in political authority?
5. What might Machiavelli's prince have in common with Castiglione's courtier?

DESIDERIUS ERASMUS OF ROTTERDAM

FROM *Ten Colloquies*

Desiderius Erasmus of Rotterdam (1476–1536) was one of the greatest scholars of his day, measured in terms of his writings and their influence. Educated at Deventer in the Netherlands and in Paris, he began his career as an editor, translator, and popularizer of classical texts. In the humanistic tradition, he used classical tropes as models for his own society, a practice that made him not only a great scholar but also a great satirist. His chief intellectual commitment, however, was the renewal of Christian piety through the study of Christian literature, the Bible and church fathers above all. In this context he is often viewed as the great exponent of Christian humanism, the northern European variant of classical Italian humanism. His translation of the Bible inspired the biblical scholarship of sixteenth-century reformers. His editions of patristic sources remain authoritative to this day. His Ten

> Colloquies *were written as popular texts to inculcate elegant Latin and to inspire Christian conduct.*

From *Ten Colloquies*, by Desiderius Erasmus, translated by Craig R. Thompson (Upper Saddle River, N.J.: Prentice Hall, 1986).

"Cyclops, or the Gospel Bearer"

CANNIUS: What's Polyphemus hunting here?

POLYPHEMUS: What could I be hunting without dogs or spear? Is that your question?

CANNIUS: Some wood nymph, perhaps.

POLYPHEMUS: A good guess. Look, here's my hunting net.

CANNIUS: What a sight! Bacchus in a lion's skin —Polyphemus with a book—a cat in a saffron gown!

POLYPHEMUS: I've painted this little book not only in saffron but bright red and blue, too.

CANNIUS: I'm not talking about saffron; I said something in Greek. Seems to be a soldierly book, for it's protected by bosses, plates, and brass clasps.

POLYPHEMUS: Take a good look at it.

CANNIUS: I'm looking. Very fine, but you haven't yet decorated it enough.

POLYPHEMUS: What's lacking?

CANNIUS: You should have added your coat of arms.

POLYPHEMUS: What coat of arms?

CANNIUS: The head of Silenus peering out of a wine jug. But what's the book about? The art of drinking?

POLYPHEMUS: Be careful you don't blurt out blasphemy.

CANNIUS: What, you don't mean it's something sacred?

POLYPHEMUS: The most sacred of all, the Gospels.

CANNIUS: By Hercules! What has Polyphemus to do with the Gospels?

POLYPHEMUS: You might as well ask what a Christian has to do with Christ.

CANNIUS: I'm not sure a halberd isn't more fitting for the likes of you. If I were at sea and met a stranger who looked like this, I'd take him for a pirate; if I met him in a wood, for a bandit.

POLYPHEMUS: Yet this very Gospel teaches us not to judge a man by appearances. Just as a haughty spirit often lurks under an ash-colored cowl, so a cropped head, curled beard, stern brow, wild eyes, plumed cap, military cloak, and slashed breeches sometimes cover a true Christian heart.

CANNIUS: Of course. Sometimes a sheep lurks in wolf's clothing, too. And if you trust fables, an ass in a lion's skin.

POLYPHEMUS: What's more, I know a man who has a sheep's head and a fox's heart. I could wish him friends as fair as his eyes are dark, and a character as shining as his complexion.

CANNIUS: If a man with a sheepskin cap has a sheep's head, what a load *you* carry, with both a sheep and an ostrich on your head. And isn't it rather ridiculous to have a bird on your head and an ass in your heart?

POLYPHEMUS: That hurt!

CANNIUS: But it would be well if, as you've decorated the Gospels with various ornaments, the Gospels in turn adorned you. You've decorated them with colors; I wish they might embellish you with good morals.

POLYPHEMUS: I'll take care of that.

CANNIUS: After your fashion, yes.

POLYPHEMUS: But insults aside, you don't condemn those who carry a volume of the Gospels about, do you?

CANNIUS: I'd be the last person in the world to do that.

POLYPHEMUS: What? I seem to you the least person in the world, when I'm taller than you by an ass's head?

CANNIUS: I don't believe you'd be that much taller even if the ass pricked up its ears.

POLYPHEMUS: Certainly by a buffalo's.

CANNIUS: I like the comparison. But I said "last"; I wasn't calling you "least."

POLYPHEMUS: What's the difference between an egg and an egg?

CANNIUS: What's the difference between middle finger and little finger?

POLYPHEMUS: The middle one's longer.

CANNIUS: Very good! What's the difference between ass ears and wolf ears?

POLYPHEMUS: Wolf ears are shorter.

CANNIUS: That's right.

POLYPHEMUS: But I'm in the habit of measuring long and short by span and ell, not by ears.

CANNIUS: Well, the man who carried Christ was called Christopher. You, who carry the Gospels, ought to be called Gospel-bearer instead of Polyphemus.

POLYPHEMUS: Don't you think it's holy to carry the Gospels?

CANNIUS: No—unless you'd agree that asses are mighty holy.

POLYPHEMUS: How so?

CANNIUS: Because one of them can carry three thousand books of this kind. I should think you'd be equal to that load if fitted with the right packsaddle.

POLYPHEMUS: There's nothing farfetched in thus crediting an ass with holiness because he carried Christ.

CANNIUS: I don't envy you that holiness. And if you like, I'll give you relics of the ass that carried Christ, so you can kiss them.

POLYPHEMUS: A gift I'll be glad to get. For by touching the body of Christ that ass was consecrated.

CANNIUS: Obviously those who smote Christ touched him too.

POLYPHEMUS: But tell me seriously, isn't carrying the Gospel about a reverent thing to do?

CANNIUS: Reverent if done sincerely, without hypocrisy.

POLYPHEMUS: Let monks have hypocrisy! What has a soldier to do with hypocrisy?

CANNIUS: But first tell me what hypocrisy is.

POLYPHEMUS: Professing something other than what you really mean.

CANNIUS: But what does carrying a copy of the Gospels profess? A gospel life, doesn't it?

POLYPHEMUS: I suppose so.

CANNIUS: Therefore, when the life doesn't correspond to the book, isn't that hypocrisy?

POLYPHEMUS: Apparently. But what is it truly to bear the Gospel?

CANNIUS: Some bear it in their hands, as the Franciscans do their Rule. Parisian porters, and asses and geldings, can do the same. There are those who bear it in their mouths, harping on nothing but Christ and the Gospel. That's pharisaical. Some bear it in their hearts. The true Gospel bearer, then, is one who carries it in hands and mouth *and* heart.

POLYPHEMUS: Where are these?

CANNIUS: In churches—the deacons, who bear the book, read it to the congregation, and have it by heart.

POLYPHEMUS: Though not all who bear the Gospel in their hearts are devout.

CANNIUS: Don't quibble. A man doesn't bear it in his heart unless he loves it through and through. Nobody loves it wholeheartedly unless he emulates the Gospel in his manner of living.

POLYPHEMUS: I don't follow these subtleties.

CANNIUS: But I'll tell you more bluntly. If you carry a jar of Beaune wine on your shoulder, it's just a burden, isn't it?

POLYPHEMUS: That's all.

CANNIUS: But if you hold the wine in your throat, and presently spit it out?

POLYPHEMUS: Useless—though, really, I'm not accustomed to doing that!

CANNIUS: But if—as you *are* accustomed—you take a long drink?

POLYPHEMUS: Nothing more heavenly.

CANNIUS: Your whole body glows; your face turns rosy; your expression grows merry.

POLYPHEMUS: Exactly.

CANNIUS: The Gospel has the same effect when it penetrates the heart. It makes a new man of you.

POLYPHEMUS: So I don't seem to you to live according to the Gospel?

CANNIUS: You can best decide that question yourself.

POLYPHEMUS: If it could be decided with a battle-ax—

CANNIUS: If someone called you a liar or a rake to your face, what would you do?

POLYPHEMUS: What would I do? He'd feel my fists.

CANNIUS: What if someone hit you hard?

POLYPHEMUS: I'd break his neck for that.

CANNIUS: But your book teaches you to repay insults with a soft answer; and "Whosoever shall smite thee on thy right cheek, turn to him the other also."

POLYPHEMUS: I've read that, but it slipped my mind.

CANNIUS: You pray frequently, I dare say.

POLYPHEMUS: That's pharisaical.

CANNIUS: Long-winded but ostentatious praying is pharisaical. But your book teaches us to pray without ceasing, yet sincerely.

POLYPHEMUS: Still, I do pray sometimes.

CANNIUS: When?

POLYPHEMUS: Whenever I think of it—once or twice a week.

CANNIUS: What do you pray?

POLYPHEMUS: The Lord's Prayer.

CANNIUS: How often?

POLYPHEMUS: Once. For the Gospel forbids vain repetitions as "much speaking."

CANNIUS: Can you concentrate on the Lord's Prayer while repeating it?

POLYPHEMUS: Never tried. Isn't it enough to say the words?

CANNIUS: I don't know, except that God hears only the utterance of the heart. Do you fast often?

POLYPHEMUS: Never.

CANNIUS: But your book recommends prayer and fasting.

POLYPHEMUS: I'd recommend them too, if my belly did not demand something else.

CANNIUS: But Paul says that those who serve their bellies aren't serving Jesus Christ. Do you eat meat on any day whatever?

POLYPHEMUS: Any day it's offered.

CANNIUS: Yet a man as tough as you are could live on hay or the bark of trees.

POLYPHEMUS: But Christ said that a man is not defiled by what he eats.

CANNIUS: True, if it's eaten in moderation, without giving offense. But Paul, the disciple of Christ, prefers starvation to offending a weak brother by his food; and he calls upon us to follow his example, in order that we may please all men in all things.

POLYPHEMUS: Paul's Paul, and I'm me.

CANNIUS: But Egon's job is to feed she-goats.

POLYPHEMUS: I'd rather eat one.

CANNIUS: A fine wish! You'll be a billygoat rather than a she-goat.

POLYPHEMUS: I said *eat* one, not *be* one.

CANNIUS: Very prettily said. Are you generous to the poor?

POLYPHEMUS: I've nothing to give.

CANNIUS: But you would have, if you lived soberly and worked hard.

POLYPHEMUS: I'm fond of loafing.

CANNIUS: Do you keep God's commandments?

POLYPHEMUS: That's tiresome.

CANNIUS: Do you do penance for your sins?

POLYPHEMUS: Christ has paid for us.

CANNIUS: Then why do you insist you love the Gospel?

POLYPHEMUS: I'll tell you. A certain Franciscan in our neighborhood kept babbling from the pulpit against Erasmus' New Testament. I met the man privately, grabbed him by the hair with my left hand, and punched him with my right. I gave him a hell of a beating; made his whole face swell. What do you say to that? Isn't that promoting the Gospel? Next I gave him absolution by banging him on the head three times with this very same book, raising three lumps, in the name of Father, Son, and Holy Ghost.

CANNIUS: The evangelical spirit, all right! This is certainly defending the Gospel with the Gospel.

POLYPHEMUS: I ran across another member of the same order who never stopped raving against Erasmus. Fired with evangelical zeal, I threatened the fellow so much he begged pardon on both knees and admitted the devil had put him up to saying what he said. If he hadn't done this, my halberd would have bounced against his head. I looked as fierce as Mars in battle. This took place before witnesses.

CANNIUS: I'm surprised the man didn't drop dead on the spot. But let's go on. Do you live chastely?

POLYPHEMUS: I may when I'm old. But shall I confess the truth to you, Cannius?

CANNIUS: I'm no priest. If you want to confess, find somebody else.

POLYPHEMUS: Usually I confess to God, but to you I admit I'm not yet a perfect follower of the Gospel; just an ordinary fellow. My kind have four Gospels. Four things above all we Gospelers seek: full bellies; plenty of work for the organs below the belly; a livelihood from somewhere or other; finally, freedom to do as we please. If we get these, we shout in our cups, "Io, triumph; Io, Paean! The Gospel flourishes! Christ reigns!"

CANNIUS: That's an Epicurean life, surely, not an evangelical one.

POLYPHEMUS: I don't deny it, but you know Christ is omnipotent and can turn us into other men in the twinkling of an eye.

CANNIUS: Into swine, too, which I think is more likely than into good men.

POLYPHEMUS: I wish there were no worse creatures in the world than swine, oxen, asses, and camels! You can meet many men who are fiercer than lions, greedier than wolves, more lecherous than sparrows, more snappish than dogs, more venomous than vipers.

CANNIUS: But now it's time for you to begin changing from brute to man.

POLYPHEMUS: You do well to warn me, for prophets these days declare the end of the world is at hand.

CANNIUS: All the more reason to hurry.

POLYPHEMUS: I await the hand of Christ.

CANNIUS: See that you are pliant material for his hand! But where do they get the notion that the end of the world is near?

POLYPHEMUS: They say it's because men are behaving now just as they did before the Flood overwhelmed them. They feast, drink, stuff themselves, marry and are given in marriage, whore, buy, sell, pay and charge interest, build buildings. Kings make war, priests are zealous to increase their wealth, theologians invent syllogisms, monks roam through the world, the commons riot, Erasmus writes colloquies. In short, no calamity is lacking: hunger, thirst, robbery, war, plague, sedition, poverty. Doesn't this prove human affairs are at an end?

CANNIUS: In this mass of woes, what worries you most?

POLYPHEMUS: Guess.

CANNIUS: That your purse is full of cobwebs.

POLYPHEMUS: Damned if you haven't hit it!— Just now I'm on my way back from a drinking party. Some other time, when I'm more sober, I'll argue with you about the Gospel, if you like.

CANNIUS: When shall I see you sober?

POLYPHEMUS: When I'm sober.

CANNIUS: When will you be so?

POLYPHEMUS: When you see me so. Meantime, my dear Cannius, good luck.

CANNIUS: I hope you, in turn, become what you're called.

POLYPHEMUS: To prevent you from outdoing me in courtesy, I pray that Cannius, as the name implies, may never be lacking a can!

REVIEW QUESTIONS

1. Why does Erasmus use the dialogue form?
2. What might he be saying, not only about his readers but also about voice and perspective?
3. What is the older mode of Christianity that Erasmus parodies?
4. What is wrong with it?
5. What ideal of Christian behavior emerges in the colloquy?
6. How might it differ from the older form?
7. How might it be better suited to the instabilities of life in Renaissance Europe?

SIR THOMAS MORE

FROM *Utopia*

Sir Thomas More (1478–1535) was born on Milk Street, in London, the "brightest star that ever shined in the via lactea*," according to Thomas Fuller. His father, John More, was a butler at Lincoln's Inn, later raised to the knighthood and made a judge first in the court of common pleas and later on the king's bench. The son was educated in the household of John Morton, archbishop of Canterbury, and at Christ Church, Oxford. Compelled by his father to study law, More entered New Inn in 1494 and Lincoln's Inn in 1496. He lived with the monks at the London Charterhouse and developed there the discipline and devotion that would serve him well in later troubles. Yet he decided on married rather than monastic life. He wed Jane Colet in 1505 and they had four children. More was an early advocate of education for women; he insisted that his son and daughters be taught by the best tutors available. Despite his many interests—intellectual, religious, and domestic—the law remained his career. City, monarchy, and church called on his services.*

He was part of a London trade delegation to the cities of the Hanse in 1515. During this service, he wrote Book II of Utopia, *describing a pagan, communist city-state in which all policies and institutions were governed by reason. Such a state contrasted notably with the polity of Christian Europe with its greed, self-interest, and violence, as More described it in Book I. The complete work, which drew heavily on descriptions of the new world as well as passages from classical literature, was published in 1516 in Louvain. It established More's international reputation as a man of letters. But public affairs constantly drew him out of his study. In 1523, he served as speaker of the House of Commons, and in 1529, he succeeded Cardinal Wolsey as lord chancellor under Henry VIII. The king favored More, keeping him in attendance, visiting him at home, and enjoying his learned conversation. They fell out over Henry's growing dispute with the Catholic Church. More resigned his office in 1532, the day after the clergy were deprived of the power to enact constitutions without royal consent. Refusal to swear the Oath of Supremacy in 1534, by which he would have recognized Henry as the supreme head of the church in England, made More guilty of treason. He was martyred in 1535, in his own words "the king's good servant but God's first."*

From *Utopia*, by Sir Thomas More, translated by Robert M. Adams, A Norton Critical Edition, 2d ed. (New York: Norton, 1975), pp. 30–33, 40–42, 50–51, 64.

*   *   *

"But as a matter of fact, my dear More, to tell you what I really think, as long as you have private property, and as long as cash money is the measure of all things, it is really not possible for a nation to be governed justly or happily. For justice cannot exist where all the best things in life are held by the worst citizens; nor can anyone be happy where property is limited to a few, since those few are always uneasy and the many are utterly wretched.

"So I reflect on the wonderfully wise and sacred institutions of the Utopians who are so well governed with so few laws. Among them virtue has its reward, yet everything is shared equally, and all men live in plenty. I contrast them with the many other nations which are constantly passing new ordinances and yet can never order their affairs satisfactorily. In these other nations, whatever a man can get he calls his own private property; but all the mass of laws old and new don't enable him to secure his own, or defend it, or even distinguish it from someone else's property. Different men lay claim, successively or all at once, to the same property; and thus arise innumerable and interminable lawsuits—fresh ones every day. When I consider all these things, I become more sympathetic to Plato and do not wonder that he declined to make laws for any people who refused to share their goods equally. Wisest of men, he easily perceived that the one and only road to the welfare of all lies through the absolute equality of goods. I doubt whether such equality can ever be achieved where property belongs to individual men. However abundant goods may be, when every man tries to get as much as he can for his own exclusive use, a handful of men end up sharing the whole thing, and the rest are left in poverty. The result generally is two sorts of people whose fortunes ought to be interchanged: the rich are rapacious, wicked, and useless, while the poor are unassuming, modest men who work hard, more for the benefit of the public than of themselves.

"Thus I am wholly convinced that unless private property is entirely done away with, there can be no fair or just distribution of goods, nor can mankind be happily governed. As long as private property remains, by far the largest and the best part of mankind will be oppressed by a heavy and inescapable burden of cares and anxieties. This load, I admit, may be lightened a little bit under the present system, but I maintain it cannot be entirely removed. Laws might be made that no one should own more than a certain amount of land or receive more than a certain income. Or laws might be passed to prevent the prince from becoming too powerful and the populace too unruly. It might be made unlawful for public offices to be solicited, or put up for sale, or made burdensome for the officeholder by great expense. Otherwise, officeholders are tempted to get their money back by fraud or extortion, and only rich men can afford to seek positions which ought to be held by wise men. Laws of this sort, I agree, may have as much effect as good and careful nursing has on men who are chronically or even terminally sick. The social evils I mentioned may be alleviated and their effects mitigated for a while, but so long as private property remains, there is no hope at all of effecting a cure and restoring society to good health. While you try to cure one part, you aggravate the disease in other parts. Suppressing one symptom causes another to break out, since you cannot give something to one man without taking it away from someone else."

"But I don't see it that way," I replied. "It seems to me that men cannot possibly live well where all things are in common. How can there be plenty of commodities where every man stops working? The hope of gain will not spur him on; he will rely on others, and become lazy. If a man is driven by want of something to produce it, and yet cannot legally protect what he has gained, what can follow but continual bloodshed and turmoil, especially when respect for magistrates and their authority has been lost? I for one cannot conceive of authority existing among men who are equal to one another in every respect."

*   *   *

"As for the relative ages of the governments," Raphael replied, "you might judge more accurately if you had read their histories. If we believe these records, they had cities before there were even human inhabitants here. What ingenuity has discovered or chance hit upon could have turned up just as well in one place as the other. As a matter of fact, I believe we surpass them in natural intelligence, but they leave us far behind in their diligence and zeal to learn.

"According to their chronicles, they had heard nothing of men-from-beyond-the-equator (that's their name for us) until we arrived, except that once, some twelve hundred years ago, a ship which a storm had blown toward Utopia was wrecked on their island. Some Romans and Egyptians were cast ashore, and never departed. Now note how the Utopians profited, through their diligence, from this one chance event. They learned every single useful art of the Roman civilization either directly from their guests, or indirectly from hints and surmises on which they based their own investigations. What benefits from the mere fact that on a single occasion some Europeans landed there! If a similar accident has hitherto brought any men here from their land, the incident has been completely forgotten, as it will be forgotten in time to come that I was ever in their country. From one such accident they made themselves masters of all our useful inventions, but I suspect it will be a long time before we accept any of their institutions which are better than ours. This willingness to learn, I think, is the really important reason for their being better governed and living more happily than we do, though we are not inferior to them in brains or resources."

*　　*　　*

Their Occupations

Agriculture is the one occupation at which everyone works, men and women alike, with no exceptions. They are trained in it from childhood, partly in the schools where they learn theory, and partly through field trips to nearby farms, which make something like a game of practical instruction. On these trips they not only watch the work being done, but frequently pitch in and get a workout by doing the jobs themselves.

Besides farm work (which, as I said, everybody performs), each person is taught a particular trade of his own, such as wool-working, linen-making, masonry, metal-work, or carpentry. There is no other craft that is practiced by any considerable number of them. Throughout the island people wear, and down through the centuries they have always worn, the same style of clothing, except for the distinction between the sexes, and between married and unmarried persons. Their clothing is attractive, does not hamper bodily movement, and serves for warm as well as cold weather; what is more, each household can make its own.

Every person (and this includes women as well as men) learns a second trade, besides agriculture. As the weaker sex, women practice the lighter crafts, such as working in wool or linen; the heavier crafts are assigned to the men. As a rule, the son is trained to his father's craft, for which most feel a natural inclination. But if anyone is attracted to another occupation, he is transferred by adoption into a family practicing the trade he prefers. When anyone makes such a change, both his father and the authorities make sure that he is assigned to a grave and responsible householder. After a man has learned one trade, if he wants to learn another, he gets the same permission. When he has learned both, he pursues whichever he likes better, unless the city needs one more than the other.

The chief and almost the only business of the syphogrants is to manage matters so that no one sits around in idleness, and assure that everyone works hard at his trade. But no one has to exhaust himself with endless toil from early morning to late at night, as if he were a beast of burden. Such wretchedness, really worse than slavery, is the common lot of workmen in all countries, except Utopia. Of the day's twenty-four hours, the Utopians devote only six to work. They work three hours before noon, when they go to dinner. After dinner they rest for a couple of hours, then go to work for another three hours. Then they have supper, and at eight o'clock (counting the first hour after noon as one), they go to bed and sleep eight hours.

The other hours of the day, when they are not working, eating, or sleeping, are left to each man's individual discretion, provided he does not waste them in roistering or sloth, but uses them busily in some occupation that pleases him. Generally these periods are devoted to intellectual activity.

For they have an established custom of giving public lectures before daybreak; attendance at these lectures is required only of those who have been specially chosen to devote themselves to learning, but a great many other people, both men and women, choose voluntarily to attend. Depending on their interests, some go to one lecture, some to another. But if anyone would rather devote his spare time to his trade, as many do who don't care for the intellectual life, this is not discouraged; in fact, such persons are commended as especially useful to the commonwealth.

*   *   *

But in all this, you may get a wrong impression, if we don't go back and consider one point more carefully. Because they allot only six hours to work, you might think the necessities of life would be in scant supply. This is far from the case. Their working hours are ample to provide not only enough but more than enough of the necessities and even the conveniences of life. You will easily appreciate this if you consider how large a part of the population in other countries exists without doing any work at all. In the first place, hardly any of the women, who are a full half of the population, work; or, if they do, then as a rule their husbands lie snoring in the bed. Then there is a great lazy gang of priests and so-called religious men. Add to them all the rich, especially the landlords, who are commonly called gentlemen and nobility. Include with them their retainers, that mob of swaggering bullies. Finally, reckon in with these the sturdy and lusty beggars, who go about feigning some disease as an excuse for their idleness. You will certainly find that the things which satisfy our needs are produced by far fewer hands than you had supposed.

And now consider how few of those who do work are doing really essential things. For where money is the standard of everything, many superfluous trades are bound to be carried on simply to satisfy luxury and licentiousness. Suppose the multitude of those who now work were limited to a few trades, and set to producing more and more of those conveniences and commodities that nature really requires. They would be bound to produce so much that the prices would drop, and the workmen would be unable to gain a living. But suppose again that all the workers in useless trades were put to useful ones, and that all the idlers (who now guzzle twice as much as the working-men who make what they consume) were assigned to productive tasks—well, you can easily see how little time each man would have to spend working, in order to produce all the goods that human needs and conveniences require—yes, and human pleasure too, as long as it's true and natural pleasure.

*   *   *

Their Gold and Silver

For these reasons, therefore, they have accumulated a vast treasure, but they do not keep it like a treasure. I'm really quite ashamed to tell you how they do keep it, because you probably won't believe me. I would not have believed it myself if someone had just told me about it; but I was there, and saw it with my own eyes. It is a general rule that the more different anything is from what people are used to, the harder it is to accept. But, considering that all their other customs are so unlike ours, a sensible man will not be surprised that they use gold and silver quite differently than we do. After all, they never do use money among themselves, but keep it only for a contingency which may or may not actually arise. So in the meanwhile they take care that no one shall over-value gold and silver, of which money is made, beyond what the metals themselves deserve. Anyone can see, for example, that iron is far superior to either; men could not live without iron, by heaven, any more than without fire or water. But gold and silver have, by nature, no function that we cannot easily dispense with. Human folly has made them precious because they are rare. Like a most wise and generous mother, nature has placed the best things everywhere and in the open, like air, water, and the earth itself; but she has hidden away in remote places all vain and unprofitable things.

If in Utopia gold and silver were kept locked up in some tower, foolish heads among the common people might well concoct a story that the prince and the senate were out to cheat ordinary folk and get some advantage for themselves. They might indeed put the gold and silver into beautiful plate-ware and rich handiwork, but then in case of necessity the people would not want to give up such articles, on which they had begun to fix their hearts, only to melt them down for soldiers' pay. To avoid all these inconveniences, they thought of a plan which conforms with their institutions as clearly as it contrasts with our own. Unless we've actually seen it working, their plan may seem ridiculous to us, because we prize gold so highly and are so careful about protecting it. With them it's just the other way. While they eat from pottery dishes and drink from glass cups, well made but inexpensive, their chamber pots and stools—all their humblest vessels, for use in the common halls and private homes—are made of gold and silver. The chains and heavy fetters of slaves are also made of these metals. Finally, criminals who are to bear through life the mark of some disgraceful act are forced to wear golden rings on their ears, golden bands on their fingers, golden chains around their necks, and even golden crowns on their heads. Thus they hold gold and silver up to scorn in every conceivable way. As a result, when they have to part with these metals, which other nations give up with as much agony as if they were being disemboweled, the Utopians feel it no more than the loss of a penny.

*   *   *

Slaves

The Utopians enslave prisoners of war only if they are captured in wars fought by the Utopians themselves. The children of slaves are not automatically enslaved, nor are any men who were enslaved in a foreign country. Most of their slaves are either their own former citizens, enslaved for some heinous offense, or else men of other nations who were condemned to death in their own land. Most are of the latter sort. Sometimes the Utopians buy them at a very modest rate, more often they ask for them, get them for nothing, and bring them home in considerable numbers. These kinds of slaves are kept constantly at work, and are always fettered. The Utopians deal with their own people more harshly than with others, feeling that their crimes are worse and deserve stricter punishment because, as it is argued, they had an excellent education and the best of moral training, yet still couldn't be restrained from wrongdoing. A third class of slaves consists of hardworking penniless drudges from other nations who voluntarily choose to become slaves in Utopia. Such people are treated well, almost as well as citizens, except that they are given a little extra work, on the score that they're used to it. If one of them wants to leave, which seldom happens, no obstacles are put in his way, nor is he sent off empty-handed.

*   *   *

REVIEW QUESTIONS

1. Why did More choose to call the place *Utopia*, literally "Nowhere"?
2. What possibilities created by the discovery of a new world does More explore in *Utopia*?
3. How are More's Utopians different from what medieval Europeans would have considered Christian?
4. How does More's attitude toward the people of Utopia reflect attitudes of the Renaissance?
5. How might *Utopia* be critical of Renaissance society?
6. What do More's Utopians have in common with the kind of Christian Erasmus described in his colloquy "Cyclops, or the Gospel-Bearer"?

13 &ens; THE AGE OF DISSENT AND DIVISION, 1500–1600

The year 1492 marked both the end of the expansion of Christianity in Europe, with the final expulsion of the Jews and Muslims from the Iberian Peninsula, and the beginning of the expansion of European Christianity across the globe. So, too, it marked the nadir of papal ambition, venality, and corruption, and thereby the medieval Christian hierarchy. In that year, the Borgia pope, Alexander VI, whom contemporaries such as Machiavelli knew to be rapacious, murderous, treacherous, and ambitious, was elected.

Within a generation of the Reconquista of Spain, the German lands of the grandson of Ferdinando and Isabella of Spain would be split between two very different understandings of Christianity: what it meant to be a Christian, what the Church was and how it was to be constituted, and what the nature of worship was. In part, the Reformation arose in response to perceptions of papal bellicosity and immorality; it belonged to an older tradition of reformatio. *Equally, however, the Reformation was heir to the Renaissance: the philological skills and discoveries of fifteenth-century humanists enabled new approaches to the study of the Bible, and the humanist emphasis on historical accuracy led to a call for a return to apostolic Christianity. That return to the text of Scripture, along with a new sensitivity to historical periods, brought theologians such as Martin Luther to reconsider not only devotional practices but the very structure of authority of medieval Christendom—the papal hierarchy—and others, such as John Calvin, to return to the Acts of the Apostles for a vision of the true church.*

Even as Christendom divided against itself in Europe, it expanded through the persons of conquistadores to create worlds unimagined in the European tradition. Reformation and expansion both came through bloodshed. In Germany, peasants and artisans fought lords and emperor to institute the godly law they found in the Bible, only to be massacred. In France, the Low Countries, and England, as well as the Holy Roman Empire, Christians executed Christians over questions of the Eucharist, the place of images in worship, and the cult of the saints. Churches divided from one another, each defining itself against the others, even as all confronted worlds for which neither the Bible nor the classical tradition had prepared them.

MARTIN LUTHER

FROM *The Large Catechism,* 1530

Martin Luther (1483–1546), one of the founders of Protestantism, was born of peasant stock. His father had left his fields for the copper mines of Mansfeld in Saxon, where he flourished economically and rose to the status of town councilor. His son, Martin, received a primary education from the Brethren of the Common Life and enrolled at the University of Erfurt in 1501, where he earned his bachelor of arts in 1502 and his master of arts in 1505. His father hoped that his son would continue the family's rise to prominence by pursuing a legal career. These aspirations were shattered when Luther unexpectedly entered a monastery in 1505. As a member of the order of Augustinian Hermits, he began formal training in theology. Selected for advanced training in theology, he made his way to the University of Wittenberg, where he received his doctorate in 1512 and occupied the chair of biblical theology. Even as his academic career prospered, his inner life suffered. Luther was beset by doubts about his own salvation, the result of a consciousness both of his own weakness and of divine righteousness. Long study and meditation led him to a resolution that became the basis for his theology of justification. Salvation was the result of divine grace, freely given; the forgiven conscience could be at peace; the soul could serve God joyfully. Luther having experienced this new conviction, it is not surprising that the extravagant claims surrounding the sale of indulgences in 1517 provoked him to public protest. The form and text of that protest became known as the "95 Theses." His objection to the claim that the pope could remit the temporal punishment of sins led him deeper and deeper into controversy and ultimately to schism. By 1520, the rift between Luther and the Catholic Church had become irreparable and extended to far more issues than papal power. His The Large Catechism, whose Preface follows, reveals another dimension of Luther's reform: his engagement in the care of souls. Through catechism, a process of recitation and repetition, young people were to be brought to a proper understanding of God's Will and Word. It reveals Luther's familiarity with the Christian Church's past and his hope for its future.

From *The Large Catechism of Martin Luther,* translated by Robert H. Fischer (Philadelphia: Augsburg Fortress Press, 1959).

Martin Luther's Preface[1]

It is not for trivial reasons that we constantly treat the Catechism and strongly urge others to do the same. For we see to our sorrow that many pastors and preachers[2] are very negligent in this respect and despise both their office and this teaching itself. Some because of their great and lofty learning, others because of sheer laziness and gluttony, behave in this matter as if they were pastors or preachers for their bellies' sake and had nothing to do but live off the fat of the land all their days, as they used to do under the papacy.

Everything that they are to teach and preach is now available to them in clear and simple form in the many excellent books which are in reality what the old manuals claimed in their titles to be: "Sermons That Preach Themselves," "Sleep Soundly," "Prepared!" and "Treasury."[3] However, they are not so upright and honest as to buy these books, or if they have them, to examine and read them. Such shameful gluttons and servants of their bellies would make better swineherds or dogkeepers than spiritual guides and pastors.

Now that they are free from the useless, bothersome babbling of the Seven Hours,[4] it would be fine if every morning, noon, and evening they would read, instead, at least a page or two from the Catechism, the Prayer Book,[5] the New Testament, or something else from the Bible and would pray the Lord's Prayer for themselves and their parishioners. In this way they might show honor and gratitude to the Gospel, through which they have been delivered from so many burdens and troubles, and they might feel a little shame because, like pigs and dogs, they remember no more of the Gospel than this rotten, pernicious, shameful, carnal liberty. As it is, the common people take the Gospel altogether too lightly, and even our utmost exertions accomplish but little. What, then, can we expect if we are sluggish and lazy, as we used to be under the papacy?

Besides, a shameful and insidious plague of security and boredom has overtaken us. Many regard the Catechism as a simple, silly teaching which they can absorb and master at one reading. After reading it once they toss the book into a corner as if they are ashamed to read it again. Indeed, even among the nobility there are some louts and skinflints who declare that we can do without pastors and preachers from now on because we have everything in books and can learn it all by ourselves. So they blithely let parishes fall into decay, and brazenly allow both pastors and preachers to suffer distress and hunger. This is what one can expect of crazy Germans. We Germans have such disgraceful people among us and must put up with them.

As for myself, let me say that I, too, am a doctor and a preacher—yes, and as learned and experienced as any of those who act so high and mighty. Yet I do as a child who is being taught the Catechism. Every morning, and whenever else I have time, I read and recite word for word the Lord's Prayer, the Ten Commandments, the Creed, the Psalms, etc. I must still read and study the Catechism daily, yet I cannot master it as I wish, but must remain a child and pupil of the Catechism, and I do it gladly. These dainty, fastidious fellows would like quickly, with one reading, to become doctors above all doctors, to know all there is to be known. Well, this, too, is a sure sign that they despise both their office and the people's souls, yes, even God and his Word. They need not fear a fall, for they have already fallen all too horribly. What they need is to become children and begin learning their ABC's, which they think they have outgrown long ago.

---

[1] In the German edition of the Book of Concord, 1580, this Longer Preface (which dates from 1530) appeared after the Shorter Preface in accordance with the order observed in the fourth German volume of the Jena edition of Luther's Works (1556).

[2] Preachers (*Prediger*) were limited to preaching; pastors (*Pfarrherren*) exercised the full ministerial office.

[3] Titles of medieval sermon books.

[4] The seven canonical hours, daily prayers prescribed by the medieval Breviary.

[5] Luther published the "Little Prayer Book" (*Betbüchlein*) in 1522 to replace Roman Catholic devotional books.

Therefore, I beg these lazy-bellies and presumptuous saints, for God's sake, to get it into their heads that they are not really and truly such learned and great doctors as they think. I implore them not to imagine that they have learned these parts of the Catechism perfectly, or at least sufficiently, even though they think they know them ever so well. Even if their knowledge of the Catechism were perfect (though that is impossible in this life), yet it is highly profitable and fruitful daily to read it and make it the subject of meditation and conversation. In such reading, conversation, and meditation the Holy Spirit is present and bestows ever new and greater light and fervor, so that day by day we relish and appreciate the Catechism more greatly. This is according to Christ's promise in Matt. 18:20, "Where two or three are gathered in my name, there am I in the midst of them."

Nothing is so effectual against the devil, the world, the flesh, and all evil thoughts as to occupy oneself with the Word of God, talk about it, and meditate on it. Psalm 1 calls those blessed who "meditate on God's law day and night."[6] You will never offer up any incense or other savor more potent against the devil than to occupy yourself with God's commandments and words and to speak, sing, and meditate on them. This, indeed, is the true holy water, the sign which routs the devil and puts him to flight.[7]

For this reason alone you should eagerly read, recite, ponder, and practice the Catechism, even if the only blessing and benefit you obtain from it is to rout the devil and evil thoughts. For he cannot bear to hear God's Word. God's Word is not like some empty tale, such as the one about Dietrich of Bern,[8] but as St. Paul says in Rom. 1:16, it is "the power of God," indeed, the power of God which burns the devil and gives us immeasurable strength, comfort, and help.

Why should I waste words? Time and paper would fail me if I were to recount all the blessings that flow from God's Word. The devil is called the master of a thousand arts. What, then, shall we call God's Word, which routs and destroys this master of a thousand arts with all his wiles and might? It must, indeed, be master of more than a hundred thousand arts. Shall we frivolously despise this might, blessing, power, and fruit—especially we who would be pastors and preachers? If so, we deserve not only to be refused food but also to be chased out by dogs and pelted with dung. Not only do we need God's Word daily as we need our daily bread; we also must use it daily against the daily, incessant attacks and ambushes of the devil with his thousand arts.

If this were not enough to admonish us to read the Catechism daily, there is God's command. That alone should be incentive enough. Deut. 6:7, 8 solemnly enjoins that we should always meditate upon his precepts whether sitting, walking, standing, lying down, or rising, and keep them before our eyes and in our hands as a constant token and sign. Certainly God did not require and command this so solemnly without good reason. He knows our danger and need. He knows the constant and furious attacks and assaults of the devil. So he wishes to warn, equip, and protect us against them with good "armor" against their "flaming darts,"[9] and with a good antidote against their evil infection and poison. O what mad, senseless fools we are! We must ever live and dwell in the midst of such mighty enemies as the devils, and yet we despise our weapons and armor, too lazy to give them a thought!

Look at these bored, presumptuous saints who will not or cannot read and study the Catechism daily. They evidently consider themselves much wiser than God himself, and wiser than all his holy angels, prophets, apostles, and all Christians! God himself is not ashamed to teach it daily, for he knows of nothing better to teach, and he always keeps on teaching this one thing without varying it with anything new or different. All the saints know

---

[6] Ps. 1:2.

[7] I.e., the Word of God really does what holy water was formerly believed to accomplish.

[8] Luther frequently cited the legend of Dietrich of Bern as an example of lies and fables.

[9] Eph. 6:11, 16.

of nothing better or different to learn, though they cannot learn it to perfection. Are we not most marvelous fellows, therefore, if we imagine, after reading or hearing it once, that we know it all and need not read or study it any more? Most marvelous fellows, to think we can finish learning in one hour what God himself cannot finish teaching! Actually, he is busy teaching it from the beginning of the world to the end, and all prophets and saints have been busy learning it and have always remained pupils, and must continue to do so.

This much is certain: anyone who knows the Ten Commandments perfectly knows the entire Scriptures. In all affairs and circumstances he can counsel, help, comfort, judge, and make decisions in both spiritual and temporal matters. He is qualified to sit in judgment upon all doctrines, estates, persons, laws, and everything else in the world.

What is the whole Psalter but meditations and exercises based on the First Commandment? Now, I know beyond a doubt that such lazy-bellies and presumptuous fellows do not understand a single Psalm, much less the entire Scriptures, yet they pretend to know and despise the Catechism, which is a brief compend and summary of all the Holy Scriptures.

Therefore, I once again implore all Christians, especially pastors and preachers, not to try to be doctors prematurely and to imagine that they know everything. Vain imaginations, like new cloth, suffer shrinkage! Let all Christians exercise themselves in the Catechism daily, and constantly put it into practice, guarding themselves with the greatest care and diligence against the poisonous infection of such security or vanity. Let them continue to read and teach, to learn and meditate and ponder. Let them never stop until they have proved by experience that they have taught the devil to death and have become wiser than God himself and all his saints.

If they show such diligence, then I promise them—and their experience will bear me out—that they will gain much fruit and God will make excellent men of them. Then in due time they themselves will make the noble confession that the longer they work with the Catechism, the less they

know of it and the more they have to learn. Only then, hungry and thirsty, will they truly relish what now they cannot bear to smell because they are so bloated and surfeited. To this end may God grant his grace! Amen.

Preface[10]

This sermon has been undertaken for the instruction of children and uneducated people. Hence from ancient times it has been called, in Greek, a "catechism"—that is, instruction for children. Its contents represent the minimum of knowledge required of a Christian. Whoever does not possess it should not be reckoned among Christians nor admitted to a sacrament,[11] just as a craftsman who does not know the rules and practices of his craft is rejected and considered incompetent. For this reason young people should be thoroughly instructed in the various parts of the Catechism or children's sermons and diligently drilled in their practice.

Therefore, it is the duty of every head of a household to examine his children and servants at least once a week and ascertain what they have learned of it, and if they do not know it, to keep them faithfully at it. I well remember the time when there were old people who were so ignorant that they knew nothing of these things—indeed, even now we find them daily—yet they come to Baptism and the Sacrament of the Altar and exercise all the rights of Christians, although those who come to the sacrament ought to know more and have a fuller understanding of all Christian doctrine than children and beginners at school. As for the common people, however, we should be satisfied if they learned the three parts[12] which

---

[10] The Shorter Preface is based on a sermon of May 18, 1528 (*WA*, 301:2).

[11] This was not only a proposal of Luther, but also a medieval prescription; cf. John Surgant, *Manuale Curatorum* (1502), etc.

[12] Ten Commandments, Creed, Lord's Prayer. From 1525 on catechetical instruction in Wittenberg was expanded to include material on Baptism and the Lord's Supper.

have been the heritage of Christendom from ancient times, though they were rarely taught and treated correctly, so that all who wish to be Christians in fact as well as in name, both young and old, may be well-trained in them and familiar with them.

I. THE TEN COMMANDMENTS OF GOD

1. You shall have no other gods before me.
2. You shall not take the name of God in vain.
3. You shall keep the Sabbath day holy.
4. You shall honor father and mother.
5. You shall not kill.
6. You shall not commit adultery.
7. You shall not steal.
8. You shall not bear false witness against your neighbor.
9. You shall not covet your neighbor's house.
10. You shall not covet his wife, man-servant, maid-servant, cattle, or anything that is his.[13]

II. THE CHIEF ARTICLES OF OUR FAITH

I believe in God, the Father almighty, maker of heaven and earth:

And in Jesus Christ, his only Son, our Lord: who was conceived by the Holy Spirit, born of the virgin Mary, suffered under Pontius Pilate, was crucified, dead, and buried: he descended into hell, the third day he rose from the dead, he ascended into heaven, and sits on the right hand of God, the Father almighty, whence he shall come to judge the living and the dead.

I believe in the Holy Spirit, the holy Christian church,[14] the communion of saints, the forgiveness of sins, the resurrection of the body, and the life everlasting. Amen.

III. THE PRAYER, OR OUR FATHER, WHICH CHRIST TAUGHT

Our Father who art in heaven, hallowed be thy name. Thy kingdom come, thy will be done, on earth as it is in heaven. Give us this day our daily bread; and forgive us our debts, as we also have forgiven our debtors; and lead us not into temptation, but deliver us from evil. For thine is the kingdom and the power and the glory, forever. Amen.[15]

These are the most necessary parts of Christian instruction. We should learn to repeat them word for word. Our children should be taught the habit of reciting them daily when they rise in the morning, when they go to their meals, and when they go to bed at night; until they repeat them they should not be given anything to eat or drink. Every father has the same duty to his household; he should dismiss man-servants and maid-servants if they do not know these things and are unwilling to learn them. Under no circumstances should a person be tolerated if he is so rude and unruly that he refuses to learn these three parts in which everything contained in Scripture is comprehended in short, plain, and simple terms, for the dear fathers or apostles, whoever they were,[16] have thus summed up the doctrine, life, wisdom, and learning which constitute the Christian's conversation, conduct, and concern.

When these three parts are understood, we ought also to know what to say about the sacraments which Christ himself instituted, Baptism and the holy Body and Blood of Christ, according to the texts of Matthew and Mark at the end of their Gospels where they describe how Christ said farewell to his disciples and sent them forth.

BAPTISM

"Go and teach all nations, and baptize them in the name of the Father and of the Son and of the Holy

---

[13] Ex. 20:2–17; cf. Deut. 5:6–21.

[14] The translation of *ecclesiam catholicam* by *eine christliche Kirche* was common in fifteenth-century Germany.

[15] Matt. 6:9–13; cf. Luke 11:2–4.

[16] Luther was not interested in defending the apostolic authorship of the Creed.

Spirit" (Matt. 28:19). "He who believes and is baptized will be saved; but he who does not believe will be condemned" (Mark 16:16).

It is enough for an ordinary person to know this much about Baptism from the Scriptures. The other sacrament may be dealt with similarly, in short, simple words according to the text of St. Paul.

THE SACRAMENT [OF THE ALTAR]

"Our Lord Jesus Christ on the night when he was betrayed took bread, gave thanks, and broke it and gave it to his disciples, saying, 'Take and eat, this is my body, which is given for you. Do this in remembrance of me.'

"In the same way also the cup, after supper, saying, 'This cup is the new testament in my blood, which is shed for you for the forgiveness of sins. Do this, as often as you drink it, in remembrance of me' " (I Cor. 11:23–25).

Thus we have, in all, five parts covering the whole of Christian doctrine, which we should constantly teach and require young people to recite word for word. Do not assume that they will learn and retain this teaching from sermons alone. When these parts have been well learned, you may assign them also some Psalms or some hymns,[17] based on these subjects, to supplement and confirm their knowledge. Thus our youth will be led into the Scriptures so that they make progress daily.

However, it is not enough for them simply to learn and repeat these parts verbatim. The young people should also attend preaching, especially at the time designated for the Catechism,[18] so that they may hear it explained and may learn the meaning of every part. Then they will also be able to repeat what they have heard and give a good, correct answer when they are questioned, and thus the preaching will not be without benefit and fruit. The reason we take such care to preach on the Catechism frequently is to impress it upon our youth, not in a lofty and learned manner but briefly and very simply, so that it may penetrate deeply into their minds and remain fixed in their memories.

Now we shall take up the above-mentioned parts one by one and in the plainest possible manner say about them as much as is necessary.

REVIEW QUESTIONS

1. Why is the catechism so important to Martin Luther?
2. To whom is the catechism to be taught, and by whom is it to be taught?
3. What matters, issues, or ideas does the catechism teach?
4. What purposes does the catechism serve in the reformation of Luther?
5. What concerns on the part of Luther do these purposes reflect?

---

[17] Luther himself wrote six hymns based on the parts of the Catechism.

[18] Preaching and instruction on the Catechism especially during Lent.

SEBASTIAN LOTZER

The Twelve Articles of the Peasants of Swabia

The Twelve Articles of the Peasants of Swabia, adopted at the free imperial city of Memmingen in 1525, is one of the signal documents of the great agrarian revolt known as the Peasants' War of 1525. More than any other such document, it specifically linked the

THE HOLY COMMUNION BY THE PROTESTANTS AND
RIDE TO HELL OF THE CATHOLICS (date unknown)   LUCAS CRANACH THE YOUNGER

Lucas Cranach the Younger (1515–1586) developed his art while apprenticed to his father, Lucas Cranach the Elder. So well did he learn that his paintings and woodcuts, usually individual portraits or allegorical scenes, are difficult to distinguish from those of his father. This particular woodcut, whose date is unknown, captures the potential of this print medium to communicate through images meaning beyond words. Cranach the Younger was an early master. What activities occur on each side of the image? What does Cranach want his viewers to know? How does the Renaissance aesthetic of balance and symmetry reinforce the central message of the image? What central themes of the Reformation appear before your eyes?

social and political grievances of the peasants with the evangelical principles of the Reformation. Ironically, this document was not composed by a peasant but by a townsman, the journeyman furrier and lay preacher Sebastian Lotzer. To do so, he summarized and condensed the long (several hundred articles) list of demands put forward by the peasants of Baltringen. The Memmingen preacher Christoph Schappeler added a preamble and supplied biblical references in the margins. This document acquired its importance because it was quickly printed and widely disseminated. In many areas of the revolt, it was adopted as the basis for lists of grievances and proposals for settlement.

From *The Revolution of 1525: The German Peasants' War from a New Perspective*, translated by Thomas A. Brady Jr. (Baltimore: Johns Hopkins University Press, 1981), pp. 195–201.

The Just and Fundamental Articles of All the Peasantry and Tenants of Spiritual and Temporal Powers by Whom They Think Themselves Oppressed

To the Christian reader, the peace and grace of God through Jesus Christ.

There are many antichrists who, now that the peasants are assembled together, seize the chance to mock the gospel, saying, "Is this the fruit of the new gospel: to band together in great numbers and plot conspiracies to reform and even topple the spiritual and temporal powers—yes, even to murder them?" The following articles answer all these godless, blasphemous critics. We want two things: first, to make them stop mocking the word of God; and second, to establish the Christian justice of the current disobedience and rebellion of all the peasants.

First of all, the gospel does not cause rebellions and uproars, because it tells of Christ, the promised Messiah, whose words and life teach nothing but love, peace, patience, and unity. And all who believe in this Christ become loving, peaceful, patient, and one in spirit. This is the basis of all the articles of the peasants (as we will clearly show): to hear the gospel and to live accordingly. How then can the antichrists call the gospel a cause of rebellion and of disobedience? It is not the gospel that drives some antichrists and foes of the gospel to resist and reject these demands and require-

ments, but the devil, the deadliest foe of the gospel, who arouses through unbelief such opposition in his own followers. His aim is to suppress and abolish the word of God, which teaches love, peace, and unity.

Second, it surely follows that the peasants, whose articles demand this gospel as their doctrine and rule of life, cannot be called "disobedient" or "rebellious." For if God deigns to hear the peasants' earnest plea that they may be permitted to live according to his word, who will dare deny his will? Who indeed will dare question his judgment? Who will dare oppose his majesty? Did he not hear the children of Israel crying to him and deliver them out of Pharaoh's hand? And can he not save his own today as well? Yes, he will save them, and soon! Therefore, Christian reader, read these articles diligently, and then judge for yourself.

These are the Articles.

THE FIRST ARTICLE

First of all, we humbly ask and beg—and we all agree on this—that henceforth we ought to have the authority and power for the whole community to elect and appoint its own pastor. We also want authority to depose a pastor who behaves improperly. This elected pastor should preach to us the holy gospel purely and clearly, without human additions or human doctrines or precepts. For constant preaching of the true faith impels us to beg God for his grace, that he may instill in us and confirm in us that same true faith. Unless we have his grace in us, we remain mere, useless flesh and blood. For the Scripture clearly teaches that we may come to God only through true faith and can be saved only through His mercy. This is why we need such a guide and pastor; and thus our demand is grounded in Scripture.

THE SECOND ARTICLE

Second, although the obligation to pay a just tithe prescribed in the Old Testament is fulfilled in the New, yet we will gladly pay the large tithe on grain—but only in just measure. Since the tithe should be given to God and distributed among his servants, so the pastor who clearly preaches the word of God deserves to receive it. From now on we want to have our church wardens, appointed by the community, collect and receive this tithe and have our elected pastor draw from it, with the whole community's consent, a decent and adequate living for himself and his. The remainder should be distributed to the village's own poor, again with the community's consent and according to need. What then remains should be kept in case some need to be called up to defend the country; and then the costs can be met from this reserve, so that no general territorial tax will be laid upon the poor folk.

Wherever one or more villages have sold off the tithe to meet some emergency, those purchasers who can show that they bought the tithe with the consent of the whole village shall not be simply expropriated. Indeed we hope to reach fair compromises with such persons, according to the facts of the case, and to redeem the tithe in installments. But wherever the tithe holder—be he clergyman or layman—did not buy the tithe from the whole village but has it from ancestors who simply seized it from the village, we will not, ought not, and do not intend to pay it any longer, except (as we said above) to support our elected pastor. And we will reserve the rest or distribute it to the poor, as the Bible commands. As for the small tithe, we

will not pay it at all, for the Lord God created cattle for man's free use; and it is an unjust tithe invented by men alone. Therefore, we won't pay it anymore.

THE THIRD ARTICLE

Third, it has until now been the custom for the lords to own us as their property. This is deplorable, for Christ redeemed and bought us all with his precious blood, the lowliest shepherd as well as the greatest lord, with no exceptions. Thus the Bible proves that we are free and want to be free. Not that we want to be utterly free and subject to no authority at all; God does not teach us that. We ought to live according to the commandments, not according to the lusts of the flesh. But we should love God, recognize him as our Lord in our neighbor, and willingly do all things God commanded us at his Last Supper. This means we should live according to his commandment, which does not teach us to obey only the rulers, but to humble ourselves before everyone. Thus we should willingly obey our elected and rightful ruler, set over us by God, in all proper and Christian matters. Nor do we doubt that you, as true and just Christians, will gladly release us from bondage or prove to us from the gospel that we must be your property.

THE FOURTH ARTICLE

Fourth, until now it has been the custom that no commoner might catch wild game, wildfowl, or fish in the running waters, which seems to us altogether improper, unbrotherly, selfish, and contrary to God's Word. In some places the rulers protect the game to our distress and great loss, for we must suffer silently while the dumb beasts gobble up the crops God gave for man's use, although this offends both God and neighbor. When the Lord God created man, he gave him dominion over all animals, over the birds of the air, and the fish in the waters. Thus we demand that if someone owns a stream, lake, or pond, he should have to produce documentary proof of ownership and show that it was sold to him with the consent of the whole village. In that case we do not want to seize it from him with force but only to review the matter in a Christian way for the sake of brotherly love. But whoever cannot produce adequate proof of ownership and sale should surrender the waters to the community, as is just.

THE FIFTH ARTICLE

Fifth, we have another grievance about woodcutting, for our lords have seized the woods for themselves alone; and when the poor commoner needs some wood, he has to pay twice the price for it. We think that those woods whose lords, be they clergymen or laymen, cannot prove ownership by purchase should revert to the whole community. And the community should be able to allow in an orderly way each man to gather firewood for his home and building timber free, though only with permission of the community's elected officials. If all the woods have been fairly purchased, then a neighborly and Christian agreement should be reached with their owners about their use. Where the woods were simply seized and then sold to a third party, however, a compromise should be reached according to the facts of the case and the norms of brotherly love and Holy Writ.

THE SIXTH ARTICLE

Sixth, there is our grievous burden of labor services, which the lords daily increase in number and kind. We demand that these obligations be properly investigated and lessened. And we should be allowed, graciously, to serve as our forefathers did, according to God's word alone.

THE SEVENTH ARTICLE

Seventh, in the future we will not allow the lords to oppress us any more. Rather, a man shall have his holding on the proper terms on which it has been leased, that is, by the agreement between lord and peasant. The lord should not force or press the tenant to perform labor or any other service without

pay, so that the peasant may use and enjoy his land unburdened and in peace. When the lord needs labor services, however, the peasant should willingly serve his own lord before others; yet a peasant should serve only at a time when his own affairs do not suffer and only for a just wage.

THE EIGHTH ARTICLE

Eighth, we have a grievance that many of us hold lands that are overburdened with rents higher than the land's yield. Thus the peasants lose their property and are ruined. The lords should have honorable men inspect these farms and adjust the rents fairly, so that the peasant does not work for nothing. For every laborer is worthy of his hire.

THE NINTH ARTICLE

Ninth, we have a grievance against the way serious crimes are punished, for they are constantly making new laws. We are not punished according to the severity of the case but sometimes out of great ill will and sometimes out of favoritism. We think that punishments should be dealt out among us according to the ancient written law and the circumstances of the case, and not according to the judge's bias.

THE TENTH ARTICLE

Tenth, we have a grievance that some people have seized meadows and fields belonging to the community. We shall restore these to the community, unless a proper sale can be proved. If they were improperly bought, however, then a friendly and brotherly compromise should be reached, based on the facts.

THE ELEVENTH ARTICLE

Eleventh, we want the custom called death taxes totally abolished. We will not tolerate it or allow widows and orphans to be so shamefully robbed of their goods, as so often happens in various ways, against God and all that is honorable. The very ones who should be guarding and protecting our goods have skinned and trimmed us of them instead. Had they the slightest legal pretext, they would have grabbed everything. God will suffer this no longer but will wipe it all out. Henceforth no one shall have to pay death taxes, whether small or large.

CONCLUSION

Twelfth, we believe and have decided that if any one or more of these articles is not in agreement with God's Word (which we doubt), then this should be proved to us from Holy Writ. We will abandon it, when this is proved by the Bible. If some of our articles should be approved and later found to be unjust, they shall be dead, null, and void from that moment on. Likewise, if Scripture truly reveals further grievances as offensive to God and a burden to our neighbor, we will reserve a place for them and declare them included in our list. We, for our part, will live and exercise our-

selves in all Christian teachings, for which we will pray to the Lord God. For he alone, and no other, can give us the truth. The peace of Christ be with us all.

REVIEW QUESTIONS

1. What do the Twelve Articles tell you about relations between the common man and his lords?
2. What are the priorities of the Twelve Articles?
3. What is most important to the petitioners?
4. Why is it so important?
5. What is second in importance?
6. What changes are the petitioners asking for the tithe?
7. What is Godly Law?
8. What might be its applications?
9. What are the implications of Godly Law for the lords?

JOHN CALVIN

FROM Draft of Ecclesiastical Ordinances, September and October 1541

John (Jean) Calvin (1509–1564) was born of bourgeois parents in the city of Noyon in Picardy. Destined by his father for an ecclesiastical career, he received several benefices to finance his education as early as 1521. In 1523, he transferred to the University of Paris, where he imbibed the spirit of humanism from such teachers as Mathurin Cordier and Guillaume Bude. Calvin earned a master of arts degree at Paris and, without abandoning his study of classical languages and literature, turned to law at Orléans in 1528. By 1532, he had earned a doctorate of law. Sometime during his legal training or shortly thereafter, Calvin converted to Protestantism. The year 1534 was decisive for Calvin. Forced to flee Paris because of the proscription of Protestantism, he made his way to Basel, where he began work on his great systematic theology, Institutes of the Christian Religion (1536). It was immediately recognized as a superb normative statement of reformed theology and established Calvin's stature as a leader among Protestants despite his youth. As the first edition went to press, Calvin made his way to Geneva, where Guillaume Farel enlisted his aid in the

THE CRUCIFIXION (c. 1596–1600)   EL GRECO

Domenikos Theotokopoulos, better known as El Greco, "the Greek" (1541–1614), is one of the most recognizable and puzzling masters of the Late Renaissance. His dramatic, expressionistic style combined elements of the mannerist and Venetian schools in ways utterly unique. He settled in Toledo, the religious capital of Spain in 1577, after spending his early career in Italy, and received a number of large commissions to decorate some of the churches of the city, as well as the monumental palace of El Escorial. A private commission, executed as part of a retable for the Lady María of Aragon, The Crucifixion *is one of his most famous and powerful works. As you view the painting, what do you think are its most striking elements? Can you identify the figures grouped around the cross? What do their postures, gestures and expressions seem to indicate? How does this painting capture the central themes of the Counter-Reformation?*

reform of the city. The early years of the Reformation in Geneva were stormy, and the doctrines advocated by Calvin met with considerable opposition. In a dispute over church discipline, the city council banished the Protestant pastors. Calvin made his way to Strasbourg, where he remained as a colleague of Martin Bucer and minister to the French refugee church until 1541. Meanwhile, political and religious chaos in Geneva eventually forced the government to seek the return of Calvin. He reluctantly consented, but only with the assurance that his entire original scheme of church polity would be instituted. The ecclesiastical ordinance adopted in 1541 encapsulated that polity and became influential for reformed churches throughout Europe. Written four years later, his Catechism of the Church of Geneva *offers a different vision of the reformer's range of activity. He was no less deeply committed to the inner life of the faithful than he was to the explication of doctrine or the organization of the church. The dedication summarizes the role of education in preserving an embattled and isolated religious community. Calvin remained in Geneva from 1541 until his death in 1564, by which time the city that had accepted reform so reluctantly had been transformed into the center of an international Reformation.*

From *John Calvin*, by G. R. Potter and M. Greengrass (London: Edward Arnold, 1983), pp. 71–76.

First there are four orders of offices instituted by our Saviour for the government of his Church: namely, the pastors, then the doctors, next the elders [*nominated and appointed by the government,*] and fourthly the deacons. If we wish to see the Church well-ordered and maintained we ought to observe this form of government.

The Duty of Pastors

Pastors are sometimes named in the Bible as overseers, elders and ministers. Their work is to proclaim the Word of God, to teach, admonish, exhort and reprove publicly and privately, to administer the sacraments and, with the elders or their deputies, to issue fraternal warnings.

The Examination of Pastors

This consists of two parts. The first concerns doctrine—to find out if the candidate has a good and sound knowledge of the Bible; and, secondly, comes his suitability for expounding this to the people for their edification.

Further, to avoid any danger of his having any wrong ideas, it is fitting that he should profess to accept and uphold the teaching approved by the Church.

Questions must be asked to find out if he is a good teacher and he must privately set forth the teaching of our Lord.

Next, it must be ascertained that he is a man of good principles without any known faults.

The Selection of Pastors

First the ministers should choose someone suitable for the position [*and notify the government*]. Then he is to be presented to the council. If he is approved, he will be accepted and received by the council [*as it thinks fit*]. He is then given a certificate to be produced when he preaches to the people, so that he can be received by the common consent of the faithful. If he is found to be unsuitable and this is demonstrated by evidence, there must be a new selection to find another.

As to the manner of introducing him, because the ceremonies previously used led to a great deal of superstition, all that is needed is that a minister should explain the nature of the position to which he has been appointed and then prayers and pleas should be made that our Lord will give him grace to do what is needed.

After election he must take an oath of allegiance to the government following a written form as required of a minister.

Weekly Meetings to be Arranged

In the first place it is desirable that all ministers should meet together once a week. This is to maintain purity and agreement in their teaching and to hold Bible discussions. Attendance shall be compulsory unless there is good reason for absence. . . . As for the preachers in the villages under the control of the government, it is for the city ministers to urge them to attend whenever possible. . . .

What Should be Done in Cases of Difference About Doctrine

If any differences of opinion concerning doctrine should arise, the ministers should gather together and discuss the matter. If necessary, they should call in the elders and commissioners [*appointed by the government*] to assist in the settlement of any difficulties.

There must be some means available to discipline ministers . . . to prevent scandalous living. In this way, respect for the ministry can be maintained and the Word of God not debased by any minister bringing it into scorn and derision. Those who deserve it must be corrected, but at the same time care must be taken to deal with gossip and malicious rumours which can bring harm to innocent parties.

But it is of first importance to notice that certain crimes are quite incompatible with the ministry and cannot be dealt with by fraternal rebuke. Namely heresy, schism, rebellion against Church discipline, open blasphemy deserving civil punishment, simony and corrupt inducement, intriguing to take over one another's position, leaving the Church without special permission, forgery.

There Follows the Second Order Which We Have Called the Doctors

The special duty of the doctors is to instruct the faithful in sound doctrine so that the purity of the gospel is not corrupted by ignorance or wrong opinion.

As thing stand at present, every agent assisting in the upholding of God's teaching is included so that the Church is not in difficulties from a lack of pastors and ministers. This is in common parlance the order of school teachers. The degree nearest the minister and closely joined to the government of the Church is the lecturer in theology.

Establishment of a College

Because it is only possible to profit from such teaching if one is first instructed in languages and humanities, and also because it is necessary to lay the foundations for the future . . . a college should be instituted for instructing children to prepare them for the ministry as well as for civil government.

In the first place suitable accommodation needs to be provided for the teaching of children and others who want to take advantage of it. We also need a literate, scholarly and trained teacher who can take care of the establishment and their education. He should be chosen and paid on the understanding that he should have under his charge teachers in languages and logic, if they can be found. He should also have some student teachers (*bacheliers*) to teach the little ones. . . .

All who are engaged must be subject to the same ecclesiastical ordinances as apply to the ministers.

There is to be no other school in the city for small children, although the girls are to have a separate school of their own as has been the case up to now.

No one is to be appointed without the approval of the ministers—essential to avoid trouble. [*The candidate must first have been notified to the government and then presented to the council. Two members of the 'council of 24' should be present at all interviews.*]

Here Follows the Third Order, or Elders

Their duty is to supervise every person's conduct. In friendly fashion they should warn backsliders and those of disorderly life. After that, where necessary, they should report to the Company [of pastors] who will arrange for fraternal correction. . . .

As our Church is now arranged, it would be most suitable to have two elected from the 'council of 24', four from the 'council of 60' and six from the 'council of 200'. They should be men of good repute and conduct. . . . They should be chosen from each quarter of the city so that they can keep an eye on the whole of it.

Method of Choosing the Elders

Further we have decided upon the machinery for choosing them. The 'council of 24' will be asked to nominate the most suitable and adequate men they can discover. In order to do this, they should discuss the matter with the ministers and then present their suggestions to the 'council of 200' for approval. If they are found worthy [and approved], they must take an oath in the same form as it is presented to the ministers. At the end of the year and after the elections to the council, they should present themselves to the government so that a decision can be made as to whether they shall be reappointed or not, but they should not be changed frequently and without good cause provided that they are doing their work faithfully.

The Fourth Order of Ecclesiastical Government, Namely, the Deacons

There have always been two kinds of these in the early Church. One has to receive, distribute and care for the goods of the poor (i.e. daily alms as well as possessions, rents and pensions); the other has to tend and look after the sick and administer the allowances to the poor as is customary. [*In order to avoid confusion*], since we have officials and hospital staff, [*one of the four officials of the said hospital should be responsible for the whole of its*

property and revenues and he should have an adequate salary in order to do his work properly].

Concerning the Hospital[1]

Care should be taken to see that the general hospital is properly maintained. This applies to the sick, to old people no longer able to work, to widows, orphans, children and other poor people. These are to be kept apart and separate from others and to form their own community.

Care for the poor who are scattered throughout the city shall be the responsibility of the officials. In addition to the hospital for those visiting the city, which is to be kept up, separate arrangements are to be made for those who need special treatment. To this end a room must be set apart to act as a reception room for those that are sent there by the officials. . . .

Further, both for the poor people in the hospital and for those in the city who have no means, there must be a good physician and surgeon provided at the city's expense. . . .

As for the plague hospital, it must be kept entirely separate.

Begging

In order to stop begging, which is contrary to good order, the government should use some of its officers to remove any beggars who are obstinately present when people come out of Church.

And this especially if it should happen that the city is visited by this sourge of God.

Of the Sacraments

Baptism is to take place only at sermon time and is to be administered only by ministers or their assistants. A register is to be kept of the names of the

---

[1] The Geneva general hospital had been established in 1535 in one of the series of measures by which the city had broken all connections with the Roman Catholic Church, and which consolidated the various confraternities and eight charitable foundations of the city.

children and of their parents: the justice department is to be informed of any bastard.

Since the Supper was instituted by our Lord to be more often observed by us and also since this was the case in the early Church until such time as the devil upset everything by setting up the mass in its place, the defect ought to be remedied by celebrating it a little more frequently. All the same, for the time being we have agreed and ordained that it should be administered four times a year, i.e. at Christmas, Easter, Pentecost and the first Sunday in September in the autumn.

The ministers shall distribute the bread in orderly and reverent fashion and no other person shall offer the chalice except those appointed (or the deacons) along with the ministers and for this reason there is no need for many plates and cups.

The tables should be set up close to the pulpit so that the mystery can be more suitably set forth near by.

Celebration should take place only in church and at the most suitable time.

Of the Order Which Must be Observed in Obedience to Those in Authority, for the Maintenance of Supervision in the Church

A day should be fixed for the consistory. The elders should meet once a week with the ministers, on a Thursday, to ensure that there is no disorder in the Church and to discuss together any necessary remedial action.

Since they have neither the power nor the authority to use force, we have agreed to assign one of our officials to them to summon those whom they wish to admonish.

If any one should deliberately refuse to appear, the council is to be informed so as to take action.

If any one teaches things contrary to the received doctrine he shall be summoned to a conference. If he listens to reason, let him be sent back without any scandal or disgrace. If he is obstinate,

he should be admonished several times until it is apparent that greater severity is needed: then he shall be forbidden to attend the communion of the Supper and he shall be reported to the magistrates.

If any one fails to come to church to such a degree that there is real dislike for the community of believers manifested, or if any one shows that he cares nothing for ecclesiastical order, let him be admonished, and if he is tractable let him be amicably sent back. If however he goes from bad to worse, after having been warned three times, let him be cut off from the Church and be denounced to the magistrate. . . .

[*All this must be done in such a way that the ministers have no civil jurisdiction nor use anything but the spiritual sword of the word of God as St Paul commands them; nor is the authority of the consistory to diminish in any way that of the magistrate or ordinary justice. The civil power must remain unimpaired. In cases where, in future, there may be a need to impose punishments or constrain individuals, then the ministers and the consistory, having heard the case and used such admonitions and exhortations as are appropriate, should report the whole matter to the council which, in turn, will judge and sentence according to the needs of the case.*]

*   *   *

REVIEW QUESTIONS

1. What is the church according to Calvin?
2. What is its structure?
3. What do the four offices tell us about the function of the church?
4. What is the purpose of the church?
5. What are its goals?
6. What are the practices of the church and the relation of those practices to the process of becoming a Christian?
7. What is the relation between the church and salvation?

JOHN CALVIN

FROM Catechism of the Church of Geneva, Being a Form of Instruction for Children in the Doctrine of Christ, 1545

From *Tracts Relating to the Reformation*, vol. 2, by John Calvin, translated by Henry Beveridge (Edinburgh: The Calvin Translation Society, 1844–1851), pp. 34–37.

Dedication.

JOHN CALVIN TO THE FAITHFUL MINISTERS OF CHRIST THROUGHOUT EAST FRIESLAND, WHO PREACH THE PURE DOCTRINE OF THE GOSPEL.

Seeing it becomes us to endeavour by all means that unity of faith, which is so highly commended by Paul, shine forth among us, to this end chiefly ought the formal profession of faith which accompanies our common baptism to have reference. Hence it were to be wished, not only that a perpetual consent in the doctrine of piety should appear among all, but also that one CATECHISM were common to all the Churches. But as, from many causes, it will scarcely ever obtain otherwise than that each Church shall have its own Catechism, we should not strive too keenly to prevent this; provided, however, that the variety in the mode of teaching is such, that we are all directed to one Christ, in whose truth being united together, we may grow up into one body and one spirit, and with the same mouth also proclaim whatever belongs to the sum of faith. Catechists not intent on this end, besides fatally injuring the Church, by sowing the materials of dissension in religion, also introduce an impious profanation of baptism. For where can any longer be the utility of baptism unless this remain as its foundation—that we all agree in one faith?

Wherefore, those who publish Catechisms ought to be the more carefully on their guard, lest, by producing anything rashly, they may not for the present only, but in regard to posterity also, do grievous harm to piety, and inflict a deadly wound on the Church.

This much I wished to premise, as a declaration to my readers, that I myself too, as became me, have made it my anxious care not to deliver any thing in this Catechism of mine that is not agreeable to the doctrine received among all the pious. This declaration will not be found vain by those who will read with candour and sound judgment. I trust I have succeeded at least so far that my labour, though it should not satisfy, will be acceptable to all good men, as being in their opinion useful.

In writing it in Latin, though some perhaps will not approve of the design, I have been influenced by many reasons, all of which it is of no use to detail at present. I shall only select such as seem to me sufficient to obviate censure.

First, In this confused and divided state of Christendom, I judge it useful that there should be public testimonies, whereby churches which, though widely separated by space, agree in the doctrine of Christ, may mutually recognise each other. For besides that this tends not a little to mutual confirmation, what is more to be desired than that mutual congratulations should pass between them, and that they should devoutly commend each other to the Lord? With this view, bishops were wont in old time, when as yet consent in faith existed and flourished among all, to send Synodal Epistles beyond sea, by which, as a kind of badges, they might maintain sacred communion among the churches. How much more necessary is it now, in this fearful devastation of the Christian world, that the few churches which duly worship God, and they too scattered and hedged round on all sides by the profane synagogues of Antichrist, should mutually give and receive this token of holy union, that they may thereby be incited to that fraternal embrace of which I have spoken?

But if this is so necessary in the present day, what shall our feelings be concerning posterity, about which I am so anxious, that I scarcely dare to think? Unless God miraculously send help from heaven, I cannot avoid seeing that the world is threatened with the extremity of barbarism. I wish our children may not shortly feel, that this has been rather a true prophecy than a conjecture. The more, therefore, must we labour to gather together, by our writings, whatever remains of the Church shall continue, or even emerge, after our death. Writings of a different class will show what were our views on all subjects in religion, but the agreement which our churches had in doctrine cannot be seen with clearer evidence than from catechisms. For therein will appear, not only what one man or other once taught, but with what rudiments learned and unlearned alike amongst us, were constantly imbued from childhood, all the faithful holding them as their formal symbol of Christian communion. This was indeed my principal reason for publishing this Catechism.

A second reason, which had no little weight with me, was, because I heard that it was desired by very many who hoped it would not be unworthy of perusal. Whether they are right or wrong in so judging is not mine to decide, but it became me to yield to their wish. Nay, necessity was almost laid upon me, and I could not with impunity decline it. For having seven years before published a brief summary of religion, under the name of a Catechism, I feared that if I did not bring forward this one, I should cause (a thing I wished not) that the former should on the other hand be excluded. Therefore if I wished to consult the public good, it behoved me to take care that this one which I preferred should occupy the ground.

Besides, I deem it of good example to testify to the world, that we who aim at the restitution of the Church, are everywhere faithfully exerting ourselves, in order that, at least, the use of the Catechism which was abolished some centuries ago under the Papacy, may now resume its lost rights. For neither can this holy custom be sufficiently commended for its utility, nor can the Papists be sufficiently condemned for the flagrant corruption, by which they not only set it aside, by converting it into puerile trifles, but also basely abuse it to purposes of impure and impious superstition. That spurious Confirmation, which they have substituted in its stead, they deck out like a harlot, with great splendour of ceremonies, and gorgeous shows without number; nay, in their wish to adorn it, they speak of it in terms of execrable blasphemy, when they give out that it is a sacrament of greater dignity than baptism, and call those only half Christians who have not been besmeared with their oil. Meanwhile, the whole proceeding consists of nothing but theatrical gesticulations, or rather the wanton sporting of apes, without any skill in imitation.

To you, my very dear brethren in the Lord, I have chosen to inscribe this work, because some of your body, besides informing me that you love me, and that the most of you take delight in my writings, also expressly requested me by letter to undertake this labour for their sake. Independently of this, it would have been reason sufficient, that what I learned of you long ago, from the statement of grave and pious men, had bound me to you with my whole soul. I now ask what I am confident you will of your own accord do—have the goodness to consult for the utility of this token of my goodwill towards you! Farewell. May the Lord increase you more and more in the spirit of wisdom, prudence, zeal, and fortitude, to the edification of his Church.

GENEVA, 2d December, 1545.

TO THE READER.

It has ever been the practice of the Church, and one carefully attended to, to see that children should be duly instructed in the Christian religion.

That this might be done more conveniently, not only were schools opened in old time, and individuals enjoined properly to teach their families, but it was a received public custom and practice, to question children in the churches on each of the heads, which should be common and well known to all Christians. To secure this being done in order, there was written out a formula, which was called a Catechism or Institute. Thereafter the devil miserably rending the Church of God, and bringing upon it fearful ruin, (of which the marks are still too visible in the greater part of the world,) overthrew this sacred policy, and left nothing behind but certain trifles, which only beget superstition, without any fruit of edification. Of this description is that confirmation, as they call it, full of gesticulations which, worse than ridiculous, are fitted only for apes, and have no foundation to rest upon. What we now bring forward, therefore, is nothing else than the use of things which from ancient times were observed by Christians, and the true worshippers of God, and which never were laid aside until the Church was wholly corrupted.

REVIEW QUESTIONS

1. What is the purpose of catechism for John Calvin, and how does his purpose differ from that of Martin Luther?
2. Who, according to Calvin, should be taught catechism, and who should do the teaching?
3. How did Calvin reconcile the unity of faith, which he hoped his catechism would serve, and the diversity of local circumstances and observances, which he expected would be the case?
4. What do this hope for unity and this admission of diversity tell us about the Reformation as Calvin understood it?
5. Use the catechism as a measure of the reformers' concerns and goals to explain how had these changed between 1530, when Luther published his *Large Catechism*, and 1545, when Calvin dedicated the *Catechism of the Church of Geneva*. Do the titles reveal anything?
6. Why did Calvin compose his catechism in Latin rather than a vernacular language, as did Martin Luther?

SAINT IGNATIUS OF LOYOLA

FROM *The Spiritual Exercises*

Saint Ignatius of Loyola (1491–1556), the great mystic and founder of the Society of Jesus, was born into a hidalgo family and spent his early manhood in military service to the king of Spain. Wounded in battle, he spent his convalescence reading the lives of saints, which awoke in him a sense of spiritual inadequacy not unlike those which fired the religious engagements of Martin Luther and John Calvin. His early attempts at reconciliation, in the form of physical austerities practiced on pilgrimage to Montserrat and in the hermitage at Manresa, failed to reassure him of his soul's salvation, just as they failed to ease the spiritual torments of the young Luther. The scholastically trained Luther sought solace in the systematic study of the Bible; the uneducated Loyola found it in visions of God. Loyola spent the next decade educating himself and seeking his mission. After a pilgrimage to the Holy Land in 1523, Loyola began his formal education by studying elementary Latin with schoolboys in Barcelona. He attended the universities in Alcalá and Salamanca, preached in the streets, and was arrested by the Inquisition on suspicion of heresy. He attended the University of Paris from 1528 to 1535 and began to gather around him the companions who would form the initial core of the Society of Jesus. In 1534, he and nine companions swore an oath of poverty and chastity and promised either to undertake a crusade to the Holy Land or, failing that, to offer absolute obedience to the pope. At the center of this group was not only the man Loyola but his series of devotions and meditations that would later be published as The Spiritual Exercises *(1548). These exercises offered a practical and ascetic meditation on the life and death of Christ that drew much from the systematic meditations of the* devotio moderna *("modern devotions"). This system instructed those who made or directed a religious retreat in order to stimulate an imitation of Christ that would be expressed in apostolic action as well as religious devotion. In 1535, Loyola and his company left for Italy. He was ordained in Venice in 1537. Finding no passage to the Holy Land, they continued to Rome, where they preached in the streets and ministered to the poor. Introduced to Pope Paul III by Gasparo Contarini, a great advocate of monastic reform, the company received a charter of foundation as the Society of Jesus in 1540. Constituted an order of clerks regular, devoted to educating the young and propagating the faith, sworn to poverty and obedience, the Jesuits grew quickly to become one of the most influential Catholic orders of the early modern period, a model of piety, discipline, education, and service.*

From *The Spiritual Exercises of St. Ignatius of Loyola*, translated from the *Autograph* by Father Elder Mullen, S. J. (New York: P. J. Kennedy and Sons, 1914).

To Have the True Sentiment Which We Ought to Have in the Church Militant

Let the following Rules be observed.

First Rule. All judgment laid aside, we ought to have our mind ready and prompt to obey, in all, the true Spouse of Christ our Lord, which is our holy Mother the Church Hierarchical.

Second Rule. To praise confession to a Priest, and the reception of the most Holy Sacrament of the Altar once in the year, and much more each month, and much better from week to week, with the conditions required and due.

Third Rule. To praise the hearing of Mass often, likewise hymns, psalms, and long prayers, in the church and out of it; likewise the hours set at the time fixed for each Divine Office and for all prayer and all Canonical Hours.

Fourth Rule. To praise much Religious Orders, virginity and continence, and not so much marriage as any of these.

Fifth Rule. To praise vows of Religion, of obedience, of poverty, of chastity and of other perfections of supererogation. And it is to be noted that as the vow is about the things which approach to Evangelical perfection, a vow ought not to be made in the things which withdraw from it, such as to be a merchant, or to be married, etc.

Sixth Rule. To praise relics of the Saints, giving veneration to them and praying to the Saints; and to praise Stations, pilgrimages, Indulgences, pardons, Cruzadas, and candles lighted in the churches.

Seventh Rule. To praise Constitutions about fasts and abstinence, as of Lent, Ember Days, Vigils, Friday and Saturday; likewise penances, not only interior, but also exterior.

Eighth Rule. To praise the ornaments and the buildings of churches; likewise images, and to venerate them according to what they represent.

Ninth Rule. Finally, to praise all precepts of the Church, keeping the mind prompt to find reasons in their defence and in no manner against them.

Tenth Rule. We ought to be more prompt to find good and praise as well the Constitutions and recommendations as the ways of our Superiors. Because, although some are not or have not been such, to speak against them, whether preaching in public or discoursing before the common people, would rather give rise to fault-finding and scandal than profit; and so the people would be incensed against their Superiors, whether temporal or spiritual. So that, as it does harm to speak evil to the common people of Superiors in their absence, so it can make profit to speak of the evil ways to the persons themselves who can remedy them.

Eleventh Rule. To praise positive and scholastic learning. Because, as it is more proper to the Positive Doctors, as St. Jerome, St. Augustine and St. Gregory, etc., to move the heart to love and serve God our Lord in everything; so it is more proper to the Scholastics, as St. Thomas, St. Bonaventure, and to the Master of the Sentences, etc., to define or explain for our times the things necessary for eternal salvation; and to combat and explain better all errors and all fallacies. For the Scholastic Doctors, as they are more modern, not only help themselves with the true understanding of the Sacred Scripture and of the Positive and holy Doctors, but also, they being enlightened and clarified by the Divine virtue, help themselves by the Councils, Canons and Constitutions of our holy Mother the Church.

Twelfth Rule. We ought to be on our guard in making comparison of those of us who are alive to the blessed passed away, because error is committed not a little in this; that is to say, in saying, this one knows more than St. Augustine; he is another, or greater than, St. Francis; he is another St. Paul in goodness, holiness, etc.

Thirteenth Rule. To be right in everything, we ought always to hold that the white which I see, is black, if the Hierarchical Church so decides it, believing that between Christ our Lord, the Bridegroom, and the Church, His Bride, there is the same Spirit which governs and directs us for the salvation of our souls. Because by the same Spirit and our Lord Who gave the ten Commandments, our holy Mother the Church is directed and governed.

Fourteenth Rule. Although there is much truth in the assertion that no one can save himself without being predestined and without having faith and grace; we must be very cautious in the manner of speaking and communicating with others about all these things.

Fifteenth Rule. We ought not, by way of custom, to speak much of predestination; but if in some way and at some times one speaks, let him so speak that the common people may not come into any error, as sometimes happens, saying: Whether I have to be saved or condemned is already determined, and no other thing can now be, through my doing well or ill; and with this, growing lazy, they become negligent in the works which lead to the salvation and the spiritual profit of their souls.

Sixteenth Rule. In the same way, we must be on our guard that by talking much and with much insistence of faith, without any distinction and explanation, occasion be not given to the people to be lazy and slothful in works, whether before faith is formed in charity or after.

Seventeenth Rule. Likewise, we ought not to speak so much with insistence on grace that the poison of discarding liberty be engendered. So that of faith and grace one can speak as much as is possible with the Divine help for the greater praise of His Divine Majesty, but not in such way, nor in such manners, especially in our so dangerous times, that works and free will receive any harm, or be held for nothing.

Eighteenth Rule. Although serving God our Lord much out of pure love is to be esteemed above all; we ought to praise much the fear of His Divine Majesty, because not only filial fear is a thing pious and most holy, but even servile fear—when the man reaches nothing else better or more useful—helps much to get out of mortal sin. And when he is out, he easily comes to filial fear, which is all acceptable and grateful to God our Lord: as being at one with the Divine Love.

REVIEW QUESTIONS

1. What do you suppose Loyola means by the *Church Militant?*
2. How might the Jesuits have been soldiers of Christ?
3. Loyola asks the members of his order to "praise" in order to be "thinking with the Church." How does this serve the Church?
4. What specifically does Loyola ask the Jesuits to praise?
5. What do the "Rules for Thinking with the Church" tell us about the Church?

SAINT FRANCIS XAVIER

FROM **"Letter from India"**

Saint Francis Xavier (1506–1552) was one of the original companions of Saint Ignatius of Loyola and one of the original members of the Society of Jesus. The two became friends during their student years at the University of Paris. Shortly after the founding of the Society, Loyola sent Xavier on a mission to Portugal's mercantile empire in South Asia. After a voyage that lasted more than a year, he arrived in Goa on the Coromandel coast of India, accompanied by the Portuguese governor, Don Martin Alfonso de Sousa, and two fellow missionaries, Father Paul and Francis Mancias, not yet in holy orders. It was at Sousa's behest that Xavier turn his attention to the pearl-fishing villages of Cape Comorin, in an effort to spread Christianity among those peoples and, so, bring them more fully into the Portuguese sphere of influence. It was from Comorin that Xavier wrote the following letter. He would remain there two years before spreading his mission to the East Indies and Japan. He died in 1552, waiting to extend his work to China. His was a life of extraordinary hardship and danger as well as extraordinary activity and achievement. To him belongs credit for extending Roman Christianity and Western ideas to Asian peoples.

From *The Life and Letters of St Francis Xavier*, vol. 1, edited by Henry James Coleridge, 2d ed. (London: Burns and Oates, 1890), pp. 151–63.

To the Society at Rome

May the grace and charity of Christ our Lord always help and favour us! Amen.

It is now the third year since I left Portugal. I am writing to you for the third time, having as yet received only one letter from you, dated February 1542. God is my witness what joy it caused me. I only received it two months ago—later than is usual for letters to reach India, because the vessel which brought it had passed the winter at Mozambique.

I and Francis Mancias are now living amongst the Christians of Comorin. They are very numerous, and increase largely every day. When I first came I asked them, if they knew anything about our Lord Jesus Christ? but when I came to the points of faith in detail and asked them what they thought of them, and what more they believed now than when they were Infidels, they only replied that they were Christians, but that as they are ignorant of Portuguese, they know nothing of the precepts and mysteries of our holy religion. We could not understand one another, as I spoke Castilian and they Malabar; so I picked out the most intelligent and well read of them, and then sought out with the greatest diligence men who knew both languages. We held meetings for several days, and by our joint efforts and with infinite difficulty we translated the Catechism into the Malabar tongue. This I learnt by heart, and then I began to go through all the villages of the coast, calling around me by the sound of a bell as many as I could, children and men. I asembled them twice a day and taught them the Christian doctrine: and thus, in the space of a month, the children had it well by heart. And all the time I kept telling them to go on teaching in their turn whatever they had learnt to their parents, family, and neighbours.

Every Sunday I collected them all, men and women, boys and girls, in the church. They came with great readiness and with a great desire for instruction. Then, in the hearing of all, I began by calling on the name of the most holy Trinity, Father, Son, and Holy Ghost, and I recited aloud the Lord's Prayer, the *Hail Mary*, and the Creed in the language of the country: they all followed me in the same words, and delighted in it wonderfully. Then I repeated the Creed by myself, dwelling upon each article singly. Then I asked them as to each article, whether they believed it unhesitatingly; and all, with a loud voice and their hands crossed over their breasts, professed aloud that they truly believed it. I take care to make them repeat the Creed oftener than the other prayers; and I tell them that those who believe all that is contained therein are called Christians. After explaining the Creed I go on to the Commandments, teaching them that the Christian law is contained in those ten precepts, and that every one who observes them all faithfully is a good and true Christian and is certain of eternal salvation, and that, on the other hand, whoever neglects

a single one of them is a bad Christian, and will be cast into hell unless he is truly penitent for his sin. Converts and heathen alike are astonished at all this, which shows them the holiness of the Christian law, its perfect consistency with itself, and its agreement with reason. . . .

* * *

The fruit that is reaped by the baptism of infants, as well as by the instruction of children and others, is quite incredible. These children, I trust heartily, by the grace of God, will be much better than their fathers. They show an ardent love for the Divine law, and an extraordinary zeal for learning our holy religion and imparting it to others. Their hatred for idolatry is marvellous. They get into feuds with the heathen about it, and whenever their own parents practise it, they reproach them and come off to tell me at once. Whenever I hear of any act of idolatrous worship, I go to the place with a large band of these children, who very soon load the devil with a greater amount of insult and abuse than he has lately received of honour and worship from their parents, relations, and acquaintances. The children run at the idols, upset them, dash them down, break them to pieces, spit on them, trample on them, kick them about, and in short heap on them every possible outrage.

I had been living for nearly four months in a Christian village, occupied in translating the Catechism. A great number of natives came from all parts to entreat me to take the trouble to go to their houses and call on God by the bedsides of their sick relatives. Such numbers also of sick made their own way to us, that I had enough to do to read a Gospel over each of them. At the same time we kept on with our daily work, instructing the children, baptizing converts, translating the Catechism, answering difficulties, and burying the dead. For my part I desired to satisfy all, both the sick who came to me themselves, and those who came to beg on the part of others, lest if I did not, their confidence in, and zeal for, our holy religion should relax, and I thought it wrong not to do what I could in answer to their prayers. But the thing grew to such a pitch that it was impossible for me myself to satisfy all, and at the same time to avoid their quarrelling among themselves, every one striving to be the first to get me to his own house; so I hit on a way of serving all at once. As I could not go myself, I sent round children whom I could trust in my place. They went to the sick persons, assembled their families and neighbours, recited the Creed with them, and encouraged the sufferers to conceive a certain and wellfounded confidence of their restoration. Then after all this, they recited the prayers of the Church. To make my tale short, God was moved by the faith and piety of these children and of the others, and restored to a great number of sick persons health both of body and soul. How good He was to them! He made the very disease of their bodies the occasion of calling them to salvation, and drew them to the Christian faith almost by force!

I have also charged these children to teach the rudiments of Christian doctrine to the ignorant in private houses, in the streets, and the crossways. As soon as I see that this has been well started in one village, I go on to another and give the same instructions and the same commission to the children, and so I go through in order the whole number of their villages. When I have done this and am going away, I leave in each place a copy of the Christian doctrine, and tell all those who know how to write to copy it out, and all the others are to learn it by heart and to recite it from memory every day. Every feast day I bid them meet in one place and sing all together the elements of the faith. For this purpose I have appointed in each of the thirty Christian villages men of intelligence and character who are to preside over these meetings, and the Governor, Don Martin Alfonso, who is so full of love for our Society and of zeal for religion, has been good enough at our request to allot a yearly revenue of 4000 gold *fanams* for the salary of these catechists. He has an immense friendship for ours, and desires with all his heart that some of them should be sent hither, for which he is always asking in his letters to the King.

*   *   *

We have in these parts a class of men among the pagans who are called Brahmins. They keep up the worship of the gods, the superstitious rites of religion, frequenting the temples and taking care of the idols. They are as perverse and wicked a set as can anywhere be found, and I always apply to them the words of holy David, "from an unholy race and a wicked and crafty man deliver me, O Lord." They are liars and cheats to the very backbone. Their whole study is, how to deceive most cunningly the simplicity and ignorance of the people. They give out publicly that the gods command certain offerings to be made to their temples, which offerings are simply the things that the Brahmins themselves wish for, for their own maintenance and that of their wives, children, and servants. Thus they make the poor folk believe that the images of their gods eat and drink, dine and sup like men, and some devout persons are found who really offer to the idol twice a day, before dinner and supper, a certain sum of money. The Brahmins eat sumptuous meals to the sound of drums, and make the ignorant believe that the gods are banqueting. When they are in need of any supplies, and even before, they give out to the people that the gods are angry because the things they have asked for have not been sent, and that if the people do not take care, the gods will punish them by slaughter, disease, and the assaults of the devils. And the poor ignorant creatures, with the fear of the gods before them, obey them implicitly. * * *

The heathen inhabitants of the country are commonly ignorant of letters, but by no means ignorant of wickedness. All the time I have been here in this country I have only converted one Brahmin, a virtuous young man, who has now undertaken to teach the Catechism to children. As I go through the Christian villages, I often pass by the temples of the Brahmins, which they call pagodas. One day lately, I happened to enter a pagoda where there were about two hundred of them, and most of them came to meet me. We had a long conversation, after which I asked them what their gods enjoined them in order to obtain the life of the blessed. There was a long discussion amongst them as to who should answer me. At last, by common consent, the commission was given to one of them, of greater age and experience than the rest, an old man, of more than eighty years. He asked me in return, what commands the God of the Christians laid on them. I saw the old man's perversity, and I refused to speak a word till he had first answered my question. So he was obliged to expose his ignorance, and replied that their gods required two duties of those who desired to go to them hereafter, one of which was to abstain from killing cows, because under that form the gods were adored; the other was to show kindness to the Brahmins, who were the worshippers of the gods. This answer moved my indignation, for I could not but grieve intensely at the thought of the devils being worshipped instead of God by these blind heathen, and I asked them to listen to me in turn. Then I, in a loud voice, repeated the Apostles' Creed and the Ten Commandments. After this I gave in their own language a short explanation, and told them what Paradise is, and what Hell is, and also who they are who go to Heaven to join the company of the blessed, and who are to be sent to the eternal punishments of hell. Upon hearing these things they all rose up and vied with one another in embracing me, and in confessing that the God of the Christians is the true God, as His laws are so agreeable to reason. Then they asked me if the souls of men like those of other animals perished together with the body. God put into my mouth arguments of such a sort, and so suited to their ways of thinking, that to their great joy I was able to prove to them the immortality of the soul. I find, by the way, that the arguments which are to convince these ignorant people must by no means be subtle, such as those which are found in the books of learned schoolmen, but must be such as their minds can understand. They asked me again how the soul of a dying person goes out of the body, how it was, whether it was as happens to us in dreams, when we seem to be conversing with our friends and acquaintance? (Ah, how often this happens to me, dearest brothers, when I am dreaming of you!) Was this because the soul then leaves the body? And again, whether God was black or white? For as there is so great a variety of colour among men, and the Indians being black themselves, consider their own colour the best, they believe that their gods are black. On this account the great majority of their idols are as black

as black can be, and moreover are generally so rubbed over with oil as to smell detestably, and seem to be as dirty as they are ugly and horrible to look at. To all these questions I was able to reply so as to satisfy them entirely. But when I came to the point at last, and urged them to embrace the religion which they felt to be true, they made that same objection which we hear from many Christians when urged to change their life,—that they would set men talking about them if they altered their ways and their religion, and besides, they said that they should be afraid that, if they did so, they would have nothing to live on and support themselves by.

I have found just one Brahmin and no more in all this coast who is a man of learning: he is said to have studied in a very famous Academy. Knowing this, I took measures to converse with him alone. He then told me at last, as a great secret, that the students of this Academy are at the outset made by their masters to take an oath not to reveal their mysteries, but that, out of friendship for me, he would disclose them to me. One of these mysteries was that there only exists one God, the Creator and Lord of heaven and earth, whom men are bound to worship, for the idols are simply images of devils, The Brahmins have certain books of sacred literature which contain, as they say, the laws of God. The masters teach in a learned tongue, as we do in Latin. He also explained to me these divine precepts one by one; but it would be a long business to write out his commentary, and indeed not worth the trouble. Their sages keep as a feast our Sunday. On this day they repeat at different hours this one player: "I adore Thee, O God; and I implore Thy help for ever." They are bound by oath to repeat this prayer frequently, and in a low voice. My friend added, that the law of nature permitted them to have more wives than one, and their sacred books predicted that the time would come when all men should embrace the same religion. After all this he asked me in my turn to explain the principal mysteries of the Christian religion, promising to keep them secret. I replied, that I would not tell him a word about them unless he promised beforehand to publish abroad what I should tell him of the religion of Jesus Christ. He made the promise, and then I carefully explained to him those words of Jesus Christ in which our religion is summed up: "He who believes and is baptized shall be saved." This text, with my commentary on it, which embraced the whole of the Apostles' Creed, he wrote down carefully, as well as the Commandments, on account of their close connection with the Creed. He told me also that one night he had dreamt that he had been made a Christian to his immense delight, and that he had become my brother and companion. He ended by begging me to make him a Christian secretly. But as he made certain conditions opposed to right and justice, I put off his baptism. I don't doubt but that by God's mercy he will one day be a Christian. I charged him to teach the ignorant and unlearned that there is only one God, Creator of heaven and earth; but he pleaded the obligation of his oath, and said he could not do so, especially as he was much afraid that if he did it he should become possessed by an evil spirit. ✶ ✶ ✶

REVIEW QUESTIONS

1. What was involved in the conversion of Asian peoples to Christianity?
2. What were the greatest challenges that Xavier and his fellows confronted?
3. How did Xavier's values shape his perception of Asian peoples?
4. How would you describe the reception of Christian missionaries and Christianity among the people of Cape Comorin?
5. How might Xavier and his mission have shaped the interaction and understanding of East and West?

SAINT TERESA OF ÁVILA

FROM *The Life of Teresa of Jesus*

Saint Teresa of Ávila (1515–1582) was a Spanish mystic, spiritual author, and monastic reformer. Her worldly achievements were great, to which the Discalced Carmelites still bear witness; in addition, the beauty of her inner life, as revealed in her writings, earned her recognition as one of the world's great female religious authors. Teresa was born in central Spain, the daughter of a wealthy hidalgo. At age fourteen, she was sent to a boarding school, where she became ill and began to consider her life's vocation. Despite paternal opposition, Teresa became a novice in a Carmelite convent around 1535. Her health collapsed again, leaving her an invalid for three years. During her convalescence, she began the series of meditations that would establish her reputation as a mystic. It took her fifteen years to perfect the prayers and meditations that would lead to her ecstatic visions and conversations with God. Her most celebrated work, The Life, *written in obedience to her confessors and directors, captured this process as the history of a soul, much like Augustine's* Confessions. *They combine religious ardor with human candor, an insistence that her experiences were a gift of God with an unwillingness to claim any spiritual distinction.*

In 1558, Teresa began to consider the restoration of Carmelite life to its original observance of austerity. It required complete separation from the world to promote prayerful meditation, such as was enjoined in the Primitive Carmelite Rule of 1247. In 1562, with the authorization of Pope Pius IV, Teresa and four companions opened the first convent of the Carmelite reform. Despite intense opposition from secular and ecclesiastical officials, her efforts eventually won the approval of the Carmelite general as well as his mandate to extend her reform to men. In 1567, she met a young Carmelite priest, Juan de Yepes, later canonized as Saint John of the Cross, a brilliant friar who helped her initiate the Carmelite reform for men. In her lifetime, she saw sixteen convents and twelve monasteries established. The last decades of her life were given to this work. Forty years after her death, she was canonized; in 1970, she was made a doctor of the Church.

From *The Life of Theresa of Jesus: The Autobiography of Teresa of Avila*, translated by E. Allison Peters (New York: Bantam Doubleday Dell, 1991), pp. 68–71.

*　　*　　*

I have strayed far from any intention, for I was trying to give the reasons why this kind of vision cannot be the work of the imagination. How could we picture Christ's Humanity by merely studying the subject or form any impression of His great beauty by means of the imagination? No little time would be necessary if such a reproduction was to be in the least like the original. One can indeed make such a picture with one's imagination, and spend time in regarding it, and considering the form and the brilliance of it; little by little one may even learn to perfect such an image and store it up in the memory. Who can prevent this? Such a picture can undoubtedly be fashioned with the understanding. But with regard to the vision which we are discussing there is no way of doing this: we have to look at it when the Lord is pleased to reveal it to us—to look as He wills and at whatever He wills. And there is no possibility of our subtracting from it or adding to it, or any way in which we can obtain it, whatever we may do, or look at it when we like or refrain from looking at it. If we try to look at any particular part of it, we at once lose Christ.

For two years and a half things went on like this and it was quite usual for God to grant me this favour. It must now be more than three years since He took it from me as a continually recurring favour, by giving me something else of a higher kind, which I shall describe later. Though I saw that He was speaking to me, and though I was looking upon that great beauty of His, and experiencing the sweetness with which He uttered those words—sometimes stern words—with that most lovely and Divine mouth, and though, too, I was extremely desirous of observing the colour of His eyes, or His height, so that I should be able to describe it, I have never been sufficiently worthy to see this, nor has it been of any use for me to attempt to do so; if I tried, I lost the vision altogether. Though I sometimes see Him looking at me compassionately, His gaze has such power that my soul cannot endure it and remains in so sublime a rapture that it loses this beauteous vision in order to have the greater fruition of it all. So there is no question here of our wanting or not wanting to see the vision. It is clear that the Lord wants of us only humility and shame, our acceptance of what is given us and our praise of its Giver.

This refers to all visions, none excepted. There is nothing that we can do about them; we cannot see more or less of them at will; and we can neither call them up nor banish them by our own efforts. The Lord's will is that we shall see quite clearly that they are produced, not by us but by His Majesty. Still less can we be proud of them: on the contrary, they make us humble and fearful, when we find that, just as the Lord takes from us the power of seeing what we desire, so He can also take from us these favours and His grace, with the result that we are completely lost. So while we live in this exile let us always walk with fear.

Almost invariably the Lord showed Himself to me in His resurrection body, and it was thus, too, that I saw Him in the Host. Only occasionally, to strengthen me when I was in tribulation, did He show me His wounds, and then He would appear sometimes as He was on the Cross and sometimes as in the Garden. On a few occasions I saw Him wearing the crown of thorns and sometimes He would also be carrying the Cross—because of my necessities, as I say, and those of others—but always in His glorified flesh. Many are the affronts and trials that I have suffered through telling this and many are the fears and persecutions that it has brought me. So sure were those whom I told of it that I had a devil that some of them wanted to exorcize me. This troubled me very little, but I was sorry when I found that my confessors were afraid to hear my confessions or when I heard that people were saying things to them against me. None the less, I could never regret having seen these heavenly visions and I would not exchange them for all the good things and delights of this world. I always considered them a great favour from the Lord, and I think they were the greatest of treasures; often the Lord Himself would reassure me about them. I found my love for Him growing exceedingly: I used to go to Him and tell Him about all these trials and I always came away from prayer comforted and with new strength. I did not dare to argue with my critics, because I saw that that made things worse, as they thought me lacking in humility. With my confessor, however, I did discuss these matters; and whenever he saw that I was troubled he would comfort me greatly.

As the visions became more numerous, one of those who had previously been in the habit of helping me and who used sometimes to hear my confessions when the minister was unable to do so, began to say that it was clear I was being deceived by the devil. So, as I was quite unable to resist it, they commanded me to make the sign of the Cross whenever I had a vision, and to snap my fingers at it so as to convince myself that it came from the devil, whereupon it would not come again: I was not to be afraid, they said, and God would protect me and take the vision away. This caused me great distress: as I could not help believing that my visions came from God, it was a terrible thing to have to do; and, as I have said, I could not possibly wish them to be taken from me. However, I did as they commanded me. I besought God often to set me free from deception; indeed, I was continually doing so and with many tears. I would also invoke Saint Peter and Saint Paul, for the Lord had told me (it was on their festival that He had first appeared to me) that they would prevent me from being deluded; and I used often to see them very clearly on my left hand, though not in an imaginary vision. These glorious Saints were in a very real sense my lords.

To be obliged to snap my fingers at a vision in which I saw the Lord caused me the sorest distress. For, when I saw Him before me, I could not have believed that the vision had come from the devil even if the alternative were my being cut to pieces. So this was a kind of penance to me, and a heavy one. In order not to have to be so continually crossing myself, I would carry a cross in my hand. This I did almost invariably; but I was not so particular about snapping my fingers at the vision, for it hurt me too much to do that. It reminded me of the way the Jews had insulted Him, and I would beseech Him to forgive me, since I did it out of obedience to him who was in His own place, and not to blame me, since he was one of the ministers whom He had placed in His Church. He told me not to worry about it and said I was quite right to obey, but He would see that my confessor learned the truth. When they made me stop my prayer He seemed to me to have become angry, and He told me to tell them that this was tyranny. He used to show me ways of knowing that the visions were not of the devil; some of these I shall describe later.

*   *   *

REVIEW QUESTIONS

1. What distinguishes Teresa's spirituality from that of Ignatius of Loyola?

2. Might we call her spirituality feminine?
3. Is Teresa's piety private or public? In what ways?
4. Are visions portable?
5. Are they entirely private?
6. How does language fail Teresa?

FROM *Canons and Decrees of the Council of Trent*

The great centerpiece of Catholic reform and reaction was the ecumenical Council of Trent, held in several sessions between 1545 and 1563. From the beginning of the sixteenth century, Catholic clergy, secular leaders, and Protestant reformers had called for an ecumenical council to address the inadequacies of the Catholic Church. Popes had resisted the tactic just as insistently for fear that such a council might be used to limit papal authority, as, indeed, had been the case in the fifteenth century. Pope Paul III, however, realized that a council might serve the cause of papal authority as well as that of church reform and accordingly called a council to meet in the city of Trent, located in imperial territory but still close to Rome. Agreements on procedures and the leadership of papal legates assured that the council remained firmly under papal direction and set a tone of doctrinal and disciplinary conservatism. Its deliberations and decisions divide themselves into three great periods. The first period, 1545–47, was devoted to dogma. The council rejected the Protestant teaching on Scripture as the sole source of religious truth and insisted that Scripture and tradition were equally authoritative. It retained the traditional seven sacraments. Most important, it rejected the Protestant doctrine of justification. During the second period, 1551–52, the council reasserted the traditional Catholic teaching on the Eucharist, rejecting the interpretations of Luther, Zwingli, and Calvin. Long delayed by political events and papal indifference, the council reconvened for the third and last time in 1562. In its final year, the council defined the Mass, addressed various liturgical issues, and resolved disciplinary issues such as clerical residency and training. Viewed in its entirety, the Council of Trent strengthened the authority of the papacy in the Catholic Church. If its decrees and canons were largely conservative, they were also unmistakable in their clarity and uniformity. In its pronouncements on discipline, it laid the foundations for a better-educated, more conscientious clergy. The Council of Trent clearly defined Catholic Christianity in opposition to Protestantism.

From *Canons and Decrees of the Council of Trent,* translated by H. J. Schroeder (London: Herder, 1941).

* * *

Fourth Session
Celebrated on the Eighth Day
of April 1546

DECREE CONCERNING THE CANONICAL SCRIPTURES

The holy, ecumenical and general Council of Trent, lawfully assembled in the Holy Ghost, the same three legates of the Apostolic See presiding, keeps this constantly in view, namely, that the purity of the Gospel may be preserved in the Church after the errors have been removed. This, of old promised through the Prophets in the Holy Scriptures, our Lord Jesus Christ, the Son of God, promulgated first with His own mouth, and then commanded it to be preached by His Apostles to every creature as the source at once of all saving truth and rules of conduct. It also clearly perceives that these truths and rules are contained in the written books and in the unwritten traditions, which, received by the Apostles from the mouth of Christ Himself, or from the Apostles themselves, the Holy Ghost dictating, have come down to us, transmitted as it were from hand to hand. Following, then, the examples of the orthodox Fathers, it receives and venerates with a feeling of piety and reverence all the books both of the Old and New Testaments, since one God is the author of both; also the traditions, whether they relate to faith or to morals, as having been dictated either orally by Christ or by the Holy Ghost, and preserved in the Catholic Church in unbroken succession. It has thought it proper, moreover, to insert in this decree a list of the sacred books, lest a doubt might arise in the mind of someone as to which are the books received by this council. They are the following: of the Old Testament, the five books of Moses, namely, Genesis, Exodus, Leviticus, Numbers, Deuteronomy; Josue, Judges, Ruth, the four books of Kings, two of Paralipomenon, the first and second of Esdras, the latter of which is called Nehemias, Tobias, Judith, Esther, Job, the Davidic Psalter of 150 Psalms, Proverbs, Ecclesiastes, the Canticle of Canticles, Wisdom, Ecclesiasticus, Isaias, Jeremias, with Baruch, Ezechiel, Daniel, the twelve minor Prophets, namely, Osee, Joel, Amos, Abdias, Jonas, Micheas, Nahum, Habacuc, Sophonias, Aggeus, Zacharias, Malachias; two books of Machabees, the first and second. Of the New Testament, the four Gospels, according to Matthew, Mark, Luke and John; the Acts of the Apostles written by Luke the Evangelist; fourteen Epistles of Paul the Apostle, to the Romans, two to the Corinthians, to the Galatians, to the Ephesians, to the Philippians, to the Colossians, two to the Thessalonians, two to Timothy, to Titus, to Philemon, to the Hebrews; two of Peter the Apostle, three of John the Apostle, one of James the Apostle, one of Jude the Apostle, and the Apocalypse of John the Apostle. If anyone does not accept as sacred and canonical the aforesaid books in their entirety and with all their parts, as they have been accustomed to be read in the Catholic Church and as they are contained in the old Latin Vulgate Edition, and knowingly and deliberately rejects the aforesaid traditions, let him be anathema. Let all understand, therefore, in what order and manner the council, after having laid the foundation of the confession of faith, will proceed, and who are the chief witnesses and supports to whom it will appeal in confirming dogmas and in restoring morals in the Church.

DECREE CONCERNING THE EDITION AND USE
OF THE SACRED BOOKS

Moreover, the same holy council considering that not a little advantage will accrue to the Church of God if it be made known which of all the Latin editions of the sacred books now in circulation is to be regarded as authentic, ordains and declares that the old Latin Vulgate Edition, which, in use for so many hundred years, has been approved by the Church, be in public lectures, disputations, sermons and expositions held as authentic, and that no one dare or presume under any pretext whatsoever to reject it.

Furthermore, to check unbridled spirits, it decrees that no one relying on his own judgment shall, in matters of faith and morals pertaining to the edification of Christian doctrine, distorting the

Holy Scriptures in accordance with his own conceptions, presume to interpret them contrary to that sense which holy mother Church, to whom it belongs to judge of their true sense and interpretation, has held and holds, or even contrary to the unanimous teaching of the Fathers, even though such interpretations should never at any time be published. Those who act contrary to this shall be made known by the ordinaries and punished in accordance with the penalties prescribed by the law.

And wishing, as is proper, to impose a restraint in this matter on printers also, who, now without restraint, thinking what pleases them is permitted them, print without the permission of ecclesiastical superiors the books of the Holy Scriptures and the notes and commentaries thereon of all persons indiscriminately, often with the name of the press omitted, often also under a fictitious press-name, and what is worse, without the name of the author, and also indiscreetly have for sale such books printed elsewhere, this council decrees and ordains that in the future the Holy Scriptures, especially the old Vulgate Edition, be printed in the most correct manner possible, and that it shall not be lawful for anyone to print or to have printed any books whatsoever dealing with sacred doctrinal matters without the name of the author, or in the future to sell them, or even to have them in possession, unless they have first been examined and approved by the ordinary, under penalty of anathema and fine prescribed by the last Council of the Lateran. If they be regulars they must in addition to this examination and approval obtain permission also from their own superiors after these have examined the books in accordance with their own statutes. Those who lend or circulate them in manuscript before they have been examined and approved, shall be subject to the same penalties as the printers, and those who have them in their possession or read them, shall, unless they make known the authors, be themselves regarded as the authors. The approbation of such books, however, shall be given in writing and shall appear authentically at the beginning of the book, whether it be written or printed, and all this, that is, both the examination and approbation, shall be done gratuitously, so that what ought to be approved may be approved and what ought to be condemned may be condemned.

Furthermore, wishing to repress that boldness whereby the words and sentences of the Holy Scriptures are turned and twisted to all kinds of profane usages, namely, to things scurrilous, fabulous, vain, to flatteries, detractions, superstitions, godless and diabolical incantations, divinations, the casting of lots and defamatory libels, to put an end to such irreverence and contempt, and that no one may in the future dare use in any manner the words of Holy Scripture for these and similar purposes, it is commanded and enjoined that all people of this kind be restrained by the bishops as violators and profaners of the word of God, with the penalties of the law and other penalties that they may deem fit to impose.

*   *   *

Twenty-third Session
Which Is the Seventh under the Supreme Pontiff, Pius IV, Celebrated on the Fifteenth Day of July 1563 The True and Catholic Doctrine Concerning the Sacrament of Order, Defined and Published by the Holy Council of Trent in the Seventh Session in Condemnation of Current Errors

FROM CHAPTER I
THE INSTITUTION OF THE PRIESTHOOD
OF THE NEW LAW

Sacrifice and priesthood are by the ordinance of God so united that both have existed in every law. Since therefore in the New Testament the Catholic Church has received from the institution of Christ the holy, visible sacrifice of the Eucharist, it must also be confessed that there is in that Church a new, visible and external priesthood, into which the old has been translated. That this was instituted by the same Lord our Savior, and that to the Apostles and their successors in the priesthood was given the power of consecrating, offering and administering His body and blood, as also of forgiving and retaining sins, is shown by the Sacred Scriptures and has always been taught by the tradition of the Catholic Church.

CHAPTER II
THE SEVEN ORDERS

But since the ministry of so holy a priesthood is something divine, that it might be exercised in a more worthy manner and with greater veneration, it was consistent that in the most well-ordered arrangement of the Church there should be several distinct orders of ministers, who by virtue of their office should minister to the priesthood, so distributed that those already having the clerical tonsure should ascend through the minor to the major orders. For the Sacred Scriptures mention unmistakably not only the priests but also the deacons, and teach in the most definite words what is especially to be observed in their ordination; and from the very beginning of the Church the names of the following orders and the duties proper to each one are known to have been in use, namely, those of the subdeacon, acolyte, exorcist, lector and porter, though these were not of equal rank; for the subdiaconate is classed among the major orders by the Fathers and holy councils, in which we also read very often of other inferior orders.

CHAPTER III
THE ORDER OF THE PRIESTHOOD IS TRULY A SACRAMENT

Since from the testimony of Scripture, Apostolic tradition and the unanimous agreement of the Fathers it is clear that grace is conferred by sacred ordination, which is performed by words and outward signs, no one ought to doubt that order is truly and properly one of the seven sacraments of holy Church. For the Apostle says: *I admonish thee*

that thou stir up the grace of God which is in thee by the imposition of my hands. For God has not given us the spirit of fear, but of power and of love and of sobriety.

CHAPTER IV
THE ECCLESIASTICAL HIERARCHY AND ORDINATION

But since in the sacrament of order, as also in baptism and confirmation, a character is imprinted which can neither be effaced nor taken away, the holy council justly condemns the opinion of those who say that the priests of the New Testament have only a temporary power, and that those who have once been rightly ordained can again become laymen if they do not exercise the ministry of the word of God. And if anyone should assert that all Christians without distinction are priests of the New Testament, or that they are all *inter se* endowed with an equal spiritual power, he seems to do nothing else than derange the ecclesiastical hierarchy, which is *an army set in array*; as if, contrary to the teaching of St. Paul, all are apostles, all prophets, all evangelists, all pastors, all doctors. Wherefore, the holy council declares that, besides the other ecclesiastical grades, the bishops, who have succeeded the Apostles, principally belong to this hierarchical order, and have been placed, as the same Apostle says, by the Holy Ghost to rule the Church of God; that they are superior to priests, administer the sacrament of confirmation, ordain ministers of the Church, and can perform many other functions over which those of an inferior order have no power. The council teaches furthermore, that in the ordination of bishops, priests and the other orders, the consent, call or authority, whether of the people or of any civil power or magistrate is not required in such wise that without this the ordination is invalid; rather does it decree that all those who, called and instituted only by the people or by the civil power or magistrate, ascend to the exercise of these offices, and those who by their rashness assume them, are not ministers of the Church, but are to be regarded as thieves and robbers, who have not entered by the door. These are the things which in general it has seemed good to the holy council to teach to the faithful of Christ regarding the sacrament of order. The contrary, however, it has resolved to condemn in definite and appropriate canons in the following manner, in order that all, making use with the help of Christ of the rule of faith, may in the midst of the darkness of so many errors recognize more easily the Catholic truth and adhere to it.

CANONS ON THE SACRAMENT OF ORDER

Canon 1. If anyone says that there is not in the New Testament a visible and external priesthood, or that there is no power of consecrating and offering the true body and blood of the Lord and of forgiving and retaining sins, but only the office and bare ministry of preaching the Gospel; or that those who do not preach are not priests at all, let him be anathema.

Canon 2. If anyone says that besides the priesthood there are not in the Catholic Church other orders, both major and minor, by which, as by certain steps, advance is made to the priesthood, let him be anathema.

Canon 3. If anyone says that order or sacred ordination is not truly and properly a sacrament instituted by Christ the Lord, or that it is some human contrivance devised by men unskilled in ecclesiastical matters, or that it is only a certain rite for choosing ministers of the word of God and of the sacraments, let him be anathema.

Canon 4. If anyone says that by sacred ordination the Holy Ghost is not imparted and that therefore the bishops say in vain: *Receive ye the Holy Ghost*, or that by it a character is not imprinted, or that he who has once been a priest can again become a layman, let him be anathema.

Canon 5. If anyone says that the holy unction which the Church uses in ordination is not only not required but is detestable and pernicious, as also are the other ceremonies of order, let him be anathema.

Canon 6. If anyone says that in the Catholic Church there is not instituted a hierarchy by di-

vine ordinance, which consists of bishops, priests and ministers, let him be anathema.

Canon 7. If anyone says that bishops are not superior to priests, or that they have not the power to confirm and ordain, or that the power which they have is common to them and to priests, or that orders conferred by them without the consent or call of the people or of the secular power are invalid, or that those who have been neither rightly ordained nor sent by ecclesiastical and canonical authority, but come from elsewhere, are lawful ministers of the word and of the sacraments, let him be anathema.

Canon 8. If anyone says that the bishops who are chosen by the authority of the Roman pontiff are not true and legitimate bishops, but merely human deception, let him be anathema.

*   *   *

Twenty-fifth Session Which Is the Ninth and Last under the Supreme Pontiff, Pius IV, Begun on the Third and Closed on the Fourth Day of December 1563

DECREE CONCERNING PURGATORY

Since the Catholic Church, instructed by the Holy Ghost, has, following the sacred writings and the ancient tradition of the Fathers, taught in sacred councils and very recently in this ecumenical council that there is a purgatory, and that the souls there detained are aided by the suffrages of the faithful and chiefly by the acceptable sacrifice of the altar, the holy council commands the bishops that they strive diligently to the end that the sound doctrine of purgatory, transmitted by the Fathers and sacred councils, be believed and maintained by the faithful of Christ, and be everywhere taught and preached. The more difficult and subtle questions, however, and those that do not make for edification and from which there is for the most part no increase in piety, are to be excluded from popular instructions to uneducated people. Likewise, things that are uncertain or that have the appearance of falsehood they shall not permit to be made known publicly and discussed. But those things that tend to a certain kind of curiosity or superstition, or that savor of filthy lucre, they shall prohibit as scandals and stumbling blocks to the faithful. The bishops shall see to it that the suffrages of the living, that is, the sacrifice of the mass, prayers, alms and other works of piety which they have been accustomed to perform for the faithful departed, be piously and devoutly discharged in accordance with the laws of the Church, and that whatever is due on their behalf from testamentary bequests or other ways, be discharged by the priests and ministers of the Church and others who are bound to render this service not in a perfunctory manner, but diligently and accurately.

ON THE INVOCATION, VENERATION, AND RELICS OF SAINTS, AND ON SACRED IMAGES

The holy council commands all bishops and others who hold the office of teaching and have charge of the *cura animarum,* that in accordance with the usage of the Catholic and Apostolic Church, received from the primitive times of the Christian religion, and with the unanimous teaching of the holy Fathers and the decrees of sacred councils, they above all instruct the faithful diligently in matters relating to intercession and invocation of the saints, the veneration of relics, and the legitimate use of images, teaching them that the saints who reign together with Christ offer up their prayers to God for men, that it is good and beneficial suppliantly to invoke them and to have recourse to their prayers, assistance and support in order to obtain favors from God through His Son, Jesus Christ our Lord, who alone is our redeemer and savior; and that they think impiously who deny that the saints who enjoy eternal happiness in heaven are to be invoked, or who assert that they do not pray for men, or that our invocation of them to pray for each of us individually is idolatry, or that it is opposed to the word of God and inconsistent with the honor of the *one mediator of God and men, Jesus Christ,* or that it is foolish to pray vocally or mentally to those who reign in heaven. Also, that the holy bodies of the holy martyrs and of others living with Christ, which were the living members of Christ and the temple of the Holy Ghost, to be awakened by Him to eternal life and to be glorified, are to be venerated by the faithful, through which many benefits are bestowed by God on men, so that those who maintain that veneration and honor are not due to the relics of the saints, or that these and other memorials are honored by the faithful without profit, and that the places dedicated to the memory of the saints for the purpose of obtaining their aid are visited in vain, are to be utterly condemned, as the Church has already long since condemned and now again condemns them. Moreover, that the images of Christ, of the Virgin Mother of God, and of the other saints are to be placed and retained especially in the churches, and that due honor and veneration is to be given them; not, however, that any divinity or virtue is believed to be in them by reason of which they are to be venerated, or that something is to be asked of them, or that trust is to be placed in images, as was done of old by the Gentiles who placed their hope in idols; but because the honor which is shown them is referred to the prototypes which they represent, so that by means of the images which we kiss and before which we uncover the head and prostrate ourselves, we adore Christ and venerate the saints whose likeness they bear. That is what was defined by the decrees of the councils, especially of the Second Council of Nicaea, against the opponents of images.

Moreover, let the bishops diligently teach that by means of the stories of the mysteries of our redemption portrayed in paintings and other representations the people are instructed and confirmed in the articles of faith, which ought to be borne in mind and constantly reflected upon; also that great profit is derived from all holy images, not only because the people are thereby reminded of the benefits and gifts bestowed on them by Christ, but also because through the saints the miracles of God and salutary examples are set before the eyes of the faithful, so that they may give God thanks for those things, may fashion their own life and conduct in imitation of the saints and be moved to adore and love God and cultivate piety. But if anyone should teach or maintain any thing contrary to these decrees, let him be anathema. If any abuses shall have found their way into these holy and salutary observances, the holy council desires earnestly that they be completely removed, so that no representation of false doctrines and such as might be the occasion of grave error to the uneducated be exhibited. And if at times it happens, when this is beneficial to the illiterate, that the stories and narratives of the Holy Scriptures are portrayed and exhibited, the people should be instructed that not for that reason is the divinity represented in picture as if it can be seen with bodily eyes or expressed in colors or figures. Furthermore, in the invocation of the saints, the veneration of relics, and the sacred use of images, all superstition shall be removed, all filthy quest for gain eliminated, and all lasciviousness avoided, so that images shall not be painted and adorned with a seductive charm, or the celebration of saints and the visitation of relics be perverted by the people into boisterous festivities and drunkenness, as if the festivals in honor of the saints are to be celebrated with revelry and with no sense of decency. Finally, such zeal and care should be exhibited by the bishops with regard to these things that nothing may appear that is disorderly or unbecoming and confusedly arranged, nothing that is profane, nothing disrespectful, since holiness becometh the house of God. That these things may be the more faithfully observed, the holy council decrees that no one is permitted to erect or cause to be erected in any place or church, howsoever exempt, any unusual image unless it has been approved by the bishop; also that no new miracles be accepted and no relics recognized unless they have been investigated and approved by the same bishop, who, as soon as he has obtained any knowledge of such matters, shall, after consulting theologians and other pious men, act thereon as he shall judge consonant with truth and piety. But if any doubtful or grave abuse is to be eradicated, or if indeed any graver question concerning these matters should arise, the bishop, before he settles the controversy, shall await the decision of the metropolitan and of the bishops of the province in a provincial synod; so, however, that nothing new or anything that has not hitherto been in use in the Church, shall be decided upon without having first consulted the most holy Roman pontiff.

*   *   *

REVIEW QUESTIONS

1. How does the Council of Trent approach the question of the authority of Scripture?
2. Why did it set that discussion in terms of a list of books the council recognized as sacred?
3. On what basis might the council claim the authority to name the books of the Bible and determine the correct translation?
4. What are the seven orders? What is their place in Christianity and their function? What is the nature of their authority?
5. What do these decrees suggest about the practice of Catholicism in the years following the Reformation?

14 ❧ RELIGION, WARFARE, AND SOVEREIGNTY, 1540–1660

The challenge to the authority of classical culture that the new worlds posed, combined with the fragmentation of the medieval Christian Church—the "body of all believers"—laid the foundation in the second half of the sixteenth century for profound crises of political and social order and of epistemology, the very foundation of human knowledge. In their efforts to describe what they saw in the Americas, European conquistadores and clergy were forced to adopt analogies: hundreds of species of plants and animals were not to be found in the writings of Pliny, the great and trusted botanist and zoologist of the ancient world, or in the Bible. The cultures of the Americas posed new models of social and political relations, opening new possibilities for the ordering of political relations and calling into question the very nature of political authority.

Within Europe, civil wars arose in the wake of the fragmentation of the Christian Church. The wars of religion in France, 1562–98, led astute observers such as Montaigne to question the claim of each side to know the truth, and to question whether human reason was sufficient to discern the truth. In all the religious wars, beginning with the German Peasants' War of 1525 and culminating in the Thirty Years' War, 1618–48, the social order was overthrown, as peasant killed lord, brother killed brother, son killed father, and neighbor killed neighbor. What was it to be human? To be savage? And where was God while Christian slaughtered Christian?

The crisis of the seventeenth century was not simply intellectual and spiritual but also had real material aspects. The expansion of Europe into new worlds changed patterns of consumption and production, thus contributing to the overthrow of traditional work processes and lifestyles. It created a tremendous influx of wealth that aided the rise of new economic and political powers, both social groups and nation-states, and that contributed to chronic inflation. Changes in society, economy, and politics created tensions that found expression in the violence of the period. Religious wars were seldom entirely religious in cause or in consequence. The almost constant march and countermarch of armies not only destroyed life and property but also disrupted agriculture and spread disease. The struggle for existence, difficult under the best of circumstances in the early modern period, became much more difficult in the age of crisis.

By 1660, peasants had risen in unprecedented numbers against their lords; common Englishmen had executed their king; Europeans had witnessed multiple incidents of cannibalism in their own villages; and the medieval epistemology, that very base by which Europeans could be certain of the veracity of what they knew, had collapsed. New formulations were being tentatively put forward, but they did not yet replace the old certainties that had been irrecoverably lost.

GIOVANNI MICHIEL

FROM A Venetian Ambassador's Report on the St. Bartholomew's Day Massacre

The struggle for supremacy in northern Italy, which marked the last half of the fifteenth century, gave rise to a new form of diplomacy, including structures and procedures that would be fundamental to relations among all modern states. Requiring continuous contact and communication, Renaissance states turned to permanent diplomacy, distinguished by the use of accredited resident ambassadors rather than ad hoc missions of medieval legates. The tasks of a permanent ambassador were to represent his government at state ceremonies, to gather information, and, occasionally, to enter into negotiations. Nowhere was this system more fully and expertly articulated than by the Republic of Venice in the late fifteenth and sixteenth centuries. Its ambassadors were chosen with unusual care from the most prominent families of the city. They were highly educated, and their duties were carefully defined. Among the latter were weekly dispatches reporting all matters of any interest to Venice. These reports were regularly read and debated in the senate, which replied with questions, instructions, and information of its own. As a result, Venetian ambassadors were among the most skilled and respected in early modern Europe. In this report, Giovanni Michiel interprets the events of St. Bartholomew's Day in 1572. The massacre of Huguenots, instigated by the Queen Mother, Catherine de Medici, outraged Protestant Europe and dashed all hopes for peace in France. Of particular interest is the ambassador's harshly realistic account of the political motives for so violent an act of statecraft.

From *Pursuit of Power: Venetian Ambassadors' Reports on Spain, Turkey and France in the Age of Phillip II, 1560–1600*, by James C. Davis (New York: HarperCollins, 1970), pp. 72–76, 78–79.

*   *   *

Turning to the queen, Admiral de Coligny said, "Madame, the king refuses to involve himself in one war. God grant that he may not be caught up in another which he cannot avoid."

By these words he meant, some say, that if they abandoned the prince of Orange things might go badly for him, and there would be a danger that if the prince failed to win or was actually driven out by the Spanish or for some other reason, then he might enter France with his French and German followers and it might be necessary to drive him out by force. However, everyone understood his words in a very different sense, namely that he was giving notice that he planned to stir up new storms and renew the rioting and civil war. When the queen carefully pondered this it became the chief reason, taken together with the other considerations, why she hurried to prepare that fate for him which he eventually met.

*   *   *

Then, at the dinner hour on Friday, while the admiral was returning on foot from the court to his lodgings and reading a letter, someone fired an arquebus at him. The shot came from a window which faced a bit obliquely on the street, near the royal palace called the Louvre. But it did not strike him in the chest as intended because it so happened that the admiral was wearing a pair of slippers which made walking difficult and, wanting to take them off and hand them to a page, he had just started to turn around. So the arquebus shot tore off a finger on his left hand and then hit his right arm near the wrist and passed through it to the other side near the elbow. If he had simply walked straight ahead it would have hit him in the chest and killed him.

As you can imagine, news of the event caused great excitement, especially at court. Everyone supposed it had been done by order of the duke of Guise to avenge his family, because the window from which the shot was fired belonged to his mother's house, which had purposely been left empty after she had gone to stay in another. When the news was reported to the king, who happened to be playing tennis with the duke of Guise, they say he turned white and looked thunderstruck. Without saying a word he withdrew into his chambers and made it obvious that he was extremely angry.

*   *   *

On Saturday the admiral's dressings were changed and the word was given out—which may or may not have been true—that the wound was not a mortal one and that there was no danger even that he would lose the arm. The Huguenots only blustered all the more, and everyone waited to see what would happen next. The duke of Guise knew he might be attacked, so he armed himself and stuck close to his uncle, the duke of Aumale, and as many relatives, friends and servants as possible.

But before long the situation changed. Late Saturday night, just before the dawn of Saint Bartholomew's Day, the massacre or slaughter was carried out. The French say the king ordered it. How wild and terrifying it was in Paris (which has a larger population than any other city in Europe), no one can imagine. Nor can one imagine the rage and frenzy of those who slaughtered and sacked, as the king ordered the people to do. Nor what a marvel, not to say a miracle, it was that the common people did not take advantage of this freedom to loot and plunder from Catholics as well as Huguenots, and ravenously take whatever they could get their hands on, especially since the city is incredibly wealthy. No one would ever imagine that a people could be armed and egged on by their ruler, yet not get out of control once they were worked up. But it was not God's will that things should reach such a pass.

The slaughter went on past Sunday for two or three more days, despite the fact that edicts were issued against it and the duke of Nevers was sent riding through the city along with the king's natural brother to order them to stop the killing. The massacre showed how powerfully religion can affect men's minds. On every street one could see the barbarous sight of men cold-bloodedly outraging others of their own people, and not just men who had never done them any harm but in most cases people they knew to be their neighbors and even their relatives. They had no feeling, no mercy on anyone, even those who kneeled before them and humbly begged for their lives. If one man hated another because of some argument or lawsuit all he had to say was "This man is a Huguenot" and he was immediately killed. (That happened to many Catholics.) If their victims threw themselves in the river as a last resort and tried to swim to safety, as many did, they chased them in boats and then drowned them. There was a great deal of looting and pillaging and they say the goods taken amounted to two million because many Huguenots, including some of the richest of them, had come to live in Paris after the most recent edict of pacification. Some estimate the number who were killed as high as four thousand, while others put it as low as two thousand.

The killing spread to all the provinces and most of the major cities and was just as frenzied there, if not more so. They attacked anyone, even the gentry, and as a result all the leaders who did not escape have been killed or thrown in prison. It is true that Montgomery and some others who were pursued by the duke of Guise escaped to England, but they are not major figures. And the king has terrified them enough so they won't make any trouble.

*   *   *

REVIEW QUESTIONS

1. According to the report, at what level of society did the St. Bartholomew's Day Massacre originate?
2. How was a person identified as Huguenot or Catholic?
3. What does that say about religious identity in early modern France?
4. Do we know from this report who ordered the assassination of Admiral de Coligny?
5. Who caused the massacre?
6. What do we learn about the relation of religion to politics and political action?

REGINALD SCOT

FROM *Discoverie of Witchcraft*

Reginald Scot (1538–1599) was a Kentish squire who witnessed a number of fraudulent accusations of witchcraft in the villages of his shire during the reign of Elizabeth I. In 1584, he wrote his Discoverie of Witchcraft, *which contains a remarkable exposition of magical elements in medieval Catholicism and a protest against the persecution of harmless old women. Scot doubted that God could ever have allowed witches to exercise supernatural powers, much less demand that they be persecuted for it. In this regard, he deserves to be ranked among the skeptics on the question of witchcraft, although he never denied the existence of witches. According to Scot, all "witches" fell into one of four categories. First were the innocent, those falsely accused. Second were the deluded, those convinced through their own misery that they were witches. Third were the malefactors, those who harmed people and damaged property, though not by supernatural means. Fourth were imposters, those who posed as witches and conjurers. Scot denied that any of these "witches" had access to supernatural powers. Malefactors and imposters were, in fact, the witches named in the Bible as not being suffered to live. They were the only witches Scot admitted. His work is said to have made a great impression in the magistracy and clergy of his day. Nonetheless, his remained a minority opinion. Most contemporaries understood as tantamount to atheism any denial of the reality of spirits or the possibility of the supernatural. The persecution of witches continued unabated into the eighteenth century; many thousands, mostly harmless old women, fell victim to the rage.*

From *Discoverie of Witchcraft*, by Reginald Scot, 1584, edited by Brinsley Nicholson (London: E. Stock, 1886).

*   *   *

The inconvenience growing by mens credulitie herein, with a reproofe of some churchmen, which are inclined to the common conceived opinion of witches omnipotencie, and a familiar example thereof. But the world is now so bewitched and over-run with this fond error, that even where a man shuld seeke comfort and counsell, there shall hee be sent (in case of necessitie) from God to the divell; and from the Physician, to the coosening witch, who will not sticke to take upon hir, by wordes to heale the lame (which was proper onelie to Christ: and to them whom he assisted with his divine power) yea, with hir familiar & charmes she will take upon hir to cure the blind: though in the tenth of S. *Johns* Gospell it be written, that the divell cannot open the eies of the blind. And they attaine such credit as I have heard (to my greefe) some of the ministerie affirme, that they have had in their parish at one instant, xvii. or xviii. witches: meaning such as could worke miracles supernaturallie. Whereby they manifested as well their infidelitie and ignorance, in conceiving Gods word; as their negligence and error in instructing their flocks. For they themselves might understand, and also teach their parishoners, that God onelie worketh great woonders; and that it is he which sendeth such punishments to the wicked, and such trials to the elect: according to the saieng of the Prophet *Haggai*, I smote you with blasting and mildeaw, and with haile, in all the labours of your hands; and yet you turned not unto me, saith the Lord. And therefore saith the same Prophet in another place; You have sowen much, and bring in little. And both in *Joel* and *Leviticus*, the like phrases and proofes are used and made. But more shalbe said of this hereafter.

*   *   *

At the assises holden at *Rochester*, Anno 1581, one *Margaret Simons*, the wife of *John Simons*, of *Brenchlie* in *Kent*, was araigned for witchcraft, at the instigation and complaint of divers fond and malicious persons; and speciallie by the meanes of one *John Ferrall* vicar of that parish: with whom I talked about that matter, and found him both fondlie assotted in the cause, and enviouslie bent towards hir: and (which is worse) as unable to make a good account of his faith, as shee whom he accused. That which he, for his part, laid to the poore womans charge, was this.

His sonne (being an ungratious boie, and prentise to one *Robert Scotchford* clothier, dwelling in that parish of *Brenchlie*) passed on a daie by hir house; at whome by chance hir little dog barked. Which thing the boie taking in evill part, drewe his knife, & pursued him therewith even to hir doore: whom she rebuked with some such words as the boie disdained, & yet nevertheless would not be persuaded to depart in a long time. At the last he returned to his maisters house, and within five or sixe daies fell sicke. Then was called to mind the fraie betwixt the dog and the boie: insomuch as the vicar (who thought himselfe so privileged, as he little mistrusted that God would visit his children with sicknes) did so calculate; as he found, partlie through his owne judgement, and partlie (as he himselfe told me) by the relation of other witches, that his said sonne was by hir bewitched. Yea, he also told me, that this his sonne (being as it were past all cure) received perfect health at the hands of another witch.

He proceeded yet further against hir, affirming, that alwaies in his parish church, when he desired to read most plainelie, his voice so failed him, as he could scant be heard at all. Which hee could impute, he said, to nothing else, but to hir inchantment. When I advertised the poore woman hereof, as being desirous to heare what she could saie for hir selfe; she told me, that in verie deed his voice did much faile him, speciallie when he strained himselfe to speake lowdest. How beit, she said that at all times his voice was hoarse and lowe: which thing I perceived to be true. But sir, said she, you shall understand, that this our vicar is diseased with such a kind of hoarsenesse, as divers of our neighbors in this parish, not long since, doubted that he had the French pox; & in that respect utterly refused to communicate with him: untill such time as (being therunto injoined by M. D. *Lewen* the Ordinarie) he had brought frō *London* a certificat, under the hands of two physicians, that his hoarsenes proceeded from a disease in the lungs. Which certificat he published in the church, in the presence of the whole congregation: and by this meanes hee was cured, or rather excused of the shame of his disease. And this I knowe to be true by the relation of divers honest men of that parish. And truelie, if one of the Jurie had not beene wiser than the other, she had beene condemned thereupon, and upon other as ridiculous matters as this. For the name of a

witch is so odious, and hir power so feared among the common people, that if the honestest bodie living chance to be arraigned thereupon, she shall hardlie escape condemnation.

A Confutation of the Common Conceived Opinion of Witches and Witchcraft, and How Detestable a Sinne It Is to Repaire to Them for Counsell or Helpe in Time of Affliction

But whatsoever is reported or conceived of such manner of witchcrafts, I dare avow to be false and fabulous (coosinage, dotage, and poisoning excepted:) neither is there any mention made of these kind of witches in the Bible. If Christ had knowne them, he would not have pretermitted to invaie against their presumption, in taking upon them his office: as, to heale and cure diseases; and to worke such miraculous and supernaturall things, as whereby he himselfe was speciallie knowne, beleeved, and published to be God; his actions and cures consisting (in order and effect) according to the power of our witchmoongers imputed to witches. Howbeit, if there be any in these daies afflicted in such strange sort, as Christs cures and patients are described in the new testament to have beene: we flie from trusting in God to trusting in witches, who doo not onelie in their coosening art take on them the office of Christ in this behalfe; but use his verie phrase of speech to such idolators, as com to seeke divine assistance at their hands, saieng; Go thy waies, thy sonne or thy daughter, &c. shall doo well, and be whole.

*   *   *

In like manner I say, he that attributeth to a witch, such divine power, as dulie and onelie apperteineth unto GOD (which all witchmongers doo) is in hart a blasphemer, an idolater, and full of grosse impietie, although he neither go nor send to hir for assistance.

A Further Confutation of Witches Miraculous and Omnipotent Power, by Invincible Reasons and Authorities, with Dissuasions from Such Fond Credulitie

If witches could doo anie such miraculous things, as these and other which are imputed to them, they might doo them againe and againe, at anie time or place, or at anie mans desire: for the divell is as strong at one time as at another, as busie by daie as by night, and readie enough to doo all mischeefe, and careth not whom he abuseth. And in so much as it is confessed, by the most part of witchmoongers themselves, that he knoweth not the cogitation of mans heart, he should (me thinks) sometimes appeere unto honest and credible persons, in such grosse and corporall forme, as it is said he dooth unto witches: which you shall never heare to be justified by one sufficient witnesse. For the divell indeed entreth into the mind, and that waie seeketh mans confusion.

The art alwaies presupposeth the power; so as, if they saie they can doo this or that, they must shew how and by what meanes they doo it; as neither the witches, nor the witchmoongers are able to doo. For to everie action is required the facultie and abilitie of the agent or dooer; the aptnes of the patient or subject; and a convenient and possible application. Now the witches are mortall, and their power dependeth upon the analogie and consonancie of their minds and bodies; but with their minds they can but will and understand; and with their bodies they can doo no more, but as the bounds and ends of terrene sense will suffer: and therefore their power extendeth not to doo such miracles, as surmounteth their owne sense, and the understanding of others which are wiser than they; so as here wanteth the vertue and power of the efficient. And in reason, there can be no more vertue in the thing caused, than in the cause, or that which proceedeth of or from the benefit of the cause. And we see, that ignorant and impotent women, or witches, are the causes of in-

cantations and charmes; wherein we shall perceive there is none effect, if we will credit our owne experience and sense unabused, the rules of philosophie, or the word of God. For alas! What an unapt instrument is a toothles, old, impotent, and unweldie woman to flie in the aier? Truelie, the divell little needs such instruments to bring his purposes to passe.

It is strange, that we should suppose, that such persons can worke such feates: and it is more strange, that we will imagine that to be possible to be doone by a witch, which to nature and sense is impossible; speciallie when our neighbours life dependeth upon our credulitie therein; and when we may see the defect of abilitie, which alwaies is an impediment both to the act, and also to the presumption thereof. And bicause there is nothing possible in lawe, that in nature is impossible; therefore the judge dooth not attend or regard what the accused man saith; or yet would doo: but what is prooved to have beene committed, and naturallie falleth in mans power and will to doo. For the lawe saith, that To will a thing unpossible, is a signe of a mad man, or of a foole, upon whom no sentence or judgement taketh hold. Furthermore, what Jurie will condemne, or what Judge will give sentence or judgement against one for killing a man at *Berwicke;* when they themselves, and manie other sawe that man at *London,* that verie daie, wherein the murther was committed; yea though the partie confesse himself guiltie therein, and twentie witnesses depose the same? But in this case also I saie the judge is not to weigh their testimonie, which is weakened by lawe; and the judges authoritie is to supplie the imperfection of the case, and to mainteine the right and equitie of the same.

Seeing therefore that some other things might naturallie be the occasion and cause of such calamities as witches are supposed to bring; let not us that professe the Gospell and knowledge of Christ, be bewitched to beleeve that they doo such things, as are in nature impossible, and in sense and reason incredible. If they saie it is doone through the divels helpe, who can work miracles; whie do not theeves bring their busines to passe miraculouslie, with whom the divell is as conversant as with the other? Such mischeefes as are imputed to witches, happen where no witches are; yea and continue when witches are hanged and burnt: whie then should we attribute such effect to that cause, which being taken awaie, happeneth neverthelesse?

*   *   *

What Testimonies and Witnesses Are Allowed to Give Evidence against Reputed Witches, by the Report and Allowance of the Inquisitors Themselves, and Such as Are Speciall Writers Heerein

Excommunicat persons, partakers of the falt, infants, wicked servants, and runnawaies are to be admitted to beare witnesse against their dames in this mater of witchcraft: bicause (saith *Bodin* the champion of witchmoongers) none that be honest are able to detect them. Heretikes also and witches shall be received to accuse, but not to excuse a witch. And finallie, the testimonie of all infamous persons in this case is good and allowed. Yea, one lewd person (saith *Bodin*) may be received to accuse and condemne a thousand suspected witches. And although by lawe, a capitall enimie may be challenged; yet *James Sprenger*, and *Henrie Institor*, (from whom *Bodin*, and all the writers that ever I have read, doo receive their light, authorities and arguments) saie (upon this point of lawe) that The poore frendlesse old woman must proove, that hir capitall enimie would have killed hir, and that hee hath both assalted & wounded hir; otherwise she pleadeth all in vaine. If the judge aske hir, whether she have anie capitall enimies; and she rehearse other, and forget hir accuser; or else answer that he was hir capital enimie, but now she hopeth he is not so: such a one is nevertheles admitted for a witnes. And though by lawe, single witnesses are not admittable; yet if one depose she hath bewitched hir cow; another, hir sow; and the third, hir butter:

these saith (saith *M. Mal.* and *Bodin*) are no single witnesses; bicause they agree that she is a witch.

The Fifteene Crimes Laid to the Charge of Witches, by Witchmongers, Speciallie by Bodin, in Dæmonomania

They denie God, and all religion.

Answere. Then let them die therefore, or at the least be used like infidels, or apostataes.

They cursse, blaspheme, and provoke God with all despite.

Answere. Then let them have the law expressed in *Levit.* 24. and *Deut.* 13 & 17.

They give their faith to the divell, and they worship and offer sacrifice unto him.

Ans. Let such also be judged by the same lawe.

They doo solemnelie vow and promise all their progenie unto the divell.

Ans. This promise proceedeth from an unsound mind, and is not to be regarded; bicause they cannot performe it, neither will it be prooved true. Howbeit, if it be done by anie that is sound of mind, let the cursse of *Jeremie*, 32.36. light upon them, to wit, the sword, famine and pestilence.

They sacrifice their owne children to the divell before baptisme, holding them up in the aire unto him, and then thrust a needle into their braines.

Ans. If this be true, I maintaine them not herein: but there is a lawe to judge them by. Howbeit, it is so contrarie to sense and nature, that it were follie to beleeve it; either upon *Bodins* bare word, or else upon his presumptions; speciallie when so small commoditie and so great danger and inconvenience insueth to the witches thereby.

They burne their children when they have sacrificed them.

Ans. Then let them have such punishment, as they that offered their children unto *Moloch: Levit.* 20. But these be meere devises of witchmoongers and inquisitors, that with extreame tortures have wroong such confessions from them; or else with false reports have beelied them; or by flatterie & faire words and promises have woon it at their hands, at the length.

They sweare to the divell to bring as manie into that societie as they can.

Ans. This is false, and so prooved elsewhere.

They sweare by the name of the divell.

Ans. I never heard anie such oth, neither have we warrant to kill them that so doo sweare; though indeed it be verie lewd and impious.

They use incestuous adulterie with spirits.

Ans. This is a stale ridiculous lie, as is prooved apparentlie hereafter.

They boile infants (after they have murthered them unbaptised) untill their flesh be made potable.

Ans. This is untrue, incredible, and impossible.

They eate the flesh and drinke the bloud of men and children openlie.

Ans. Then are they kin to the *Anthropophagi* and *Canibals.* But I beleeve never an honest man in *England* nor in *France,* will affirme that he hath seene any of these persons, that are said to be witches, do so; if they shuld, I beleeve it would poison them.

They kill men with poison.

Ans. Let them be hanged for their labour.

They kill mens cattell.

Ans. Then let an action of trespasse be brought against them for so dooing.

They bewitch mens corne, and bring hunger and barrennes into the countrie; they ride and flie in the aire, bring stormes, make tempests, &c.

Ans. Then will I worship them as gods; for those be not the works of man nor yet of witch: as I have elsewhere prooved at large.

They use venerie with a divell called *Incubus,* even when they lie in bed with their husbands, and have children by them, which become the best witches.

Ans. This is the last lie, verie ridiculous, and confuted by me elsewhere.

Of Foure Capitall Crimes Objected against Witches, All Fullie Answered and Confuted as Frivolous

First therefore they laie to their charge idolatrie. But alas without all reason: for such are properlie knowne to us to be idolaters, as doo externall worship to idols or strange gods. The furthest point that idolatrie can be stretched unto, is, that they, which are culpable therein, are such as hope for and seeke salvation at the hands of idols, or of anie other than God; or fixe their whole mind and love upon anie creature, so as the power of God be neglected and contemned thereby. But witches neither seeke nor beleeve to have salvation at the hands of divels, but by them they are onlie deceived; the instruments of their phantasie being corrupted, and so infatuated, that they suppose, confesse, and saie they can doo that, which is as farre beyond their power and nature to doo, as to kill a man at *Yorke* before noone, when they have beene seene at *London* in that morning, &c. But if these latter idolaters, whose idolatrie is spirituall, and committed onelie in mind, should be punished by death; then should everie covetous man, or other, that setteth his affection anie waie too much upon an earthlie creature, be executed, and yet perchance the witch might escape scotfree.

Secondlie, apostasie is laid to their charge, whereby it is inferred, that they are worthie to die. But apostasie is, where anie of sound judgement forsake the gospell, learned and well knowne unto them; and doo not onelie embrace impietie and infidelitie; but oppugne and resist the truth erstwhile by them professed. But alas these poore women go not about to defend anie impietie, but after good admonition repent.

Thirdlie, they would have them executed for seducing the people. But God knoweth they have small store of Rhetorike or art to seduce; except to tell a tale of Robin good-fellow be to deceive and seduce. Neither may their age or sex admit that opinion or accusation to be just: for they themselves are poore seduced soules. I for my part (as else-where I have said) have prooved this point to be false in most apparent sort.

Fourthlie, as touching the accusation, which all the writers use herein against them for their carnall copulation with *Incubus:* the follie of mens credulitie is as much to be woondered at and derided, as the others vaine and impossible confessions. For the divell is a spirit, and hath neither flesh nor bones, which were to be used in the performance of this action. And since he also lacketh all instruments, substance, and seed ingendred of bloud; it were follie to staie overlong in the confutation of that, which is not in the nature of things. And yet must I saie somewhat heerein, bicause the opinion hereof is so stronglie and universallie received, and the fables thereupon so innumerable; wherby *M. Mal. Bodin, Hemingius, Hyperius, Danaeus, Erastus,* and others that take upon them to write heerein, are so abused, or rather seeke to abuse others; as I woonder at their fond credulitie in this behalfe. For they affirme undoubtedlie, that the divell plaieth *Succubus* to the man, and carrieth from him the seed of generation, which he delivereth as *Incubus* to the woman, who manie times that waie is gotten with child; which will verie naturallie (they saie) become a witch, and such one they affirme *Merline* was.

*   *   *

By What Meanes the Common People Have Beene Made Beleeve in the Miraculous Works of Witches, a Definition of Witchcraft, and a Description Thereof

The common people have beene so assotted and bewitched, with whatsoever poets have feigned of witchcraft, either in earnest, in jest, or else in derision; and with whatsoever lowd liers and couseners for their pleasures heerein have invented, and with whatsoever tales they have heard from old doting women, or from their mothers maids, and with whatsoever the grandfoole their ghostlie father, or anie other morrow masse preest had informed them; and finallie with whatsoever they have swallowed up through tract of time, or through their owne timerous nature or ignorant conceipt, concerning these matters of hagges and witches: as they have so settled their opinion and credit thereupon, that they thinke it heresie to doubt in anie part of the matter; speciallie bicause they find this word

witchcraft expressed in the scriptures; which is as to defend praieng to saincts, bicause *Sanctus, Sanctus, Sanctus* is written in *Te Deum.*

And now to come to the definition of witchcraft, which hitherto I did deferre and put off purposelie: that you might perceive the true nature thereof, by the circumstances, and therefore the rather to allow of the same, seeing the varietie of other writers. Witchcraft is in truth a cousening art, wherin the name of God is abused, prophaned and blasphemed, and his power attributed to a vile creature. In estimation of the vulgar people, it is a supernaturall worke, contrived betweene a corporall old woman, and a spirituall divell. The maner thereof is so secret, mysticall, and strange, that to this daie there hath never beene any credible witnes thereof. It is incomprehensible to the wise, learned or faithfull; a probable matter to children, fooles, melancholike persons and papists. The trade is thought to be impious. The effect and end thereof to be sometimes evill, as when thereby man or beast, grasse, trees, or corne, &c; is hurt: sometimes good, as whereby sicke folkes are healed, theeves bewraied, and true men come to their goods, &c. The matter and instruments, wherewith it is accomplished, are words, charmes, signes, images, characters, &c; the which words although any other creature do pronounce, in manner and forme as they doo, leaving out no circumstance requisite or usually for that action: yet none is said to have the grace or gift to performe the matter, except she be a witch, and so taken either by hir owne consent, or by others imputation.

Reasons to Proove That Words and Characters Are But Bables, and That Witches Cannot Doo Such Things as the Multitude Supposeth They Can, Their Greatest Woonders Prooved Trifles, of a Yoong Gentleman Cousened

That words, characters, images, and such other trinkets, which are thought so necessarie instruments for witchcraft (as without the which no such thing can be accomplished) are but bables, devised by couseners, to abuse the people withall; I trust I have sufficientlie prooved. And the same maie be further and more plainelie perceived by these short and compendious reasons following.

First, in that *Turkes* and infidels, in their witchcraft, use both other words, and other characters than our witches doo and also such as are most contrarie. In so much as, if ours be bad, in reason theirs should be good. If their witches can doo anie thing, ours can doo nothing. For as our witches are said to renounce Christ, and despise his sacraments: so doo the other forsake *Mahomet,* and his lawes, which is one large step to christianitie.

It is also to be thought, that all witches are couseners; when mother *Bungie,* a principall witch, so reputed, tried, and condemned of all men, and continuing in that exercise and estimation manie yeares (having cousened & abused the whole realme, in so much as there came to hir, witchmongers from all the furthest parts of the land, she being in diverse bookes set out with authoritie, registred and chronicled by the name of the great witch of *Rochester,* and reputed among all men for the cheefe ringleader of all other witches) by good proofe is found to be a meere cousener; confessing in hir death bed freelie, without compulsion or inforcement, that hir cunning consisted onlie in deluding and deceiving the people: saying that she had (towards the maintenance of hir credit in that cousening trade) some sight in physicke and surgerie, and the assistance of a freend of hirs, called *Heron,* a professor thereof. And this I know, partlie of mine owne knowledge, and partlie by the testimonie of hir husband, and others of credit, to whome (I saie) in hir death bed, and at sundrie other times she protested these things; and also that she never had indeed anie materiall spirit or divell (as the voice went) nor yet knew how to worke anie supernaturall matter, as she in hir life time made men beleeve she had and could doo.

*   *   *

Againe, who will mainteine, that common witchcrafts are not cousenages, when the great and famous witchcrafts, which had stolne credit not onlie from all the common people, but from men of great wisdome and authoritie, are discovered to be beggerlie slights of cousening varlots? Which otherwise might and would have remained a perpetuall objection against me. Were there not three images of late yeeres found in a doonghill, to the terror & astonishment of manie thousands? In so much as great matters were thought to have beene pretended to be doone by witchcraft. But if the Lord preserve those persons (whose destruction was doubted to have beene intended thereby) from all other the lewd practises and attempts of their enimies; I feare not, but they shall easilie withstand these and such like devises, although they should indeed be practised against them. But no doubt, if such bables could have brought those matters of mischeefe to passe, by the hands of traitors, witches, or papists; we should long since have beene deprived of the most excellent jewell and comfort that we enjoy in this world. Howbeit, I confesse, that the feare, conceipt, and doubt of such mischeefous pretenses may breed inconvenience to them that stand in awe of the same. And I wish, that even for such practises, though they never can or doo take effect, the practisers be punished with all extremitie: bicause therein is manifested a traiterous heart to the Queene, and a presumption against God.

*   *   *

REVIEW QUESTIONS

1. What is witchcraft?
2. How does Scot depict it?
3. According to Scot, what characterizes witches and witchcraft?
4. How does Scot confound the very notion of witchcraft?
5. Where does he locate the source of all power to override the laws of nature?
6. What sort of power is left to witches?
7. What, according to Scot, is the relation of witches to the natural world?

THE PLUNDERING AND BURNING OF A VILLAGE, A HANGING, AND
PEASANTS AVENGE THEMSELVES (1633)

JACQUES CALLOT

These three prints, often referred to as The Horrors of War, powerfully reveal commonplace events of the early seventeenth century: the ravages of war on a small village, the punishment of unruly troops, and the violence of the violated. How does Callot portray rural life? What general aspects of the Iron Century does Callot capture in his images? Why do you think Callot decided to reveal the underbelly of 17th-century warfare rather than portraying it in more heroic terms?

HANS JAKOB CHRISTOPH VON GRIMMELSHAUSEN

FROM *Simplicissimus*

Hans Jakob Christoph von Grimmelshausen (1621–1676), author of Simplicissimus, *the greatest German novel of the seventeenth century and one of the great works of all German literature, was born at Gelnhausen, near Hanau in Hesse Kassel. The troubled times of the Thirty Years' War (1618–1648), which found eloquent consideration in his writing, are reflected in his life. He lost his parents early, probably in the 1634 sack of Gelnhausen by troops under Ferdinand, cardinal-infante of Spain, and was himself kidnapped by marauding Hessian troops the following year. His experiences became the stuff of his novel. In 1636, he joined the imperial army. In 1639, he became secretary to Reinhard von Schauenburg, the commandant at Offenburg, on whose staff he served until 1647. At the end of the war, he was commandant on the Inn. Soon after the war he became the steward of the Schauenburg estates, married, and converted to Catholicism. In 1667, Grimmelshausen was appointed magistrate and tax collector at Renchen, a town belonging to the bishopric of Strasbourg. His duties evidently left him free to write; he published his masterpiece,* Simplicissimus, *in 1669. Modeled on the Spanish picaresque romance,* Simplicissimus *sketched the development of a human soul measured against the background of a land riven by warfare. It gave free rein to its author's narrative gifts: his realist detail, coarse humor, and social criticism.* Simplicissimus *is widely considered a historical document for its vivid picture of seventeenth-century Germany. Grimmelshausen's life ended as it began, in the shadow of war. In 1674, Renchen was occupied by French troops, and his household was broken up. He died in 1676, once more in military service.*

From *Simplicissimus*, by Hans Jakob Christoph von Grimmelshausen, translated by A. T. S. Goodrich (London: Heinemann, 1912).

Book I

CHAPTER I
TREATS OF SIMPLICISSIMUS'S RUSTIC DESCENT AND OF HIS UPBRINGING ANSWERING THERETO

There appeareth in these days of ours (of which many do believe that they be the last days) among the common folk, a certain disease which causeth those who do suffer from it (so soon as they have either scraped and higgled together so much that they can, besides a few pence in their pocket, wear a fool's coat of the new fashion with a thousand bits of silk ribbon upon it, or by some trick of fortune have become known as men of parts) forthwith to give themselves out gentlemen and nobles of ancient descent. Whereas it doth often happen that their ancestors were day-labourers, carters, and porters, their cousins donkey-drivers, their brothers turnkeys and catchpolls, their sisters harlots, their mothers bawds—yea, witches even: and in a word, their whole pedigree of thirty-two quarterings as full of dirt and stain as ever was the sugarbakers' guild of Prague. Yea, these new sprigs of nobility be often themselves as black as if they had been born and bred in Guinea.

With such foolish folk I desire not to even myself, though 'tis not untrue that I have often fancied I must have drawn my birth from some great lord or knight at least, as being by nature disposed to follow the nobleman's trade had I but the means and the tools for it. 'Tis true, moreover, without jesting, that my birth and upbringing can be well compared to that of a prince if we overlook the one great difference in degree. How! did not my dad (for so they call fathers in the Spessart) have his own palace like any other, so fine as no king could build with his own hands, but must let that alone for ever. 'Twas painted with lime, and in place of unfruitful tiles, cold lead and red copper, was roofed with that straw whereupon the noble corn doth grow, and that he, my dad, might make a proper show of nobility and riches, he had his wall round his castle built, not of stone, which men do find upon the road or dig out of the earth in barren places, much less of miserable baked bricks that in a brief space can be made and burned (as other great lords be wont to do), but he did use oak, which noble and profitable tree, being such that smoked sausage and fat ham doth grow upon it, taketh for its full growth no less than a hundred years; and where is the monarch that can imitate him therein? His halls, his rooms, and his chambers did he have thoroughly blackened with smoke, and for this reason only, that 'tis the most lasting colour in the world, and doth take longer to reach to real perfection than an artist will spend on his most excellent paintings. The tapestries were of the most delicate web in the world, wove for us by her that of old did challenge Minerva to a spinning match. His windows were dedicated to St. Papyrius for no other reason than that that same paper doth take longer to come to perfection, reckoning from the sowing of the hemp or flax whereof 'tis made, than doth the finest and clearest glass of Murano: for his trade made him apt to believe that whatever was produced with much paint was also more valuable and more costly; and what was most costly was best suited to nobility. Instead of pages, lackeys, and grooms, he had sheep, goats, and swine, which often waited upon me in the pastures till I drove them home. His armoury was well furnished with ploughs, mattocks, axes, hoes, shovels, pitch-

forks, and hayforks, with which weapons he daily exercised himself; for hoeing and digging he made his military discipline, as did the old Romans in time of peace. The yoking of oxen was his generalship, the piling of dung his fortification, tilling of the land his campaigning, and the cleaning out of stables his princely pastime and exercise. By this means did he conquer the whole round world so far as he could reach, and at every harvest did draw from it rich spoils. But all this I account nothing of, and am not puffed up thereby, lest any should have cause to jibe at me as at other new-fangled nobility, for I esteem myself no higher than was my dad, which had his abode in a right merry land, to wit, in the Spessart, where the wolves do howl good-night to each other. But that I have as yet told you nought of my dad's family, race and name is for the sake of precious brevity, especially since there is here no question of a foundation for gentlefolks for me to swear myself into; 'tis enough if it be known that I was born in the Spessart.

Now as my dad's manner of living will be perceived to be truly noble, so any man of sense will easily understand that my upbringing was like and suitable thereto: and whoso thinks that is not deceived, for in my tenth year had I already learned the rudiments of my dad's princely exercises: yet as touching studies I might compare with the famous Amphistides, of whom Suidas reports that he could not count higher than five: for my dad had perchance too high a spirit, and therefore followed the use of these days, wherein many persons of quality trouble themselves not, as they say with bookworms' follies, but have their hirelings to do their inkslinging for them. Yet was I a fine performer on the bagpipe, whereon I could produce most dolorous strains. But as to knowledge of things divine, none shall ever persuade me that any lad of my age in all Christendom could there beat me, for I knew nought of God or man, of Heaven or hell, of angel or devil, nor could discern between good and evil. So may it be easily understood that I, with such knowledge of theology, lived like our first parents in Paradise, which in their innocence knew nought of sickness or death or dying, and still less of the Resurrection. O noble life! (or, as one might better say, O noodle's life!) in which none troubles himself about medicine. And by this measure ye can estimate my proficiency in the study of jurisprudence and all other arts and sciences. Yea, I was so perfected in ignorance that I knew not that I knew nothing. So say I again, O noble life that once I led! But my dad would not suffer me long to enjoy such bliss, but deemed it right that as being nobly born, I should nobly act and nobly live: and therefore began to train me up for higher things and gave me harder lessons.

*   *   *

CHAPTER IV
HOW SIMPLICISSIMUS'S PALACE WAS STORMED, PLUNDERED, AND RUINATED, AND IN WHAT SORRY FASHION THE SOLDIERS KEPT HOUSE THERE

Although it was not my intention to take the peaceloving reader with these troopers to my dad's house and farm, seeing that matters will go ill therein, yet the course of my history demands that I should leave to kind posterity an account of what manner of cruelties were now and again practised in this our German war: yea, and moreover testify by my own example that such evils must often have been sent to us by the goodness of Almighty God for our profit. For, gentle reader, who would ever have taught me that there was a God in Heaven if these soldiers had not destroyed my dad's house, and by such a deed driven me out among folk who gave me all fitting instruction thereupon? Only a little while before, I neither knew nor could fancy to myself that there were any people on earth save only my dad, my mother and me, and the rest of our household, nor did I know of any human habitation but that where I daily went out and in. But soon thereafter I understood the way of men's coming into this world, and how they must leave it again. I was only in shape a man and in name a Christian: for the rest I was but a beast. Yet the Almighty looked upon my innocence with a pitiful eye, and would bring me to a knowledge both of Himself and of myself. And although He had a thousand ways to lead me thereto, yet would He doubtless use that one only by which my dad and my mother should be punished: and that for an example to all others by reason of their heathenish upbringing of me.

The first thing these troopers did was, that they stabled their horses: thereafter each fell to his appointed task: which task was neither more nor less than ruin and destruction. For though some began to slaughter and to boil and to roast so that it looked as if there should be a merry banquet forward, yet others there were who did but storm through the house above and below stairs. Others stowed together great parcels of cloth and apparel and all manner of household stuff, as if they would set up a frippery market. All that they had no mind to take with them they cut in pieces. Some thrust their swords through the hay and straw as if they had not enough sheep and swine to slaughter: and some shook the feathers out of the beds and in their stead stuffed in bacon and other dried meat and provisions as if such were better and softer to sleep upon. Others broke the stove and the windows as if they had a never-ending summer to promise. Houseware of copper and tin they beat flat, and packed such vessels, all bent and spoiled, in with the rest. Bedsteads, tables, chairs, and benches they burned, though there lay many cords of dry wood in the yard. Pots and pipkins must all go to pieces, either because they would eat none but roast flesh, or because their purpose was to make there but a single meal.

Our maid was so handled in the stable that she could not come out; which is a shame to tell of. Our man they laid bound upon the ground, thrust a gag into his mouth, and poured a pailful of filthy water into his body: and by this, which they called a Swedish draught, they forced him to lead a party of them to another place where they captured men and beasts, and brought them back to our farm, in which company were my dad, my mother, and our Ursula.

And now they began: first to take the flints out of their pistols and in place of them to jam the peasants' thumbs in and so to torture the poor rogues as if they had been about the burning of witches: for one of them they had taken they thrust into the baking oven and there lit a fire under him, although he had as yet confessed no crime: as for another, they put a cord round his head and so twisted it tight with a piece of wood that the blood gushed from his mouth and nose and ears. In a word each had his own device to torture the peasants, and each peasant his several torture. But as it seemed to me then, my dad was the luckiest, for he with a laughing face confessed what others must out with in the midst of pains and miserable lamentations: and such honour without doubt fell to him because he was the householder. For they set him before a fire and bound him fast so that he could neither stir hand nor foot, and smeared the soles of his feet with wet salt, and this they made our old goat lick off, and so tickle him that he well nigh burst his sides with laughing. And this seemed to me so merry a thing that I must needs laugh with him for the sake of fellowship, or because I knew no better. In the midst of such laughter he must needs confess all that they would have of him, and indeed revealed to them a secret treasure, which proved far richer in pearls, gold, and trinkets than any would have looked for among peasants. Of the women, girls, and maidservants whom they took, I have not much to say in particular, for the soldiers would not have me see how they dealt with them. Yet this I know, that one heard some of them scream most piteously in divers corners of the house; and well I can judge it fared no better with my mother and our Ursel than with the rest. Yet in the midst of all this miserable ruin I helped to turn the spit, and in the afternoon to give the horses drink, in which employ I encountered our maid in the stable, who seemed to me wondrously tumbled, so that I knew her not, but with a weak voice she called to me, "O lad, run away, or the troopers will have thee away with them. Look to it well that thou get hence: thou seest in what plight . . ." And more she could not say.

*   *   *

CHAPTER XV

HOW SIMPLICISSIMUS WAS PLUNDERED, AND HOW HE DREAMED OF THE PEASANTS AND HOW THEY FARED IN TIMES OF WAR

Now when I came home I found that my fireplace and all my poor furniture, together with my store of provisions, which I had grown during the summer in my garden and had kept for the coming winter, were all gone. "And whither now?" thought I. And then first did need teach me heartily to pray: and I must summon all my small wits together, to devise what I should do. But as my knowledge of the world was both small and evil, I could come to no proper conclusion, only that 'twas best to commend myself to God and to put my whole confidence in Him: for otherwise I must perish. And besides all this those things which I had heard and seen that day lay heavy on my mind: and I pondered not so much upon my food and my sustenance as upon the enmity which there is ever between soldiers and peasants. Yet could my foolish mind come to no other conclusion than this—that there must of a surety be two races of men in the world, and not one only, descended from Adam, but two, wild and tame, like other unreasoning beasts, and therefore pursuing one another so cruelly.

With such thoughts I fell asleep, for mere misery and cold, with a hungry stomach. Then it seemed to me, as if in a dream, that all the trees which stood round my dwelling suddenly changed and took on another appearance: for on every treetop sat a trooper, and the trunks were garnished, in place of leaves, with all manner of folk. Of these, some had long lances, others musquets, hangers, halberts, flags, and some drums and fifes. Now this was merry to see, for all was neatly distributed and each according to his rank. The roots, moreover, were made up of folk of little worth, as mechanics and labourers, mostly, however, peasants and the like; and these nevertheless gave its strength to the tree and renewed the same when it was lost: yea more, they repaired the loss of any fallen leaves from among themselves to their own great damage: and all the time they lamented over them that sat on the tree, and that with good reason, for the whole weight of the tree lay upon them and pressed them so that all the money was squeezed out of their pockets, yea, though it was behind seven locks and keys: but if the money would not out, then did the commissaries so handle them with rods (which thing they call military execution) that sighs came from their heart, tears from their eyes, blood from their nails, and the marrow from their bones. Yet among these were some whom men call light o' heart; and these made but little ado, took all with a shrug, and in the midst of their torment had, in place of comfort, mockery for every turn.

CHAPTER XVI
OF THE WAYS AND WORKS OF SOLDIERS
NOWADAYS, AND HOW HARDLY A COMMON
SOLDIER CAN GET PROMOTION

So must the roots of these trees suffer and endure toil and misery in the midst of trouble and complaint, and those upon the lower boughs in yet greater hardship: yet were these last mostly merrier than the first named, yea and moreover, insolent and swaggering, and for the most part godless folk, and for the roots a heavy unbearable burden at all times. And this was the rhyme upon them:

Hunger and thirst, and cold and heat, and work
    and woe, and all we meet;
And deeds of blood and deeds of shame, all may
    ye put to the landsknecht's name.

Which rhymes were the less like to be lyingly invented in that they answered to the facts. For gluttony and drunkenness, hunger and thirst, wenching and dicing and playing, riot and roaring, murdering and being murdered, slaying and being slain, torturing and being tortured, hunting and being hunted, harrying and being harried, robbing and being robbed, frighting and being frighted, causing trouble and suffering trouble, beating and being beaten: in a word, hurting and harming, and in turn being hurt and harmed—this was their whole life. And in this career they let nothing hinder them: neither winter nor summer, snow nor ice, heat nor cold, rain nor wind, hill nor dale, wet nor dry; ditches, mountain-passes, ramparts and walls, fire and water, were all the same to them. Father nor mother, sister nor brother, no, nor the danger to their own bodies, souls, and consciences, nor even loss of life and of heaven itself, or aught else that can be named, will ever stand in their way, for ever they toil and moil at their own strange work, till at last, little by little, in battles, sieges, attacks, campaigns, yea, and in their winter quarters too (which are the soldiers' earthly paradise, if they can but happen upon fat peasants) they perish, they die, they rot and consume away, save but a few, who in their old age, unless they have been right thrifty rievers and robbers, do furnish us with the best of all beggars and vagabonds.

Next above these hard-worked folk sat old henroost-robbers, who, after some years and much peril of their lives, had climbed up the lowest branches and clung to them, and so far had had the luck to escape death. Now these looked more serious, and somewhat more dignified than the lowest, in that they were a degree higher ascended: yet above them were some yet higher, who had yet loftier imaginings because they had to command the very lowest. And these people did call coat-beaters, because they were wont to dust the jackets of the poor pikemen, and to give the musketeers oil enough to grease their barrels with.

Just above these the trunk of the tree had an interval or stop, which was a smooth place without branches, greased with all manner of ointments and curious soap of disfavour, so that no man save of noble birth could scale it, in spite of courage and skill and knowledge, God knows how clever he might be. For 'twas polished as smooth as a marble pillar or a steel mirror. Just over that smooth spot sat they with the flags: and of these some were young, some pretty well in years: the young folk their kinsmen had raised so far: the older people had either mounted on a silver ladder which is called the Bribery Backstairs or else on a step which Fortune, for want of a better client, had left for them. A little further up sat higher folk, and these had also their toil and care and annoyance: yet had they this advantage, that they could fill their pokes with the fattest slices which they could cut out of the roots, and that with a knife which they called "War-contribution." And these were at their best and happiest when there came a commissary-bird flying overhead, and shook out a whole panfull of gold over the tree to cheer them: for of that they caught as much as they could, and let but little or nothing at all fall to the lowest branches: and so of these last more died of hunger than of the enemy's attacks, from which danger those placed above seemed to be free. Therefore was there a perpetual climbing and swarming going on on those trees; for each would needs sit in those highest and happiest places: yet were there some idle, worthless rascals, not worth their commissariat-bread, who troubled themselves little about higher places, and only did their duty. So the lowest, being ambitious, hoped for the fall of the highest, that they might sit in their place, and if it happened to one among ten thousand of them that he got so far, yet would such good luck come to him only in his miserable old age when he was more fit to sit in the chimney-corner and roast apples than to meet the foe in the field. And if any man dealt honestly and carried himself well, yet was he ever envied by others,

and perchance by reason of some unlucky chance of war deprived both of office and of life. And nowhere was this more grievous than at the before-mentioned smooth place on the tree: for there an officer who had had a good sergeant or corporal under him must lose him, however unwillingly, because he was now made an ensign. And for that reason they would take, in place of old soldiers, ink-slingers, footmen, overgrown pages, poor noblemen, and at times poor relations, tramps and vagabonds. And these took the very bread out of the mouths of those that had deserved it, and forthwith were made Ensigns.

*   *   *

REVIEW QUESTIONS

1. Who is Simplicissimus?
2. What is his relation to nature?
3. What does he consider noble and base?
4. What does Grimmelshausen tell us about the conduct of the Thirty Years' War?
5. What happens to the character of Simplicissimus when he witnesses the violence of war?
6. What did the Thirty Years' War do to the land and its occupants?

MICHEL EYQUEM DE MONTAIGNE

FROM "Of Cannibals"

Michel Eyquem de Montaigne (1533–1592) originated the essay as a literary form. Born of a wealthy family at the Château de Montaigne, near Libourne, he was first educated by a tutor who spoke to him in Latin but no French. Until he was six years old, Montaigne learned the classical language as his native tongue. He was further educated at the Collège du Guyenne, where his fluency intimidated some of the finest Latinists in France, and studied law at Toulouse. In 1554, his father purchased an office in the Cour des Aides of Périgeaux, a fiscal court later incorporated into the Parlement of Bordeaux, a position he soon resigned to his son. Montaigne spent thirteen years in office at work he found neither pleasant nor useful. In 1571, he retired to the family estate. Apart from brief visits to Paris and Rouen, periods of travel, and two terms as mayor of Bordeaux (1581–85), Montaigne spent the rest of his life as a country gentleman. His life was not all leisure. He became gentleman-in-ordinary to the king's chamber and spent the period 1572–76 trying to broker a peace between Catholics and Huguenots. His first two books of the Essais *appeared in 1580; the third and last volume appeared in 1588. These essays are known for their discursive, conversational style, in which Montaigne undertook explorations of custom, opinion, and institutions. They gave voice to his opposition to all forms of dogmatism that were without rational basis. He observed life with a degree of skepticism, emphasizing the limits of human knowledge and the contradictions in human behavior. Indeed, Montaigne's essays are often cited as examples of an epistemological crisis borne of the new discoveries, theological debates, and social tensions that marked the early modern period.*

From *The Complete Essays of Montaigne,* translated by Donald M. Frame (Stanford: Stanford University Press, 1958).

W hen King Pyrrhus passed over into Italy, after he had reconnoitered the formation of the army that the Romans were sending to meet him, he said: "I do not know what barbarians these are" (for so the Greeks called all foreign nations), "but the formation of this army that I see is not at all barbarous." The Greeks said as much of the army that Flamininus brought into their country, and so did Philip, seeing from a knoll the order and distribution of the Roman camp, in his kingdom, under Publius Sulpicius Galba. Thus we should beware of clinging to vulgar opinions, and judge things by reason's way, not by popular say.

I had with me for a long time a man who had lived for ten or twelve years in that other world which has been discovered in our century, in the place where Villegaignon landed, and which he called Antarctic France. This discovery of a boundless country seems worthy of consideration. I don't know if I can guarantee that some other such discovery will not be made in the future, so many personages greater than ourselves having been mistaken about this one. I am afraid we have eyes bigger than our stomachs, and more curiosity than capacity. We embrace everything, but we clasp only wind.

*   *   *

This man I had was a simple, crude fellow—a character fit to bear true witness; for clever people observe more things and more curiously, but they interpret them; and to lend weight and conviction to their interpretation, they cannot help altering history a little. They never show you things as they are, but bend and disguise them according to the way they have seen them; and to give credence to their judgment and attract you to it, they are prone to add something to their matter, to stretch it out and amplify it. We need a man either very honest, or so simple that he has not the stuff to build up false inventions and give them plausibility; and wedded to no theory. Such was my man; and besides this, he at various times brought sailors and merchants, whom he had known on that trip, to see me. So I content myself with his information, without inquiring what the cosmographers say about it.

*   *   *

Now, to return to my subject, I think there is nothing barbarous and savage in that nation, from what I have been told, except that each man calls barbarism whatever is not his own practice; for indeed it seems we have no other test of truth and reason than the example and pattern of the opinions and customs of the country we live in. *There is always the perfect religion, the perfect government, the perfect and accomplished manners in all things.* Those people are wild, just as we call wild the fruits that Nature has produced by herself and in her normal course; whereas really it is those that we have changed artificially and led astray from the common order, that we should rather call wild. The former retain alive and vigorous their genuine, their most useful and natural, virtues and properties, which we have debased in the latter in adapting them to gratify our corrupted taste. And yet for all that, the savor and delicacy of some uncultivated fruits of those countries is quite as excellent, even to our taste, as that of our own. It is not reasonable that art should win the place of honor over our great and powerful mother Nature. We have so overloaded the beauty and richness of her works by our inventions that we have quite smothered her. Yet wherever her purity shines forth, she wonderfully puts to shame our vain and frivolous attempts:

> Ivy comes readier without our care;
> In lonely caves the arbutus grows more fair;
> No art with artless bird song can compare.
>   Propertius

All our efforts cannot even succeed in reproducing the nest of the tiniest little bird, its contexture, its beauty and convenience; or even the web of the puny spider. All things, says Plato, are produced by nature, by fortune, or by art; the greatest and most beautiful by one or the other of the first two, the least and most imperfect by the last.

These nations, then, seem to me barbarous in this sense, that they have been fashioned very little by the human mind, and are still very close to their original naturalness. The laws of nature still rule them, very little corrupted by ours; and they are in such a state of purity that I am sometimes vexed that they were unknown earlier, in the days when there were men able to judge them better than we. I am sorry that Lycurgus and Plato did not know of them; for it seems to me that what

we actually see in these nations surpasses not only all the pictures in which poets have idealized the golden age and all their inventions in imagining a happy state of man, but also the conceptions and the very desire of philosophy. They could not imagine a naturalness so pure and simple as we see by experience; nor could they believe that our society could be maintained with so little artifice and human solder. This is a nation, I should say to Plato, in which there is no sort of traffic, no knowledge of letters, no science of numbers, no name for a magistrate or for political superiority, no custom of servitude, no riches or poverty, no contracts, no successions, no partitions, no occupations but leisure ones, no care for any but common kinship, no clothes, no agriculture, no metal, no use of wine or wheat. The very words that signify lying, treachery, dissimulation, avarice, envy, belittling, pardon—unheard of. How far from this perfection would he find the republic that he imagined: *Men fresh sprung from the gods.*

These manners nature first ordained.

                                                                                    Virgil

For the rest, they live in a country with a very pleasant and temperate climate, so that according to my witnesses it is rare to see a sick man there; and they have assured me that they never saw one palsied, bleary-eyed, toothless, or bent with age. They are settled along the sea and shut in on the land side by great high mountains, with a stretch about a hundred leagues wide in between. They have a great abundance of fish and flesh which bear no resemblance to ours, and they eat them with no other artifice than cooking. The first man who rode a horse there, though he had had dealings with them on several other trips, so horrified them in this posture that they shot him dead with arrows before they could recognize him.

Their buildings are very long, with a capacity of two or three hundred souls; they are covered with the bark of great trees, the strips reaching to the ground at one end and supporting and leaning on one another at the top, in the manner of some of our barns, whose covering hangs down to the ground and acts as a side. They have wood so hard that they cut with it and make of it their swords and grills to cook their food. Their beds are of a cotton weave, hung from the roof like those in our ships, each man having his own; for the wives sleep apart from their husbands.

They get up with the sun, and eat immediately upon rising, to last them through the day; for they take no other meal than that one. Like some other Eastern peoples, of whom Suidas tells us, who drank apart from meals, they do not drink then; but they drink several times a day, and to capacity. Their drink is made of some root, and is of the color of our claret wines. They drink it only lukewarm. This beverage keeps only two or three days; it has a slightly sharp taste, is not at all heady, is good for the stomach, and has a laxative effect upon those who are not used to it; it is a very pleasant drink for anyone who is accustomed to it. In place of bread they use a certain white substance like preserved coriander. I have tried it; it tastes sweet and a little flat.

The whole day is spent in dancing. The younger men go to hunt animals with bows. Some of the women busy themselves meanwhile with warming their drink, which is their chief duty. Some one of the old men, in the morning before they begin to eat, preaches to the whole barnful in common, walking from one end to the other, and repeating one single sentence several times until he has completed the circuit (for the buildings are fully a hundred paces long). He recommends to them only two things: valor against the enemy and love for their wives. And they never fail to point out this obligation, as their refrain, that it is their wives who keep their drink warm and seasoned.

There may be seen in several places, including my own house, specimens of their beds, of their ropes, of their wooden swords and the bracelets with which they cover their wrists in combats, and of the big canes, open at one end, by whose sound they keep time in their dances. They are close shaven all over, and shave themselves much more cleanly than we, with nothing but a wooden or stone razor. They believe that souls are immortal, and that those who have deserved well of the gods are lodged in that part of heaven where the sun rises, and the damned in the west.

They have some sort of priests and prophets, but they rarely appear before the people, having their home in the mountains. On their arrival there is a great feast and solemn assembly of several villages—each barn, as I have described it, makes up a village, and they are about one French league from each other. The prophet speaks to them in public, exhorting them to virtue and their duty; but their whole ethical science contains only these two articles: resoluteness in war and affection for their wives. He prophesies to them things to come and the results they are to expect from their undertakings, and urges them to war or holds them back from it; but this is on the condition that when he fails to prophesy correctly, and if things turn out otherwise than he has predicted, he is cut into a thousand pieces if they catch him, and condemned as a false prophet. For this reason, the prophet who has once been mistaken is never seen again.

*   *   *

They have their wars with the nations beyond the mountains, further inland, to which they go quite naked, with no other arms than bows or wooden swords ending in a sharp point, in the manner of the tongues of our boar spears. It is astonishing what firmness they show in their combats, which never end but in slaughter and bloodshed; for as to routs and terror, they know nothing of either.

Each man brings back as his trophy the head of the enemy he has killed, and sets it up at the entrance to his dwelling. After they have treated their prisoners well for a long time with all the hospitality they can think of, each man who has a prisoner calls a great assembly of his acquaintances. He ties a rope to one of the prisoner's arms, by the end of which he holds him, a few steps away, for fear of being hurt, and gives his dearest friend the other arm to hold in the same way; and these two, in the presence of the whole assembly, kill him with their swords. This done, they roast him and eat him in common and send some pieces to their absent friends. This is not, as people think, for nourishment, as of old the Scythians used to do; it is to betoken an extreme revenge. And the proof of this came when they saw the Portuguese, who had joined forces with their adversaries, inflict a different kind of death on them when they took them prisoner, which was to bury them up to the waist, shoot the rest of their body full of arrows, and afterward hang them. They thought that these people from the other world, being men who had sown the knowledge of many vices among their neighbors and were much greater masters than themselves in every sort of wickedness, did not adopt this sort of vengeance without some reason, and that it must be more painful than their own; so they began to give up their old method and to follow this one.

I am not sorry that we notice the barbarous horror of such acts, but I am heartily sorry that, judging their faults rightly, we should be so blind to our own. I think there is more barbarity in eating a man alive than in eating him dead; and in tearing by tortures and the rack a body still full of feeling, in roasting a man bit by bit, in having him bitten and mangled by dogs and swine (as we have not only read but seen within fresh memory, not among ancient enemies, but among neighbors and fellow citizens, and what is worse, on the pretext of piety and religion), than in roasting and eating him after he is dead.

*   *   *

So we may well call these people barbarians, in respect to the rules of reason, but not in respect to ourselves, who surpass them in every kind of barbarity.

Their warfare is wholly noble and generous, and as excusable and beautiful as this human disease can be; its only basis among them is their rivalry in valor. They are not fighting for the conquest of new lands, for they still enjoy that natural abundance that provides them without toil and trouble with all necessary things in such profusion that they have no wish to enlarge their boundaries. They are still in that happy state of desiring only

as much as their natural needs demand; anything beyond that is superfluous to them.

They generally call those of the same age, brothers; those who are younger, children; and the old men are fathers to all the others. These leave to their heirs in common the full possession of their property, without division or any other title at all than just the one that Nature gives to her creatures in bringing them into the world.

If their neighbors cross the mountains to attack them and win a victory, the gain of the victor is glory, and the advantage of having proved the master in valor and virtue; for apart from this they have no use for the goods of the vanquished, and they return to their own country, where they lack neither anything necessary nor that great thing, the knowledge of how to enjoy their condition happily and be content with it. These men of ours do the same in their turn. They demand of their prisoners no other ransom than that they confess and acknowledge their defeat. But there is not one in a whole century who does not choose to die rather than to relax a single bit, by word or look, from the grandeur of an invincible courage; not one who would not rather be killed and eaten than so much as ask not to be. They treat them very freely, so that life may be all the dearer to them, and usually entertain them with threats of their coming death, of the torments they will have to suffer, the preparations that are being made for that purpose, the cutting up of their limbs, and the feast that will be made at their expense. All this is done for the sole purpose of extorting from their lips some weak or base word, or making them want to flee, so as to gain the advantage of having terrified them and broken down their firmness. For indeed, if you take it the right way, it is in this point alone that true victory lies:

It is no victory
Unless the vanquished foe admits your mastery.
                                                Claudian

The Hungarians, very bellicose fighters, did not in olden times pursue their advantage beyond putting the enemy at their mercy. For having wrung a confession from him to this effect, they let him go unharmed and unransomed, except, at most, for exacting his promise never again to take up arms against them.

We win enough advantages over our enemies that are borrowed advantages, not really our own. It is the quality of a porter, not of valor, to have sturdier arms and legs; agility is a dead and corporeal quality; it is a stroke of luck to make our enemy stumble, or dazzle his eyes by the sunlight; it is a trick of art and technique, which may be found in a worthless coward, to be an able fencer. The worth and value of a man is in his heart and his will; there lies his real honor. Valor is the strength, not of legs and arms, but of heart and soul; it consists not in the worth of our horse or our weapons, but in our own. He who falls obstinate in his courage, *if he has fallen, he fights on his knees.* He who relaxes none of his assurance, no matter how great the danger of imminent death; who, giving up his soul, still looks firmly and scornfully at his enemy—he is beaten not by us, but by fortune; he is killed, not conquered.

*   *   *

To return to our story. These prisoners are so far from giving in, in spite of all that is done to them, that on the contrary, during the two or three months that they are kept, they wear a gay expression; they urge their captors to hurry and put them to the test; they defy them, insult them, reproach them with their cowardice and the number of battles they have lost to the prisoners' own people.

I have a song composed by a prisoner which contains this challenge, that they should all come boldly and gather to dine off him, for they will be eating at the same time their own fathers and grandfathers, who have served to feed and nourish his body. "These muscles," he says, "this flesh and these veins are your own, poor fools that you are. You do not recognize that the substance of your ancestors' limbs is still contained in them. Savor them well; you will find in them the taste of your own flesh." An idea that certainly does not smack of barbarity. Those that paint these people dying, and who show the execution, portray the prisoner spitting in the face of his slayers and scowling at them. Indeed, to the last gasp they never stop braving and defying their enemies by word and look. Truly here are real savages by our standards; for either they must be thoroughly so, or we must be; there is an amazing distance between their character and ours.

The men there have several wives, and the higher their reputation for valor the more wives they have. It is a remarkably beautiful thing about their marriages that the same jealousy our wives have to keep us from the affection and kindness of other women, theirs have to win this for them. Being more concerned for their husbands' honor than for anything else, they strive and scheme to have as many companions as they can, since that is a sign of their husbands' valor.

*   *   *

Three of these men, ignorant of the price they will pay some day, in loss of repose and happiness, for gaining knowledge of the corruptions of this side of the ocean; ignorant also of the fact that of this intercourse will come their ruin (which I suppose is already well advanced: poor wretches, to let themselves be tricked by the desire for new things, and to have left the serenity of their own sky to come and see ours!)—three of these men were at Rouen, at the time the late King Charles IX was there. The king talked to them for a long time; they were shown our ways, our splendor, the aspect of a fine city. After that, someone asked their opinion, and wanted to know what they had found most amazing. They mentioned three things, of which I have forgotten the third, and I am very sorry for it; but I still remember two of them. They said that in the first place they thought it very strange that so many grown men, bearded, strong, and armed, who were around the king (it is likely that they were talking about the Swiss of his guard) should submit to obey a child, and that one of them was not chosen to command instead. Second (they have a way in their language of speaking of men as halves of one another), they had noticed that there were among us men full

THE "ARMADA PORTRAIT" OF QUEEN ELIZABETH (c. 1588)   GEORGE GOWER

The English portraitist George Gower (1540–1596) became Sergeant Painter to Queen Eliza-beth I of England in 1581. This, his most famous painting notwithstanding, we know little of the artist or his career. A number of portraits survive from the period before his court ap-pointment. Thereafter, he created portraits of many English aristocrats and supervised the decoration of the royal palace at Hampton Court. The "Armada Portrait" commemorates the defeat of the Spanish Armada in 1588. What elements of the painting indicate the importance of the sea and of naval power for England? Given that warfare was commonly understood to be "man's work," how does Gower handle the apparent contradiction of a warrior queen? How does he signal his patroness's firmness of command without making her masculine? How does he glorify Glorianna?

and gorged with all sorts of good things, and that their other halves were beggars at their doors, emaciated with hunger and poverty; and they thought it strange that these needy halves could endure such an injustice, and did not take the others by the throat, or set fire to their houses.

I had a very long talk with one of them; but I had an interpreter who followed my meaning so badly, and who was so hindered by his stupidity in taking in my ideas, that I could get hardly any satisfaction from the man. When I asked him what profit he gained from his superior position among his people (for he was a captain, and our sailors called him king), he told me that it was to march foremost in war. How many men followed him? He pointed to a piece of ground, to signify as many as such a space could hold; it might have been four or five thousand men. Did all his authority expire with the war? He said that this much remained, that when he visited the villages dependent on him, they made paths for him through the underbrush by which he might pass quite comfortably.

All this is not too bad—but what's the use? They don't wear breeches.

* * *

REVIEW QUESTIONS

1. What lessons does Montaigne draw from accounts of the New World?
2. Why do you suppose Montaigne chose cannibalism, of all possible topics, to compare European and American cultures?
3. How do Montaigne's ideas reflect the crisis of the iron century?
4. Are there any human constants for Montaigne?
5. Does he believe in a single human nature, a single ideal of virtue?

HUGO GROTIUS

FROM *On the Law of War and Peace*

Hugo Grotius (1583–1645) was a Dutch statesman, jurist, theologian, poet, philologist, and historian, a man of all-embracing knowledge whose writings were of fundamental importance in the formulation of international law. He was born in Delft, the son of the burgomaster and curator at the University of Leiden. Grotius was precocious; he matriculated at the University of Leiden at age eleven. By age fifteen, he had edited the encyclopedia of Martianus Capella and accompanied a diplomatic mission to the king of France, who described Grotius as the "miracle of Holland." He earned his doctorate in law at the University of Orléans and became a distinguished jurist at The Hague. In 1601, he was appointed historiographer of the States of Holland.

He wrote a number of minor but memorable legal treatises before publishing his great work, On the Law of War and Peace, *in 1625. Grotius argued that the entire law of humankind was based on four fundamental precepts: neither a state nor an individual may attack another state or individual, neither a state nor an individual may appropriate what belongs to another state or individual, neither a state nor an individual may disregard treaties or contracts, and neither a state nor an individual may commit a crime. In the case of a violation of one of these precepts, compensation might be sought either by war or by individual action. These principles and the arguments that surrounded them significantly aided the development of a theory of state sovereignty and international relations in the early modern period. During the remainder of his life, Grotius remained involved in the political as well as the intellectual affairs of his day. Besides creating a vast corpus of written works, he participated in the government of the United Provinces of the Netherlands. He was eventually imprisoned for his support of Arminianism and managed to escape hidden in a trunk. He spent the rest of his life in exile, honored as one of the great intellectuals of the seventeenth century but unacknowledged by his own country.*

From *The Rights of War and Peace*, by Hugo Grotius (Washington and London: M. Walter Dunne, 1901).

*   *   *

VIII

And here is the proper place for refuting the opinion of those, who maintain that, every where and without exception, the sovereign power is vested in the people, so that they have a right to restrain and punish kings for an abuse of their power. However there is no man of sober wisdom, who does not see the incalculable mischiefs, which such opinions have occasioned, and may still occasion; and upon the following grounds they may be refuted.

From the Jewish, as well as the Roman Law, it appears that any one might engage himself in private servitude to whom he pleased. Now if an individual may do so, why may not a whole people, for the benefit of better government and more certain protection, completely transfer their sovereign rights to one or more persons, without reserving any portion to themselves? Neither can it be alledged that such a thing is not to be presumed, for the question is not, what is to be presumed in a doubtful case, but what may lawfully be done. Nor is it any more to the purpose to object to the inconveniences, which may, and actually do arise from a people's thus surrendering their rights. For it is not in the power of man to devise any form of government free from imperfections and dangers. As a dramatic writer says, "you must either

take these advantages with those imperfections, or resign your pretensions to both."

Now as there are different ways of living, some of a worse, and some of a better kind, left to the choice of every individual; so a nation, "under certain circumstances, WHEN for instance, the succession to the throne is extinct, or the throne has by any other means become vacant," may choose what form of government she pleases. Nor is this right to be measured by the excellence of this or that form of government, on which there may be varieties of opinion, but by the will of the people.

There may be many reasons indeed why a people may entirely relinquish their rights, and surrender them to another: for instance, they may have no other means of securing themselves from the danger of immediate destruction, or under the pressure of famine it may be the only way, through which they can procure support. For if the Campanians, formerly, when reduced by necessity surrendered themselves to the Roman people in the following terms:—"Senators of Rome, we consign to your dominion the people of Campania, and the city of Capua, our lands, our temples, and all things both divine and human," and if another people as Appian relates, offered to submit to the Romans, and were refused, what is there to prevent any nation from submitting in the same manner to one powerful sovereign? It may also happen that a master of a family, having large possessions, will suffer no one to reside upon them on any other terms, or an owner, having many slaves, may give them their liberty upon condition of their doing certain services, and paying certain rents; of which examples may be produced. Thus Tacitus, speaking of the German slaves, says, "Each has his own separate habitation, and his own household to govern. The master considers him as a tenant, bound to pay a certain rent in corn, cattle, and wearing apparel. And this is the utmost extent of his servitude."

Aristotle, in describing the requisites, which fit men for servitude, says, that "those men, whose powers are chiefly confined to the body, and whose principal excellence consists in affording bodily service, are naturally slaves, because it is their interest to be so." In the same manner some nations are of such a disposition that they are more calculated to obey than to govern, which seems to have been the opinion which the Cappadocians held of themselves, who when the Romans offered them a popular government, refused to accept it, because the nation they said could not exist in safety without a king. Thus Philostratus in the life of Apollonius, says, that it was foolish to offer liberty to the Thracians, the Mysians, and the Getae, which they were not capable of enjoying. The example of nations, who have for many ages lived happily under a kingly government, has induced many to give the preference to that form. Livy says, that the cities under Eumenes would not have changed their condition for that of any free state whatsoever. And sometimes a state is so situated, that it seems impossible it can preserve its peace and existence, without submitting to the absolute government of a single person, which many wise men thought to be the case with the Roman Republic in the time of Augustus Cæsar. From these, and causes like these it not only may, but generally does happen, that men, as Cicero observes in the second book of his offices, willingly submit to the supreme authority of another.

Now as property may be acquired by what has been already styled just war, by the same means the rights of sovereignty may be acquired. Nor is the term sovereignty here meant to be applied to monarchy alone, but to government by nobles, from any share in which the people are excluded. For there never was any government so purely popular, as not to require the exclusion of the poor, of strangers, women, and minors from the public councils. Some states have other nations under them, no less dependent upon their will, than subjects upon that of their sovereign princes. From whence arose that question, Are the Collatine people in their own power? And the Campanians, when they submitted to the Romans, are said to have passed under a foreign dominion. In the same manner Acarnania and Amphilochia are said to have been under the dominion of the Aetolians; Peraea and Caunus under that of the Rhodians; and Pydna was ceded by Philip to the Olynthians. And those towns, that had been under the Spartans, when they were delivered from their dominion, received the name of the free Laconians. The city of Cotyora is said by Xenophon to have belonged to the people of Sinope. Nice in Italy, according to Strabo, was adjudged to the people of Marseilles; and the island of Pithecusa to the Neapolitans. We find in Frontinus, that the towns of Calati and Caudium with their territories were adjudged, the one to the colony of Capua, and the other to that of Beneventum. Otho, as Tacitus relates, gave the cities of the Moors to the Province of Baetia. None of these instances, any more than the cessions of other conquered countries could be admitted, if it were a received rule that the rights of sovereigns are under the controul and direction of subjects.

Now it is plain both from sacred and profane history, that there are kings, who are not subject to the controul of the people in their collective body; God addressing the people of Israel, says, if thou shalt say, "I will place a king over me"; and to Samuel "Shew them the manner of the king, who shall reign over them." Hence the King is said to be anointed over the people, over the inheritance of the Lord, over Israel. Solomon is styled King over all Israel. Thus David gives thanks to God, for subduing the people under him. And Christ says, "the Kings of the nations bear rule over them." There is a well known passage in Horace, "Powerful sovereigns reign over their own subjects, and the supreme being over sovereigns themselves." Seneca thus describes the three forms of government, "Sometimes the supreme power is lodged in the people, sometimes in a senate composed of the leading men of the state, sometimes this power of the people, and dominion over the people themselves is vested in a single person." Of the last description are those, who, as Plutarch says, exercise authority not according to the laws, but over the laws. And in Herodutus, Otanes describes a monarch as one whose acts are not subject to controul. Dion Prusaeensis also and Pausanias define a monarchy in the same terms.

Aristotle says there are some kings, who have the same right, which the nation elsewhere possesses over persons and property. Thus when the Roman Princes began to exercise regal power, the people it was said had transferred all their own personal sovereignty to them, which gave rise to the saying of Marcus Antoninus the Philosopher, that no one but God alone can be judge of the Prince. Dion. L. liii. speaking of such a prince, says, "he is perfectly master of his own actions, to do whatever he pleases, and cannot be obliged to do any thing against his will." Such anciently was the power of the Inachidae established at Argos in Greece. For in the Greek Tragedy of the Suppliants, Aeschylus has introduced the people thus addressing the King: "You are the state, you the people; you the court from which there is no appeal, you preside over the altars, and regulate all affairs by your supreme will." King Theseus himself in Euripides speaks in very different terms of the Athenian Republic; "The city is not governed by one man, but in a popular form, by an annual succession of magistrates." For according to Plutarch's explanation, Theseus was the general in war, and the guardian of the laws; but in other respects nothing more than a citizen. So that they who are limited by popular controul are improperly called kings. Thus after the time of Lycurgus, and more particularly after the institution of the

Ephori, the Kings of the Lacedaemonians are said by Polybius, Plutarch, and Cornelius Nepos, to have been Kings more in name than in reality. An example which was followed by the rest of Greece. Thus Pausanias says of the Argives to the Corinthians, "The Argives from their love of equality have reduced their kingly power very low; so that they have left the posterity of Cisus nothing more than the shadow of Kings." Aristotle denies such to be proper forms of government, because they constitute only a part of an Aristocracy or Democracy.

Examples also may be found of nations, who have not been under a perpetual regal form, but only for a time under a government exempt from popular controul. Such was the power of the Amimonians among the Cnidians, and of the Dictators in the early periods of the Roman history, when there was no appeal to the people, from whence Livy says, the will of the Dictator was observed as a law. Indeed they found this submission the only remedy against imminent danger, and in the words of Cicero, the Dictatorship possessed all the strength of royal power.

It will not be difficult to refute the arguments brought in favour of the contrary opinion. For in the first place the assertion that the constituent always retains a controul over the sovereign power, which he has contributed to establish, is only true in those cases where the continuance and existence of that power depends upon the will and pleasure of the constituent: but not in cases where the power, though it might derive its origin from that constituent, becomes a necessary and fundamental part of the established law. Of this nature is that authority to which a woman submits when she gives herself to a husband. Valentinian the Emperor, when the soldiers who had raised him to the throne, made a demand of which he did not approve, replied; "Soldiers, your election of me for your emperor was your own voluntary choice; but since you have elected me, it depends upon my pleasure to grant your request. It becomes you to obey as subjects, and me to consider what is proper to be done."

Nor is the assumption true, that all kings are made by the people, as may be plainly seen from the instances adduced above, of an owner admitting strangers to reside upon his demesnes on condition of their obedience, and of nations submitting by right of conquest. Another argument is derived from a saying of the Philosophers, that all power is conferred for the benefit of the governed and not of the governing party. Hence from the nobleness of the end, it is supposed to follow, that subjects have a superiority over the sovereign. But it is not universally true, that all power is conferred for the benefit of the party governed. For some powers are conferred for the sake of the governor, as the right of a master over a slave, in which the advantage of the latter is only a contingent and adventitious circumstance. In the same manner the gain of a Physician is to reward him for his labour; and not merely to promote the good of his art. There are other kinds of authority established for the benefit of both parties, as for instance, the authority of a husband over his wife. Certain governments also, as those which are gained by right of conquest, may be established for the benefit of the sovereign; and yet convey no idea of tyranny, a word which in its original signification, implied nothing of arbitrary power or injustice, but only the government or authority of a Prince. Again, some governments may be formed for the advantage both of subjects and sovereign, as when a people, unable to defend themselves, put themselves under the protection and dominion of any powerful king. Yet it is not to be denied, but that in most governments the good of the subject is the chief object which is regarded: and that what Cicero has said after Herodotus, and Herodotus after Hesiod, is true, that Kings were appointed in order that men might enjoy complete justice.

Now this admission by no means goes to establish the inference that kings are amenable to the people. For though guardianships were invented for the benefit of wards, yet the guardian has a right to authority over the ward. Nor, though a guardian may for mismanagement be removed from his trust, does it follow that a king may for the same reason be deposed. The cases are quite different, the guardian has a superior to judge him; but in governments, as there must be some dernier resort, it must be vested either in an individual, or in some public body, whose misconduct, as there is no superior tribunal before which they can be called, God declares that he himself will judge. He either punishes their offences, should he deem it necessary; or permits them for the chastisement of his people.

This is well expressed by Tacitus: he says, "you should bear with the rapacity or luxury of rulers, as you would bear with drought, or excessive rains, or any other calamities of nature. For as long as men exist there will be faults and imperfections; but these are not of uninterrupted continuance, and they are often repaired by the succession of better times." And Marcus Aurelius speaking of subordinate magistrates, said, that they were under the controul of the sovereign: but that the sovereign was amenable to God. There is a remarkable passage in Gregory of Tours, where that Bishop thus addresses the King of France, "If any of us, Sir, should transgress the bounds of justice, he may be punished by you. But if you exceed them, who can call you to account? For when we address you, you may hear us if you please; but if you will not, who can judge you, except him, who has declared himself to be righteousness?" Among the maxims of the Essenes, Porphyry cites a passage, that "no one can reign without the special appointment of divine providence." Irenaeus has expressed this well, "Kings are appointed by him at whose command men are created; and their appointment is suited to the condition of those, whom they are called to govern." There is the same thought in the Constitutions of Clement, "You shall fear the King, for he is of the Lord's appointment."

Nor is it an objection to what has been said, that some nations have been punished for the offences of their kings, for this does not happen, because they forbear to restrain their kings, but because they seem to give, at least a tacit consent to their vices, or perhaps, without respect to this, God may use that sovereign power which he has over the life and death of every man to inflict a punishment upon the king by depriving him of his subjects.

*   *   *

REVIEW QUESTIONS

1. What is the relation between political power and will according to Grotius?

2. How does Grotius define the state? The sovereign state?
3. Where does Grotius locate sovereignty?
4. Does sovereignty have a moral component?
5. What is sovereignty's relation to property? To the good of the people?

FROM The Religious Peace of Augsburg

On September 25, 1555, the Religious Peace of Augsburg officially ended the religious struggle between the Catholic authorities, led by the Holy Roman emperor Charles V, and the forces of the Schmalkaldic League, an alliance of Lutheran princes. It made permanent the division of Christian church within the Holy Roman Empire by establishing the principle that each ruling authority could determine the official religion of its realm, either Lutheranism in accordance with the Augsburg Confession or Catholicism. This principle was later referred to as cuius regio, eius religio. *Subjects had to submit or migrate.*

From *Select Documents*, edited by E. Reich (London: P. S. King: 1905), pp. 230–32.

*   *   *

15. In order to bring peace to the Holy Roman Empire of the Germanic Nation between the Roman Imperial Majesty and the Electors, Princes and Estates, let neither his Imperial Majesty nor the Electors, Princes, etc., do any violence or harm to any estate of the empire on the account of the Augsburg Confession, but let them enjoy their religious belief, liturgy and ceremonies as well as their estates and other rights and privileges in peace; and complete religious peace shall be obtained only by Christian means of amity, or under threat of punishment of the Imperial ban.

16. Likewise the Estates espousing the Augsburg Confession shall let all the Estates and Princes who cling to the old religion live in absolute peace and in the enjoyment of all their estates, rights, and privileges.

17. However, all such as do not belong to the two above named religions shall not be included in the present peace but be totally excluded from it.

18. And since it has proved to be a matter of great dispute what was to happen with the bishoprics, priories and other ecclesiastical benefices of such Catholic priests who would in course of time abandon the old religion, we have in virtue of the powers of Roman Emperors ordained as follows: where an archbishop, bishop or prelate or any other priest of our old religion shall abandon the same, his archbishopric, bishopric, prelacy and other benefices together with all their income and rev-

enues which he has so far possessed, shall be abandoned by him without any further objection or delay. The chapter and such [as] are entitled to it by common law or the custom of the place shall elect a person espousing the old religion who may enter on the possession and enjoyment of all the rights and incomes of the place without any further hindrance and without prejudging any ultimate amicable transaction of religion.

19. Some of the abbeys, monasteries and other ecclesiastical estates having been confiscated and turned into churches, schools, and charitable institutions, it is herewith ordained that such estates which their original owners had not possessed at the time of the Treaty of Passau [1552] shall be comprised in the present treaty of peace.

20. The ecclesiastical jurisdiction over the Augsburg Confession, dogma, appointment of ministers, church ordinances, and ministries hitherto practiced (but apart from all the rights of Electors, Princes and Estates colleges and monasteries to taxes in money or tithes) shall from now cease and the Augsburg Confession shall be left to the free and untrammeled enjoyment of their religion, ceremonies, appointment of ministers, as is stated in a subsequent separate article, until the final transaction of religion will take place.

*   *   *

23. No Estate shall try to persuade the subjects of other Estates to abandon their religion or protect them against their own magistrates. Such as had from olden times the rights of patronage are not included in the present article.

24. In case our subjects whether belonging to the old religion or the Augsburg confession should intend leaving their homes with their wives and children in order to settle in another, they shall be hindered neither in the sale of their estates after due payment of the local taxes nor injured in their honor.

REVIEW QUESTIONS

1. Why do we call this document a "religious peace"?
2. What does the Religious Peace specifically allow?
3. What does the Religious Peace specifically disallow?
4. Does the Religious Peace constitute an act of toleration?
5. What is the particular significance of Article 18, the so-called ecclesiastical reservation?
6. What grounds for future conflicts does this "religious peace" contain?

15 ∾ ABSOLUTISM AND EMPIRE, 1660–1789

The word transition *best characterizes the economy and society of early modern Europe. Although the forms of production and exchange remained corporatist and traditional, elements of individualism and capitalism exerted increasingly strong influence. Accordingly, European society, which remained in large part hierarchical and patriarchal, showed signs of an emergent class structure. Evidence of these changes remained regional, being more marked in certain places and times than in others. Nonetheless, the evidence of such a transition can be seen nearly everywhere in Europe, driven by forces that gripped the entire continent.*

For much of this period, the population remained locked in a struggle to survive. Beset by periodic famine and disease, life seemed tenuous and expectancies were short. Given high and early mortality, marriages occurred relatively late in life, and truncated families were commonplace. Beginning in the late seventeenth century, however, mortality began to decline. By the eighteenth century, populations were expanding across Europe.

The principal cause of the change in demographic dynamics was an increase in food supply that can be attributed in turn to a gradual change in agricultural techniques. Throughout the early modern period, traditional agricultural practices gradually yielded to techniques known generally as scientific farming. Landowners who sought gain in the marketplaces of Europe needed more direct control over land use and the ability to respond flexibly to market conditions. As a result, they enclosed communal lands and turned to the kinds of husbandry that would increase harvests and profits. The result was an increased food supply that eventually freed Europe from its age-old cycle of feast and famine.

An increasing population put new pressures on industry by raising the demand for manufactured goods and supplying a ready labor force to produce them. Rural manufacturing in the form of extensive production networks, known as the putting-out system, increased industrial productivity and captured surplus population in industrial work processes. Those who could not find such employment fled to the cities, which also grew rapidly. It is interesting that urban manufacturing remained largely traditional, that is, highly regulated and guild based, throughout the early modern period.

The greatest single force for change between 1500 and 1800 was the expansion of long-distance commerce based on the development of overseas empires and the consolidation of central states. Capitalist practices had existed since the late fourteenth century at least, but the possibility of large profits from direct trade with Asia and the Americas offered new scope for their application. The development of mercantilist theories, which advocated the expansion of trade as a source of political power, combined with capitalist ambitions to facilitate global commerce. As a result, enterprises such as charter companies emerged on a larger scale. The supplies of goods traded and their profitability promoted the refinement of commercial facilities such as commodity exchanges, stock markets, and banking techniques. Moreover, the activities of these enterprises introduced new commodities in such volumes that new tastes emerged and old patterns of consumption were transformed.

Growing populations and expanding economies notwithstanding, the society of early modern Europe remained traditional. It was hierarchical in structure; each individual's place was fixed by birthright. Authority was patriarchal in nature, modeled on the supposedly absolute authority of the father within his family. Yet transition was also evident here. Economic change created mobility. New wealth encouraged social and political aspirations as bourgeois everywhere chafed under the exclusivity of the aristocracy and sought admission to their ranks. New poverty created a class of have-nots that challenged the established order and threatened its security.

Observers and theorists viewed the transformation of Europe's economy and society with some trepidation. In most instances, their responses were reactionary. They returned to notions of fatherhood for a model of authority that could withstand the changing times. As the period progressed, however, more and more theorists turned to philosophical reason to find general laws of human interaction that might be applied to govern economic and social behavior.

Absolutism refers to a particular conception of political authority that emerged in the wake of this transition and its attendant disorders in the later sixteenth century. It asserted order, where Europeans felt order had been undermined in political and social relations, by positing a vision of a society that had its apex in the person of a single ruler. At the center of all conceptions of absolutism was the will of the ruler: For all theorists, that will was absolute, not merely sovereign but determinative of all political relations. Such an understanding of the nature and operation of political power required a number of developments, not the least of which were a military and a bureaucracy to carry out the king's will.

By the end of the period, there would be calls for enlightened absolutism, whereby reason guided the will of the sovereign, but the will of the monarch was still the agent of political life. Among theorists, several emerged who countered the notion of absolute monarchy with that of sovereignty placed in the hands of property owners. Moreover, they argued persuasively that the exercise of sovereignty was limited in accordance with the principles of natural law.

No monarch in this period was truly absolute—such an effective expression of the will of the ruler requires greater technological and military support than any ruler prior to the nineteenth century could have. Many, however, were largely successful in representing themselves as the center of all political life in their states, nurturing courts and bureaucracies that reflected images of omniscient and powerful rulers. These same courts provided both a milieu and the financial support for philosophes such as Voltaire and scientists such as Galileo, even as those intellectuals were calling into question the ethics of and the social bases for absolutism.

JEAN BODIN

FROM *On Sovereignty*

Jean Bodin (1529–1596) was born a bourgeois in Angers. He entered a Carmelite monastery in 1545, apparently set on an ecclesiastical career, but obtained release from his vows around 1549. He pursued a course of study at the royal Collège de Quatre Langues in Paris. By 1550, he was well trained in humanist studies and went on to become one of the greatest scholars of his day. His continual search for religious truth placed him repeatedly under suspicion of heresy, but no clear evidence exists to support a conversion to Calvinism. Bodin continued his studies and attended the University of Toulouse, where he studied law during the 1550s. In 1561, he launched his public career by serving as an advocate before the parliament in Paris. Bodin soon came to the attention of high officials and dignitaries and received special commissions from the king as early as 1570. In 1571, he entered the service of Francis, duke of Alençon, a prince of the blood. During his service to Alençon, and in the aftermath of the St. Bartholomew's Day massacre, Bodin published his great work, Six livres de la république *(1576), a systematic exposition of public law. It included an absolutist theory of royal government, from which the following selection is drawn. Bodin's theory was based on the controversial notion, which proved highly influential in the development of royal absolutism, that sovereignty was indivisible and that high powers of government could not be shared by separate agents or agencies. His notion that all governmental powers were concentrated in the king of France can be seen as a direct response to the anarchy of civil war that gripped the kingdom during the second half of the sixteenth century. In 1576, Bodin was chosen as a deputy for the Third Estate of the Estates-General of Blois. Though a royalist, Bodin opposed the civil wars that raged in France and became a leading spokesperson against royal requests for increased taxation and religious uniformity. It cost him royal favor and high office. With the death in 1584 of his patron, the duke of Alençon, Bodin's career in high politics ended. He retired to Laon, where he died.*

From *On Sovereignty*, by Jean Bodin, edited by Julian H. Franklin (Cambridge: Cambridge University Press, 1992), pp. 46–50.

Book I

*   *   *

CHAPTER 8
ON SOVEREIGNTY

Sovereignty is the absolute and perpetual power of a commonwealth, which the Latins call *maiestas;* the Greeks *akra exousia, kurion arche,* and *kurion politeuma;* and the Italians *segnioria,* a word they use for private persons as well as for those who have full control of the state, while the Hebrews call it *tomech shévet*—that is, the highest power of command. We must now formulate a definition of sovereignty because no jurist or political philosopher has defined it, even though it is the chief point, and the one that needs most to be explained, in a treatise on the commonwealth. Inasmuch as we have said that a commonwealth is a just government, with sovereign power, of several households and of that which they have in common, we need to clarify the meaning of sovereign power.

*   *   *

We shall conclude, then, that the sovereignty of the monarch is in no way altered by the presence of the Estates. On the contrary, his majesty is all the greater and more illustrious when all his people publicly acknowledge him as sovereign, even though, in an assembly like this, princes, not wishing to rebuff their subjects, grant and pass many things that they would not consent to had they not been overcome by the requests, petitions, and just complaints of a harassed and afflicted people which has most often been wronged without the knowledge of the prince, who sees and hears only through the eyes, ears, and reports of others.

We thus see that the main point of sovereign majesty and absolute power consists of giving the law to subjects in general without their consent. Not to go to other countries, we in this kingdom have often seen certain general customs repealed by edicts of our kings without hearing from the Estates when the injustice of the rules was obvious. Thus the custom concerning the inheritance by mothers of their children's goods, which was observed in this kingdom throughout the entire region governed by customary law, was changed without assembling either the general or local estates. Nor is this something new. In the time of King Philip the Fair, the general custom of the entire kingdom, by which the losing party in a case could not be required to pay expenses, was suppressed by an edict without assembling the Estates.

*   *   *

CHAPTER 10
ON THE TRUE MARKS OF SOVEREIGNTY

Since there is nothing greater on earth, after God, than sovereign princes, and since they have been established by Him as His lieutenants for commanding other men, we need to be precise about their status so that we may respect and revere their majesty in complete obedience, and do them honor in our thoughts and in our speech. Contempt for one's sovereign prince is contempt toward God, of whom he is the earthly image. That is why God, speaking to Samuel, from whom the people had demanded a different prince, said "It is me that they have wronged."

To be able to recognize such a person—that is, a sovereign—we have to know his attributes, which are properties not shared by subjects. For if they were shared, there would be no sovereign prince. Yet the best writers on this subject have not treated this point with the clarity it deserves, whether from flattery, fear, hatred, or forgetfulness.

We read that Samuel, after consecrating the king that God had designated, wrote a book about the rights of majesty. But the Hebrews have written that the kings suppressed his book so that they could tyrannize their subjects. Melanchthon thus went astray in thinking that the rights of majesty were the abuses and tyrannical practices that Samuel pointed out to the people in a speech. "Do you wish to know," said Samuel, "the ways of tyrants? It is to seize the goods of subjects to dispose of at his pleasure, and to seize their women and their children in order to abuse them and to make them slaves." The word *mishpotim* as it is used in this passage does not mean rights, but rather practices and ways of doing things. Otherwise this good prince, Samuel, would have contradicted himself. For when accounting to the people for the stewardship that God had given him, he said, "Is there anyone among you who can say that I ever took gold or silver from him, or any present whatsoever?" And thereupon the whole people loudly praised him for never having done a wrong or taken anything from anyone no matter who.

*   *   *

We may thus conclude that the first prerogative of a sovereign prince is to give law to all in general and each in particular. But this is not sufficient. We have to add "without the consent of any other, whether greater, equal, or below him." For if the prince is obligated to make no law without the consent of a superior, he is clearly a subject; if of an equal, he has an associate; if of subjects, such as the senate or the people, he is not sovereign. The names of grandees that one finds affixed to edicts are not put there to give the law its force, but to witness it and to add weight to it so that the enactment will be more acceptable. For there are very ancient edicts, extant at Saint Denys in France, issued by Philip I and Louis the Fat in 1060 and 1129 respectively, to which the seals of their queens Anne and Alix, and of Robert and Hugh, were affixed. For Louis the Fat, it was year twelve of his reign; for Adelaide, year six.

When I say that the first prerogative of sovereignty is to give law to all in general and to each in particular, the latter part refers to privileges, which are in the jurisdiction of sovereign princes to the exclusion of all others. I call it a privilege when a law is made for one or a few private individuals, no matter whether it is for the profit or the loss of the person with respect to whom it is decreed. Thus Cicero said, *Privilegium de meo capite latum est.* "They have passed," he said, "a capital privilege against me." He is referring to the authorization to put him on trial decreed against him by the commoners at the request of the tribune Clodius. He calls this the *lex Clodia* in many places, and he bitterly protests that privileges could be decreed only by the great Estates of the people as it was laid down by the laws of the Twelve Tables in the words: *Privilegia, nisi comitiis centuriatis irroganto, qui secus faxit capital esto.*[1] And all those who have written of regalian rights agree that only the sovereign can grant privileges, exemptions, and immunities, and grant dispensations from edicts and ordinances. In monarchies, however, privileges last only for the lifetime of the monarchs, as the emperor Tiberius, Suetonius re-

---

[1] "Let no privileges be imposed except in the *comita centuriata;* let him who has done otherwise be put to death."

ports, informed all those who had received privileges from Augustus.

*   *   *

Book II

CHAPTER 5

WHETHER IT IS LAWFUL TO MAKE AN ATTEMPT
UPON THE TYRANT'S LIFE AND TO NULLIFY AND
REPEAL HIS ORDINANCES AFTER HE IS DEAD

Ignorance of the exact meaning of the term "tyrant" has led many people astray, and has been the cause of many inconveniences. We have said that a tyrant is someone who makes himself into a sovereign prince by his own authority—without election, or right of succession, or lot, or a just war, or a special calling from God. This is what is understood by tyrant in the writings of the ancients and in the laws that would have him put to death. Indeed, the ancients established great prizes and rewards for those who killed tyrants, offering titles of nobility, prowess, and chivalry to them along with statues and honorific titles, and even all the tyrant's goods, because they were taken as true liberators of the fatherland, or of the motherland, as the Cretans say. In this they did not distinguish, between a good and virtuous prince and a bad and wicked one, for no one has the right to seize the sovereignty and make himself the master of those who had been his companions, no matter what pretenses of justice and virtue he may offer. In strictest law, furthermore, use of the prerogatives reserved to sovereignty is punishable by death. Hence if a subject seeks, by whatever means, to invade the state and steal it from his king or, in a democracy or aristocracy, to turn himself from a fellow-citizen into lord and master, he deserves to be put to death. In this respect our question does not pose any difficulty.

*   *   *

At this point there are many questions one may ask, such as whether a tyrant, who I said may be justly killed without form or shape of trial, be-

comes legitimate if, after having encroached upon sovereignty by force or fraud, he has himself elected by the Estates. For it seems that the solemn act of election is an authentic ratification of the tyranny, an indication that the people have found it to their liking. But I say that it is nevertheless permissible to kill him, and to do so by force unless the tyrant, stripping off his authority, has given up his arms and put power back into the hands of the people in order to have its judgment. What tyrants force upon a people stripped of power cannot be called consent. Sulla, for example, had himself made dictator for eighty years by the Valerian law, which he got published with a powerful army camped inside the city of Rome. But Cicero said that this was not a law. Another example is Caesar, who had himself made permanent dictator by the Servian law; and yet another is Cosimo de Medici who, having an army inside Florence, had himself elected duke. When objections were raised, he set off a volley of gunfire in front of the palace, which induced the lords and magistrates to get on with it more quickly.

*   *   *

So much then for the tyrant, whether virtuous or wicked, who makes himself a sovereign lord on his own authority. But the chief difficulty arising from our question is whether a sovereign prince who has come into possession of the state by way of election, or lot, or right of succession, or just war, or by a special calling from God, can be killed if he is cruel, oppressive, or excessively wicked. For that is the meaning given to the word tyrant. Many doctors and theologians, who have touched upon this question, have resolved that it is permissible to kill a tyrant without distinction, and some, putting two words together that are incompatible, have spoken of a king-tyrant (*roi tyran*), which has caused the ruin of some very fine and flourishing monarchies.

But to decide this question properly we need to distinguish between a prince who is absolutely sovereign and one who is not, and between subjects and foreigners. It makes a great difference whether we say that a tyrant can be lawfully killed by a foreign prince or by a subject. For just as it is glorious and becoming, when the gates of justice have been shut, for someone, whoever he may be, to use force in defense of the goods, honor, and life of those who have been unjustly oppressed—as Moses did when he saw his brother being beaten and mistreated and had no way of getting justice—so is it a most beautiful and magnificent thing for a prince to take up arms in order to avenge an entire people unjustly oppressed by a tyrant's cruelty, as did Hercules, who traveled all over the world exterminating tyrant-monsters and was deified for his great feats. The same was done by Dion, Timoleon, Aratus, and other generous princes, who obtained the title of chastisers and correctors of tyrants. This, furthermore, was the sole cause for which Tamerlane, prince of the Tartars, declared war on Bajazet, who was then besieging Constantinople, Tamerlane saying that he had come to punish him for tyranny and to deliver the afflicted peoples. He defeated Bajazet in a battle fought on the plateau of Mount Stella, and after he had killed and routed three hundred thousand Turks, he had the tyrant chained inside a cage until he died. In this case it makes no difference whether this virtuous prince proceeds against a tyrant by force, deception, or judicial means. It is however true that if a virtuous prince has seized a tyrant, he will obtain more honor by putting him on trial and punishing him as a murderer, parricide, and thief, rather than acting against him by the common law of peoples (*droit des gens*).

But as for subjects, and what they may do, one has to know whether the prince is absolutely sovereign, or is properly speaking not a sovereign. For if he is not absolutely sovereign, it follows necessarily that sovereignty is in the people or the aristocracy. In this latter case there is no doubt that it is permissible to proceed against the tyrant either by way of law if one can prevail against him, or else by way of fact and open force, if one cannot otherwise have justice. Thus the Senate took the first way against Nero, the second against Maximinus inasmuch as the Roman emperors were no more than princes of the republic, in the sense of first persons and chief citizens, with sovereignty remaining in the people and the Senate.

* * *

But if the prince is sovereign absolutely, as are the genuine monarchs of France, Spain, England, Scotland, Ethiopia, Turkey, Persia, and Moscovy—whose power has never been called into question and whose sovereignty has never been shared with subjects—then it is not the part of any subject individually, or all of them in general, to make an attempt on the honor or the life of the monarch, either by way of force or by way of law, even if he has committed all the misdeeds, impieties, and cruelties that one could mention. As to the way of law, the subject has no right of jurisdiction over his prince, on whom all power and authority to command depends; he not only can revoke all the power of his magistrates, but in his presence, all the power and jurisdiction of all magistrates, guilds and corporations, Estates and communities, cease, as we have said and will say again even more elaborately in the proper place. And if it is not permissible for a subject to pass judgment on his prince, or a vassal on his lord, or a servant on his master—in short, if it is not permissible to proceed against one's king by way of law—how could it be licit to do so by way of force? For the question here is not to discover who is the strongest, but only whether it is permissible in law, and whether a subject has the power to condemn his sovereign prince.

A subject is guilty of treason in the first degree not only for having killed a sovereign prince, but also for attempting it, advising it, wishing it, or even thinking it. And the law finds this so monstrous [as to subject it to a special rule of sentencing]. Ordinarily, if someone who is accused, seized, and convicted dies before he has been sentenced, his personal status is not diminished, no matter what his crime, even if it was treason. But treason in the highest degree can never be purged by the death of the person accused of it, and even someone who was never accused is considered in law as having been already sentenced. And although evil thoughts are not subject to punishment, anyone who has thought of making an attempt on the life of his sovereign prince is held to be guilty of a capital crime, no matter whether he repented of it. In fact there was a gentleman from Normandy who confessed to a Franciscan friar that he had wanted to kill King Francis I but had repented of this evil wish. The Franciscan gave him absolution, but still told the king about it; he had the gentleman sent before the Parlement of Paris to stand trial, where he was condemned to death by its verdict and thereupon executed. And one cannot say that the court acted from fear, in view of the fact that it often refused to verify edicts and letters patent even when the king commanded it. And in Paris a man, named Caboche, who was completely mad and out of his senses, drew a sword against King Henry II without any effect or even attempt. He too was condemned to die without consideration of his insanity, which the law ordinarily excuses no matter what murder or crime the madman may have committed.

*　*　*

As for Calvin's remark that if there existed in these times magistrates especially constituted for the defense of the people and to restrain the licentiousness of kings, like the ephors in Sparta, the tribunes in Rome, and the demarchs in Athens, then those magistrates should resist, oppose, and prevent their licentiousness and cruelty—it clearly shows that it is never licit, in a proper monarchy, to attack a sovereign king, or defend one's self against him, or to make an attempt upon his life or honor, for he spoke only of democratic and aristocratic states. I have shown above that the kings of Sparta were but simple senators and captains. And when he speaks of the Estates, he says "possible," not daring to be definite. In any event there is an important difference between attacking the honor of one's prince and resisting his tyranny, between killing one's king and opposing his cruelty.

We thus read that the Protestant princes of Germany, before taking up arms against the emperor, asked Martin Luther if it were permissible. He frankly replied that it was not permissible no mat-

ter how great the charge of impiety or tyranny. But he was not heeded; and the outcome of the affair was miserable, bringing with it the ruin of some great and illustrious houses of Germany. *Quia nulla iusta causa videri potest,* said Cicero, *adversus patriam arma capiendi.*[2] Admittedly, it is quite certain that the sovereignty of the German Empire does not lie in the person of the emperor, as we shall explain in due course. But since he is the chief, they could have taken up arms against him only with the consent of the Estates or its majority, which was not obtained. It would have been even less permissible against a sovereign prince.

I can give no better parallel than that of a son with respect to his father. The law of God says that he who speaks evil of his father or his mother shall be put to death. If the father be a murderer, a thief, a traitor to his country, a person who has committed incest or parricide, a blasphemer, an atheist, and anything else one wants to add, I confess that the entire gamut of penalties will not suffice for his punishment; but I say that it is not for his son to lay hands on him, *quia nulla tanta impietas, nullum tantum factum est quod sit parricidio vindicandum,*[3] as it was put by an orator of ancient times. And yet Cicero, taking up this question, says that love of country is even greater. Hence the prince of our country, being ordained and sent by God, is always more sacred and ought to be more inviolable than a father.

I conclude then that it is never permissible for a subject to attempt anything against a sovereign prince, no matter how wicked and cruel a tyrant he may be. It is certainly permissible not to obey him in anything that is against the law of God or nature—to flee, to hide, to evade his blows, to suffer death rather than make any attempt upon his life or honor. For oh, how many tyrants there would be if it were lawful to kill them! He who taxes too heavily would be a tyrant, as the vulgar understand it; he who gives commands that the

---

[2] "Because there can never be a just cause to take up arms against one's country."

[3] "Because there is no impiety so great, and no crime so great that it ought to be avenged by patricide."

people do not like would be a tyrant, as Aristotle defined a tyrant in the *Politics;* he who maintains guards for his security would be a tyrant; he who punishes conspirators against his rule would be a tyrant. How then should good princes be secure in their lives? I would not say that it is illicit for other princes to proceed against tyrants by force of arms, as I have stated, but it is not for subjects.

*　　*　　*

REVIEW QUESTIONS

1. What, according to Bodin, is the definition of *sovereignty?*
2. In describing its prerogatives, would Bodin have agreed with Machiavelli?
3. Can sovereignty be mixed? Why?
4. Is it permissible to resist a tyrant?
5. Can a sovereign ruler be a tyrant?
6. May one resist a sovereign?

THOMAS HOBBES

FROM *Leviathan*

Thomas Hobbes (1588–1679) was an English philosopher whose mechanistic and deterministic theories of political life were highly controversial in his own time. Born in Malmesbury, Hobbes attended Magdalen Hall, Oxford, and became tutor to William Cavendish, later the Earl of Devonshire, in 1608. With his student, he undertook several tours of the Continent, where he met and spoke with leading intellectual lights of the day, including Galileo and Descartes. Around 1637, he became interested in the constitutional struggle between Parliament and Charles I and set to work writing a "little treatise in English" in defense of the royal prerogative. Before its publication in 1650, the book circulated privately in 1640 under the title Elements of Law, Natural and Politic. *Fearing arrest by Parliament, Hobbes fled to Paris, where he remained for the next eleven years. While in exile, he served as math tutor to the Prince of Wales, later Charles II, from 1646 to 1648. His great work,* Leviathan *(1651), was a forceful argument for political absolutism. Its title, taken from the horrifying sea monster of the Old Testament, suggested the power and authority Hobbes thought necessary to compel obedience and order in human society. Strongly influenced by mechanical philosophy, he treated human beings as matter in motion, subject to certain physical, rational laws. According to Hobbes, people feared one another and lived in a state of constant competition and conflict. For this reason, they must submit to the absolute, supreme authority of the state, a social contract among selfish individuals moved by fear and necessity. Once delegated, that authority was irrevocable and indivisible. Ironically, these theories found favor neither with royalists nor with antiroyalists. Charles II believed that it was written in justification of the Commonwealth. The French feared its attacks on the papacy. After the Restoration, Parliament added* Leviathan *to a list of books to be investigated for atheistic tendencies.*

Despite frustrations over the reception of his political theories, Hobbes retained his intellectual vigor. At age eighty-four, he wrote an autobiography in Latin and translated the works of Homer into English. He died at age ninety-one.

From *Leviathan*, by Thomas Hobbes, edited by E. Hershey Sneath (Needham, Eng.: Ginn Press, 1898).

*   *   *

Of the Causes, Generation, and Definition of a Commonwealth

The final cause, end, or design of men, who naturally love liberty and dominion over others, in the introduction of that restraint upon themselves in which we see them live in commonwealths is the foresight of their own preservation, and of a more contented life thereby; that is to say, of getting themselves out from that miserable condition of war which is necessarily consequent . . . to the natural passions of men when there is no visible power to keep them in awe and tie them by fear of punishment to the performance of their covenants, and observation of the laws of nature. . . .

For the laws of nature, as "justice," "equity," "modesty," "mercy," and, in sum, "doing to others as we would be done to," of themselves, without the terror of some power to cause them to be observed, are contrary to our natural passions, that carry us to partiality, pride, revenge, and the like. And covenants without the sword are but words, and of no strength to secure a man at all. Therefore, notwithstanding the laws of nature, which every one has then kept when he has the will to keep them, when he can do it safely, if there be no power erected, or not great enough for our security; every man will, and may lawfully rely on his own strength and art, for protection against all other men. And in all places where men have lived by small families, to rob and spoil one another has been a trade, and so far from being reputed against the law of nature that the greater spoils they gained, the greater was their honor; and men observed no other laws therein but the laws of honor; that is, to abstain from cruelty, leaving to men their lives and instruments of livelihood. And as small families did then, so now do cities and kingdoms, which are but greater families, for their own security enlarge their dominions upon all pretenses of danger and fear of invasion or assistance that may be given to invaders, and endeavor as much as they can to subdue or weaken their neighbors by open force and secret arts, for lack of other protection, justly; and are remembered for it in later ages with honor.

Nor is it the joining together of a small number of men that gives them this security, because in small numbers small additions on the one side or the other make the advantage of strength so great as is sufficient to carry the victory; and therefore gives encouragement to an invasion. The multitude sufficient to confide in for our security is not determined by any certain number but by comparison with the enemy we fear; and is then sufficient when the advantage of the enemy is not so visible and conspicuous to determine the event of war as to move him to attempt it.

And should there not be so great a multitude, even if their actions be directed according to their particular judgments and particular appetites, they can expect thereby no defense nor protection, neither against a common enemy nor against the injuries of one another. For being distracted in opinions concerning the best use and application of their strength, they do not help but hinder one another, and reduce their strength by mutual opposition to nothing; whereby they are easily not only subdued by a very few that agree together, but also, when there is no common enemy, they make war upon each other for their particular interests. For if we could suppose a great multitude of men to consent in the observation of justice and other laws of nature without a common power to keep them all in awe, we might as well suppose all mankind to do the same; and then there neither would be, nor need to be, any civil government or commonwealth at all, because there would be peace without subjection.

Nor is it enough for the security which men desire should last all the time of their life that they be governed and directed by one judgment for a limited time, as in one battle or one war. For though they obtain a victory by their unanimous endeavor against a foreign enemy, yet afterwards, when either they have no common enemy or he that by one group is held for an enemy is by another group held for a friend, they must needs, by the difference of their interests, dissolve, and fall again into a war among themselves.

It is true that certain living creatures, as bees and ants, live sociably one with another, which are therefore by Aristotle numbered among political creatures, and yet have no other direction, than their particular judgments and appetites; nor speech whereby one of them can signify to another what he thinks expedient for the common benefit; and therefore some man may perhaps desire to know why mankind cannot do the same. To which I answer:

First, that men are continually in competition for honor and dignity, which these creatures are not; and consequently among men there arises on the ground envy and hatred and finally war, but among these not so.

Secondly, that among these creatures the common good differ not from the private; and being by nature inclined to their private, they procure thereby the common benefit. But man, whose joy consists in comparing himself with other men, can relish nothing but what is eminent.

Thirdly, that these creatures, having not, as man, the use of reason, do not see nor think they see any fault, in the administration of their common business; whereas among men, there are very many that think themselves wiser and abler to govern the public better than the rest; and these strive to reform and innovate, one this way, another that way, and thereby bring it into distraction and civil war.

Fourthly, that these creatures, though they have some use of voice in making known to one another their desires and other affections, yet they lack that art of words by which some men can represent to others that which is good in the likeness of evil; and evil in the likeness of good; and augment or diminish the apparent greatness of good and evil, making men discontented and troubling their peace at their pleasure.

Fifthly, irrational creatures cannot distinguish between "injury" and "damage"; and, therefore, as long as they be at ease they are not offended with their fellows; whereas man is then most troublesome when he is most at ease; for then it is that he loves to show his wisdom and control the actions of them that govern the commonwealth.

Lastly, the agreement of these creatures is natural, that of men is by covenant only, which is artificial; and therefore, it is no wonder if there be somewhat else required besides covenant to make their agreement constant and lasting, which is a common power to keep them in awe and to direct their actions to the common benefit.

The only way to erect such a common power which may be able to defend them from the invasion of foreigners and the injuries of one another, and thereby to secure them in such sort so that by their own industry and by the fruits of the earth they may nourish themselves and live contentedly, is to confer all their power and strength upon one man, or upon one assembly of men that may reduce all their wills, by plurality of voices, unto one will; which is as much as to say, to appoint one man or assembly of men to bear their person; and every one to accept and acknowledge himself to be author of whatsoever he that so bears their person shall act or cause to be acted in those things which concern the common peace and safety, and therein to submit their wills every one to his will, and their judgments to his judgment. This is more than consent or concord; it is a real unity of them all in one and the same person, made by covenant of every man with every man, in such manner as if every man should say to every man, "I authorize and give up my right of governing myself to this man, or to this assembly of men, on this condition, that you give up your right to him and authorize all his actions in like manner." This done, the multitude so united in one person is called a "commonwealth," in Latin *civitas*. This is the generation of that great "leviathan," or rather, to speak more reverently, of that "mortal god," to which we owe, under the "immortal God," our peace and defense. For by this authority, given him by every particular man in the commonwealth, he has the use of so much power and strength conferred on him that, by terror thereof, he is enabled to form the wills of them all to peace at home and mutual aid against their enemies abroad. And in him consists the essence of the commonwealth, which, to define it, is "one person, of whose acts a great multitude, by mutual covenants one with another, have made themselves the author, to the end he may use the strength and means of them all as he shall think expedient for their peace and common defense."

And he that carries this person is called "sovereign" and said to have "sovereign power"; and every one besides, his "subject."

The attaining to this sovereign power is by two ways. One, by natural force, as when a man makes his children to submit themselves and their children to his government, as being able to destroy them if they refuse; or by war subdues his enemies to his will, giving them their lives on that condition. The other is when men agree among themselves to submit to some man or assembly of men voluntarily, on confidence that they will be protected by him against all others. This latter, may be called a political commonwealth, or commonwealth by "institution," and the former, a commonwealth by "acquisition." * * *

Of the Office of the Sovereign Representative

The office of the sovereign, be it a monarch or an assembly, consists in the end for which he was trusted with the sovereign power, namely, the securing of "the safety of the people"; to which he is obliged by the law of nature, and to render an account thereof to God, the author of that law, and to none but him. But by safety here is not meant a bare preservation but also all other contentments of life which every man by lawful industry, without danger or hurt to the commonwealth, shall acquire to himself.

And this is to be done, not by care applied to individuals further than their protection from injuries when they shall complain, but by a general provision contained in public instruction, both of doctrine and example, and in the making and executing of good laws to which individual persons may apply their own cases.

And because, if the essential rights of sovereignty . . . be taken away, the commonwealth is thereby dissolved and every man returns into the condition and calamity of a war with every other man, which is the greatest evil that can happen in this life; it is the office of the sovereign, to maintain those rights entire, and consequently against his duty, first, to transfer to another or to lay from himself any of them. For he that deserts the means deserts the ends; and he deserts the means when, being the sovereign, he acknowledges himself subject to the civil laws and renounces the power of supreme judicature, or of making war or peace by his own authority; or of judging of the necessities of the commonwealth; or of levying money and soldiers when and as much as in his own conscience he shall judge necessary; or of making officers and ministers both of war and peace; or of appointing teachers and examining what doctrines are conformable or contrary to the defense, peace, and good of the people. Secondly, it is against his duty to let the people be ignorant or misinformed of the grounds and reasons of those his essential rights, because thereby men are easy to be seduced and drawn to resist him when the commonwealth shall require their use and exercise.

And the grounds of these rights have the need to be diligently and truly taught, because they cannot be maintained by any civil law or terror of legal punishment. For a civil law that shall forbid rebellion (and such is all resistance to the essential rights of the sovereignty), is not, as a civil law, any obligation, but by virtue only of the law of nature that forbids the violation of faith; which natural obligation if men know not, they cannot know the right of any law the sovereign makes. And for the punishment, they take it but for an act of hostility which when they think they have strength enough, they will endeavor by acts of hostility, to avoid. * * *

To the care of the sovereign belongs the making of good laws. But what is a good law? By a good law I mean not a just law; for no law can be unjust. The law is made by the sovereign power, and all that is done by such power is warranted and owned by every one of the people; and that which every man will have so, no man can say is unjust. It is in the laws of a commonwealth as in the laws of gaming; whatsoever the gamesters all agree on is injustice to none of them. A good law is that which is "needed" for the "good of the people" and "perspicuous."

For the use of laws, which are but rules authorized, is not to bind the people from all voluntary actions but to direct and keep them in such a motion as not to hurt themselves by their own impetuous desires, rashness, or indiscretion; as hedges are set not to stop travellers, but to keep them in their way. And, therefore, a law that is not needed, having not the true end of a law, is not good. A law may be conceived to be good when it is for the benefit of the sovereign, though it be not necessary for the people, but it is not so. For the good of the sovereign and people cannot be separated. It is a weak sovereign, that has weak subjects, and a weak people, whose sovereign lacks power to rule them at his will. Unnecessary laws are not good laws but traps for money; which, where the right of sovereign power is acknowledged, are superfluous, and where it is not acknowledged, insufficient to defend the people. * * *

It belongs also to the office of the sovereign to make a right application of punishments and rewards. And seeing the end of punishing is not revenge and discharge of anger, but correction, either of the offender, or of others by his example; the severest punishments are to be inflicted for those crimes that are of most danger to the public; such as are those which proceed from malice to the government established; those that spring from contempt of justice; those that provoke indignation in the multitude; and those which, unpunished, seem authorized, as when they are committed by sons, servants, or favorites of men in authority. For indignation carries men not only against the actors and authors of injustice, but against all power that is likely to protect them; as in the case of Tarquin, when for the insolent act of one of his sons he was driven out of Rome and the monarchy itself dissolved. But crimes of infirmity, such as are those which proceed from great provocation, from great fear, great need, or from ignorance, whether the fact be a great crime or not, there is place many times for leniency without prejudice to the commonwealth; and leniency, when there is such place for it, is required by the law of nature. The punishment of the leaders and teachers in a commotion, not the poor seduced people, when they are punished, can profit the commonwealth by their example. To be severe to the people is to punish that ignorance which may in great part be imputed to the sovereign, whose fault it was that they were no better instructed.

In like manner it belongs to the office and duty of the sovereign, to apply his rewards so that there may arise from them benefit to the commonwealth, wherein consists their use, and end; and is then done when they that have well served the commonwealth are, with as little expense of the common treasure as is possible, so well recompensed as others thereby may be encouraged both to serve the same as faithfully as they can and to study the arts by which they may be enabled to do it better. To buy with money or preferment from a popular ambitious subject to be quiet and desist from making ill impressions in the minds of the people has nothing of the nature of reward (which is ordained not for disservice, but for service past), nor a sign of gratitude, but of fear; nor does it tend to the benefit but to the damage of the public. It is a contention with ambition like that of Hercules with the monster Hydra which, having many heads, for every one that was vanquished there grew up three. For in like manner, when the stubbornness of one popular man is overcome with reward there arise many more, by the example, that do the same mischief in hope of like benefit; and as all sorts of manufacture, so also malice increases by being salable. And though sometimes a civil war may be deferred by such ways as that, yet the danger grows still the greater and the public ruin more assured. It is therefore against the duty of the sovereign, to whom the public safety is committed, to reward those that aspire to greatness by disturbing the peace of their country, and not rather to oppose the beginnings of such men with a little danger than after a longer time with greater. ✶ ✶ ✶

When the sovereign himself is popular, that is, revered and beloved of his people, there is no danger at all from the popularity of a subject. For soldiers are never so generally unjust as to side with their captain though they love him, against their sovereign, when they love not only his person but also his cause. And therefore those who by violence have at any time suppressed the power of their lawful sovereign, before they could settle themselves in his place have been always put to the trouble of contriving their titles to save the people from the shame of receiving them. To have a known right to sovereign power is so popular a quality as he that has it needs no more, for his own part, to turn the hearts of his subjects to him but that they see him able absolutely to govern his own family; nor, on the part of his enemies, but a disbanding of their armies. For the greatest and most active part of mankind has never hitherto been well contented with the present.

Concerning the offices of one sovereign to another, which are comprehended in that law which is commonly called the "law of nations," I need not say anything in this place because the law of nations and the law of nature is the same thing. And every sovereign has the same right, in securing the safety of his people that any particular man can have in securing the safety of his own body. And the same law that dictates to men that have no civil government what they ought to do and what to avoid in regard of one another dictates the same to commonwealths, that is, to the consciences of sovereign princes and sovereign assemblies, there being no court of natural justice but in the conscience only; where not man but God reigns whose laws, such of them as oblige all mankind, in respect of God as he is the author of nature are "natural," and in respect of the same God as he is King of kings are "laws."

✶   ✶   ✶

REVIEW QUESTIONS

1. What is Hobbes's view of human nature?
2. What, according to Hobbes, motivates human beings?
3. What, according to Hobbes, is the purpose of the state?
4. Why do human beings come together to form a political society?
5. What are the responsibilities of the sovereign?
6. What is the sovereign's highest obligation?
7. Does Hobbes hold out any hope that the state can improve human nature?

SIAMESE EMBASSY TO LOUIS XIV, IN 1686 (1686)   NICOLAS III DE LARMESSIN

Nicolas III Larmessin (c. 1640–1725) was a member of the de Larmessin (also: de L'Armessin) family, a famous French dynasty of engravers, printers and booksellers, who were active during the seventeenth and eighteenth centuries. Art historians attribute a number of important portraits to him as well as the many engravings for books, calendars, almanacs and decorative purposes, for which he is best known. Here he commemorates the Siamese embassy to the court of Louis XIV in 1686. What might have made this event a fit subject for an engraving? How does the artist glorify the French king? What elements of court ritual in an age of absolutism are readily visible? In a period of burgeoning imperialism, what propaganda purposes might this image have served?

Coffee House Society

Coffee is an example of the impact of overseas trade and colonial empire on the consumption and lifestyle of ordinary Europeans. The bean's historical origins are shrouded in legend. What seems clear is that they were taken to Arabia from Africa during the fifteenth century and placed under cultivation. Introduced into Europe during the sixteenth and seventeenth centuries, they gained almost immediate popularity. Served at coffeehouses, the first of which was established in London around 1650, coffee's consumption became an occasion for transacting political, social, commercial, or literary business. So great was the demand for coffee that European merchants took it from the Arabian Peninsula to Java, Indonesia, and the Americas. The following descriptions by two anonymous authors give some sense of the ways in which colonial products shaped European culture in the seventeenth century.

From *Selections from the Sources of English History*, edited by Charles W. Colby (New York: Longmans, Green, 1899), pp. 208–12.

*   *   *

1673

A coffee-house is a lay conventicle, good-fellowship turned puritan, ill-husbandry in masquerade, whither people come, after toping all day, to purchase, at the expense of their last penny, the repute of sober companions: A Rota [club] room, that, like Noah's ark, receives animals of every sort, from the precise diminutive band, to the hectoring cravat and cuffs in folio: a nursery for training up the smaller fry of virtuosi in confident tattling, or a cabal of kittling [carping] critics that have only learned to spit and mew; a mint of intelligence, that, to make each man his pennyworth, draws out into petty parcels, what the merchant receives in bullion: he, that comes often, saves twopence a week in Gazettes, and has his news and his coffee for the same charge, as at a threepenny ordinary they give in broth to your chop of mutton; it is an exchange, where haberdashers of political small-wares meet, and mutually abuse each other, and the public, with bottomless stories, and headless notions; the rendezvous of idle pamphlets, and persons more idly employed to read them; a high court of justice, where every little fellow in a camlet cloak takes upon him to transpose affairs both in church and state, to show reasons against acts of parliament, and condemn the decrees of general councils.

*   *   *

As you have a hodge-podge of drinks, such too is your company, for each man seems a leveller, and ranks and files himself as he lists, without regard to degrees or order; so that often you may see a silly fop and a worshipful justice, a griping rook and a grave citizen, a worthy lawyer and an errant pickpocket, a reverend nonconformist and a canting mountebank, all blended together to compose an oglio [medley] of impertinence.

If any pragmatic, to show himself witty or eloquent, begin to talk high, presently the further tables are abandoned, and all the rest flock round (like smaller birds, to admire the gravity of the madge-howlet [barn-owl]). They listen to him awhile with their mouths, and let their pipes go out, and coffee grow cold, for pure zeal of attention, but on the sudden fall all a yelping at once with more noise, but not half so much harmony, as a pack of beagles on the full cry. To still this bawling, up starts Capt. All-man-sir, the man of mouth, with a face as blustering as that of Æolus and his four sons, in painting, and a voice louder than the speaking trumpet, he begins you the story of a sea-fight; and though he never were further, by water, than the Bear-garden, . . . yet, having pirated the names of ships and captains, he persuades you himself was present, and performed miracles; that he waded knee-deep in blood on the upper-deck, and never thought to serenade his mistress so pleasant as the bullets whistling; how he stopped a vice-admiral of the enemy's under full sail; till she was boarded, with his single arm, instead of grappling-irons, and puffed out with his breath a fire-ship that fell foul on them. All this he relates, sitting in a cloud of smoke, and belching so many common oaths to vouch it, you can scarce guess whether the real engagement, or his romancing account of it, be the more dreadful: however, he concludes with railing at the conduct of some eminent officers (that, perhaps, he never saw), and protests, had they taken his advice at the council of war, not a sail had escaped us.

He is no sooner out of breath, but another begins a lecture on the Gazette, where, finding several prizes taken, he gravely observes, if this trade hold, we shall quickly rout the Dutch, horse and foot, by sea: he nicknames the Polish gentlemen wherever he meets them, and enquires whether Gayland and Taffaletta be Lutherans or Calvinists? *stilo novo* he interprets a vast new stile, or turnpike, erected by his electoral highness on the borders of Westphalia, to keep Monsieur Turenne's cavalry from falling on his retreating troops: he takes words by the sound, without examining their sense: Morea he believes to be the country of the Moors, and Hungary a place where famine always keeps her court, nor is there anything more certain, than that he made a whole room full of fops, as wise as himself, spend above two hours in searching the map for Aristocracy and Democracy, not doubting but to have found them there, as well as Dalmatia and Croatia.

1675

Though the happy Arabia, nature's spicery, prodigally furnishes the voluptuous world with all kinds of aromatics, and divers other rarities; yet I scarce know whether mankind be not still as much obliged to it for the excellent fruit of the humble coffee-shrub, as for any other of its more specious productions: for, since there is nothing we here enjoy, next to life, valuable beyond health, certainly those things that contribute to preserve us in good plight and eucrasy, and fortify our weak bodies against the continual assaults and batteries of disease, deserve our regards much more than those which only gratify a liquorish palate, or otherwise prove subservient to our delights. As for this salutiferous berry, of so general a use through all the regions of the east, it is sufficiently known, when prepared, to be moderately hot, and of a very drying attenuating and cleansing quality; whence reason infers, that its decoction must contain many good physical properties, and cannot but be an incomparable remedy to dissolve crudities, comfort the brain, and dry up ill humours in the stomach. In brief, to prevent or redress, in those that frequently drink it, all cold drowsy rheumatic distempers whatsoever, that proceed from excess of moisture, which are so numerous, that but to name them would tire the tongue of a mountebank.

*　　*　　*

Lastly, for diversion. It is older than Aristotle, and will be true, when Hobbes is forgot, that man is a sociable creature, and delights in company. Now, whither shall a person, wearied with hard study, or the laborious turmoils of a tedious day, repair to refresh himself? Or where can young gentlemen, or shop-keepers, more innocently and advantageously spend an hour or two in the evening, than at a coffee-house? Where they shall be sure to meet company, and, by the custom of the house, not such as at other places, stingy and reserved to themselves, but free and communicative; where every man may modestly begin his story, and propose to, or answer another, as he thinks fit. Discourse is *pabulum animi, cos ingenii;* the mind's best diet, and the great whetstone and incentive of ingenuity; by that we come to know men better than by their physiognomy. *Loquere, ut te videam,* speak, that I may see thee, was the philosopher's adage. To read men is acknowledged more useful than books; but where is there a better library for that study, generally, than here, amongst such a variety of humours, all expressing themselves on divers subjects, according to their respective abilities?

*   *   *

In brief, it is undeniable, that, as you have here the most civil, so it is, generally, the most intelligent society; the frequenting whose converse, and observing their discourses and department, cannot but civilise our manners, enlarge our understandings, refine our language, teach us a generous confidence and handsome mode of address, and brush off that *pudor rubrusticus* (as, I remember, Tully somewhere calls it), that clownish kind of modesty frequently incident to the best natures, which renders them sheepish and ridiculous in company.

So that, upon the whole matter, spite of the idle sarcasms and paltry reproaches thrown upon it, we may, with no less truth than plainness, give this brief character of a well-regulated coffeehouse (for our pen disdains to be an advocate for any sordid holes, that assume that name to cloak the practice of debauchery), that it is the sanctuary of health, the nursery of temperance, the delight of frugality, an academy of civility, and free-school of ingenuity.

*   *   *

REVIEW QUESTIONS

1. How would you describe coffeehouse society in the late seventeenth century?
2. What is the attitude of each of our two anonymous authors? How and why do they differ?
3. What is the significance of reading the gazette?
4. What are the virtues of coffee?
5. How could coffee drinking be considered a vice in early modern Europe?

JOHN LOCKE

FROM *Two Treatises on Government*

John Locke (1632–1704) was an English philosopher whose thought contributed to the Enlightenment. He grew up in a liberal Puritan family, the son of an attorney who fought in the civil war against Charles I, and attended Christ Church College, Oxford. He received his bachelor of arts in 1656, lectured in classical languages while earning his master of arts, and entered Oxford's medical school to avoid being forced to join the clergy. In 1666, Locke attached himself to the household of the Earl of Shaftesbury and his fortunes to the liberal Whig Party. Between 1675 and 1679, he lived in France, where he made contact with leading intellectuals of the late seventeenth century. On his return to England, he plunged into the controversy

*surrounding the succession of James II, an avowed Catholic with absolutist preten-
sions, to the throne of his brother, Charles II. Locke's patron, Shaftesbury, was imprisoned for his opposition, and Locke went into exile in 1683. Though he was
involved to some extent in the Glorious Revolution of 1688, he returned to England
in 1689, in the entourage of Mary, Princess of Orange, who would assume the
throne with her husband, William. The* Two Treatises on Government *(1690) were
published anonymously, although readers commonly assumed Locke's authorship.
More interesting is the time at which they were written. Most scholars assume that
they were written immediately before publication, as a justification of the revolution
just completed. Other scholars believe, however, that the treatises were written from
exile as a call to revolution, a riskier, much more inflammatory project. The first
treatise comprises a long attack on Robert Filmer's* Patriarcha, *a denial of the patriarchal justification of the absolute monarch. The second treatise constructs in the
place of patriarchy a theory of politics based on natural law, which provides the foundation of human freedom. The social contract creates a political structure by consent
of the governed and designed to preserve those freedoms established in natural law.
Locke's treatises inspired the political theories of the Enlightenment.*

From *First Treatise* in *Two Treatises on Government*, edited by Ernst Rhys (New York: Dutton, 1993).

*   *   *

Chapter VI
Of Paternal Power

It may perhaps be censured an impertinent criticism in a discourse of this nature to find fault with words and names that have obtained in the world. And yet possibly it may not be amiss to offer new ones when the old are apt to lead men into mistakes, as this of paternal power probably has done, which seems so to place the power of parents over their children wholly in the father, as if the mother had no share in it; whereas if we consult reason or revelation, we shall find she has an equal title, which may give one reason to ask whether this might not be more properly called parental power? For whatever obligation Nature and the right of generation lays on children, it must certainly bind them equal to both the concurrent causes of it. And accordingly we see the positive law of God everywhere joins them together without distinction, when it commands the obedience of children: "Honour thy father and thy mother"; "Whosoever curseth his father or his mother"; "Ye shall fear every man his mother and his father"; "Children, obey your parents" etc., is the style of the Old and New Testament.

*   *   *

Though I have said above "That all men by nature are equal," I cannot be supposed to understand all sorts of "equality." Age or virtue may give men a just precedency. Excellency of parts and merit may place others above the common level. Birth may subject some, and alliance or benefits others, to pay an observance to those to whom Nature, gratitude, or other respects, may have made it due; and yet all this consists with the equality which all men are in in respect of jurisdiction or dominion one over another, which was the equality I there spoke of as proper to the business in hand, being that equal right that every man hath to his natural freedom, without being subjected to the will or authority of any other man.

Children, I confess, are not born in this full state of equality, though they are born to it. Their

PALACE AND GARDENS OF VERSAILLES (1668)   PIERRE PATEL

Patel's famous print of the palace at Versailles captures the grand scale of monarchy in the seventeenth century. Note not only the size of the palace but also its location in the center of carefully planned gardens, boulevards, and buildings. Versailles was truly a theater for the display of political power. Why was such a theater of power necessary? What can be learned from the iconography of power that was built into Versailles, such as the function of gardens or the location of boulevards or alleys or broad open spaces? How might Versailles have functioned not only as a theater of power but also as a prison for the powerful?

parents have a sort of rule and jurisdiction over them when they come into the world, and for some time after, but it is but a temporary one. The bonds of this subjection are like the swaddling clothes they are wrapt up in and supported by in the weakness of their infancy. Age and reason as they grow up loosen them, till at length they drop quite off, and leave a man at his own free disposal.

Adam was created a perfect man, his body and mind in full possession of their strength and reason, and so was capable from the first instance of his being to provide for his own support and preservation, and govern his actions according to the dictates of the law of reason God had implanted in him. From him the world is peopled with his descendants, who are all born infants, weak and helpless, without knowledge or understanding. But to supply the defects of this imperfect state till the improvement of growth and age had removed them, Adam and Eve, and after them all parents were, by the law of Nature, under an obligation to preserve, nourish and educate the children they had begotten, not as their own workmanship, but the workmanship of their own Maker, the Almighty, to whom they were to be accountable for them.

The law that was to govern Adam was the same that was to govern all his posterity, the law of reason. But his offspring having another way of entrance into the world, different from him, by a natural birth, that produced them ignorant, and without the use of reason, they were not presently under that law. For nobody can be under a law that is not promulgated to him; and this law being promulgated or made known by reason only, he that is not come to the use of his reason cannot be said to be under this law; and Adam's children being not presently as soon as born under this law of reason, were not presently free. For law, in its true notion, is not so much the limitation as the direction of a free and intelligent agent to his proper interest, and prescribes no farther than is for the general good of those under that law. Could they be happier without it, the law, as a useless thing, would of itself vanish; and that ill deserves the name of confinement which hedges us in only from bogs and precipices. So that how-

ever it may be mistaken, the end of law is not to abolish or restrain, but to preserve and enlarge freedom. For in all the states of created beings, capable of laws, where there is no law there is no freedom. For liberty is to be free from restraint and violence from others, which cannot be where there is no law; and is not, as we are told, "a liberty for every man to do what he lists." For who could be free, when every other man's humour might domineer over him? But a liberty to dispose and order freely as he lists his person, actions, possessions, and his whole property within the allowance of those laws under which he is, and therein not to be subject to the arbitrary will of another, but freely follow his own.

The power, then, that parents have over their children arises from that duty which is incumbent on them, to take care of their offspring during the imperfect state of childhood. To inform the mind, and govern the actions of their yet ignorant nonage, till reason shall take its place and ease them of that trouble, is what the children want, and the parents are bound to. For God having given man an understanding to direct his actions, has allowed him a freedom of will and liberty of acting, as properly belonging thereunto within the bounds of that law he is under. But whilst he is in an estate wherein he has no understanding of his own to direct his will, he is not to have any will of his own to follow. He that understands for him must will for him too; he must prescribe to his will, and regulate his actions, but when he comes to the estate that made his father a free man, the son is a free man too.

This holds in all the laws a man is under, whether natural or civil. Is a man under the law of Nature? What made him free of that law? what gave him a free disposing of his property, according to his own will, within the compass of that law? I answer, an estate wherein he might be supposed capable to know that law, that so he might keep his actions within the bounds of it. When he has acquired that state, he is presumed to know how far that law is to be his guide, and how far he may make use of his freedom, and so comes to have it; till then, somebody else must guide him, who is presumed to know how far the law allows a liberty. If such a state of reason, such an age of discretion made him free, the same shall make his son free too. Is a man under the law of England? what made him free of that law—that is, to have the liberty to dispose of his actions and possessions, according to his own will, within the permission of that law? a capacity of knowing that law. Which is supposed, by that law, at the age of twenty-one, and in some cases sooner. If this made the father free, it shall make the son free too. Till then, we see the law allows the son to have no will, but he is to be guided by the will of his father or guardian, who is to understand for him. And if the father die and fail to substitute a deputy in this trust, if he hath not provided a tutor to govern his son during his minority, during his want of understanding, the law takes care to do it: some other must govern him and be a will to him till he hath attained to a state of freedom, and his understanding be fit to take the government of his will. But after that the father and son are equally free, as much as tutor and pupil, after nonage, equally subjects of the same law together, without any dominion left in the father over the life, liberty, or estate of his son, whether they be only in the state and under the law of Nature, or under the positive laws of an established government.

*   *   *

The freedom then of man, and liberty of acting according to his own will, is grounded on his having reason, which is able to instruct him in that law he is to govern himself by, and make him know how far he is left to the freedom of his own will. To turn him loose to an unrestrained liberty, before he has reason to guide him, is not the allowing him the privilege of his nature to be free, but to thrust him out amongst brutes, and abandon him to a state as wretched and as much beneath that of a man as theirs. This is that which puts the authority into the parents' hands to govern the minority of their children. God hath made it their business to employ this care on their offspring, and hath placed in them suitable inclinations of tenderness

and concern to temper this power, to apply it as His wisdom designed it, to the children's good as long as they should need to be under it.

But what reason can hence advance this care of the parents due to their offspring into an absolute, arbitrary dominion of the father, whose power reaches no farther than by such a discipline as he finds most effectual to give such strength and health to their bodies, such vigour and rectitude to their minds, as may best fit his children to be most useful to themselves and others, and, if it be necessary to his condition, to make them work when they are able for their own subsistence; but in this power the mother, too, has her share with the father.

Nay, this power so little belongs to the father by any peculiar right of Nature, but only as he is guardian of his children, that when he quits his care of them he loses his power over them, which goes along with their nourishment and education, to which it is inseparably annexed, and belongs as much to the foster-father of an exposed child as to the natural father of another. So little power does the bare act of begetting give a man over his issue, if all his care ends there, and this be all the title he hath to the name and authority of a father. And what will become of this paternal power in that part of the world where one woman hath more than one husband at a time? or in those parts of America where, when the husband and wife part, which happens frequently, the children are all left to the mother, follow her, and are wholly under her care and provision? And if the father die whilst the children are young, do they not naturally everywhere owe the same obedience to their mother, during their minority, as to their father, were he alive? And will any one say that the mother hath a legislative power over her children that she can make standing rules which shall be of perpetual obligation, by which they ought to regulate all the concerns of their property, and bound their liberty all the course of their lives, and enforce the observation of them with capital punishments? For this is the proper power of the magistrate, of which the father hath not so much as the shadow. His command over his children is but temporary, and reaches not their life or property. It is but a help to the weakness and imperfection of their nonage, a discipline necessary to their education. And though a father may dispose of his own possessions as he pleases when his children are out of danger of perishing for want, yet his power extends not to the lives or goods which either their own industry, or another's bounty, has made theirs, nor to their liberty neither, when they are once arrived to the enfranchisement of the years of discretion. The father's empire then ceases, and he can from thenceforward no more dispose of the liberty of his son than that of any other man. And it must be far from an absolute or perpetual jurisdiction from which a man may withdraw himself, having licence from Divine authority to "leave father and mother and cleave to his wife."

*   *   *

Chapter VII
Of Political or Civil Society

God, having made man such a creature that, in His own judgment, it was not good for him to be alone, put him under strong obligations of necessity, convenience, and inclination, to drive him into society, as well as fitted him with understanding and language to continue and enjoy it. The first society was between man and wife, which gave beginning to that between parents and children, to which, in time, that between master and servant came to be added. And though all these might, and commonly did, meet together, and make up but one family, wherein the master or mistress of it had some sort of rule proper to a family, each of these, or all together, came short of "political society," as we shall see if we consider the different ends, ties, and bounds of each of these.

Conjugal society is made by a voluntary compact between man and woman, and though it consist chiefly in such a communion and right in one another's bodies as is necessary to its chief end, procreation, yet it draws with it mutual support

and assistance, and a communion of interests too, as necessary not only to unite their care and affection, but also necessary to their common offspring, who have a right to be nourished and maintained by them till they are able to provide for themselves.

For the end of conjunction between male and female being not barely procreation, but the continuation of the species, this conjunction betwixt male and female ought to last, even after procreation, so long as is necessary to the nourishment and support of the young ones, who are to be sustained by those that got them till they are able to shift and provide for themselves. This rule, which the infinite wise Maker hath set to the works of His hands, we find the inferior creatures steadily obey. In those vivaporous animals which feed on grass the conjunction between male and female lasts no longer than the very act of copulation, because the teat of the dam being sufficient to nourish the young till it be able to feed on grass, the male only begets, but concerns not himself for the female or young, to whose sustenance he can contribute nothing. But in beasts of prey the conjunction lasts longer, because the dam, not being able well to subsist herself and nourish her numerous offspring by her own prey alone (a more laborious as well as more dangerous way of living than by feeding on grass), the assistance of the male is necessary to the maintenance of their common family, which cannot subsist till they are able to prey for themselves, but by the joint care of male and female. The same is observed in all birds (except some domestic ones, where plenty of food excuses the cock from feeding and taking care of the young brood), whose young, needing food in the nest, the cock and hen continue mates till the young are able to use their wings and provide for themselves.

And herein, I think, lies the chief, if not the only reason, why the male and female in mankind are tied to a longer conjunction than other creatures—viz., because the female is capable of conceiving, and, *de facto*, is commonly with child again, and brings forth too a new birth, long before the former is out of a dependency for support on his parents' help and able to shift for himself, and has all the assistance due to him from his parents, whereby the father, who is bound to take care for those he hath begot, is under an obligation to continue in conjugal society with the same woman longer than other creatures, whose young, being able to subsist of themselves before the time of procreation returns again, the conjugal bond dissolves of itself, and they are at liberty till Hymen, at his usual anniversary season, summons them again to choose new mates. Wherein one cannot but admire the wisdom of the great Creator, who, having given to man an ability to lay up for the future as well as supply the present necessity, hath made it necessary that society of man and wife should be more lasting than of male and female amongst other creatures, that so their industry might be encouraged, and their interest better united, to make provision and lay up goods for their common issue, which uncertain mixture, or easy and frequent solutions of conjugal society, would mightily disturb.

But though these are ties upon mankind which make the conjugal bonds more firm and lasting in a man than the other species of animals, yet it would give one reason to inquire why this compact, where procreation and education are secured and inheritance taken care for, may not be made determinable, either by consent, or at a certain time, or upon certain conditions, as well as any other voluntary compacts, there being no necessity, in the nature of the thing, nor to the ends of it, that it should always be for life—I mean, to such as are under no restraint of any positive law which ordains all such contracts to be perpetual.

But the husband and wife, though they have but one common concern, yet having different understandings, will unavoidably sometimes have different wills too. It therefore being necessary that the last determination (i.e., the rule) should be placed somewhere, it naturally falls to the man's share as the abler and the stronger. But this, reaching but to the things of their common interest and property, leaves the wife in the full and true possession of what by contract is her peculiar right, and at least gives the husband no more power over

her than she has over his life; the power of the husband being so far from that of an absolute monarch that the wife has, in many cases, a liberty to separate from him where natural right or their contract allows it, whether that contract be made by themselves in the state of Nature or by the customs or laws of the country they live in, and the children, upon such separation, fall to the father or mother's lot as such contract does determine.

For all the ends of marriage being to be obtained under politic government, as well as in the state of Nature, the civil magistrate doth not abridge the right or power of either, naturally necessary to those ends—viz., procreation and mutual support and assistance whilst they are together, but only decides any controversy that may arise between man and wife about them. If it were otherwise, and that absolute sovereignty and power of life and death naturally belonged to the husband, and were necessary to the society between man and wife, there could be no matrimony in any of these countries where the husband is allowed no such absolute authority. But the ends of matrimony requiring no such power in the husband, it was not at all necessary to it. The condition of conjugal society put it not in him; but whatsoever might consist with procreation and support of the children till they could shift for themselves—mutual assistance, comfort, and maintenance—might be varied and regulated by that contract which first united them in that society, nothing being necessary to any society that is not necessary to the ends for which it is made.

*   *   *

Let us therefore consider a master of a family with all these subordinate relations of wife, children, servants and slaves, united under the domestic rule of a family, with what resemblance soever it may have in its order, offices, and number too, with a little commonwealth, yet is very far from it both in its constitution, power, and end; or if it must be thought a monarchy, and the paterfamilias the absolute monarch in it, absolute monarchy will have but a very shattered and short power, when it is plain by what has been said before, that the master of the family has a very distinct and differently limited power both as to time and extent over those several persons that are in it; for excepting the slave (and the family is as much a family, and his power as paterfamilias as great, whether there be any slaves in his family or no) he has no legislative power of life and death over any of them, and none too but what a mistress of a family may have as well as he. And he certainly can have no absolute power over the whole family who has but a very limited one over every individual in it. But how a family, or any other society of men, differ from that which is properly political society, we shall best see by considering wherein political society itself consists.

Man being born, as has been proved, with a title to perfect freedom and an uncontrolled enjoyment of all the rights and privileges of the law of Nature, equally with any other man, or number of men in the world, hath by nature a power not only to preserve his property—that is, his life, liberty, and estate, against the injuries and attempts of other men, but to judge of and punish the breaches of that law in others, as he is persuaded the offence deserves, even with death itself, in crimes where the heinousness of the fact, in his opinion, requires it. But because no political society can be, nor subsist, without having in itself the power to preserve the property, and in order thereunto punish the offences of all those of that society, there, and there only, is political society where every one of the members hath quitted this natural power, resigned it up into the hands of the community in all cases that exclude him not from appealing for protection to the law established by it. And thus all private judgment of every particular member being excluded, the community comes to be umpire, and by understanding indifferent rules and men authorised by the community for their execution, decides all the differences that may happen between any members of that society concerning any matter of right, and punishes those offences which any member hath committed against the society with such penalties as the law has established; whereby it is easy to discern who are, and are not, in political society together. Those who are united into

one body, and have a common established law and judicature to appeal to, with authority to decide controversies between them and punish offenders, are in civil society one with another; but those who have no such common appeal, I mean on earth, are still in the state of Nature, each being where there is no other, judge for himself and executioner; which is, as I have before showed it, the perfect state of Nature.

And thus the commonwealth comes by a power to set down what punishment shall belong to the several transgressions they think worthy of it, committed amongst the members of that society (which is the power of making laws), as well as it has the power to punish any injury done unto any of its members by any one that is not of it (which is the power of war and peace); and all this for the preservation of the property of all the members of that society, as far as is possible. But though every man entered into society has quitted his power to punish offences against the law of Nature in prosecution of his own private judgment, yet with the judgment of offences which he has given up to the legislative, in all cases where he can appeal to the magistrate, he has given up a right to the commonwealth to employ his force for the execution of the judgments of the commonwealth whenever he shall be called to it, which, indeed, are his own judgments, they being made by himself or his representative. And herein we have the original of the legislative and executive power of civil society, which is to judge by standing laws how far offences are to be punished when committed within the commonwealth; and also by occasional judgments founded on the present circumstances of the fact, how far injuries from without are to be vindicated, and in both these to employ all the force of all the members when there shall be need.

Wherever, therefore, any number of men so unite into one society as to quit every one his executive power of the law of Nature, and to resign it to the public, there and there only is a political or civil society. And this is done wherever any number of men, in the state of Nature, enter into society to make one people one body politic under one supreme government: or else when any one joins himself to, and incorporates with any government already made. For hereby he authorises the society, or which is all one, the legislative thereof, to make laws for him as the public good of the society shall require, to the execution whereof his own assistance (as to his own decrees) is due. And this puts men out of a state of Nature into that of a commonwealth, by setting up a judge on earth with authority to determine all the controversies and redress the injuries that may happen to any member of the commonwealth, which judge is the legislative or magistrates appointed by it. And wherever there are any number of men, however associated, that have no such decisive power to appeal to, there they are still in the state of Nature.

And hence it is evident that absolute monarchy, which by some men is counted for the only government in the world, is indeed inconsistent with civil society, and so can be no form of civil government at all. For the end of civil society being to avoid and remedy those inconveniencies of the state of Nature which necessarily follow from every man's being judge in his own case, by setting up a known authority to which every one of that society may appeal upon any injury received, or controversy that may arise, and which every one of the society ought to obey. Wherever any persons are who have not such an authority to appeal to, and decide any difference between them there, those persons are still in the state of Nature. And so is every absolute prince in respect of those who are under his dominion.

For he being supposed to have all, both legislative and executive, power in himself alone, there is no judge to be found, no appeal lies open to any one, who may fairly and indifferently, and with authority decide, and from whence relief and redress may be expected of any injury or inconveniency that may be suffered from him, or by his order. So that such a man, however entitled, Czar, or Grand Signior, or how you please, is as much in the state of Nature, with all under his dominion, as he is with the rest of mankind. For wherever any two men are, who have no standing rule and common judge to appeal to on earth, for the determination of controversies of right betwixt them, there they are still in the state of Nature, and under all the inconveniencies of it, with only this woeful difference to the subject, or rather slave of an absolute prince. That whereas, in the ordinary state of Nature, he has a liberty to judge of his right, according to the best of his power to maintain it; but whenever his property is invaded by the will and order of his monarch, he has not only no appeal, as those in society ought to have, but, as if he were degraded from the common state of rational creatures, is denied a liberty to judge of, or defend his right, and so is exposed to all the misery and inconveniencies that a man can fear from one, who being in the unrestrained state of Nature, is yet corrupted with flattery and armed with power.

*   *   *

Chapter VIII
Of the Beginning of Political Societies

Men being, as has been said, by nature all free, equal, and independent, no one can be put out of this estate and subjected to the political power of another without his own consent, which is done by agreeing with other men, to join and unite into a community for their comfortable, safe, and peaceable living, one amongst another, in a secure enjoyment of their properties, and a greater security against any that are not of it. This any number of men may do, because it injures not the freedom of the rest; they are left, as they were, in the liberty of the state of Nature. When any number of men have so consented to make one community or government, they are thereby presently incorporated, and make one body politic, wherein the majority have a right to act and conclude the rest.

For, when any number of men have, by the consent of every individual, made a community, they have thereby made that community one body, with a power to act as one body, which is only by the will and determination of the majority.

For that which acts any community, being only the consent of the individuals of it, and it being one body, must move one way, it is necessary the body should move that way whither the greater force carries it, which is the consent of the majority, or else it is impossible it should act or continue one body, one community, which the consent of every individual that united into it agreed that it should; and so every one is bound by that consent to be concluded by the majority. And therefore we see that in assemblies empowered to act by positive laws where no number is set by that positive law which empowers them, the act of the majority passes for the act of the whole, and of course determines as having, by the law of Nature and reason, the power of the whole.

And thus every man, by consenting with others to make one body politic under one government, puts himself under an obligation to every one of that society to submit to the determination of the majority, and to be concluded by it; or else this original compact, whereby he with others incorporates into one society, would signify nothing, and be no compact if he be left free and under no other ties than he was in before in the state of Nature. For what appearance would there be of any compact? What new engagement if he were no farther tied by any decrees of the society than he himself thought fit and did actually consent to? This would be still as great a liberty as he himself had before his compact, or any one else in the state of Nature, who may submit himself and consent to any acts of it if he thinks fit.

*　　*　　*

Whosoever, therefore, out of a state of Nature unite into a community, must be understood to give up all the power necessary to the ends for which they unite into society to the majority of the community, unless they expressly agreed in any number greater than the majority. And this is done by barely agreeing to unite into one political society, which is all the compact that is, or needs be, between the individuals that enter into or make up a commonwealth. And thus, that which begins and actually constitutes any political so-ciety is nothing but the consent of any number of freemen capable of majority, to unite and incorporate into such a society. And this is that, and that only, which did or could give beginning to any lawful government in the world.

*　　*　　*

Every man being, as has been showed, naturally free, and nothing being able to put him into subjection to any earthly power, but only his own consent, it is to be considered what shall be understood to be a sufficient declaration of a man's consent to make him subject to the laws of any government. There is a common distinction of an express and a tacit consent, which will concern our present case. Nobody doubts but an express consent of any man, entering into any society, makes him a perfect member of that society, a subject of that government. The difficulty is, what ought to be looked upon as a tacit consent, and how far it binds—*i.e.*, how far any one shall be looked on to have consented, and thereby submitted to any government, where he has made no expressions of it at all. And to this I say, that every man that hath any possession or enjoyment of any part of the dominions of any government doth hereby give his tacit consent, and is as far forth obliged to obedience to the laws of that government, during such enjoyment, as any one under it, whether this his possession be of land to him and his heirs for ever, or a lodging only for a week; or whether it be barely travelling freely on the highway; and, in effect, it reaches as far as the very being of any one within the territories of that government.

To understand this the better, it is fit to consider that every man when he at first incorporates himself into any commonwealth, he, by his uniting himself thereunto, annexes also, and submits to the community those possessions which he has, or shall acquire, that do not already belong to any other government. For it would be a direct contradiction for any one to enter into society with others for the securing and regulating of property, and yet to suppose his land, whose property is to be regulated by the laws of the society, should be exempt from the jurisdiction of that government to which he himself, and the property of the land, is a subject. By the same act, therefore, whereby any one unites his person, which was before free, to any commonwealth, by the same he unites his possessions, which were before free, to it also; and they become, both of them, person and possession, subject to the government and dominion of that commonwealth as long as it hath a being. Whoever therefore, from thenceforth, by inheritance, purchases permission, or otherwise enjoys any part of the land so annexed to, and under the government of that commonweal, must take it with the condition it is under—that is, of submitting to the government of the commonwealth, under whose jurisdiction it is, as far forth as any subject of it.

But since the government has a direct jurisdiction only over the land and reaches the possessor of it (before he has actually incorporated himself in the society) only as he dwells upon and enjoys that, the obligation any one is under by virtue of such enjoyment to submit to the government begins and ends with the enjoyment; so that whenever the owner, who has given nothing but such a tacit consent to the government will, by donation, sale or otherwise, quit the said possession, he is at liberty to go and incorporate himself into any other commonwealth, or agree with others to begin a new one *in vacuis locis,* in any part of the world they can find free and unpossessed; whereas he that has once, by actual agreement and any express declaration, given his consent to be of any commonweal, is perpetually and indispensably obliged to be, and remain unalterably a subject to it, and can never be again in the liberty of the state of Nature, unless by any calamity the government he was under comes to be dissolved.

But submitting to the laws of any country, living quietly and enjoying privileges and protection under them, makes not a man a member of that society; it is only a local protection and homage due to and from all those who, not being in a state of war, come within the territories belonging to any government, to all parts whereof the force of its law extends. But this no more makes a man a member of that society, a perpetual subject of that commonwealth, than it would make a man a sub-

ject to another in whose family he found it convenient to abide for some time, though, whilst he continued in it, he were obliged to comply with the laws and submit to the government he found there. And thus we see that foreigners, by living all their lives under another government, and enjoying the privileges and protection of it, though they are bound, even in conscience, to submit to its administration as far forth as any denizen, yet do not thereby come to be subjects or members of that commonwealth. Nothing can make any man so but his actually entering into it by positive engagement and express promise and compact. This is that which, I think, concerning the beginning of political societies, and that consent which makes any one a member of any commonwealth.

Chapter IX
Of the Ends of Political Society and Government

If man in the state of Nature be so free as has been said, if he be absolute lord of his own person and possessions, equal to the greatest and subject to nobody, why will he part with his freedom, this empire, and subject himself to the dominion and control of any other power? To which it is obvious to answer, that though in the state of Nature he hath such a right, yet the enjoyment of it is very uncertain and constantly exposed to the invasion of others; for all being kings as much as he, every man his equal, and the greater part no strict observers of equity and justice, the enjoyment of the property he has in this state is very unsafe, very insecure. This makes him willing to quit this condition which, however free, is full of fears and continual dangers; and it is not without reason that he seeks out and is willing to join in society with others who are already united, or have a mind to unite for the mutual preservation of their lives, liberties and estates, which I call by the general name—property.

The great and chief end, therefore, of men uniting into commonwealths, and putting themselves under government, is the preservation of their property; to which in the state of Nature there are many things wanting.

Firstly, there wants an established, settled, known law, received and allowed by common consent to be the standard of right and wrong, and the common measure to decide all controversies between them. For though the law of Nature be plain and intelligible to all rational creatures, yet men, being biased by their interest, as well as ignorant for want of study of it, are not apt to allow of it as a law binding to them in the application of it to their particular cases.

Secondly, in the state of Nature there wants a known and indifferent judge, with authority to determine all differences according to the established law. For every one in that state being both judge and executioner of the law of Nature, men being partial to themselves, passion and revenge is very apt to carry them too far, and with too much heat in their own cases, as well as negligence and unconcernedness, make them too remiss in other men's.

Thirdly, in the state of Nature there often wants power to back and support the sentence when right, and to give it due execution. They who by any injustice offended will seldom fail where they are able by force to make good their injustice. Such resistance many times makes the punishment dangerous, and frequently destructive to those who attempt it.

*   *   *

REVIEW QUESTIONS

1. According to Locke, what is the nature of political society?
2. How does political society come into being?
3. How does Locke's notion of a social contract compare with that of Hobbes?
4. What are the ends of political society?
5. What are the implications of Locke's reasoning for early modern economic thinking?

ADAM SMITH

FROM *The Wealth of Nations*

Though best remembered for his towering system of political economy, An Inquiry into the Nature and Causes of the Wealth of Nations *(1776), Adam Smith (1723–1790) was one of the most important social philosophers of the eighteenth century. His economic writings constitute only a part of his larger view of social and political development. Born the son of a minor government official, he entered the University of Glasgow in 1737, already a center of what became known as the Scottish Enlightenment, where he was deeply influenced by another great moral and economic philosopher, Francis Hutcheson. After completing his education at Oxford, he returned to Scotland, where he embarked on a series of public lectures in Edinburgh. In 1752, he was appointed professor of logic at Glasgow, and in 1754, he assumed the chair in moral philosophy. He would look on his tenure as the happiest and most honorable of his life. It was certainly the most productive. There he made the acquaintance of some of the leading intellectual lights of his day: James Watt, of steam-engine fame; David Hume, the great philosopher; and Andrew Cochrane. The last was the founder of the Political Economy Club and the likely source of much of*

Smith's information on business and commerce. In 1759, Smith published his first important work, The Theory of Moral Sentiments, *in which he attempted to describe universal principles of human nature. His answer to the question of moral judgment was the thesis of the "inner man," or "impartial spectator," which is the conscience in each human being and whose pronouncements cannot be ignored. Thus, human beings can be driven by passions and self-interests and simultaneously capable of ethics and generosity. This principle foreshadowed the "invisible hand" that would guide economic behavior in* The Wealth of Nations. *He began work on this classic text after resigning his post at Glasgow to serve as tutor to the young Duke of Buccleuch. When it finally appeared, it continued the themes first addressed in* The Theory of Moral Sentiments, *the resolution of passion and reason in human behavior, and now, human history. According to Smith, society evolves through four broad stages, each with appropriate institutions: simple hunters, nomadic herders, feudal farmers, and commercial workers. The guiding force in this development is human nature, motivated by self-interest but guided by disinterested reason. Most of the book is given over to a discussion of the function of the invisible hand in the final, current stage. Whereas conscience provided the necessary guidance in* The Theory of Moral Sentiments, *competition assumes that function in* The Wealth of Nations. *Competition rendered markets self-regulating and ensured that prices and wages never stray far from their "natural" levels. Much of the book, especially Book IV, where he places his discussion of colonies, is given over to a polemic against restriction, through both regulation and monopoly, in economic life.* The Wealth of Nations *appeared to great acclaim and earned its author fame and fortune. He published nothing more.*

From *An Inquiry into the Nature and Causes of the Wealth of Nations*, by Adam Smith (Edinburgh: Thomas Nelson, 1838).

*   *   *

Of the Motives for Establishing New Colonies

The interest which occasioned the first settlement of the different European colonies in America and the West Indies, was not altogether so plain and distinct as that which directed the establishment of those of ancient Greece and Rome.

GREEK COLONIES WERE SENT OUT WHEN THE POPULATION GREW TOO GREAT AT HOME.

All the different states of ancient Greece possessed, each of them, but a very small territory, and when the people in any one of them multiplied beyond what that territory could easily maintain, a part of them were sent in quest of a new habitation in some remote and distant part of the world; the warlike neighbours who surrounded them on all sides, rendering it difficult for any of them to enlarge very much its territory at home. * * *

THE MOTHER CITY CLAIMED NO AUTHORITY.

The mother city, though she considered the colony as a child, at all times entitled to great favour and assistance, and owing in return much gratitude and respect, yet considered it as an emancipated child, over whom she pretended to claim no direct authority or jurisdiction.

The colony settled its own form of government, enacted its own laws, elected its own magistrates, and made peace or war with its neighbours as an independent state, which had no occasion to wait for the approbation or consent of the mother city. Nothing can be more plain and distinct than the interest which directed every such establishment.

ROMAN COLONIES WERE SENT OUT TO SATISFY THE DEMAND FOR LANDS AND TO ESTABLISH GARRISONS IN CONQUERED TERRITORIES.

Rome, like most of the other ancient republics, was originally founded upon an Agrarian law, which divided the public territory in a certain proportion among the different citizens who composed the state. The course of human affairs, by marriage, by succession, and by alienation, necessarily deranged this original division, and frequently threw the lands, which had been allotted for the maintenance of many different families into the possession of a single person. To remedy this disorder, for such it was supposed to be, a law was made, restricting the quantity of land which any citizen could possess to five hundred jugera, about three hundred and fifty English acres. This law, however, though we read of its having been executed upon one or two occasions, was either neglected or evaded, and the inequality of fortunes went on continually increasing. The greater part of the citizens had no land, and without it the manners and customs of those times rendered it difficult for a freeman to maintain his independency. * * * The people became clamorous to get land, and the rich and the great, we may believe, were perfectly determined not to give them any part of theirs. To satisfy them in some measure, therefore, they frequently proposed to send out a new colony.

THEY WERE ENTIRELY SUBJECT TO THE MOTHER CITY.

But conquering Rome was, even upon such occasions, under no necessity of turning out her citizens to seek their fortune, if one may say so, through the wide world, without knowing where they were to settle. She assigned them lands generally in the conquered provinces of Italy, where,

being within the dominions of the republic, they could never form any independent state; but were at best but a sort of corporation, which, though it had the power of enacting bye-laws for its own government, was at all times subject to the correction, jurisdiction, and legislative authority of the mother city. The sending out a colony of this kind, not only gave some satisfaction to the people, but often established a sort of garrison too in a newly conquered province, of which the obedience might otherwise have been doubtful. A Roman colony, therefore, whether we consider the nature of the establishment itself, or the motives for making it, was altogether different from a Greek one. The words accordingly, which in the original languages denote those different establishments, have very different meanings. The Latin word (*Colonia*) signifies simply a plantation. The Greek word (αποιηια), on the contrary, signifies a separation of dwelling, a departure from home, a going out of the house. But, though the Roman colonies were in many respects different from the Greek ones, the interest which prompted to establish them was equally plain and distinct. Both institutions derived their origin either from irresistible necessity, or from clear and evident utility.

THE UTILITY OF THE AMERICAN COLONIES IS NOT SO EVIDENT.

The establishment of the European colonies in America and the West Indies arose from no necessity: and though the utility which has resulted from them has been very great, it is not altogether so clear and evident. It was not understood at their first establishment, and was not the motive either of that establishment or of the discoveries which gave occasion to it; and the nature, extent, and limits of that utility are not, perhaps, well understood at this day.

THE VENETIANS HAD A PROFITABLE TRADE IN EAST INDIA GOODS.

The Venetians, during the fourteenth and fifteenth centuries, carried on a very advantageous commerce in spiceries, and other East India goods, which they distributed among the other nations of Europe. They purchased them chiefly in Egypt, at that time under the dominion of the Mammeluks, the enemies of the Turks, of whom the Venetians were the enemies; and this union of interest, assisted by the money of Venice, formed such a connection as gave the Venetians almost a monopoly of the trade.

THIS WAS ENVIED BY THE PORTUGUESE AND LED THEM TO DISCOVER THE CAPE OF GOOD HOPE PASSAGE.

The great profits of the Venetians tempted the avidity of the Portuguese. They had been endeavouring, during the course of the fifteenth century, to find out by sea a way to the countries from which the Moors brought them ivory and gold dust across the Desart. They discovered the Madeiras, the Canaries, the Azores, the Cape de Verd islands, the coast of Guinea, that of Loango, Congo, Angola, and Benguela, and finally, the Cape of Good Hope. They had long wished to share in the profitable traffic of the Venetians, and this last discovery opened to them a probable prospect of doing so. In 1497, Vasco de Gama sailed from the port of Lisbon with a fleet of four ships, and, after a navigation of eleven months, arrived upon the coast of Indostan, and thus completed a course of discoveries which had been pursued with great steadiness, and with very little interruption, for near a century together.

COLUMBUS ENDEAVOURED TO REACH THE EAST INDIES BY SAILING WESTWARDS.

Some years before this, while the expectations of Europe were in suspense about the projects of the Portuguese, of which the success appeared yet to be doubtful, a Genoese pilot formed the yet more daring project of sailing to the East Indies by the West. The situation of those countries was at that time very imperfectly known in Europe. The few European travellers who had been there had magnified the distance; perhaps through simplicity and ignorance, what was really very great, appearing almost infinite to those who could not measure it;

or, perhaps, in order to increase somewhat more the marvellous of their own adventures in visiting regions so immensely remote from Europe. The longer the way was by the East, Columbus very justly concluded, the shorter it would be by the West. He proposed, therefore, to take that way, as both the shortest and the surest, and he had the good fortune to convince Isabella of Castile of the probability of his project. He sailed from the port of Palos in August 1492, near five years before the expedition of Vasco de Gama set out from Portugal, and, after a voyage of between two and three months, discovered first some of the small Bahama or Lucayan islands, and afterwards the great island of St. Domingo.

COLUMBUS MISTOOK THE COUNTRIES HE FOUND FOR THE INDIES.

But the countries which Columbus discovered, either in this or in any of his subsequent voyages, had no resemblance to those which he had gone in quest of. Instead of the wealth, cultivation and populousness of China and Indostan, he found, in St. Domingo, and in all the other parts of the new world which he ever visited, nothing but a country quite covered with wood, uncultivated, and inhabited only by some tribes of naked and miserable savages. He was not very willing, however, to believe that they were not the same with some of the countries described by Marco Polo, the first European who had visited, or at least had left behind him any description of China or the East Indies; and a very slight resemblance, such as that which he found between the name of Cibao, a mountain in St. Domingo, and that of Cipango, mentioned by Marco Polo, was frequently sufficient to make him return to this favourite prepossession, though contrary to the clearest evidence. In his letters to Ferdinand and Isabella he called the countries which he had discovered, the Indies. He entertained no doubt but that they were the extremity of those which had been described by Marco Polo, and that they were not very distant from the Ganges, or from the countries which had been conquered by Alexander. Even when at last convinced that they were different, he still flattered himself that those rich countries were at no great distance, and in a subsequent voyage, accordingly, went in quest of them along the coast of Terra Firma, and towards the isthmus of Darien.

HENCE THE NAMES EAST AND WEST INDIES.

In consequence of this mistake of Columbus, the name of the Indies has stuck to those unfortunate countries ever since; and when it was at last clearly discovered that the new were altogether different from the old Indies, the former were called the West, in contradistinction to the latter, which were called the East Indies.

THE COUNTRIES DISCOVERED WERE NOT RICH.

It was of importance to Columbus, however, that the countries which he had discovered, whatever they were, should be represented to the court of Spain as of very great consequence; and, in what constitutes the real riches of every country, the animal and vegetable productions of the soil, there was at that time nothing which could well justify such a representation of them.

*   *   *

SO COLUMBUS RELIED ON THE MINERALS.

Finding nothing either in the animals or vegetables of the newly discovered countries, which could justify a very advantageous representation of them, Columbus turned his view towards their minerals; and in the richness of the productions of this third kingdom, he flattered himself, he had found a full compensation for the insignificancy of those of the other two. The little bits of gold with which the inhabitants ornamented their dress, and which, he was informed, they frequently found in the rivulets and torrents that fell from the mountains, were sufficient to satisfy him that those mountains abounded with the richest gold mines. St. Domingo, therefore, was represented as a country abounding with gold, and upon that account (according to the prejudices not only of the present times, but of those times), an inexhausti-

ble source of real wealth to the crown and kingdom of Spain.

THE COUNCIL OF CASTILE WAS ATTRACTED BY THE GOLD, COLUMBUS PROPOSING THAT THE GOVERNMENT SHOULD HAVE HALF THE GOLD AND SILVER DISCOVERED.

In consequence of the representations of Columbus, the council of Castile determined to take possession of countries of which the inhabitants were plainly incapable of defending themselves. The pious purpose of converting them to Christianity sanctified the injustice of the project. But the hope of finding treasures of gold there, was the sole motive which prompted to undertake it; and to give this motive the greater weight, it was proposed by Columbus that the half of all the gold and silver that should be found there should belong to the crown. This proposal was approved of by the council.

*   *   *

THE SUBSEQUENT SPANISH ENTERPRISES WERE ALL PROMPTED BY THE SAME MOTIVE.

All the other enterprises of the Spaniards in the new world, subsequent to those of Columbus, seem to have been prompted by the same motive. It was the sacred thirst of gold that carried Oieda, Nicuessa, and Vasco Nugnes de Balboa, to the isthmus of Darien, that carried Cortez to Mexico, and Almagro and Pizarro to Chile and Peru. When those adventurers arrived upon any unknown coast, their first enquiry was always if there was any gold to be found there; and according to the information which they received concerning this particular, they determined either to quit the country or to settle in it.

*   *   *

IN THIS CASE EXPECTATIONS WERE TO SOME EXTENT REALISED, SO FAR AS THE SPANIARDS WERE CONCERNED.

In the countries first discovered by the Spaniards, no gold or silver mines are at present known which are supposed to be worth the working. The quantities of those metals which the first adventurers are said to have found there, had probably been very much magnified, as well as the fertility of the mines which were wrought immediately after the first discovery. What those adventurers were reported to have found, however, was sufficient to inflame the avidity of all their countrymen. Every Spaniard who sailed to America expected to find an Eldorado. Fortune too did upon this what she has done upon very few other occasions. She realized in some measure the extravagant hopes of her votaries, and in the discovery and conquest of Mexico and Peru (of which the one happened about thirty, the other about forty years after the first expedition of Columbus), she presented them with something not very unlike that profusion of the precious metals which they sought for.

A project of commerce to the East Indies, therefore, gave occasion to the first discovery of the West. A project of conquest gave occasion to all the establishments of the Spaniards in those newly discovered countries. The motive which excited them to this conquest was a project of gold and silver mines; and a course of accidents, which no human wisdom could foresee, rendered this project much more successful than the undertakers had any reasonable grounds for expecting.

BUT THE OTHER NATIONS WERE NOT SO SUCCESSFUL.

The first adventures of all the other nations of Europe, who attempted to make settlements in America, were animated by the like chimerical views; but they were not equally successful. It was more than a hundred years after the first settlement of the Brazils, before any silver, gold, or diamond mines were discovered there. In the English, French, Dutch, and Danish colonies, none have ever yet been discovered; at least none that are at present supposed to be worth the working. The first English settlers in North America, however, offered a fifth of all the gold and silver which should be found there to the king, as a motive for granting them their patents. In the patents to Sir Walter Raleigh, to the London and Plymouth companies, to the council of Plymouth, &c. this fifth was accordingly reserved to the crown. To the expectation of finding gold and silver mines, those first settlers too joined that of discovering a northwest passage to the East Indies. They have hitherto been disappointed in both.

Causes of the Prosperity of New Colonies

The colony of a civilized nation which takes possession either of a waste country, or of one so thinly inhabited, that the natives easily give place to the new settlers, advances more rapidly to wealth and greatness than any other human society.

COLONISTS TAKE OUT KNOWLEDGE AND REGULAR GOVERNMENT.

The colonists carry out with them a knowledge of agriculture and of other useful arts, superior to what can grow up of its own accord in the course of many centuries among savage and barbarous nations. They carry out with them too the habit of subordination, some notion of the regular government which takes place in their own country, of the system of laws which supports it, and of a regular administration of justice; and they naturally establish something of the same kind in the new settlement. But among savage and barbarous nations, the natural progress of law and government is still slower than the natural progress of arts, after law and government have been so far established, as is necessary for their protection.

LAND IS PLENTIFUL AND CHEAP.

Every colonist gets more land than he can possibly cultivate. He has no rent, and scarce any taxes to pay. No landlord shares with him in its produce, and the share of the sovereign is commonly but a trifle. He has every motive to render as great as possible a produce, which is thus to be almost entirely his own. But his land is commonly so extensive, that with all his own industry, and with all the industry of other people whom he can get to employ, he can seldom make it produce the tenth part of what it is capable of producing.

WAGES ARE HIGH.

He is eager, therefore, to collect labourers from all quarters, and to reward them with the most liberal wages. But those liberal wages, joined to the plenty and cheapness of land, soon make those labourers leave him, in order to become landlords themselves, and to reward, with equal liberality, other labourers, who soon leave them for the same reason that they left their first master.

*   *   *

Of the Advantages Which Europe Has Derived from the Discovery of America, and from That of a Passage to the East Indies by the Cape of Good Hope

THE ADVANTAGES DERIVED BY EUROPE FROM AMERICA ARE (1) THE ADVANTAGES OF EUROPE IN GENERAL, AND (2) THE ADVANTAGES OF THE PARTICULAR COUNTRIES WHICH HAVE COLONIES.

Such are the advantages which the colonies of America have derived from the policy of Europe.

What are those which Europe has derived from the discovery and colonization of America?

Those advantages may be divided, first, into the general advantages which Europe, considered as one great country, has derived from those great events; and, secondly, into the particular advantages which each colonizing country has derived from the colonies which particularly belong to it, in consequence of the authority or dominion which it exercises over them.

(1) THE GENERAL ADVANTAGES TO EUROPE ARE (A) AN INCREASE OF ENJOYMENTS.

The general advantages which Europe, considered as one great country, has derived from the dis-

covery and colonization of America, consist, first, in the increase of its enjoyments; and, secondly, in the augmentation of its industry.

The surplus produce of America, imported into Europe, furnishes the inhabitants of this great continent with a variety of commodities which they could not otherwise have possessed, some for conveniency and use, some for pleasure, and some for ornament, and thereby contributes to increase their enjoyments.

(B) AN AUGMENTATION OF INDUSTRY NOT ONLY IN THE COUNTRIES WHICH TRADE WITH AMERICA DIRECTLY, BUT ALSO IN OTHER COUNTRIES WHICH DO NOT SEND THEIR PRODUCE TO AMERICA OR EVEN RECEIVE ANY PRODUCE FROM AMERICA.

The discovery and colonization of America, it will readily be allowed, have contributed to augment the industry, first, of all the countries which trade to it directly; such as Spain, Portugal, France, and England; and, secondly, of all those which, without trading to it directly, send, through the medium of other countries, goods to it of their own produce; such as Austrian Flanders, and some provinces of Germany, which, through the medium of the countries before mentioned, send to it a considerable quantity of linen and other goods. All such countries have evidently gained a more extensive market for their surplus produce, and must consequently have been encouraged to increase its quantity.

*   *   *

Those great events may even have contributed to increase the enjoyments, and to augment the industry of countries which, not only never sent any commodities to America, but never received any from it. Even such countries may have received a greater abundance of other commodities from countries of which the surplus produce had been augmented by means of the American trade. This greater abundance, as it must necessarily have increased their enjoyments, so it must likewise have augmented their industry. A greater number of new equivalents of some kind or other must have been presented to them to be exchanged for the surplus produce of that industry. A more extensive market must have been created for that surplus produce, so as to raise its value, and thereby encourage its increase. The mass of commodities annually thrown into the great circle of European commerce, and by its various revolutions annually distributed among all the different nations comprehended within it, must have been augmented by the whole surplus produce of America. A greater share of this greater mass, therefore, is likely to have fallen to each of those nations, to have increased their enjoyments, and augmented their industry.

*   *   *

(2) THE PARTICULAR ADVANTAGES OF THE COLONISING COUNTRIES ARE (A) THE COMMON ADVANTAGES DERIVED FROM PROVINCES, (B) THE PECULIAR ADVANTAGES DERIVED FROM PROVINCES IN AMERICA.

The particular advantages which each colonizing country derives from the colonies which particularly belong to it, are of two different kinds; first, those common advantages which every empire derives from the provinces subject to its dominion; and, secondly, those peculiar advantages which are supposed to result from provinces of so very peculiar a nature as the European colonies of America.

The common advantages which every empire derives from the provinces subject to its dominion, consist, first, in the military force which they furnish for its defence; and, secondly, in the revenue which they furnish for the support of its civil government. * * *

(A) THE COMMON ADVANTAGES ARE CONTRIBUTIONS OF MILITARY FORCES AND REVENUE, BUT NONE OF THE COLONIES HAVE EVER FURNISHED MILITARY FORCE.

The European colonies of America have never yet furnished any military force for the defence of the mother country. Their military force has never yet been sufficient for their own defence; and in the different wars in which the mother countries have been engaged, the defence of their colonies has generally occasioned a very considerable distraction of the military force of those countries. In this respect, therefore, all the European colonies have, without exception, been a cause rather of weakness than of strength to their respective mother countries.

AND THE COLONIES OF SPAIN AND PORTUGAL ALONE HAVE CONTRIBUTED REVENUE.

The colonies of Spain and Portugal only have contributed any revenue towards the defence of the mother country, or the support of her civil government. The taxes which have been levied upon those of other European nations, upon those of England in particular, have seldom been equal to the expence laid out upon them in time of peace, and never sufficient to defray that which they occasioned in time of war. Such colonies, therefore, have been a source of expence and not of revenue to their respective mother countries.

(B) THE EXCLUSIVE TRADE IS THE SOLE PECULIAR ADVANTAGE.

The advantages of such colonies to their respective mother countries, consist altogether in those peculiar advantages which are supposed to result from provinces of so very peculiar a nature as the European colonies of America; and the exclusive trade, it is acknowledged, is the sole source of all those peculiar advantages.

THE EXCLUSIVE TRADE OF EACH COUNTRY IS A DISADVANTAGE TO THE OTHER COUNTRIES.

In consequence of this exclusive trade, all that part of the surplus produce of the English colonies, for example, which consists in what are called enumerated commodities, can be sent to no other country but England. Other countries must afterwards buy it of her. It must be cheaper therefore in England than it can be in any other country, and must contribute more to increase the enjoyments of England than those of any other country. It must likewise contribute more to encourage her industry. For all those parts of her own surplus produce which England exchanges for those enumerated commodities, she must get a better price than any other countries can get for the like parts of theirs, when they exchange them for the same commodities. The manufactures of England, for example, will purchase a greater quantity of the sugar and tobacco of her own colonies, than the like manufactures of other countries can purchase of that sugar and tobacco. So far, therefore, as the manufactures of England and those of other countries are both to be exchanged for the sugar and tobacco of the English colonies, this superiority of price gives an encouragement to the former, beyond what the latter can in these circumstances enjoy. The exclusive trade of the colonies, therefore, as it diminishes, or, at least, keeps down below what they would otherwise rise to, both the enjoyments and the industry of the countries which do not possess it; so it gives an evident advantage to the countries which do possess it over those other countries.

*　　*　　*

REVIEW QUESTIONS

1. How, according to Smith, did the colonial empires of early modern Europe differ from those of the ancient world?
2. What was the motive force of empire?
3. How does Smith explain the eventual success of the colonies in America?
4. What benefits does he think derive from empire? What costs?
5. How do we explain Smith's apparent indifference to the exploitation of native or slave populations?

CATHERINE THE GREAT

FROM **Proposals for a New Code of Law**

Catherine II (1729–1796), a German princess who became Tsarina of Russia after disposing of her ineffectual husband, was one of the most successful European monarchs of the eighteenth century and one of the most remarkable female rulers of all time. She followed Peter the Great in regarding Russia as a European power. Among her many achievements was the addition of some 200,000 square miles to the territory of the Russian Empire. Nor were her interests limited to expansion. She also took effective measures to modernize the empire's administration and improve its society. In 1767 Catherine summoned an assembly to draft a new code of laws for Russia and gave detailed instructions to the members about the principles they should apply. The proposed code never went into effect, but the proposal breathes the spirit of the Enlightenment.

From *Documents of Catherine the Great: The Correspondence with Voltaire and the Instruction of 1767 in the English Text of 1768*, translated by W. F. Reddaway (Cambridge: Cambridge University Press, 1931), pp. 216–17, 219, 231, 241, 244, 256, 258.

*   *   *

6. Russia is a European State.

7. This is clearly demonstrated by the following Observations: The Alterations which *Peter the Great* undertook in Russia succeeded with the greater Ease, because the Manners, which prevailed at that Time, and had been introduced amongst us by a Mixture of different Nations, and the Conquest of foreign Territories, were quite unsuitable to the Climate. *Peter the First*, by introducing the Manners and Customs of Europe among the European People in his Dominions, found at that Time such Means as even he himself was not sanguine enough to expect. . . .

8. The Possessions of the Russian Empire extend upon the terrestrial Globe to 32 Degrees of Latitude, and to 165 of Longitude.

9. The Sovereign is absolute; for there is no other Authority but that which centers in his single Person, that can act with a Vigor proportionate to the Extent of such a vast Dominion.

10. The Extent of the Dominion requires an absolute Power to be vested in that Person who rules over it. It is expedient so to be, that the quick Dispatch of Affairs, sent from distant Parts, might make ample Amends for the Delay occasioned by the great Distance of the Places.

11. Every other Form of Government whatsoever would not only have been prejudicial to Russia, but would even have proved its entire Ruin.

12. Another Reason is: That it is better to be subject to the Laws under one Master, than to be subservient to many.

13. What is the true End of Monarchy? Not to deprive People of their natural Liberty; but to correct their Actions, in order to attain the *supreme Good*.

14. The Form of Government, therefore, which best attains this End, and at the same Time sets less Bounds than others to natural Liberty, is that which coincides with the Views and Purposes of rational Creatures, and answers the End, upon which we ought to fix a steadfast Eye in the Regulations of civil Polity.

15. The Intention and the End of Monarchy, is the Glory of the Citizens, of the State, and of the Sovereign.

16. But, from this Glory, a Sense of Liberty arises in a People governed by a Monarch; which may produce in these States as much Energy in transacting the most important Affairs, and may contribute as much to the Happiness of the Subjects, as even Liberty itself. . . .

33. The Laws ought to be so framed, as to secure the Safety of every Citizen as much as possible.

34. The Equality of the Citizens consists in this; that they should all be subject to the same Laws.

35. This Equality requires Institutions so well adapted, as to prevent the Rich from oppressing those who are not so wealthy as themselves, and converting all the Charges and Employments entrusted to them as Magistrates only, to their own private Emolument. . . .

37. In a State or Assemblage of People that live together in a Community, where there are Laws, Liberty can only consist *in doing that which every One ought to do*, and *not to be constrained to do that which One ought not to do*.

38. A Man ought to form in his own Mind an exact and clear Idea of what Liberty is. *Liberty is the Right of doing whatsoever the Laws allow*: And if any one Citizen could do what the Laws forbid, there would be no more Liberty; because others would have an equal Power of doing the same.

39. The political Liberty of a Citizen is the Peace of Mind arising from the Consciousness, that every Individual enjoys his peculiar Safety; and in order that the People might attain this Liberty, the Laws ought to be so framed, that no one Citizen should stand in Fear of another; but that all of them should stand in Fear of the same Laws. . . .

123. The Usage of Torture is contrary to all the Dictates of Nature and Reason; even Mankind itself cries out against it, and demands loudly the total Abolition of it. . . .

180. That Law, therefore, is highly beneficial to the Community where it is established, which ordains that every Man shall be judged by his Peers and Equals. For when the Fate of a Citizen is in Question, all Prejudices arising from the Difference of Rank or Fortune should be stifled; because they ought to have no Influence between the Judges and the Parties accused. . . .

194. (1.) No Man ought to be looked upon as *guilty*, before he has received his judicial Sentence; nor can the Laws deprive him of *their* Protection, before it is proved that he *has forfeited all Right* to it. What Right therefore can Power give to any to inflict Punishment upon a Citizen at a Time, when it is yet dubious, whether he is *Innocent* or *guilty*? . . .

250. A Society of Citizens, as well as every Thing else, requires a certain fixed Order: There ought to be *some to govern*, and *others to obey*.

251. And this is the Origin of every Kind of Subjection; which feels itself more or less alleviated, in Proportion to the Situation of the Subjects. . . .

252. And, consequently, as the Law of Nature commands Us to take as much Care, as lies in *Our* Power, of the Prosperity of all the People; we are obliged to alleviate the Situation of the Subjects, as much as sound Reason will permit.

253. And therefore, to shun all Occasions of reducing People to a State of Slavery, except the *utmost* Necessity should *inevitably* oblige us to do it; in that Case, it ought not to be done for our own Benefit; but for the Interest of the State: Yet even that Case is extremely uncommon.

254. Of whatever Kind Subjection may be, the civil Laws ought to guard, on the one Hand, against the *Abuse* of Slavery, and, on the other, against the *Dangers* which may arise from it. . . .

269. It seems too, that the Method of exacting their Revenues, *newly* invented by the Lords, diminishes both the *Inhabitants*, and the *Spirit of Agriculture* in Russia. Almost all the Villages are *heavily* taxed. The Lords, who seldom or never *reside* in their Villages, lay an Impost on every Head of one, two, and even five Rubles, without the least Regard to the *Means* by which their Peasants may be able to *raise* this Money.

270. It is highly necessary that the Law should prescribe a Rule to the Lords, for a more judicious Method of raising their Revenues; and oblige them to levy *such* a Tax, as *tends least* to separate the Peasant from his House and Family; this would be the Means by which Agriculture would become more extensive, and Population be more increased in the Empire.

REVIEW QUESTIONS

1. Which articles and which instructions, coincide with the liberal or enlightened principles that were spreading across Europe in the late seventeenth and eighteenth centuries?

2. These liberal sentiments notwithstanding, what makes this document a classic exercise in absolute monarchy?

3. Why does Catherine include the curious instruction in Article 6?

4. How does Catherine understand such concepts as "society" and the "laws of nature"?

5. How does Catherine understand monarchy? How do her ideas differ from those of other absolute monarchs you may have studied?

DANIEL DEFOE

FROM *The Complete English Tradesman*

Daniel Defoe (c. 1659–1731) was an English writer who gained fame as an early proponent of the novel, helping to popularize its form through the success of Robinson Crusoe. *He was a prolific writer on an extraordinary range of subjects, publishing more than five hundred novels, pamphlets, essays and journals in his lifetime. He is also considered a pioneer of economic journalism, of which the following excerpt from his book* The Complete English Tradesman *might be considered a prime example. It reflects an unusually exact, practical knowledge of trade, its potentials and pitfalls. Defoe's knowledge reflects the fact that he actively engaged in many enterprises. In it he attempts to defend trade as practiced by the English, which he clearly sees as the cornerstone of national prosperity, power, and glory.*

From *The Complete English Tradesman*, by Daniel Defoe (London, 1724), chap. XXV as reprinted in *The Western Tradition: From the Ancient World to Louis XIV*, edited by Eugen Weber (Lexington, Mass.: D. C. Heath, 1995), pp. 476–81.

The instances which we have given in the last chapter abundantly make for the honor of the British traders; and we may venture to say, at the same time, are very far from doing dishonor to the nobility who have from time to time entered into alliance with them; for it is very well known that, besides the benefit which we reap by being a trading nation, which is our principal glory, trade is a very different thing in England than it is in many other countries and is carried on by persons who, both in their education and descent, are far from being the dregs of the people.

King Charles II, who was perhaps the prince of all the kings that ever reigned in England, who best understood the country and the people he governed, used to say, that the tradesmen were the only gentry in England. His majesty spoke it merrily, but it had a happy signification in it, such as was peculiar to the bright genius of that prince, who, though he was not the best governor, was the best acquainted with the world of all the princes of his age, if not of all the men in it; and I make no scruple to advance these three points in honor of our country; viz.

1. That we are the greatest trading country in the world because we have the greatest exportation of the growth and product of our land and of the manufacture and labor of our people; and the greatest importation and consumption of the growth, product, and manufactures of other countries from abroad, of any nation in the world.

2. That our climate is the best and most agreeable to live in because a man can be more out of doors in England than in other countries.

3. That our men are the stoutest and best because, strip them naked from the waist upwards, and give them no weapons at all but their hands and heels, and turn them into a room or stage, and lock them in with the like number of other men of any nation, man for man, and they shall beat the best men you shall find in the world.

As so many of our noble and wealthy families, as we have shown, are raised by and derived from trade, so it is true, and indeed it cannot well be otherwise, that many of the younger branches of our gentry, and even of the nobility itself, have descended again into the spring from whence they flowed and have become tradesmen; and thence it is that, as I said above, our tradesmen in England are not, as it generally is in other countries, always of the meanest of our people. Nor is trade itself in England, as it generally is in other countries, the meanest thing the men can turn their hand to; but, on the contrary, trade is the readiest way for men to raise their fortunes and families; and therefore it is a field for men of figure and of good families to enter upon.

Having thus done a particular piece of justice to ourselves, in the value we put upon trade and tradesmen in England, it reflects very much upon the understandings of those refined heads who pretend to depreciate that part of the nation which is so infinitely superior in wealth to the families who call themselves gentry, and so infinitely more numerous.

As to the wealth of the nation, that undoubtedly lies chiefly among the trading part of the people; and though there are a great many families raised within few years, in the late war, by great employments and by great actions abroad, to the honor of the English gentry, yet how many more families among the tradesmen have been raised to immense estates, even during the same time, by the attending circumstances of the war; such as the clothing, the paying, the victualling and furnishing, etc., both army and navy? And by whom have the prodigious taxes been paid, the loans supplied, and money advanced upon all occasions? By whom are the banks and companies carried on, and on whom are the customs and excises levied? Have not the trade and tradesmen borne the burden of the war? And do they not still pay four millions a year interest for the public debts? On whom are the funds levied, and by whom the public credit supported? Is not trade the unexhausted fund of all funds, and upon which all the rest depend?

As is the trade, so in proportion are the tradesmen; and how wealthy are tradesmen in almost all the several parts of England, as well as in London? How common is it to see a tradesman go off the stage, even but from mere shop-keeping, with from ten to forty thousand pounds' estate to divide among his family! When, on the contrary, take the gentry in England, from one end to the other, except a few here and there, what with excessive high living, which is of late grown so much into a disease, and the other ordinary circumstances of families, we find few families of the lower gentry, that is to say from six or seven hundred a year downwards, but they are in debt, and in necessitous circumstances, and a great many of greater estates also.

On the other hand, let any one who is acquainted with England, look but abroad into the several counties, especially near London, or within fifty miles of it; how are the ancient families worn out by time and family misfortunes, and the estates possessed by a new race of tradesmen, grown up into families of gentry, and established by the immense wealth gained, as I may say, behind the counter; that is, in the shop, the warehouse, and the counting-house.

How many noble seats, superior to the palaces of sovereign princes, in some countries, do we see erected within few miles of this city by tradesmen, or the sons of tradesmen, while the seats and castles of the ancient gentry, like their families, look worn out and fallen into decay!

Again, in how superior a port do our tradesmen live, to what the middling gentry either do or can support! An ordinary tradesman now, not in the city only, but in the country, shall spend more money by the year, than a gentleman of four or five hundred pounds a year too; whereas the gentleman shall, at the best, stand stock still just where he began, nay, perhaps, decline: and as for the lower gentry, from a hundred pounds a year to three hundred, or thereabouts, though they are often as proud and high in their appearance as the other; as to them, I say, a shoemaker in London shall keep a better house, spend more money, clothe his family better, and yet grow rich too. It is evident where the difference lies; an estate's a pond, but trade's a spring: the first, if it keeps full, and the water wholesome, by the ordinary supplies and drains from the neighboring grounds, it is well, and it is all that is expected; but the other is an unexhausted current, which not only fills the pond and keeps it full, but is continually running over, and fills all the lower ponds and places about it.

This being the case in England, and our trade being so vastly great, it is no wonder that the tradesmen in England fill the lists of our nobility and gentry; no wonder that the gentlemen of the best families marry tradesmen's daughters, and put their younger sons apprentices to tradesmen; and how often do these younger sons come to buy the elder sons' estates, and restore the family, when the elder and head of the house, proving rakish and extravagant, has wasted his patrimony, and is obliged to make out the blessing of Israel's family, where the younger son bought the birthright, and the elder was doomed to serve him!

Trade is so far here from being inconsistent with a gentleman, that, in short, trade in England makes gentlemen, and has peopled this nation with gentlemen; for, after a generation or two, the tradesman's children, or at least their grandchildren, come to be as good gentlemen, statesmen, parliament-men, privy-counselors, judges, bishops, and noblemen, as those of the highest birth and the most ancient families; as we have shown. Nor do we find any defect either in the genius or capacities of the posterity of tradesmen, arising from any remains of mechanic blood, which, it is pretended, should influence them; but all the gallantry of spirit, greatness of soul, and all the generous principles that can be found in any of the ancient families, whose blood is the most untainted, as they call it, with the low mixtures of a mechanic race, are found in these; and, as is said before, they generally go beyond them in knowledge of the world, which is the best education.

We see the tradesmen of England, as they grow wealthy, coming every day to the herald's office to search for the coats of arms of their ancestors, in order to paint them upon their coaches, and grave them upon their plate, embroider them upon their furniture, or carve them upon the pediments of their new houses; and how often do we see them trace the registers of their families up to the prime nobility, or the most ancient gentry of the kingdom!

In this search we find them often qualified to raise new families, if they do not descend from old; as was said of a certain tradesman of London, that if he could not find the ancient race of gentlemen, from which he came, he would begin a new race, who should be as good gentlemen as any that went before him.

Thus, in the late wars between England and France, how was our army full of excellent officers, who went from the shop, and behind the counter, into the camp, and who distinguished themselves there by their merits and gallant behavior! And several such came to command regiments, and even to be general officers, and to gain as much reputation in the service as any, as Colonel Pierce, Wood, Richards, and several others that may be named.

All this confirms what I have said before, viz., that trade in England neither is or ought to be compared with what it is in other countries; or the tradesmen depreciated as they are abroad, and as some of our gentry would pretend to do in England; but that as many of our best families rose from trade, so many branches of the best families in England, under the nobility, have stooped so low as to put apprentices to tradesmen in London, and to set up and follow those trades when they have come out of their times, and have thought it no dishonor to their blood.

To bring this once more home to the ladies, who are scandalized at that mean step, which they call it, of marrying a tradesman, it may be told them, for their humiliation, that, however they think fit to act, sometimes those tradesmen come of better families than their own; and oftentimes, when they have refused them to their loss, those very tradesmen have married ladies of superior fortune to them, and have raised families of their own, who, in one generation, have been superior to those nice ladies both in dignity and estate; and have, to their great mortification, been ranked above them upon all public occasions.

The word "tradesman," in England, does not sound so harsh as it does in other countries; and to say a gentleman-tradesman, is not so much nonsense as some people would persuade us to reckon it; and, indeed, the very name of an English tradesman, will and does already obtain in the world; and as our soldiers, by the late war, gained the reputation of being some of the best troops in the world; and our seamen are at this day, and very justly too, esteemed the best sailors in the world; so the English tradesman may be allowed to rank with the best gentlemen in Europe.

And hence it is natural to ask, whence comes all this to be so? How is it produced? War has not done it; no, nor so much as helped or assisted to it; it is not by any martial exploits; we have made no conquests abroad, added no new kingdoms to the British Empire, reduced no neighboring nations, or extended the possession of our monarchs into the properties of others; we have gained nothing by war and encroachment; nay, we have lost all the dominions which our ancient kings for some hundreds of years held in France; and, instead of being enriched by war and victory, on the contrary, we have been torn in pieces by civil wars and rebellions, and that several times, to the ruin of our richest families, and the slaughter of our nobility and gentry.

These things prove abundantly that the greatness of the British nation is not owing to war and conquests, to enlarging its dominions by the sword, or subjecting the people of other countries to our power; but it is allowing to trade, to the increase of our commerce at home, and the extending it abroad.

It is owing to trade that new discoveries have been made in lands unknown, and new settlements and plantations made, new colonies planted, and new governments formed in the uninhabited islands and the uncultivated continent of America; and those plantings and settlements have again enlarged and increased the trade, and thereby the wealth and power of the nation by whom they were discovered and planted. We have not increased our power, or the number of our subjects, by subduing the nations which possess those countries, and incorporating them into our own, but have entirely planted our colonies, and peopled the countries with our own subjects. Excepting the Negroes, which we transport from Africa to America as slaves to work in the sugar and tobacco plantations, all our colonies, as well in the islands as on the continent of America, are entirely peopled from Great Britain and Ireland, and chiefly the former; the natives having either removed further up into the country, or, by their own folly and treachery raising war against us, been destroyed and cut off.

As trade has thus extended our colonies abroad, so it has (except those colonies) kept our people at home, where they are multiplied to that prodigious degree, and do still continue to multiply in such a manner that, if it goes on so, time may come that all the lands in England will do little more than serve for gardens for them and to feed their cows, and their corn and cattle be supplied from Scotland and Ireland.

What is the reason that we see numbers of French, and of Scots, and Germans, in all the foreign nations in Europe, and especially filling up their armies and courts, and that you see few or no English there?

What is the reason that, when we want to raise armies, or to man navies, in England, we are obliged to press the seamen, and to make laws, and empower the justices of peace and magistrates of towns, to force men to go for soldiers, and enter into the service, or allure them by giving bounty-money as an encouragement to men to list themselves; whereas the people of other nations, and even the Scots and Irish, travel abroad and run into all the neighbor-nations, to seek service and to be admitted into their pay?

What is it but trade, the increase of business at home, and the employment of the poor in the business and manufactures of this kingdom, by which the poor get so good wages, and live so well, that they will not list for soldiers; and have so good pay in the merchants' service, that they will not serve on board the ships of war, unless they are forced to do it?

What is the reason that, in order to supply our colonies and plantations with people, besides the encouragement given in those colonies to all people that will come hither to plant and to settle, we are obliged to send away thither all our petty offenders, and all the criminals that we think fit to spare from the gallows, besides what we formerly called the kidnapping trade, that is to say, the arts made use of to wheedle and draw away young, vagrant, and indigent people, and people of desperate fortunes, to sell themselves, that is, bind themselves for servants, the number of which are very great?

Poverty fills armies, mans navies, and peoples colonies. In vain the drums beat for soldiers to serve in the armies for five pence a day, and the king's captains invite seamen to serve in the royal navy for twenty-three shillings per month, in a country where the ordinary laborer can have nine shillings a week for his labor, and the manufacturers earn from twelve to sixteen shillings a week for their work, and while trade gives thirty shillings per month wages to the seamen on board merchant ships, men will always stay or go, as the pay gives them encouragement; and this is the reason why it has been so much more difficult to raise and recruit armies in England, than it has been in Scotland and Ireland, France and Germany.

The same trade that keeps our people at home, is the cause of the well-living of the people here;

for as frugality is not the national virtue of England, so the people that get much, spend much; and as they work hard, so they live well, eat and drink well, clothe warm, and lodge soft. In a word, the working, manufacturing people of England eat the fat, drink the sweet, live better, and fare better, than the working poor of any other nation in Europe; they make better wages of their work; and spend more of the money upon their backs and bellies than in any other country. This expense of the poor, as it causes a prodigious consumption both of the provisions and of the manufactures of our country at home, so two things are undeniably the consequence of that part.

1. The consumption of provisions increases the rent and value of the lands; and this raises the gentlemen's estates, and that again increases the employment of people, and consequently the numbers of them, as well those that are employed in the husbandry of land, breeding and feeding of cattle, etc., as of servants to the gentlemen's families, who as their estates increase in value, so they increase their families and equipages.

2. As the people get greater wages, so they, I mean the same poorer part of the people, clothe better, and furnish better; and this increases the consumption of the very manufactures they make; then that consumption increases the quantity made; and this creates what we call inland trade, by which innumerable families are employed, and the increase of the people maintained; and by which increase of trade and people the present growing prosperity of this nation is produced.

The whole glory and greatness of England then, being thus raised by trade, it must be unaccountable folly and ignorance in us to lessen that one article in our own esteem, which is the only fountain from whence we all, take us as a nation, are raised, and by which we are enriched and maintained. The Scripture says, speaking of the riches and glory of the city of Tyre, which was indeed at that time the great port or emporium of the world for foreign commerce, from whence all the silks and fine manufactures of Persia and India were exported all over the western world, "that her merchants were princes," and in another place, "by thy traffic thou hast increased thy riches." Certain it is, that our traffic has increased our riches; and it is also certain, that the flourishing of our manufacture is the foundation of all our traffic, as well our merchandise as our inland trade.

REVIEW QUESTIONS

1. Why, according to Defoe, is English trade so prosperous?
2. How does trade contribute to the wealth of England?
3. How does trade contribute to the well-being of Englishmen?
4. Why is trade the best means to combat poverty?
5. How does empire contribute to English trade and prosperity?
6. How does Defoe's understanding of trade differ from that of Adam Smith, who believed that the unrestrained pursuit of profit by individuals actually created prosperity for all?

FROM The Charter of the Dutch West India Company

A chartered company of Dutch merchants, the Dutch West India Company received its charter from the Dutch Republic for a trade monopoly in the West Indies on June 2, 1621. The monopoly included all trade to and from the Caribbean, especially the slave trade between Africa and the Americas. The company intended to displace all competition, of which the Spanish and Portuguese were the greatest, from its monopoly region. Although it enjoyed only mixed success in this regard, the company and its charter became the vehicles for Dutch colonization in the New World.

From *Van Rensselaer Bowier Manuscripts*, translated by A. J. F. van Laer (Albany, NY: University of the State of New York, 1908), pp. 87–115.

Charter granted by the High and Mighty Lords the States General to the West India Company, dated the 3d of June 1621.

The States General of the United Netherlands to all who shall see these presents or hear them read, greeting, Be it known, that we, noticing that the prosperity of this country and the welfare of its inhabitants consist principally in navigation and trade, which from time immemorial has been carried on by this country with good fortune and great blessing with all countries and kingdoms; and desiring that the aforesaid inhabitants not only be maintained in their former navigation, commerce and trade, but also that their commerce may be increased as much as possible, especially in conformity with the treaties, alliances, conventions and covenants concerning commerce and navigation formerly made with other princes, republics and nations, which we intend shall be punctually kept and observed in all their parts; and finding by experience that without the common help, aid and means of a general company, no profitable business can be carried on, protected and maintained in the parts hereafter designated on account of the great risk from pirates, extortions and the like, which are incurred on such long and distant voyages; we, therefore, many other and different pregnant reasons and considerations also us thereunto moving, after mature deliberation of Council, and for very pressing causes, have resolved that the navigation, trade and commerce in the West Indies, Africa and other countries hereafter designated, shall henceforth not be carried on otherwise than with the common united strength of the merchants and inhabitants of this country and that to this end there shall be established a general company, which, on account of our great love for the common weal and in order to conserve the trade and welfare of the inhabitants of this country, we will maintain and strengthen with our help, favor and assistance, so far as the present state and condition of this country will in any way admit, and for that purpose furnish with a proper charter and endow with the privileges and exemptions hereafter enumerated, to wit:

I. That for the period of twenty-four years no native or inhabitant of this country shall be permitted, except in the name of this United Company, from these United Netherlands nor even from any place outside of them, to sail to or trade with the coasts and countries of Africa, from the Tropic of Cancer to the Cape of Good Hope; nor to or with the countries of America, or the West Indies, beginning at the south end of *Terra Nova*, through the Straits of Magellan, *le Maire*, and other straits and passages situated thereabouts, to the Strait of *Anjan*, neither on the North Sea nor on the South Sea, nor to or with any islands situated on the one side or the other, or between both; nor to or with the Australian or South Lands, extending and lying between the two meridians of the Cape of Good Hope in the east, and of the east end of New Guinea in the west, inclusive. And whoever shall venture, without the consent of this Company, to sail to or to traffic with any places within the aforesaid limits granted to this Company, shall forfeit the ships and goods which shall be found trading upon the aforesaid coasts and lands, the which in the name of the aforesaid Company may immediately and everywhere be attached, seized and held as confiscated property for the behoof of the same. And in case such ship or goods shall have been sold or taken to other countries or ports, the owners and partners may be levied on for the value of those ships and goods; except only, that they, who before the date of this charter shall have sailed from these or other countries to any of the aforesaid coasts, shall be permitted to continue their trade till they have sold their goods and come back to this country, or otherwise until the expiration of their charter if they have been granted any before this date, and no longer. Provided, that after the first of July, sixteen hundred and twenty-one, the day and time of the commencement of this charter, no one shall be permitted to send any ships or goods to the places comprehended in this charter even if this Company should not be fully organized before that date; but proper provision shall be made against those who knowingly and fraudulently seek to frustrate our good intentions for the common weal; it being understood that the salt trade at *Ponte del Ré* may be continued according to the conditions and instructions already given, or to be given by us respecting it, without being in any way restricted by this charter.

II. That further the aforesaid Company, in our name and by our authority, within the limits hereinbefore set forth, shall have power to make contracts, leagues and alliances with the princes and natives of the countries therein comprised also to build any fortresses and strongholds there; to appoint, transfer, discharge and replace governors, troops and officers of justice and for other necessary services, for the preservation of the places, the maintenance of good order, police and justice, in general for the furtherance of trade, as according to circumstances they shall see fit; moreover, they may promote the settlement of fertile and uninhabited districts, and do all that the service of this country and the profit and increase of trade shall require. And the [directors] of the Company shall regularly communicate to us and transmit such contracts and alliances as they shall have made with the aforesaid princes and nations, likewise [report] the situation of the fortresses, strongholds and settlements by them begun.

III. Provided that when they have chosen a governor general and prepared instructions for him,

the same must be approved, and the commission given by us; and further, that such governor general, as also other vice governors, commanders and officers, shall be obliged to take the oath of allegiance to us and also to the Company.

IV. And if the aforesaid Company in any of the aforesaid places be cheated under the pretense of friendship or badly treated, or if any money or goods entrusted by them be kept without their receiving restitution or payment, they may according to circumstances and the best of their ability cause the loss to be made good by all such means as can properly be employed.

V. And as it will also be necessary for the establishment, security and defense of this trade to take some troops along, we will, according to the condition of the country and the situation of affairs, furnish the said Company with such troops for field and garrison duty as shall be necessary, provided they be paid and supported by the Company.

VI. Which troops, besides the oath already taken to us and to his Excellency, shall swear to obey the commands of the said Company and to help promote their interests to the utmost of their ability.

VII. That the provosts of the Company on shore shall have power to apprehend any soldiers or other of the military that have enlisted in the service of the aforesaid Company and to confine them on board ship in whatever city, place or jurisdiction of this country they may be found; provided the provosts first inform the officers and magistrates of the cities and places where this occurs.

VIII. That we will not take any ships, ordnance or ammunition belonging to the Company, for the use of this country, except with the consent of the said Company.

IX. We have further granted, privileged and conceded this Company, and do hereby grant and concede, that they may pass freely with all their ships and goods without paying toll to any of the United Provinces and that they may use this freedom in the same manner as the free inhabitants of the cities of this country enjoy their freedom, notwithstanding some persons who are not free should be members of this Company.

X. That all the goods which this Company during the eight next ensuing years shall carry out of this country to the West Indies and Africa, and other places comprised within the aforesaid limits, and those which they shall bring thence into this country shall be exempt from outgoing and ingoing convoy charges; provided, that if at the expiration of the aforesaid eight years, the state and condition of this country will not admit of this eight years' freedom's continuing for another term of years, then outgoing convoy charges and license fees on the said goods and merchandise coming from the places mentioned in this charter and again exported from this country, during the whole term of this charter shall not be rated higher by us than they are rated at present; unless we should be again engaged in war, in which case all the aforesaid goods and merchandises shall not be rated higher by us than they were in the last list in time of war.

XI. And in order that this Company may have a good government, to the greatest profit and satisfaction of all the participants, we have ordained that the said government shall be vested in five Chambers of directors—one at Amsterdam which shall have the management of four ninths; one Chamber in Zealand, of two ninths; one Chamber on the *Maze*, of one ninth; one Chamber in the *Noorder-quartier*; of one ninth; and the fifth Chamber in Friesland together with *Stadt ende Landen*, also of one ninth—upon the conditions set forth in the register of our resolutions and the agreement drawn up respecting it. And the provinces in which there are no Chambers shall be accommodated with as many directors, divided among the respective Chambers, as the number of hundred thousand guilders which they shall furnish to the Company.

XII. That the Chamber of Amsterdam shall consist of twenty directors; the Chamber of Zealand of twelve; the Chambers of the *Maze* and of the *Noorder-quartier* each of fourteen; and the Chamber of Friesland together with *Stadt ende Landen* also of fourteen directors. If it shall hereafter appear that this work can not be carried on

without a greater number of persons, then more may be added after notice to the Nineteen and our approbation, but not otherwise.

XIII. And the States of the respective united provinces are authorized to make such regulations, either for their Noble Mightinesses' ordinary deputies or for the magistrates of the cities of their province, concerning the registration of the participants and the election of directors, as they think proper, according to the constitution of their province; provided that no person in the Chamber of Amsterdam shall be chosen a director who shall not in his own name participate in the Company for the sum of six thousand guilders; in the Chamber of Zealand for four thousand guilders; and in the Chambers of the *Maze*, of the *Noorder-quartier*, and of Friesland, with *Stadt ende Landen*, for the like sum of four thousand guilders.

XIV. That the first directors shall serve for the term of six years and that at the expiration of the said term, first one third part of the number of directors, selected by lot, shall be changed; and two years after a like third part; and again after two years, the last third part; and thenceforth successively, the oldest in the service shall be retired; and in the place of [each] retiring director or of such as shall at any time die, or for other reason leave a vacancy, three others shall be nominated by the directors, both remaining and retiring, together with those chief participants who in person and at their own expense shall care to join them, from which number the aforesaid respective provinces, deputies or magistrates, shall elect new directors and successively supply the vacancies; and they shall be considered chief participants who in their own name participate for the same amount as the respective directors.

XV. That the accounts of the equipment and fitting out of the ships, with their appurtenances, shall be rendered three months after the departure of the ships and that one month thereafter copies shall be sent to us and to the respective Chambers; and the Chambers shall (as often as we see fit or they are requested by the [other] Chambers) send to us and to each other an account of the returns and also of the sales of the same.

XVI. That every six years a general accounting shall be made of all outfits and returns, as also of all gains and losses of the Company, to wit, one relating to trade and one relating to war, each separate; which accounts shall be rendered publicly, notices being previously posted, to the end that every one who is interested may attend the hearing of the said accounts; and if before the expiration of the seventh year the accounts are not rendered in the manner aforesaid, the directors shall forfeit their commissions, which shall be appropriated to the use of the poor, and they shall nevertheless be held to render their accounts as aforesaid within such time and under such penalty as shall be fixed by us respecting the delinquents. And none the less a dividend shall meantime be declared from the profits of the trade as often as it shall be found that ten per cent has been gained.

XVII. No one shall be permitted during the continuance of this charter to withdraw his capital or sums advanced from this Company; nor shall any new participants be admitted. If at the expiration of twenty-four years it shall be judged well to continue this Company or to erect a new one, a final accounting and estimate shall be made by the Nineteen, with our approval, of all that belongs to the Company, and also of their necessary expenses, and after the aforesaid settlement and estimate any one may withdraw his money or, in proportion thereof, in whole or in part, continue and share in the succeeding Company; and the succeeding Company shall in such case take the remainder, which shall be found according to the accounting and estimate, and pay the participants who do not think fit to continue in the Company their share at such times at the Nineteen, with our knowledge and approbation, shall think proper.

XVIII. That so often as it shall be necessary to have a general Assembly of the aforesaid Chambers, it shall be by Nineteen persons, of whom eight shall come from the Chamber of Amsterdam, four from Zealand, two from the *Maze*, two from the *Noorder-quartier*, two from Friesland and *Stadt ende Landen*; provided, that the nineteenth person, or so many more as we shall at any time think fit, shall be deputed by us for the purpose of helping to direct the affairs of the Company in the aforesaid Assembly.

XIX. By which general Assembly of the aforesaid Chambers, all matters relating to this Company shall be considered and decided; provided, that in matters of war, our approbation of their resolution shall be asked.

XX. The aforesaid general Assembly being summoned, it shall meet, whenever they are about to fit out, to resolve how many ships they shall send to each place for the account of the Company in general, and no individual Chamber shall be permitted to undertake anything not included in the aforesaid common resolution but [all] shall be bound to carry it into effect and to execute it. And if any Chamber should fail to comply with the common resolution, or be found to act in violation thereof, we have authorized, and by these presents do authorize, the said Assembly immediately to cause reparation to be made for such failure or violation, wherein, on request, we will assist them.

XXI. The said general Assembly shall be held the first six years in the city of Amsterdam, and the following two years in Zealand; and so on alternately in the aforesaid two places.

XXII. The directors who by commission of the Company shall go from home to attend the aforesaid Assembly or otherwise, shall have for their expenses and daily allowance four guilders a day, besides boat and stage fare; it being understood that those who go from one city to another to attend the meetings of the Chambers as directors and managers shall receive no allowance or traveling expenses at the charge of the Company.

XXIII. And if it should happen that in the aforesaid general Assembly any weighty matter came before them, wherein they could not agree, or even in which one side should scruple to impose its decision on the other, the same shall be left to our decision; and whatever shall be determined upon shall be followed and carried into execution.

XXIV. And all the inhabitants of this country, and also of other countries, shall be notified by public posting of notices within the month after the date hereof that they may be admitted into this Company during five months from the first of July, this year, sixteen hundred and twenty-one, and that they may pay the money they wish to invest in three payments; to wit, one third at the expiration of the aforesaid five months and the other two thirds within the three next succeeding years, unless the aforesaid general Assembly shall find it necessary to extend the time, whereof the participants shall be notified by posting of notices.

XXV. The ships returning from a voyage shall come to the place they sailed from; and if, by stress of wind and weather, the vessels which sailed out from one district shall arrive in another—as those from Amsterdam or the *Noorder-quartier* in Zealand or the *Maze*; or from Zealand in Holland; or those from Friesland, with *Stadt ende Landen*, in another district—each Chamber shall nevertheless retain the direction and management of the ships and goods it sent out and be allowed to send and transport the goods to the places whence the vessels sailed, either in the same or other vessels; provided that the directors of that Chamber shall be required to be present in person at the place where the vessels and goods shall have arrived and not to appoint factors to superintend the business; but in case it shall not be convenient for them to travel, they shall commit this business to the Chamber in whose district the vessels arrived.

XXVI. If any Chamber shall have obtained any goods or returns from the places included within the limits of this charter with which another is not provided, it shall be required to send such goods on request to the Chamber which is unprovided, according to the situation of the case; and when they have sold out to send more. And in like manner, if the managers of the respective Chambers have need of any persons for crews or other purposes, from the cities where there are Chambers or directors, they shall request and employ [the aid of] the directors of this Company therefore and not make use of any factors.

XXVII. And if any of the provinces think fit to appoint an agent to collect the money from their inhabitants, deposit the amount in bulk in any Chamber, and receive the payment of dividends, the Chamber shall be required to give such agent access, that he may obtain information of the state of the disbursements and receipts, and of the debts

and assets; provided that the money brought in by such agent shall amount to fifty thousand guilders or upwards.

XXVIII. The directors shall have for commissions one per cent on the outfits and returns, and also on the prizes, and a half per cent on gold and silver; which commissions shall be divided—to the Chamber of Amsterdam, four ninths; the Chamber of Zealand, two ninths; the *Maze*, one ninth; the *Noorder-quartier*, one ninth; and Friesland with *Stadt ende Landen*, a like ninth.

XXIX. Provided that they shall not receive commissions on the ordnance and value of the ships more than once. They shall, moreover, have no commission on the ships, ordnance and other things with which we shall strengthen the Company, nor on the money which they shall collect for the Company, nor on the profits they receive from the goods; nor shall they charge the Company with any salaries, expenses of traveling or board of those to whom they shall commit the fitting out and purchasing of goods necessary therefore.

XXX. The bookkeepers and cashiers shall have a salary paid them by the directors out of their commissions.

XXXI. The directors shall not deliver or sell to the Company any ships, merchandise, or goods belonging to themselves in whole or in part, nor buy or cause to be bought of the said Company, directly or indirectly, any goods or merchandise, nor have any portion or part therein, on forfeiture by those who shall be found to have acted to the contrary of one year's commissions for the use of the poor and on pain of being deposed from their directorship.

XXXII. The directors shall be obliged to give notice, by posting of bills, as often as they have a fresh importation of goods and merchandise, to the end that every one may have seasonable knowledge of it before they proceed to a final sale.

XXXIII. And if it should happen that in one Chamber or another any of the directors should get into such a situation that he could not make good what was entrusted to him for his administration and in consequence thereof any loss should occur, said loss shall be charged against the money which such directors have in the Company, which [investment] is also especially pledged for their administration; the same shall also be the case as to all the participants who, on account of goods purchased or otherwise, shall become debtors to the Company, and to all intents it shall be reckoned as if the money which they put in had from the beginning been counterbalanced and wiped out by what they owe the Company.

XXXIV. The directors of the respective Chambers shall be responsible for their cashiers and bookkeepers.

XXXV. That all the goods of this Company which shall be disposed of by weight shall be sold by one standard of weight, to wit, that of the weight of Amsterdam; and that all such goods may be sold on board ship, or in store, without paying any excise, impost or weigh money; provided that, once being sold, they shall not be delivered in any other way than at the Weigh-house and that the impost and weigh money shall be paid as often as they are alienated in the same manner as other goods subject to weigh money.

XXXVI. That the persons or goods of the directors shall not be arrested, attached or encumbered in order to obtain from them an account of the administration of the Company nor for the payment of the salaries or wages of those whom they have employed in the service of the Company; but those who wish to make any such demands upon them must bring the matter before the ordinary judges.

XXXVII. Whenever any ship shall return from a voyage, the admirals or commanders of the fleets, ship or ships shall be obliged to come and report to us the success of the voyage within ten days after their arrival and shall make out and deliver a report in writing, if the case requires it.

XXXVIII. And if it should happen (which we by no means expect) that any one ventured to injure or hinder in any way the navigation, commerce, trade or traffic of this Company, contrary to the common law or to the contents of the aforesaid treaties, leagues and covenants, they shall have the right to protect themselves against such actions and shall govern themselves according to the instructions to be issued by us concerning them.

XXXIX. We have, moreover, promised, and do promise, that we will maintain and defend this Company against every person in [their rights of] free navigation and trade, and to that end will assist them with a sum of ten hundred thousand guilders, to be paid in five years, whereof the first two hundred thousand guilders shall be paid them when the first payment shall be made by the participants; provided, that we, with half the aforesaid ten hundred thousand guilders, shall receive and bear profit and risk in the same manner as the other participants of this Company.

XL. And if by a powerful and continued obstruction of the aforesaid navigation and trade, the affairs within the limits of this Company should be brought to a state of open war, we will, if the situation of this country will in any wise admit of it, give them for their assistance sixteen ships of war, the smallest one of one hundred and fifty lasts burden, with four good, well-sailing yachts, the smallest of forty lasts burden, which shall be properly mounted and provided in all respects, both with brass and other cannon, and a proper quantity of ammunition, together with double suits of running and standing rigging, sails, cables, anchors and other things thereto belonging, such as are proper to be provided and used in all great expeditions; upon condition that they shall be manned, victualed and supported at the expense of the Company and that the Company shall be obliged to add thereto sixteen like ships of war and four yachts, mounted and provided as above, to be used in like manner for the defense of trade and all exploits of war; provided that all the ships of war and merchantmen (which likewise shall be provided and manned as is fitting) shall be under an admiral appointed by us after previous advice of the aforesaid general Assembly and shall obey our commands, together with the resolutions of the Company, and if need be, shall be used together for purposes of war, in such manner, however, that the merchantmen shall not unnecessarily hazard their lading.

XLI. And if it should happen that the country should be greatly eased of its burdens and that this Company should be put to the heavy charges of war, we have further promised, and do promise, to increase the aforesaid subsidy in such manner as the situation of this country will permit and the affairs of the Company shall require.

XLII. We have moreover ordained that in case of war all the prizes which may be taken from enemies and pirates within the aforesaid limits by the Company or those who have been sent to its assistance; also the goods which shall be seized by virtue of our proclamations—after deducting all necessary expenses and the damage which the Company may have suffered in taking each prize, together with the dues of His Excellency as admiral in chief agreeable to our resolution to that effect adopted on the first of April, sixteen hundred and two, and the tenth part for the officers, sailors and soldiers who have taken the prize—shall remain at the disposal of the directors of the aforesaid Company; provided that the account of them shall be kept separate and distinct from the account of trade and commerce, that the net proceeds of the said prizes shall be employed in fitting out ships, paying the troops, fortifications, garrisons and like matters of war and defense, by sea and land, and that there shall be no distribution unless the said proceeds shall amount to so much that a notable share may be distributed without weakening the said defense and after paying the expenses of the war, which distribution shall be made separately and apart from that on account of trade; and the distribution shall be made, one tenth part for the use of the United Netherlands and the remainder for the participants of this Company, in exact proportion to their invested capital.

XLIII. Provided, however, that all the prizes and goods taken by virtue of our proclamations shall be brought and tried before the council of the admiralty of the district to which they are brought, that it may take cognizance of them and determine the legality or illegality of the said prizes, the administration of the goods brought in remaining, nevertheless, with the Company, pending the process, and that under a proper inventory, and saving to those who might be injured by the sentence of the admiralty the right of appeal, agreeable to the instructions given the admiralty; provided that the vendue masters and other officers of the admiralty shall neither receive nor claim any fees from prizes which shall be sold for the benefit of this Company and in [connection with] which they are not employed.

XLIV. The directors of this Company shall solemnly promise and swear that they will act well and faithfully in their administration and render good and just accounts of their transactions; that they will in all things consult the greatest profit of the Company and, as much as possible, prevent its meeting with losses; that they will not give the greatest participant any greater advantage in the payments or distribution of money than the least; that, in collecting and receiving outstanding debts, they will not excuse one more than another; that they, for their own account, will invest, and during the continuance of their administration will continue the investment of all such sums of money as by this charter are stipulated; and moreover, that they will, as far as concerns them, to the utmost of their power, observe and keep all and every the particulars and articles herein contained.

XLV. All of which privileges, freedoms and exemptions, together with the assistance above mentioned, in all their points and articles, we have granted, allowed, promised and pledged to the aforesaid Company, and do hereby grant, allow and pledge with full knowledge of the matter, promising to allow them to enjoy the same quietly and peaceably. We likewise order that the same shall be kept and observed by all magistrates, officers and subjects of these United Netherlands and that they shall not do anything contrary to the same directly or indirectly, either within or without the said United Netherlands, upon pain of being punished therefore both in person and property as disturbers of the common welfare of this country and transgressors of our ordinance. We further promise that we will maintain and uphold the Company in the contents of this our charter, by all treaties of peace, alliances and covenants with the neighboring princes, kingdoms and countries, without suffering anything to be done or transacted that might tend to diminish its value. Wherefore we expressly charge and command all governors, justiciaries, officers, magistrates and inhabitants of these United Netherlands to permit and suffer the Company and its directors to enjoy quietly and peaceably all the benefits of this charter, license and privilege, ceasing all opposition and obstruction to it. And in order that none may pretend ignorance of this, we have ordered a summary of the contents of this charter to be publicly proclaimed and placarded wherever necessary, for we have found this to be for the best interests of the country. Given under our great seal, paraph and the signature of our secretary, at the Hague, on the third day of the month of June, in the year sixteen hundred and twenty-one.

Was paraphed, *I. Magnus*

By order of the aforesaid Honorable Lords the States General.

C. Aersscn

[Having a seal pendent of red wax, on a cord of white silk.]

REVIEW QUESTIONS

1. Why did the West India Company receive a charter from the Dutch Republic?
2. How is the company structured? What does that structure tell you about its decision making?
3. Why does the company wish to exercise a monopoly?
4. What unusual powers are granted to the company to protect its monopoly?
5. Does the company suffer from any obvious weaknesses in its organization?
6. Given the content of this charter, how would you describe the relationship between trade and politics?

16 ✸ THE NEW SCIENCE OF THE SEVENTEENTH CENTURY

The term scientific revolution *is commonly applied to the changes in scientific theory and practice that took root in the early seventeenth century and promoted the advance of science as we know it today. It grew initially out of changes in astronomy and physics, the creation of mechanical philosophy as a general theory of nature, and the adoption of mathematics as a basic language of science. Natural phenomena were conceived to be regular and rational. Because nature was subject to reason, human beings could uncover its laws, which were assumed to be few in number and universal in application, by the right exercise of their own rational capacities. Among these laws were those of mechanics, which altered the scientific vision of the universe. They explained all physical phenomena in terms of matter and assumed that motion was the natural state of the universe. Mechanical philosophy posited that all bodies were composed of a single, universal substance, matter. These natural phenomena, matter and motion, were so defined as to be measurable and translatable into numbers that could be manipulated in mathematical formulas. As a form of reason, therefore, mathematics could become the language of scientific inquiry. Reason and mathematics, scientists believed, could teach reliable truths about nature. Thus the scientific revolution created the basic intellectual milieu for enlightened thinking.*

NICOLAUS COPERNICUS

FROM Six Books Concerning the Revolutions of the Heavenly Orbs

The Polish cleric and astronomer Nicolaus Copernicus (1473–1543) is generally credited as the discoverer of the heliocentric solar system. He proposed and demonstrated mathematically how the observed motions of stars and planets might be reconciled by assuming that the sun was a fixed point and that the earth rotated around the Sun while revolving on its own axis. His interest in the heavens probably began during a period of study at the University of Bologna, where he came into contact with Domenic Maria de Novara, the university's leading astronomer. Although his principal interests were scientific, his career remained ecclesiastical. He served as a church canon, involved in administrative matters, and pursued astronomy in his spare time. Troubled by the discrepancies between theoretical descriptions and direct observations of planetary motion, Copernicus overturned Aristotle's earth-centered universe by proposing instead that the sun remained stationary and that the earth revolved around it. If this were true, it would mean that the remaining planets also revolved around the sun at fixed distances and in mathematically predictable time frames. Though he is thought to have developed his theory between 1508 and 1514, De revolutionibus orbium coelestium libri vi *("Six Books Concerning the Revolutions of the Heavenly Orbs") did not appear until the year of his death, 1543. Its full implications as a new theory of the fundamental structure of the universe would not be recognized until Johannes Kepler published his own theories a century later.*

From *On the Revolutions of the Heavenly Spheres*, by Nicolaus Copernicus, translated by Charles Glenn Wallis (Amherst, Mass.: Prometheus Books, 1996), pp. 4–7, 15–19.

*   *   *

Preface and Dedication to Pope Paul III

I can reckon easily enough, Most Holy Father, that as soon as certain people learn that in these books of mine which I have written about the revolutions of the spheres of the world I attribute certain motions to the terrestrial globe, they will immediately shout to have me and my opinion hooted off the stage. For my own works do not please me so much that I do not weigh what judgments others will pronounce concerning them. And although I realize that the conceptions of a philosopher are placed beyond the judgment of the crowd, because it is his loving duty to seek the truth in all things, in so far as God has granted that to human reason; nevertheless I think we should avoid opinions utterly foreign to rightness. And when I considered how absurd this "lecture" would be held by those who know that the opinion that the Earth rests immovable in the middle of the heavens as if their centre had been confirmed by the judgments of many ages—if I were to assert to the contrary that the Earth moves; for a long time I was in great difficulty as to whether I should bring to light my commentaries written to demonstrate the Earth's movement, or whether it would not be better to follow the example of the Pythagoreans and certain others who used to hand down the mysteries of their philosophy not in writing but by word of mouth and only to their relatives and friends—witness the letter of Lysis to Hipparchus. They however seem to me to have done that not, as some judge, out of a jealous unwillingness to communicate their doctrines but in order that things of very great beauty which have been investigated by the loving care of great men should not be scorned by those who find it a bother to expend any great energy on letters—except on the money-making variety—or who are provoked by the exhortations and examples of others to the liberal study of philosophy but on account of their natural stupidity hold the position among philosophers that drones hold among bees. Therefore, when I weighed these things in my mind, the scorn which I had to fear on account of the newness and absurdity of my opinion almost drove me to abandon a work already undertaken.

*   *   *

But perhaps Your Holiness will not be so much surprised at my giving the results of my nocturnal study to the light—after having taken such care in working them out that I did not hesitate to put in writing my conceptions as to the movement of the Earth—as you will be eager to hear from me what came into my mind that in opposition to the general opinion of mathematicians and almost in opposition to common sense I should dare to imagine some movement of the Earth. And so I am unwilling to hide from Your Holiness that nothing except my knowledge that mathematicians have not agreed with one another in their researches moved me to think out a different scheme of drawing up the movements of the spheres of the world. For in the first place mathematicians are so uncertain about the movements of the sun and moon that they can neither demonstrate nor observe the unchanging magnitude of the revolving year. Then in setting up the solar and lunar movements and those of the other five wandering stars, they do not employ the same principles, assumptions, or demonstrations for the revolutions and apparent movements. * * * Moreover, they have not been able to discover or to infer the chief point of all, i.e., the form of the world and the certain commensurability of its parts. But they are in exactly the same fix as someone taking from different places hands, feet, head, and the other limbs—shaped very beautifully but not with reference to one body and without correspondence to one another—so that such parts made up a monster rather than a man. And so, in the process of demonstration which they call "method," they are found either to have omitted something necessary or to have admitted something foreign which by no means pertains to the matter; and they would by no means have been in this fix, if they had followed sure principles. For if the hypotheses they assumed were not false, everything which followed from the hypotheses would have been verified without fail; and though what I am saying may be obscure right now, nevertheless it will become clearer in the proper place.

Accordingly, when I had meditated upon this lack of certitude in the traditional mathematics concerning the composition of movements of the spheres of the world, I began to be annoyed that the philosophers, who in other respects had made a very careful scrutiny of the least details of the world, had discovered no sure scheme for the movements of the machinery of the world, which has been built for us by the Best and Most Orderly Workman of all. Wherefore, I took the trouble to reread all the books by philosophers which I could get hold of, to see if any of them even supposed that the movements of the spheres of the world were different from those laid down by those who taught mathematics in the schools. And as a matter of fact, I found first in Cicero that Nicetas thought that the Earth moved. And afterwards I found in Plutarch that there were some others of the same opinion: I shall copy out his words here, so that they may be known to all:

Some think that the Earth is at rest; but Philolaus the Pythagorean says that it moves around the fire with an obliquely circular motion, like the sun and moon. Herakleides of Pontus and Ekphantus the Pythagorean do not give the Earth any movement of locomotion, but rather a limited movement of rising and setting around its centre, like a wheel.

Therefore I also, having found occasion, began to meditate upon the mobility of the Earth. And although the opinion seemed absurd, nevertheless because I knew that others before me had been granted the liberty of constructing whatever circles they pleased in order to demonstrate astral phenomena, I thought that I too, would be readily permitted to test whether or not, by the laying down that the Earth had some movement, demonstrations less shaky than those of my predecessors could be found for the revolutions of the celestial spheres.

And so, having laid down the movements which I attribute to the Earth farther on in the work, I finally discovered by the help of long and numerous observations that if the movements of the other wandering stars are correlated with the circular movement of the Earth, and if the movements are computed in accordance with the revolution of each planet, not only do all their phenomena follow from that but also this correlation binds together so closely the order and magnitudes of all the planets and of their spheres or orbital circles and the heavens themselves that nothing can be shifted around in any part of them without disrupting the remaining parts and the universe as a whole.

Accordingly, in composing my work I adopted the following order: in the first book I describe all the locations of the spheres or orbital circles together with the movements which I attribute to the earth, so that this book contains as it were the general set-up of the universe. But afterwards in the remaining books I correlate all the movements of the other planets and their spheres or orbital circles with the mobility of the Earth, so that it can be gathered from that how far the apparent movements of the remaining planets and their orbital circles can be saved by being correlated with the movements of the Earth. And I have no doubt that talented and learned mathematicians will agree with me, if—as philosophy demands in the first place—they are willing to give not superficial but profound thought and effort to what I bring forward in this work in demonstrating these things. And in order that the unlearned as well as the learned might see that I was not seeking to flee from the judgment of any man, I preferred to dedicate these results of my nocturnal study to Your Holiness rather than to anyone else; because, even in this remote corner of the earth where I live, you are held to be most eminent both in the dignity of your order and in your love of letters and even of mathematics; hence, by the authority of your judgment you can easily provide a guard against the bites of slanderers, despite the proverb that there is no medicine for the bite of a sycophant.

But if perchance there are certain "idle talkers" who take it upon themselves to pronounce judgment, although wholly ignorant of mathematics, and if by shamelessly distorting the sense of some passage in Holy Writ to suit their purpose, they dare to reprehend and to attack my work; they worry me so little that I shall even scorn their judgments as foolhardy. For it is not unknown that Lactantius, otherwise a distinguished writer but hardly a mathematician, speaks in an utterly childish fashion concerning the shape of the Earth, when he laughs at those who have affirmed that the Earth has the form of a globe. And so the studious need not be surprised if people like that laugh at us. Mathematics is written for mathematicians; and among them, if I am not mistaken, my labours will be seen to contribute something to the ecclesiastical commonwealth, the principate of which Your Holiness now holds. For not many years ago under Leo X when the Lateran Council was considering the question of reforming the Ecclesiastical Calendar, no decision was reached, for the sole reason that the magnitude of the year and the months and the movements of the sun and moon had not yet been measured with sufficient accuracy. From that time on I gave attention to making more exact observations of these things and was encouraged to do so by that most distinguished man, Paul, Bishop of Fossombrone, who had been present at those deliberations. But what have I accomplished in this matter I leave to the judgment of Your Holiness in particular and to that of all other learned mathematicians. And so as not to appear to Your Holiness to make more promises concerning the utility of this book than I can fulfill, I now pass on to the body of the work.

*   *   *

7. Why the Ancients Thought the Earth Was at Rest at the Middle of the World as Its Centre

Wherefore for other reasons the ancient philosophers have tried to affirm that the Earth is at rest at the middle of the world, and as principal cause they put forward heaviness and lightness. For Earth is the heaviest element; and all things of any weight are borne towards it and strive to move towards the very centre of it.

For since the Earth is a globe towards which from every direction heavy things by their own nature are borne at right angles to its surface, the heavy things would fall on one another at the centre if they were not held back at the surface; since a straight line making right angles with a plane surface where it touches a sphere leads to the centre. And those things which are borne toward the centre seem to follow along in order to be at rest at the centre. All the more then will the Earth be at rest at the centre; and, as being the receptacle for falling bodies, it will remain immovable because of its weight.

They strive similarly to prove this by reason of movement and its nature. For Aristotle says that the movement of a body which is one and simple is simple, and the simple movements are the rectilinear and the circular. And of rectilinear movements, one is upward, and the other is downward. As a consequence, every simple movement is either toward the centre, i.e., downward, or away from the centre, i.e., upward, or around the cen-

tre, i.e., circular. Now it belongs to earth and water, which are considered heavy, to be borne downward, i.e., to seek the centre: for air and fire, which are endowed with lightness, move upward, i.e., away from the centre. It seems fitting to grant rectilinear movement to these four elements and to give the heavenly bodies a circular movement around the centre. So Aristotle. Therefore, said Ptolemy of Alexandria, if the Earth moved, even if only by its daily rotation, the contrary of what was said above would necessarily take place. For this movement which would traverse the total circuit of the Earth in twenty-four hours would necessarily be very headlong and of an unsurpassable velocity. Now things which are suddenly and violently whirled around are seen to be utterly unfitted for reuniting, and the more unified are seen to become dispersed, unless some constant force constrains them to stick together. And a long time ago, he says, the scattered Earth would have passed beyond the heavens, as is certainly ridiculous; and *a fortiori* so would all the living creatures and all the other separate masses which could by no means remain unshaken. Moreover, freely falling bodies would not arrive at the places appointed them, and certainly not along the perpendicular line which they assume so quickly. And we would see clouds and other things floating in the air always borne toward the west.

8. Answer to the Aforesaid Reasons and Their Inadequacy

For these and similar reasons they say that the Earth remains at rest at the middle of the world and that there is no doubt about this. But if someone opines that the Earth revolves, he will also say that the movement is natural and not violent. Now things which are according to nature produce effects contrary to those which are violent. For things to which force or violence is applied get broken up and are unable to subsist for a long time. But things which are caused by nature are in a right condition and are kept in their best organization. Therefore Ptolemy had no reason to fear that the Earth and all things on the Earth would be scattered in a revolution caused by the efficacy of nature, which is greatly different from that of art or from that which can result from the genius of man. But why didn't he feel anxiety about the world instead, whose movement must necessarily be of greater velocity, the greater the heavens are than the Earth? Or have the heavens become so immense, because an unspeakably vehement motion has pulled them away from the centre, and because the heavens would fall if they came to rest anywhere else?

Surely if this reasoning were tenable, the magnitude of the heavens would extend infinitely. For the farther the movement is borne upward by the vehement force, the faster will the movement be, on account of the ever-increasing circumference which must be traversed every twenty-four hours: and conversely, the immensity of the sky would increase with the increase in movement. In this way, the velocity would make the magnitude increase infinitely, and the magnitude the velocity. And in accordance with the axiom of physics that *that which is infinite cannot be traversed or moved in any way,* then the heavens will necessarily come to rest.

But they say that beyond the heavens there isn't any body or place or void or anything at all; and accordingly it is not possible for the heavens to move outward: in that case it is rather surprising that something can be held together by nothing. But if the heavens were infinite and were finite only with respect to a hollow space inside, then it will be said with more truth that there is nothing outside the heavens, since anything which occupied any space would be in them; but the heavens will remain immobile. For movement is the most powerful reason wherewith they try to conclude that the universe is finite.

But let us leave to the philosophers of nature the dispute as to whether the world is finite or infinite, and let us hold as certain that the Earth is held together between its two poles and terminates in a spherical surface. Why therefore should we hesitate any longer to grant to it the movement which accords naturally with its form, rather than put the whole world in a commotion—the world whose limits we do not and cannot know? And why not admit that the appearance of daily revolution belongs to the heavens but the reality belongs to the Earth? And things are as when Aeneas said in Virgil: "We sail out of the harbor, and the land and the cities move away." As a matter of fact, when a ship floats on over a tranquil sea, all the things outside seem to the voyagers to be moving in a movement which is the image of their own, and they think on the contrary that they themselves and all the things with them are at rest. So it can easily happen in the case of the movement of the Earth that the whole world should be believed to be moving in a circle. Then what would we say about the clouds and the other things floating in the air or falling or rising up, except that not only the Earth and the watery element with which it is conjoined are moved in this way but also no small part of the air and whatever other things have a similar kinship with the Earth? whether because the neighbouring air, which is mixed with earthly and watery matter, obeys the same nature as the Earth or because the movement of the air is an acquired one, in which it participates without resistance on account of the contiguity and perpetual rotation of the Earth. Conversely, it is no less astonishing for them to say that the highest region of the air follows the celestial movement, as is shown by those stars which appear suddenly—I mean those called "comets" or "bearded stars" by the Greeks. For that place is assigned for their generation; and like all the other stars they rise and set. We can say that that part of the air is deprived of terrestrial motion on account of its great distance from the Earth. Hence the air which is nearest to the Earth and the things floating in it will appear tranquil, unless they are driven to and fro by the wind or some other force, as happens. For how is the wind in the air different from a current in the sea?

But we must confess that in comparison with the world the movement of falling and of rising bodies is twofold and is in general compounded of the rectilinear and the circular. As regards things which move downward on account of their weight because they have very much earth in them, doubtless their parts possess the same nature as the whole, and it is for the same reason that fiery bodies are drawn upward with force. For even this earthly fire feeds principally on earthly matter; and they define flame as glowing smoke. Now it is a property of fire to make that which it invades to expand; and it does this with such force that it can be stopped by no means or contrivance from breaking prison and completing its job. Now expanding movement moves away from the centre to the circumference; and so if some part of the Earth caught on fire, it would be borne away from the centre and upward. Accordingly, as they say, a simple body possesses a simple movement—this is first verified in the case of circular movement —as long as the simple body remain in its unity in its natural place. In this place, in fact, its movement is none other than the circular, which remains entirely in itself, as though at rest. Rectilinear movement, however, is added to those bodies which journey away from their natural place or are shoved out of it or are outside it somehow. But nothing is more repugnant to the order of the whole and to the form of the world than for anything to be outside of its place. Therefore rectilinear movement belongs only to bodies which are not in the right condition and are not perfectly conformed to their nature—when they are separated from their whole and abandon its unity. Furthermore, bodies which are moved upward or downward do not possess a simple, uniform, and regular movement—even without taking into account circular movement. For they cannot be in equilibrium with their lightness or their force of weight. And those which fall downward possess a slow movement at the beginning but increase their velocity as they fall. And conversely we note that this earthly fire—and we have experience of no other—when carried high up immediately dies down, as if through the acknowledged agency of the violence of earthly matter.

Now circular movement always goes on regularly, for it has an unfailing cause; but [in rectilinear movement] the acceleration stops, because, when the bodies have reached their own place,

they are no longer heavy or light, and so the movement ends. Therefore, since circular movement belongs to wholes and rectilinear to parts, we can say that the circular movement stands with the rectilinear, as does animal with sick. And the fact that Aristotle divided simple movement into three genera: away from the centre, toward the centre, and around the centre, will be considered merely as an act of reason, just as we distinguish between line, point, and surface, though none of them can subsist without the others or without body.

In addition, there is the fact that the state of immobility is regarded as more noble and godlike than that of change and instability, which for that reason should belong to the Earth rather than to the world. I add that it seems rather absurd to ascribe movement to the container or to that which provides the place and not rather to that which is contained and has a place, i.e., the Earth. And lastly, since it is clear that the wandering stars are sometimes nearer and sometimes farther away from the Earth, then the movement of one and the same body around the centre—and they mean the centre of the Earth—will be both away from the centre and toward the centre. Therefore it is necessary that movement around the centre should be taken more generally; and it should be enough if each movement is in accord with its own centre. You see therefore that for all these reasons it is more probably that the Earth moves than that it is at rest—especially in the case of the daily revolution, as it is the Earth's very own. And I think that is enough as regards the first part of the question.

9. Whether Many Movements Can Be Attributed to the Earth, and Concerning the Centre of the World

Therefore, since nothing hinders the mobility of the Earth, I think we should now see whether more than one movement belongs to it, so that it can be regarded as one of the wandering stars. For the apparent irregular movement of the planets and their variable distances from the Earth—which cannot be understood as occurring in circles homocentric with the Earth—make it clear that the Earth is not the centre of their circular movements. Therefore, since there are many centres, it is not foolhardy to doubt whether the centre of gravity of the Earth rather than some other is the centre of the world. I myself think that gravity or heaviness is nothing except a certain natural appetency implanted in the parts by the divine providence of the universal Artisan, in order that they should unite with one another in their oneness and wholeness and come together in the form of a globe. It is believable that this affect is present in the sun, moon, and the other bright planets and that through its efficacy they remain in the spherical figure in which they are visible, though they nevertheless accomplish their circular movements in many different ways. Therefore if the Earth too possesses movements different from the one around its centre, then they will necessarily be movements which similarly appear on the outside in the many bodies; and we find the yearly revolution among these movements. For if the annual revolution were changed from being solar to being terrestrial, and immobility were granted to the sun, the risings and settings of the signs and of the fixed stars—whereby they become morning or evening stars—will appear in the same way; and it will be seen that the stoppings, retrogressions, and progressions of the wandering stars are not their own, but are a movement of the Earth and that they borrow the appearances of this movement. Lastly, the sun will be regarded as occupying the centre of the world. And the ratio of order in which these bodies succeed one another and the harmony of the whole world teaches us their truth, if only—as they say—we would look at the thing with both eyes.

*   *   *

REVIEW QUESTIONS

1. Why did Copernicus dedicate his great work to Pope Paul III?
2. What assumptions about the nature of scientific knowledge caused Copernicus to revisit and revise the received natural philosophy?
3. How does Copernicus refute in this work the notion that the Earth is at rest in the universe?
4. What does this reveal about his scientific method?
5. What benefits would arise from the establishment of scientific truth?

GALILEO GALILEI

FROM *The Starry Messenger* AND *The Assayer*

Galileo Galilei (1564–1642), an Italian astronomer, mathematician, and physicist, was a major contributor to the shift in scientific practice commonly called the scientific revolution. Born the son of a musician, Vincenzo Galilei, Galileo received his primary education from a tutor in Pisa and later from the monks of Santa Maria at Vallambrosa in Florence. From 1581 to 1585, he studied medicine at the University of Pisa and supplemented his education with private lessons in mathematics. Without formal instruction in that field, Galileo occupied the chair in mathematics at the University of Pisa from 1589 to 1591 and at the University of Padua from

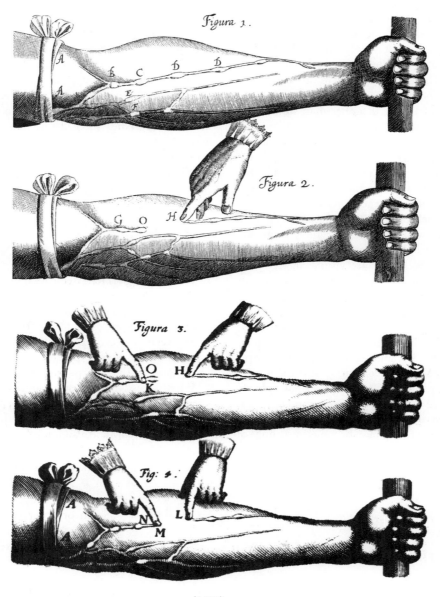

ON THE CIRCULATION OF THE BLOOD (1628)   WILLIAM HARVEY

This illustration depicts one of William Harvey's experiments in his On the Circulation of the Blood (1628). Venal valves had already been discovered, but here Harvey shows that venal blood flows only toward the heart. He ligatured an arm to make obvious the veins and their valves, then pressed blood away from the heart and showed that the vein would remain empty because it was blocked by the valve. How is Harvey's work representative of the revolution in science? What does the image suggest about the connection between advances in scientific discovery and mechanistic philosophy in early modern Europe?

1592 until 1610, when he was appointed court philosopher and mathematician to the grand duke of Tuscany. During his tenure at court, he published The Starry Messenger *(1610) and* The Assayer *(1619). The former presented evidence to confirm the heliocentric theory of the solar system. The latter offered a strong defense of the empirical basis of scientific reasoning. It was his advocacy of the Copernican theory that led Galileo into conflict with the Roman Catholic Inquisition. Galileo was forced to abjure his scientific findings and was sentenced to perpetual house arrest. His books were burned. His trial, no less than his discoveries, secured his fame, and his books continued to circulate clandestinely throughout Europe.*

From *Discoveries and Opinions of Galileo*, translated by Stillman Drake (New York: Bantam Doubleday Dell, 1957), pp. 27–31, 237–38.

FROM *The Starry Messenger*

from ASTRONOMICAL MESSAGE
WHICH CONTAINS AND EXPLAINS RECENT
OBSERVATIONS MADE WITH THE AID OF A NEW
SPYGLASS CONCERNING THE SURFACE OF THE
MOON, THE MILKY WAY, NEBULOUS STARS, AND
INNUMERABLE FIXED STARS, AS WELL AS FOUR
PLANETS NEVER BEFORE SEEN, AND NOW NAMED
THE MEDICEAN STARS

Great indeed are the things which in this brief treatise I propose for observation and consideration by all students of nature. I say great, because of the excellence of the subject itself, the entirely unexpected and novel character of these things, and finally because of the instrument by means of which they have been revealed to our senses.

Surely it is a great thing to increase the numerous host of fixed stars previously visible to the unaided vision, adding countless more which have never before been seen, exposing these plainly to the eye in numbers ten times exceeding the old and familiar stars.

It is a very beautiful thing, and most gratifying to the sight, to behold the body of the moon, distant from us almost sixty earthly radii, as if it were no farther away than two such measures— its diameter appears almost thirty times larger, its surface nearly nine hundred times, and its volume twenty-seven thousand times as large

as when viewed with the naked eye. In this way one may learn with all the certainty of sense evidence that the moon is not robed in a smooth and polished surface but is in fact rough and uneven, covered everywhere, just like the earth's surface, with huge prominences, deep valleys, and chasms.

Again, it seems to me a matter of no small importance to have ended the dispute about the Milky Way by making its nature manifest to the very senses as well as to the intellect. Similarly it will be a pleasant and elegant thing to demonstrate that the nature of those stars which astronomers have previously called "nebulous" is far different from what has been believed hitherto. But what surpasses all wonders by far, and what particularly moves us to seek the attention of all astronomers and philosophers, is the discovery of four wandering stars not known or observed by any man before us. Like Venus and Mercury, which have their own periods about the sun, these have theirs about a certain star that is conspicuous among those already known, which they sometimes precede and sometimes follow, without ever departing from it beyond certain limits. All these facts were discovered and observed by me not many days ago with the aid of a spyglass which I devised, after first being illuminated by divine grace. Perhaps other things, still more remarkable, will in time be discovered by me or by other observers with the aid of such an instrument, the form and construction of which I shall first briefly explain, as well as the occasion of its having been devised. Afterwards I shall relate the story of the observations I have made.

About ten months ago a report reached my ears that a certain Fleming had constructed a spyglass by means of which visible objects, though very distant from the eye of the observer, were distinctly seen as if nearby. Of this truly remarkable effect several experiences were related, to which some persons gave credence while others denied them. A few days later the report was confirmed to me in a letter from a noble Frenchman at Paris, Jacques Badovere, which caused me to apply myself wholeheartedly to inquire into the means by which I might arrive at the invention of a similar instrument. This I did shortly afterwards, my basis being the theory of refraction. First I prepared a tube of lead, at the ends of which I fitted two glass lenses, both plane on one side while on the other side one was spherically convex and the other concave. Then placing my eye near the concave lens I perceived objects satisfactorily large and near, for they appeared three times closer and nine times larger than when seen with the naked eye alone. Next I constructed another one, more accurate, which represented objects as enlarged more than sixty times. Finally, sparing neither labor nor expense, I succeeded in constructing for myself so excellent an instrument that objects seen by means of it appeared nearly one thousand times larger and over thirty times closer than when regarded with our natural vision.

It would be superfluous to enumerate the number and importance of the advantages of such an instrument at sea as well as on land. But forsaking terrestrial observations, I turned to celestial ones, and first I saw the moon from as near at hand as if it were scarcely two terrestrial radii away. After that I observed often with wondering delight both the planets and the fixed stars, and since I saw these latter to be very crowded, I began to seek (and eventually found) a method by which I might measure their distances apart.

Here it is appropriate to convey certain cautions to all who intend to undertake observations of this sort, for in the first place it is necessary to prepare quite a perfect telescope, which will show all objects bright, distinct, and free from any haziness, while magnifying them at least four hundred times and thus showing them twenty times closer. Unless the instrument is of this kind it will be vain to attempt to observe all the things which I have seen in the heavens, and which will presently be set forth. Now in order to determine without much trouble the magnifying power of an instrument, trace on paper the contour of two circles or two squares of which one is four hundred times as large as the other, as it will be when the diameter of one is twenty times that of the other. Then, with both these figures attached to the same wall, observe them simultaneously from a distance, looking at the smaller one through the telescope and at the larger one with the other eye unaided. This may be done without inconvenience while holding both eyes open at the same time; the two figures will appear to be of the same size if the instrument magnifies objects in the desired proportion.

Such an instrument having been prepared, we seek a method of measuring distances apart. This we shall accomplish by the following contrivance.

Let ABCD be the tube and E be the eye of the observer. Then if there were no lenses in the tube, the rays would reach the object FG along the straight lines ECF and EDG. But when the lenses have been inserted, the rays go along the refracted lines ECH and EDI; thus they are brought closer together, and those which were previously directed freely to the object FG now include only the portion of it HI. The ratio of the distance EH to the line HI then being found, one may by means of a table of sines determine the size of the angle formed at the eye by the object HI, which we shall find to be but a few minutes of arc. Now, if to the lens CD we fit thin plates, some pierced with larger and some with smaller apertures, putting now one plate and now another over the lens as required, we may form at pleasure different angles subtending more or fewer minutes of arc, and by this means we may easily measure the intervals between stars which are but a few minutes apart, with no greater error than one or two minutes. And for the present let it suffice that we have touched lightly on these matters and scarcely more than mentioned them, as on some other occasion we shall explain the entire theory of this instrument.

*   *   *

Deserving of notice also is the difference between the appearances of the planets and of the fixed stars. The planets show their globes perfectly round and definitely bounded, looking like little moons, spherical and flooded all over with light; the fixed stars are never seen to be bounded by a circular periphery, but have rather the aspect of blazes whose rays vibrate about them and scintillate a great deal. Viewed with a telescope they appear of a shape similar to that which they present to the naked eye, but sufficiently enlarged so that a star of the fifth or sixth magnitude seems to equal the Dog Star, largest of all the fixed stars. Now, in addition to stars of the sixth magnitude, a host of other stars are perceived through the telescope which escape the naked eye; these are so numerous as almost to surpass belief. One may, in fact, see more of them than all the stars included among the first six magnitudes. The largest of these, which we may call stars of the seventh magnitude, or the first magnitude of invisible stars, appear through the telescope as larger and brighter than stars of the second magnitude when the latter are viewed with the naked eye. In order to give one or two proofs of their almost inconceivable number, I have adjoined pictures of two constellations. With these as samples, you may judge of all the others.

FROM *The Assayer*

*   *   *

In Sarsi I seem to discern the firm belief that in philosophizing one must support oneself upon the opinion of some celebrated author, as if our minds ought to remain completely sterile and barren unless wedded to the reasoning of some other person. Possibly he thinks that philosophy is a book of fiction by some writer, like the *Iliad* or *Orlando Furioso*, productions in which the least important thing is whether what is written there is true. Well, Sarsi, that is not how matters stand. Philosophy is written in this grand book, the universe, which stands continually open to our gaze. But the book cannot be understood unless one first learns to comprehend the language and read the letters in which it is composed. It is written in the language of mathematics, and its characters are triangles, circles, and other geometric figures without which it is humanly impossible to understand a single word of it; without these, one wanders about in a dark labyrinth.

Sarsi seems to think that our intellect should be enslaved to that of some other man. . . . But even on that assumption, I do not see why he selects Tycho. . . . Tycho could not extricate himself from his own explanation of diversity in the apparent motion of his comet; but now Sarsi expects my mind to be satisfied and set at rest by a little poetic flower that is not followed by any fruit at all. It is this that Guiducci rejected when he quite rightly said that nature takes no delight in poetry. That is a very true statement, even though Sarsi appears to disbelieve it and acts as if acquainted with neither nature nor poetry. He seems not to know that fables and fictions are in a way essential to poetry, which could not exist without them, while any sort of falsehood is so abhorrent to nature that it is as absent there as darkness is in light.

*   *   *

REVIEW QUESTIONS

1. How does a telescope work? What is its relation to human sight?
2. What does Galileo see? What does he discern?
3. What are the two books for Galileo?
4. What is the relation of one to the other?
5. What are the implications of Galileo's assertion that understanding depends on how one reads the book of the universe?

FRANCIS BACON

FROM *The Great Instauration*

With Francis Bacon (1561–1626) we enter the so-called Age of Reason, the era of science and enlightenment. The son of Sir Nicholas Bacon, lord keeper of the Great Seal of England, Bacon attended Trinity College, Cambridge, and entered the legal profession in 1582. His public life was not that of a natural philosopher but that of a statesman. Beginning his career under Elizabeth I, he rose to the position of lord chancellor and was created Lord Verulam and Viscount St. Albans in 1621 by James I. His Great Instauration (1620) was published on the eve of his advancement. After the collapse of his career in 1622, when he pleaded guilty to charges of bribery, Bacon withdrew into enforced retirement and, like Machiavelli, pursued his intellectual passion. In his writings, he envisioned the transformation of the human mind through the right use of reason. He called for the close observation of nature and scientific collaboration in the cause of human improvement. In this, Bacon was the prophet of the revolution in science.

From *Works of Francis Bacon*, edited by Robert L. Ellis, James Spedding, and D. D. Heath (London: Longman, 1857–1874).

Preface

That the state of knowledge is not prosperous nor greatly advancing; and that a way must be opened for the human understanding entirely different from any hitherto known, and other helps provided, in order that the mind may exercise over the nature of things the authority which properly belongs to it.

It seems to me that men do not rightly understand either their store or their strength, but overrate the one and underrate the other. Hence it follows, that either from an extravagant estimate of the value of the arts which they possess, they seek no further; or else from too mean an estimate of their own powers, they spend their strength in small matters and never put it fairly to the trial in those which go to the main. These are as the pillars of fate set in the path of knowledge; for men have neither desire nor hope to encourage them to penetrate further. And since opinion of store is one of the chief causes of want, and satisfaction with the present induces neglect of provision for the future, it becomes a thing not only useful, but absolutely necessary, that the excess of honour and admiration with which our existing stock of inventions is regarded be in the very entrance and threshold of the work, and that frankly and without circumlocution, stripped off, and men be duly warned not to exaggerate or make too much of them. For let a man look carefully into all that variety of books with which the arts and sciences abound, he will find everywhere endless repetitions of the same thing, varying in the method of treatment, but not new in substance, insomuch that the whole stock, numerous as it appears at first view, proves on examination to be but scanty. And for its value and utility it must be plainly avowed that that wisdom which we have derived principally from the Greeks is but like the boyhood of knowledge, and has the characteristic property of boys: it can talk, but it cannot generate; for it is fruitful of controversies but barren of works.

So that the state of learning as it now is appears to be represented to the life in the old fable of Scylla, who had the head and face of a virgin, but her womb was hung round with barking monsters, from which she could not be delivered. For in like manner the sciences to which we are accustomed have certain general positions which are specious and flattering; but as soon as they come to particulars, which are as the parts of generation, when they should produce fruit and works, then arise contentions and barking disputations, which are the end of the matter and all the issue they can yield. Observe also, that if sciences of this kind had any life in them, that could never have come to pass which has been the case now for many ages— that they stand almost at a stay, without receiving any augmentations worthy of the human race; insomuch that many times not only what was asserted once is asserted still, but what was a question once is a question still, and instead of being resolved by discussion is only fixed and fed; and all the tradition and succession of schools is still a succession of masters and scholars, not of inventors and those who bring to further perfection the things invented. In the mechanical arts we do not find it so; they, on the contrary, as having in them some breath of life, are continually growing and becoming more perfect. As originally invented they are commonly rude, clumsy, and shapeless; afterwards they acquire new powers and more commodious arrangements and constructions; in so far that men shall sooner leave the study and pursuit of them and turn to something else, than they arrive at the ultimate perfection of which they are capable. Philosophy and the intellectual sciences, on the contrary, stand like statues, worshipped and celebrated, but not moved or advanced. Nay, they sometimes flourish most in the hands of the first author, and afterwards degenerate. For when men have once made over their judgments to others' keeping, and (like those senators whom they called *Pedarii*) have agreed to support some one person's opinion, from that time they make no enlargement of the sciences themselves, but fall to the servile office of embellishing certain individual authors and increasing their retinue.

And let it not be said that the sciences have been growing gradually till they have at last reached their full stature, and so (their course being completed) have settled in the works of a few writers; and that there being now no room for the invention of better, all that remains is to embellish and cultivate those things which have been invented already. Would it were so! But the truth is that this appropriating of the sciences had its origin in nothing better than the confidence of a few persons and the sloth and indolence of the rest. For after the sciences had been in several parts perhaps cultivated and handled diligently, there has risen up some man of bold disposition, and famous for methods and short ways which people like, who has in appearance reduced them to an art, while he has in fact only spoiled all that the others had done. And yet this is what posterity like, because it makes the work short and easy, and saves further inquiry, of which they are weary and impatient. And if any one take this general acquiescence and consent for an argument of weight, as being the judgment of Time, let me tell him that the reasoning on which he relies is most fallacious and weak. For, first, we are far from knowing all that in the matter of sciences and arts has in various ages and places been brought to light and published; much less, all that has been by private persons secretly attempted and stirred; so neither the births nor the miscarriages of Time are entered in our records. Nor, secondly, is the consent itself and the time it has continued a consideration of much worth. For however various are the forms of civil polities, there is but one form of polity in the sciences; and that always has been and always will be popular. Now the doctrines which find most favour with the populace are those which are either contentious and pugnacious, or specious and empty; such, I say, as either entangle assent or tickle it. And therefore no doubt the greatest wits in each successive age have been forced out of their own course; men of capacity and intellect above the vulgar having been fain, for reputation's sake, to bow to the judgment of the time and the multitude; and thus if any contemplations of a higher order took light anywhere, they were presently blown out by the winds of vulgar opinions. So that Time is like a river, which has brought down to us things light and puffed up, while those which are weighty and solid have sunk. Nay, those very authors who have usurped a kind of dictatorship in the sciences and taken upon them to lay down the law with such confidence, yet when from time to time they come to themselves again, they fall to complaints of the subtlety of nature, the hiding-places of truth, the obscurity of things, the entanglement of causes, the weakness of the human mind; wherein nevertheless they show themselves never the more modest, seeing that they will rather lay the blame upon the common condition of men and nature than upon themselves. And then whatever any art fails to attain, they ever set it down upon the authority of that art itself as impossible of attainment; and how can art be found guilty when it is judge in its own cause? So it is but a device for exempting ignorance from ignominy. Now for those things which are delivered and received, this is their condition: barren of works, full of questions; in point of enlargement slow and languid; carrying a show of perfection in the whole, but in the parts ill filled up; in selection popular, and unsatisfactory even to those who propound them; and therefore fenced round and set forth with sundry artifices. And if there be any who have determined to make trial for themselves, and put their own strength to the work of advancing the boundaries of the sciences, yet have they not ventured to cast themselves completely loose from received opinions or to seek their knowledge at the fountain; but they think they have done some great thing if they do but add and introduce into the existing sum of science something of their own; prudently considering with themselves that by making the addition they can assert their liberty, while they retain the credit of modesty by assenting to the rest. But these mediocrities and middle ways so much praised, in deferring to opinions and customs, turn to the great detriment of the sciences. For it is hardly possible at once to admire an author and to go beyond him; knowledge being as water, which will not rise above the

level from which it fell. Men of this kind, therefore, amend some things, but advance little; and improve the condition of knowledge, but do not extend its range. Some, indeed, there have been who have gone more boldly to work, and taking it all for an open matter and giving their genius full play, have made a passage for themselves and their own opinions by pulling down and demolishing former ones; and yet all their stir has but little advanced the matter; since their aim has been not to extend philosophy and the arts in substance and value, but only to change doctrines and transfer the kingdom of opinions to themselves; whereby little has indeed been gained, for though the error be the opposite of the other, the causes of erring are the same in both. And if there have been any who, not binding themselves either to other men's opinions or to their own, but loving liberty, have desired to engage others along with themselves in search, these, though honest in intention, have been weak in endeavour. For they have been content to follow probable reasons, and are carried round in a whirl of arguments, and in the promiscuous liberty of search have relaxed the severity of inquiry. There is none who has dwelt upon experience and the facts of nature as long as is necessary. Some there are indeed who have committed themselves to the waves of experience, and almost turned mechanics; yet these again have in their very experiments pursued a kind of wandering inquiry, without any regular system of operations. And besides they have mostly proposed to themselves certain petty tasks, taking it for a great matter to work out some single discovery— a course of proceeding at once poor in aim and unskilful in design. For no man can rightly and successfully investigate the nature of anything in the thing itself; let him vary his experiments as laboriously as he will, he never comes to a resting-place, but still finds something to seek beyond. And there is another thing to be remembered; namely, that all industry in experimenting has begun with proposing to itself certain definite works to be accomplished, and has pursued them with premature and unseasonable eagerness; it has sought, I say, experiments of Fruit, not experiments of Light; not imitating the divine procedure, which in its first day's work created light only and assigned to it one entire day; on which day it produced no material work, but proceeded to that on the days following. As for those who have given the first place to Logic, supposing that the surest helps to the sciences were to be found in that, they have indeed most truly and excellently perceived that the human intellect left to its own course is not to be trusted; but then the remedy is altogether too weak for the disease; nor is it without evil in itself. For the Logic which is received, though it be very properly applied to civil business and to those arts which rest in discourse and opinion, is not nearly subtle enough to deal with nature; and in offering at what it cannot master, has done more to establish and perpetuate error than to open the way to truth.

Upon the whole therefore, it seems that men have not been happy hitherto either in the trust which they have placed in others or in their own industry with regard to the sciences; especially as neither the demonstrations nor the experiments as yet known are much to be relied upon. But the universe to the eye of the human understanding is framed like a labyrinth; presenting as it does on every side so many ambiguities of way, such deceitful resemblances of objects and signs, natures so irregular in their lines, and so knotted and entangled. And then the way is still to be made by the uncertain light of the sense, sometimes shining out, sometimes clouded over, through the woods of experience and particulars; while those who offer themselves for guides are (as was said) themselves also puzzled, and increase the number of errors and wanderers. In circumstances so difficult neither the natural force of man's judgment nor even any accidental felicity offers any chance of success. No excellence of wit, no repetition of chance experiments, can overcome such difficulties as these. Our steps must be guided by a clue, and the whole way from the very first perception of the senses must be laid out upon a sure plan. Not that I would be understood to mean that nothing whatever has been done in so many ages by so great labours. We have no reason to be ashamed of the discoveries which have been made, and no doubt the ancients proved themselves in everything that turns on wit and abstract meditation, wonderful men. But as in former ages when men sailed only by observation of the stars, they could indeed coast along the shores of the old continent or cross a few small and mediterranean seas; but before the ocean could be traversed and the new world discovered, the use of the mariner's needle, as a more faithful and certain guide, had to be found out; in like manner the discoveries which have been hitherto made in the arts and sciences are such as might be made by practice, meditation, observation, argumentation,—for they lay near to the senses, and immediately beneath common notions; but before we can reach the remoter and more hidden parts of nature, it is necessary that a more perfect use and application of the human mind and intellect be introduced.

For my own part at least, in obedience to the everlasting love of truth, I have committed myself to the uncertainties and difficulties and solitudes of the ways, and relying on the divine assistance have upheld my mind both against the shocks and embattled ranks of opinion, and against my own private and inward hesitations and scruples, and against the fogs and clouds of nature, and the phantoms flitting about on every side; in the hope of providing at last for the present and future generations guidance more faithful and secure. Wherein if I have made any progress, the way has been opened to me by no other means than the true and legitimate humiliation of the human spirit. For all those who before me have applied themselves to the invention of arts have but cast a glance or two upon facts and examples and experience, and straightway proceeded, as if invention were nothing more than an exercise of thought, to invoke their own spirits to give them oracles. I, on the contrary, dwelling purely and constantly among the facts of nature, withdraw my intellect from them no further than may suffice to let the images and rays of natural objects meet in a point, as they do in the sense of vision; whence it follows that the strength and excellency of the wit has but little to do in the matter. And the same humility which I use in inventing I employ likewise in teaching. For I do not endeavour either by triumphs of confutation, or pleadings of antiquity, or assumption of authority, or even by the veil of obscurity, to invest these inventions of mine with any majesty; which might easily be done by one who sought to give lustre to his own name rather than light to other men's minds. I have not sought (I say) nor do I seek either to force or ensnare men's judgments, but I lead them to things themselves and the concordances of things, that they may see for themselves what they have, what they can dispute, what they can add and contribute to the common stock. And for myself, if in anything I have been either too credulous or too little awake and attentive, or if I have fallen off by the way and left the inquiry incomplete, nevertheless I so present these things naked and open that my errors can be marked and set aside before the mass of knowledge be further infected by them: and it will be easy also for others to continue and carry on my labours. And by these means I suppose that I have established for ever a true and lawful marriage between the empirical and the rational faculty, the unkind and ill-starred divorce and separation of which has thrown into confusion all the affairs of the human family.

Wherefore, seeing that these things do not depend upon myself, at the outset of the work I most humbly and fervently pray to God the Father, God the Son, and God the Holy Ghost, that remembering the sorrows of mankind and the pilgrimage of this our life wherein we wear out days few and evil, they will vouchsafe through my hands to endow the human family with new mercies. This likewise I humbly pray, that things human may not interfere with things divine, and that from the opening of the ways of sense and the increase of natural light there may arise in our minds no incredulity or darkness with regard to the divine mysteries; but rather that the understanding being thereby purified and purged of fancies and vanity, and yet not the less subject and entirely submissive to the divine oracles, may give to faith that which is faith's. Lastly, that knowledge being now dis-

charged of that venom which the serpent infused into it, and which makes the mind of man to swell, we may not be wise above measure and sobriety, but cultivate truth in charity.

And now having said my prayers I turn to men; to whom I have certain salutary admonitions to offer and certain fair requests to make. My first admonition (which was also my prayer) is that men confine the sense within the limits of duty in respect of things divine: for the sense is like the sun, which reveals the face of earth, but seals and shuts up the face of heaven. My next, that in flying from this evil they fall not into the opposite error, which they will surely do if they think that the inquisition of nature is in any part interdicted or forbidden. For it was not that pure and uncorrupted natural knowledge whereby Adam gave names to the creatures according to their propriety, which gave occasion to the fall. It was the ambitious and proud desire of moral knowledge to judge of good and evil, to the end that man may revolt from God and give laws to himself, which was the form and manner of the temptation. Whereas of the sciences which regard nature, the divine philosopher declares that "it is the glory of God to conceal a thing, but it is the glory of the King to find a thing out." Even as though the divine nature took pleasure in the innocent and kindly sport of children playing at hide and seek, and vouchsafed of his kindness and goodness to admit the human spirit for his playfellow at that game. Lastly, I would address one general admonition to all; that they consider what are the true ends of knowledge, and that they seek it not either for pleasure of the mind, or for contention, or for superiority to others, or for profit, or fame, or power, or any of these inferior things; but for the benefit and use of life; and that they perfect and govern it in charity. For it was from lust of power that the angels fell, from lust of knowledge that man fell; but of charity there can be no excess, neither did angel or man ever come in danger by it.

The requests I have to make are these. Of myself I say nothing; but in behalf of the business which is in hand I entreat men to believe that it is not an opinion to be held, but a work to be done; and to be well assured that I am labouring to lay the foundation, not of any sect or doctrine, but of human utility and power. Next, I ask them to deal fairly by their own interests, and laying aside all emulations and prejudices in favour of this or that opinion, to join in consultation for the common good; and being now freed and guarded by the securities and helps which I offer from the errors and impediments of the way, to come forward themselves and take part in that which remains to be done. Moreover, to be of good hope, nor to imagine that this Instauration of mine is a thing infinite and beyond the power of man, when it is in fact the true end and termination of infinite error; and seeing also that it is by no means forgetful of the conditions of mortality and humanity, (for it does not suppose that the work can be altogether completed within one generation, but provides for its being taken up by another); and finally that it seeks for the sciences not arrogantly in the little cells of human wit, but with reverence in the greater world. But it is the empty things that are vast: things solid are most contracted and lie in little room. And now I have only one favour more to ask (else injustice to me may perhaps imperil the business itself)—that men will consider well how far, upon that which I must needs assert (if I am to be consistent with myself), they are entitled to judge and decide upon these doctrines of mine; inasmuch as all that premature human reasoning which anticipates inquiry, and is abstracted from the facts rashly and sooner than is fit, is by me rejected (so far as the inquisition of nature is concerned), as a thing uncertain, confused, and ill built up; and I cannot be fairly asked to abide by the decision of a tribunal which is itself on its trial.

*   *   *

REVIEW QUESTIONS

1. What does Bacon believe to be the wrong relation to the past and to past authors?
2. Why does he think so?
3. What relation to the past and to past authors does he think a true scientist should hold?
4. Why does Bacon propose the necessity of a method? What method does he propose?
5. According to Bacon, what is invention? What is its relation to experience and prior knowledge?

BLAISE PASCAL

FROM *Pensées*

Blaise Pascal (1623–1662) was the son of a French official. Over the course of his life, he dabbled in many subjects, including science, religion, and literature. His conversion to Jansenism plunged him into controversy with the Jesuits, giving rise to his Lettres provinciales. *These, along with his* Pensées, *from which the following selection is drawn, established his literary fame. His thought contained a fascinating blend of confidence in human reason and consciousness of its limits. Descartes viewed Pascal as the embodiment of a mentality of intellectual and spiritual crisis. Be that as it may, Pascal raised profound questions about the purpose and potential of human knowledge.*

From *Pensées*, by Blaise Pascal, translated by A. J. Krailsheimer (New York: Penguin, 1995), pp. 58–64, 121–25.

*   *   *

XV. Transition from Knowledge of Man to Knowledge of God

DISPROPORTION OF MAN

*   *   *

This is where unaided knowledge brings us. If it is not true, there is no truth in man, and if it is true, he has good cause to feel humiliated; in either case he is obliged to humble himself.

And, since he cannot exist without believing this knowledge, before going on to a wider inquiry concerning nature, I want him to consider nature just once, seriously and at leisure, and to look at himself as well, and judge whether there is any proportion between himself and nature by comparing the two.

Let man then contemplate the whole of nature in her full and lofty majesty, let him turn his gaze away from the lowly objects around him; let him behold the dazzling light set like an eternal lamp to light up the universe, let him see the earth as a mere speck compared to the vast orbit described by this star, and let him marvel at finding this vast orbit itself to be no more than the tiniest point compared to that described by the stars revolving in the firmament. But if our eyes stop there, let our imagination proceed further; it will grow weary of conceiving things before nature tires of producing them. The whole visible world is only an imperceptible dot in nature's ample bosom. No idea comes near it; it is no good inflating our conceptions beyond imaginable space, we only bring forth atoms compared to the reality of things. Nature is an infinite sphere whose centre is everywhere and circumference nowhere. In short it is

the greatest perceptible mark of God's omnipotence that our imagination should lose itself in that thought.

Let man, returning to himself, consider what he is in comparison with what exists; let him regard himself as lost, and from this little dungeon, in which he finds himself lodged, I mean the universe, let him learn to take the earth, its realms, its cities, its houses and himself at their proper value.

What is a man in the infinite?

But, to offer him another prodigy equally astounding, let him look into the tiniest things he knows. Let a mite show him in its minute body incomparably more minute parts, legs with joints, veins in its legs, blood in the veins, humours in the blood, drops in the humours, vapours in the drops: let him divide these things still further until he has exhausted his powers of imagination, and let the last thing he comes down to now be the subject of our discourse. He will perhaps think that this is the ultimate of minuteness in nature.

I want to show him a new abyss. I want to depict to him not only the visible universe, but all the conceivable immensity of nature enclosed in this miniature atom. Let him see there an infinity of universes, each with its firmament, its planets, its earth, in the same proportions as in the visible world, and on that earth animals, and finally mites, in which he will find again the same results as in the first; and finding the same thing yet again in the others without end or respite, he will be lost in such wonders, as astounding in their minuteness as the others in their amplitude. For who will not marvel that our body, a moment ago imperceptible in a universe, itself imperceptible in the bosom of the whole, should now be a colossus, a world, or rather a whole, compared to the nothingness beyond our reach? Anyone who considers himself in this way will be terrified at himself, and, seeing his mass, as given him by nature, supporting him between these two abysses of infinity and nothingness, will tremble at these marvels. I believe that with his curiosity changing into wonder he will be more disposed to contemplate them in silence than investigate them with presumption.

For, after all, what is man in nature? A nothing compared to the infinite, a whole compared to the nothing, a middle point between all and nothing, infinitely remote from an understanding of the extremes; the end of things and their principles are unattainably hidden from him in impenetrable secrecy.

Equally incapable of seeing the nothingness from which he emerges and the infinity in which he is engulfed.

What else can he do, then, but perceive some semblance of the middle of things, eternally hopeless of knowing either their principles or their end? All things have come out of nothingness and are carried onwards to infinity. Who can follow these astonishing processes? The author of these wonders understands them: no one else can.

Because they failed to contemplate these infinities, men have rashly undertaken to probe into nature as if there were some proportion between themselves and her.

Strangely enough they wanted to know the principles of things and go on from there to know everything, inspired by a presumption as infinite as their object. For there can be no doubt that such a plan could not be conceived without infinite presumption or a capacity as infinite as that of nature.

When we know better, we understand that, since nature has engraved her own image and that of her author on all things, they almost all share her double infinity. Thus we see that all the sciences are infinite in the range of their researches, for who can doubt that mathematics, for instance, has an infinity of infinities of propositions to expound? They are infinite also in the multiplicity and subtlety of their principles, for anyone can see that those which are supposed to be ultimate do not stand by themselves, but depend on others, which depend on others again, and thus never allow of any finality.

But we treat as ultimate those which seem so to our reason, as in material things we call a point indivisible when our senses can perceive nothing beyond it, although by its nature it is infinitely divisible.

Of these two infinites of science, that of greatness is much more obvious, and that is why it has occurred to few people to claim that they know everything. 'I am going to speak about everything,' Democritus used to say.

But the infinitely small is much harder to see. The philosophers have much more readily claimed to have reached it, and that is where they have all tripped up. This is the origin of such familiar titles as *Of the principles of things*, *Of the principles of philosophy*, and the like, which are really as pretentious, though they do not look it, as this blatant one: *Of all that can be known*.

We naturally believe we are more capable of reaching the centre of things than of embracing their circumference, and the visible extent of the world is visibly greater than we. But since we in our turn are greater than small things, we think we are more capable of mastering them, and yet it takes no less capacity to reach nothingness than the whole. In either case it takes an infinite capacity, and it seems to me that anyone who had understood the ultimate principles of things might also succeed in knowing infinity. One depends on the other, and one leads to the other. These extremes touch and join by going in opposite directions, and they meet in God and God alone.

Let us then realize our limitations. We are something and we are not everything. Such being as we have conceals from us the knowledge of first principles, which arise from nothingness, and the smallness of our being hides infinity from our sight.

Our intelligence occupies the same rank in the order of intellect as our body in the whole range of nature.

Limited in every respect, we find this intermediate state between two extremes reflected in all our faculties. Our senses can perceive nothing extreme; too much noise deafens us, too much light dazzles; when we are too far or too close we cannot see properly; an argument is obscured by being too long or too short; too much truth bewilders us. I know people who cannot understand that 4 from 0 leaves 0. First principles are too obvious for us; too much pleasure causes discomfort; too much harmony in music is displeasing; too much kindness annoys us: we want to be able to pay back the debt with something over. *Kindness is welcome to the extent that it seems the debt can be paid back. When it goes too far gratitude turns into hatred.*

We feel neither extreme heat nor extreme cold. Qualities carried to excess are bad for us and cannot be perceived; we no longer feel them, we suffer them. Excessive youth and excessive age impair thought; so do too much and too little learning.

In a word, extremes are as if they did not exist for us nor we for them; they escape us or we escape them.

Such is our true state. That is what makes us incapable of certain knowledge or absolute ignorance. We are floating in a medium of vast extent, always drifting uncertainly, blown to and fro; whenever we think we have a fixed point to which we can cling and make fast, it shifts and leaves us behind; if we follow it, it eludes our grasp, slips away, and flees eternally before us. Nothing stands still for us. This is our natural state and yet the state most contrary to our inclinations. We burn with desire to find a firm footing, an ultimate, lasting base on which to build a tower rising up to infinity, but our whole foundation cracks and the earth opens up into the depth of the abyss.

Let us then seek neither assurance nor stability; our reason is always deceived by the inconsistency of appearances; nothing can fix the finite between the two infinites which enclose and evade it.

Once that is clearly understood, I think that each of us can stay quietly in the state in which nature has placed him. Since the middle station allotted to us is always far from the extremes, what does it matter if someone else has a slightly better understanding of things? If he has, and if he takes them a little further, is he not still infinitely remote from the goal? Is not our span of life equally infinitesimal in eternity, even if it is extended by ten years?

In the perspective of these infinites, all finites are equal and I see no reason to settle our imagination on one rather than another. Merely comparing ourselves with the finite is painful.

If man studied himself, he would see how incapable he is of going further. How could a part possibly know the whole? But perhaps he will aspire to know at least the parts to which he bears some proportion. But the parts of the world are all so related and linked together that I think it is impossible to know one without the other and without the whole.

There is, for example, a relationship between man and all he knows. He needs space to contain him, time to exist in, motion to be alive, elements to constitute him, warmth and food for nourishment, air to breathe. He sees light, he feels bodies, everything in short is related to him. To understand man therefore one must know why he needs air to live, and to understand air one must know how it comes to be thus related to the life of man, etc.

Flame cannot exist without air, so, to know one, one must know the other.

Thus, since all things are both caused or causing, assisted and assisting, mediate and immediate, providing mutual support in a chain linking together naturally and imperceptibly the most distant and different things, I consider it as impossible to know the parts without knowing the whole as to know the whole without knowing the individual parts.

The eternity of things in themselves or in God must still amaze our brief span of life.

The fixed and constant immobility of nature, compared to the continual changes going on in us, must produce the same effect.

And what makes our inability to know things absolute is that they are simple in themselves, while we are composed of two opposing natures of different kinds, soul and body. For it is impossible for the part of us which reasons to be anything but spiritual, and even if it were claimed that we are simply corporeal, that would still more preclude us from knowing things, since there is nothing so inconceivable as the idea that matter knows itself. We cannot possibly know how it could know itself.

Thus, if we are simply material, we can know nothing at all, and, if we are composed of mind and matter, we cannot have perfect knowledge of things which are simply spiritual or corporeal.

That is why nearly all philosophers confuse their ideas of things, and speak spiritually of corporeal things and corporeally of spiritual ones, for they boldly assert that bodies tend to fall, that they aspire towards their centre, that they flee from destruction, that they fear a void, that they have inclinations, sympathies, antipathies, all things pertaining only to things spiritual. And when they speak of minds, they consider them as being in a place, and attribute to them movement from one place to another, which are things pertaining only to bodies.

Instead of receiving ideas of these things in their purity, we colour them with our qualities and stamp our own composite being on all the simple things we contemplate.

Who would not think, to see us compounding everything of mind and matter, that such a mixture is perfectly intelligible to us? Yet this is the thing we understand least; man is to himself the greatest prodigy in nature, for he cannot conceive what body is, and still less what mind is, and least of all how a body can be joined to a mind. This is his supreme difficulty, and yet it is his very being. *The way in which minds are attached to bodies is beyond man's understanding, and yet this is what man is.*

*   *   *

REVIEW QUESTIONS

1. According to Pascal, what is the relation between universality and infinity?
2. Why does Pascal argue in favor of the former?
3. Why cannot humans know everything? What does Pascal's contention that nature is an infinite sphere teach us about human knowledge?
4. Why does nature hold abysses that human knowledge cannot penetrate?
5. How has Pascal's concept of infinity, which he uses first as a concept by which human beings might approach knowledge of God, changed in this passage?

RENÉ DESCARTES

FROM *Discourse on Method and Meditations on First Philosophy*

René Descartes (1596–1650) was born of a family of the judicial nobility. He graduated in 1612 from the Collège La Flèche and received a law degree in 1616 from the University of Poitiers. From 1616 until 1624, he saw military service in the Thirty Years' War. During the winter of 1620, while quartered near Ulm, Descartes claimed to have achieved the philosophical insights that would form the basis of his entire system of rational thought. In 1628 he left France, for reasons that are not clear, and returned only for relatively brief periods of time. Until 1649, he lived in the United Provinces of the Netherlands. There, with the publication of the Dis-course on Method *in 1637, he began to make public the ideas first glimpsed in 1620, the systematic philosophy that would make him famous. His was one of the three great systems of rationalism of the seventeenth century, along with those created by Baruch Spinoza and Gottfried Leibniz. Reacting to the skepticism of the early seventeenth century, represented by the thought of philosophers such as Pascal, Descartes decided to subject every idea to critical scrutiny and retain as true only those ideas that were self-evident. The result was a geometric method of reasoning that consisted of four simple rules: to start only with clear and distinct ideas, to simplify any difficulty in thinking by dividing it into small parts, to think in an orderly process from simplest to most complex, and to make thorough evaluations that overlook no part of the problem. The Cartesian method gained enthusiastic popular support and became an important stimulus for the science of the Enlightenment.*

From *The Philosophical Works of Descartes*, translated by Elizabeth S. Haldane and G. R. T. Ross (Cambridge: Cambridge University Press, 1911).

*   *   *

Part 2

I was then in Germany, to which country I had been attracted by the wars which are not yet at an end. And as I was returning from the coronation of the Emperor to join the army, the setting in of winter detained me in a quarter where, since I found no society to divert me, while fortunately I had also no cares or passions to trouble me, I remained the whole day shut up alone in a stove-heated room, where I had complete leisure to occupy myself with my own thoughts. One of the first of the considerations that occurred to me was that there is very often less perfection in works composed of several portions, and carried out by the hands of various masters, than in those on which one individual alone has worked. Thus we see that buildings planned and carried out by one architect alone are usually more beautiful and better proportioned than those which many have tried to put in order and improve, making use of old walls that were built with other ends in view. * * * And similarly I thought that the sciences found in books—in those at least whose reasonings are only probable and which have no demonstrations, composed as they are of the grad-

ually accumulated opinions of many different individuals—do not approach so near to the truth as the simple reasoning that a man of common sense can quite naturally carry out respecting the things which come immediately before him. Again I thought that since we have all been children before being men, and since it has for long fallen to us to be governed by our appetites and by our teachers (who often enough contradicted one another, and none of whom perhaps counselled us always for the best), it is almost impossible that our judgments should be so excellent or solid as they would have been had we had complete use of our Reason since our birth, and had we been guided by it alone.

It is true that we do not find that all the houses in a town are razed to the ground for the sole reason that the town is to be rebuilt in another fashion, with streets made more beautiful; but at the same time we see that many people cause their own houses to be knocked down in order to rebuild them, and that sometimes they are forced to do so where there is danger of the houses falling of themselves, and when the foundations are not secure. From such examples I argued to myself that there was no plausibility in the claim of any private individual to reform a state by altering everything, and by overturning it throughout, in order to set it right again. Nor is it likewise probable that the whole body of the Sciences, or the order of teaching established by the Schools, should be reformed. But as regards all the opinions which up to this time I had embraced, I thought I could not do better than endeavor once for all to sweep them completely away, so that they might later on be replaced, either by others that were better, or by the same, when I had made them conform to the uniformity of a rational scheme. And I firmly believed that by this means I should succeed in directing my life much better than if I had only built on old foundations, and relied on principles of which I allowed myself to be in youth persuaded without having inquired into their truth. For although in so doing I recognized various difficulties, these were at the same time not unsurmountable, nor comparable to those which are found in reformation of the most insignificant kind in matters which concern the public. ✳ ✳ ✳

✳ ✳ ✳ My design has never extended beyond trying to reform my own opinion and to build on a foundation that is entirely my own. If my work has given me a certain satisfaction, so that I here present to you a draft of it, I do not so do because I wish to advise anybody to imitate it. Those to whom God has been most beneficent in the bestowal of His grace will perhaps form designs that are more elevated; but I fear much that this particular one will seem too venturesome for many. The simple resolve to strip oneself of all opinions and beliefs formerly received is not to be regarded as an example that each man should follow, and the world may be said to be mainly composed of two classes of minds neither of which could prudently adopt it. There are those who, believing themselves to be cleverer than they are, cannot restrain themselves from being precipitate in judgment and have not sufficient patience to arrange their thoughts in proper order; hence, once a man of this description had taken the liberty of doubting the principles he formerly accepted, and had deviated from the beaten track, he would never be able to maintain the path which must be followed to reach the appointed end more quickly, and he would hence remain wandering astray all through

his life. Secondly, there are those who having reason or modesty enough to judge that they are less capable of distinguishing truth from falsehood than some others from whom instruction might be obtained, are right in contenting themselves with following the opinions of these others rather than in searching better ones for themselves.

For myself I should doubtless have been of these last if I had never had more than a single master, or had I never known the diversities that have from all time existed between the opinions of men of the greatest learning. But I had been taught, even in my College days, that there is nothing imaginable so strange or so little credible that it has not been maintained by one philosopher or other, and I further recognized in the course of my travels that all those whose sentiments are very contrary to ours are yet not necessarily barbarians or savages, but may be possessed of Reason in as great or even a greater degree than ourselves. I also considered how very different the self-same man, identical in mind and spirit, may become, according as he is brought up from childhood amongst the French or Germans, or has passed his whole life amongst Chinese or cannibals. I likewise noticed how even in the fashions of one's clothing the same thing that pleased us ten years ago, and that will perhaps please us once again before ten years are passed, seems at the present time extravagant and ridiculous. I thus concluded that it is much more custom and example that persuade us than any certain knowledge, and yet in spite of this the voice of the majority is valueless as a proof of any truths that are a little difficult to discover, because such truths are much more likely to have been discovered by one man than by a nation. I could not, however, put my finger on a single person whose opinions seemed preferable to those of others, and I found that I was, so to speak, constrained myself to undertake the direction of my procedure.

But like one who walks alone and in the twilight I resolved to go so slowly, and to use so much circumspection in all things, that if my advance was but very small, at least I guarded myself well from falling. I did not wish to set about the final rejection of any single opinion which might formerly have crept into my beliefs without having been introduced there by means of Reason, until I had first of all employed sufficient time in planning out the task which I had undertaken, and in seeking the true Method of arriving at a knowledge of all the things of which my mind was capable.

Among the different branches of Philosophy, I had in my younger days to a certain extent studied Logic; and in those of Mathematics, Geometrical Analysis and Algebra—three arts or sciences which seemed as though they ought to contribute something to the design I had in view. But in examining them I observed in respect to Logic that the syllogisms and the greater part of the other teaching served better in explaining to others those things that one knows (or like the art of Lully, in enabling one to speak without judgment of those things of which one is ignorant) than in learning what is new. And although in reality Logic contains many precepts that are very true and very good, there are at the same time mingled with them so many others that are hurtful or superfluous, that it is almost as difficult to separate the two as to draw a Diana or a Minerva out of a block of marble that is not yet roughly hewn. And as to the Analysis of the ancients and the Algebra of the moderns, besides the fact that they embrace only matters the most abstract, such as appear to have no actual use, the former is always so restricted to the consideration of symbols that it cannot exercise the Understanding without greatly fatiguing the Imagination; and in the latter one is so subjected to certain rules and formulas that the result is the construction of an art that is confused and obscure, and that embarrasses the mind, instead of a science that contributes to its cultivation. This made me feel that some other Method must be found, which, comprising the advantages of the three, is yet exempt from their faults. And as a multiplicity of laws often furnishes excuses for evil-doing, and as a State is hence much better ruled when, having but very few laws, these are most strictly observed; so, instead of the great number of precepts of which Logic is composed, I believed that I should find the

four which I shall state quite sufficient, provided that I adhered to a firm and constant resolve never on any single occasion to fail in their observance.

The first of these was to accept nothing as true which I did not clearly recognize to be so: that is to say, carefully to avoid precipitation and prejudice in judgments, and to accept in them nothing more than what was presented to my mind so clearly and distinctly that I could have no occasion to doubt it.

The second was to divide up each of the difficulties that I examined into as many parts as possible, and as seemed requisite in order that it might be resolved in the best manner possible.

The third was to carry on my reflections in due order, commencing with objects that were the most simple and easy to understand, in order to rise little by little, or by degrees, to knowledge of the most complex, assuming an order, even if a fictitious one, among those which do not follow a natural sequence relatively to one another.

The last was in all cases to make enumerations so complete and reviews so general that I should be certain of having omitted nothing.

Those long chains of reasoning, simple and easy as they are, of which geometricians make use in order to arrive at the most difficult demonstrations, had caused me to imagine that all those things which fall under the cognizance of man might very likely be mutually related in the same fashion; and that, provided only that we abstain from receiving anything as true that is not so, and always retain the order that is necessary in order to deduce the one conclusion from the other, there can be nothing so remote that we cannot reach to it, nor so recondite that we cannot discover it. And I had not much trouble in discovering which objects it was necessary to begin with, for I already knew that I must begin with the most simple and most easy to apprehend. Considering also that of all those who have hitherto sought for the truth in the Sciences, it has been the mathematicians alone who have been able to succeed in making any demonstrations, that is to say producing reasons that are evident and certain, I did not doubt that it had been by means of a similar kind that they carried on their investigations. I did not at the same time hope for any practical result in so doing, except that my mind would become accustomed to the nourishment of truth and would not content itself with false reasoning. But for all that I had no intention of trying to master all those particular sciences that receive in common the name of Mathematics; but observing that, although their objects are different, they do not fail to agree in this, that they take nothing under consideration but the various relationships or proportions that are present in these objects, I thought it would be better if I only examined these proportions in their general aspect, and without viewing them otherwise than in the objects that would serve most to facilitate a knowledge of them. Not that I should in any way restrict them to these objects, for I might later on all the more easily apply them to all other objects to which they were applicable. Then, having carefully noted that in order to comprehend the proportions I should sometimes require to consider each one in particular, and sometimes merely keep them in mind, or take them in groups, I thought that, in order the better to consider them in detail, I should picture them in the form of lines, because I could find no method more simple nor more capable of being distinctly represented to my imagination and senses. I considered, however, that in order to keep them in my memory or to embrace several at once, it would be essential that I should explain them by means of certain formulas, the shorter the better. And for this purpose it was requisite that I should borrow all that is best in Geometrical Analysis and Algebra, and correct the errors of the one by the other.

*   *   *

But what pleased me most in this Method was that I was certain by its means of exercising my reason in all things, if not perfectly, at least as well as was in my power. And besides this, I felt in making use of it that my mind gradually accus-

tomed itself to conceive of its objects more accurately and distinctly; and not having restricted this Method to any particular matter, I promised myself to apply it as usefully to the difficulties of other sciences as I had done to those of Algebra. Not that on this account I dared undertake to examine just at once all those which might present themselves; for that would itself have been contrary to the order that the Method prescribes. But having noticed that the knowledge of these difficulties must be dependent on principles derived from Philosophy in which I yet found nothing to be certain, I thought that it was requisite above all to try to establish certainty in it. I considered also that since this endeavor is the most important in all the world, and that in which precipitation and prejudice were most to be feared, I should not try to grapple with it till I had attained to a much riper age than that of three and twenty, which was the age I had reached. I thought, too, that I should first of all employ much time in preparing myself for the work by eradicating from my mind all the wrong opinions that I had up to this time accepted, and accumulating a variety of experiences fitted later on to afford matter for my reasonings, and by ever exercising myself in the Method I had prescribed, in order more and more to fortify myself in the power of using it.

*   *   *

REVIEW QUESTIONS

1. Why does Descartes reject the received knowledge of the past?
2. Why does Descartes not trust his own mind as a reasoning instrument?
3. What method does he propose, and what relationship does he see between experience and knowledge?
4. How does Descartes's epistemology compare with those of Montaigne (pp. 116–123)?

ISAAC NEWTON

FROM *Mathematical Principles of Natural Philosophy*

Isaac Newton (1642–1727) created the great reformulation of seventeenth-century mechanical philosophy. He was born of yeoman stock. His intellectual gifts were recognized early by a teacher and an uncle, who urged that Newton be prepared for a university education. He entered Trinity College, Cambridge, in 1661 and received his bachelor of arts in 1665 and his master of arts in 1668. The next year, Newton was appointed Lucasian Professor, a position he held until 1701. As a natural philosopher, Newton agreed with Bacon that empiricism, that is, the gathering of experimental data, was the starting point for scientific inquiry. Yet he reserved a role for Cartesian rationalism by demonstrating the theoretical utility of mathematics in mechanical philosophy. In Mathematical Principles of Natural Philosophy, *Newton laid out the quantitative framework of his mechanical philosophy and showed how it was possible, experimentally, to work with invisible bodies. In the following rules of reason, he offered a methodological guide to the study of reality.*

From *Mathematical Principles of Natural Philosophy*, vol. 2, by Isaac Newton, translated by Andrew Motte (London: Sherwood, Neely and Jones, 1919).

*   *   *

Book III

In the preceding books I have laid down the principles of philosophy; principles not philosophical, but mathematical; such, to wit, as we may build our reasonings upon in philosophical enquiries. These principles are the laws and conditions of certain motions, and powers or forces, which chiefly have respect to philosophy; but, lest they should have appeared of themselves dry and barren, I have illustrated them here and there with some philosophical scholiums, giving an account of such things as are of more general nature, and which philosophy seems chiefly to be founded on; such as the density and the resistance of bodies, spaces void of all bodies, and the motion of light

and sounds. It remains that, from the same principles, I now demonstrate the frame of the System of the World. Upon this subject I had, indeed, composed the third book in a popular method, that it might be read by many; but afterwards, considering that such as had not sufficiently entered into the principles could not easily discern the strength of the consequences, nor lay aside the prejudices to which they had been many years accustomed, therefore, to prevent the disputes which might be raised upon such accounts, I chose to reduce the substance of this book into the form of propositions (in the mathematical way), which should be read by those only who had first made themselves masters of the principles established in the preceding books: not that I would advise any one to the previous study of every proposition of those books; for they abound with such as might cost too much time, even to readers of good mathematical learning. It is enough if one carefully reads the definitions, the laws of motions, and the first three sections of the first book. He may then pass on to this book, and consult such of the remaining propositions of the *first two books,* as the references in this, and his occasions, shall require.

Rules of Reasoning in Philosophy

RULE I

WE ARE TO ADMIT NO MORE CAUSES OF NATURAL THINGS THAN SUCH AS ARE BOTH TRUE AND SUFFICIENT TO EXPLAIN THEIR APPEARANCES.

To this purpose the philosophers say that Nature does nothing in vain, and more is in vain when less will serve; for Nature is pleased with simplicity, and affects not the pomp of superfluous causes.

RULE II

THEREFORE TO THE SAME NATURAL EFFECTS WE MUST, AS FAR AS POSSIBLE, ASSIGN THE SAME CAUSES.

As to respiration in a man and in a beast; the descent of stones in Europe and in America; the light of our culinary fire and of the sun; the reflection of light in the earth and in the planets.

RULE III

THE QUALITIES OF BODIES, WHICH ADMIT NEITHER INTENSION OR REMISSION OF DEGREES, AND WHICH ARE FOUND TO BELONG TO ALL BODIES WITHIN THE REACH OF OUR EXPERIMENTS, ARE TO BE ESTEEMED THE UNIVERSAL QUALITIES OF ALL BODIES WHATSOEVER.

For since the qualities of bodies are only known to us by experiments, we are to hold for universal all such as universally agree with experiments; and such as are not liable to diminution can never be quite taken away. We are certainly not to relinquish the evidence of experiments for the sake of dreams and vain fictions of our own devising; nor are we to recede from the analogy of Nature, which is wont to be simple, and always consonant to itself. We no other way know the extension of bodies than by our senses, nor do these reach it in all bodies; but because we perceive extension in all that are sensible, therefore we ascribe it universally to all others also. That abundance of bodies are hard, we learn by experience; and because the hardness of the whole arises from the hardness of the parts, we therefore justly infer the hardness of the undivided particles not only of the bodies we feel but of all others. That all bodies are impenetrable, we gather not from reason, but from sensation. The bodies which we handle we find impenetrable, and thence conclude impenetrability to be an universal property of all bodies whatsoever. That all bodies are moveable, and endowed with certain powers (which we call *vires inertiæ*) of persevering in their motion, or in their rest, we only infer from the like properties observed in the bodies which we have seen. The extension, hardness, impenetrability, mobility, and *vis inertiæ* of the whole, result from the extension, hardness, impenetrability, mobility, and *vires inertiæ* of the parts; and thence we conclude the least particles of all bodies to be also all extended, and hard, and impenetrable, and moveable, and endowed with their proper *vires inertiæ*. And this is the foundation of all philosophy. Moreover, that the divided but continuous particles of bodies may be separated from one another, is matter of observation; and, in the particles that remain undivided, our minds are able to distinguish yet lesser parts, as is mathematically demonstrated. But whether the parts so distinguished, and not yet divided, may, by the powers of Nature, be actually divided and separated from one another, we cannot certainly determine. Yet, had we the proof of but one experiment that any undivided particle, in breaking a hard and solid body, suffered a division, we might by virtue of this rule conclude that the undivided as well as the divided particles may be divided and actually separated to infinity.

DETAIL FROM THE FRONTISPIECE OF DE HUMANI CORPORIS FABRICA (1543)   ANDREAS VESALIUS

Andreas Vesalius (Andreas van Wesel, 1514–1564) came from a family of physicians. Educated in Leuven, Paris, and Padua, he was appointed explicator chirurgiae *(professor of surgery) at the University of Padua in 1537, at twenty-three years of age. There he began teaching, not simply by lecturing but also by demonstrating. He also prepared drawings as aids to memory for his students. De Fabrica, as it is often called, was published in 1543, when Vesalius was only twenty-eight years old. It became not only the most influential book in the history of medicine but also one of the most important books ever published. It overturned fourteen centuries of Galenic teaching and tradition in medicine. It was also the first printed book to integrate every aspect of book design: content, art, layout and typography. What does this image reveal about science and education in the sixteenth century? Why are the architectural elements and figures of animals so prominent? Can you identify Vesalius? Why is he represented, posing and gesturing, as he is? Looking carefully, what can you determine about the corpse? Given what you see, why would this image have been particularly daring? What purpose might that daring have served?*

Lastly, if it universally appears, by experiments and astronomical observations, that all bodies about the earth gravitate towards the earth, and that in proportion to the quantity of matter which they severally contain; that the moon likewise, according to the quantity of its matter, gravitates towards the earth; that, on the other hand, our sea gravitates towards the moon; and all the planets mutually one towards another; and the comets in like manner towards the sun; we must, in consequence of this rule, universally allow that all bodies whatsoever are endowed with a principle of mutual gravitation. For the argument from the appearances concludes with more force for the universal gravitation of all bodies than for their impenetrability; of which, among those in the celestial regions, we have no experiments, nor any manner of observation. Not that I affirm gravity to be essential to bodies: by their *vis insita* I mean nothing but their *vis inertiæ*. This is immutable. Their gravity is diminished as they recede from the earth.

RULE IV

IN EXPERIMENTAL PHILOSOPHY WE ARE TO LOOK UPON PROPOSITIONS COLLECTED BY GENERAL INDUCTION FROM PHÆNOMENA AS ACCURATELY OR VERY NEARLY TRUE, NOTWITHSTANDING ANY CONTRARY HYPOTHESES THAT MAY BE IMAGINED, TILL SUCH TIME AS OTHER PHÆNOMENA OCCUR, BY WHICH THEY MAY EITHER BE MADE MORE ACCURATE, OR LIABLE TO EXCEPTIONS.

This rule we must follow, that the argument of induction may not be evaded by hypotheses.

*   *   *

REVIEW QUESTIONS

1. Why does Newton take mathematical principles as the principles of philosophy?
2. If nature, as Newton asserts, is "pleased with simplicity," what is the origin of "superfluous causes"?
3. What is the relation between cause and law?
4. How does Newton arrive at the universal?
5. How does his method differ from that of Pascal?

JOHN LOCKE

FROM *An Essay Concerning Human Understanding*

John Locke (1632–1704) was an English philosopher whose thought contributed to the Enlightenment. He grew up in a liberal, Puritan family, the son of an attorney who fought in the Civil War against Charles I, and attended Christ Church College, Oxford. He received his bachelor of arts in 1656, lectured in classical languages while earning his master of arts, and entered Oxford's medical school to avoid being forced to join the clergy. In 1666, Locke attached himself to the household of the Earl of Shaftesbury and his fortunes to the liberal Whig Party. Between 1675 and 1679, he lived in France, where he made contact with leading intellectuals of the late seventeenth century. On his return to England, he plunged into the controversy sur-

rounding the succession of James II, an avowed Catholic with absolutist pretensions, to the throne of his brother, Charles II. Locke's patron, Shaftesbury, was imprisoned for his opposition, and Locke went into exile in 1683. Though he was involved to some extent in the Glorious Revolution of 1688, he returned to England in 1689, in the entourage of Mary, Princess of Orange, who would assume the throne with her husband William. This was a period of intense political engagement for Locke, the fruits of which would be the publication of the Two Treatises on Government *(1690). Yet he was also engaged in broader philosophical study. Locke's great work on epistemology,* An Essay Concerning Human Understanding, *appeared in the same year. It was a complete account of human knowledge, its source and its reliability. His argument was as simple as it was revolutionary. Rejecting all appeals to authority and theory, he showed that all knowledge derives from sensory perception and experience as considered and elaborated by reason. It was one of the most influential works in all of Western philosophy and had an immediate impact on enlightened thinkers. As Voltaire himself announced, "No Man ever had a more judicious or more methodical Genius . . . than Mr. Locke."*

From *The Works of John Locke* (London: Thomas Tegg et al., 1823).

*   *   *

Book II
Of Ideas

Chapter I
Of Ideas in General, and Their Original

IDEA IS THE OBJECT OF THINKING.

Every man being conscious to himself, that he thinks, and that which his mind is applied about, whilst thinking, being the ideas, that are there, 'tis past doubt, that men have in their minds several ideas, such as are those expressed by the words, *whiteness, hardness, sweetness, thinking, motion, man, elephant, army, drunkenness,* and others: it is in the first place then to be inquired, how he comes by them? I know it is a received doctrine, that men have native ideas, and original characters stamped upon their minds, in their very first be-

ing. This opinion I have at large examined already; and, I suppose, what I have said in the foregoing book, will be much more easily admitted, when I have shown, whence the understanding may get all the ideas it has, and by what ways and degrees they may come into the mind; for which I shall appeal to everyone's own observation and experience.

ALL IDEAS COME FROM SENSATION OR REFLECTION.

Let us then suppose the mind to be, as we say, white paper, void of all characters, without any ideas; how comes it to be furnished? Whence comes it by that vast store, which the busy and boundless fancy of man has painted on it, with an almost endless variety? Whence has it all the materials of reason and knowledge? To this I answer, in one world, from *experience* in that, all our knowledge is founded; and from that it ultimately derives itself. Our observation employed either about *external sensible objects; or about the internal operations of our minds, perceived and reflected on by ourselves, is that, which supplies our understandings with all the materials of thinking.* These two are the fountains of knowledge, from whence all the ideas we have, or can naturally have, do spring.

THE OBJECTS OF SENSATION ONE SOURCE OF IDEAS.

First, *our senses,* conversant about particular sensible objects, do *convey into the mind,* several distinct *perceptions* of things, according to those various ways, wherein those objects do affect them: and thus we come by those ideas, we have of *yellow, white, heat, cold, soft, hard, bitter, sweet,* and all those which we call sensible qualities, which when I say the senses convey into the mind, I mean, they from external objects convey into the mind what produces there those *perceptions.* This great source, of most of the ideas we have, depending wholly upon our senses, and derived by them to the understanding, I call *sensation.*

THE OPERATIONS OF OUR MINDS, THE OTHER SOURCE OF THEM.

Secondly, the other fountain, from which experience furnisheth the understanding with ideas, is the *perception of the operations of our own minds* within us, as it is employed about the ideas it has got; which operations, when the soul comes to reflect on, and consider, do furnish the understanding with another set of ideas, which could not be had from things without; and such are, *perception, thinking, doubting, believing, reasoning, knowing, willing,* and all the different actings of our own minds; which we being conscious of, and observing in ourselves, do from these receive into our understandings, as distinct ideas, as we do from bodies affecting our senses. This source of ideas, every man has wholly in himself: and though it be not sense, as having nothing to do with external objects; yet it is very like it, and might properly enough be called internal sense. But as I call the other *sensation,* so I call this *reflection,* the ideas it affords being such only, as the mind gets by reflecting on its own operations within itself. By *reflection* then, in the following part of this discourse, I would be understood to mean, that

notice which the mind takes of its own operations, and the manner of them, by reason whereof, there come to be ideas of these operations in the understanding. These two, I say, *viz.* external, material things, as the objects of *sensation;* and the operations of our own minds within, as the objects of *reflection,* are, to me, the only originals, from whence all our ideas take their beginnings. The term *operations* here, I use in a large sense, as comprehending not barely the actions of the mind about its ideas, but some sort of passions arising sometimes from them, such as is the satisfaction or uneasiness arising from any thought.

ALL OUR IDEAS ARE OF THE ONE OR THE OTHER OF THESE.

The understanding seems to me, not to have the least glimmering of any ideas, which it doth not receive from one of these two. *External objects furnish the mind with the ideas of sensible qualities,* which are all those different perceptions they produce in us: and the *mind furnishes the understanding with ideas of its own operations.*

These, when we have taken a full survey of them, and their several modes, combinations, and relations, we shall find to contain all our whole stock of ideas; and that we have nothing in our minds, which did not come in, one of these two ways. Let anyone examine his own thoughts, and throughly search into his understanding, and then let him tell me, whether all the original ideas he has there, are any other than of the objects of his *senses;* or of the operations of his mind, considered as objects of his *reflection:* and how great a mass of knowledge soever he imagines to be lodged there, he will, upon taking a strict view, see, that he has *not any idea in his mind, but what one of these two have imprinted;* though, perhaps, with infinite variety compounded and enlarged by the understanding, as we shall see hereafter.

OBSERVABLE IN CHILDREN.

He that attentively considers the state of a *child,* at his first coming into the world, will have little reason to think him stored with plenty of ideas, that are to be the matter of his future knowledge. 'Tis by degrees he comes to be furnished with them: and though the ideas of obvious and familiar qualities, imprint themselves, before the memory begins to keep a register of time and order, yet 'tis often so late, before some unusual qualities come in the way, that there are few men that cannot recollect the beginning of their acquaintance with them: and if it were worthwhile, no doubt a child might be so ordered, as to have but a very few, even of the ordinary ideas, till he were grown up to a man. But all that are born into the world being surrounded with bodies, that perpetually and diversely affect them, variety of ideas, whether care be taken about it or no, are imprinted on the minds of children. *Light,* and *colours,* are busy at hand everywhere, when the eye is but open; *sounds,* and some *tangible qualities* fail not to solicit their proper senses, and force an entrance to the mind; but yet, I think, it will be granted easily, that if a child were kept in a place, where he never saw any other but black and white, till he were a man, he would have no more ideas of scarlet or green, than he that from his childhood never tasted an oyster, or a pineapple, has of those particular relishes.

MEN ARE DIFFERENTLY FURNISHED WITH THESE, ACCORDING TO THE DIFFERENT OBJECTS THEY CONVERSE WITH.

Men then come to be furnished with fewer or more simple ideas from without, according as the *objects,* they converse with, afford greater or less variety; and from the operation of their minds within, according as they more or less *reflect* on them. For, though he that contemplates the operations of his mind, cannot but have plain and clear *ideas* of them; yet unless he turn his thoughts that way, and considers them *attentively,* he will no more have clear and distinct ideas of all the *operations of his mind,* and all that may be observed therein, than he will have all the particular ideas of any landscape, or of the parts and motions of a clock, who will not turn his eyes to it, and

with attention heed all the parts of it. The picture, or clock may be so placed, that they may come in his way every day; but yet he will have but a confused idea of all the parts they are made up of, till he *applies himself with attention,* to consider them each in particular.

IDEAS OF REFLECTION LATER, BECAUSE THEY NEED ATTENTION.

And hence we see the reason, why 'tis pretty late, before most children get ideas of the operations of their own minds; and some have not any very clear, or perfect ideas of the greatest part of them all their lives. Because, though they pass there continually; yet like floating visions, they make not deep impressions enough, to leave in the mind clear distinct lasting ideas, till the understanding turns inwards upon itself, *reflects* on its own *operations,* and makes them the object of its own contemplation. Children, when they come first into it, are surrounded with a world of new things, which, by a constant solicitation of their senses, draw the mind constantly to them, forward to take notice of new, and apt to be delighted with the variety of changing objects. Thus the first years are usually employed and diverted in looking abroad. Men's business in them is to acquaint themselves with what is to be found without; and so growing up in a constant attention to outward sensations, seldom make any considerable reflection on what passes within them, till they come to be of riper years; and some scarce ever at all.

THE SOUL BEGINS TO HAVE IDEAS, WHEN IT BEGINS TO PERCEIVE.

To ask, *at what time a man has first any ideas,* is to ask, when he begins to perceive; having ideas, and perception, being the same thing. I know it is an opinion, that the soul always thinks, and that it has the actual perception of ideas in itself constantly, as long as it exists; and that actual thinking is as inseparable from the soul, as actual extension is from the body; which if true, to inquire after the beginning of a man's ideas, is the same, as to inquire after the beginning of his soul. For by this account, soul and its ideas, as body and its extension, will begin to exist both at the same time.

*   *   *

REVIEW QUESTIONS

1. What, according to Locke, is the source of human knowledge? How does this compare with the philosophy of Descartes?

2. How reliable is human knowledge as a source of truth?
3. What does Locke mean by the "soul"?
4. How does Locke arrive at his epistemology?

17 ❧ THE ENLIGHTENMENT

The Enlightenment continued and extended the work begun by the revolution in science by spreading its new ideas to the general reading public and by extending those ideas to new disciplines devoted to the study of human nature. As an intellectual and cultural movement of the eighteenth century, it was characterized by faith in the power of human reason to solve the basic problems of existence. Though centered in Paris, the Enlightenment was international in scope, manifesting itself throughout Europe and North America. Enlightened intellectuals turned critical reason on all received institutions and traditions with an eye to rebuilding human society according to the natural order of things. This natural order was born of three scientific cornerstones: mechanics, reason, and empiricism. Reason provided both an analogy for the universe and a tool for its analysis. Nature was assumed to be rational, to be ordered according to knowable, controllable relations—fundamental laws that could be discovered through observation and experimentation. Confidence in the existence of natural laws encouraged the search for similar laws governing human relations. Knowledge of these laws would benefit humankind by making possible practical reforms at all levels of life.

By popularizing and extending the ideas of the scientific revolution, the Enlightenment encouraged a secular view of the world. In this way, it helped bring Europe into the modern era.

ABBÉ GUILLAUME-THOMAS RAYNAL

FROM *A Philosophical and Political History of the Settlements and Trade of the Europeans in the East and West Indies*

The Abbé Guillaume-Thomas Raynal (1713–1796) was an author and propagan-dist who helped set the intellectual climate for the French Revolution. Educated by the Jesuits, he initially joined the Society of Jesus but later left the religious life to concentrate on his writing. The author of several popular histories and the editor of the Mercure de France, *he established himself with the publication in 1770 of a six-volume history of the European colonies in the East Indies and North America, from which this passionate denunciation of slavery is drawn. The work's popularity can be measured by the fact that it went through thirty editions before the revolu-tion. Elected to the Estates General in 1789, he refused to serve because of his oppo-sition to violence. He later renounced radicalism in favor of a constitutional monarchy. Raynal's property was expropriated by the revolutionary regime he op-posed, and he died in poverty.*

From *A Philosophical and Political History of the Settlements and Trade of the Europeans in the East and West Indies*, by Abbé Raynal (Glasgow: M'Kenzie, 1812), pp. 311–17.

*   *   *

Slavery Is Entirely Contrary to Humanity, Reason, and Justice.

We will not here so far demean ourselves, as to en-large the ignominious list of those writers who devote their abilities to justify, by policy, what morality condemns. In an age where so many errors are boldly laid open, it would be unpardon-able to conceal any truth that is interesting to hu-manity. If, whatever we have hitherto advanced, hath seemingly tended only to alleviate the burden of slavery, the reason is, that it was first necessary to give some comfort to those unhappy beings, whom we cannot set free; and convince their oppressors, that they are cruel, to the prejudice of real interests. But, in the meantime, until some great revolution makes the evidence of this great truth felt, it is proper to go on with the subject. We shall then first prove, that there is no reason of state that can au-thorise slavery. We shall not be afraid to cite to the tribunal of reason and justice, those governments which tolerate this cruelty, or which even are not ashamed to make it the basis of their power.

Montesquieu could not resolve with himself to treat seriously the question concerning slavery. In reality it is degrading reason to employ it, I will not say in defending, but even in refuting an abuse so repugnant to it. Whoever justifies so odi-ous a system, deserves the utmost contempt from a philosopher, and from the negro a stab with his dagger.

*   *   *

Will it be said, that he who wants to make me a slave does me no injury, but that he only makes use of his rights? Where are those rights? Who hath stamped upon them so sacred a character as to silence mine? From Nature I hold the right of self-defence; Nature, therefore, has not given to another the right of attacking me. If thou thinkest thyself authorised to oppress me, because thou art stronger and more ingenious than I am; do not complain if my vigorous arm shall plunge a dagger into thy breast; do not complain when in thy tortured entrails thou shalt feel the pangs of death conveyed by poison into thy food: I am stronger and more ingenious than thou; fall a victim, therefore, in thy turn, and expiate the crime of having been an oppressor.

He who supports the system of slavery, is the enemy of the whole human race. He divides it into two societies of legal assassins; the oppressors, and the oppressed. It is the same thing as proclaiming to the world, if you would preserve your life, instantly take away mine, for I want to have yours.

But the right of slavery, you say, extends only to the right of labour and the privation of liberty, not of life. What! does not the master, who disposes of my strength at his pleasure, likewise dispose of my life, which depends on the voluntary and moderate use of my faculties. What is existence to him, who has not the disposal of it? I cannot kill my slave, but I can make him bleed under the whip of an excutioner; I can overwhelm him with sorrows, drudgery, and want; I can injure him every way, and secretly undermine the principles and springs of his life; I can smother, by slow punishments, the wretched infant, which a negro woman carries in her womb. Thus the laws protect the slave against violent death, only to leave to my cruelty the right of making him die by degrees.

Let us proceed a step farther: the right of slavery is that of perpetrating all sorts of crimes: those crimes which invade property; for slaves are not suffered to have any, even in their own persons: those crimes which destroy personal safety; for the slave may be sacrificed to the caprice of his master:

those crimes, which make modesty shudder. My blood rises at these horrid images. I detest, I abhor the human species, made up only of victims and executioners; and, if it is never to become better, may it be anihilated!

*   *   *

But these negroes, say they, are a race of men born for slavery; their dispositions are narrow, treacherous, and wicked; they themselves allow the superiority of our understandings, and almost acknowledge the justice of our authority.

The minds of the negroes are contracted; because slavery spoils all the springs of the soul. They are wicked; but not half so wicked as you. They are treacherous, because they are under no obligation to speak truth to their tyrants. They acknowledge the superiority of our understandings, because we have abused their ignorance. They allow the justice of our authority, because we have abused their weakness. I might as well say, that the Indians are a species of men born to be crushed to death, because there are fanatics among them who throw themselves under the wheels of their idol's car, before the temple of Jaguernat.

But these negroes, it is farther urged, were born as slaves. Barbarians, will you persuade me, that a man can be the property of a sovereign, a son the property of a father, a wife the property of an husband, a domestic the property of a master, a negro the property of a planter?

But these slaves have sold themselves. Could ever a man, by compact, or by an oath, permit another to use and abuse him? If he assented to this compact, or confirmed it by an oath, it were a transport of ignorance or folly; and he is released from it, the moment that he either knows himself, or his reason returns.

But they had been taken in war. What have you to do with that? Suffer the conqueror to make what ill use he pleases of his own victory. Why do you make yourselves his accomplices?

But they were criminals, condemned in their own country to slavery. Who was it that condemned them? Do you not know, that in a despotic state there is no criminal but the despot?

The subject of a despotic prince is the same as the slave in a state repugnant to Nature. Every thing that contributes to keep a man in such a state, is an attempt against his person. Every power, which fixes him to the tyranny of one man, is the power of his enemies; and all those who are about him, are the authors or abettors of this violence. His mother, who taught him the first lessons of disobedience; his neighbour, who set him the example of it; his superiors, who compelled him into this state; and his equals, who led him into it by their opinion: All these are the ministers and instruments of tyranny. The tyrant can do nothing of himself; he is only the first mover of those efforts which all his subjects exert to their mutual oppression. He keeps them in a state of perpetual war, which renders robberies, treasons, and even assassinations, lawful. Thus, like the blood which flows in his veins, all crimes originate from his heart, and return thither, as to their primary source. Caligula used to say, that he wished the whole human race had but one head, that he might have the pleasure of cutting it off. Socrates would have said, that if all crimes were heaped upon one head, that should be the one which ought to be struck off.

Let us, therefore, endeavour to make the light of reason, and the sentiments of Nature, take place of the blind ferocity of our ancestors. Let us break the bonds of so many victims to our mercenary principles, should we even be obliged to discard a commerce which is founded only on injustice, and whose object is luxury.

But even this is not necessary. There is no occasion to give up those conveniences which custom hath so much endeared to us. We may draw them from our colonies, without peopling them with the slaves. These productions may be cultivated by the hands of free men, and then be reaped without remorse.

The islands are filled with blacks, whose fetters have been broken. They successfully clear the small plantations that have been given them, or which they have acquired by their industry. Such of these unhappy men, as should recover their independence, would live in quiet upon the same manual labours, that would then be free and advantageous to them. The vassals of Denmark, who have lately been made free, have not abandoned their ploughs.

Is it then apprehended, that the facility of acquiring subsistence without labour, on a soil naturally fertile, and of dispensing with the want of clothes under a burning sky, would plunge these men in idleness? Why then do not the inhabitants of Europe confine themselves to such labours as are of the first necessity? Why do they exhaust their powers in laborious employments, which tend only to the transient gratifications of a frivolous imagination? There are amongst us a thousand professions, some more laborious than others, which owe their origin to our institutions. Human laws have given rise to a variety of fictitious wants which otherwise would never have had an existence. By disposing of every species of property according to their capricious institutions, they have subjected an infinite number of people to the imperious will of their fellow-creatures, so far as even to make them sing and dance for a living. We have amongst us beings formed like ourselves, who have consented to inter themselves under mountains, to furnish us with metals and with copper, perhaps to poison us: Why do we imagine that the negroes are less dupes and less foolish than the Europeans?

At the time that we gradually confer liberty on these unhappy beings as a reward for their economy, their good behaviour, and their industry, we must be careful to subject them to our laws and manners, and to offer them our superfluities. We must give to them a country, give them interest to study, productions to cultivate, and an object adequate to their respective tastes, and our colonies will never want men, who, being eased of their chains, will be more active and robust.

To what tribunal shall we refer the cause of humanity, which so many men are in confederacy to betray, in order to over turn the whole system of slavery, which is supported by passions so universal, by laws so authentic, by the emulations of such powerful nations, and by prejudices still more powerful? Sovereigns of the earth, you alone can bring about this revolution. If you do not sport with the rest of mortals, if you do not regard the power of kings as the right of a successful plunder, and the obedience of subjects as artfully obtained from their ignorance, reflect on your own obligations. Refuse the sanction of your authority to the infamous and criminal traffic of men, turned into so many herds of cattle, and this trade will cease. For once unite, for the happiness of the world, those powers and designs which have been so often exerted for its ruin. If some one amongst you would venture to found the expectation of his opulence and grandeur on the generosity of all the rest, he instantly becomes an enemy of mankind, who ought to be destroyed. You may carry fire and sword into his territories. Your armies will soon be inspired with the sacred enthusiasm of humanity. You will then perceive what difference virtue makes between men who succour the oppressed, and mercenaries who serve tyrants.

But, what am I saying? Let the ineffectual calls of humanity be no longer pleaded with the people and their masters; perhaps they have never been consulted in any public transactions. If then, ye nations of Europe, interest alone can exert its influence over you, listen to me once more: Your slaves stand in no need either of your generosity or of your counsels, in order to break the sacrilegious yoke which oppresses them. Nature speaks a more powerful language than philosophy, or interest. Some white people, already massacred, have expiated a part of our crimes; already have two colonies of fugitive negroes been established, to whom treaties and power give a perfect security from your attempts. Poison hath at different times been the instrument of their vengeance. Several have eluded your oppression by a voluntary death. These enterprizes are so many indications of the impending storm; and the negroes only want a chief, sufficiently courageous, to lead them on to vengeance and slaughter.

Where is this great man to be found, whom Nature, perhaps, owes to the honour of the human species? Where is this new Spartacus, who will not find a Crassus? Then will the *black code* be no more; and the *white code* will be dreadful, if the conqueror only regards the right of reprisals.

Till this revolution takes place, the negroes will groan under the yoke of oppression, the description of which cannot, but interest us more and more in their destiny.

*　　*　　*

REVIEW QUESTIONS

1. What is the philosophical basis of Raynal's condemnation of slavery?
2. According to Raynal, what abuses arise as a result of slavery?
3. What is the consequence of slavery for the enslaved?
4. What would be the consequence of emancipation for the colonial powers?

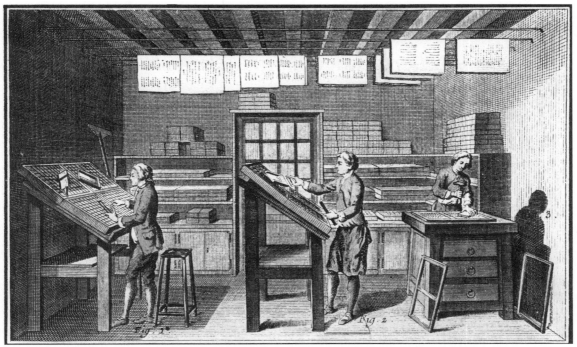

"ENGRAVINGS OF A PRINTSHOP"   DENIS DIDEROT AND JEAN D'ALEMBERT
FROM ENCYCLOPÉDIE, OU DICTIONNAIRE RAISONNÉ DES SCIENCES, DES ARTS ET DES MÉTIERS (1751–72)

*Intended to be a systematic dictionary of the sciences, arts and crafts, as the subtitle indicates,
the* Encyclopédie *was innovative as well as ambitious. It was the first compendium of knowledge to include contributions from many named authors, a model that is followed to this day.
It was also the first encyclopedia to pay particular attention to the mechanical arts. Its purpose, according to Diderot, who wrote the article on* encyclopédie, *was "to change the way
people think." How might the engravings before you help to achieve that purpose? What do
the engravings reveal about their creator's understanding of mechanical arts and mechanics
in a world dominated by reason? Why would representations of the mechanical arts, such as
printing, have been particularly important to Enlightenment thinkers?*

VOLTAIRE

FROM *Letters Concerning the English Nation*

François-Marie Arouet (1694–1778) was the son of a Parisian notary and royal official at the Cour des Comptes and became one of the fathers of the Enlightenment in France. As a youngster, he attached himself to his godfather, the abbé de Chateauneuf, a freethinker who introduced him to progressive circles in the French capital. He attended the Jesuit Collège Louis-le-Grand, where he graduated in 1711 with a degree in philosophy. Though he enrolled in law school, he decided on a literary career and frequented the salons of Paris. His first success came in 1718 with the staging of Oedipus. *At this point, he adopted the pen name of Voltaire. Legal difficulties that followed a brawl with the servants of the chevalier de Rohan resulted in Voltaire's exile to England. From 1726 to 1729 he was brought into direct contact with English philosophy, science, politics, and culture. Voltaire considered English thought and institutions the best in human history and devoted himself to their introduction to France on his return. His* Letters Concerning the English Nation *(1734) brought fame and notoriety. A warrant for his arrest forced him to flee once again. In fact, his career was marked by a series of legal difficulties and exiles: to Circey in Champagne in 1734, to Berlin and the court of Frederick II in 1750, to Geneva in 1752, and to Ferney in 1757. His lifelong commitments to freedom, toleration, reform, and empiricism made Voltaire one of the great figures of the Enlightenment.*

From *Letters Concerning the English Nation*, by F. Arouet, edited by Nicholas Cronk (Oxford: Oxford University Press, 1994), pp. 61–66.

*   *   *

Letter 13
On Mr. Locke

Perhaps no Man ever had a more judicious or more methodical Genius, or was a more acute Logician than Mr. *Locke,* and yet he was not deeply skill'd in the Mathematicks. This great Man could never subject himself to the tedious Fatigue of Calculations, nor to the dry Pursuit of Mathematical Truths, which do not at first present any sensible Objects to the Mind; and no one has given better Proofs than he, that 'tis possible for a Man to have a geometrical Head without the Assistance of Geometry. Before his Time, several great Philosophers had declar'd, in the most positive Terms, what the Soul of Man is; but as these absolutely knew nothing about it, they might very well be allow'd to differ entirely in opinion from one another.

In *Greece,* the infant Seat of Arts and of Errors, and where the Grandeur as well as Folly of the human Mind went such prodigious Lengths, the People us'd to reason about the Soul in the very same Manner as we do.

The divine *Anaxagoras,* in whose Honour an Altar was erected, for his having taught Mankind that the Sun was greater than *Peloponnesus,* that Snow was black, and that the Heavens were of

Stone; affirm'd that the Soul was an aerial Spirit, but at the same Time immortal. *Diogenes,* (not he who was a cynical Philosopher after having coyn'd base Money) declar'd that the Soul was a Portion of the Substance of God; an Idea which we must confess was very sublime. *Epicurus* maintain'd that it was compos'd of Parts in the same Manner as the Body.

Aristotle who has been explain'd a thousand Ways, because he is unintelligible, was of the Opinion, according to some of his Disciples, that the Understanding in all Men is one and the same Substance.

The divine *Plato,* Master of the divine *Aristotle,* and the divine *Socrates* Master of the divine *Plato,* us'd-to say that the Soul was corporeal and eternal. No doubt but the Demon of *Socrates* had instructed him in the Nature of it. Some People, indeed, pretend, that a Man who boasted his being attended by a familiar Genius, must infallibly be either a Knave or a Madman, but this kind of People are seldom satisfied with any Thing but Reason.

With regard to the Fathers of the Church, several in the primitive Ages believ'd that the Soul was human, and the Angels and God corporeal. Men naturally improve upon every System. St. *Bernard,* as Father *Mabillon* confesses, taught that the Soul after Death does not see God in the celestial Regions, but converses with *Christ's* human Nature only. However, he was not believ'd this Time on his bare Word; the Adventure of the Crusade having a little sunk the Credit of his Oracles. Afterwards a thousand Schoolmen arose, such as the irrefragable Doctor, the subtil Doctor, the angelic Doctor, the seraphic Doctor, and the cherubic Doctor, who were all sure that they had a very clear and distinct Idea of the Soul, and yet wrote in such a Manner, that one would conclude they were resolv'd no one should understand a Word in their Writings. Our *Des Cartes,* born not to discover the Errors of Antiquity, but to substitute his own in the Room of them; and hurried away by that systematic Spirit which throws a Cloud over the Minds of the greatest Men, thought he had demonstrated that the Soul is the same Thing as

Thought, in the same Manner as Matter, in his Opinion, is the same as Extension. He asserted, that Man thinks eternally, and that the Soul, at its coming into the Body, is inform'd with the whole Series of metaphysical Notions; knowing God, infinite Space, possessing all abstract Ideas; in a Word, completely endued with the most sublime Lights, which it unhappily forgets at its issuing from the Womb.

Father *Malbranche,* in his sublime Illusions, not only admitted innate Ideas, but did not doubt of our living wholly in God, and that God is, as it were, our Soul.

Such a Multitude of Reasoners having written the Romance of the Soul, a Sage at last arose, who gave, with an Air of the greatest Modesty, the History of it. Mr. *Locke* has display'd the human Soul, in the same Manner as an excellent Anatomist explains the Springs of the human Body. He every where takes the Light of Physicks for his Guide. He sometimes presumes to speak affirmatively, but then he presumes also to doubt. Instead of concluding at once what we know not, he examines gradually what we wou'd know. He takes an Infant at the Instant of his Birth; he traces, Step by Step, the Progress of his Understanding; examines what Things he has in common with Beasts, and what he possesses above them. Above all he consults himself; the being conscious that he himself thinks.

I shall leave, says he, to those who know more of this Matter than my self, the examining whether the Soul exists before or after the Organization of our Bodies. But I confess that 'tis my Lot to be animated with one of those heavy Souls which do not think always; and I am even so unhappy as not to conceive, that 'tis more necessary the Soul should think perpetually, than that Bodies shou'd be for ever in Motion.

With regard to my self, I shall boast that I have the Honour to be as stupid in this Particular as Mr. *Locke.* No one shall ever make me believe, that I think always; and I am as little inclin'd as he cou'd be, to fancy that some Weeks after I was conceiv'd, I was a very learned Soul; knowing at that Time a thousand Things which I forgot at my

Birth; and possessing when in the Womb, (tho' to no Manner of Purpose,) Knowledge which I lost the Instant I had occasion for it; and which I have never since been able to recover perfectly.

Mr. *Locke* after having destroy'd innate Ideas; after having fully renounc'd the Vanity of believing that we think always; after having laid down, from the most solid Principles, that Ideas enter the Mind through the Senses; having examin'd our simple and complex Ideas; having trac'd the human Mind through its several Operations; having shew'd that all the Languages in the World are imperfect, and the great Abuse that is made of Words every Moment; he at last comes to consider the Extent or rather the narrow Limits of human Knowledge. 'Twas in this Chapter he presum'd to advance, but very modestly, the following Words, 'We shall, perhaps, never be capable of knowing, whether a Being, purely material, thinks or not.' This sage Assertion was, by more Divines than one, look'd upon as a scandalous Declaration that the Soul is material and mortal. Some *Englishmen,* devout after their Way, sounded an Alarm. The Superstitious are the same in Society as Cowards in an Army; they themselves are seiz'd with a panic Fear, and communicate it to others. 'Twas loudly exclaim'd, that Mr. *Locke* intended to destroy Religion; nevertheless, Religion had nothing to do in the Affair, it being a Question purely Philosophical, altogether independent on Faith and Revelation. Mr. *Locke*'s Opponents needed but to examine, calmly and impartially, whether the declaring that Matter can think, implies a Contradiction; and whether God is able to communicate Thought to Matter. But Divines are too apt to begin their Declarations with saying, that God is offended when People differ from them in Opinion; in which they too much resemble the bad Poets, who us'd to declare publickly that *Boileau* spake irreverently of *Lewis* the Fourteenth, because he ridicul'd their stupid Productions. Bishop *Stillingfleet* got the Reputation of a calm and unprejudic'd Divine, because he did not expressly make use of injurious Terms in his Dispute with Mr. *Locke.* That Divine entred the Lists against him, but was defeated; for he argued as a Schoolman, and *Locke* as a Philosopher who was perfectly acquainted with the strong as well as the weak Side of the human Mind, and who fought with Weapons whose Temper he knew. If I might presume to give my Opinion on so delicate a Subject after Mr. *Locke,* I would say, that Men have long disputed on the Nature and the Immortality of the Soul. With regard to its Immortality tis impossible to give a Demonstration of it, since its Nature is still the Subject of Controversy; which however must be thoroughly understood, before a Person can be able to determine whether it be immortal or not. Human Reason is so little able, merely by its own Strength, to demonstrate the Immortality of the Soul, that 'twas absolutely necessary Religion should reveal it to us. 'Tis of Advantage to Society in general, that Mankind should believe the Soul to be immortal; Faith commands us to do this; nothing more is requir'd, and the Matter is clear'd up at once. But 'tis otherwise with respect to its Nature; 'tis of little Importance to Religion, which only requires the Soul to be virtuous, what Substance it may be made of. 'Tis a Clock which is given us to regulate, but the Artist has not told us of what Materials the Spring of this Clock is compos'd.

I am a Body and, I think, that's all I know of the Matter. Shall I ascribe to an unknown Cause, what I can so easily impute to the only second Cause I am acquainted with? Here all the School Philosophers interrupt me with their Arguments, and declare that there is only Extension and Solidity in Bodies, and that there they can have nothing but Motion and Figure. Now Motion, Figure, Extension and Solidity cannot form a Thought, and consequently the Soul cannot be Matter. All this, so often repeated, mighty Series of Reasoning, amounts to no more than this; I am absolutely ignorant what Matter is; I guess, but imperfectly, some Properties of it; now, I absolutely cannot tell whether these Properties may be joyn'd to Thought. As I therefore know nothing, I maintain positively that Matter cannot think. In this Manner do the Schools reason.

Mr. *Locke* address'd these Gentlemen in the candid, sincere Manner following. At least confess your selves to be as ignorant as I. Neither your Imaginations nor mine are able to comprehend in what manner a Body is susceptible of Ideas; and do you conceive better in what manner a Substance, of what kind soever, is susceptible of them? As you cannot comprehend either Matter or Spirit, why will you presume to assert any thing?

The superstitious Man comes afterwards, and declares, that all those must be burnt for the Good of their Souls, who so much as suspect that 'tis possible for the Body to think without any foreign Assistance. But what would these People say should they themselves be prov'd irreligious? And indeed, what Man can presume to assert, without being guilty at the same time of the greatest Impiety, that 'tis impossible for the Creator to form Matter with Thought and Sensation? Consider only, I beg you, what a Dilemma you bring yourselves into; you who confine in this Manner the Power of the Creator. Beasts have the same Organs, the same Sensations, the same Perceptions as we; they have Memory, and combine certain Ideas. In case it was not in the Power of God to animate Matter, and inform it with Sensation, the Consequence would be, either that Beasts are mere Machines, or that they have a spiritual Soul.

Methinks 'tis clearly evident that Beasts cannot be mere Machines, which I prove thus. God has given them the very same Organs of Sensation as to us: If therefore they have no Sensation, God has created a useless Thing; now according to your own Confession God does nothing in vain; he therefore did not create so many Organs of Sensation, merely for them to be uninform'd with this Faculty; consequently Beasts are not mere Machines. Beasts, according to your Assertion, cannot be animated with a spiritual Soul; you will therefore, in spight of your self, be reduc'd to this only Assertion, *viz.* that God has endued the Organs of Beasts, who are mere Matter, with the Faculties of Sensation and Perception, which you call Instinct in them. But why may not God if he pleases, communicate to our more delicate Organs, that Faculty of feeling, perceiving, and thinking, which we call human Reason? To whatever Side you turn, you are forc'd to acknowledge your own Ignorance, and the boundless Power of the Creator. Exclaim therefore no more against the sage, the modest Philosophy of Mr. *Locke*, which so far from interfering with Religion, would be of use to demonstrate the Truth of it, in case Religion wanted any such Support. For what Philosophy can be of a more religious Nature than that, which affirming nothing but what it conceives clearly; and conscious of its own Weakness, declares that we must always have recourse to God in our examining of the first Principles.

Besides, we must not be apprehensive, that any philosophical Opinion will ever prejudice the Religion of a Country. Tho' our Demonstrations clash directly with our Mysteries, that's nothing to the Purpose, for the latter are not less rever'd upon that Account by our Christian Philosophers, who know very well that the Objects of Reason and those of Faith are of a very different Nature. Philosophers will never form a religious Sect, the Reason of which is, their Writings are not calculated for the Vulgar, and they themselves are free from Enthusiasm. If we divide Mankind into twenty Parts, 'twill be found that nineteen of these consist of Persons employ'd in manual Labour, who will never know that such a Man as Mr. *Locke* existed. In the remaining twentieth Part how few are Readers? And among such as are so, twenty amuse themselves with Romances to one who studies Philosophy. The thinking Part of Mankind are confin'd to a very small Number, and these will never disturb the Peace and Tranquillity of the World.

Neither *Montagne, Locke, Bayle, Spinoza, Hobbes,* the Lord *Shaftsbury, Collins* nor *Toland* lighted up the Firebrand of Discord in their Countries; this has generally been the Work of Divines, who being at first puff'd up with the Ambition of becoming Chiefs of a Sect, soon grew very desirous of being at the Head of a Party. But what do I say? All the Works of the modern Philosophers put together will never make so much Noise as even the Dispute which arose among the *Franciscans,* merely about the Fashion of their Sleeves and of their Cowls.

Letter XIV

ON *DES CARTES* AND SIR *ISAAC NEWTON*.

A Frenchman who arrives in *London,* will find Philosophy, like every Thing else, very much chang'd there. He had left the World a *plenum,* and he now finds it a *vacuum.* At *Paris* the Universe is seen, compos'd of Vortices of subtile Matter; but nothing like it is seen in *London.* In *France,* 'tis the Pressure of the Moon that causes the Tides; but in *England* 'tis the Sea that gravitates towards the Moon; so that when you think that the Moon should make it Flood with us, those Gentlemen fancy it should be Ebb, which, very unluckily, cannot be prov'd. For to be able to do this, 'tis necessary the Moon and the Tides should have been enquir'd into, at the very instant of the Creation.

You'll observe farther, that the Sun, which in *France* is said to have nothing to do in the Affair, comes in here for very near a quarter of its Assistance. According to your *Cartesians,* every Thing is perform'd by an Impulsion, of which we have very little Notion; and according to Sir *Isaac Newton,* 'tis by an Attraction, the Cause of which is as much unknown to us. At *Paris* you imagine that the Earth is shap'd like a Melon, or of an oblique Figure; at *London* it has an oblate one. A *Cartesian* declares that Light exists in the Air; but a *Newtonian* asserts that it comes from the Sun in six Minutes and a half. The several Operations of your Chymistry are perform'd by Acids, Alkalies and subtile Matter; but Attraction prevails even in Chymistry among the *English.*

The very Essence of Things is totally chang'd. You neither are agreed upon the Definition of the Soul, nor on that of Matter. *Descartes,* as I observ'd in my last, maintains that the Soul is the same Thing with Thought, and Mr. *Locke* has given a pretty good Proof of the contrary.

Descartes asserts farther, that Extension alone constitutes Matter, but Sir *Isaac* adds Solidity to it.

How furiously contradictory are these Opinions!
Non nostrum inter vos tantas componere lites.
                    VIRGIL, Eclogue III.
'Tis not for us to end such great Disputes.

This famous *Newton,* this Destroyer of the *Cartesian* System, died in *March Anno* 1727. His Countrymen honour'd him in his Life-Time, and interr'd him as tho' he had been a King who had made his People happy.

The *English* read with the highest Satisfaction, and translated into their Tongue, the Elogium of Sir *Isaac Newton,* which Mr. *de Fontenelle,* spoke in the Academy of Sciences. Mr. *de Fontenelle* presides as Judge over Philosophers; and the *English* expected his Decision, as a solemn Declaration of the Superiority of the *English* Philosophy over that of the *French.* But when 'twas found that this Gentleman had compar'd *Des Cartes* to Sir *Isaac,* the whole Royal Society in *London* rose up in Arms. So far from acquiescing with Mr. *Fontenelle*'s Judgment, they criticis'd his Discourse. And even several (who however were not the ablest Philosophers in that Body) were offended at the Comparison; and for no other Reason but because *Des Cartes* was a *Frenchman.*

It must be confess'd that these two great Men differ'd very much in Conduct, in Fortune, and in Philosophy.

Nature had indulg'd *Des Cartes* a shining and strong Imagination, whence he became a very singular Person both in private Life, and in his Manner of Reasoning. This Imagination could not conceal itself even in his philosophical Works, which are every where adorn'd with very shining, ingenious Metaphors and Figures. Nature had almost made him a Poet; and indeed he wrote a Piece of Poetry for the Entertainment of *Christina* Queen of *Sweden,* which however was suppress'd in Honour to his Memory.

He embrac'd a Military Life for some Time, and afterwards becoming a complete Philosopher, he did not think the Passion of Love derogatory to his Character. He had by his Mistress a Daughter call'd *Froncine,* who died young, and was very much regretted by him. Thus he experienc'd every Passion incident to Mankind.

He was a long Time of Opinion, that it would be necessary for him to fly from the Society of his Fellow Creatures, and especially from his native Country, in order to enjoy the Happiness of cultivating his philosophical Studies in full Liberty.

Des Cartes was very right, for his Cotemporaries were not knowing enough to improve and enlighten his Understanding, and were capable of little else than of giving him Uneasiness.

He left *France* purely to go in search of Truth, which was then persecuted by the wretched Philosophy of the Schools. However, he found that Reason was as much disguis'd and deprav'd in the Universities of *Holland,* into which he withdrew, as in his own Country. For at the Time that the *French* condemn'd the only Propositions of his Philosophy which were true, he was persecuted by the pretended Philosophers of *Holland,* who understood him no better; and who, having a nearer View of his Glory, hated his Person the more, so that he was oblig'd to leave *Utrecht. Des Cartes* was injuriously accus'd of being an Atheist, the last Refuge of religious Scandal: And he who had employ'd all the Sagacity and Penetration of his Genius, in searching for new Proofs of the Existence of a God, was suspected to believe there was no such Being.

Such a Persecution from all Sides, must necessarily suppose a most exalted Merit as well as a very distinguish'd Reputation, and indeed he possess'd both. Reason at that Time darted a Ray upon the World thro' the Gloom of the Schools, and the Prejudices of popular Superstition. At last his Name spread so universally, that the *French* were desirous of bringing him back into his native Country by Rewards, and accordingly offer'd him an annual Pension of a thousand Crowns. Upon these Hopes *Des Cartes* return'd to *France;* paid the Fees of his Patent, which was sold at that Time, but no Pension was settled upon him. Thus disappointed, he return'd to his Solitude in *North-Holland,* where he again pursued the Study of Philosophy, whilst the great *Galileo,* at fourscore

Years of Age, was groaning in the Prisons of the Inquisition, only for having demonstrated the Earth's Motion.

At last *Des Cartes* was snatch'd from the World in the Flower of his Age at·*Stockholm.* His Death was owing to a bad Regimen, and he expir'd in the Midst of some *Literati* who were his Enemies, and under the Hands of a Physician to whom he was odious.

The Progress of Sir *Isaac Newton*'s Life was quite different. He liv'd happy, and very much honour'd in his native Country, to the Age of fourscore and five Years.

'Twas his peculiar Felicity, not only to be born in a Country of Liberty, but in an Age when all scholastic Impertinencies were banish'd from the World. Reason alone was cultivated, and Mankind cou'd only be his Pupil, not his Enemy.

One very singular Difference in the Lives of these two great Men is, that Sir *Isaac,* during the long Course of Years he enjoy'd was never sensible to any Passion, was not subject to the common Frailties of Mankind, nor ever had any Commerce with Women; a Circumstance which was assur'd me by the Physician and Surgeon who attended him in his last Moments.

We may admire Sir *Isaac Newton* on this Occasion, but then we must not censure *Des Cartes.*

The Opinion that generally prevails in *England* with regard to these two Philosophers is, that the latter was a Dreamer, and the former a Sage.

Very few People in *England* read *Descartes,* whose Works indeed are now useless. On the other Side, but a small Number peruse those of Sir *Isaac,* because to do this the Student must be deeply skill'd in the Mathematicks, otherwise those Works will be unintelligible to him. But notwithstanding this, these great Men are the Subject of every One's Discourse. Sir *Isaac Newton* is allow'd every Advantage, whilst *Des Cartes* is not indulg'd a single one. According to some, 'tis to the former that we owe the Discovery of a *Vacuum,* that the Air is a heavy Body, and the Invention of Telescopes. In a Word, Sir *Isaac Newton* is here as the *Hercules* of fabulous Story, to whom the Ignorant ascrib'd all the Feats of ancient Heroes.

In a Critique that was made in *London* on Mr. *de Fontenelle*'s Discourse, the Writer presum'd to assert that *Des Cartes* was not a great Geometrician. Those who make such a Declaration may justly be reproach'd with flying in their Master's Face. *Des Cartes* extended the Limits of Geometry as far beyond the Place where he found them, as Sir *Isaac* did after him. The former first taught the Method of expressing Curves by Equations. This Geometry which, Thanks to him for it, is now grown common, was so abstruse in his Time, that not so much as one Professor would undertake to explain it; and *Schotten* in *Holland,* and *Format* in *France,* were the only Men who understood it.

He applied this geometrical and inventive Genius to Dioptricks, which, when treated of by him, became a new Art. And if he was mistaken in some Things, the Reason of that is, a Man who discovers a new Tract of Land cannot at once know all the Properties of the Soil. Those who come after him, and make these Lands fruitful, are at least oblig'd to him for the Discovery. I will not deny but that there are innumerable Errors in the rest of *Des Cartes*'s Works.

Geometry was a Guide he himself had in some Measure fashion'd, which would have conducted him safely thro' the several Paths of natural Philosophy. Nevertheless he at last abandon'd this Guide, and gave entirely into the Humour of forming Hypotheses; and then Philosophy was no more than an ingenious Romance, fit only to amuse the Ignorant. He was mistaken in the Nature of the Soul, in the Proofs of the Existence of a God, in Matter, in the Laws of Motion, and in the Nature of Light. He admitted innate Ideas, he invented new Elements, he created a World; he made Man according to his own Fancy; and 'tis justly said, that the Man of *Des Cartes* is in Fact that of *Des Cartes* only, very different from the real one.

He push'd his metaphysical Errors so far, as to declare that two and two make four, for no other Reason but because God would have it so. How-

ever, 'twill not be making him too great a Compliment if we affirm that he was valuable even in his Mistakes. He deceiv'd himself, but then it was at least in a methodical Way. He destroy'd all the absurd Chimæra's with which Youth had been infatuated for two thousand Years. He taught his Contemporaries how to reason, and enabled them to employ his own Weapons against himself. If *Des Cartes* did not pay in good Money, he however did great Service in crying down that of a base Alloy.

I indeed believe, that very few will presume to compare his Philosophy in any respect with that of Sir *Isaac Newton.* The former is an Essay, the latter a Master-Piece: But then the Man who first brought us to the Path of Truth, was perhaps as great a Genius as he who afterwards conducted us through it.

Des Cartes gave Sight to the Blind. These saw the Errors of Antiquity and of the Sciences. The Path he struck out is since become boundless. *Rohault*'s little Work was during some Years a complete System of Physicks; but now all the Transactions of the several Academies in *Europe* put together do not form so much as the Beginning of a System. In fathoming this Abyss no Bottom has been found. We are now to examine what Discoveries Sir *Isaac Newton* has made in it.

*   *   *

REVIEW QUESTIONS

1. How does Voltaire describe the scientific revolution?
2. What are its consequences?
3. What, according to Voltaire, was the particular contribution of John Locke?
4. Why does Voltaire single out Descartes and Newton?
5. What differentiates their methods?
6. Why, according to Voltaire, was Descartes persecuted and Newton not?

DAVID HUME

FROM *A Treatise of Human Nature*

David Hume (1711–1776) was born the younger son of a gentry family in Scotland. Though he attended the University of Edinburgh, he found formal education distasteful and applied himself instead to an intense program of reading. After a nervous breakdown in 1729 and an unsuccessful foray into business, Hume moved to France in 1734. During his stay there, which lasted until 1737, he devoted himself to studying and to writing A Treatise of Human Nature *(1739–1740). Though he later dismissed it as immature, it became his most influential work. In it, he introduced his notion of skepticism, which restricted human knowledge to the experience of ideas and impressions and denied the ability to verify their ultimate truth. Nonetheless, given the cautious, persistent exercise of reason, humankind could gather knowledge that was reliable and useful. As a historian, economist, and essayist, Hume was one of the most influential figures of the middle years of the Enlightenment.*

From *A Treatise of Human Nature*, by David Hume, edited by L. A. Selby-Biggs (Oxford: Clarendon Press, 1888), pp. xvii–xxiii.

Introduction

Nothing is more usual and more natural for those, who pretend to discover any thing new to the world in philosophy and the sciences, than to insinuate the praises of their own systems, by decrying all those, which have been advanced before them. And indeed were they content with lamenting that ignorance, which we still lie under in the most important questions, that can come before the tribunal of human reason, there are few, who have an acquaintance with the sciences, that would not readily agree with them. 'Tis easy for one of judgment and learning, to perceive the weak foundation even of those systems, which have obtained the greatest credit, and have carried their pretensions highest to accurate and profound reasoning. Principles taken upon trust, consequences lamely deduced from them, want of coherence in the parts, and of evidence in the whole, these are every where to be met with in the systems of the most eminent philosophers, and seem to have drawn disgrace upon philosophy itself.

Nor is there requir'd such profound knowledge to discover the present imperfect condition of the sciences, but even the rabble without doors may judge from the noise and clamour, which they hear, that all goes not well within. There is nothing which is not the subject of debate, and in which men of learning are not of contrary opinions. The most trivial question escapes not our controversy, and in the most momentous we are not able to give any certain decision. Disputes are multiplied, as if every thing was uncertain; and these disputes are managed with the greatest warmth, as if every thing was certain. Amidst all this bustle 'tis not reason, which carries the prize, but eloquence; and no man needs ever despair of gaining proselytes to the most extravagant hypothesis, who has art enough to represent it in any favourable colours. The victory is not gained by the men at arms, who manage the pike and the sword; but by the trumpeters, drummers, and musicians of the army.

From hence in my opinion arises that common prejudice against metaphysical reasonings of all kinds, even amongst those, who profess themselves scholars, and have a just value for every other part of literature. By metaphysical reasonings, they do not understand those on any particular branch of science, but every kind of argument, which is any way abstruse, and requires some attention to be comprehended. We have so often lost our labour in such researches, that we commonly reject them without hesitation, and resolve, if we must for ever be a prey to errors and delusions, that they shall at least be natural and entertaining. And indeed nothing but the most determined scepticism, along with a great degree of indolence, can justify this aversion to metaphysics. For if truth be at all within the reach of human capacity, 'tis certain it must lie very deep and abstruse; and to hope we shall arrive at it without pains, while the greatest geniuses have failed with the utmost pains, must certainly be esteemed sufficiently vain and presumptuous. I pretend to no such advantage in the philosophy I am going to unfold, and would esteem it a strong presumption against it, were it so very easy and obvious.

'Tis evident, that all the sciences have a relation, greater or less, to human nature; and that however wide any of them may seem to run from it, they still return back by one passage or another. Even *Mathematics, Natural Philosophy, and Natural Religion,* are in some measure dependent on the science of Man; since they lie under the cognizance of men, and are judged of by their powers and faculties. 'Tis impossible to tell what changes and improvements we might make in these sciences were we thoroughly acquainted with the extent and force of human understanding, and cou'd explain the nature of the ideas we employ, and of the operations we perform in our reasonings. And these improvements are the more to be hoped for in natural religion, as it is not content with instructing us in the nature of superior powers, but carries its views farther, to their disposition towards us, and our duties towards them; and consequently we ourselves are not only the beings, that reason, but also one of the objects, concerning which we reason.

If therefore the sciences of Mathematics, Natural Philosophy, and Natural Religion, have such a dependence on the knowledge of man, what may be expected in the other sciences, whose connexion with human nature is more close and intimate? The sole end of logic is to explain the principles and operations of our reasoning faculty, and the nature of our ideas: morals and criticism regard our tastes and sentiments: and politics consider men as united in society, and dependent on each other. In these four sciences of *Logic, Morals, Criticism, and Politics,* is comprehended almost every thing, which it can any way import us to be acquainted with, or which can tend either to the improvement or ornament of the human mind.

Here then is the only expedient, from which we can hope for success in our philosophical researches, to leave the tedious ling'ring method, which we have hitherto followed, and instead of taking now and then a castle or village on the frontier, to march up directly to the capital or center of these sciences, to human nature itself; which being once masters of, we may every where else hope for an easy victory. From this station we may extend our conquests over all those sciences, which more intimately concern human life, and may afterwards proceed at leisure to discover more fully those, which are the objects of pure curiosity. There is no question of importance, whose decision is not compriz'd in the science of man; and there is none, which can be decided with any certainty, before we become acquainted with that science. In pretending therefore to explain the principles of human nature, we in effect propose a compleat system of the sciences, built on a foundation almost entirely new, and the only one upon which they can stand with any security.

And as the science of man is the only solid foundation for the other sciences, so the only solid foundation we can give to this science itself must be laid on experience and observation. 'Tis no astonishing reflection to consider, that the application of experimental philosophy to moral subjects should come after that to natural at the distance of above a whole century; since we find in fact, that there was about the same interval betwixt the origins of these sciences; and that reckoning from Thales to Socrates, the space of time is nearly equal to that betwixt my Lord Bacon and some late philosophers in *England,* who have begun to put the science of man on a new footing, and have engaged the attention, and excited the curiosity of the public. So true it is, that however other nations may rival us in poetry, and excel us in some other agreeable arts, the improvements in reason and philosophy can only be owing to a land of toleration and of liberty.

Nor ought we to think, that this latter improvement in the science of man will do less honour to our native country than the former in natural philosophy, but ought rather to esteem it a greater glory, upon account of the greater importance of that science, as well as the necessity it lay under of such a reformation. For to me it seems evident, that the essence of the mind being equally unknown to us with that of external bodies, it must be equally impossible to form any notion of its powers and qualities otherwise than from careful and exact experiments, and the observation of those particular effects, which result from its different circumstances and situations. And tho' we must endeavour to render all our principles as universal as possible, by tracing up our experiments to the utmost, and explaining all effects from the simplest and fewest causes, 'tis still certain we cannot go beyond experience; and any hypothesis, that pretends to discover the ultimate original qualities of human nature, ought at first to be rejected as presumptuous and chimerical.

I do not think a philosopher, who would apply himself so earnestly to the explaining the ultimate principles of the soul, would show himself a great master in that very science of human nature, which he pretends to explain, or very knowing in what is naturally satisfactory to the mind of man. For nothing is more certain, than that despair has almost the same effect upon us with enjoyment, and that we are no sooner acquainted with the impossibility of satisfying any desire, than the desire itself vanishes. When we see, that we have arrived at the utmost extent of human reason, we sit down contented; tho' we be perfectly satisfied in the main of our ignorance, and perceive that we can give no reason for our most general and most refined principles, beside our experience of their reality; which is the reason of the mere vulgar, and what it required no study at first to have discovered for the most particular and most extraordinary phaenomenon. And as this impossibility of making any farther progress is enough to satisfy the reader, so the writer may derive a more delicate satisfaction from the free confession of his ignorance, and from his prudence in avoiding that error, into which so many have fallen, of imposing their conjectures and hypotheses on the world for the most certain principles. When this mutual contentment and satisfaction can be obtained betwixt the master and scholar, I know not what more we can require of our philosophy.

But if this impossibility of explaining ultimate principles should be esteemed a defect in the science of man, I will venture to affirm, that 'tis a defect common to it with all the sciences, and all the arts, in which we can employ ourselves, whether they be such as are cultivated in the schools of the philosophers, or practised in the shops of the meanest artizans. None of them can go beyond experience, or establish any principles which are not founded on that authority. Moral philosophy has, indeed, this peculiar disadvantage, which is not found in natural, that in collecting its experiments, it cannot make them purposely, with premeditation, and after such a manner as to satisfy itself concerning every particular difficulty which may arise. When I am at a loss to know the effects of one body upon another in any situation, I need only put them in that situation, and observe what results from it. But should I endeavour to clear up after the same manner any doubt in moral philosophy, by placing myself in the same case with that which I consider, 'tis evident this reflection and premeditation would so disturb the operation of my natural principles, as must render it impossible to form any just conclusion from the phaenomenon. We must therefore glean up our experiments in this science from a cautious observation of human life, and take them as they appear in the common course of the world, by men's behaviour in company, in affairs, and in their pleasures. Where experiments of this kind are judiciously collected and compared, we may hope to establish on them a science, which will not be inferior in certainty, and will be much superior in utility to any other of human comprehension.

*   *   *

REVIEW QUESTIONS

1. To what does Hume attribute all the disputes in the sciences?
2. According to Hume, what is the science of man? What are its methods and goals?
3. Why must one understand human reason before studying the science of man?

BARON DE LA BRÈDE ET DE MONTESQUIEU

FROM *The Spirit of Laws*

Charles-Louis de Secondat, baron de La Brède et de Montesquieu (1689–1755), was a French philosopher, historian, and satirist. He was born at the family chateau of La Brède near Bordeaux. His great-grandfather, a Calvinist, had been rewarded with a title of nobility for his service to Henry IV. In the next generation, however, the family had converted to Catholicism and had entered the judicial nobility by purchasing offices in the Parlement of Bordeaux. Charles-Louis de Secondat inherited one of these offices, that of presiding judge of the criminal division, in 1712 and held it for eleven years. Montesquieu studied law at the University of Bordeaux and married Jeanne de Lartique, a practicing Calvinist who risked persecution for her faith. This and his own background may explain Montesquieu's lifelong championship of religious toleration. He entered the literary world with the publication of his Persian Letters *(1721). Shortly thereafter Montesquieu moved to Paris and joined the intellectual world of the salon. His most influential work, at least among his contemporaries, was* The Spirit of Laws *(1748). By 1750, twenty-two editions had appeared, and it had been translated into every major European language. Montesquieu explored the role of law in shaping political society and sought theoretical and practical responses to the problem of despotism. He envisioned political order as a human body, possessed of a dynamic balance among its various parts. A healthy political order contained inner mechanisms to maintain its balance. An ideal example of such separation and balance of power was the English system of monarch and Parliament. These ideas made Montesquieu one of the most widely read and influential figures of the Enlightenment.*

From *The Spirit of Laws*, vol. 1, translated by Thomas Nugent (London: Bell, 1901).

Book XII
Of the Laws that Establish Political Liberty, in Relation to the Subject

I. It is not sufficient to have treated of political liberty in relation to the constitution; we must examine it likewise in the relation it bears to the subject.

We have observed that in the former case it arises from a certain distribution of the three powers; but in the latter we must consider it in another light. It consists in security, or in the opinion people have of their country.

The constitution may happen to be free, and the subject not. The subject may be free, and not the constitution. In those cases, the constitution will be free by right, and not in fact; the subject will be free in fact, and not by right.

It is the disposition only of the laws, and even of the fundamental laws, that constitutes liberty in relation to the constitution. But as it regards the subject: manners, customs, or received examples may give rise to it, and particular civil laws may encourage it, as we shall presently observe.

Further, as in most states liberty is more checked or depressed than their constitution requires, it is proper to treat of the particular laws that in each constitution are apt to assist or check the principle of liberty which each state is capable of receiving.

II. Philosophic liberty consists in the free exercise of the will; or at least, if we must speak agreeably to all systems, in an opinion that we have the free exercise of our will. Political liberty consists in securing, or, at least, in the opinion that we enjoy security.

This security is never more dangerously attacked than in public or private accusations. It is, therefore, on the goodness of criminal laws that the liberty of the subject principally depends.

Criminal laws did not receive their full perfection all at once. Even in places where liberty has been most sought after, it has not been always found. Aristotle informs us that at Cumae the parents of the accuser might be witnesses. So imperfect was the law under the kings of Rome, that

Servius Tullius pronounced sentence against the children of Ancus Martius, who were charged with having assassinated the king, his father-in-law. Under the first kings of France, Clotarius made a law that nobody should be condemned without being heard, which shows that a contrary custom had prevailed in some particular case or among some barbarous people. It was Charondas that first established penalties against false witnesses. When the subject has no fence to secure his innocence, he has none for his liberty.

The knowledge already acquired in some countries, or that may be hereafter attained in others, concerning the surest rules to be observed in criminal judgments, is more interesting to mankind than any other thing in the world.

Liberty can be founded on the practice of this knowledge only; and supposing a state to have the best laws imaginable in this respect, a person tried under that state, and condemned to be hanged the next day, would have much more liberty than a pasha enjoys in Turkey.

Those laws which condemn a man to death on the deposition of a single witness are fatal to liberty. In reason there should be two, because a witness who affirms, and the accused who denies, make an equal balance, and a third must incline the scale.

The Greeks and Romans required one voice more to condemn; but our French laws insist upon two. The Greeks pretend that their custom was established by the gods; but this more justly may be said of ours.

III. Liberty is in perfection when criminal laws derive each punishment from the particular nature of the crime. There are then no arbitrary decisions; the punishment does not flow from the capriciousness of the legislator, but from the very nature of the thing; and man uses no violence to man.

There are four sorts of crimes. Those of the first species are prejudicial to religion, the second to morals, the third to the public tranquillity, and the fourth to the security of the subject. The punishments inflicted for these crimes ought to proceed from the nature of each of these species.

In the class of crimes that concern religion, I rank only those which attack it directly, such as all simple sacrileges. For as to crimes that disturb the exercise of it, they are of the nature of those which prejudice the tranquillity or security of the subject, and ought to be referred to those classes.

In order to derive the punishment of simple sacrileges from the nature of the thing, it should consist in depriving people of the advantages conferred by religion in expelling them out of the temples, in a temporary or perpetual exclusion from the society of the faithful, in shunning their presence, in execrations, comminations, and conjurations.

In things that prejudice the tranquillity or security of the state, secret actions are subject to human jurisdiction. But in those which offend the Deity, where there is no public act, there can be no criminal matter; the whole passes between man and God, who knows the measure and time of his vengeance. Now, if magistrates confounding things should inquire also into hidden sacrileges, this inquisition would be directed to a kind of action that does not at all require it; the liberty of the subject would be subverted by arming the zeal of timorous as well as of presumptuous consciences against him.

The mischief arises from a notion which some people have entertained of revenging the cause of the Deity. But we must honor the Deity and leave him to avenge his own cause. And, indeed, were we to be directed by such a notion, where would be the end of punishments? If human laws are to avenge the cause of an infinite Being, they will be directed by his infinity, and not by the weakness, ignorance, and caprice of man.

A historian of Provence relates a fact which furnishes us with an excellent description of the consequences that may arise in weak capacities from the notion of avenging the Deity's cause. A Jew was accused of having blasphemed against the Virgin Mary, and upon conviction was condemned to be flayed alive. A strange spectacle was then exhibited: gentlemen masked, with knives in their hands, mounted the scaffold, and drove away the executioner, in order to be the avengers them-

selves of the honor of the blessed Virgin. I do not here choose to anticipate the reflections of the reader.

The second class consists of those crimes which are prejudicial to morals. Such is the violation of public or private continence—that is, of the police directing the manner in which the pleasure annexed to the conjunction of the sexes is to be enjoyed. The punishment of those crimes ought to be also derived from the nature of the thing; the privation of such advantages as society has attached to the purity of morals, fines, shame, necessity of concealment, public infamy, expulsion from home and society, and, in fine, all such punishments as belong to a corrective jurisdiction, are sufficient to repress the temerity of the two sexes. In effect these things are less founded on malice than on carelessness and self-neglect.

We speak here of none but crimes which relate merely to morals, for as to those that are also prejudicial to the public security, such as rapes, they belong to the fourth species.

The crimes of the third class are those which disturb the public tranquillity. The punishments ought therefore to be derived from the nature of the thing, and to be in relation to this tranquillity; such as imprisonment, exile, and other like chastisements, proper for reclaiming turbulent spirits, and obliging them to conform to the established order.

I confine those crimes that injure the public tranquillity to things which imply a bare offense against the police; for as to those which by disturbing the public peace attack at the same time the security of the subject, they ought to be ranked in the fourth class.

The punishments inflicted upon the latter crimes are such as are properly distinguished by that name. They are a kind of retaliation, by which the society refuses security to a member who has actually or intentionally deprived another of his security. These punishments are derived from the nature of the thing, founded on reason, and drawn from the very source of good and evil. A man deserves death when he has violated the security of the subject so far as to deprive, or attempt to deprive, another man of his life. This punishment of death is the remedy, as it were, of a sick society. When there is a breach of security with regard to property, there may be some reasons for inflicting a capital punishment; but it would be much better, and perhaps more natural, that crimes committed against the security of property should be punished with the loss of property; and this ought, indeed, to be the case if men's fortunes were common or equal. But as those who have no property of their own are generally the readiest to attack that of others, it has been found necessary, instead of a pecuniary, to substitute a corporal, punishment.

All that I have here advanced is founded in Nature, and extremely favorable to the liberty of the subject.

IV. It is an important maxim that we ought to be very circumspect in the prosecution of witchcraft and heresy. The accusation of these two crimes may be vastly injurious to liberty, and productive of infinite oppression, if the legislator knows not how to set bounds to it. For as it does not directly point at a person's actions, but at his character, it grows dangerous in proportion to the ignorance of the people; and then a man is sure to be always in danger, because the most exceptional conduct, the purest morals, and the constant practice of every duty in life are not a sufficient security against the suspicion of his being guilty of the like crimes.

Under Manuel Comnenus, the Protestator was accused of having conspired against the emperor, and of having employed for that purpose some secrets that render men invisible. It is mentioned in the life of this emperor that Aaron was detected as he was poring over a book of Solomon's, the reading of which was sufficient to conjure up whole legions of devils. Now, by supposing a power in witchcraft to rouse the infernal spirits to arms, people look upon a man whom they call a sorcerer as the person in the world most likely to disturb and subvert society, and of course they are disposed to punish him with the utmost severity.

But their indignation increases when witchcraft is supposed to have the power of subverting religion. The history of Constantinople informs us that in consequence of a revelation made to a bishop of a miracle having ceased because of the magic practices of a certain person, both that person and his son were put to death. On how many surprising things did not this single crime depend!—that revelations should not be uncommon, that the bishop should be favored with one, that it was real, that there had been a miracle in the case, that this miracle had ceased, that there was an art magic, that magic could subvert religion, that this particular person was a magician, and, in fine, that he had committed that magic act.

The Emperor Theodorus Lascarus attributed his illness to witchcraft. Those who were accused of this crime had no other resource left than to handle a red-hot iron without being hurt. Thus among the Greeks a person ought to have been a sorcerer to be able to clear himself of the imputation of witchcraft. Such was the excess of their stupidity that to the most dubious crime in the world they joined the most dubious proofs of innocence.

Under the reign of Philip the Long, the Jews were expelled from France, being accused of having poisoned the springs with their lepers. So absurd an accusation ought to make us doubt all those that are founded on public hatred.

I have not here asserted that heresy ought not to be punished; I said only that we ought to be extremely circumspect in punishing it.

V. God forbid that I should have the least inclination to diminish the public horror against a crime which religion, morality, and civil government equally condemn. It ought to be proscribed, were it only for its communicating to one sex the weaknesses of the other, and for leading people by a scandalous prostitution of their youth to an ignominious old age. What I shall say concerning it will in no way diminish its infamy, being leveled only against the tyranny that may abuse the very horror we ought to have against the vice.

As a natural circumstance of this crime is secrecy, there are frequent instances of its having been punished by legislators upon the deposition of a child. This was opening a very wide door to calumny. "Justinian," says Procopius, "published a law against this crime; he ordered an inquiry to be made not only against those who were guilty of it, after the enacting of that law, but even before. The deposition of a single witness, sometimes of a child, sometimes of a slave, was sufficient, especially against such as were rich, and against those of the green faction."

It is very odd that these three crimes—witchcraft, heresy, and that against Nature, of which the first might easily be proved not to exist, the second to be susceptible of an infinite number of distinctions, interpretations, and limitations, the third to be often obscure and uncertain—it is very odd, I say, that these three crimes should among us be punished with fire.

I may venture to affirm that the crime against Nature will never make any great progress in society, unless people are prompted to it by some particular custom, as among the Greeks, where the youths of that country performed all their exercises naked; as among us, where domestic education is disused; as among the Asiatics, where particular persons have a great number of women whom they despise, while others can have none at all. Let there be no customs preparatory to this crime; let it, like every other violation of morals, be severely proscribed by the civil magistrate; and Nature will soon defend or resume her rights. Nature, that fond, that indulgent parent, has strewed her pleasures with a bounteous hand, and while she fills us with delights she prepares us, by means of our issue, in whom we see ourselves, as it were, reproduced—she prepares us, I say, for future satisfactions of a more exquisite kind than those very delights.

VI. It is determined by the laws of China that whosoever shows any disrespect to the emperor is to be punished with death. As they do not mention in what this disrespect consists, everything may furnish a pretext to take away a man's life, and to exterminate any family whatsoever.

Two persons of that country who were employed to write the court gazette, having inserted some circumstances relating to a certain fact that was not true, it was pretended that to tell a lie in the court gazette was a disrespect shown to the court, in consequence of which they were put to death. A prince of the blood having inadvertently made some mark on a memorial signed with the red pencil by the emperor, it was determined that he had behaved disrespectfully to the sovereign, which occasioned one of the most terrible persecutions against that family that ever was recorded in history.

If the crime of high treason be indeterminate, this alone is sufficient to make the government degenerate into arbitrary power. I shall descant more largely on this subject when I come to treat of the composition of laws.

VII. It is likewise a shocking abuse to give the appellation of high treason to an action that does not deserve it. By an imperial law it was decreed that those who called in question the prince's judgment, or doubted the merit of such as he had chosen for a public office, should be prosecuted as guilty of sacrilege. Surely it was the cabinet council and the prince's favorites who invented that crime. By another law it was determined that whosoever made any attempt to injure the ministers and officers belonging to the sovereign should be deemed guilty of high treason, as if he had attempted to injure the sovereign himself. This law is owing to two princes remarkable for their weaknesses—princes who were led by their ministers as flocks by shepherds; princes who were slaves in the palace, children in the council, strangers to the army; princes, in fine, who preserved their authority only by giving it away every day. Some of those favorites conspired against their sovereigns. Nay, they did more, they conspired against the empire—they called in barbarous nations; and when the emperors wanted to stop their progress the state was so enfeebled as to be under a necessity of infringing the law, and of exposing itself to the crime of high treason in order to punish those favorites.

And yet this is the very law which the judge of Monsieur de Cinq-Mars built upon when endeavoring to prove that the latter was guilty of the crime of high treason for attempting to remove

Cardinal Richelieu from the ministry. He says: "Crimes that aim at the persons of ministers are deemed by the imperial constitutions of equal consequence with those which are leveled against the emperor's own person. A minister discharges his duty to his prince and to his country; to attempt, therefore, to remove him is endeavoring to deprive the former one of his arms, and the latter of part of its power." It is impossible for the meanest tools of power to express themselves in more servile language.

By another law of Valentinian, Theodosius, and Arcadius, false coiners are declared guilty of high treason. But is not this confounding the ideas of things? Is not the very horror of high treason diminished by giving that name to another crime?

Paulinus having written to the Emperor Alexander that "he was preparing to prosecute for high treason a judge who had decided contrary to his edict," the emperor answered that "under his reign there was no such thing as indirect high treason."

Faustinian wrote to the same emperor, that as he had sworn by the prince's life never to pardon his slave, he found himself thereby obliged to perpetuate his wrath, lest he should incur the guilt of *laesa majestas*. Upon which the emperor made answer, "Your fears are groundless, and you are a stranger to my principles."

It was determined by a senatus-consultum that whosoever melted down any of the emperor's statues which happened to be rejected should not be deemed guilty of high treason. The Emperors Severus and Antoninus wrote to Pontius that those who sold unconsecrated statues of the emperor should not be charged with high treason. The same princes wrote to Julius Cassianus that if a person in flinging a stone should by chance strike one of the emperor's statues he should not be liable to a prosecution for high treason. The Julian law requires this sort of limitations; for in virtue of this law the crime of high treason was charged not only upon those who melted down the emperor's statues, but likewise on those who committed any suchlike action, which made it an arbitrary crime. When a number of crimes of *laesa*

majestas had been established, they were obliged to distinguish the several sorts. Hence Ulpian, the civilian, after saying that the accusation of *laesa majestas* did not die with the criminal, adds that this does not relate to all the treasonable acts established by the Julian law, but only to that which implies an attempt against the empire, or against the emperor's life.

There was a law passed in England under Henry VIII, by which whoever predicted the king's death was declared guilty of high treason. This law was extremely vague; the terror of despotic power is so great that it recoils upon those who exercise it. In this king's last illness, the physicians would not venture to say he was in danger; and surely they acted very right.

VIII. Marsyas dreamed that he had cut Dionysius' throat. Dionysius put him to death, pretending that he would never have dreamed of such a thing by night if he had not thought of it by day. This was a most tyrannical action, for though it had been the subject of his thoughts, yet he had made no attempt toward it. The laws do not take upon them to punish any other than overt acts.

IX. Nothing renders the crime of high treason more arbitrary than declaring people guilty of it for indiscreet speeches. Speech is so subject to interpretation; there is so great a difference between indiscretion and malice; and frequently so little is there of the latter in the freedom of expression, that the law can hardly subject people to a capital punishment for words unless it expressly declares what words they are.

Words do not constitute an overt act; they remain only in idea. When considered by themselves, they have generally no determinate signification, for this depends on the tone in which they are uttered. It often happens that in repeating the same words they have not the same meaning; this depends on their connection with other things, and sometimes more is signified by silence than by any expression whatever. Since there can be nothing so equivocal and ambiguous as all this, how is it possible to convert it into a crime of high treason? Wherever this law is established, there is an end not only of liberty, but even of its very shadow.

In the manifesto of the late Czarina against the family of the Dolgorukis, one of these princes is condemned to death for having uttered some indecent words concerning her person; another, for having maliciously interpreted her imperial laws, and for having offended her sacred person by disrespectful expressions.

Not that I pretend to diminish the just indignation of the public against those who presume to stain the glory of their sovereign; what I mean is, that if despotic princes are willing to moderate their power, a milder chastisement would be more proper on those occasions than the charge of high treason—a thing always terrible even to innocence itself.

Overt acts do not happen every day; they are exposed to the eye of the public, and a false charge with regard to matters of fact may be easily detected. Words carried into action assume the nature of that action. Thus a man who goes into a public marketplace to incite the subject to revolt incurs the guilt of high treason, because the words are joined to the action, and partake of its nature. It is not the words that are punished, but an action in which words are employed. They do not become criminal but when they are annexed to a criminal action; everything is confounded if words are construed into a capital crime, instead of considering them only as a mark of that crime.

The Emperors Theodosius, Arcadius, and Honorius wrote thus to Rufinus, who was *praefectus praetorio*: "Though a man should happen to speak amiss of our person or government, we do not intend to punish him. If he has spoken through levity, we must despise him; if through folly, we must pity him; and if he wrongs us, we must forgive him. Therefore, leaving things as they are, you are to inform us accordingly, that we may be able to judge of words by persons, and that we may duly consider whether we ought to punish or overlook them."

X. In writings there is something more permanent than in words, but when they are in no way preparative to high treason they cannot amount to that charge. . . .

*　　*　　*

REVIEW QUESTIONS

1. What kinds of liberty does Montesquieu distinguish?
2. On what basis does he make his distinctions?
3. What is the relation between liberty and reason?
4. What is the relation between crime and nature?
5. What role does a concept of nature play in Montesquieu's differentiation of crimes?

CESARE, MARCHESE DI BECCARIA BONESANA

FROM *An Essay on Crimes and Punishments*

Cesare, marchese di Beccaria Bonesana (1738–1794), was an economist and criminologist and one of the best-known Italian thinkers of the Enlightenment. Born the son of a Milanese aristocrat, he was educated by Jesuits and received a degree in law from the University of Pavia in 1755. He gravitated into the enlightened circle around Count Pietro Verri, who encouraged him in 1763 to take up the study of criminal law. Beccaria's great work, An Essay on Crimes and Punishments, *appeared a year later. Arguing on the basis of utilitarian principles—the greatest good for the greatest number—he excoriated the barbaric and ineffective legal practices of his day, such as judicial torture, extreme punishment, and magisterial corruption. The effectiveness of the law, he reasoned, depended ultimately on its certainty rather than its severity. Thus, torture should be abolished and punishments made proportional to the crimes. For the same reason Beccaria became the first modern writer to advocate the abolition of capital punishment. The work proved tremendously influential, guiding legal reforms across Europe and winning champions such as Jeremy Bentham.*

From *An Essay on Crimes and Punishments*, by Cesare Beccaria Bonesana (Stanford: Academic Reprints, 1953), pp. 15–19, 47, 59–67, 95–96.

Chapter 1
Of the Origin of Punishments

Laws are the conditions under which men, naturally independent, united themselves in society. Weary of living in a continual state of war, and of enjoying a liberty, which became of little value, from the uncertainty of its duration, they sacrificed one part of it, to enjoy the rest in peace and security. The sum of all these portions of the liberty of each individual constituted the sovereignty of a nation and was deposited in the hands of the sovereign, as the lawful administrator. But it was not sufficient only to establish this deposit; it was also necessary to defend it from the usurpation of each individual, who will always endeavour to take away from the mass, not only his own portion, but to encroach on that of others. Some motives therefore, that strike the senses were necessary to prevent the despotism of each individual from plunging society into its former chaos. Such motives are the punishments established against the infractors of the laws. I say that motives of this kind are necessary; because experience shows, that the multitude adopt no established principle of conduct; and because society is prevented from approaching to that dissolution, (to which, as well as all other parts of the physical and moral world, it naturally tends,) only by motives that are the immediate objects of sense, and which being continually presented to the mind, are sufficient to counterbalance the effects of the passions of the individual which oppose the general good. Neither the power of eloquence nor the sublimest truths are sufficient to restrain, for any length of time, those passions which are excited by the lively impressions of present objects.

Chapter 2
Of the Right to Punish

Every punishment which does not arise from absolute necessity, says the great Montesquieu, is tyrannical. A proposition which may be made more general thus: every act of authority of one man over another, for which there is not an absolute necessity, is tyrannical. It is upon this then that the sovereign's right to punish crimes is founded; that is, upon the necessity of defending the public liberty, entrusted to his care, from the usurpation of individuals; and punishments are just in proportion, as the liberty, preserved by the sovereign, is sacred and valuable.

Let us consult the human heart, and there we shall find the foundation of the sovereign's right to punish, for no advantage in moral policy can be lasting which is not founded on the indelible sentiments of the heart of man. Whatever law deviates from this principle will always meet with a resistance which will destroy it in the end; for the smallest force continually applied will overcome the most violent motion communicated to bodies.

No man ever gave up his liberty merely for the good of the public. Such a chimera exists only in romances. Every individual wishes, if possible, to be exempt from the compacts that bind the rest of mankind.

The multiplication of mankind, though slow, being too great, for the means which the earth, in its natural state, offered to satisfy necessities which every day became more numerous, obliged men to separate again, and form new societies. These naturally opposed the first, and a state of war was transferred from individuals to nations.

Thus it was necessity that forced men to give up a part of their liberty. It is certain, then, that every individual would choose to put into the public stock the smallest portion possible, as much only as was sufficient to engage others to defend it. The aggregate of these, the smallest portions possible, forms the right of punishing; all that extends beyond this, is abuse, not justice.

Observe that by *justice* I understand nothing more than that bond which is necessary to keep the interest of individuals united, without which men would return to their original state of barbarity. All punishments which exceed the necessity of preserving this bond are in their nature unjust. We should be cautious how we associate with the word *justice* an idea of any thing real, such as a physical power, or a being that actually exists. I do not, by any means, speak of the justice of God, which is of another kind, and refers immediately to rewards and punishments in a life to come.

*   *   *

Chapter 12
Of the Intent of Punishments

From the foregoing considerations it is evident that the intent of punishments is not to torment a sensible being, nor to undo a crime already committed. Is it possible that torments and useless cruelty, the instrument of furious fanaticism or the impotency of tyrants, can be authorised by a political body, which, so far from being influenced by passion, should be the cool moderator of the passions of individuals? Can the groans of a tortured wretch recall the time past, or reverse the crime he has committed?

The end of punishment, therefore, is no other than to prevent the criminal from doing further injury to society, and to prevent others from committing the like offence. Such punishments, therefore, and such a mode of inflicting them, ought to be chosen, as will make the strongest and most lasting impressions on the minds of others, with the least torment to the body of the criminal.

*   *   *

Chapter 16
Of Torture

The torture of a criminal during the course of his trial is a cruelty consecrated by custom in most nations. It is used with an intent either to make him confess his crime, or to explain some contradictions into which he had been led during his examination, or discover his accomplices, or for some kind of metaphysical and incomprehensible purgation of infamy, or, finally, in order to discover other crimes of which he is not accused, but of which he may be guilty.

No man can be judged a criminal until he be found guilty nor can society take from him the public protection until it have been proved that he has violated the conditions on which it was granted. What right, then, but that of power, can authorise the punishment of a citizen so long as there remains any doubt of his guilt? This dilemma is frequent. Either he is guilty, or not guilty. If guilty, he should only suffer the punishment ordained by the laws, and torture becomes useless, as his confession is unnecessary. If he be not guilty, you torture the innocent; for, in the eye of the law, every man is innocent whose crime has not been proved. Besides, it is confounding all relations to expect that a man should be both the accuser and accused; and that pain should be the test of truth, as if truth resided in the muscles and fibres of a wretch in torture. By this method the robust will escape, and the feeble be condemned. These are the inconveniencies of this pretended test of truth, worthy only of a cannibal, and which the Romans, in many respects barbarous, and whose savage virtue has been too much admired, reserved for the slaves alone.

What is the political intention of punishments? To terrify and be an example to others. Is this intention answered by thus privately torturing the guilty and the innocent? It is doubtless of importance that no crime should remain unpunished; but it is useless to make a public example of the author of a crime hid in darkness. A crime already committed, and for which there can be no remedy, can only be punished by a political society with an intention that no hopes of impunity should induce others to commit the same. If it be true, that the number of those who from fear or virtue respect the laws is greater than of those by whom they are violated, the risk of torturing an innocent person is greater, as there is a greater probability that, *cæteris paribus,* an individual hath observed, than that he hath infringed the laws.

There is another ridiculous motive for torture, namely, *to purge a man from infamy.* Ought such an abuse to be tolerated in the eighteenth century? Can pain, which is a sensation, have any connection with a moral sentiment, a matter of opinion? Perhaps the rack may be considered as the refiner's furnace.

It is not difficult to trace this senseless law to its origin; for an absurdity, adopted by a whole nation, must have some affinity with other ideas established and respected by the same nation. This custom seems to be the offspring of religion, by which mankind, in all nations and in all ages, are so generally influenced. We are taught by our infallible church, that those stains of sin contracted through human frailty, and which have not deserved the eternal anger of the Almighty, are to be purged away in another life by an incomprehensible fire. Now infamy is a stain, and if the punishments and fire of purgatory can take away all spiritual stains, why should not the pain of torture take away those of a civil nature? I imagine, that the confession of a criminal, which in some tribunals is required as being essential to his condemnation, has a similar origin, and has been taken from the mysterious tribunal of penitence, where the confession of sins is a necessary part of the sacrament. Thus have men abused the unerring light of revelation; and, in the times of tractable ignorance, having no other, they naturally had recourse to it on every occasion, making the most remote and absurd applications. Moreover, infamy is a sentiment regulated neither by the laws nor by reason, but entirely by opinion; but torture renders the victim infamous, and therefore cannot take infamy away.

Another intention of torture is to oblige the supposed criminal to reconcile the contradictions into which he may have fallen during his examination; as if the dread of punishment, the uncertainty of his fate, the solemnity of the court, the majesty of the judge, and the ignorance of the accused, were not abundantly sufficient to account for contradictions, which are so common to men even in a state of tranquility, and which must necessarily be multiplied by the perturbation of the mind of a man entirely engaged in the thoughts of saving himself from imminent danger.

This infamous test of truth is a remaining monument of that ancient and savage legislation, in which trials by fire, by boiling water, or the uncertainty of combats, were called *judgments of God;* as if the links of that eternal chain, whose beginning is in the breast of the first cause of all things, could ever be disunited by the institutions of men. The only difference between torture and trials by fire and boiling water is, that the event of the first depends on the will of the accused, and of the second on a fact entirely physical and external: but this difference is apparent only, not real. A man on the rack, in the convulsions of torture, has it as little in his power to declare the truth, as, in former times, to prevent without fraud the effects of fire or boiling water.

Every act of the will is invariably in proportion to the force of the impression on our senses. The impression of pain, then, may increase to such a degree, that, occupying the mind entirely, it will compel the sufferer to use the shortest method of freeing himself from torment. His answer, therefore, will be an effect as necessary as that of fire or boiling water, and he will accuse himself of crimes of which he is innocent: so that the very means employed to distinguish the innocent from the guilty will most effectually destroy all difference between them.

It would be superfluous to confirm these reflections by examples of innocent persons who, from the agony of torture, have confessed themselves guilty: innumerable instances may be found in all nations, and in every age. How amazing that mankind have always neglected to draw the natural conclusion! Lives there a man who, if he has carried his thoughts ever so little beyond the necessities of life, *when he reflects on such cruelty, is not tempted to fly from society, and return to his natural state of independence?*

The result of torture, then, is a matter of calculation, and depends on the constitution, which differs in every individual, and it is in proportion to his strength and sensibility; so that to discover truth by this method, is a problem which may be better solved by a mathematician than by a judge, and may be thus stated: *The force of the muscles and the sensibility of the nerves of an innocent person being given, it is required to find the degree of pain necessary to make him confess himself guilty of a given crime.*

The examination of the accused is intended to find out the truth: but if this be discovered with so much difficulty in the air, gesture, and countenance of a man at ease, how can it appear in a countenance distorted by the convulsions of torture? Every violent action destroys those small alterations in the features which sometimes disclose the sentiments of the heart.

These truths were known to the Roman legislators, amongst whom, as I have already observed, slaves only, who were not considered as citizens, were tortured. They are known to the English a nation in which the progress of science, superiority in commerce, riches, and power, its natural consequences, together with the numerous examples of virtue and courage, leave no doubt of the excellence of its laws. They have been acknowledged in Sweden, where torture has been abolished. They are known to one of the wisest monarchs in Europe, who, having seated philos-

ophy on the throne by his beneficent legislation, has made his subjects free, though dependent on the laws; the only freedom that reasonable men can desire in the present state of things. In short, torture has not been thought necessary in the laws of armies, composed chiefly of the dregs of mankind, where its use should seem most necessary. Strange phenomenon! that a set of men, hardened by slaughter, and familiar with blood, should teach humanity to the sons of peace.

It appears also that these truths were known, though imperfectly, even to those by whom torture has been most frequently practised; for a confession made during torture, is null, if it be not afterwards confirmed by an oath, which if the criminal refuses, he is tortured again. Some civilians and some nations permit this infamous *petitio principii* to be only three times repeated, and others leave it to the discretion of the judge; therefore, of two men equally innocent, or equally guilty, the most robust and resolute will be acquitted, and the weakest and most pusillanimous will be condemned, in consequence of the following excellent mode of reasoning. *I, the judge, must find some one guilty. Thou, who art a strong fellow, hast been able to resist the force of torment; therefore I acquit thee. Thou, being weaker, hast yielded to it; I therefore condemn thee. I am sensible, that the confession which was extorted from thee has no weight; but if thou dost not confirm by oath what thou hast already confessed, I will have thee tormented again.*

A very strange but necessary consequence of the use of torture is, that the case of the innocent is worse than that of the guilty. With regard to the first, either he confesses the crime which he has not committed, and is condemned, or he is acquitted, and has suffered a punishment he did not deserve. On the contrary, the person who is really guilty has the most favourable side of the question; for, if he supports the torture with firmness and resolution, he is acquitted, and has gained, having exchanged a greater punishment for a less.

The law by which torture is authorised, says, *Men, be insensible to pain. Nature has indeed given you an irresistible self-love, and an unalienable right of self-preservation; but I create in you a contrary sentiment, an heroical hatred of yourselves. I command you to accuse yourselves, and to declare the truth, amidst the tearing of your flesh and the dislocation of your bones.*

*   *   *

Chapter 27
Of the Mildness of Punishments

The course of my ideas has carried me away from my subject, to the elucidation of which I now return. Crimes are more effectually prevented by the *certainty* than the *severity* of punishment. Hence in a magistrate the necessity of vigilance, and in a judge of implacability, which, that it may become an useful virtue, should be joined to a mild legislation. The certainty of a small punishment will make a stronger impression than the fear of one more severe, if attended with the hopes of escaping; for it is the nature of mankind to be terrified at the approach of the smallest inevitable evil, whilst hope, the best gift of Heaven, hath the power of dispelling the apprehension of a greater, especially if supported by examples of impunity, which weakness or avarice too frequently afford.

If punishments be very severe, men are naturally led to the perpetration of other crimes, to avoid the punishment due to the first. The countries and times most notorious for severity of punishments were always those in which the most bloody and inhuman actions and the most atrocious crimes were committed for the hand of the legislator and the assassin were directed by the same spirit of ferocity, which on the throne dictated laws of iron to slaves and savages, and in private instigated the subject to sacrifice one tyrant to make room for another.

In proportion as punishments become more cruel, the minds of men, as a fluid rises to the same height with that which surrounds it, grow hardened and insensible; and the force of the passions still continuing, in the space of an hundred years the *wheel* terrifies no more than formerly the *prison*. That a punishment may produce the effect required, it is sufficient that the *evil* it occasions should exceed the *good* expected from the crime, including in the calculation the certainty of the punishment, and the privation of the expected advantage. All severity beyond this is superfluous, and therefore tyrannical.

Men regulate their conduct by the repeated impression of evils they know, and not by those with which they are unacquainted. Let us, for example, suppose two nations, in one of which the greatest punishment is *perpetual slavery,* and in the other *the wheel:* I say, that both will inspire the same degree of terror, and that there can be no reasons for increasing the punishments of the first, which are not equally valid for augmenting those of the second to more lasting and more ingenious modes of tormenting, and so on to the most exquisite refinements of a science too well known to tyrants.

There are yet two other consequences of cruel punishments, which counteract the purpose of their institution, which was, to prevent crimes. The *first* arises from the impossibility of establishing an exact proportion between the crime and punishment; for though ingenious cruelty hath greatly multiplyed the variety of torments, yet the human frame can suffer only to a certain degree, beyond which it is impossible to proceed, be the enormity of the crime ever so great. The *second* consequence is impunity. Human nature is limited no less in evil than in good. Excessive barbarity can never be more than temporary, it being impossible that it should be supported by a permanent system of legislation; for if the laws be too cruel, they must be altered, or anarchy and impunity will succeed.

Is it possible without shuddering with horror, to read in history of the barbarous and useless torments that were cooly invented and executed by men who were called sages? Who does not tremble at the thoughts of thousands of wretches, whom their misery, either caused or tolerated by the laws, which favoured the few and outraged the many, had forced in despair to return to a state of nature, or accused of impossible crimes, the fabric of ignorance and superstition, or guilty only of having been faithful to their own principles; who, I say, can, without horror, think of their being torn to pieces, with slow and studied barbarity, by men endowed with the same passions and the same feelings? A delightful spectacle to a fanatic multitude!

REVIEW QUESTIONS

1. According to Beccaria, what is the proper basis of law in human society?

2. What is the legal purpose and function of punishment?
3. Why is torture irrational?
4. What does Beccaria's criminal theory reveal about his assumptions concerning human nature and human society?
5. What aspects of Beccaria's thought qualify as *enlightened* in the strict, historical sense of the term?

JEAN-JACQUES ROUSSEAU

FROM *The Social Contract*

Jean-Jacques Rousseau (1712–1778) was one of the most original writers of the Enlightenment. A native of Geneva, he was raised by his father, a watchmaker. At sixteen years of age, he left home and eventually settled in Paris. His first attempts to penetrate the world of philosophes and encyclopedists were not very successful. In 1750, however, he won a literary award from the Academy of Dijon for an essay that contrasted the corruption of modern civilization with the natural goodness of simple, uncivilized human beings. Rousseau eventually settled in the town of Montmorency. His years there proved to be the most fruitful of his life. In a two-year span he wrote his most significant works: La nouvelle Héloïse *(1761),* Émile *(1761), and* Le contrat social *(1762).*

In The Social Contract, *as well as his other works, Rousseau sought to balance the freedom of the individual against the needs of the collectivity. He believed the preservation of liberty depended on the creation of a new society by means of a social contract. The idea was not new, having been adopted by other enlightened thinkers from the political theory of John Locke. Rousseau's interpretation was highly original, however. Locke believed that the social contract preserved freedom; Rousseau argued that the social contract preserved equality. Under his social contract, people voluntarily relinquished certain rights and submitted to the general will, a vague entity that found expression in a set of positive laws under a virtuous legislator. These laws had absolute authority and would preserve absolute equality between people.*

From *The Social Contract*, by Jean-Jacques Rousseau, translated by Henry J. Tozer (New York: Scribner's, 1898).

Book I

I mean to inquire if, in the civil order, there can be any sure and legitimate rule of administration, men being taken as they are and laws as they might be. In this inquiry I shall endeavour always to unite what right sanctions with what is prescribed by interest, in order that justice and utility may in no case be divided.

I enter upon my task without proving the importance of the subject. I shall be asked if I am a prince or a legislator, to write on politics. I answer that I am neither, and that is why I do so. If I were a prince or a legislator, I should not waste time in saying what wants doing; I should do it, or hold my peace.

As I was born a citizen of a free State, and a member of the Sovereign, I feel that, however feeble the influence my voice can have on public affairs, the right of voting on them makes it my duty to study them: and I am happy, when I reflect upon governments, to find my inquiries always furnish me with new reasons for loving that of my own country.

CHAPTER I
SUBJECT OF THE FIRST BOOK

Man is born free; and everywhere he is in chains. One thinks himself the master of others, and still remains a greater slave than they. How did this change come about? I do not know. What can make it legitimate? That question I think I can answer.

If I took into account only force, and the effects derived from it, I should say: "As long as a people is compelled to obey, and obeys, it does well; as soon as it can shake off the yoke, and shakes it off, it does still better; for, regaining its liberty by the same right as took it away, either it is justified in resuming it, or there was no justification for those who took it away." But the social order is a sacred right which is the basis of all rights. Nevertheless, this right does not come from nature, and must therefore be founded on conventions. Before coming to that, I have to prove what I have just asserted.

CHAPTER II
THE FIRST SOCIETIES

The most ancient of all societies, and the only one that is natural, is the family: and even so the children remain attached to the father only so long as they need him for their preservation. As soon as this need ceases, the natural bond is dissolved. The children, released from the obedience they owed to the father, and the father, released from the care he owed his children, return equally to independence. If they remain united, they continue so no longer naturally, but voluntarily; and the family itself is then maintained only by convention.

This common liberty results from the nature of man. His first law is to provide for his own preservation, his first cares are those which he owes to himself; and, as soon as he reaches years of discretion, he is the sole judge of the proper means of preserving himself, and consequently becomes his own master.

The family then may be called the first model of political societies: the ruler corresponds to the father, and the people to the children; and all, being born free and equal, alienate their liberty only for their own advantage. The whole difference is that, in the family, the love of the father for his children repays him for the care he takes of them, while, in the State, the pleasure of commanding takes the place of the love which the chief cannot have for the peoples under him.

Grotius denies that all human power is established in favour of the governed, and quotes slavery as an example. His usual method of reasoning is constantly to establish right by fact. It would be possible to employ a more logical method, but none could be more favourable to tyrants.

It is then, according to Grotius, doubtful whether the human race belongs to a hundred men, or that hundred men to the human race: and, throughout his book, he seems to incline to the former alternative, which is also the view of Hobbes. On this showing, the human species is divided into so many herds of cattle, each with its ruler, who keeps guard over them for the purpose of devouring them.

As a shepherd is of a nature superior to that of his flock, the shepherds of men, i.e. their rulers, are of a nature superior to that of the peoples under them. Thus, Philo tells us, the Emperor Caligula reasoned, concluding equally well either that kings were gods, or that men were beasts.

The reasoning of Caligula agrees with that of Hobbes and Grotius. Aristotle, before any of them, had said that men are by no means equal naturally, but that some are born for slavery, and others for dominion.

Aristotle was right; but he took the effect for the cause. Nothing can be more certain than that every man born in slavery is born for slavery. Slaves lose everything in their chains, even the desire of escaping from them: they love their servitude, as the comrades of Ulysses loved their brutish condition. If then there are slaves by nature, it is because there have been slaves against nature. Force made the first slaves, and their cowardice perpetuated the condition.

I have said nothing of King Adam, or Emperor Noah, father of the three great monarchs who shared out the universe, like the children of Saturn, whom some scholars have recognized in them. I trust to getting due thanks for my moderation; for, being a direct descendant of one of these princes, perhaps of the eldest branch, how do I know that a verification of titles might not leave me the legitimate king of the human race? In any case, there can be no doubt that Adam was sovereign of the world, as Robinson Crusoe was of his island, as long as he was its only inhabitant; and this empire had the advantage that the monarch, safe on his throne, had no rebellions, wars, or conspirators to fear.

CHAPTER III
THE RIGHT OF THE STRONGEST

The strongest is never strong enough to be always the master, unless he transforms strength into right, and obedience into duty. Hence the right of the strongest, which, though to all seeming meant ironically, is really laid down as a fundamental principle. But are we never to have an explanation of this phrase? Force is a physical power, and I fail to see what moral effect it can have. To yield to force is an act of necessity, not of will—at the most, an act of prudence. In what sense can it be a duty?

Suppose for a moment that this so-called "right" exists. I maintain that the sole result is a mass of inexplicable nonsense. For, if force creates right, the effect changes with the cause: every force that is greater than the first succeeds to its right. As soon as it is possible to disobey with impunity, disobedience is legitimate; and, the strongest being always in the right, the only thing that matters is to act so as to become the strongest. But what kind of right is that which perishes when force fails? If we must obey perforce, there is no need to obey because we ought; and if we are not forced to obey, we are under no obligation to do so. Clearly, the word "right" adds nothing to force: in this connection, it means absolutely nothing.

Obey the powers that be. If this means yield to force, it is a good precept, but superfluous: I can answer for its never being violated. All power comes from God, I admit; but so does all sickness; does that mean that we are forbidden to call in the doctor? A brigand surprises me at the edge of a wood: must I not merely surrender my purse on compulsion; but, even if I could withhold it, am I in conscience bound to give it up? For certainly the pistol he holds is also a power.

Let us then admit that force does not create right, and that we are obliged to obey only legitimate powers. In that case, my original question recurs.

CHAPTER IV
SLAVERY

Since no man has a natural authority over his fellow, and force creates no right, we must conclude that conventions form the basis of all legitimate authority among men.

If an individual, says Grotius, can alienate his liberty and make himself the slave of a master, why could not a whole people do the same and make itself subject to a king? There are in this passage plenty of ambiguous words which would need explaining; but let us confine ourselves to the word *alienate*. To alienate is to give or to sell. Now, a man who becomes the slave of another does not give himself; he sells himself, at the least for his subsistence: but for what does a people sell itself? A king is so far from furnishing his subjects with their subsistence that he gets his own only from them; and, according to Rabelais, kings do not live on nothing. Do subjects then give their persons on condition that the king takes their goods also? I fail to see what they have left to preserve.

It will be said that the despot assures his subjects civil tranquillity. Granted; but what do they gain, if the wars his ambition brings down upon them, his insatiable avidity, and the vexatious conduct of his ministers press harder on them than their own dissensions would have done? What do they gain, if the very tranquillity they enjoy is one of their miseries? Tranquillity is found also in dungeons; but is that enough to make them desirable places to live in? The Greeks imprisoned in the cave of the Cyclops lived there very tranquilly, while they were awaiting their turn to be devoured.

To say that a man gives himself gratuitously, is to say what is absurd and inconceivable; such an act is null and illegitimate, from the mere fact that he who does it is out of his mind. To say the same of a whole people is to suppose a people of madmen; and madness creates no right.

Even if each man could alienate himself, he could not alienate his children: they are born men and free; their liberty belongs to them, and no one but they has the right to dispose of it. Before they come to years of discretion, the father can, in their name, lay down conditions for their preservation and well-being, but he cannot give them irrevocably and without conditions: such a gift is contrary to the ends of nature, and exceeds the rights of paternity. It would therefore be necessary, in order to legitimize an arbitrary government, that in every generation the people should be in a position to accept or reject it; but, were this so, the government would be no longer arbitrary.

To renounce liberty is to renounce being a man, to surrender the rights of humanity and even its duties. For him who renounces everything no indemnity is possible. Such a renunciation is incompatible with man's nature; to remove all liberty from his will is to remove all morality from his acts. Finally, it is an empty and contradictory convention that sets up, on the one side, absolute authority, and, on the other, unlimited obedience. Is it not clear that we can be under no obligation to a person from whom we have the right to exact everything? Does not this condition alone, in the absence of equivalence or exchange, in itself involve the nullity of the act? For what right can my slave have against me, when all that he has belongs to me, and, his right being mine, this right of mine against myself is a phrase devoid of meaning?

Grotius and the rest find in war another origin for the so-called right of slavery. The victor having, as they hold, the right of killing the vanquished, the latter can buy back his life at the price of his liberty; and this convention is the more legitimate because it is to the advantage of both parties.

But it is clear that this supposed right to kill the conquered is by no means deducible from the state of war. Men, from the mere fact that, while they are living in their primitive independence, they have no mutual relations stable enough to constitute either the state of peace or the state of war, cannot be naturally enemies. War is constituted by a relation between things, and not between persons; and, as the state of war cannot arise out of simple personal relations, but only out of real relations, private war, or war of man with man, can exist neither in the state of nature, where there is no constant property, nor in the social state, where everything is under the authority of the laws.

Individual combats, duels, and encounters, are acts which cannot constitute a state; while the private wars, authorized by the Establishments of Louis IX, King of France, and suspended by the Peace of God, are abuses of feudalism, in itself an absurd system if ever there was one, and contrary to the principles of natural right and to all good polity.

War then is a relation, not between man and

man, but between State and State, and individuals are enemies only accidentally, not as men, nor even as citizens, but as soldiers; not as members of their country, but as its defenders. Finally, each State can have for enemies only other States, and not men; for between things disparate in nature there can be no real relation.

Furthermore, this principle is in conformity with the established rules of all times and the constant practice of all civilized peoples. Declarations of war are intimations less to powers than to their subjects. The foreigner, whether king, individual, or people, who robs, kills, or detains the subjects, without declaring war on the prince, is not an enemy, but a brigand. Even in real war, a just prince, while laying hands, in the enemy's country, on all that belongs to the public, respects the lives and goods of individuals: he respects rights on which his own are founded. The object of the war being the destruction of the hostile State, the other side has a right to kill its defenders, while they are bearing arms; but as soon as they lay them down and surrender, they cease to be enemies or instruments of the enemy, and become once more merely men, whose life no one has any right to take. Sometimes it is possible to kill the State without killing a single one of its members; and war gives no right which is not necessary to the gaining of its object. These principles are not those of Grotius: they are not based on the authority of poets, but derived from the nature of reality and based on reason.

The right of conquest has no foundation other than the right of the strongest. If war does not give the conqueror the right to massacre the conquered peoples, the right to enslave them cannot be based upon a right which does not exist. No one has a right to kill an enemy except when he cannot make him a slave, and the right to enslave him cannot therefore be derived from the right to kill him. It is accordingly an unfair exchange to make him buy at the price of his liberty his life, over which the victor holds no right. Is it not clear that there is a vicious circle in founding the right of life and death on the right of slavery, and the right of slavery on the right of life and death?

Even if we assume this terrible right to kill everybody, I maintain that a slave made in war, or a conquered people, is under no obligation to a master, except to obey him as far as he is compelled to do so. By taking an equivalent for his life, the victor has not done him a favour; instead of killing him without profit, he has killed him usefully. So far then is he from acquiring over him any authority in addition to that of force, that the state of war continues to subsist between them: their mutual relation is the effect of it, and the usage of the right of war does not imply a treaty of peace. A convention has indeed been made; but this convention, so far from destroying the state of war, presupposes its continuance.

So, from whatever aspect we regard the question, the right of slavery is null and void, not only as being illegitimate, but also because it is absurd and meaningless. The words *slave* and *right* contradict each other, and are mutually exclusive. It will always be equally foolish for a man to say to a man or to a people: "I make with you a convention wholly at your expense and wholly to my advantage; I shall keep it as long as I like, and you will keep it as long as I like."

*   *   *

CHAPTER VI
THE SOCIAL COMPACT

I suppose men to have reached the point at which the obstacles in the way of their preservation in the state of nature show their power of resistance to be greater than the resources at the disposal of each individual for his maintenance in that state. That primitive condition can then subsist no longer; and the human race would perish unless it changed its manner of existence.

But, as men cannot engender new forces, but only unite and direct existing ones, they have no other means of preserving themselves than the formation, by aggregation, of a sum of forces great enough to overcome the resistance. These they have to bring into play by means of a single motive power, and cause to act in concert.

This sum of forces can arise only where several persons come together: but, as the force and liberty of each man are the chief instruments of his self-preservation, how can he pledge them without harming his own interests, and neglecting the care he owes to himself? This difficulty, in its bearing on my present subject, may be stated in the following terms:

"The problem is to find a form of association which will defend and protect with the whole common force the person and goods of each associate, and in which each, while uniting himself with all, may still obey himself alone, and remain as free as before." This is the fundamental problem of which the *Social Contract* provides the solution.

The clauses of this contract are so determined by the nature of the act that the slightest modification would make them vain and ineffective; so that, although they have perhaps never been formally set forth, they are everywhere the same and everywhere tacitly admitted and recognized, until, on the violation of the social compact, each regains his original rights and resumes his natural liberty, while losing the conventional liberty in favour of which he renounced it.

These clauses, properly understood, may be reduced to one—the total alienation of each associate, together with all his rights, to the whole community; for, in the first place, as each gives himself absolutely, the conditions are the same for all; and, this being so, no one has any interest in making them burdensome to others.

Moreover, the alienation being without reserve, the union is as perfect as it can be, and no associate has anything more to demand: for, if the individuals retained certain rights, as there would be no common superior to decide between them and the public, each, being on one point his own judge, would ask to be so on all; the state of nature would thus continue, and the association would necessarily become inoperative or tyrannical.

Finally, each man, in giving himself to all, gives himself to nobody; and as there is no associate over which he does not acquire the same right as he yields others over himself, he gains an equivalent for everything he loses, and an increase of force for the preservation of what he has.

If then we discard from the social compact what is not of its essence, we shall find that it reduces itself to the following terms:

"*Each of us puts his person and all his power in common under the supreme direction of the general will, and, in our corporate capacity, we receive each member as an indivisible part of the whole.*"

At once, in place of the individual personality of each contracting party, this act of association creates a moral and collective body, composed of as many members as the assembly contains voters, and receiving from this act its unity, its common identity, its life, and its will. This public person, so formed by the union of all other persons, formerly took the name of *city,* and now takes that of *Republic* or *body politic;* it is called by its members *State* when passive, *Sovereign* when active, and *Power* when compared with others like itself. Those who are associated in it take collectively the name of *people,* and severally are called *citizens,* as sharing in the sovereign power, and *subjects,* as being under the laws of the State. But these terms are often confused and taken one for another: it is enough to know how to distinguish them when they are being used with precision.

CHAPTER VII
THE SOVEREIGN

This formula shows us that the act of association comprises a mutual undertaking between the public and the individuals, and that each individual, in making a contract, as we may say, with himself, is bound in a double capacity; as a member of the Sovereign he is bound to the individuals, and as a member of the State to the Sovereign. But the maxim of civil right, that no one is bound by undertakings made to himself, does not apply in this case; for there is a great difference between incurring an obligation to yourself and incurring one to a whole of which you form a part.

Attention must further be called to the fact that public deliberation, while competent to bind all the subjects to the Sovereign, because of the two different capacities in which each of them may be regarded, cannot, for the opposite reason, bind the Sovereign to itself; and that it is consequently against the nature of the body politic for the Sovereign to impose on itself a law which it cannot infringe. Being able to regard itself in only one capacity, it is in the position of an individual who makes a contract with himself; and this makes it clear that there neither is nor can be any kind of fundamental law binding on the body of the people—not even the social contract itself. This does not mean that the body politic cannot enter into undertakings with others, provided the contract is not infringed by them; for in relation to what is external to it, it becomes a simple being, an individual.

But the body politic or the Sovereign, drawing its being wholly from the sanctity of the contract, can never bind itself, even to an outsider, to do anything derogatory to the original act, for instance, to alienate any part of itself, or to submit to another Sovereign. Violation of the act by which it exists would be self-annihilation; and that which is itself nothing can create nothing.

As soon as this multitude is so united in one body, it is impossible to offend against one of the members without attacking the body, and still more to offend against the body without the members resenting it. Duty and interest therefore equally oblige the two contracting parties to give each other help; and the same men should seek to combine, in their double capacity, all the advantages dependent upon that capacity.

Again, the Sovereign, being formed wholly of the individuals who compose it, neither has nor can have any interest contrary to theirs; and consequently the sovereign power need give no guarantee to its subjects, because it is impossible for the body to wish to hurt all its members. We shall also see later on that it cannot hurt any in particular. The Sovereign, merely by virtue of what it is, is always what it should be.

This, however, is not the case with the relation of the subjects to the Sovereign, which, despite the common interest, would have no security that they would fulfil their undertakings, unless it found means to assure itself of their fidelity.

In fact, each individual, as a man, may have a particular will contrary or dissimilar to the general will which he has as a citizen. His particular interest may speak to him quite differently from the common interest: his absolute and naturally independent existence may make him look upon what he owes to the common cause as a gratuitous contribution, the loss of which will do less harm to others than the payment of it is burdensome to himself; and, regarding the moral person which constitutes the State as a *persona ficta,* because not a man, he may wish to enjoy the rights of citizenship without being ready to fulfil the duties of a subject. The continuance of such an injustice could not but prove the undoing of the body politic.

In order then that the social compact may not be an empty formula, it tacitly includes the undertaking, which alone can give force to the rest, that whoever refuses to obey the general will shall be compelled to do so by the whole body. This means nothing less than that he will be forced to be free; for this is the condition which, by giving each citizen to his country, secures him against all personal dependence. In this lies the key to the working of the political machine; this alone legitimizes civil undertakings, which, without it, would be absurd, tyrannical, and liable to the most frightful abuses.

CHAPTER VIII
THE CIVIL STATE

The passage from the state of nature to the civil state produces a very remarkable change in man, by substituting justice for instinct in his conduct, and giving his actions the morality they had formerly lacked. Then only, when the voice of duty takes the place of physical impulses and right of appetite, does man, who so far had considered only himself, find that he is forced to act on different principles, and to consult his reason before listening to his inclinations. Although, in this state, he deprives himself of some advantages which he got from nature, he gains in return others so great, his faculties are so stimulated and developed, his ideas so extended, his feelings so ennobled, and his whole soul so uplifted, that, did not the abuses of this new condition often degrade him below that which he left, he would be bound to bless continually the happy moment which took him from it for ever, and, instead of a stupid and unimaginative animal, made him an intelligent being and a man.

Let us draw up the whole account in terms easily commensurable. What man loses by the social contract is his natural liberty and an unlimited right to everything he tries to get and succeeds in getting; what he gains is civil liberty and the proprietorship of all he possesses. If we are to avoid mistake in weighing one against the other, we must clearly distinguish natural liberty, which is bounded only by the strength of the individual, from civil liberty, which is limited by the general will; and possession, which is merely the effect of force or the right of the first occupier, from property which can be founded only on a positive title.

We might, over and above all this, add, to what man acquires in the civil state, moral liberty, which alone makes him truly master of himself; for the mere impulse of appetite is slavery, while obedience to a law which we prescribe to ourselves is liberty. But I have already said too much on this head, and the philosophical meaning of the word liberty does not now concern us.

*   *   *

Book II

*   *   *

CHAPTER III
WHETHER THE GENERAL WILL IS FALLIBLE

It follows from what has gone before that the general will is always right and tends to the pub-

lic advantage; but it does not follow that the deliberations of the people are always equally correct. Our will is always for our own good, but we do not always see what that is; the people is never corrupted, but it is often deceived, and on such occasions only does it seem to will what is bad.

There is often a great deal of difference between the will of all and the general will; the latter considers only the common interest, while the former takes private interest into account, and is no more than a sum of particular wills: but take away from these same wills the pluses and minuses that cancel one another, and the general will remains as the sum of the differences.

If, when the people, being furnished with adequate information, held its deliberations, the citizens had no communication one with another, the grand total of the small differences would always give the general will, and the decision would always be good. But when factions arise, and partial associations are formed at the expense of the great association, the will of each of these associations becomes general in relation to its members, while it remains particular in relation to the State; it may then be said that there are no longer as many votes as there are men, but only as many as there are associations. The differences become less numerous and give a less general result. Lastly, when one of these associations is so great as to prevail over all the rest, the result is no longer a sum of small differences, but a single difference; in this case there is no longer a general will, and the opinion which prevails is purely particular.

It is therefore essential, if the general will is to be able to express itself, that there should be no partial society within the State, and that each citizen should think only his own thoughts: which was indeed the sublime and unique system established by the great Lycurgus. But if there are partial societies, it is best to have as many as possible and to prevent them from being unequal, as was done by Solon, Numa, and Servius. These precautions are the only ones that can guarantee that the general will shall be always enlightened, and that the people shall in no way deceive itself.

*   *   *

CHAPTER IV
THE LIMITS OF THE SOVEREIGN POWER

If the State is a moral person whose life is in the union of its members, and if the most important of its cares is the care for its own preservation, it must have a universal and compelling force, in order to move and dispose each part as may be most advantageous to the whole. As nature gives each man absolute power over all his members, the social compact gives the body politic absolute power over all its members also; and it is this power which, under the direction of the general will, bears, as I have said, the name of Sovereignty.

But, besides the public person, we have to consider the private persons composing it, whose life and liberty are naturally independent of it. We are bound then to distinguish clearly between the respective rights of the citizens and the Sovereign, and between the duties the former have to fulfil as subjects, and the natural rights they should enjoy as men.

Each man alienates, I admit, by the social compact, only such part of his powers, goods, and liberty as it is important for the community to control; but it must also be granted that the Sovereign is sole judge of what is important.

Every service a citizen can render the State he ought to render as soon as the Sovereign demands it; but the Sovereign, for its part, cannot impose upon its subjects any fetters that are useless to the community, nor can it even wish to do so; for no more by the law of reason than by the law of nature can anything occur without a cause.

The undertakings which bind us to the social body are obligatory only because they are mutual; and their nature is such that in fulfilling them we cannot work for others without working for ourselves. Why is it that the general will is always in the right, and that all continually will the happiness of each one, unless it is because there is not a man who does not think of "each" as meaning him, and consider himself in voting for all? This proves that equality of rights and the idea of justice which such equality creates originate in the preference each man gives to himself, and accordingly in the very nature of man. It proves that the general will, to be really such, must be general in its object as well as its essence; that it must both come from all and apply to all; and that it loses its natural rectitude when it is directed to some particular and determinate object, because in such a case we are judging of something foreign to us, and have no true principle of equity to guide us.

Indeed, as soon as a question of particular fact or right arises on a point not previously regulated by a general convention, the matter becomes contentious. It is a case in which the individuals concerned are one party, and the public the other, but in which I can see neither the law that ought to be followed nor the judge who ought to give the decision. In such a case, it would be absurd to propose to refer the question to an express decision of the general will, which can be only the conclusion reached by one of the parties and in consequence will be, for the other party, merely an external and particular will, inclined on this occasion to injustice and subject to error. Thus, just as a particular will cannot stand for the general will, the general will, in turn, changes its nature, when its object is particular, and, as general, cannot pronounce on a man or a fact. When, for instance, the people of Athens nominated or displaced its rulers, decreed honours to one, and imposed penalties on another, and, by a multitude of particular decrees, exercised all the functions of government indiscriminately, it had in such cases no longer a general will in the strict sense; it was acting no longer as Sovereign, but as magistrate. This will seem contrary to current views; but I must be given time to expound my own.

It should be seen from the foregoing that what makes the will general is less the number of voters than the common interest uniting them; for, under this system, each necessarily submits to the conditions he imposes on others: and this admirable agreement between interest and justice gives to the common deliberations an equitable character which at once vanishes when any particular question is discussed, in the absence of a common interest to unite and identify the ruling of the judge with that of the party.

From whatever side we approach our principle, we reach the same conclusion, that the social compact sets up among the citizens an equality of such a kind, that they all bind themselves to observe the same conditions and should therefore all enjoy the same rights. Thus, from the very nature of the compact, every act of Sovereignty, i.e. every authentic act of the general will, binds or favours all the citizens equally; so that the Sovereign recognizes only the body of the nation, and draws no distinctions between those of whom it is made up. What, then, strictly speaking, is an act of Sovereignty? It is not a convention between a superior and an inferior, but a convention between the body and each of its members. It is legitimate, because based on the social contract, and equitable, because common to all; useful, because it can have no other object than the general good, and stable, because guaranteed by the public force and the supreme power. So long as the subjects have to submit only to conventions of this sort, they obey no one but their own will; and to ask how far the respective rights of the Sovereign and the citizens extend, is to ask up to what point the latter can enter into undertakings with themselves, each with all, and all with each.

We can see from this that the sovereign power, absolute, sacred, and inviolable as it is, does not and cannot exceed the limits of general conventions, and that every man may dispose at will of such goods and liberty as these conventions leave him; so that the Sovereign never has a right to lay more charges on one subject than on another, because, in that case, the question becomes particular, and ceases to be within its competency.

When these distinctions have once been admitted, it is seen to be so untrue that there is, in the social contract, any real renunciation on the part of the individuals, that the position in which they find themselves as a result of the contract is really preferable to that in which they were before. Instead of a renunciation, they have made an advantageous exchange: instead of an uncertain and precarious way of living they have got one that is better and more secure; instead of natural independence they have got liberty, instead of the power to harm others security for themselves, and instead of their strength, which others might overcome, a right which social union makes invincible. Their very life, which they have devoted to the State, is by it constantly protected; and when they risk it in the State's defence, what more are they doing than giving back what they have received from it? What are they doing that they would not do more often and with greater danger in the state of nature, in which they would inevitably have to fight battles at the peril of their lives in defence of that which is the means of their preservation? All have indeed to fight when their country needs them; but then no one has ever to fight for himself. Do we not gain something by running, on behalf of what gives us our security, only some of the risks we should have to run for ourselves, as soon as we lost it?

*   *   *

REVIEW QUESTIONS

1. How does Rousseau's conception of the origin of political society compare with that of Locke?
2. According to Rousseau, what is the relation between human slavery and human nature?
3. How do relations of subject and ruler come into being?
4. What is the social contract?
5. What is its relation to nature? To reason? To will?

A READING IN THE SALON OF MME GEOFFRIN (1755)   ANICET CHARLES GABRIEL LEMONNIER

Anicet Charles Gabriel Lemonnier (1743–1824) received his initial training at the School of Fine Arts in his native Rouen. Like many artists and intellectuals of his day, he was drawn to Paris, where his connections soon gained him introductions to Enlightened individuals and their patronage. The subjects of his paintings tended toward allegorical representations of classical myth and antiquity. These proved highly acceptable to the Académie Royale de Peinture, which awarded him the Prix de Rome *in 1772 and granted him membership in 1789. He held a series of lucrative government pensions throughout his career. He became director of the Gobelins Manufactory in 1801 and helped to found the Musée des Beaux-Arts in his hometown of Rouen. His best-known work depicts the salon of Mme. Geoffrin, a circle of which he may have been a regular member. An imaginary reconstruction, this painting includes a number of noteworthy figures of the day, Diderot and Montesquieu among others, gathered under a bust of Voltaire. What seems to be happening in this painting? What can you tell about the nature of the gathering? What role did such salons play in the Enlightenment? What role did women play in such salons?*

254

IMMANUEL KANT

"What Is Enlightenment?"

*Immanuel Kant (1724–1804) was born, lived, and died in Königsberg, eastern Prussia, but wandered much more widely in his mind. A rationalist and disciple of Christian von Wolff, he set himself the task of working out the philosophical implications of Newtonian physics. Appointed to the chair of logic and metaphysics at the University of Königsberg in 1770, he began work on his great system of critical thought. His trilogy—*Critique of Pure Reason *(1781),* Critique of Practical Reason *(1788), and* Critique of Judgment *(1790)—showed how rational thought serves as the foundation for gaining human knowledge. In addition, he penned popular shorter essays that explained aspects of his thought. One of the most famous of these appears here. Publication of his last great work,* Religion in the Bounds of Reason *(1793), earned the censure of the Prussian government. Alone and silent, he died a decade later.*

From "What Is Enlightenment?" translated by Peter Gay, in *Introduction to Contemporary Civilization*, vol. 1 (New York: Columbia University Press, 1954), pp. 1071–76.

Enlightenment is man's emergence from his self-imposed nonage. Nonage is the inability to use one's own understanding without another's guidance. This nonage is self-imposed if its cause lies not in lack of understanding but in indecision and lack of courage to use one's own mind without another's guidance. *Dare to know!* "Have the courage to use your own understanding," is therefore the motto of the enlightenment.

Laziness and cowardice are the reasons why such a large part of mankind gladly remain minors all their lives, long after nature has freed them from external guidance. They are the reasons why it is so easy for others to set themselves up as guardians. It is so comfortable to be a minor. If I have a book that thinks for me, a pastor who acts as my conscience, a physician who prescribes my diet, and so on—then I have no need to exert myself. I have no need to think, if only I can pay; others will take care of that disagreeable business for me. Those guardians who have kindly taken supervision upon themselves see to it that the overwhelming majority of mankind—among them the entire fair sex—should consider the step

to maturity not only as hard, but as extremely dangerous. First, these guardians make their domestic cattle stupid and carefully prevent the docile creatures from taking a single step without the leading-strings to which they have fastened them. Then they show them the danger that would threaten them if they should try to walk by themselves. Now, this danger is really not very great; after stumbling a few times they would, at last, learn to walk. However, examples of such failures intimidate and generally discourage all further attempts.

Thus it is very difficult for the individual to work himself out of the nonage which has become almost second nature to him. He has even grown to like it and is at first really incapable of using his own understanding, because he has never been permitted to try it. Dogmas and formulas, these mechanical tools designed for reasonable use—or rather abuse—of his natural gifts, are the fetters of an everlasting nonage. The man who casts them off would make an uncertain leap over the narrowest ditch, because he is not used to such free movement. That is why there are only a few men who walk firmly, and who have emerged from nonage by cultivating their own minds.

It is more nearly possible, however, for the public to enlighten itself; indeed, if it is only given freedom, enlightenment is almost inevitable. There will always be a few independent thinkers, even among the self-appointed guardians of the multitude. Once such men have thrown off the yoke of nonage, they will spread about them the spirit of a reasonable appreciation of man's value and of his duty to think for himself. It is especially to be noted that the public which was earlier brought under the yoke by these men afterward forces these very guardians to remain in submission, if it is so incited by some of its guardians who are themselves incapable of any enlightenment. That shows how pernicious it is to implant prejudices: they will eventually revenge themselves upon their authors or their authors' descendants. Therefore, a public can achieve enlightenment only slowly. A revolution may bring about the end of a personal despotism or of avaricious and tyrannical oppression, but never a true reform of modes of thought. New prejudices will serve, in place of the old, as guidelines for the unthinking multitude.

This enlightenment requires nothing but *freedom*—and the most innocent of all that may be called "freedom": freedom to make public use of one's reason in all matters. Now I hear the cry from all sides: "Do not argue!" The officer says: "Do not argue—drill!" The tax collector: "Do not argue—pay!" The pastor: "Do not argue—believe!" Only one ruler in the world says: "Argue as much as you please, and about what you please, but obey!" We find restrictions on freedom everywhere. But which restriction is harmful to enlightenment? Which restriction is innocent, and which advances enlightenment? I reply: the public use of one's reason must be free at all times, and this alone can bring enlightenment to mankind.

On the other hand, the private use of reason may frequently be narrowly restricted without especially hindering the progress of enlightenment. By "public use of one's reason" I mean that use which a man, as *scholar*, makes of it before the reading public. I call "private use" that use which a man makes of his reason in a civic post that has been entrusted to him. In some affairs affecting the interest of the community a certain governmental mechanism is necessary in which some members of the community remain passive. This creates an artificial unanimity which will serve the fulfillment of public objectives, or at least keep these objectives from being destroyed. Here arguing is not permitted: one must obey. Insofar as a part of this machine considers himself at the same time a member of a universal community— a world society of citizens—(let us say that he thinks of himself as a scholar rationally addressing his public through his writings) he may indeed argue, and the affairs with which he is associated in part as a passive member will not suffer. Thus, it would be very unfortunate if an officer on duty and under orders from his superiors should want to criticize the appropriateness or utility of his orders. He must obey. But as a scholar he could not rightfully be prevented from taking notice of the mistakes in the military service and from submitting his views to his public for its judgment. The citizen cannot refuse to pay the taxes levied upon him; indeed, impertinent censure of such taxes could be punished as a scandal that might cause general disobedience. Nevertheless, this man does not violate the duties of a citizen if, as a scholar, he publicly expresses his objections to the impropriety or possible injustice of such levies. A pastor too is bound to preach to his congregation in accord with the doctrines of the church which he serves, for he was ordained on that condition. But as a scholar he has full freedom, indeed the obligation, to communicate to his public all his carefully examined and constructive thoughts concerning errors in that doctrine and his proposals concerning improvement of religious dogma and church institutions. This is nothing that could burden his conscience. For what he teaches in pursuance of his office as representative of the church, he represents as something which he is not free to teach as he sees it. He speaks as one who is employed to speak in the name and under the orders of another. He will say: "Our church teaches this or that; these are the proofs which it employs." Thus he will benefit his congregation as much as possible by presenting doctrines to which he may not subscribe with full conviction. He can commit himself to teach them because it is not completely impossible that they may contain hidden truth. In any event, he has found nothing in the doctrines that contradicts the heart of religion. For if he believed that such contradictions existed he would not be able to administer his office with a clear conscience. He would have to resign it. Therefore the use which a scholar makes of his reason before the congregation that employs him is only a private use, for, no matter how sizable, this is only a domestic audience. In view of this he, as preacher, is not free and ought not to be free, since he is carrying out the orders of others. On the other hand, as the scholar who speaks to his own public (the world) through his writings, the minister in the public use of his reason enjoys unlimited freedom to use his own reason and to speak for himself. That the spiritual guardians of the people should themselves be treated as minors is an absurdity which would result in perpetuating absurdities.

But should a society of ministers, say a Church Council, . . . have the right to commit itself by oath to a certain unalterable doctrine, in order to secure perpetual guardianship over all its members and through them over the people? I say that this is quite impossible. Such a contract, concluded to keep all further enlightenment from humanity, is simply null and void even if it should be confirmed by the sovereign power, by parliaments, and by the most solemn treaties. An epoch cannot conclude a pact that will commit succeeding ages, prevent them from increasing their significant insights, purging themselves of errors, and generally progressing in enlightenment. That would be a crime against human nature, whose proper destiny lies precisely in such progress. Therefore, succeeding ages are fully entitled to repudiate such decisions as unauthorized and outrageous. The touchstone of all those decisions that may be made into law for a people lies in this question: Could a people impose such a law upon itself? Now, it might be possible to introduce a certain order for a definite short period of time in expectation of a better order. But while this provisional order continues, each citizen (above all, each pastor acting as a scholar) should be left free to publish his criticisms of the faults of existing institutions. This should continue until public understanding of these matters has gone so far that, by uniting the voices of many (although not necessarily all) scholars, reform proposals could be brought before the sovereign to protect those congregations which had decided according to their best lights upon an altered religious order, without, however, hindering those who want to remain true to the old institutions. But to agree to a perpetual religious constitution which is not to be publicly questioned by anyone would be, as it were, to annihilate a period of time in the progress of man's improvement. This must be absolutely forbidden.

A man may postpone his own enlightenment, but only for a limited period of time. And to give up enlightenment altogether, either for oneself or one's descendants, is to violate and to trample upon the sacred rights of man. What a people may not decide for itself may even less be decided for it by a monarch, for his reputation as a ruler consists precisely in the way in which he unites the will of the whole people within his own. If he only sees to it that all true or supposed improvement remains in step with the civic order, he can for the rest leave his subjects alone to do what they find necessary for the salvation of their souls. Salvation is none of his business; it *is* his business to prevent one man from forcibly keeping another from determining and promoting his salvation to the best of his ability. Indeed, it would be prejudicial to his majesty if he meddled in these matters and supervised the writings in which his subjects seek to bring their views into the open, even when he does this from his own highest insight, because then he exposes himself to the reproach: *Caesar non est supra grammaticos.*[1] It is worse when he debases his sovereign power so far as to support the spiritual despotism of a few tyrants in his state over the rest of his subjects.

---

[1] "Caesar is not above grammarians."

When we ask, Are we now living in an enlightened age? the answer is, No, but we live in an age of enlightenment. As matters now stand it is still far from true that men are already capable of using their own reason in religious matters confidently and correctly without external guidance. Still, we have some obvious indications that the field of working toward the goal of religious truth is now being opened. What is more, the hindrances against general enlightenment or the emergence from self-imposed nonage are gradually diminishing. In this respect this is the age of the enlightenment and the century of Frederick.

A prince ought not to deem it beneath his dignity to state that he considers it his duty not to dictate anything to his subjects in religious matters, but to leave them complete freedom. If he repudiates the arrogant word *tolerant,* he is himself enlightened; he deserves to be praised by a grateful world and posterity as that man who was the first to liberate mankind from dependence, at least on the government, and let everybody use his own reason in matters of conscience. Under his reign, honorable pastors, acting as scholars and regardless of the duties of their office, can freely and openly publish their ideas to the world for inspection, although they deviate here and there from accepted doctrine. This is even more true of every other person not restrained by any oath of office. This spirit of freedom is spreading beyond the boundaries of Prussia, even where it has to struggle against the external hindrances established by a government that fails to grasp its true interest. Frederick's Prussia is a shining example that freedom need not cause the least worry concerning public order or the unity of the community. When one does not deliberately attempt to keep men in barbarism, they will gradually work out of that condition by themselves.

I have emphasized the main point of the enlightenment—man's emergence from his self-imposed nonage—primarily in religious matters, because our rulers have no interest in playing the guardian to their subjects in the arts and sciences. Above all, nonage in religion is not only the most harmful but the most dishonorable. But the dis-position of a sovereign ruler who favors freedom in the arts and sciences goes even further: he knows that there is no danger in permitting his subjects to make public use of their reason and to publish their ideas concerning a better constitution, as well as candid criticism of existing basic laws. We already have a striking example [of such freedom], and no monarch can match the one whom we venerate.

But only the man who is himself enlightened, who is not afraid of shadows, and who commands at the same time a well-disciplined and numerous army as guarantor of public peace—only he can say what a free state cannot dare to say: "Argue as much as you like, and about what you like, but obey!" Thus we observe here as elsewhere in human affairs, in which almost everything is paradoxical, a surprising and unexpected course of events: a large degree of civic freedom appears to be of advantage to the intellectual freedom of the people, yet at the same time it establishes insurmountable barriers. A lesser degree of civic freedom, however, creates room to let that free spirit expand to the limits of its capacity. Nature, then, has carefully cultivated the seed within the hard core—namely, the urge for and the vocation of free thought. And this free thought gradually reacts back on the modes of thought of the people, and men become more and more capable of acting in freedom. At last free thought acts even on the fundamentals of government, and the state finds it agreeable to treat man, who is now more than a machine, in accord with his dignity.

REVIEW QUESTIONS

1. According to Kant, what is enlightenment?
2. What is its relation to habit? To freedom? To revolution?
3. What is the relation of enlightenment to argument? Why?
4. Why should reasoning be public?
5. How does Kant define "public"?
6. Does Kant consider the church public or private?

MARQUIS DE CONDORCET

FROM *Sketch for a Historical Picture on the Progress of the Human Mind*

Marie-Jean-Antoine-Nicolas de Caritat, marquis de Condorcet (1734–1794), came from an old noble family of the principality of Orange. His ancestors had converted to Calvinism and settled in the Dauphiné. During the repression of French Protestantism under Louis XIV, they reconverted to Roman Catholicism. While still an infant, he lost his father and was raised by his mother in an atmosphere of intense Catholic piety. He was educated by Jesuits in Reims and at the Collège de Navare. In his adulthood, Condorcet's thought showed strains of anticlericalism, and he opposed the Jesuit tradition of education. In 1758, he defied his family's wishes by traveling to Paris to pursue studies in mathematics. His work on integral calculus won him a seat in the French Academy of Sciences, where he advanced to assistant to the perpetual secretary in 1774 and became perpetual secretary himself in 1775. He retained this post until 1793. Condorcet espoused revolutionary ideas and was an early supporter of the goals of the French Revolution. Yet he attacked the constitution proposed in the National Convention of 1793. This earned him the enmity of radicals, including a fellow academician, Chabot, who denounced him as an enemy of the revolution. He went into hiding and eventually fled Paris only to be caught and imprisoned. He committed suicide while in prison. Condorcet was a champion of the improvement of humankind through the proper use of reason, believing that rational laws governed human affairs just as they did nature. These laws could be discovered by reason and applied to improve the human condition. Condorcet's Sketch for a Historical Picture on the Progress of the Human Mind *(1795) was published posthumously, one year after his death.*

From *Sketch for a Historical Picture on the Progress of the Human Mind*, by Marie-Jean-Antoine-Nicolas de Caritat, Marquis de Condorcet, translated by June Barraclough (London: Weidenfeld and Nicolson, 1955).

The Tenth Stage
The Future Progress of the Human Mind

If man can, with almost complete assurance, predict phenomena when he knows their laws, and if, even when he does not, he can still, with great expectation of success, forecast the future on the basis of his experience of the past, why, then, should it be regarded as a fantastic undertaking to sketch, with some pretence to truth, the future destiny of man on the basis of his history? The sole foundation for belief in the natural sciences is this idea, that the general laws directing the phenomena of the universe, known or unknown, are necessary and constant. Why should this principle be any less true for the development of the intellectual and moral faculties of man than for the other operations of nature? Since beliefs founded on past experience of like conditions provide the only rule of conduct for the wisest of men, why should the philosopher be forbidden to base his conjectures on these same foundations, so long as he does not attribute to them a certainty superior to that warranted by the number, the constancy, and the accuracy of his observations?

Our hopes for the future condition of the human race can be subsumed under three important heads: the abolition of inequality between nations, the progress of equality within each nation, and the true perfection of mankind. Will all nations one day attain that state of civilization which the most enlightened, the freest and the least burdened by prejudices, such as the French and the Anglo-Americans, have attained already? Will the vast gulf that separates these peoples from the slavery of nations under the rule of monarchs, from the barbarism of African tribes, from the ignorance of savages, little by little disappear?

Is there on the face of the earth a nation whose inhabitants have been debarred by nature herself from the enjoyment of freedom and the exercise of reason?

Are those differences which have hitherto been seen in every civilized country in respect of the enlightenment, the resources, and the wealth enjoyed by the different classes into which it is divided, is that inequality between men which was aggravated or perhaps produced by the earliest progress of society, are these part of civilization itself, or are they due to the present imperfections of the social art? Will they necessarily decrease and ultimately make way for a real equality, the final end of the social art, in which even the effects of the natural differences between men will be mitigated and the only kind of inequality to persist will be that which is in the interests of all and which favours the progress of civilization, of education, and of industry, without entailing either poverty, humiliation, or dependence? In other words, will men approach a condition in which everyone will have the knowledge necessary to conduct himself in the ordinary affairs of life, according to the light of his own reason, to preserve

his mind free from prejudice, to understand his rights and to exercise them in accordance with his conscience and his creed; in which everyone will become able, through the development of his faculties, to find the means of providing for his needs; and in which at last misery and folly will be the exception, and no longer the habitual lot of a section of society?

Is the human race to better itself, either by discoveries in the sciences and the arts, and so in the means to individual welfare and general prosperity; or by progress in the principles of conduct or practical morality; or by a true perfection of the intellectual, moral, or physical faculties of man, an improvement which may result from a perfection either of the instruments used to heighten the intensity of these faculties and to direct their use or of the natural constitution of man?

In answering these three questions we shall find in the experience of the past, in the observation of the progress that the sciences and civilization have already made, in the analysis of the progress of the human mind and of the development of its faculties, the strongest reasons for believing that nature has set no limit to the realization of our hopes.

If we glance at the state of the world today we see first of all that in Europe the principles of the French constitution are already those of all enlightened men. We see them too widely propagated, too seriously professed, for priests and despots to prevent their gradual penetration even into the hovels of their slaves; there they will soon awaken in these slaves the remnants of their common sense and inspire them with that smouldering indignation which not even constant humiliation and fear can smother in the soul of the oppressed.

As we move from nation to nation, we can see in each what special obstacles impede this revolution and what attitudes of mind favour it. We can distinguish the nations where we may expect it to be introduced gently by the perhaps belated wisdom of their governments, and those nations where its violence intensified by their resistance must involve all alike in a swift and terrible convulsion.

Can we doubt that either common sense or

the senseless discords of European nations will add to the effects of the slow but inexorable progress of their colonies, and will soon bring about the independence of the New World? And then will not the European population in these colonies, spreading rapidly over that enormous land, either civilize or peacefully remove the savage nations who still inhabit vast tracts of its land?

Survey the history of our settlements and commercial undertakings in Africa or in Asia, and you will see how our trade monopolies, our treachery, our murderous contempt for men of another colour or creed, the insolence of our usurpations, the intrigues or the exaggerated proselytic zeal of our priests, have destroyed the respect and goodwill that the superiority of our knowledge and the benefits of our commerce at first won for us in the eyes of the inhabitants. But doubtless the moment approaches when, no longer presenting ourselves as always either tyrants or corrupters, we shall become for them the beneficent instruments of their freedom.

*   *   *

The time will therefore come when the sun will shine only on free men who know no other master but their reason; when tyrants and slaves, priests and their stupid or hypocritical instruments will exist only in works of history and on the stage; and when we shall think of them only to pity their victims and their dupes; to maintain ourselves in a state of vigilance by thinking on their excesses; and to learn how to recognize and so to destroy, by force of reason, the first seeds of tyranny and superstition, should they ever dare to reappear amongst us.

In looking at the history of societies we shall have had occasion to observe that there is often a great difference between the rights that the law allows its citizens and the rights that they actually enjoy, and, again, between the equality established by political codes and that which in fact exists amongst individuals: and we shall have noticed that these differences were one of the principal causes of the destruction of freedom in the Ancient republics, of the storms that troubled them,

and of the weakness that delivered them over to foreign tyrants.

These differences have three main causes: inequality in wealth; inequality in status between the man whose means of subsistence are hereditary and the man whose means are dependent on the length of his life, or, rather, on that part of his life in which he is capable of work; and, finally, inequality in education.

We therefore need to show that these three sorts of real inequality must constantly diminish without however disappearing altogether: for they are the result of natural and necessary causes which it would be foolish and dangerous to wish to eradicate; and one could not even attempt to bring about the entire disappearance of their effects without introducing even more fecund sources of inequality, without striking more direct and more fatal blows at the rights of man.

It is easy to prove that wealth has a natural tendency to equality, and that any excessive disproportion could not exist or at least would rapidly disappear if civil laws did not provide artificial ways of perpetuating and uniting fortunes; if free trade and industry were allowed to remove the advantages that accrued wealth derives from any restrictive law or fiscal privilege; if taxes on covenants, the restrictions placed on their free employment, their subjection to tiresome formalities and the uncertainty and inevitable expense involved in implementing them did not hamper the activity of the poor man and swallow up his meagre capital; if the administration of the country did not afford some men ways of making their fortune that were closed to other citizens; if prejudice and avarice, so common in old age, did not preside over the making of marriages; and if, in a society enjoying simpler manners and more sensible institutions, wealth ceased to be a means of satisfying vanity and ambition, and if the equally misguided notions of austerity, which condemn spending money in the cultivation of the more delicate pleasures, no longer insisted on the hoarding of all one's earnings.

Let us turn to the enlightened nations of Europe, and observe the size of their present populations in relation to the size of their territories. Let us consider, in agriculture and industry the proportion that holds between labour and the means of subsistence, and we shall see that it would be impossible for those means to be kept at their present level and consequently for the population to be kept at its present size if a great number of individuals were not almost entirely dependent for the maintenance of themselves and their family either on their own labour or on the interest from capital invested so as to make their labour more productive. Now both these sources of income depend on the life and even on the health of the head of the family. They provide what is rather like a life annuity, save that it is more dependent on chance; and in consequence there is a very real difference between people living like this and those whose resources are not at all subject to the same risks, who live either on revenue from land, or on the interest on capital which is almost independent of their own labour.

Here then is a necessary cause of inequality, of dependence and even of misery, which ceaselessly threatens the most numerous and most active class in our society.

We shall point out how it can be in great part eradicated by guaranteeing people in old age a means of livelihood produced partly by their own savings and partly by the savings of others who make the same outlay, but who die before they need to reap the reward; or, again, on the same principle of compensation, by securing for widows and orphans an income which is the same and costs the same for those families which suffer an early loss and for those which suffer it later; or again by providing all children with the capital necessary for the full use of their labour, available at the age when they start work and found a family, a capital which increases at the expense of those whom premature death prevents from reaching this age. It is to the application of the calculus to the probabilities of life and the investment of money that we owe the idea of these methods which have already been successful, although they have not been applied in a sufficiently comprehensive and exhaustive fashion to render

them really useful, not merely to a few individuals, but to society as a whole, by making it possible to prevent those periodic disasters which strike at so many families and which are such a recurrent source of misery and suffering.

We shall point out that schemes of this nature, which can be organized in the name of the social authority and become one of its greatest benefits, can also be the work of private associations, which will be formed without any real risk, once the principles for the proper working of these schemes have been widely diffused and the mistakes which have been the undoing of a large number of these associations no longer hold terrors for us.

[We shall reveal other methods of ensuring this equality, either by seeing that credit is no longer the exclusive privilege of great wealth, but that it has another and no less sound foundation; or by making industrial progress and commercial activity more independent of the existence of the great capitalists. And once again, it is to the application of the calculus that we shall be indebted for such methods.]

The degree of equality in education that we can reasonably hope to attain, but that should be adequate, is that which excludes all dependence, either forced or voluntary. We shall show how this condition can be easily attained in the present state of human knowledge even by those who can study only for a small number of years in childhood, and then during the rest of their life in their few hours of leisure. We shall prove that, by a suitable choice of syllabus and of methods of education, we can teach the citizen everything that he needs to know in order to be able to manage his household, administer his affairs and employ his labour and his faculties in freedom; to know his rights and to be able to exercise them; to be acquainted with his duties and fulfil them satisfactorily; to judge his own and other men's actions according to his own lights and to be a stranger to none of the high and delicate feelings which honour human nature; not to be in a state of blind dependence upon those to whom he must entrust his affairs or the exercise of his rights; to be in a proper condition to choose and supervise them; to be no longer the dupe of those popular errors which torment man with superstitious fears and chimerical hopes; to defend himself against prejudice by the strength of his reason alone; and, finally, to escape the deceits of charlatans who would lay snares for his fortune, his health, his freedom of thought and his conscience under the pretext of granting him health, wealth and salvation.

From such time onwards the inhabitants of a single country will no longer be distinguished by their use of a crude or refined language; they will be able to govern themselves according to their own knowledge; they will no longer be limited to a mechanical knowledge of the procedures of the arts or of professional routine; they will no longer depend for every trivial piece of business, every insignificant matter of instruction on clever men who rule over them in virtue of their necessary superiority; and so they will attain a real equality, since differences in enlightenment or talent can no longer raise a barrier between men who understand each other's feelings, ideas and language, some of whom may wish to be taught by others but, to do so, will have no need to be controlled by them, or who may wish to confide the care of government to the ablest of their number but will not be compelled to yield them absolute power in a spirit of blind confidence.

This kind of supervision has advantages even for those who do not exercise it, since it is employed for them and not against them. Natural differences of ability between men whose understanding has not been cultivated give rise, even in savage tribes, to charlatans and dupes, to clever men and men readily deceived. These same differences are truly universal, but now they are differences only between men of learning and upright men who know the value of learning without being dazzled by it; or between talent or genius and the common sense which can appreciate and benefit from them; so that even if these natural differences were greater, and more extensive than they are, they would be only the more influential in improving the relations between men and promoting what is advantageous for their independence and happiness.

These various causes of equality do not act in isolation; they unite, combine and support each other and so their cumulative effects are stronger, surer and more constant. With greater equality of education there will be greater equality in industry and so in wealth; equality in wealth necessarily leads to equality in education: and equality between the nations and equality within a single nation are mutually dependent.

So we might say that a well directed system of education rectifies natural inequality in ability instead of strengthening it, just as good laws remedy natural inequality in the means of subsistence, and just as in societies where laws have brought about this same equality, liberty, though subject to a regular constitution, will be more widespread, more complete than in the total independence of savage life. Then the social art will have fulfilled its aim, that of assuring and extending to all men enjoyment of the common rights to which they are called by nature.

The real advantages that should result from this progress, of which we can entertain a hope that is almost a certainty, can have no other term than that of the absolute perfection of the human race; since, as the various kinds of equality come to work in its favour by producing ampler sources of supply, more extensive education, more complete liberty, so equality will be more real and will embrace everything which is really of importance for the happiness of human beings.

It is therefore only by examining the progress and the laws of this perfection that we shall be able to understand the extent or the limits of our hopes.

*   *   *

The progress of the sciences ensures the progress of the art of education which in turn advances that of the sciences. This reciprocal influence, whose activity is ceaselessly renewed, deserves to be seen as one of the most powerful and active causes working for the perfection of mankind. At the present time a young man on leaving school may know more of the principles of mathematics than Newton ever learnt in years of study or discovered by dint of genius, and he may use the calculus with a facility then unknown. The same observation, with certain reservations, applies to all the sciences. As each advances, the methods of expressing a large number of proofs in a more economical fashion and so of making their comprehension an easier matter, advance with it. So, in spite of the progress of science, not only do men of the same ability find themselves at the same age on a level with the existing state of science, but with every generation, that which can be acquired in a certain time with a certain degree of intelligence and a certain amount of concentration will be permanently on the increase, and, as the elementary part of each science to which all men may attain grows and grows, it will more and more include all the knowledge necessary for each man to know for the conduct of the ordinary events of his life, and will support him in the free and independent exercise of his reason.

In the political sciences there are some truths that, with free people (that is to say, with certain generations in all countries) can be of use only if they are widely known and acknowledged. So the influence of these sciences upon the freedom and prosperity of nations must in some degree be measured by the number of truths that, as a result of elementary instruction, are common knowledge; the swelling progress of elementary instruction, connected with the necessary progress of these sciences promises us an improvement in the destiny of the human race, which may be regarded as indefinite, since it can have no other limits than that of this same progress.

We have still to consider two other general methods which will influence both the perfection of education and that of the sciences. One is the more extensive and less imperfect use of what we might call technical methods; the other is the setting up of a universal language.

I mean by technical methods the art of arranging a large number of subjects in a system so that we may straightway grasp their relations, quickly perceive their combinations, and readily form new combinations out of them.

We shall develop the principles and examine the utility of this art, which is still in its infancy, and which, as it improves, will enable us, within the compass of a small chart, to set out what could possibly not be expressed so well in a whole book, or, what is still more valuable, to present isolated facts in such a way as to allow us to deduce their general consequences. We shall see how by means of a small number of these charts, whose use can easily be learned, men who have not been sufficiently educated to be able to absorb details useful to them in ordinary life, may now be able to master them when the need arises; and how these methods may likewise be of benefit to elementary education itself in all those branches where it is concerned either with a regular system of truths or with a series of observations and facts.

A universal language is that which expresses by signs either real objects themselves, or well-defined collections composed of simple and general ideas, which are found to be the same or may arise in a similar form in the minds of all men, or the general relations holding between these ideas, the operations of the human mind, or the operations peculiar to the individual sciences, or the procedures of the arts. So people who become acquainted with these signs, the ways to combine them and the rules for forming them will understand what is written in this language and will be able to read it as easily as their own language.

It is obvious that this language might be used to set out the theory of a science or the rules of an art, to describe a new observation or experiment, the invention of a procedure, the discovery of a truth or a method; and that, as in algebra, when one has to make use of a new sign, those already known provide the means of explaining its import.

Such a language has not the disadvantages of a scientific idiom different from the vernacular. We have already observed that the use of such an idiom would necessarily divide society into two unequal classes, the one composed of men who, understanding this language, would possess the key to all the sciences, the other of men who, unable to acquire it, would therefore find themselves almost completely unable to acquire enlightenment. In contrast to this, a universal language would be learnt, like that of algebra, along with the science itself; the sign would be learnt at the same time as the object, idea or operation that it designates. He who, having mastered the elements of a science, would like to know more of it, would find in books not only truths he could understand by means of the signs whose import he has learnt, but also the explanation of such further signs as he needs in order to go on to other truths.

We shall show that the formation of such a language, if confined to the expression of those simple, precise propositions which form the system of a science or the practice of an art, is no chimerical scheme; that even at the present time it could be readily introduced to deal with a large number of objects; and that, indeed, the chief obstacle that would prevent its extension to others would be the humiliation of having to admit how very few precise ideas and accurate, unambiguous notions we actually possess.

We shall show that this language, ever improving and broadening its scope all the while, would be the means of giving to every subject embraced by the human intelligence, a precision and a rigour that would make knowledge of the truth easy and error almost impossible. Then the progress of every science would be as sure as that of mathematics, and the propositions that compose it would acquire a geometrical certainty, as far, that is, as is possible granted the nature of its aim and method.

All the causes that contribute to the perfection of the human race, all the means that ensure it must by their very nature exercise a perpetual influence and always increase their sphere of action. The proofs of this we have given and in the great work they will derive additional force from elaboration. We may conclude then that the perfectibility of man is indefinite. Meanwhile we have considered him as possessing the natural faculties and organization that he has at present. How much greater would be the certainty, how must vaster the scheme of our hopes if we could believe that these natural faculties themselves and this organization could also be improved? This is the last question that remains for us to ask ourselves.

Organic perfectibility or deterioration amongst the various strains in the vegetable and animal kingdom can be regarded as one of the general laws of nature. This law also applies to the human race. No-one can doubt that, as preventitive medicine improves and food and housing become healthier, as a way of life is established that develops our physical powers by exercise without ruining them by excess, as the two most virulent causes of deterioration, misery and excessive wealth, are eliminated, the average length of human life will be increased and a better health and a stronger physical constitution will be ensured. The improvement of medical practice, which will become more efficacious with the progress of reason and of the social order, will mean the end of infectious and hereditary diseases and illnesses brought on by climate, food, or working conditions. It is reasonable to hope that all other diseases may likewise disappear as their distant causes are discovered. Would it be absurd then to suppose that this perfection of the human species might be capable of indefinite progress; that the day will come when death will be due only to extraordinary accidents or to the decay of the vital forces, and that ultimately the average span between birth and decay will have no assignable value? Certainly man will not become immortal, but will not the interval between the first breath that he draws and the time when in the natural course of events, without disease or accident, he expires, increase indefinitely? Since we are now speaking of a progress that can be represented with some accuracy in figures or on a graph, we shall take this opportunity of explaining the two meanings that can be attached to the word *indefinite*.

In truth, this average span of life which we suppose will increase indefinitely as time passes, may grow in conformity either with a law such that it continually approaches a limitless length but without ever reaching it, or with a law such that through the centuries it reaches a length greater than any determinate quantity that we may assign to it as its limit. In the latter case such an increase is truly indefinite in the strictest sense of the word, since there is no term on this side of which it must of necessity stop. In the former case it is equally indefinite in relation to us, if we cannot fix the limit it always approaches without ever reaching, and particularly if, knowing only that it will never stop, we are ignorant in which of the two senses the term 'indefinite' can be applied to it. Such is the present condition of our knowledge as far as the perfectibility of the human race is concerned; such is the sense in which we may call it indefinite.

So, in the example under consideration, we are bound to believe that the average length of human life will for ever increase unless this is prevented by physical revolutions; we do not know what the limit is which it can never exceed. We cannot tell even whether the general laws of nature have determined such a limit or not.

But are not our physical faculties and the strength, dexterity and acuteness of our senses, to be numbered among the qualities whose perfection in the individual may be transmitted? Observation of the various breeds of domestic animals inclines us to believe that they are, and we can confirm this by direct observation of the human race.

Finally may we not extend such hopes to the intellectual and moral faculties? May not our parents, who transmit to us the benefits or disadvantages of their constitution, and from whom we receive our shape and features, as well as our tendencies to certain physical affections, hand on to us also that part of the physical organization which determines the intellect, the power of the brain, the ardour of the soul or the moral sensibility? Is it not probable that education, in perfecting these qualities, will at the same time influence, modify and perfect the organization itself? Analogy, investigation of the human faculties and the study of certain facts, all seem to give substance to such conjectures which would further push back the boundaries of our hopes.

These are the questions with which we shall conclude this final stage. How consoling for the philosopher who laments the errors, the crimes, the injustices which still pollute the earth and of which he is often the victim is this view of the human race, emancipated from its shackles, released from the empire of fate and from that of the enemies of its progress, advancing with a firm and sure step along the path of truth, virtue and happiness! It is the contemplation of this prospect that rewards him for all his efforts to assist the progress of reason and the defence of liberty. He dares to regard these strivings as part of the eternal chain of human destiny; and in this persuasion he is filled with the true delight of virtue and the pleasure of having done some lasting good which fate can never destroy by a sinister stroke of revenge, by calling back the reign of slavery and prejudice. Such contemplation is for him an asylum, in which the memory of his persecutors cannot pursue him; there he lives in thought with man restored to his natural rights and dignity, forgets man tormented and corrupted by greed, fear or envy; there he lives with his peers in an Elysium created by reason and graced by the purest pleasures known to the love of mankind.

*   *   *

REVIEW QUESTIONS

1. On what does Condorcet found his ability to predict the future?
2. Would Newton agree "that nature has set no limit to the realization of one's hopes"?
3. In what areas of human endeavor does Condorcet measure progress?
4. What are the standards by which he measures it?
5. What does Condorcet see as the end point of Enlightenment?
6. According to Condorcet, what is the nature of freedom? Of equality?
7. How does Condorcet measure equality?
8. What is its relation to a universal language?

OLAUDAH EQUIANO

FROM *The Interesting Narrative of the Life of Olaudah Equiano, or Gustavus Vassa, the African*

One of the most notable records of the slave trade, which dominated African-European relations into the nineteenth century, was the autobiography of Equiano, an ex-slave living in London. He was remarkable not only because he survived the experience of capture, transportation, and exploitation but also because he obtained sufficient education and opportunity to record his experiences. The extract provided here describes his first encounter with white men aboard a slave ship. Freed in 1766, he toured widely, speaking and writing against the slave trade until his death sometime between 1797 and 1801.

From *The Interesting Narrative of the Life of Olaudah Equiano, or Gustavus Vassa, the African, written by himself,* edited by Werner Sollers, a Norton Critical Edition (New York: Norton, 2001), pp. 38–43.

*   *   *

The first object which saluted my eyes when I arrived on the coast was the sea, and a slave ship, which was then riding at anchor, and waiting for its cargo. These filled me with astonishment, which was soon converted into terror when I was carried on board. I was immediately handled and tossed up to see if I were sound by some of the crew; and I was now persuaded that I had gotten into a world of bad spirits, and that they were going to kill me. Their complexions too differing so much from ours, their long hair, and the language they spoke, (which was very different from any I had ever heard) united to confirm me in this belief. Indeed such were the horrors of my views and fears at the moment, that, if ten thousand worlds had been my own, I would have freely parted with them all to have exchanged my condition with that of the meanest slave in my own country. When I looked round the ship too and saw a large furnace or copper boiling, and a multitude of black people of every description chained together, every one of their countenances expressing dejection and sorrow, I no longer doubted of my fate; and, quite overpowered with horror and anguish, I fell motionless on the deck and fainted. When I recovered a little I found some black people about me, who I believed were some of those who brought me on board, and had been receiving their pay; they talked to me in order to cheer me, but all in vain. I asked them if we were not to be eaten by those white men with horrible looks, red faces, and loose hair. They told me I was not; and one of the crew brought me a small portion of spirituous liquor in a wine glass; but, being afraid of him, I would not take it out of his hand. One of the blacks therefore took it from him and gave it to me, and I took a little down my palate, which, instead of reviving me, as they thought it would, threw me into the greatest consternation at the strange feeling it produced, having never tasted any such liquor before. Soon after this the blacks who brought me on board went off, and left me abandoned to despair. I now saw myself deprived of all chance of returning to my native country, or even the least glimpse of hope of gaining the shore, which I now considered as friendly; and I even wished for my former slavery in preference to my present situation, which was filled with horrors of every kind, still heightened by my ignorance of what I was to undergo. I was not long suffered to indulge my grief; I was soon put down under the decks, and there I received such a salutation in my nostrils as I had never experienced in my life: so that, with the loathsomeness of the stench, and crying together, I became so sick and low that I was not able to eat, nor had I the least desire to taste any thing. I now wished for the last friend, death, to relieve me; but soon, to my grief, two of the white men offered me eatables; and, on my refusing to eat, one of them held me fast by the hands, and laid me across I think the windlass,[1] and tied my feet, while the other flogged me severely. I had never experienced any thing of this kind before; and although, not being used to the water, I naturally feared that element the first time I saw it, yet nevertheless, could I have got over the nettings, I would have jumped over the side, but I could not; and, besides, the crew used to watch us very closely who were not chained down to the decks, lest we should leap into the water: and I have seen some of these poor African prisoners most severely cut for attempting to do so, and hourly whipped for not eating. This indeed was often the case with myself. In a little time after, amongst the poor chained men, I found some of my own nation, which in a small degree gave ease to my mind. I inquired of these what was to be done with us; they gave me to understand we were to be carried to these white people's country to work for them. I then was a little revived, and thought, if it were no worse than working, my situation was not so desperate: but still I feared I should be put to death, the white people looked and acted, as I thought, in so savage a manner; for I had never seen among any people such instances of brutal cruelty; and this not only shewn towards us blacks, but also to some of the whites themselves. One white man in particular I saw, when we were permitted to be on deck, flogged so unmercifully with a large rope near the

foremast, that he died in consequence of it; and they tossed him over the side as they would have done a brute. This made me fear these people the more; and I expected nothing less than to be treated in the same manner. I could not help expressing my fears and apprehensions to some of my countrymen: I asked them if these people had no country, but lived in this hollow place (the ship): they told me they did not, but came from a distant one. "Then," said I, "how comes it in all our country we never heard of them?" They told me because they lived so very far off. I then asked where were their women? had they any like themselves? I was told they had: "and why," said I, "do we not see them?" they answered, because they were left behind. I asked how the vessel could go? they told me they could not tell; but that there were cloths put upon the masts by the help of the ropes I saw, and then the vessel went on; and the white men had some spell or magic they put in the water when they liked in order to stop the vessel. I was exceedingly amazed at this account, and really thought they were spirits. I therefore wished much to be from amongst them, for I expected they would sacrifice me: but my wishes were vain; for we were so quartered that it was impossible for any of us to make our escape. While we stayed on the coast I was mostly on deck; and one day, to my great astonishment, I saw one of these vessels coming in with the sails up. As soon as the whites saw it, they gave a great shout, at which we were amazed; and the more so as the vessel appeared larger by approaching nearer. At last she came to an anchor in my sight, and when the anchor was let go I and my countrymen who saw it were lost in astonishment to observe the vessel stop; and were now convinced it was done by magic. Soon after this the other ship got her boats out, and they came on board of us, and the people of both ships seemed very glad to see each other. Several of the strangers also shook hands with us black people, and made motions with their hands, signifying I suppose we were to go to their country; but we did not understand them. At last, when the ship we were in had got in all her cargo, they made ready

---

[1] An apparatus for winding rope.

with many fearful noises, and we were all put under deck, so that we could not see how they managed the vessel. But this disappointment was the least of my sorrow. The stench of the hold while we were on the coast was so intolerably loathsome, that it was dangerous to remain there for any time, and some of us had been permitted to stay on the deck for the fresh air; but now that the whole ship's cargo were confined together, it became absolutely pestilential. The closeness of the place, and the heat of the climate, added to the number in the ship, which was so crowded that each had scarcely room to turn himself, almost suffocated us. This produced copious perspirations, so that the air soon became unfit for respiration, from a variety of loathsome smells, and brought on a sickness among the slaves, of which many died, thus falling victims to the improvident avarice, as I may call it, of their purchasers. This wretched situation was again aggravated by the galling of the chains, now become insupportable; and the filth of the necessary tubs,[2] into which the children often fell, and were almost suffocated. The shrieks of the women, and the groans of the dying, rendered the whole a scene of horror almost inconceivable. Happily perhaps for myself I was soon reduced so low here that it was thought necessary to keep me almost always on deck; and from my extreme youth I was not put in fetters. In this situation I expected every hour to share the fate of my companions, some of whom were almost daily brought upon deck at the point of death, which I began to hope would soon put an end to my miseries. Often did I think many of the inhabitants of the deep much more happy than myself. I envied them the freedom they enjoyed, and as often wished I could change my condition for theirs. Every circumstance I met with served only to render my state more painful, and heighten my apprehensions, and my opinion of the cruelty of the whites. One day they had taken a number of fishes; and when they had killed and satisfied themselves with as many as they thought fit, to our astonishment who were on the deck, rather than give any of them to us to eat as we expected, they tossed the remaining fish into the sea again, although we begged and prayed for some as well as we could, but in vain; and some of my countrymen, being pressed by hunger, took an opportunity when they thought no one saw them, of trying to get a little privately; but they were discovered, and the attempt procured them some very severe floggings. One day, when we had a smooth sea and moderate wind, two of my wearied countrymen who were chained together (I was near them at the time), preferring death to such a life of misery, somehow made through the nettings and jumped into the sea: immediately another quite dejected fellow, who, on one account of his illness, was suffered to be out of irons, also followed their example; and I believe many more would very soon have done the same if they had not been prevented by the ship's crew, who were instantly alarmed. Those of us that were the most active were in a moment put down under the deck, and here was such a noise and confusion amongst the people of the ship as I never heard before, to stop her, and get the boat out to go after the slaves. However two of the wretches drowned, but they got the other, and afterwards flogged him unmercifully for thus attempting to prefer death to slavery. In this manner we continued to undergo more hardships than I can now relate, hardships which are inseparable from this accursed trade. Many a time we were near suffocation from the want of fresh air, which we were often without for whole days together. This, and the stench of the necessary tubs, carried off many. During our passage I first saw flying fishes, which surprised me very much: they used frequently to fly across the ship, and many of them fell on the deck. I also now first saw the use of the quadrant;[3] I had often with astonishment seen the mariners make observations with it, and I could not think what it meant. They at last took notice of my surprise; and one of them, willing to increase

---

[2] Latrines.

[3] Instrument used to determine geographical latitude.

it, as well as to gratify my curiosity, made me one day look through it. The clouds appeared to me to be land, which disappeared as they passed along. This heightened my wonder; and I was now more persuaded than ever that I was in another world, and that every thing about me was magic. At last we came in sight of the island of Barbadoes,[4] at which the whites on board gave a great shout, and made many signs of joy to us. We did not know what to think of this; but as the vessel drew nearer we plainly saw the harbour, and other ships of different kinds and sizes; and we soon anchored amongst them off Bridge Town.[5] Many merchants and planters now came on board, though it was in the evening. They put us in separate parcels, and examined us attentively. They also made us jump, and pointed to the land, signifying we were to go there. We thought by this we should be eaten by these ugly men, as they appeared to us; and, when soon after we were all put down under the deck again, there was much dread and trembling among us, and nothing but bitter cries to be heard all the night from these apprehensions, insomuch that at last the white people got some old slaves from the land to pacify us. They told us we were not to be eaten, but to work, and were soon to go on land, where we should see many of our country people. This report eased us much; and sure enough, soon after we were landed, there came to us Africans of all languages. We were conducted immediately to the merchant's yard, where we were all pent up together like so many sheep in a fold, without regard to sex or age. As every object was new to me every thing I saw filled me with surprise. What struck me first was that the houses were built with stories, and in every other respect different from those in Africa: but I was still more astonished on seeing people on horseback. I did not know what this could mean; and indeed I thought these people were full of nothing but magical arts. While I was in this astonishment one of my fellow prisoners spoke to a countryman of his about the horses, who said they were the same kind they had in their country. I understood them, though they were from a distant part of Africa, and I thought it odd I had not seen any horses there; but afterwards, when I came to converse with different Africans, I found they had many horses amongst them, and much larger than those I then saw. We were not many days in the merchant's custody before we were sold after their usual manner, which is this:— On a signal given, (as the beat of a drum) the buyers rush at once into the yard where the slaves are confined, and make choice of that parcel they like best. The noise and clamour with which this is attended, and the eagerness visible in the countenances of the buyers, serve not a little to increase the apprehensions of the terrified Africans, who may well be supposed to consider them as the ministers of that destruction to which they think themselves devoted. In this manner, without scruple, are relations and friends separated, most of them never to see each other again. I remember in the vessel in which I was brought over, in the men's apartment, there were several brothers, who, in the sale, were sold in different lots; and it was very moving on this occasion to see and hear their cries at parting. O, ye nominal Christians! might not an African ask you, learned you this from your God, who says unto you, Do unto all men as you would men should do unto you? Is it not enough that we are torn from our country and friends to toil for your luxury and lust of gain? Must every tender feeling be likewise sacrificed to your avarice? Are the dearest friends and relations, now rendered more dear by their separation from their kindred, still to be parted from each other, and thus prevented from cheering the gloom of slavery with the small comfort of being together and mingling their sufferings and sorrows? Why are parents to lose their children, brothers their sisters, or husbands their wives? Surely this is a new refinement in cruelty, which, while it has no advantage to atone for it, thus aggravates distress, and adds fresh horrors even to the wretchedness of slavery.

---

[4] Or Barbados, the most easterly of the Caribbean islands.
[5] Capital of Barbados.

REVIEW QUESTIONS

1. What things capture Equiano's attention aboard the slave ship?
2. How would you characterize his reactions?
3. What is his view of his captors?
4. For whom is Equiano writing?
5. How does his writing reflect the general principles and goals of the Enlightenment?
6. Does the Enlightenment inform Equiano's view of slavery?

18 ∞ THE FRENCH REVOLUTION

The French revolutionary and Napoleonic eras, 1789–1815, launched the modern period in European history. Europe had so irrevocably changed after 1815 that contemporaries distinguished the period before 1789 as the old regime. To be sure, many features of the old regime continued into the new era, but the sentiment of sudden rupture was largely valid. In various dimensions of public life, the radical transformations of the French Revolution rendered many prerevolutionary attitudes toward society and politics obsolete. Following the abolition of feudalism, the declaration of civic equality, and the subordination of monarchy to national political sovereignty, traditional authority became irretrievable.

The areas of French society (aristocrats, civil servants, professionals, merchants, artisans, urban workers, peasants) willing to reform, if not dismantle, absolutist monarchy established the revolution's legitimacy. The wide range of grievances that had accumulated in the French provinces and cities provided the broad social base for the upheaval of 1789, just as the prevailing emphasis of eighteenth-century letters on applying reason, natural law, and social utility to public affairs offered a general intellectual framework. To understand the revolution's development, however, one must recognize that although the revolution inaugurated a new era of political rights and citizenship ideals, the specific content of "liberty, equality, fraternity" remained contested. Consequently, the freshly constituted polity of France embarked on an uncharted course of political experimentation, the prominent milestones of which (dissolution of the monarchy, regicide, radical republicanism, political terror, abolition of the slave trade, republican imperialism) subsequently defined the parameters of the modern political landscape.

The revolutionary impulses in Paris resonated throughout Europe. Because France was the largest and most powerful continental state in Europe (one out of five Europeans lived in France), French politics affected all Europeans. The precedent of French constitutionalism and the Declaration of the Rights of Man and

Citizen reconfigured the domestic political cultures of all European states. The level of political disputation intensified; contemporaries alternately celebrated or denounced the potential of widened political participation. Even Great Britain's stable political establishment of limited monarchy and parliamentary rule perceived French republicanism as a threat. The decision of Austria and Prussia to invade France in 1792 not only radicalized French politics but also expanded the revolutionary political arena. Napoleon's military prowess further embedded French revolutionary influence abroad with the creation of new kingdoms, the appointment of new rulers, the institution of new laws, and the transmission of a new political outlook. Although the European great powers attempted to eradicate most of Napoleon's political reordering after 1815, the revolutionary challenge to traditional elites remained a permanent feature of European political life.

ARTHUR YOUNG

FROM *Travels in France during the Years 1787, 1788, 1789*

Arthur Young (1741–1820), an established author and one of the "improving landlords" of English agriculture, traveled through France prior to and during the French Revolution. His acute observations of the conditions of French society offer invaluable contemporary testimony to the many problems that hindered both agricultural prosperity and political stability.

From *Travels in France during the Years 1787, 1788, 1789*, by Arthur Young (London: G. Bell, 1890).

*   *   *

Of all the subjects of political economy, I know not one that has given rise to such a cloud of errors as this of population. It seems, for some centuries, to have been considered as the only sure test of national prosperity. I am clearly of opinion from the observations I made in every province of the Kingdom, that her population is so much beyond the proportion of her industry and labour, that she would be much more powerful, and infinitely more flourishing, if she had five or six millions less of inhabitants. From her too great population, she presents in every quarter such spectacles of wretchedness as are absolutely inconsistent with that degree of national felicity which she was capable of attaining even under her old government. A traveller much less attentive than I was to objects of this kind must see at every turn most unequivocal signs of distress.

That these should exist, no one can wonder who considers the price of labour, and of provisions, and the misery into which a small rise in the price of wheat throws the lower classes. The causes of this great population were certainly not to be found in the benignity of the old government yielding a due protection to the lower classes, for, on the contrary, it abandoned them to the mercy of the privileged orders. This great populousness of France I attribute very much to the division of the lands into small properties, which takes place in that country to a degree of which we have in England but little conception. Whatever promises the appearance even of subsistence induces men to marry. The inheritance of 10 or 12 acres to be divided amongst the children of the proprietor will be looked to with the views of a permanent settlement, and either occasions a marriage, the infants of which die young for want of sufficient nourishment, or keeps children at home, distressing their relations, long after the time that they should have emigrated to towns.

*   *   *

V. MÉTAYERS is the tenure under which perhaps seven-eighths of the lands of France are held.

*   *   *

At the first blush, the great disadvantage of the *métayage* system[1] is to landlords; but on a nearer examination, the tenants are found in the lowest state of poverty, and some of them in misery. At Vatan, in Berry, I was assured that the *métayers* almost every year borrowed their bread of the landlord before the harvest came round, yet hardly worth borrowing, for it was made of rye and barley mixed. I tasted enough of it to pity sincerely the poor people. In Limousin the *métayers* are considered as little better than menial servants, removable at pleasure, and obliged to conform in all things to the will of the landlords. It is commonly computed that half the tenantry are deeply

---

[1] The *métayage* system can be likened to sharecropping: the lord or proprietor provided land to tenant farmers, who in return surrendered a portion of their harvest.

in debt to the proprietor, so that he is often obliged to turn them off with the loss of these debts, in order to save his land from running waste.

In all the modes of occupying land, the great evil is the smallness of farms. There are large ones in Picardy, the Isle of France, the Pays de Beauce, Artois and Normandy; but in the rest of the kingdom such are not general. The division of the farms and population is so great, that the misery flowing from it is in many places extreme; the idleness of the people is seen the moment you enter a town on market day; the swarms of people are incredible. At Landivisiau in Bretagne, I saw a man who walked 7 miles to bring 2 chickens, which would not sell for 24 *sous* the couple, as he told me himself. At Avranches, men attending each a horse, with a pannier load of sea ooze, not more than 4 bushels. Near Isenheim in Alsace, a rich country, women, in the midst of harvest, where their labour is nearly as valuable as that of men, reaping grass by the road side to carry home to their cows.

*   *   *

In this most miserable of all the modes of letting land, after running the hazard of such losses, fatal in many instances, the defrauded landlord receives a contemptible rent; the farmer is in the lowest state of poverty; the land is miserably cultivated; and the nation suffers as severely as the parties themselves.

*   *   *

The abuses attending the levy of taxes were heavy and universal. The kingdom was parcelled into *généralités*, with an Intendant at the head of each, into whose hands the whole power of the Crown was delegated for everything except the military authority; but particularly for all affairs of finance. The *généralités* were sub-divided into *élections*, at the head of which was a *subdélégué*, appointed by the Intendant. The rolls of the *taille, capitation, vingtièmes,* and other taxes, were distributed among districts, parishes, and individuals, at the pleasure of the Intendant, who could exempt, change, add, or diminish, at pleasure. Such an enormous power, constantly acting, and from which no man was free, must, in the nature of things, degenerate in many cases into absolute tyranny. It must be obvious, that the friends, acquaintances, and dependents of the Intendant, and of all his *subdélégués,* and the friends of these friends, to a long chain of dependence, might be favoured in taxation at the expense of their miserable neighbours; and that noblemen, in favour at court, to whose protection the Intendant himself would naturally look up, could find little difficulty in throwing much of the weight of their taxes on others, without a similar support. Instances, and even gross ones, have been reported to me in many parts of the kingdom, that made me shudder at the oppression to which numbers must have been condemned, by the undue favours granted to such crooked influence.

*   *   *

The *corvées,* or police of the roads, were annually the ruin of many hundreds of farmers; more than 300 were reduced to beggary in filling up one vale in Lorraine. All these oppressions fell on the *tiers état* only; the nobility and clergy having been equally exempted from *tailles,* militia, and *corvées.*

The penal code of finance makes one shudder at the horrors of punishment inadequate to the crime. A few features will sufficiently characterize the old government of France.

1. Smugglers of salt, armed and assembled to the number of five, in Provence, a *fine of 500 livres and nine years galleys*; in all the rest of the kingdom, *death.*

2. Smugglers armed, assembled, but in number under five, *a fine of 300 livres and three years galleys.* Second offence, *death.*

3. Smugglers, without arms, but with horses, carts, or boats, *a fine of 300 livres; if not paid, three years galleys.* Second offence, *400 livres and nine years galleys.* In Dauphiné, second offence, *galleys for life.* In Provence, *five years galleys.*

4. Smugglers, who carry the salt on their backs, and without arms, *a fine of 200 livres, and, if not paid, are flogged and branded.* Second offence, *a fine of 300 livres and six years galleys.*

5. Women, married and single, smugglers, first offence, *a fine of 100 livres.* Second, *300 livres.* Third, *flogged, and banished the kingdom for life. Husbands responsible both in fine and body.*

6. Children smugglers, the same as women. *Fathers and mothers responsible; and for defect of payment flogged.*

*   *   *

But these were not all the evils with which the people struggled. The administration of justice was partial, venal, infamous. I have, in conversation with many very sensible men, in different parts of the kingdom, met with something of content with their government, in all other respects than this; but upon the question of expecting justice to be really and fairly administered, everyone confessed there was no such thing to be looked for. The conduct of the parliaments was profligate and atrocious. Upon almost every cause that came before them, interest was openly made with the judges; and woe betided the man who, with a cause to support, had no means of conciliating favour, either by the beauty of a handsome wife, or by other methods. It has been said, by many writers, that property was as secure under the old government of France as it is in England; and the assertion might possibly be true, as far as any violence from the King, his ministers, or the great was concerned; but for all that mass of property, which comes in every country to be litigated in courts of justice, there was not even the shadow of security, unless the parties were totally and equally unknown, and totally and equally honest; in every other case, he who had the best interest with the judges was sure to be the winner. To reflecting minds, the cruelty and abominable practice attending such courts are sufficiently apparent.

*   *   *

The true judgment to be formed of the French revolution must surely be gained from an attentive consideration of the evils of the old government. When these are well understood, and when the extent and universality of the oppression under which the people groaned, oppression which bore upon them from every quarter, it will scarcely be attempted to be urged that a revolution was not absolutely necessary to the welfare of the kingdom. Not one opposing voice can, with reason, be raised against this assertion; abuses ought certainly to be corrected, and corrected effectually. This could not be done without the establishment of a new form of government; whether the form that has been adopted were the best, is another question absolutely distinct.

*   *   *

REVIEW QUESTIONS

1. For Arthur Young, what are the chief problems in the French countryside?
2. What were the specific problems imposed on the small farmer by the nobility, the legal system, and the government?
3. How were public affairs conducted?
4. How did these problems in the countryside contribute to the success of the revolution?

THOMAS JEFFERSON

The Declaration of Independence

The successful attempt of the original thirteen colonies to break their allegiance to Great Britain was an important antecedent to the French Revolution. Not only did France's financial support of the insurgent colonies precipitate the financial crisis that would compel Louis XVI to convene the Estates General but the American War of Independence also produced a political culture that celebrated principles of popular sovereignty and "unalienable" individual liberties. The Declaration of Independence, among the noblest of U.S. documents, arose out of the need to attach a preamble to a resolution by Congress, which moved in June 1776 "that these United Colonies are, and of right ought to be, free and independent States." Congress appointed a committee of five representatives to write the preamble, but one member, Thomas Jefferson (1743–1826), actually drafted the document, which was adopted by Congress on July 4, 1776.

When in the course of human events, it becomes necessary for one people to dissolve the political bands which have connected them with another, and to assume among the Powers of the earth, the separate and equal station to which the Laws of Nature and of Nature's God entitle them, a decent respect to the opinions of mankind requires that they should declare the causes which impel them to the separation.

We hold these truths to be self-evident, that all men are created equal, that they are endowed by their Creator with certain unalienable rights, that among these are Life, Liberty, and the pursuit of Happiness. That to secure these rights, Governments are instituted among Men, deriving their just powers from the consent of the governed. That whenever any Form of Government becomes destructive of these ends, it is the Right of the

People to alter or to abolish it, and to institute new Government, laying its foundation on such principles and organizing its powers in such form, as to them shall seem most likely to effect their Safety and Happiness. Prudence, indeed, will dictate that Governments long established should not be changed for light and transient causes; and accordingly all experience hath shown, that mankind are more disposed to suffer, while evils are sufferable, than to right themselves by abolishing the forms to which they are accustomed. But when a long train of abuses and usurpations, pursuing invariably the same Object evinces a design to reduce them under absolute Despotism, it is their right, it is their duty, to throw off such Government, and to provide new Guards for their future security—Such has been the patient sufferance of these Colonies; and such is now the necessity which constrains them to alter their former Systems of Government. The history of the present King of Great Britain is a history of repeated injuries and usurpations, all having in direct object the establishment of an absolute Tyranny over these States. To prove this, let Facts be submitted to a candid world.

He has refused his Assent to Laws, the most wholesome and necessary for the public good.

He has forbidden his Governors to pass Laws of immediate and pressing importance, unless suspended in their operation till his Assent should be obtained; and when so suspended, he has utterly neglected to attend to them.

He has refused to pass other Laws for the accommodation of large districts of people, unless those people would relinquish the right of Representation in the Legislature, a right inestimable to them and formidable to tyrants only.

He has called together legislative bodies at places unusual, uncomfortable, and distant from the depository of their public Records, for the sole purpose of fatiguing them into compliance with his measures.

He has dissolved Representative Houses repeatedly, for opposing with manly firmness his invasions on the rights of the people.

He has refused for a long time, after such dissolutions, to cause others to be elected; whereby the Legislative powers, incapable of Annihilation, have returned to the People at large for their exercise; the State remaining in the mean time exposed to all dangers of invasion from without, and convulsions within.

He has endeavoured to prevent the population of these States; for that purpose obstructing the Laws of Naturalization of Foreigners; refusing to pass others to encourage their migrations hither, and raising the conditions of new Appropriations of Lands.

He has obstructed the Administration of Justice, by refusing his Assent to Laws for establishing Judiciary powers.

He has made Judges dependent on his Will alone, for the tenure of their offices, and the amount and payment of their salaries.

He has erected a multitude of New Offices, and sent hither swarms of Officers to harass our People, and eat out their substance.

He has kept among us, in times of peace, Standing Armies without the Consent of our legislature.

He has affected to render the Military independent of and superior to the Civil Power.

He has combined with others to subject us to a jurisdiction foreign to our constitution, and unacknowledged by our laws; giving his Assent to their Acts of pretended Legislation:

For quartering large bodies of armed troops among us:

For protecting them, by a mock Trial, from Punishment for any Murders which they should commit on the Inhabitants of these States:

For cutting off our Trade with all parts of the world:

For imposing taxes on us without our Consent:

For depriving us in many cases, of the benefits of Trial by jury:

For transporting us beyond Seas to be tried for pretended offences:

For abolishing the free System of English Laws in a neighbouring Province, establishing therein an Arbitrary government, and enlarging its Boundaries so as to render it at once an example and fit instrument for introducing the same absolute rule into these Colonies:

For taking away our Charters, abolishing our most valuable Laws, and altering fundamentally the Forms of our Governments:

For suspending our own Legislatures, and declaring themselves invested with Power to legislate for us in all cases whatsoever.

He has abdicated Government here, by declaring us out of his Protection and waging War against us.

He has plundered our seas, ravaged our Coasts, burnt our towns, and destroyed the lives of our people.

He is at this time transporting large armies of foreign mercenaries to compleat the works of death, desolation, and tyranny, already begun with circumstances of Cruelty & perfidy scarcely paralleled in the most barbarous ages, and totally unworthy the Head of a civilized nation.

He has constrained our fellow Citizens taken Captive on the high Seas to bear Arms against their Country, to become the executioners of their friends and Brethren, or to fall themselves by their Hands.

He has excited domestic insurrections amongst us, and has endeavoured to bring on the inhabitants of our frontiers, the merciless Indian Savages, whose known rule of warfare, is an undistinguished destruction of all ages, sexes, and conditions.

In every stage of these Oppressions We have Petitioned for Redress in the most humble terms: Our repeated Petitions have been answered only by repeated injury. A Prince, whose character is thus marked by every act which may define a Tyrant, is unfit to be the ruler of a free people.

Nor have We been wanting in attention to our British brethren. We have warned them from time to time of attempts by their legislature to extend an unwarrantable jurisdiction over us. We have reminded them of the circumstances of our emigration and settlement here. We have appealed to

their native justice and magnanimity, and we have conjured them by the ties of our common kindred to disavow these usurpations, which, would inevitably interrupt our connections and correspondence. They too must have been deaf to the voice of justice and of consanguinity. We must, therefore, acquiesce in the necessity, which denounces our Separation, and hold them, as we hold the rest of mankind, Enemies in War, in Peace Friends.

WE, THEREFORE, the Representatives of the UNITED STATES OF AMERICA, in General Congress, Assembled, appealing to the Supreme Judge of the world for the rectitude of our intentions, do, in the Name, and by Authority of the good People of these Colonies, solemnly publish and declare, That these United Colonies are, and of Right ought to be FREE AND INDEPENDENT STATES; that they are Absolved from all Allegiance to the British Crown, and that all political connection between them and the State of Great Britain, is and ought to be totally dissolved; and that as Free and Independent States, they have full Power to levy War, conclude Peace, contract Alliances, establish Commerce, and to do all other Acts and Things which Independent States may of right do. And for the support of this Declaration, with a firm reliance on the Protection of Divine Providence, we mutually pledge to each other our Lives, our Fortunes, and our sacred Honor.

The foregoing Declaration was, by order of Congress, engrossed, and signed by the following members: * * *

REVIEW QUESTIONS

1. On what grounds does the Declaration of Independence justify a break from Great Britain?
2. Why is this document often viewed as a prominent example of the Enlightenment's political outlook?
3. Compare Locke's *Two Treatises on Government* with the American Declaration of Independence. What Lockeian influences can be detected in the declaration?

ABBÉ EMMANUEL SIEYÈS

FROM *What Is the Third Estate?*

King Louis XVI's announcement in the summer of 1788 convening the Estates General, compounded by bread riots and widespread economic hardship, heated up political debate about reform and the future of France. Because the Estates General had not met since 1614, members of the Third Estate protested against the custom that the estates meet separately and vote by order. They insisted that the estates should instead deliberate in united sessions and vote as individuals, not as corporate bodies. Equally important, the Third Estate demanded that its votes be doubled, so that it could counter the votes of the First and Second Estates. In January 1789, Abbé Emmanuel Sieyès (1748–1836), a postmaster's son who became a radical clergyman and a leader in the revolution's early stages, sought to mobilize public support for these causes with the pamphlet, What Is the Third Estate? *Its influence was pervasive and contributed to the plan to transform the Estates General into the National Constituent Assembly.*

From *A Documentary Survey of the French Revolution*, edited by John Hall Stewart (Upper Saddle River, N.J.: Prentice-Hall, 1951).

*   *   *

The plan of this pamphlet is very simple. We have three questions to ask:

1st. What is the third estate? Everything.

2nd. What has it been heretofore in the political order? Nothing.

3rd. What does it demand? To become something therein.

We shall see if the answers are correct. Then we shall examine the measures that have been tried and those which must be taken in order that the third estate may in fact become *something*. Thus we shall state:

4th. What the ministers have *attempted*, and what the privileged classes themselves *propose* in its favor.

5th. What *ought* to have been done.

6th. Finally, what *remains* to be done in order that the third estate may take its rightful place.

Chapter I
The Third Estate Is a Complete Nation

What are the essentials of national existence and prosperity? *Private* enterprise and *public* functions.

Private enterprise may be divided into four classes: 1st. Since earth and water furnish the raw material for man's needs, the first class will comprise all families engaged in agricultural pursuits. 2nd. Between the original sale of materials and their consumption or use, further workmanship, more or less manifold, adds to these materials a second value, more or less compounded. Human industry thus succeeds in perfecting the benefits of nature and in increasing the gross produce twofold, tenfold, one hundredfold in value. Such is the work of the second class. 3rd. Between production and consumption, as well as among the different degrees of production, a group of intermediate agents, useful to producers as well as to consumers, comes into being; these are the dealers and merchants. . . . 4th. In addition to these three classes of industrious and useful citizens concerned with goods for consumption and use, a society needs many private undertakings and endeavors which are *directly* useful or agreeable to the *individual.* This fourth class includes from the most distinguished scientific and liberal professions to the least esteemed domestic services. Such are the labors which sustain society. Who performs them? The third estate.

Public functions likewise under present circumstances may be classified under four well known headings: the Sword, the Robe, the Church, and the Administration. It is unnecessary to discuss them in detail in order to demonstrate that the third estate everywhere constitutes nineteen-twentieths of them, except that it is burdened with all that is really arduous, with all the tasks that the privileged order refuses to perform. Only the lucrative and honorary positions are held by members of the privileged order. . . . nevertheless they have dared lay the order of the third estate under an interdict. They have said to it: "Whatever be your services, whatever your talents, you shall go thus far and no farther. It is not fitting that you be honored." . . .

. . .

It suffices here to have revealed that the alleged utility of a privileged order to public service is only a chimera; that without it, all that is arduous in such service is performed by the third estate; that without it, the higher positions would be infinitely better filled; that they naturally ought to be the lot of and reward for talents and recognized services; and that if the privileged classes have succeeded in usurping all the lucrative and honorary positions, it is both an odious injustice to the majority of citizens and a treason to the commonwealth.

Who, then, would dare to say that the third estate has not within itself all that is necessary to constitute a complete nation? It is the strong and robust man whose one arm remains enchained. If the privileged order were abolished, the nation would be not something less but something more. Thus, what is the third estate? Everything; but an everything shackled and oppressed. What would it

be without the privileged order? Everything; but an everything free and flourishing. Nothing can progress without it; everything would proceed infinitely better without the others. It is not sufficient to have demonstrated that the privileged classes, far from being useful to the nation, can only enfeeble and injure it; it is necessary, moreover, to prove that the nobility does not belong to the social organization at all; that, indeed, it may be a *burden* upon the nation, but that it would not know how to constitute a part thereof.

. . .

What is a nation? a body of associates living under a *common* law and represented by the same *legislature.*

Is it not exceedingly clear that the noble order has privileges, exemptions, even rights separate from the rights of the majority of citizens? Thus it deviates from the common order, from the common law. Thus its civil rights already render it a people apart in a great nation. It is indeed *imperium in imperio.*

Also, it enjoys its political rights separately. It has its own representatives, who are by no means charged with representing the people. Its deputation sits apart; and when it is assembled in the same room with the deputies of ordinary citizens, it is equally true that its representation is essentially distinct and separate; it is foreign to the nation in principle, since its mandate does not emanate from the people, and in aim, since its purpose is to defend not the general but a special interest.

The third estate, then, comprises everything appertaining to the nation; and whatever is not the third estate may not be regarded as being of the nation. What is the third estate? Everything!

Chapter III
What Does the Third Estate Demand? To Become Something

* * * The true petitions of this order may be appreciated only through the authentic claims directed to the government by the large munici-

palities of the kingdom. What is indicated therein? That the people wishes to be *something,* and, in truth, the very least that is possible. It wishes to have real representatives in the Estates General, that is to say, deputies *drawn from its order,* who are competent to be interpreters of its will and defenders of its interests. But what will it avail it to be present at the Estates General if the predominating interest there is contrary to its own! Its presence would only consecrate the oppression of which it would be the eternal victim. Thus, it is indeed certain that it cannot come to vote at the Estates General unless it is to have in that body *an influence at least equal to that of the privileged classes;* and it demands a number of representatives equal to that of the first two orders together. Finally, this equality of representation would become completely illusory if every chamber voted separately. The third estate demands, then, that votes be taken *by head and not by order.* This is the essence of those claims so alarming to the privileged classes, because they believed that thereby the reform of abuses would become inevitable. The real intention of the third estate is to have an influence in the Estates General equal to that of the privileged classes. I repeat, can it ask less? And is it not clear that if its influence therein is less than equality, it cannot be expected to emerge from its political nullity and become *something*?

But what is indeed unfortunate is that the three articles constituting the demand of the third estate are insufficient to give it this equality of influence which it cannot, in reality, do without. In vain will it obtain an equal number of representatives drawn from its order; the influence of the privileged classes will establish itself and dominate even in the sanctuary of the third estate. . . .

· · ·

Besides the influence of the aristocracy . . . there is the influence of property. This is natural. I do not proscribe it at all; but one must agree that it is still all to the advantage of the privileged classes . . .

· · ·

The more one considers this matter, the more obvious the insufficiency of the three demands of the third estate becomes. But finally, such as they are, they have been vigorously attacked. Let us examine the pretexts for this hostility.

*   *   *

I have only one observation to make. Obviously there are abuses in France; these abuses are profitable to someone; they are scarcely advantageous to the third estate—indeed, they are injurious to it in particular. Now I ask if, in this state of affairs, it is possible to destroy any abuse so long as those who profit therefrom control the *veto*? All justice would be powerless; it would be necessary to rely entirely on the sheer generosity of the privileged classes. Would that be your idea of what constitutes the social order?

*   *   *

REVIEW QUESTIONS

1. What is Sieyès's tone of voice? How does it affect his argument?
2. What reasons does Sieyès provide for his claim that the Third Estate constitutes the nation?
3. What kind of political and social order does he advocate?

THIRD ESTATE OF DOURDAN

FROM Grievance Petitions

After summoning the Estates General, the king charged each estate with the task of drawing up grievance petitions, which in turn acted as suggestions for reform. Local assemblies throughout France, which appointed the Third Estate's deputies for the Estates General, wrote the grievance petitions, which are among the most valuable documents for assessing the moods of France's many regions and social groups just prior to the revolution. This particular petition is from the Third Estate of Dourdan, a town north of Paris.

From *A Documentary Survey of the French Revolution*, edited by John Hall Stewart (Upper Saddle River, N.J.: Prentice-Hall, 1951).

*   *   *

The order of the third estate of the City, *Bailliage*, and County of Dourdan, imbued with gratitude prompted by the paternal kindness of the King, who deigns to restore its former rights and its former constitution, forgets at this moment its misfortunes and impotence, to harken only to its foremost sentiment and its foremost duty, that of sacrificing everything to the glory of the *Patrie* and the service of His Majesty. It supplicates him to accept the grievances, complaints, and remonstrances which it is permitted to bring to the foot of the throne, and to see therein only the expression of its zeal and the homage of its obedience.

It wishes:

1. That his subjects of the third estate, equal by such status to all other citizens, present themselves before the common father without other distinction which might degrade them.

2. That all the orders, already united by duty and a common desire to contribute equally to the needs of the State, also deliberate in common concerning its needs.

3. That no citizen lose his liberty except according to law; that, consequently, no one be arrested by virtue of special orders, or, if imperative circumstances necessitate such orders, that the prisoner be handed over to the regular courts of justice within forty-eight hours at the latest.

4. That no letters or writings intercepted in the post be the cause of the detention of any citizen, or be produced in court against him, except in case of conspiracy or undertaking against the State.

5. That the property of all citizens be inviolable, and that no one be required to make sacrifice thereof for the public welfare, except upon assurance of indemnification based upon the statement of freely selected appraisers.

*   *   *

9. That the national debt be verified; that the payment of arrears of said debt be assured by such indirect taxes as may not be injurious to the husbandry, industry, commerce, liberty, or tranquillity of the citizens.

10. That an annual reimbursement fund be established to liquidate the capital of the debt.

11. That as one part of the debt is liquidated, a corresponding part of the indirect tax also be liquidated.

12. That every tax, direct or indirect, be granted only for a limited time, and that every collection

beyond such term be regarded as peculation, and punished as such.

13. That no loan be contracted, under any pretext or any security whatsoever, without the consent of the Estates General. ✳ ✳ ✳

15. That every personal tax be abolished; that thus the *capitation* and the *taille* and its accessories be merged with the *vingtièmes* in a tax on land and real or nominal property.

16. That such tax be borne equally, without distinction, by all classes of citizens and by all kinds of property, even feudal and contingent rights.

17. That the tax substituted for the *corvée* be borne by all classes of citizens equally and without distinction. That said tax, at present beyond the capacity of those who pay it and the needs to which it is destined, be reduced by at least one-half.

18. That provincial Estates, subordinate to the Estates General, be established and charged with the assessment and levying of subsidies, with their deposit in the national treasury, with the administration of all public works, and with the examination of all projects conducive to the prosperity of lands situated within the limits of their jurisdiction.

19. That such Estates be composed of freely elected deputies of the three orders from the cities, boroughs, and parishes subject to their administration, and in the proportion established for the next session of the Estates General.

✳   ✳   ✳

Justice

1. That the administration of justice be reformed, either by restoring strict execution of ordinances, or by reforming the sections thereof that are contrary to the dispatch and welfare of justice.

2. That every royal *bailliage* have such jurisdiction that persons be not more than three or four leagues distant from their judges, and that these pass judgment in the last resort up to the value of 300 *livres*.

3. That seigneurial courts of justice created by purely gratuitous right be suppressed.

4. That seigneurial courts of justice separated from the jurisdiction of royal *bailliages* . . . be returned thereto.

5. That seigneurial courts of justice, the creation of which has not been gratuitous, or usurpation of which is not proved, be suppressed with reimbursement.

✳   ✳   ✳

8. That the excessive number of offices in the necessary courts be reduced in just measure, and that no one be given an office of magistracy if he is not at least twenty-five years of age, and until after a substantial public examination has verified his morality, integrity, and ability.

✳   ✳   ✳

10. That the study of law be reformed; that it be directed in a manner analogous to our legislation, and that candidates for degrees be subjected to rigorous tests which may not be evaded; that no dispensation of age or time be granted.

✳   ✳   ✳

12. That deliberations of courts and companies of magistracy which tend to prevent entry of the third estate thereto be rescinded and annulled as injurious to the citizens of that order, in contempt of the authority of the King, whose choice they limit, and contrary to the welfare of justice, the administration of which would become the patrimony of those of noble birth instead of being entrusted to merit, enlightenment, and virtue.

13. That military ordinances which restrict entrance to the service to those possessing nobility be reformed.

✳   ✳   ✳

Finances

1. That if the Estates General considers it necessary to preserve the fees of *aides*, such fees be made uniform throughout the entire kingdom and reduced to a single denomination; that, accordingly, all ordinances and declarations in force be

revoked . . . ; that the odious tax of *trop-bu* especially, a source of constant annoyance in rural districts, be abolished forever.

2. That the tax of the *gabelle* be eliminated if possible, or that it be regulated among the several provinces of the kingdom . . .

*   *   *

Agriculture

1. That exchange fees, disastrous to husbandry, . . . be suppressed.

*   *   *

3. That the privilege of hunting be restricted within its just limits; that the decrees of the *parlement* of the years 1778 and 1779, which tend rather to obstruct the claims of the cultivator than to effect his indemnification, be rescinded and annulled; that after having declared the excessive amount of game and summoned the seignieur to provide therefor, the landowner and the cultivator be authorized to destroy said game on their own lands and in their own woods—without permission, however, to use firearms, the carrying of which is forbidden by ordinances; that, moreover, a simple and easy method be established whereby every cultivator may have the damage verified and obtain compensation therefor.

4. That the right to hunt may never affect the property of the citizen; that, accordingly, he may at all times travel over his lands, have injurious herbs uprooted, and cut *luzernes, sainfoins,* and other produce whenever it suits him; and that stubble may be freely raked immediately after the harvest.

5. That, in conformity with former ordinances, gamekeepers be forbidden to carry arms, even in the retinue of their masters.

6. That hunting offences be punished only by pecuniary fines.

7. That His Majesty be supplicated to have enclosed the parks and forests which are reserved for his enjoyment; also to authorize elsewhere the destruction of wild beasts which ruin the rural districts, and particularly that bordering on this forest of Dourdan.

8. That every individual who, without title or valid occupancy, has dovecotes or aviaries, be required to destroy them; that those who have title or valid occupancy be required to confine their pigeons at seedtime and harvest.

*   *   *

10. That no cultivator be permitted . . . several farms or farmings, if the total thereof necessitates the use of more than two ploughs.

*   *   *

15. That the militia, which devastates the country, takes workers away from husbandry, produces premature and ill-matched marriages, and imposes secret and arbitrary taxes upon those who are subject thereto, be suppressed and replaced by voluntary enlistment at the expense of the provinces.

*   *   *

17. That the ordinance and regulation concerning woods and forests be reformed so as to preserve property rights, encourage plantings, and prevent deforestation.

*   *   *

Commerce

1. That every regulation which tends to impede the business of citizens be revoked.

2. That the exportation and circulation of grain be directed by the provincial Estates, which shall correspond among themselves in order to prevent sudden and artificial increases in the price of provisions.

3. That when wheat reaches the price of twenty-five *livres* per *septier* in the markets, all day laborers be forbidden to buy any, unless it be for their sustenance.

4. That if circumstances necessitate the revenue from certificates and letters of mastership in the arts and crafts, no member be admitted into corporations except upon condition of residing in the place of his establishment; that widows may carry

on the profession of their husbands without new letters; that their children be admitted thereto at a moderate price; that all persons without an established and recognized domicile be forbidden to peddle.

5. That fraudulent bankruptcy be considered a public crime; that the public prosecutor be enjoined to prosecute it as such, and that privileged positions no longer serve as a refuge for bankrupts.

6. That all toll rights and other similar ones be suppressed throughout the interior of the kingdom, that customhouses be moved back to the frontiers, and that rights of *traite* be entirely abolished.

7. That, within a given time, weights and measures be rendered uniform throughout the entire kingdom.

REVIEW QUESTIONS

1. In the petitions, what are the principal targets of criticism?
2. Which groups and institutions are cited as the recurring causes of hardship?
3. How extensive are the proposals for reform?
4. After studying this petition, how would you characterize the relationship between the French state and its people?

NATIONAL ASSEMBLY

FROM Declaration of the Rights of Man and of the Citizen

This declaration, adopted August 26, 1789, was a revolutionary clarion call to the people of France. Its subsequent impact on European political culture cannot be overestimated.

From *The Ideas That Have Influenced Civilization, in the original documents*, vol. 7, translated and edited by Oliver Joseph Thatcher (London: Roberts-Manchester, 1902), pp. 415–17.

*   *   *

The representatives of the French people, organized as a national assembly, believing that the ignorance, neglect or contempt of the rights of man are the sole causes of public calamities and of the corruption of governments, have determined to set forth in a solemn declaration, the natural, inalienable and sacred rights of man, in order that this declaration, being constantly before all the members of the social body, shall remind them continually of their rights and duties; in order that the acts of the legislative power, as well as those of the executive power, may be compared at any moment with the ends of all political institutions and may thus be more respected; in order that the grievances of the citizens, based hereafter upon simple and incontestable principles, shall tend to the maintenance of the constitution and redound to the happiness of all. Hence the National Assembly recognizes and proclaims in the presence and under the auspices of the Supreme Being the following rights of man and of the citizen:

Article 1. Men are born and remain free and equal in rights. Social distinctions can only be founded upon the general good.

2. The aim of all political association is the preservation of the natural and imprescriptible rights of man. These rights are liberty, property, security, and resistance to oppression.

3. The principle [*principe*] of all sovereignty resides essentially in the nation. No body nor

individual may exercise any authority which does not proceed directly from the nation.

4. Liberty consists in being able to do everything which injures no one else; hence the exercise of the natural rights of each man has no limits except those which assure to the other members of the society the enjoyment of the same rights. These limits can only be determined by law.

5. Law can only prohibit such actions as are hurtful to society. Nothing may be prevented which is not forbidden by law, and no one may be forced to do anything not provided for by law.

6. Law is the expression of the general will. Every citizen has a right to participate personally or through his representative in its formation. It must be the same for all, whether it protects or punishes. All citizens being equal in the eyes of the law are equally eligible to all dignities and to all public positions and occupations according to their abilities and without distinction except that of their virtues and talents.

7. No person shall be accused, arrested or imprisoned except in the cases and according to the forms prescribed by law. Any one soliciting, transmitting, executing or causing to be executed any arbitrary order shall be punished. But any citizen summoned or arrested in virtue of the law shall submit without delay, as resistance constitutes an offence.

8. The law shall provide for such punishments only as are strictly and obviously necessary, and no one shall suffer punishment except it be legally inflicted in virtue of a law passed and promulgated before the commission of the offence.

9. As all persons are held innocent until they shall have been declared guilty, if arrest shall be deemed indispensable all severity not essential to the securing of the prisoner's person shall be severely repressed by law.

10. No one shall be disquieted on account of his opinions, including his religious views, provided their manifestation does not disturb the public order established by law.

11. The free communication of ideas and opinions is one of the most precious of the rights of man. Every citizen may, accordingly, speak, write and print with freedom, being responsible, however, for such abuses of this freedom as shall be defined by law.

12. The security of the rights of man and of the citizen requires public military force. These forces are, therefore, established for the good of all and not for the personal advantage of those to whom they shall be entrusted.

13. A common contribution is essential for the maintenance of the public forces and for the cost of administration. This should be equitably distributed among all the citizens in proportion to their means.

14. All the citizens have a right to decide either personally or by their representatives as to the necessity of the public contribution, to grant this freely, to know to what uses it is put, and to fix the proportion, the mode of assessment, and of collection, and the duration of the taxes.

15. Society has the right to require of every public agent an account of his administration.

16. A society in which the observance of the law is not assured nor the separation of powers defined has no constitution at all.

17. Property being an inviolable and sacred right, no one shall be deprived thereof except where public necessity, legally determined shall clearly demand it, and then only on condition that the owner shall have been previously and equitably indemnified.

REVIEW QUESTIONS

1. What similarities in issues do you see in the grievance petitions and in this declaration?
2. What are the principal differences between this declaration and the American Declaration of Independence?
3. How does this document reconcile the rights of the individual with the rights of government?
4. Which civil liberties are missing here?
5. Assess the influence of the American Declaration of Independence on the Declaration of the Rights of Man and Citizen.

TENNIS COURT OATH (1792)   JACQUES-LOUIS DAVID

David's painting of the birth of the modern French nation strove not for authentic represen-
tation but rather for mythic grandeur. In depicting this disparate group of bourgeois men com-
mitted to take an oath to transform France into a constitutional monarchy, what was David
implying about the political foundation of the new nation?

NATIONAL CONVENTION

FROM Levée en Masse Edict

This decree of August 23, 1793 mobilized the French nation for war, marking a new era in the modern history of warfare. Numerous setbacks of the French revolutionary army after its initial victories in 1792 compelled the government to pass a universal levy to repulse the enemy. The government's ability to conscript soldiers, requisition supplies, and organize the economy for war reveals the nationalist spirit that gripped France and provides one critical reason for success in the government's subsequent military campaigns.

From *A Documentary Survey of the French Revolution*, edited by John Hall Stewart (Upper Saddle River, N.J.: Prentice-Hall, 1951).

*   *   *

1. Henceforth, until the enemies have been driven from the territory of the Republic, the French people are in permanent requisition for army service.

The young men shall go to battle; the married men shall forge arms and transport provisions; the women shall make tents and clothes, and shall serve in the hospitals; the children shall turn old linen into lint; the old men shall repair to the public places, to stimulate the courage of the warriors and preach the unity of the Republic and hatred of kings.

2. National buildings shall be converted into barracks; public places into armament workshops; the soil of cellars shall be washed in lye to extract saltpeter therefrom.

3. Arms of caliber shall be turned over exclusively to those who march against the enemy; the service of the interior shall be carried on with fowling pieces and sabers.

4. Saddle horses are called for to complete the cavalry corps; draught horses, other than those employed in agriculture, shall haul artillery and provisions.

5. The Committee of Public Safety is charged with taking all measures necessary for establishing, without delay, a special manufacture of arms of all kinds, in harmony with the *élan* and the energy of the French people. Accordingly, it is authorized to constitute all establishments, manufactories, workshops, and factories deemed necessary for the execution of such works, as well as to requisition for such purpose, throughout the entire extent of the Republic, the artists and workmen who may contribute to their success. For such purpose a sum of 30,000,000, taken from the 498,200,000 livres in *assignats* in reserve in the "Fund of the Three Keys," shall be placed at the disposal of the Minister of War. The central establishment of said special manufacture shall be established at Paris.

6. The representatives of the people dispatched for the execution of the present law shall have similar authority in their respective *arrondissements*, acting in concert with the Committee of Public Safety; they are invested with the unlimited powers attributed to the representatives of the people with the armies.

7. No one may obtain a substitute in the service to which he is summoned. The public functionaries shall remain at their posts.

8. The levy shall be general. Unmarried citizens or childless widowers, from eighteen to twenty-five years, shall go first; they shall meet, without delay, at the chief town of their districts, where they shall

practice manual exercise daily, while awaiting the hour of departure.

9. The representatives of the people shall regulate the musters and marches so as to have armed citizens arrive at the points of assembling only in so far as supplies, munitions, and all that constitutes the material part of the army exist in sufficient proportion.

10. The points of assembling shall be determined by circumstances, and designated by the representatives of the people dispatched for the execution of the present decree, upon the advice of the generals, in co-operation with the Committee of Public Safety and the provisional Executive Council.

11. The battalion organized in each district shall be united under a banner bearing the inscription: *The French people risen against tyrants.*

12. Such battalions shall be organized according to established decrees, and their pay shall be the same as that of the battalions at the frontiers.

13. In order to collect supplies in sufficient quantity, the farmers and managers of national property shall deposit the produce of such property, in the form of grain, in the chief town of their respective districts.

14. Owners, farmers, and others possessing grain shall be required to pay, in kind, arrears of taxes, even the two-thirds of those of 1793, on the rolls which have served to effect the last payment.

*   *   *

17. The Minister of War is responsible for taking all measures necessary for the prompt execution of the present decree; a sum of 50,000,000, from the 498,200,000 *livres* in *assignats* in the "Fund of the Three Keys," shall be placed at his disposal by the National Treasury.

18. The present decree shall be conveyed to the departments by special messengers.

REVIEW QUESTIONS

1. Which social groups and areas of the economy did this edict affect? What roles were they assigned?
2. How is this organization for war different from warfare under the old regime?
3. How does this document evoke the sense of emergency and crisis that characterized the early years of the republic?

NATIONAL CONVENTION

FROM The Law of Suspects

Amid the chaos wreaked by foreign invasion, internal rebellion, inflation, and intense political factionalism, the republican government, dominated by the Jacobin club, erected political machinery in the form of emergency committees to monitor and suppress antirepublican activity. In 1793–1794 the fear of enemies of the revolution reached a fever pitch, endowing the revolutionary tribunals with an almost religious fervor as they sent their victims to the guillotine. The following law of September 17, 1793 gave the government the necessary legal authorization to suspend certain civil liberties in order to proceed with extraordinary "revolutionary" measures for rescuing the republic from its actual and perceived enemies.

From *The Constitutions and Other Select Documents Illustrative of the History of France, 1789–1907*, edited and translated by Frank Maloy Anderson (Minneapolis, Minn.: H. W. Wilson, 1908), pp. 185–87.

*   *   *

1. Immediately after the publication of the present decree all the suspect-persons who are in the territory of the Republic and who are still at liberty shall be placed under arrest.

2. These are accounted suspect-persons: 1st, those who by their conduct, their connections, their remarks, or their writings show themselves the partisans of tyranny or federalism and the enemies of liberty; 2d, those who cannot, in the manner prescribed by the decree of March 21st last, justify their means of existence and the performance of their civic duties; 3d, those who have been refused certificates of civism; 4th, public functionaries suspended or removed from their functions by the National Convention or its commissioners and not reinstated, especially those who have been or shall be removed in virtue of the decree of August 14th last; 5th, those of the former nobles, all of the husbands, wives, fathers, mothers, sons or daughters, brothers, or sisters, and agents of the *émigrés* who have not constantly manifested their attachment to the revolution; 6th, those who have emigrated from France in the interval from July 1, 1789, to the publication of the decree of March 30,–April 8, 1792, although they may have returned to France within the period fixed by that decree or earlier.

3. The committees of surveillance established according to the decree of March 21st last, or those which have been substituted for them, either by the orders of the representatives of the people sent with the armies and into the departments, or in virtue of special decrees of the National Convention, are charged to prepare, each in its district, the list of suspect-persons, to issue warrants of arrest against them, and to cause seals to be put upon their papers. The commanders of the public force to whom these warrants shall be delivered shall be required to put them into execution immediately, under penalty of removal.

4. The members of the committee without being seven in number and an absolute majority of votes cannot order the arrest of any person.

5. The persons arrested as suspects shall be first conveyed to the jail of the place of their imprisonment: in default of jails, they shall be kept from view in their respective dwellings.

6. Within the eight days following they shall be transferred to the national building, which the administrations of the department, immediately after the receipt of the present decree, shall be required to designate and to cause to be prepared for that purpose.

7. The prisoners can cause to be transferred to these buildings the movables which are of absolute necessity to them; they shall remain there under guard until the peace.

8. The expenses of custody shall be at the charge of the prisoners and shall be divided among them equally; this custody shall be confided preferably to the fathers of families and the parents of the citizens who are upon or shall go to the frontiers. The salary for it is fixed for each man of the guard at the value of a day and a half of labor.

9. The committees of surveillance shall send without delay to the committee of general security of the National Convention the list of the persons whom they shall have caused to be arrested, with the reasons for their arrest and the papers which shall have been seized with them as suspect-persons.

10. The civil and criminal tribunals can, if there is need cause to be arrested and sent into the above mentioned jails persons accused of offences in respect of whom it may have been declared that there was no ground for accusation, or who may have been acquitted of the accusations brought against them.

*   *   *

REVIEW QUESTIONS

1. For which social groups was this law intended?
2. What, according to this law, was the correct procedure for arresting suspects?
3. Did the suspect have rights?
4. Are there checks against potential abuses in this law?
5. After studying this document, determine the social and political atmosphere that pervaded France during the Jacobin republic.

OLYMPE DE GOUGES

FROM Declaration of the Rights of Woman

The revolution politicized millions of French men by transforming their status from subjects to citizens, but revolutionaries of all political stripes displayed extreme reluctance to incorporate women into the national political body. Heeding the new political discourse of equality, inalienable rights, and universal liberties, Olympe de Gouges (1748–1793), the self-educated daughter of a butcher, pointed out the revolutionaries' patent contradiction of applying tenets of natural law philosophy to one half of the human race but not to the other. This pamphlet, published in September 1791, documents an important discussion during the revolution over the public roles and duties of women in civil society. Olympe de Gouges engaged her critical pen over a number of issues, which led to her arrest as a counterrevolutionary and her execution in 1793.

From *Women, The Family, and Freedom: The Debate in Documents*, edited by Susan Groag Bell and Karen M. Offen (Stanford, CA: Stanford University Press, 1983), pp. 105–09.

To be decreed by the National Assembly in its last meetings or in those of the next legislature.

Preamble

The mothers, daughters, and sisters, representatives of the nation, demand to be constituted a national assembly. Considering that ignorance, disregard of or contempt for the rights of women are the only causes of public misfortune and of governmental corruption, they have resolved to set forth in a solemn declaration, the natural, inalienable and sacred rights of woman; to the end that this declaration, constantly held up to all members of society, may always remind them of their rights and duties; to the end that the acts based on women's power and those based on the power of men, being constantly measured against the goal of all political institutions, may be more respected; and so that the demands of female citizens, henceforth founded on simple and indisputable principles, may ever uphold the constitution and good morals, and may contribute to the happiness of all.

Consequently, the sex that is superior in beauty as well as in courage of maternal suffering, recognizes and declares, in the presence and under the auspices of the Supreme Being, the following rights of woman and citizen.

Article I. Woman is born free and remains equal in rights to man. Social distinctions can be founded only on general utility.

II. The goal of every political association is the preservation of the natural and irrevocable rights of Woman and Man. These rights are liberty, property, security, and especially resistance to oppression.

III. The principle of all sovereignty resides essentially in the Nation, which is none other than the union of Woman and Man; no group, no individual can exercise any authority that is not derived expressly from it.

IV. Liberty and Justice consist of rendering to persons those things that belong to them; thus, the exercise of woman's natural rights is limited only by the perpetual tyranny with which man opposes her; these limits must be changed according to the laws of nature and reason.

V. The laws of nature and of reason prohibit all acts harmful to society; whatever is not prohibited by these wise and divine laws cannot be prevented, and no one can be forced to do anything unspecified by the law.

VI. The law should be the expression of the general will: all female and male citizens must participate in its elaboration personally or through their representatives. It should be the same for all; all female and male citizens, being equal in the eyes of the law, should be equally admissible to all public offices, places, and employments, according to their capacities and with no distinctions other than those of their virtues and talents.

VII. No woman is immune; she can be accused, arrested, and detained in such cases as determined by law. Women, like men, must obey these rigorous laws.

VIII. Only punishments strictly and obviously necessary may be established by law. No one may be punished except under a law established and promulgated before the offense occurred, and which is legally applicable to women.

IX. If any woman is declared guilty, then the law must be enforced rigorously.

X. No one should be punished for their opinions. Woman has the right to mount the scaffold; she should likewise have the right to speak in public, provided that her demonstrations do not disrupt public order as established by law.

XI. Free communication of thoughts and opinions is one of the most precious rights of woman, since this liberty assures the legitimate paternity of fathers with regard to their children. Every female citizen can therefore freely say: "I am the mother of a child that belongs to you," without a barbaric prejudice forcing her to conceal the truth; she must also answer for the abuse of this liberty in cases determined by law.

XII. Guarantee of the rights of woman and female citizens requires the existence of public services. Such guarantee should be established for the advantage of everyone, not for the personal benefit of those to whom these services are entrusted.

XIII. For the maintenance of public forces and administrative expenses, the contributions of women and men shall be equal; the woman shares in all forced labor and all painful tasks, therefore she should have the same share in the distribution of positions, tasks, assignments, honors, and industry.

XIV. Female and male citizens have the right to determine the need for public taxes, either by themselves or through their representatives. Female citizens can agree to this only if they are admitted to an equal share not only in wealth but also in public administration, and by determining the proportion and extent of tax collection.

XV. The mass of women, allied for tax purposes to the mass of men, has the right to hold every public official accountable for his administration.

XVI. Any society in which the guarantee of rights is not assured, or the separation of powers determined, has no constitution. The constitution is invalid if the majority of individuals who compose the Nation have not cooperated in writing it.

XVII. The right of property is inviolable and sacred to both sexes, jointly or separately. No one can be deprived of it, since it is a true inheritance of nature except when public necessity, certified by law, clearly requires it, subject to just and prior compensation.

Postamble

Woman, wake up! The tocsin of reason is sounding throughout the Universe; know your rights. The powerful empire of nature is no longer surrounded by prejudices, fanaticism, superstition and lies. The torch of truth has dispelled all the clouds of stupidity and usurpation. Man enslaved has multiplied his forces; he has had recourse to yours in order to break his own chains. Having become free, he has become unjust toward his mate. Oh Women! Women! when will you cease to be blind? What advantages have you gained in the Revolution? A more marked scorn, a more signal disdain. During centuries of corruption, you reigned only over the weakness of men. Your empire is destroyed; what then remains for you? The proof of man's injustice. The claim of your patrimony founded on the wise decrees of nature—what have you to fear from such a splendid enterprise? The good word of the legislator at the marriage of Canaan? Do you not fear that our French legislators, who are correcting this morality, which was for such a long time appended to the realm of politics but is no longer fashionable, will again say to you, "Women, what do we have in common with you?" You must answer, "Everything!" If, in their weakness, they are obstinate in drawing this conclusion contrary to their principles, you must courageously invoke the force of reason against their vain pretensions of superiority. Unite yourselves under the banner of philosophy; deploy all the energy of your character, and soon you will see these prideful ones, your adoring servants, no longer grovelling at your feet but proud to share with you the treasures of the Supreme Being. Whatever the obstacles that are put in your way, it is in your power to overturn them; you have only to will it. Let us turn now to the frightful picture of what you have been in society; and since there is currently a question of national education, let us see if our wise legislators will think wisely about the education of women.

*   *   *

If my attempt thus to give my sex an honorable and just stability is now considered a paradox on my part, an attempt at the impossible, I must leave to men yet to come the glory of discussing this matter; but meanwhile, one can pave the way through national education, the restoration of morals, and by conjugal contracts.

MODEL FOR A SOCIAL CONTRACT BETWEEN A MAN AND A WOMAN

We, N & N, of our own free will, unite ourselves for the remainder of our lives and for the duration of our mutual inclinations, according to the following conditions: We intend and desire to pool our fortunes as community property, while nevertheless preserving the right to divide them on behalf of our own children and those we might have with someone else, mutually recognizing that our fortune belongs directly to our children, from whatever bed they might spring, and that all of them have the right to carry the name of the fathers and mothers who have acknowledged them, and we obligate ourselves to subscribe to the law that punishes the renunciation of one's own flesh and blood. We obligate ourselves equally, in case of separation, to divide our fortune, and to set apart the portion belonging to our children as indicated by the law; and in the case of perfect union, the first to die would assign half the property to their children; and if one of us should die without children, the survivor would inherit everything, unless the dying party had disposed of his half of the common wealth in favor of someone else he might deem appropriate. * * *

*   *   *

REVIEW QUESTIONS

1. Compare de Gouges's declaration with the Declaration of the Rights of Man and Citizen. Determine the parallel and divergent aspects of the two documents.
2. How does de Gouges envision women in civil society? How does this projected role differ from the social realities of eighteenth-century France?
3. What traditional institutions and mores does de Gouges criticize? What does she exhort women to do?

AL-JABARTI

FROM *Chronicle of the French Occupation, 1798*

In May 1798, 400 French ships, carrying Napoleon and 36,000 men, set sail for Egypt. In an attempt to extend France's colonial empire and undermine Britain's economic dominance in the eastern Mediterranean, the French revolutionary army established control in Egypt in June 1798 after defeating the Mamluks, the military caste governing Egypt for the Ottoman Empire. In 1799 a superior British navy destroyed the French fleet in Alexandria, spurring Napoleon to return to France in the same year, leaving behind a trapped, defeated French army, which finally returned in 1801. Although brief, the French occupation of Egypt significantly changed Arab life, alerting the Arab world to the West's formidable military might and its advances in learning. Al-Jabarti, a learned Egyptian born into a family of religious scholars, captured the upheaval and suffering of the Egyptian population. In the following section Al-Jabarti cites and critiques Napoleon's announcement of French occupation.

From *Al-Jabarti's Chronicle of the French Occupation*, translated by S. Moreh (1798), pp. 24, 26–33.

*   *   *

On Monday news arrived that the French had reached Damanhūr and Rosetta, bringing about the flight of their inhabitants to Fuwwa and its surroundings. Contained in this news was mention of the French sending notices throughout the country demanding impost for the upkeep of the military. Furthermore they printed a large proclamation in Arabic, calling on the people to obey them and to raise their "Bandiera." In this proclamation were inducements, warnings, all manner of wiliness and stipulations. Some copies were sent from the provinces to Cairo and its text is:

In the name of God, the Merciful, the Compassionate. There is no god but God. He has no son, nor has He an associate in His Dominion.

On behalf of the French Republic which is based upon the foundation of liberty and equality, General Bonaparté, Commander-in-Chief of the French armies makes known to all the Egyptian people that for a long time the Ṣanjaqs who lorded it over Egypt have treated the French community basely and contemptuously and have persecuted its merchants with all manner of extortion and violence. Therefore the hour of punishment has now come.

Unfortunately this group of Mamluks, imported from the mountains of Circassia and Georgia have acted corruptly for ages in the fairest land that is to be found upon the face of the globe. However, the Lord of the Universe, the Almighty, has decreed the end of their power.

O ye Egyptians, they may say to you that I have not made an expedition hither for any other object than that of abolishing your religion; but this is a pure falsehood and you must not give credit to it, but tell the slanderers that I have not come to you except for the purpose of restoring your rights from the hands of the oppressors and that I more than the Mamluks, serve God—may He be praised and exalted—and revere His Prophet Muhammad and the glorious Qur'ān.

And tell them also that all people are equal in the eyes of God and the only circumstances which distinguish one from the other are reason, virtue, and knowledge. But amongst the Mamluks, what is there of reason, virtue, and knowledge, which would distinguish them from others and qualify them alone to possess everything which sweetens life in this world? Wherever fertile land is found it is appropriated to the Mamluks; and the handsomest female slaves, and the best horses, and the most desirable dwelling-places, all these belong to them exclusively. If the land of Egypt is a fief of the Mamluks, let them then produce the title-deed, which God conferred upon them. But the Lord of the Universe is compassionate and equitable toward mankind, and with the help of the Exalted, from this day forward no Egyptian shall be excluded from admission to eminent positions nor from acquiring high ranks, therefore the intelligent and virtuous and learned ("*ulamā*") amongst them, will regulate their affairs, and thus the state of the whole population will be rightly adjusted.

Formerly, in the lands of Egypt there were great cities, and wide canals and extensive commerce and nothing ruined all this but the avarice and the tyranny of the Mamluks.

O ye Qādis, Shaykhs and Imāms; O ye Shurbājiyya and men of circumstance tell your nation that the French are also faithful Muslims, and in confirmation of this they invaded Rome and destroyed there the Papal See, which was always exhorting the Christians to make war with Islam. And then they went to the island of Malta, from where they expelled the Knights, who claimed that God the Exalted required them to fight the Muslims. Furthermore, the French at all times have declared themselves to be the most sincere friends of the Ottoman Sultan and the enemy of his enemies, may God ever perpetuate his empire! And on the contrary the Mamluks have withheld their obeisance from the Sultan, and have not followed his orders. Indeed they never obeyed anything but their own greed!

Blessing on blessing to the Egyptians who will act in concert with us, without any delay, for their condition shall be rightly adjusted, and their rank raised. Blessing also, upon those who will abide in their habitations, not siding with either of the two hostile parties, yet when they know us better, they will hasten to us with all their hearts. But woe upon woe to those who will unite with the Mamlūks and assist them in the war against us, for they will not find the way of escape, and no trace of them shall remain.

First Article

All the villages, situated within three hours' distance from the places through which the French army passes, are required to send to the Commander-in-Chief some persons, deputed by them, to announce to the aforesaid, that they submit and that they have hoisted the French flag, which is white, blue, and red.

Second Article

Every village that shall rise against the French army, shall be burnt down.

Third Article

Every village that submits to the French army must hoist the French flag and also the flag of our friend the Ottoman Sultan, may he continue for ever.

Fourth Article

The Shaykh of each village must immediately seal all property, houses, and possessions, belonging to the Mamluks, making the most strenuous effort that not the least thing be lost.

Fifth Article

The Shaykhs, Qāḍīs, and Imāms must remain at their posts, and every countryman shall remain peaceably in his dwelling, and also prayers shall be performed in the mosques as customary and the Egyptians, all of them shall render thanks for God's graciousness, praise be to Him and may He be exalted, in extirpating the power of the Mamlūks, saying with a loud voice, May God perpetuate the glory of the Ottoman Sultan! May God preserve the glory of the French army! May God curse the Mamluks and rightly adjust the condition of the Egyptian people.

Written in the Camp at Alexandria on the 13th of the month Messidor [the 6th year] of the founding of the French Republic, that is to say toward the end of the month Muharram in the year [1213] of the Hijra [2 July 1798].

It ends here word for word. Here is an explanation of the incoherent words and vulgar constructions which he put into this miserable letter.

His statement "In the name of God, the Merciful, the Compassionate. There is no god but God. He has no son, nor has He an associate in His Dominion." In mentioning these three sentences there is an indication that the French agree with the three religions, but at the same time they do not agree with them, nor with any religion. They are consistent with the Muslims in stating the formula "In the name of God," in denying that He has a son or an associate. They disagree with the Muslims in not mentioning the two Articles of Faith, in rejecting the mission of Muhammad, and the legal words and deeds which are necessarily recognized by religion. They agree with the Christians in most of their words and deeds, but disagree with them by not mentioning the Trinity, and denying the mission and furthermore in rejecting their beliefs, killing the priests, and destroying the churches. Then, their statement "On behalf of the French Republic, etc.," that is, this proclamation is sent from their Republic, that means their body politic, because they have no chief or sultan with whom they all agree, like others, whose function is to speak on their behalf. For when they rebelled against their sultan six years ago and killed him, the people agreed unanimously that there was not to be a single ruler but that their state, territories, laws, and administration of their affairs, should be in the hands of the intelligent and wise men among them. They appointed persons chosen by them and made them heads of the army, and below them generals and commanders of thousands, two hundreds, and tens, administrators and advisers, on condition that they were all to be equal and none superior to any other in view of the equality of creation and nature. They made this the foundation and basis of their system. This is the meaning of their statement "based upon the foundation of liberty and equality." Their term "liberty" means that they are not slaves like the Mamluks; "equality" has the aforesaid meaning. Their officials are distinguished by the cleanliness of their garments. They wear emblems on their uniforms and upon their heads. For example an Amir of ten has a large rosette of silk upon his head, like a big rose. If he is a commander of twenty-five his rosette is of two colours, and if he is a commander of a hundred his rosette is of three colours. His hat which is known as *burnayṭa* (It. *borreta*) is embroidered with gold brocade, or he may bear upon his shoulders an emblem of the same. If he has a reputation for daring and is well-known for his heroism and has been wounded several times he receives two badges on his shoulder. They follow this rule: great and small, high and low, male and

female are all equal. Sometimes they break this rule according to their whims and inclinations or reasoning. Their women do not veil themselves and have no modesty; they do not care whether they uncover their private parts. Whenever a Frenchman has to perform an act of nature he does so wherever he happens to be, even in full view of people, and he goes away as he is, without washing his private parts after defecation. If he is a man of taste and refinement he wipes himself with whatever he finds, even with a paper with writing on it, otherwise he remains as he is. They have intercourse with any woman who pleases them and vice versa. Sometimes one of their women goes into a barber's shop, and invites him to shave her pubic hair. If he wishes he can take his fee in kind. It is their custom to shave both their moustaches and beard. Some of them leave the hair of their cheeks only.

They do not shave their heads nor their pubic hair. They mix their foods. Some might even put together in one dish coffee, sugar, arrack, raw eggs, limes, and so on. As for the name "Bonaparté" this is the title of their general, it is not a name. Its meaning is "the pleasant gathering," because *Bona* (*Būnā*) means "pleasant" and *parté* means "gathering." ＊ ＊ ＊

＊   ＊   ＊

His saying *fī hādhā 'l-taraf* (hither), means "this part of the earth." His statement *wa-qūlū li 'l-muftariyīn* (but tell the slanderers) is the plural of *muftarī* (slanderer) which means liar, and how worthy of this description they are. The proof of that is his saying "I have not come to you except for the purpose of restoring your rights from the hands of the oppressors," which is the first lie he uttered and a falsehood which he invented. Then he proceeds to something even worse than that, may God cast him into perdition, with his words: "I more than the Mamluks serve God. . . ." There is no doubt that this is a derangement of his mind, and an excess of foolishness. What a worship he is speaking about, however great its intensity, *kufr* (disbelief) had dulled his heart, and prevented him from reaching the way of his salvation. There is inversion in the words which should read *innanī a'budu Allāh akthar min al-Mamālīk* (I serve God more than the Mamluks do). However, it is possible that there is no inversion, and that the meaning is "I have more troops or more money than the Mamluks" and that the accusative of specification has been omitted. So his words "I serve God" are a new sentence and a new lie.

His statement "[I] revere His Prophet" is conjoined to what goes before, as one lie joined to another, because if he respected him he would believe in him, accept his truth, and respect his nation. His statement *al-Qur'ān al-'aẓim* (the glorious Qur'ān) is joined to "His Prophet," that is, "I respect the glorious Qur'ān," and this too is a lie, because to respect the Qur'ān means to glorify it, and one glorifies it by believing in what it contains. The Qur'ān is one of the miracles of the Prophet which proves his truth, and that he is the Prophet to the end of time, and that his nation is the most noble of all nations. These people deny all that and lie in every thing they enumerate, "And many as are the signs in the Heavens and on the Earth, yet they will pass them by, and turn aside from them."

His saying "[all people] are equal in the eyes of God" the Almighty, this is a lie and stupidity. How can this be when God has made some superior to others as is testified by the dwellers in the Heavens and on the Earth?

* * *

His statement *al-manāṣib al-sāmiya* (eminent positions), that means *al-murtafi'a* (elevated). This is in order to avert blame from themselves by giving high posts of authority to the low and vulgar people among them, as for example their appointment of Barṭulmān (Barthélemy) the artilleryman to the post of Katkhudā Mustaḥfiẓān. He says "and thus the state of the whole population will be rightly adjusted." Yes, that is to say, under the administration of wise and intelligent men. But

they did not appoint them. The word *Muslimīn* should be *Muslimūn* in the nominative. The point of putting the word in the *naṣb* (accusative) has already been mentioned. There is another point namely: that their Islam is *naṣb* (fraud).

As for his statement "and destroyed there the Papal See," by this deed they have gone against the Christians as has already been pointed out. So those people are opposed to both Christians and Muslims, and do not hold fast to any religion. You see that they are materialists, who deny all God's attributes, the Hereafter and Resurrection, and who reject Prophethood and Messengership. They believe that the world was not created, and that the heavenly bodies and the occurrences of the Universe are influenced by the movement of the stars, and that nations appear and states decline, according to the nature of the conjunctions and the aspects of the moon. Some believe in transmigration of souls, or other fantasies. For this reason they do not slaughter ritually any animal they eat, or behead any man, before having killed them, so that the parts of his soul may not be separated and scattered, so as not to be whole in another body, and similar nonsense and erroneous beliefs. * * *

* * *

REVIEW QUESTIONS

1. In what ways does the French announcement accommodate Islamic culture? Is it successful?
2. What are Al-Jabarti's political, religious, and social views of the French? How are these views interconnected?
3. What made the French invasion and colonization of an Islamic culture more difficult than conquests in Europe?
4. What is the manner and method of Al-Jabarti's critique of Napoleon's announcement?

FROM *The Code Napoleon*

The Civil Code, promulgated in 1804 and renamed the Code Napoleon *in 1807, marked a domestic triumph of the French Revolution, uniting France under one code of law that above all guaranteed civic equality and property rights. In doing so, it swept away centuries of legal privileges for the aristocracy, clergy, and government. Accompanied by commercial, criminal, penal, and civil procedure codes (1806–10), the Civil Code quickly became a legal model for modern civil society; it was widely borrowed and adapted throughout continental Europe and other regions of the world. Dubbed the "bourgeois bible," the code embodied the beliefs and values of the nineteenth-century middle classes, including their biases against women, children, and the unpropertied. The following section centers on the code's definition of women's legal status.*

From *The Code Napoleon*, translated by Bryant Barrett (London: Reed, 1811), pp. 47–50, 57–58.

Title V
Of Marriage

CHAPTER VI
OF THE RIGHTS AND RESPECTIVE DUTIES
OF HUSBAND AND WIFE

212. Husband and wife mutually owe to each other fidelity, succour, and assistance.

213. The husband owes protection to his wife, the wife obedience to her husband.

214. The wife is obliged to live with her husband, and to follow him wherever he may think proper to dwell: the husband is bound to receive her, and to furnish her with every thing necessary for the purposes of life, according to his means and condition.

215. The wife can do no act in law without the authority of her husband, even where she shall be a public trader, or not in community, or separate in property.

216. The authority of the husband is not necessary where a woman is prosecuted for criminal matters, or matters of police.

217. The wife, even not in community or separate in property, cannot give, alien, mortgage, or acquire, either gratuitously or subject to condition, without the concurrence of her husband in the acts, or his consent in writing.

218. If the husband refuses to authorize his wife to proceed at law, a judge may give authority.

219. If the husband refuse to authorize his wife to pass an act, the wife may cause her husband to be cited directly before the tribunal of first instance of the district of their common domicile, which may give or refuse the authority, after the husband shall have been heard or duly summoned to the council chamber.

220. The wife, if she is a public trader, may without the authority of her husband, bind herself in what concerns her business; and, in such case, she also binds her husband, if there is community between them. She is not reputed a public trader, if she merely retails the merchandize of her husband in his business, but only where she carries on a separate trade.

221. Where the husband has incurred a condemnation carrying afflictive or infamous punishment, although it shall only have been pronounced for contempt, the wife, even of full age, cannot, during the continuance of the punishment, do any act in law, nor contract, until after being authorized by the judge, who may, in such case, give author-

ity, without the husband being heard or summoned.

222. If the husband is interdicted or absent, the judge may, on cognizance of the matter, authorize the wife, either to do acts in law, or to contract.

223. No general authority, even though stipulated by a marriage contract, is valid but as to administration of the property of the wife.

224. If the husband is a minor, the authority of a judge is necessary to the wife, either to do acts in law, or to contract.

225. Nullity founded on want of authority can only be set up by the wife, by the husband, or by their heirs.

226. The wife may make a will without the authority of her husband.

CHAPTER VII
OF DISSOLUTION OF MARRIAGE

227. Marriage is dissolved,

By the death of one of the parties;
By divorce legally pronounced;
By the condemnation, become definitive,
   of one of the parties, to a punishment
   carrying civil death.

CHAPTER VIII
OF SECOND MARRIAGES

228. The wife cannot contract a new marriage until ten months have elapsed since the dissolution of the preceding marriage.

Title VI
Of Divorce

CHAPTER THE FIRST
OF CAUSES OF DIVORCE

229. The husband may demand divorce for cause of adultery on the part of his wife.

230. The wife may demand divorce for cause of adultery on the part of her husband, where he shall have kept his concubine in their common house.

231. The married parties may reciprocally demand divorce for cause of excess, cruelty, or grievous injuries, by the one of them towards the other.

232. Condemnation of one of the married parties to an infamous punishment, shall be to the other party a cause of divorce.

233. The mutual and persevering consent of the parties, expressed in the manner prescribed by the law, under the conditions and after the trials the law prescribes, shall sufficiently prove that living in common is insupportable to them, and that there exists, in respect to them, a peremptory cause of divorce.

CHAPTER II
OF DIVORCE FOR CAUSE DEFINED

*   *   *

Section II

Of the Provisional Measures to Which the Demand of Divorce for Cause Defined May Give Rise

267. The provisional administration of the children shall remain with the husband plaintiff or defendant in divorce, unless it shall be otherwise ordered by the tribunal, at the request either of the mother, or of the family, or of the imperial proctor, for the greater benefit of the children.

268. The wife plaintiff or defendant in divorce, may quit the domicile of her husband during the suit, and demand an alimentary pension proportioned to the means of the husband. The tribunal shall point out the house in which the wife shall be obliged to reside, and shall fix, if that is ground for it, the alimentary pension which the husband shall be obliged to pay her.

269. The wife shall be bound to prove her residence in the house pointed out for her, as often as she shall be required so to do: in default of such proof, the husband may refuse the alimentary

provision, and, if the wife is demandant in divorce, may cause her to be declared incapable to continue her suit.

270. The wife, plaintiff or defendant in divorce, being in community of property, may, in every state of the cause, commencing from the date of the order of which mention is made in article 238, require, for the preservation of her rights, the affixing of seals upon the moveable effects in community. These seals shall not be taken off without an inventory being made with a valuation, and at the charge on the part of the husband of producing the things inventoried, or making good their value as judiciary guardian.

271. Every obligation upon the community contracted by the husband, and every alienation made by him of the immoveables belonging to the community subsequently to the date of the order of which mention is made in article 238, shall be declared null, if proved to have been made or contracted in fraud of the rights of the wife.

* * *

REVIEW QUESTIONS

1. What civic rights did the code accord women?
2. How did the code fix the relationship of married women to property?
3. What were the distinctions between the rights of men and women in divorce proceedings?
4. What does this law code tell us about nineteenth-century social relations between men and women?

19 ⚬ THE INDUSTRIAL REVOLUTION AND NINETEENTH-CENTURY SOCIETY

The economic transition from mercantile to industrial capitalism in Britain and Europe constitutes one of the momentous structural revolutions in modern civilization. Industrialization not only expanded the material culture of the West but also penetrated and transformed most spheres of social and economic activity. Most fundamentally, the Industrial Revolution unleashed an unprecedented dynamism of sustained growth. It introduced a new scale and scope of economic activity whose need for new markets, better infrastructure, greater capitalization, and technological innovation characterizes a self-evident aspect of the modern world.

Early industrialization is commonly associated with laissez-faire political economy, a doctrine that championed free trade, private enterprise, meritocratic individualism, and the sanctity of private property. Grounded in the writings of the political economist Adam Smith, it roundly attacked any interference with the "natural laws" of the marketplace, thus advocating separation of government and economy. Although Adam Smith was not the first to criticize mercantilism and advocate unrestricted trade, his treatise, by associating free trade with the "natural rights" of other individual liberties, provided the philosophical underpinnings for the political demands of Great Britain's capitalist classes, whose enfranchisement after 1832 exerted influence on state policy. By dint of the vast wealth accumulated through private enterprise, the middle classes espoused the notion that commerce and industry were the twin pillars of civil society. Liberals confidently embraced the belief that these two spheres of public life provided the material basis for progress and prosperity. Industrialized sectors of Britain's economy benefitted from unfree forms of labor found in the empire. Liberal industrialists espoused rule of law and freedom of movement, hence their reliance on cotton, sugar, and other slave-driven economies posed a contradiction to their political principles. Yet in spite of Britain's self-proclaimed status as the "workshop of the world," industrialism clearly cut in both positive and negative directions. Contemporaries dubbed the new discipline of political economy the "dismal science," because its studies on population growth and wage levels suggested the impossibility of general happiness and welfare. Not all agreed that laissez-faire principles were the best way to organize industrial society. Consequently, the industrialization of Europe did not follow any single model. European governments, accustomed to directing economic activity, proved reluctant to surrender to the market's "invisible hand." In contrast to Britain, they nurtured domestic industry with subventions and protective tariffs, mobilized state capital to assist railroad construction, promoted economic development through technical education, and supervised the management of large-scale industrial enterprises. Moreover, European society remained predominantly rural throughout most of the nineteenth century. Hence, although we speak of an Industrial Revolution, we must envision small handicraft workshops alongside mechanized factories and vital rural economies serving dynamic urban centers.

The onset of early industrialization also generated an extraordinary range of criticism of the premise that capitalism would benefit the majority of society. The French comte de Saint-Simon, Robert Owen, and Karl Marx are but three observers who acknowledged capitalism's material benefits but nonetheless emphasized its elemental flaws in its emphasis on property and waged work. Their concerns for the material, moral, and creative dimensions of workers' lives compelled them to offer alternative visions to the dominant principles of competition and individual self-interest. Such critical voices sharpened the debate on ethics and social justice, thus exerting force over the next century—through rational argument and political struggle—on Europe's elites to incorporate the interests of unpropertied workers into government policy.

The transition from agricultural and handicraft economies to the new urban industrial society produced pervasive dislocation and suffering. In the countryside, the erosion of traditional authority and social stability preceded large-scale industrialization. The enclosure of common lands and the increasing demand for profitable harvests replaced the paternalistic ties that had bound lords and tenant farmers with the more contractual relationship of wages and rents. Reduced to the penury of day laborers, many farmers migrated to the young industrial towns seeking work. Yet squalor and grueling factory work offered little reward in the city. Unencumbered by any legal restraints, employers imposed insufferable working conditions on men, women, and children. In the 1830s, reformers likened the circumstances in English mill towns to colonial slavery and ridiculed the blind spots of bourgeois society, which fervently proselytized for slavery's abolition but could not see similar misery and exploitation in its own cities. Pointing to urban malnutrition, disease, alcohol abuse, prostitution, and theft, commentators questioned whether laissez-faire capitalism possessed a moral center.

The "social question" of early industrialization inexorably took on political dimensions. The legacy of revolutionary republicanism combined with the harsh economic conditions of early industrial capitalism produced a new era in social relations and political struggle. Privation in the countryside produced machine breaking, hayrick burning, and violent confrontations with masters. In the city, bloody interventions of governments against workers reflected the differences of class interests between political elites and workers, who gradually developed their own political organizations. Emerging as one of the earliest independent working-class movements, chartism was a national network of committees in Britain that agitated for workers' enfranchisement through colossal petition drives. Although unsuccessful in its immediate goals (Parliament rejected all demands), the movement alerted the nation to a mature, responsible working class, thus laying the groundwork for its eventual integration into Britain's political body. On the Continent, however, unremitting state hostility toward workers' rights produced more resolute positions against bourgeois capitalism, most vividly expressed in the classic pamphlet the Communist Manifesto *(1848). Influenced by the general immiseration of the 1840s and the growing concentration of capital, Karl Marx and Friedrich Engels asserted the axiomatic existence of class struggle and the eventual triumph of workers' socialism. The manifesto launched the political movement of Marxist socialism, which anchored class antagonism as a central issue in European political life.*

ADAM SMITH

FROM *The Wealth of Nations*

Adam Smith (1723–1790), a professor of logic and moral philosophy as well as the rector of Glasgow University, wrote on moral philosophy, rhetoric, astronomy, and the formation of languages, but his reputation rests on his work of political economy, An Inquiry into the Nature and Causes of the Wealth of Nations *(1776). The treatise's wide-ranging discussions on wages, profit, capital, and industry influenced political economists for the next century, but the book's attack on mercantilism and its corresponding advocacy of free trade heralded a new economic age. The following selections center on the division of labor, the productive "orders" of society, the "invisible hand" of individual interest, and the role of the state in political economy.*

From *An Inquiry into the Nature and Causes of the Wealth of Nations*, by Adam Smith, edited by Edwin Cannan (London: Methuen and Co., 1904).

Book I

Of the Causes of Improvement in the Productive Powers of Labour, and of the Order According to Which Its Produce Is Naturally Distributed among the Different Ranks of the People

CHAPTER I
OF THE DIVISION OF LABOUR

The greatest improvement in the productive powers of labour, and the greater part of the skill, dexterity, and judgment with which it is any where directed, or applied, seem to have been the effects of the division of labour.

*   *   *

To take an example, therefore, from a very trifling manufacture; but one in which the division of labour has been very often taken notice of, the trade of the pin-maker; a workman not educated to this business (which the division of labour has rendered a distinct trade), nor acquainted with the use of the machinery employed in it (to the invention of which the same division of labour has probably given occasion), could scarce, perhaps, with his utmost industry, make one pin in a day, and certainly could not make twenty. But in the way in which this business is now carried on, not only the whole work is a peculiar trade, but it is divided into a number of branches, of which the greater part are likewise peculiar trades. One man draws out the wire, another straights it, a third cuts it, a fourth points it, a fifth grinds it at the top for receiving the head; to make the head requires two or three distinct operations; to put it on, is a peculiar business, to whiten the pins is another; it is even a trade by itself to put them into the paper; and the important business of making a pin is, in this manner, divided into about eighteen distinct operations, which, in some manufactories, are all performed by distinct

hands, though in others the same man will sometimes perform two or three of them. I have seen a small manufactory of this kind where ten men only were employed, and where some of them consequently performed two or three distinct operations. But though they were very poor, and therefore but indifferently accommodated with the necessary machinery, they could, when they exerted themselves, make among them about twelve pounds of pins in a day. There are in a pound upwards of four thousand pins of a middling size. Those ten persons, therefore, could make among them upwards of forty-eight thousand pins in a day. Each person, therefore, making a tenth part of forty-eight thousand pins, might be considered as making four thousand eight hundred pins in a day. But if they had all wrought separately and independently, and without any of them having been educated to this peculiar business, they certainly could not each of them have made twenty, perhaps not one pin in a day; that is, certainly, not the two hundred and fortieth, perhaps not the four thousand eight hundredth part of what they are at present capable of performing, in consequence of a proper division and combination of their different operations.

*   *   *

It is the great multiplication of the productions of all the different arts, in consequence of the division of labour, which occasions, in a well-governed society, that universal opulence which extends itself to the lowest ranks of the people. Every workman has a great quantity of his own work to dispose of beyond what he himself has occasion for; and every other workman being exactly in the same situation, he is enabled to exchange a great quantity of his own goods for a great quantity, or, what comes to the same thing, for the price of a great quantity of theirs. He supplies them abundantly with what they have occasion for, and they accommodate him as amply with what he has occasion for, and a general plenty diffuses itself through all the different ranks of the society.

*   *   *

* * * The whole annual produce of the land and labour of every country, or what comes to the same thing, the whole price of that annual produce, naturally divides itself, it has already been observed, into three parts; the rent of land, the wages of labour, and the profits of stock; and constitutes a revenue to three different orders of people; to those who live by rent, to those who live by wages, and to those who live by profit. These are the three great, original and constituent orders of every civilized society, from whose revenue that of every other order is ultimately derived.

The interest of the first of those three great orders, it appears from what has been just now said, is strictly and inseparably connected with the general interest of the society. Whatever either promotes or obstructs the one, necessarily promotes or obstructs the other. When the publick deliberates concerning any regulation of commerce or police, the proprietors of land never can mislead it, with a view to promote the interest of their own particular order; at least, if they have any tolerable knowledge of that interest. They are, indeed, too often defective in this tolerable knowledge. They are the only one of the three orders whose revenue costs them neither labour nor care, but comes to them, as it were, of its own accord, and independent of any plan or project of their own. That indolence, which is the natural effect of the ease and security of their situation, renders them too often, not only ignorant, but incapable of that application of mind which is necessary in order to foresee and understand the consequences of any publick regulation.

The interest of the second order, that of those who live by wages, is as strictly connected with the interest of the society as that of the first. The wages of the labourer, it has already been shewn, are never so high as when the demand for labour is continually rising, or when the quantity employed is every year increasing considerably. When this real wealth of the society becomes stationary, his wages are soon reduced to what is barely enough to enable him to bring up a family, or to continue the race of labourers. When the society declines, they fall even below this. The order of proprietors may, perhaps, gain more by the prosperity of the society, than that of labourers: but there is no order that suffers so cruelly from its decline. But though the interest of the labourer is strictly connected with that of the society, he is incapable either of comprehending that interest, or of understanding its connection with his own. His condition leaves him no time to receive the necessary information, and his education and habits are commonly such as to render him unfit to judge even though he was fully informed. In the publick deliberations, therefore, his voice is little heard and less regarded, except upon some particular occasions, when his clamour is animated, set on, and supported by his employers, not for his, but their own particular purposes.

His employers constitute the third order, that of those who live by profit. It is the stock that is employed for the sake of profit, which puts into motion the greater part of the useful labour of every society. The plans and projects of the employers of stock regulate and direct all the most important operations of labour, and profit is the end proposed by all those plans and projects. But the rate of profit does not, like rent and wages, rise with the prosperity, and fall with the declension of the society. On the contrary, it is naturally low in rich, and high in poor countries, and it is always highest in the countries which are going fastest to ruin. The interest of this third order therefore, has not the same connection with the general interest of the society as that of the other two. Merchants and master manufacturers are, in this order, the two classes of people who commonly employ the largest capitals, and who by their weakness draw to themselves the greatest share of the publick consideration. As during their whole lives they are engaged in plans and projects, they have frequently more acuteness of understanding than the greater part of country gentlemen. As their thoughts, however, are commonly exercised rather about the interest of their own particular branch of business, than about that of the society, their judgment, even when given with the greatest candour (which it has not been upon every occasion) is much more to be depended upon with regard to the former of those two objects, than with regard to the latter. Their superiority over the country gentleman is, not so much in their knowledge of the publick interest, as in their having a better knowledge of their own interest than he has of his. It is by this superior knowledge of their own interest that they have frequently imposed upon his generosity, and persuaded him to give up both his own interest and that of the publick, from a very simple but honest conviction, that their interest, and not his, was the interest of the publick. The interest of the dealers, however, in any particular branch of trade or manufactures, is always in some respects different from, and even opposite to, that of the publick. To widen the market and to narrow the competition, is always the interest of the dealers. To widen the market may frequently be agreeable enough to the interest of the publick; but to narrow the competition must always be against it, and can serve only to enable the dealers, by raising their profits above what they naturally would be, to levy, for their own benefit, an absurd tax upon the rest of their fellow-citizens. The proposal of any new law or regulation of commerce which comes from this order, ought always to be listened to with great precaution, and ought never to be adopted till after having been long and carefully examined, not only with the most scrupulous, but with the most suspicious attention. It comes from an order of men, whose interest is never exactly the same with that of the publick, who have generally an interest to deceive and even to oppress the publick, and who accordingly have, upon many occasions, both deceived and oppressed it. * * *

* * *

But the annual revenue of every society is always precisely equal to the exchangeable value of the whole annual produce of its industry, or rather is precisely the same thing with that exchangeable value. As every individual, therefore, endeavours as much as he can both to employ his capital in the support of domestick industry, and so to direct

that industry that its produce may be of the greatest value; every individual necessarily labours to render the annual revenue of the society as great as he can. He generally, indeed, neither intends to promote the publick interest, nor knows how much he is promoting it. By preferring the support of domestick to that of foreign industry, he intends only his own security; and by directing that industry in such a manner as its produce may be of the greatest value, he intends only his own gain, and he is in this, as in many other cases, led by an invisible hand to promote an end which was no part of his intention. Nor is it always the worse for the society that it was no part of it. By pursuing his own interest he frequently promotes that of the society more effectually than when he really intends to promote it. I have never known much good done by those who affected to trade for the publick good. It is an affectation, indeed, not very common among merchants, and very few words need be employed in dissuading them from it.

What is the species of domestick industry which his capital can employ, and of which the produce is likely to be of the greatest value, every individual, it is evident, can, in his local situation, judge much better than any statesman or lawgiver can do for him. The statesman, who should attempt to direct private people in what manner they ought to employ their capitals, would not only load himself with a most unnecessary attention, but assume an authority which could safely be trusted, not only to no single person, but to no council or senate whatever, and which would nowhere be so dangerous as in the hands of a man who had folly and presumption enough to fancy himself fit to exercise it.

To give the monopoly of the home-market to the produce of domestick industry, in any particular art or manufacture, is in some measure to direct private people in what manner they ought to employ their capitals, and must, in almost all cases, be either a useless or a hurtful regulation. If the produce of domestick can be brought there as cheap as that of foreign industry, the regulation is evidently useless. If it cannot, it must generally be hurtful. It is the maxim of every prudent master of a family, never to attempt to make at home what it will cost him more to make than to buy. The taylor does not attempt to make his own shoes, but buys them of the shoemaker. The shoemaker does not attempt to make his own cloaths, but employs a taylor. The farmer attempts to make neither the one nor the other, but employs those different artificers. All of them find it for their interest to employ their whole industry in a way in which they have some advantage over their neighbours, and to purchase with a part of its produce, or what is the same thing, with the price of a part of it, whatever else they have occasion for.

What is prudence in the conduct of every private family, can scarce be folly in that of a great kingdom.

*   *   *

The expence of defending the society, and that of supporting the dignity of the chief magistrate, are both laid out for the general benefit of the whole society. It is reasonable, therefore, that they should be defrayed by the general contribution of the whole society, all the different members contributing, as nearly as possible, in proportion to their respective abilities.

The expence of the administration of justice too, may, no doubt, be considered as laid out for the benefit of the whole society. There is no impropriety, therefore, in its being defrayed by the general contribution of the whole society. The persons, however, who give occasion to this expence are those who, by their injustice in one way or another, make it necessary to seek redress or protection from the courts of justice. The persons again most immediately benefited by this expence, are those whom the courts of justice either restore to their rights, or maintain in their rights. The expence of the administration of justice, therefore, may very properly be defrayed by the particular contribution of one or other, or both of those two different sets of persons, according as different occasions may require, that is, by the fees of court. It cannot be necessary to have recourse to the general contribution of the whole society, except for the conviction of those criminals who have not themselves any estate or fund sufficient for paying those fees.

Those local or provincial expences of which the benefit is local or provincial (what is laid out, for example, upon the police of a particular town or district) ought to be defrayed by a local or provincial revenue, and ought to be no burden upon the general revenue of the society. It is unjust that the whole society should contribute towards an expence of which the benefit is confined to a part of the society.

The expence of maintaining good roads and communications is, no doubt, beneficial to the whole society, and may, therefore, without any injustice, be defrayed by the general contribution of the whole society. This expence, however, is most immediately and directly beneficial to those who travel or carry goods from one place to another, and to those who consume such goods. The turnpike tolls in England, and the duties called peages in other countries, lay it altogether upon those two different sets of people, and thereby discharge the general revenue of the society from a very considerable burden.

The expence of the institutions for education and religious instruction, is likewise, no doubt, beneficial to the whole society, and may, therefore, without injustice, be defrayed by the general contribution of the whole society. This expence, however, might perhaps with equal propriety, and even with some advantage, be defrayed altogether by those who receive the immediate benefit of such education and instruction, or by the voluntary contribution of those who think they have occasion for either the one or the other.

When the institutions or publick works which are beneficial to the whole society, either cannot be maintained altogether, or are not maintained altogether by the contribution of such particular members of the society as are most immediately benefited by them, the deficiency must in most cases be made up by the general contribution of the whole society. The general revenue of the society, over and above defraying the expence of defending the society, and of supporting the dignity of the chief magistrate, must make up for the deficiency of many particular branches of revenue. ✳ ✳ ✳

✳   ✳   ✳

REVIEW QUESTIONS

1. What is the organizational innovation of the pin factory? What, according to Smith, is its significance for society?

2. What are Smith's three productive orders? What political roles does he assign these orders?

3. How does Smith find businessmen's ability to serve the public good both praiseworthy and suspicious?

4. Why did Smith's metaphor of the "invisible hand" grip the minds of nineteenth-century capitalists?

5. Who, according to Smith, should maintain state costs?

THOMAS MALTHUS

FROM *An Essay on the Principle of Population*

In 1798 Thomas Malthus (1766–1834), a minister and an economist, published this essay, which challenged the Enlightenment's indomitable belief in the perfectibility of humankind. The essay raised much controversy in the early nineteenth century. It not only resigned some social groups to the inevitability of poverty but also encouraged them to abandon traditional charity. The custom of indiscriminately aiding all indigent people with satisfactory relief, argued Malthusians, only exacerbated the problem. The following passage on food supply and population increase laid the foundation for his bleak argument.

From *An Essay on the Principle of Population*, by Thomas Malthus (London: Murray, 1826).

In an inquiry concerning the improvement of society, the mode of conducting the subject which naturally presents itself, is,

1. To investigate the causes that have hitherto impeded the progress of mankind towards happiness; and,

2. To examine the probability of the total or partial removal of these causes in future.

To enter fully into this question, and to enumerate all the causes that have hitherto influenced human improvement, would be much beyond the power of an individual. The principal object of the present essay is to examine the effects of one great cause intimately united with the very nature of man; which, though it has been constantly and powerfully operating since the commencement of society, has been little noticed by the writers who have treated this subject. The facts which establish the existence of this cause have, indeed, been repeatedly stated and acknowledged; but its natural and necessary effects have been almost totally overlooked; though probably among these effects

POWER LOOMS IN A BRITISH COTTON FACTORY (1830)

The number of power looms in England rose from 2,400 in 1813 to 224,000 in 1850, bringing about the full mechanization of textile production. The work of spinning and weaving was now concentrated in factories, a shift that had profound consequences for urbanization and the future of industrial labor. While publicists praised the new system with words, artists illustrated the new manufacturing processes. This drawing of a cotton mill, for example, underscores the prominence of unskilled women workers, denoting a signal change in the weaving industry that excluded skilled male weavers. Yet the illustration also conveys work conditions that the viewer should question. What elements of factory life might the artist have chosen not to represent?

may be reckoned a very considerable portion of that vice and misery, and of that unequal distribution of the bounties of nature, which it has been the unceasing object of the enlightened philanthropist in all ages to correct.

The cause to which I allude, is the constant tendency in all animated life to increase beyond the nourishment prepared for it.

It is observed by Dr. Franklin, that there is no bound to the prolific nature of plants or animals, but what is made by their crowding and interfering with each other's means of subsistence. Were the face of the earth, he says, vacant of other plants, it might be gradually sowed and overspread with one kind only, as for instance with fennel: and were it empty of other inhabitants, it might in a few ages be replenished from one nation only, as for instance with Englishmen.

This is incontrovertibly true. Through the animal and vegetable kingdoms Nature has scattered the seeds of life abroad with the most profuse and liberal hand; but has been comparatively sparing in the room and the nourishment necessary to rear them. The germs of existence contained in this earth, if they could freely develop themselves, would fill millions of worlds in the course of a few thousand years. Necessity, that imperious, all-pervading law of nature, restrains them within the prescribed bounds. The race of plants and the race of animals shrink under this great restrictive law; and man cannot by any efforts of reason escape from it.

In plants and irrational animals, the view of the subject is simple. They are all impelled by a powerful instinct to the increase of their species; and this instinct is interrupted by no doubts about providing for their offspring. Wherever therefore there is liberty, the power of increase is exerted; and the superabundant effects are repressed afterwards by want of room and nourishment.

The effects of this check on man are more complicated. Impelled to the increase of his species by an equally powerful instinct, reason interrupts his career, and asks him whether he may not bring beings into the world, for whom he cannot provide the means of support. If he attend to this natural suggestion, the restriction too frequently produces vice. If he hear it not, the human race will be constantly endeavouring to increase beyond the means of subsistence. But as, by that law of our nature which makes food necessary to the life of man, population can never actually increase beyond the lowest nourishment capable of supporting it, a strong check on population, from the difficulty of acquiring food, must be constantly in operation. This difficulty must fall somewhere, and must necessarily be severely felt in some or other of the various forms of misery, or the fear of misery, by a large portion of mankind.

That population has this constant tendency to increase beyond the means of subsistence, and that it is kept to its necessary level by these causes, will sufficiently appear from a review of the different states of society in which man has existed. But, before we proceed to this review, the subject will, perhaps, be seen in a clearer light, if we endeavour to ascertain what would be the natural increase of population, if left to exert itself with perfect freedom; and what might be expected to be the rate of increase in the productions of the earth, under the most favourable circumstances of human industry.

*   *   *

According to a table of Euler, calculated on a mortality of 1 in 36, if the births be to the deaths in the proportion of 3 to 1, the period of doubling will be only 12 years and 4-5ths. And this proportion is not only a possible supposition, but has actually occurred for short periods in more countries than one.

*   *   *

It may safely be pronounced, therefore, that population, when unchecked, goes on doubling itself every twenty-five years, or increases in a geometrical ratio.

The rate according to which the productions of the earth may be supposed to increase, it will not be so easy to determine. Of this, however, we may be perfectly certain, that the ratio of their increase in a limited territory must be of a totally different nature from the ratio of the increase of population. A thousand millions are just as easily doubled every twenty-five years by the power of population as a thousand. But the food to support the increase from the greater number will by no means be obtained with the same facility. Man is necessarily confined in room. When acre has been added to acre till all the fertile land is occupied, the yearly increase of food must depend upon the melioration of the land already in possession. This is a fund, which, from the nature of all soils, instead of increasing, must be gradually diminishing. But population, could it be supplied with food, would go on with unexhausted vigour; and the increase of one period would furnish the power of a greater increase the next, and this without any limit.

*   *   *

It may be fairly pronounced, therefore, that, considering the present average state of the earth, the means of subsistence, under circumstances the most favourable to human industry, could not possibly be made to increase faster than in an arithmetical ratio.

The necessary effects of these two different rates of increase, when brought together, will be very striking. Let us call the population of this island eleven millions; and suppose the present produce equal to the easy support of such a number. In the first twenty-five years the population would be twenty-two millions, and the food being also doubled, the means of subsistence would be equal to this increase. In the next twenty-five years, the population would be forty-four millions, and the means of subsistence only equal to the support of thirty-three millions. In the next period the population would be eighty-eight millions, and the means of subsistence just equal to the support

of half that number. And, at the conclusion of the first century, the population would be a hundred and seventy-six millions, and the means of subsistence only equal to the support of fifty-five millions, leaving a population of a hundred and twenty-one millions totally unprovided for.

Taking the whole earth, instead of this island, emigration would of course be excluded; and, supposing the present population equal to a thousand millions, the human species would increase as the numbers, 1, 2, 4, 8, 16, 32, 64, 128, 256, and subsistence as 1, 2, 3, 4, 5, 6, 7, 8, 9. In two centuries the population would be to the means of subsistence as 256 to 9; in three centuries as 4096 to 13, and in two thousand years the difference would be almost incalculable.

In this supposition no limits whatever are placed to the produce of the earth. It may increase for ever and be greater than any assignable quantity; yet still the power of population being in every period so much superior, the increase of the human species can only be kept down to the level of the means of subsistence by the constant operation of the strong law of necessity, acting as a check upon the greater power.

*   *   *

REVIEW QUESTIONS

1. For Malthus, how does nature check the happiness of human society?
2. What are his assumptions regarding food supply and demography? Are they valid?
3. How might this argument affect discussions on public relief of the poor?
4. How did this essay contribute to the emerging laissez-faire philosophy of the early nineteenth century?

Rules of a Factory in Berlin

The transition for Europeans from agricultural and artisanal labor to factory work was by no means an easy change. The task-oriented world of traditional labor clashed radically with the time-oriented, strictly routinized world of industrial capitalism. The following set of rules from a Berlin foundry and engineering works in the 1840s denotes the new demands of industrial discipline.

From *Documents of Economic European History*, Vol. 1, *The Process of Industrialization, 1750–1870*, edited by Sidney Pollard and C. Holmes (New York: Arnold, 1968), pp. 534–36.

In every large works, and in the co-ordination of any large number of workmen, good order and harmony must be looked upon as the fundamentals of success, and therefore the following rules shall be strictly observed.

Every man employed in the concern named below shall receive a copy of these rules, so that no one can plead ignorance. Its acceptance shall be deemed to mean consent to submit to its regulations.

1. The normal working day begins at all seasons at 6 a.m. precisely and ends, after the usual break of half an hour for breakfast, an hour for dinner and half an hour for tea, at 7 p.m., and it shall be strictly observed.

Five minutes before the beginning of the stated hours of work until their actual commencement, a bell shall ring and indicate that every worker employed in the concern has to proceed to his place of work, in order to start as soon as the bell stops.

The doorkeeper shall lock the door punctually at 6 a.m., 8.30 a.m., 1 p.m. and 4.30 p.m.

Workers arriving 2 minutes late shall lose half an hour's wages; whoever is more than 2 minutes late may not start work until after the next break, or at least shall lose his wages until then. Any disputes about the correct time shall be settled by the clock mounted above the gatekeeper's lodge.

These rules are valid both for time- and for piece-workers, and in cases of breaches of these rules, workmen shall be fined in proportion to their earnings. The deductions from the wage shall be entered in the wage-book of the gatekeeper whose duty they are; they shall be unconditionally accepted as it will not be possible to enter into any discussions about them.

2. When the bell is rung to denote the end of the working day, every workman, both on piece- and on day-wage, shall leave his workshop and the yard, but is not allowed to make preparations for his departure before the bell rings. Every breach of this rule shall lead to a fine of five silver groschen to the sick fund. Only those who have obtained special permission by the overseer may stay on in the workshop in order to work.—If a workman has worked beyond the closing bell, he must give his name to the gatekeeper on leaving, on pain of losing his payment for the overtime.

3. No workman, whether employed by time or piece, may leave before the end of the working day, without having first received permission from the overseer and having given his name to the gatekeeper. Omission of these two actions shall lead to a fine of ten silver groschen payable to the sick fund.

4. Repeated irregular arrival at work shall lead to dismissal. This shall also apply to those who are found idling by an official or overseer, and refuse to obey their order to resume work.

5. Entry to the firm's property by any but the designated gateway, and exit by any prohibited route, e.g. by climbing fences or walls, or by crossing the Spree, shall be punished by a fine of fifteen silver groschen to the sick fund for the first offences, and dismissal for the second.

6. No worker may leave his place of work otherwise than for reasons connected with his work.

7. All conversation with fellow-workers is prohibited; if any worker requires information about his work, he must turn to the overseer, or to the particular fellow-worker designated for the pupose.

8. Smoking in the workshops or in the yard is prohibited during working hours; anyone caught smoking shall be fined five silver groschen for the sick fund for every such offence.

9. Every worker is responsible for cleaning up his space in the workshop, and if in doubt, he is to turn to his overseer.—All tools must always be kept in good condition, and must be cleaned after use. This applies particularly to the turner, regarding his lathe.

10. Natural functions must be performed at the appropriate places, and whoever is found soiling walls, fences, squares, etc., and similarly, whoever is found washing his face and hands in the workshop and not in the places assigned for the purpose, shall be fined five silver groschen for the sick fund.

11. On completion of his piece of work, every workman must hand it over at once to his foreman or superior, in order to receive a fresh piece of work. Pattern makers must on no account hand over their patterns to the foundry without express order of their supervisors. No workman may take over work from his fellow-workman without instruction to that effect by the foreman.

12. It goes without saying that all overseers and officials of the firm shall be obeyed without question, and shall be treated with due deference. Disobedience will be punished by dismissal.

13. Immediate dismissal shall also be the fate of anyone found drunk in any of the workshops.

14. Untrue allegations against superiors or officials of the concern shall lead to stern reprimand, and may lead to dismissal. The same punishment shall be meted out to those who knowingly allow errors to slip through when supervising or stock-taking.

15. Every workman is obliged to report to his superiors any acts of dishonesty or embezzlement on the part of his fellow workmen. If he omits to do so, and it is shown after subsequent discovery of a misdemeanour that he knew about it at the time, he shall be liable to be taken to court as an accessory after the fact and the wage due to him shall

be retained as punishment. Conversely, anyone denouncing a theft in such a way as to allow conviction of the thief shall receive a reward of two Thaler, and, if necessary, his name shall be kept confidential.—Further, the gatekeeper and the watchman, as well as every official, are entitled to search the baskets, parcels, aprons etc. of the women and children who are taking the dinners into the works, on their departure, as well as search any worker suspected of stealing any article whatever. * * *

* * *

18. Advances shall be granted only to the older workers, and even to them only in exceptional circumstances. As long as he is working by the piece, the workman is entitled merely to his fixed weekly wage as subsistence pay; the extra earnings shall be paid out only on completion of the whole piece contract. If a workman leaves before his piece contract is completed, either of his own free will, or on being dismissed as punishment, or because of illness, the partly completed work shall be valued by the general manager with the help of two overseers, and he will be paid accordingly. There is no appeal against the decision of these experts.

19. A free copy of these rules is handed to every workman, but whoever loses it and requires a new one, or cannot produce it on leaving, shall be fined 2½ silver groschen, payable to the sick fund.

Moabit, August, 1844.

REVIEW QUESTIONS

1. What does the specificity of these regulations suggest about the social realities of early factory work?

2. What areas of factory work are for newcomers the most difficult to learn? Base your answer on the rules' injunctions and monetary fines.

3. What kind of relationship is established between factory hands and their superiors?

4. How do these regulations distinguish the work experience of factories from those of agriculture, domestic service, or the traditional crafts?

FRIEDRICH ENGELS

FROM *The Condition of the Working-Class in England in 1844*

Friedrich Engels (1820–1895), the son of a pietistic textile manufacturer from the Ruhr Valley town of Barmen, completed his apprenticeship as a textile entrepreneur in Manchester in 1842–44. Prior to this apprenticeship, Engels read critical philosophy as a student in Berlin and published articles in the opposition Cologne paper Rheinische Zeitung. *In 1842 in Cologne, Engels met Karl Marx for the first time. Manchester nurtured Engel's radical political spirit: he joined the Chartists, the movement agitating for universal suffrage and workingmen's rights; published articles in the Owenite newspaper* The New Moral World; *and wrote "Outlines of a Critique of Political Economy," which Marx published in his new Paris-based journal,* Deutsch-Französische Jahrbücher. *In 1844 Engels gathered material for a social history of England's working class, which became* The Condition of the Working-Class in England *(first published in German in 1845), a descriptive work of English industrial life that amounted to an empirical indictment of capitalism's immorality. The following passage examines Manchester, a city whose population increase of seventy thousand between 1831 and 1841 produced deplorable living conditions for the city's poor.*

From *The Condition of the Working-Class in England in 1844,* by Friedrich Engels, translated by Florence Kelley Wischnewetzky (London: George Allen and Unwin, 1892).

*   *   *

The south bank of the Irk is here very steep and between fifteen and thirty feet high. On this declivitous hillside there are planted three rows of houses, of which the lowest rise directly out of the river, while the front walls of the highest stand on the crest of the hill in Long Millgate. Among them are mills on the river, in short, the method of construction is as crowded and disorderly here as in the lower part of Long Millgate. Right and left a multitude of covered passages lead from the main street into numerous courts, and he who turns in thither gets into a filth and disgusting grime, the equal of which is not to be found— especially in the courts which lead down to the Irk, and which contain unqualifiedly the most horrible dwellings which I have yet beheld. In one of these courts there stands directly at the entrance, at the end of the covered passage, a privy without a door, so dirty that the inhabitants can pass into and out of the court only by passing through foul pools of stagnant urine and excrement. This is the first court on the Irk above Ducie Bridge—in case any one should care to look into it. Below it on the river there are several tanneries which fill the whole neighbourhood with the stench of animal putrefaction. Below Ducie Bridge the only entrance to most of the houses is by means of narrow, dirty stairs and over heaps of refuse and filth. The first court below Ducie Bridge, known as Allen's Court, was in such a state at the time of the cholera that the sanitary police ordered it evacuated, swept, and disinfected with chloride of lime. Dr. Kay gives a terrible description of the state of this court at that time. Since then, it seems to have been partially torn away and rebuilt; at least looking down from Ducie Bridge, the passer-by sees several ruined walls and heaps of débris with some newer houses. The view from this bridge, mercifully concealed from mortals of small stature by a parapet as high as a man, is characteristic for the whole district. At the bottom flows, or rather stagnates, the Irk, a narrow, coal-black, foul-smelling stream, full of débris and refuse, which it deposits on the shallower right bank. In dry weather, a long string of the most disgusting, blackish-green, slime pools are left standing on this bank, from the depths of which bubbles of miasmatic gas constantly arise and give forth a stench unendurable even on the bridge forty or fifty feet above the surface of the stream. But besides this, the stream itself is checked every few paces by high weirs, behind which slime and refuse accumulate and rot in thick masses. Above the bridge are tanneries, bonemills, and gasworks, from which all drains and refuse find their way into the Irk, which receives further the contents of all the neighbouring sewers and privies. It may be easily imagined, therefore, what sort of residue the stream deposits. Below the bridge you look upon the piles of débris, the refuse, filth, and offal from the courts on the steep left bank; here each house is packed close behind its neighbour and a piece of each is visible, all black, smoky, crumbling, ancient, with broken panes and window frames. The background is furnished by old barrack-like factory buildings. On the lower right bank stands a long row of houses and mills; the second house being a ruin without a roof, piled with débris; the third stands so low that the lowest floor is uninhabitable, and therefore without windows or doors. Here the background embraces the pauper burial-ground, the station of the Liverpool and Leeds railway, and, in the rear of this, the Workhouse, the "Poor-Law Bastille" of Manchester, which, like a citadel, looks threateningly down from behind its high walls and parapets on the hilltop, upon the working-people's quarter below.

Above Ducie Bridge, the left bank grows more flat and the right bank steeper, but the condition of the dwellings on both banks grows worse rather than better. He who turns to the left here from the main street, Long Millgate, is lost; he wanders from one court to another, turns countless corners, passes nothing but narrow, filthy nooks and alleys, until after a few minutes he has lost all clue, and knows not whither to turn. Everywhere half or wholly ruined buildings, some of them actually uninhabited, which means a great deal here; rarely a wooden or stone floor to be seen in the houses, almost uniformly broken, ill-fitting windows and doors, and a state of filth! Everywhere heaps of débris, refuse, and offal; standing pools for gutters, and a stench which alone would make it impossible for a human being in any degree civilised to live in such a district. The newly-built extension of the Leeds railway, which crosses the Irk here, has swept away some of these courts and lanes, laying others completely open to view. Immediately under the railway bridge there stands a court, the filth and horrors of which surpass all the others by far, just because it was hitherto so shut off, so secluded that the way to it could not be found without a good deal of trouble. I should never have discovered it myself, without the breaks made by the railway, though I thought I knew this whole region thoroughly. Passing along a rough bank, among stakes and washing-lines, one penetrates into this chaos of small one-storied, one-roomed huts, in most of which there is no artificial floor; kitchen, living and sleeping-room all in one. In such a hole, scarcely five feet long by six broad, I found two beds—and such bedsteads and beds!—which, with a staircase and chimney-place, exactly filled the room. In several others I found absolutely nothing, while the door stood open, and the inhabitants leaned against it. Everywhere before the doors refuse and offal; that any sort of pavement lay underneath could not be seen but only felt, here and there, with the feet. This whole collection of cattle-sheds for human beings was surrounded on two sides by houses and a factory, and on the third by the river, and besides the narrow stair up the bank, a narrow doorway alone led out into another almost equally ill-built, ill-kept labyrinth of dwellings.

A VIEW OF MANCHESTER FROM KERSTAL MOOR, William Wyld, MANCHESTER, ENGLAND (1852)

Among the most prominent social consequences of industrialization were urbanization and mechanization. Between 1750 and 1850, the English city of Manchester swelled from twenty thousand to four hundred thousand, becoming a notorious example of overcrowding and squalor. What two ways of life are contrasted in this painting?

Enough! The whole side of the Irk is built in this way, a planless, knotted chaos of houses, more or less on the verge of uninhabitableness, whose unclean interiors fully correspond with their filthy external surroundings. And how could the people be clean with no proper opportunity for satisfying the most natural and ordinary wants? Privies are so rare here that they are either filled up every day, or are too remote for most of the inhabitants to use. How can people wash when they have only the dirty Irk water at hand, while pumps and water pipes can be found in decent parts of the city alone? In truth, it cannot be charged to the account of these helots of modern society if their dwellings are not more cleanly than the pigsties which are here and there to be seen among them. The land lords are not ashamed to let dwellings like the six or seven cellars on the quay directly below Scotland Bridge, the floors of which stand at least two feet below the low-water level of the Irk that flows not six feet away from them; or like the upper floor of the corner-house on the opposite shore directly above the bridge, where the ground floor, utterly uninhabitable, stands deprived of all fittings for doors and windows, a case by no means rare in this region, when this open ground floor is used as a privy by the whole neighbourhood for want of other facilities!

If we leave the Irk and penetrate once more on the opposite side from Long Millgate into the midst of the working-men's dwellings, we shall come into a somewhat newer quarter, which stretches from St. Michael's Church to Withy Grove and Shude Hill. Here there is somewhat better order. In place of the chaos of buildings, we find at least long straight lanes and alleys or courts, built according to a plan and usually square. But if, in the former case, every house was built according to caprice, here each lane and court is so built, without reference to the situation of the adjoining ones. The lanes run now in this direction, now in that, while every two minutes the wanderer gets into a blind alley, or, on turning a corner, finds himself back where he started from; certainly no one who has not lived a considerable time in this labyrinth can find his way through it.

If I may use the word at all in speaking of this district, the ventilation of these streets and courts is, in consequence of this confusion, quite as imperfect as in the Irk region; and if this quarter may, nevertheless, be said to have some advantage over that of the Irk, the houses being newer and the streets occasionally having gutters, nearly every house has, on the other hand, a cellar dwelling, which is rarely found in the Irk district, by reason of the greater age and more careless construction of the houses. As for the rest, the filth, débris, and offal heaps, and the pools in the streets are common to both quarters, and in the district now under discussion, another feature most injurious to the cleanliness of the inhabitants, is the multitude of pigs walking about in all the alleys, rooting into the offal heaps, or kept imprisoned in small pens. Here, as in most of the working-men's quarters of Manchester, the pork-raisers rent the courts and build pig-pens in them. In almost every court one or even several such pens may be found, into which the inhabitants of the court throw all refuse and offal, whence the swine grow fat; and the atmosphere, confined on all four sides, is utterly corrupted by putrefying animal and vegetable substances. Through this quarter, a broad and measurably decent street has been cut, Millers Street, and the background has been pretty successfully concealed. But if any one should be led by curiosity to pass through one of the numerous passages which lead into the courts, he will find this piggery repeated at every twenty paces.

Such is the Old Town of Manchester, and on re-reading my description, I am forced to admit that instead of being exaggerated, it is far from black enough to convey a true impression of the filth, ruin, and uninhabitableness, the defiance of all considerations of cleanliness, ventilation, and health which characterise the construction of this single district, containing at least twenty to thirty thousand inhabitants. And such a district exists in the heart of the second city of England, the first manufacturing city of the world. If any one wishes to see in how little space a human being can move, how little air—and *such* air!—he can breathe, how little of civilisation he may share and yet live, it is only necessary to travel hither.

*   *   *

REVIEW QUESTIONS

1. What does Engels's account of slum life tell us about the material conditions of Manchester's working class?

2. What factors contribute to the overall hazardous conditions of living in England?

3. What was Engels's purpose of writing this book for a German audience?

COMTE DE SAINT-SIMON

FROM "The Incoherence and Disorder of Industry"

European observers of early industrialization were not always enamored with the spirit of rugged individualism and minimalist governmental control. Claude Henri de Rouvroy (1760–1825), comte de Saint-Simon, roundly criticized laissez-faire political economy, advocating instead an industrialized state directed by science, and an enlightened class of industrialists to address the needs of the poor. Saint-Simon, who fought in the American Revolution, used a self-made fortune to promote numerous large-scale industrial enterprises that left him impoverished. His writings, especially The New Christianity, *had little impact during his lifetime but influenced subsequent generations of French social theorists. His most enduring legacy was perhaps his influence on Auguste Comte, who founded the doctrine of Positivism.*

From *Documents of Economic European History*, Vol. 1, *The Process of Industrialization, 1750–1870,* edited by Sidney Pollard and C. Holmes (New York: Arnold, 1968), pp. 545–46.

In industry, as in science, emphasis is centred entirely on individualism; the sole sentiment which dominates all thinking is egotism. The industrialist is very little concerned about society's interests. His family, his capital and the personal fortune he strives to attain, constitute his humanity, his universe, his god. All those pursuing the same career are inevitably enemies . . . and it is by ruining them that he attains personal happiness and glory.

Problems which are no less serious exist regarding the organisation of work. Industry possesses a theory, which it might be believed holds the key to the harmonisation of production and consumption. Now this theory itself is the principal cause of disorder; the economists seem to pose the following problem:

"If it is accepted that leaders of society are more ignorant than those they govern; if it is supposed, moreover, that far from favouring the development of industry, these leaders wished to hinder its development, and their representatives were the born enemies of the producers, what kind of industrial organisation is suited to society?"

Laissez-faire, laissez-passer! Such has been the inevitable solution; such has been the single, general principle which they have proclaimed. The economists have thought by this to resolve with a stroke of the pen all questions relating to the production and distribution of wealth; they have entrusted the realisation of their schemes to *personal interest,* without realising that the individual, irrespective of his insight, is incapable of assessing total situations. . . . Well then! what is the picture we see before us? Each industry, deprived of direction, without any guidance other than personal observation, which is always imperfect . . . strives to become informed about consumer needs. Rumour has it that a branch of production offers wonderful prospects; all endeavour and capital are directed towards it, everyone dashes blindly into it. . . . The economists immediately applaud the stampede because in it they recognise the principle of competition. . . . Alas! What results from this struggle to the death? Several fortunate individuals triumph . . . the price is the complete ruin of innumerable victims. A necessary consequence of this over-production in certain sectors, this uncoordinated activity, is that the equilibrium between production and consumption is always affected. Innumerable crises result, those commercial crises which terrify speculators and frustrate worthwhile projects. Honest and hard-working men are ruined and morale is injured by such events; such people come to believe that to succeed something more than honesty and hard work are needed. They become cunning, shrewd and sly; they even boast

about these characteristics; once they have assumed this position, they are lost to humanity.

Let us add now that the fundamental principle, *laissez-faire, laissez-passer,* assumes that personal and social interests always coincide, a supposition which is disproved by innumerable facts. To select only one example, is it not clear that if society sees its interest in the establishment of a steam engine, the worker who lives by his hands cannot share this sentiment? The reply to the workers' objection is well-known; for example, printing is cited, and it is true that today it occupies more men than there were transcribers before its invention, therefore it is concluded and stated that in the long run a new equilibrium is obtained. An admirable conclusion! And until then what will happen to the thousands of hungry men? Will our reasoning console them? Will they bear their misery patiently because statistical calculations prove that in future years they will have food to appease their hunger?

REVIEW QUESTIONS

1. How does Saint-Simon's view of individual interest differ from Adam Smith's notion of the "invisible hand"?
2. Why does Saint-Simon reject competitive capitalism?
3. What social interests should capitalists aspire to embrace?

ROBERT OWEN

FROM *A New View of Society*

Robert Owen (1771–1858), a highly successful manager and partner of a cotton mill in Manchester, grew disenchanted early in his life with the deplorable material and moral standards of factory workers. Resolved to direct a capitalist enterprise that could ameliorate the lives of factory workers, Owen convinced his partners to buy cotton mills in Lanarkshire, Scotland, and set up a model community, New Lanark.

Workers received salubrious housing, quality goods from low-cost cooperative stores, and education for their children; in turn, Owen inculcated the moral virtues of cleanliness, order, thrift, and sobriety. Because New Lanark combined moral improvement with commercial success, Owen's communitarian project achieved international fame, and it still ranks among the most important examples of utopian socialism. In 1813, Owen delineated his views on the importance of human capital in his A New View of Society. *The following speech is included in this work.*

From *A New View of Society*, by Robert Owen (Friends of the New System, 1826).

An Address To the Superintendants of Manufactories, and to Those Individuals Generally, Who, by Giving Employment to an Aggregated Population, May Easily Adopt the Means to Form the Sentiments and Manners of Such a Population

Like you, I am a manufacturer for pecuniary profit. But having for many years acted on principles the reverse in many respects of those in which you have been instructed, and having found my procedure beneficial to others and to myself, even in a pecuniary point of view, I am anxious to explain such valuable principles, that you and those under your influence may equally partake of their advantages.

In two Essays, already published, I have developed some of these principles, and in the following pages you will find still more of them explained, with some detail of their application to practice, under the particular local circumstances in which I undertook the direction of the New Lanark Mills and Establishment.

By those details you will find that from the commencement of my management I viewed the population, with the mechanism and every other part of the establishment, as a system composed of many parts, and which it was my duty and interest so to combine, as that every hand, as well as every spring, lever, and wheel, should effectually co-operate to produce the greatest pecuniary gain to the proprietors.

Many of you have long experienced in your manufacturing operations the advantages of substantial, well-contrived, and well-executed machinery.

Experience has also shewn you the difference of the results between mechanism which is neat, clean, well arranged, and always in a high state of repair; and that which is allowed to be dirty, in disorder, without the means of preventing unnecessary friction, and which therefore becomes, and works, much out of repair.

In the first case, the whole economy and management are good; every operation proceeds with ease, order, and success. In the last, the reverse must follow, and a scene be presented of counteraction, confusion, and dissatisfaction among all the agents and instruments interested or occupied in the general process, which cannot fail to create great loss.

If then due care as to the state of your inanimate machines can produce such beneficial results, what may not be expected if you devote equal attention to your vital machines, which are far more wonderfully constructed?

When you shall acquire a right knowledge of these, of their curious mechanism, of their self-adjusting powers; when the proper main spring shall be applied to their varied movements, you will become conscious of their real value, and you will be readily induced to turn your thoughts more frequently from your inanimate to your living machines; you will discover that the latter may be easily trained and directed to procure a large increase of pecuniary gain, while you may also derive from them high and substantial gratification.

Will you then continue to expend large sums of money to procure the best devised mechanism of wood, brass, or iron; to retain it in perfect repair; to provide the best substance for the prevention of unnecessary friction, and to save it from falling into premature decay? Will you also devote years of intense application to understand the connection of the various parts of these lifeless machines, to improve their effective powers, and to calculate with mathematical precision all their minute and combined movements? And when in these transactions you estimate time by minutes, and the money expended for the chance of increased gain by fractions, will you not afford some of your attention to consider whether a portion of your time and capital would not be more advantageously applied to improve your living machines?

From experience which cannot deceive me, I venture to assure you that your time and money, so applied, if directed by a true knowledge of the subject, would return you, not five, ten, or fifteen per cent. for your capital so expended, but often fifty, and in many cases a hundred per cent.

I have expended much time and capital upon improvements of the living machinery; and it will soon appear that the time and money so expended in the manufactory at New Lanark, even while such improvements are in progress only, and but half their beneficial effects attained, are now producing a return exceeding fifty per cent., and will shortly create profits equal to cent. per cent. on the original capital expended in them.

Indeed, after experience of the beneficial effects, from due care and attention to the mechanical implements, it became easy to a reflecting mind to conclude at once, that at least equal advantages would arise from the application of similar care and attention to the living instruments. And when it was perceived that inanimate mechanism was greatly improved by being made firm and substantial; that it was the essence of economy to keep it neat, clean, regularly supplied with the best substance to prevent unnecessary friction, and, by proper provision for the purpose, to preserve it in good repair; it was natural to conclude that the more delicate, complex, living mechanism, would be equally improved by being trained to strength and activity; and that it would also prove true economy to keep it neat and clean; to treat it with kindness, that its mental movements might not experience too much irritating friction; to endeavour by every means to make it more perfect; to supply it regularly with a sufficient quantity of wholesome food and other necessaries of life, that the body might be preserved in good working condition, and prevented from being out of repair, or falling prematurely to decay.

These anticipations are proved by experience to be just.

Since the general introduction of inanimate mechanism into British manufactories, man, with few exceptions, has been treated as a secondary and inferior machine; and far more attention has been given to perfect the raw materials of wood and metals than those of body and mind. Give but due reflection to the subject, and you will find that man, even as an instrument for the creation of wealth, may be still greatly improved.

But, my friends, a far more interesting and gratifying consideration remains. Adopt the means which ere long shall be rendered obvious to every understanding, and you may not only partially improve those living instruments, but learn how to impart to them such excellence as shall make them infinitely surpass those of the present and all former times.

Here then is an object which truly deserves your attention; and instead of devoting all your faculties to invent improved inanimate mechanism, let your thoughts be, at least in part, directed to discover how to combine the more excellent materials of body and mind, which, by a well devised experiment, will be found capable of progressive improvement.

Thus seeing with the clearness of noon-day light, thus convinced with the certainty of conviction itself, let us not perpetuate the really unnecessary evils which our present practices inflict on this large proportion of our fellow subjects.⋆ ⋆ ⋆ But when you may have ocular demonstration, that, instead of any pecuniary loss, a well-directed attention to form the character and increase the comforts of those who are so entirely at your mercy, will essentially add to your gains, prosperity, and happiness, no reasons, except those founded on ignorance of your self-interest, can in future prevent you from bestowing your chief care on the living machines which you employ; and by so doing you will prevent an accumulation of human misery, of which it is now difficult to form an adequate conception.

That you may be convinced of this most valuable truth, which due reflection will shew you is founded on the evidence of unerring facts, is the sincere wish of

The Author.

REVIEW QUESTIONS

1. Who is Owen's intended audience? Why is Owen's analogy of workers as machines especially effective for this social group?
2. How does Owen reconcile social improvement with capitalist principles?
3. Why was Owen's argument largely dismissed by his peers as radical and unacceptable?

KARL MARX AND FRIEDRICH ENGELS

FROM *Manifesto of the Communist Party*

Published in February 1848 to proclaim the existence of a newly constituted—and minuscule—revolutionary party, the Communist Manifesto *subsequently became the most widely read political pamphlet in modern European history. The manifesto's success is grounded in its dramatic, confident presentation of a socialist blueprint for social development and political emancipation. Divided into three sections, the pamphlet outlines the class struggle between the bourgeoisie and the proletariat, the final stage of history under communism, and, finally, the false promises of competing socialist doctrines. The passage below is an excerpt from the first section, which boldly lays out the economic process by which the bourgeoisie and the capitalist mode of production would falter and surrender to the next stage of history.*

From *The Marx-Engels Reader*, edited by Robert C. Tucker, 2d ed. (New York: Norton, 1978), pp. 56–62.

A spectre is haunting Europe—the spectre of Communism. All the Powers of old Europe have entered into a holy alliance to exorcise this spectre: Pope and Czar, Metternich and Guizot, French Radicals and German police-spies.

To this end, Communists of various nationalities have assembled in London, and sketched the following Manifesto, to be published in the English, French, German, Italian, Flemish and Danish languages.

*   *   *

I. Bourgeois and Proletarians

The history of all hitherto existing society is the history of class struggles.

Freeman and slave, patrician and plebeian, lord and serf, guild-master and journeyman, in a word, oppressor and oppressed, stood in constant opposition to one another, carried on an uninterrupted, now hidden, now open fight, a fight that each time ended, either in a revolutionary reconstitution of society at large, or in the common ruin of the contending classes.

In the earlier epochs of history, we find almost everywhere a complicated arrangement of society into various orders, a manifold gradation of social rank. In ancient Rome we have patricians, knights, plebeians, slaves; in the Middle Ages, feudal lords, vassals, guild-masters, journeymen, apprentices, serfs; in almost all of these classes, again, subordinate gradations.

The modern bourgeois society that has sprouted from the ruins of feudal society has not done away with clash antagonisms. It has but established new classes, new conditions of oppression, new forms of struggle in place of the old ones.

Our epoch, the epoch of the bourgeoisie, possesses, however, this distinctive feature: it has simplified the class antagonisms: Society as a whole is more and more splitting up into two great hostile camps, into two great classes directly facing each other: Bourgeoisie and Proletariat.

*   *   *

The feudal system of industry, under which industrial production was monopolised by closed guilds, now no longer sufficed for the growing wants of the new markets. The manufacturing system took its place. The guild-masters were pushed on one side by the manufacturing middle class; division of labour between the different corporate guilds vanished in the face of division of labour in each single workshop.

*   *   *

Modern industry has established the world market, for which the discovery of America paved the way. This market has given an immense development to commerce, to navigation, to communication by land. This development has, in its turn, reacted on the extension of industry; and in proportion as industry, commerce, navigation, railways extended, in the same proportion the bourgeoisie developed, increased its capital, and pushed into the background every class handed down from the Middle Ages.

*   *   *

The bourgeoisie, historically, has played a most revolutionary part.

The bourgeoisie, wherever it has got the upper hand, has put an end to all feudal, patriarchal, idyllic relations. It has pitilessly torn asunder the motley feudal ties that bound man to his "natural superiors," and has left remaining no other nexus between man and man than naked self-interest, than callous "cash payment." It has drowned the most heavenly ecstasies of religious fervour, of chivalrous enthusiasm, of philistine sentimentalism, in the icy water of egotistical calculation. It has resolved personal worth into exchange value, and in place of the numberless indefeasible chartered freedoms, has set up that single, unconscionable freedom—Free Trade. In one word, for exploitation, veiled by religious and political illusions, it has substituted naked, shameless, direct, brutal exploitation.

*   *   *

The bourgeoisie cannot exist without constantly revolutionising the instruments of production, and thereby the relations of production, and with them the whole relations of society. Conservation of the old modes of production in unaltered form, was, on the contrary, the first condition of existence for all earlier industrial classes. Constant revolutionising of production, uninterrupted disturbance of all social conditions, everlasting uncertainty and agitation distinguish the bourgeois epoch from all earlier ones. All fixed, fast-frozen relations, with their train of ancient and venerable prejudices and opinions, are swept away, all new-formed ones become antiquated before they can ossify. All that is solid melts into air, all that is holy is profaned, and man is at last compelled to face with sober senses, his real conditions of life, and his relations with his kind.

The need of a constantly expanding market for its products chases the bourgeoisie over the whole surface of the globe. It must nestle everywhere, settle everywhere, establish connexions everywhere.

*   *   *

The bourgeoisie, during its rule of scarce one hundred years, has created more massive and more colossal productive forces than have all preceding generations together. Subjection of Nature's forces to man, machinery, application of chemistry to industry and agriculture, steam-navigation, railways, electric telegraphs, clearing of whole continents for cultivation, canalisation of rivers, whole populations conjured out of the ground—what earlier century had even a presentiment that such productive forces slumbered in the lap of social labour?

We see then: the means of production and of exchange, on whose foundation the bourgeoisie built itself up, were generated in feudal society. At a certain stage in the development of these means of production and of exchange, the conditions under which feudal society produced and exchanged, the feudal organisation of agriculture and manufacturing industry, in one word, the feudal relations of property became no longer compatible with the already developed productive forces; they became so many fetters. They had to be burst asunder; they were burst asunder.

Into their place stepped free competition, accompanied by a social and political constitution adapted to it, and by the economical and political sway of the bourgeois class.

*   *   *

Modern bourgeois society with its relations of production, of exchange and of property, a society that has conjured up such gigantic means of production and of exchange, is like the sorcerer, who

is no longer able to control the powers of the nether world whom he has called up by his spells. For many a decade past the history of industry and commerce is but the history of the revolt of modern productive forces against modern conditions of production, against the property relations that are the conditions for the existence of the bourgeoisie and of its rule. It is enough to mention the commercial crises that by their periodical return put on its trial, each time more threateningly, the existence of the entire bourgeois society. In these crises a great part not only of the existing products, but also of the previously created productive forces, are periodically destroyed. In these crises there breaks out an epidemic that, in all earlier epochs, would have seemed an absurdity—the epidemic of over-production. Society suddenly finds itself put back into a state of momentary barbarism; it appears as if a famine, a universal war of devastation had cut off the supply of every means of subsistence; industry and commerce seem to be destroyed; and why? Because there is too much civilisation, too much means of subsistence, too much industry, too much commerce. The productive forces at the disposal of society no longer tend to further the development of the conditions of bourgeois property; on the contrary, they have become too powerful for these conditions, by which they are fettered, and so soon as they overcome these fetters, they bring disorder into the whole of bourgeois society, endanger the existence of bourgeois property. The conditions of bourgeois society are too narrow to comprise the wealth created by them. And how does the bourgeoisie get over these crises? On the one hand by enforced destruction of a mass of productive forces; on the other, by the conquest of new markets, and by the more thorough exploitation of the old ones. That is to say, by paving the way for more extensive and more destructive crises, and by diminishing the means whereby crises are prevented.

The weapons with which the bourgeoisie felled feudalism to the ground are now turned against the bourgeoisie itself.

But not only has the bourgeoisie forged the weapons that bring death to itself; it has also called into existence the men who are to wield those weapons—the modern working class—the proletarians.

In proportion as the bourgeoisie, i.e., capital, is developed, in the same proportion is the proletariat, the modern working class, developed—a class of labourers, who live only so long as they find work, and who find work only so long as their labour increases capital. These labourers, who must sell themselves piece-meal, are a commodity, like every other article of commerce, and are consequently exposed to all the vicissitudes of competition, to all the fluctuations of the market.

*   *   *

The proletariat goes through various stages of development. With its birth begins its struggle with the bourgeoisie. At first the contest is carried on by individual labourers, then by the workpeople of a factory, then by the operatives of one trade, in one locality, against the individual bourgeois who directly exploits them. They direct their attacks not against the bourgeois conditions of production, but against the instruments of production themselves; they destroy imported wares that compete with their labour, they smash to pieces machinery, they set factories ablaze, they seek to restore by force the vanished status of the workman of the Middle Ages.

*   *   *

But with the development of industry the proletariat not only increases in number; it becomes concentrated in greater masses, its strength grows, and it feels that strength more. The various interests and conditions of life within the ranks of the proletariat are more and more equalised, in proportion as machinery obliterates all distinctions of labour, and nearly everywhere reduces wages to the same low level. The growing competition among the bourgeois, and the resulting commercial crises, make the wages of the workers ever more fluctuating. The unceasing improvement of machinery, ever more rapidly developing, makes their livelihood more and more precarious; the collisions between individual workmen and

individual bourgeois take more and more the character of collisions between two classes. Thereupon the workers begin to form combinations (Trades Unions) against the bourgeois; they club together in order to keep up the rate of wages; they found permanent associations in order to make provision beforehand for these occasional revolts. Here and there the contest breaks out into riots.

*   *   *

This organisation of the proletarians into a class, and consequently into a political party, is continually being upset again by the competition between the workers themselves. But it ever rises up again, stronger, firmer, mightier. It compels legislative recognition of particular interests of the workers, by taking advantage of the divisions among the bourgeoisie itself. Thus the ten-hours' bill in England was carried.

*   *   *

Of all the classes that stand face to face with the bourgeoisie today, the proletariat alone is a really revolutionary class. The other classes decay and finally disappear in the face of Modern Industry; the proletariat is its special and essential product.

*   *   *

All previous historical movements were movements of minorities, or in the interests of minorities. The proletarian movement is the self-conscious, independent movement of the immense majority, in the interests of the immense majority. The proletariat, the lowest stratum of our present society, cannot stir, cannot raise itself up, without the whole superincumbent strata of official society being sprung into the air.

Though not in substance, yet in form, the struggle of the proletariat with the bourgeoisie is at first a national struggle. The proletariat of each country must, of course, first of all settle matters with its own bourgeoisie.

In depicting the most general phases of the development of the proletariat, we traced the more or less veiled civil war, raging within existing society, up to the point where that war breaks out into open revolution, and where the violent overthrow of the bourgeoisie lays the foundation for the sway of the proletariat.

Hitherto, every form of society has been based, as we have already seen, on the antagonism of oppressing and oppressed classes. But in order to oppress a class, certain conditions must be assured to it under which it can, at least, continue its slavish existence. The serf, in the period of serfdom, raised himself to membership in the commune, just as the petty bourgeois, under the yoke of feudal absolutism, managed to develop into a bourgeois. The modern labourer, on the contrary, instead of rising with the progress of industry, sinks deeper and deeper below the conditions of existence of his own class. He becomes a pauper, and pauperism develops more rapidly than population and wealth. And here it becomes evident, that the bourgeoisie is unfit any longer to be the ruling class in society, and to impose its conditions of existence upon society as an over-riding law. It is unfit to rule because it is incompetent to assure an existence to its slave within his slavery, because it cannot help letting him sink into such a state, that it has to feed him, instead of being fed by him. Society can no longer live under this bourgeoisie, in other words, its existence is no longer compatible with society.

The essential condition for the existence, and for the sway of the bourgeois class, is the formation and augmentation of capital; the condition for capital is wage-labour. Wage-labour rests exclusively on competition between the labourers. The advance of industry, whose involuntary promoter is the bourgeoisie, replaces the isolation of the labourers, due to competition, by their revolutionary combination, due to association. The development of Modern Industry, therefore, cuts from under its feet the very foundation on which the bourgeoisie produces and appropriates products. What the bourgeoisie, therefore, produces, above all, is its own grave-diggers. Its fall and the victory of the proletariat are equally inevitable.

*　　*　　*

REVIEW QUESTIONS

1. According to Marx and Engels, what is the role of the bourgeoisie in world history?
2. How do Marx and Engels characterize the evolution of working-class political consciousness?
3. What do Marx and Engels mean by saying the bourgeoisie are their "own gravediggers"?

ANONYMOUS

An Address by a Journeyman Cotton Spinner

The factory system in northern England brought with it new social relations and political tensions. This anonymous address of 1818, published in the radical democratic newspaper The Black Dwarf, *highlights the growing political divide between the two principal classes of Manchester: employers, who owned factories and controlled the market for commissioned work from weavers working from their homes, and workers, either factory hands or independent, reduced to accepting ever-lower rates for their skills. The article's sharp invective against the new moneyed class of Manchester points up the power of the public sphere to mobilize public opinion against wealth and political power.* The Black Dwarf, *one among a handful of prominent radical democratic newspapers, boasted a circulation of more than 12,000 in 1820, which, compared with the 7,000 of* The Times, *the newspaper of record, suggests a literate, informed working class capable of political organization.*

From *The Making of the English Working Class*, by E. P. Thompson (London: Penguin, 1968), quoting *The Black Dwarf*, 30 September 1818.

First, then, as to the employers: with very few exceptions, they are a set of men who have sprung from the cotton-shop without education or address, except so much as they have acquired by their intercourse with the little world of merchants on the exchange at Manchester; but to counterbalance that deficiency, they give you enough of appearances by an ostentatious display of elegant mansions, equipages, liveries, parks, hunters, hounds, &c. which they take care to shew off to the merchant stranger in the most pompous manner. Indeed their houses are gorgeous palaces, far surpassing in bulk and extent the neat charming retreats you see round London . . . but the chaste observer of the beauties of nature and art combined will observe a woeful deficiency of taste. They bring up their families at the most costly schools, determined to give their offspring a double portion of what they were so deficient in themselves. Thus with scarcely a second idea in their heads, they are literally petty monarchs, absolute and despotic, in their own particular districts; and to support all this, their whole time is occupied in contriving how to get the greatest quantity of work turned off with the least expence. . . . In short, I will venture to say, without fear of contradiction, that there is a greater distance observed between the master there and the spinner, than there is between the first merchant in London and his lowest servant or the lowest artisan. Indeed there is no comparison. I know it to be a fact, that the greater part of the master spinners are anxious to keep wages low for the purpose of keeping the spinners indigent and spiritless . . . as for the purpose of taking the surplus to their own pockets.

The master spinners are a class of men unlike all other master tradesmen in the kingdom. They are ignorant, proud, and tyrannical. What then must be the men or rather beings who are the instruments of such masters? Why, they have been for a series of years, with their wives and their families, patience itself—bondmen and bondwomen to their cruel taskmasters. It is in vain to insult our common understandings with the observation that such men are free; that the law protects the rich and poor alike, and that a spinner can leave his master if he does not like the wages. True; so he can: but where must he go? why to another, to be sure. Well: he goes; he is asked where did you work last: "did he discharge you?" No; we could not agree about wages. Well I shall not employ you nor anyone who leaves his master in that manner. Why is this? Because there is an abominable *combination existing amongst the masters,* first established at Stockport in 1802, and it has since become so general, as to embrace all the great masters for a circuit of many miles round Manchester, though not the little masters: they are excluded. They are the most obnoxious beings to the great ones that can be imagined. . . . When the combination first took place, one of their first articles was, that no master should take on a man until he had first ascertained whether his last master had discharged him. What then is the man to do? If he goes to the parish, that grave of all independence, he is there told—We shall not relieve you; if you dispute with your master, and don't support your family, we will send you to prison; so that the man is bound, by a combination of circumstances, to submit to his master. He cannot travel and get work in any town like a shoe-maker, joiner, or taylor; he is confined to the district.

The workmen in general are an inoffensive, unassuming, set of well-informed men, though how they acquire their information is almost a mystery to me. They are docile and tractable, if not goaded too much; but this is not to be wondered at, when we consider that they are trained to work from six years old, from five in a morning to eight and nine at night. Let one of the advocates for obedience to his master take his stand in an avenue leading to a factory a little before five o'clock in the morning, and observe the squalid appearance of the little infants and their parents taken from their beds at so early an hour in all kinds of weather; let him examine the miserable pittance of food, chiefly composed of water gruel and oatcake broken into it, a little salt, and sometimes coloured with a little milk, together with a few potatoes, and a bit of bacon or fat for dinner; would a London mechanic eat this? There they are, (and if late a few minutes, a quarter of a day is stopped in wages) locked up until night in rooms heated above the hottest days we have had this summer, and allowed no time, except three-quarters of an hour at dinner in the whole day: whatever they eat at any other time must be as they are at work. The negro slave in the West Indies, if he works under a scorching sun, has probably a little breeze of air sometimes to fan him: he has a space of ground, and time allowed to cultivate it. The English spinner slave has no enjoyment of the open atmosphere and breezes of heaven. Locked up in factories eight stories high, he has no relaxation till the ponderous engine stops, and then he goes home to get refreshed for the next day; no time for sweet association with his family; they are all alike fatigued and exhausted. This is no over-drawn picture: it is literally true. I ask again, would the mechanics in the South of England submit to this?

When the spinning of cotton was in its infancy, and before those terrible machines for superseding the necessity of human labour, called steam engines, came into use, there were a great number of what were then called *little masters*; men who with a small capital, could procure a few machines, and employ a few hands, men and boys (say to twenty or thirty), the produce of whose labour was all taken to Manchester central mart, and put into the hands of brokers. . . . The brokers sold it to the merchants, by which means the master spinner was enabled to stay at home and work and attend to his workmen. The cotton was then always given out in its raw state from the bale to the wives of the spinners at home, when they heat and cleansed it ready for the spinners in the factory. By this they could earn eight, ten, or twelve shillings a week, and cook and attend to their families. But none are thus employed now; for all the cotton is broke up by a machine, turned by the steam engine, called a devil: so that the spinners wives have no employment, except they go to work in the factory all day at what can be done by children for a few shillings, four or five per week. If a man then could not agree with his master, he left him, and could get employed elsewhere. A few years, however, changed the face of things. Steam engines came into use, to purchase which, and to erect buildings sufficient to contain them and six or seven hundred hands, required a great capital. The engine power produced a more marketable (though not a better) article than the little master could at the same price. The consequence was their ruin in a short time; and the overgrown capitalists triumphed in their fall; for they were the only obstacle that stood between them and complete control of the workmen.

Various disputes then originated between the workmen and masters as to the fineness of the work, the workmen being paid according to the number of hanks or yards of thread he produced from a given quantity of cotton, which was always to be proved by the overlooker, whose interest made it imperative on him to lean to his master, and call the material coarser than it was. If the workman would not submit *he must summon his employer before a magistrate*; the whole of the acting magistrates in that district, with the exception of two worthy clergymen, being gentlemen who have sprung from the *same* source with the master cotton spinners. The employer generally contented himself with sending his overlooker to answer any such summons, thinking it beneath him to meet his servant. The magistrate's decision was generally in favour of the master, though on the statement of the overlooker only. The workman dared not appeal to the sessions on account of the expense. . . .

These evils to the men have arisen from that dreadful monopoly which exists in those districts where wealth and power are got into the hands of the few, who, in the pride of their hearts, think themselves the lords of the universe.

REVIEW QUESTIONS

1. Why are employers characterized as "petty monarchs, absolute and despotic"?
2. Why is this a new attitude among employers?
3. How does this address compare the lives of Manchester workers with workers of prior times and with workers elsewhere in Britain?
4. What is the perceived attitude of the state in this conflict between employers and workers?

ANONYMOUS

FROM *The Life & History of Captain Swing, the Kent Rick Burner, Written by Himself*

The mechanization of spinning and weaving and the introduction of threshing machines in the English countryside brought waves of machine breakings and barn burnings in the 1820s and 1830s. Although this violence is often characterized as the futile resistance to inevitable change, these uprisings are more accurately seen as highly organized, disciplined political events. Under such fictional leaders as Ned Ludd or Captain Swing, weavers, artisans, and sharecroppers organized themselves into bands and destroyed private property that they believed had stripped them of their livelihoods and dignity. The following story, which circulated as a popular political tract in the early 1830s, compresses the major political grievances of England's agricultural workers into the life of Swing, a fictional hard-working tenant farmer driven to destitution and despair by social and political change in the early nineteenth century.

From *The Life & History of Captain Swing, the Kent Rick Burner, Written by Himself,* by Anonymous (Chubb, 1830).

I was born on the day William Pitt became Prime Minister of England. My father was one of the class of small farmers, then so numerous in England, but whom the system of large farms has now altogether extinguished in the country. My father had two sons, of whom I was the younger; and as the savings of his predecessors had rendered him wealthy in his way, he determined educating me for a profession, and sent me to a grammar school in the neighbourhood; from whence I was removed in due time to a public school, preparatory to my entering college. When I was about to enter college, my elder brother died,—in consequence of which my father changed his intention of bringing me up to a profession, and took me home to attend to the farm. As I considered my future path in life was now definitely marked out for me, I gave up my entire time and attention to acquire a thorough knowledge of agriculture, and soon became one of the best farmers in that part of the kingdom. Soon after my father died, and bequeathed to me the farm and greater part of his effects. Some time after this I became acquainted with the daughter of a neighbouring curate, * * * and after a short period I proposed marriage to her, and she became my wife. I, of course, got no fortune with her, but she had that which surpasseth riches,—a most kind and amiable disposition; and if industry and integrity on the one side, and virtue and humility on the other, were sufficient to render our union a happy one, never was there a couple bid fairer for it than we did.

A few years passed as happily as I could wish, and three little ones added to my felicity. Although working hard all day, I at night forgot my toil and trouble when I returned to my fireside and family; and as soon as my children began to lisp, the first words I taught them to utter were the same I had myself learned when I was their age, namely, "To fear God and honour the King—to give every man his due, and behave uprightly to all." A short time after the birth of my fourth child, our old landlord died, and was succeeded by his son.

About two years after our young landlord returned home, (he had been on the Continent since the death of his father) I received a notice to quit,—the receipt of which astonished me beyond measure, as I owed no rent, and had always supported the character of being the best and most improving tenant on the estate. * * * As I found it impossible to see the lord, I called on the steward, and asked him what fault I had committed, or what crime I had been guilty of, that I should be turned out of the farm where my forefathers had lived for centuries, and which they and I had done so much to improve? "There is no fault to be found with you," replied the steward, "you have always paid your rent regularly, and conducted yourself correctly; but my lord wants your

farm to make a fox-cover, and you must leave it next settling day."

"Good God!" exclaimed I, "are my wife and children to be turned out to make room for wild beasts?"—"There is no use in talking," said the steward, "your land is the best site on the estate for a fox-cover, and you must give it up."

The lord himself happened to pass by, and with tears in my eyes, I beseeched him not to turn out my family, in order to replace them with foxes. "Every man," said the lord, "*can do what he pleases with his own*," and he walked away and left me.

*   *   *

Time, which flies equally fast whether we are miserable or happy, soon brought about the settling day, and as I found all appeals to the landlord utterly useless, I was prepared to give him possession, I had not sufficient capital to take a large farm, and small ones were not to be had, so I was obliged to dispose of my horses, black cattle, and farming machinery; and as the period I sold them was one of unusual depression, I did not receive one half their value.

As soon as my first burst of grief for the loss of my farm was over, I again applied myself to labour in my garden, (which I had taken with a cottage in the neighbourhood) and by dint of industry and exertion supported my family, by supplying a neighbouring village with vegetables. Up to this period I had never attended a political meeting in my life, nor took any part whatever in politics; I thought our laws and legislators too good to require alteration or change; and if I hated one thing more than another, it was Radicalism, the abettors of which I considered no better than rebels and revolutionists, who wanted to destroy our glorious constitution, and cause anarchy in the country. I begun, however, now to think otherwise. I had seen all around me, my neighbours reduced from comfort to poverty, and from poverty to the poor-rates; and as, in the greater number of cases, it had arisen from no fault of their own, it occurred to me that some change was necessary; as had England been governed as it ought, those things could never have taken place. Reflections of this sort determined me to attend the great meeting at Manchester, then about to be held, and I accordingly went there. Every thing passed quietly off until noon, when, to my horror and surprise, a charge was made by the military and yeomanry on the peaceable and unarmed multitude that were assembled, and I, amongst others, was wounded by a sabre-cut in the arm. Bleeding profusely, and with my arm hanging uselessly by my side, I went into Manchester and got it dressed; I was kept awake the entire night by the pain of my wound, but consoled myself with the reflection that immediate and condign punishment would be inflicted on the lawless soldiery who had dared to massacre a peaceable multitude assembled to petition Parliament. "The King," said I, "will certainly send down a commission to have the monsters tried for their blood-thirsty outrage." What was my astonishment and indignation, in ten days after, when I saw a letter from the Secretary of State, thanking in the King's name, the military and magistrates, for massacring the people at Manchester.

I no longer wanted a proof that our country was sadly misgoverned—that a great change was necessary—and that the Reformers were the only real friends of the people.

*   *   *

[Swing is wrongfully accused of poaching and serves eighteen months in prison] When I was permitted to leave prison, I again commenced working in my garden, hoping my troubles were now over, and that, for the rest of my life, though poor, I should be allowed to rear my children peaceably and without persecution. A new and unexpected misfortune, however, arose; the parson of the parish considered his tithes not sufficiently productive, and made a claim for small tithes, which none of his predecessors had done, and demanded of me not only tithes for the current year, but also for that of the preceding one. I was unable to pay it, and was served with a law process, and, in a few weeks after, my cow sold by auction for the parson's tithes. I was now no

longer able to keep my cottage and garden, and gave it up to the landlord, and rented a smaller one, having half an acre of ground attached to it. My present holding, though situated in the same parish, was two miles farther in the country than the former one, and adjoining it was a slip of uncultivated land, containing about an acre. My present landlord proposed that I should take this piece of land, in addition to what I had already; and, as an encouragement to me to do so, told me that he would not ask rent for the two first years, as during that time, he was perfectly well aware, the land would produce nothing. As I considered his proposal a fair one, I accepted it, and became his tenant for the piece of land, which I immediately set about enclosing with a ditch: having no person to assist me in making it, it was a considerable time before I had it finished: and I then commenced digging it with a spade, as I had no money to pay for getting it ploughed. In this way I fallowed it for two successive seasons; and in the beginning of the third spring I contrived, by parting with a good deal of my furniture to purchase some manure, which I carried in a basket on my head to the land: thus prepared, I sowed a crop in it, and nothing could succeed better than it did. When the time nearly came for gathering it, I was one day standing admiring it, with a gratification proportionate to the immense labour and time I had expended in bringing it about. "Although it had cost me three years labour," said I, "to grow this crop, it will nevertheless amply remunerate me." I had scarcely uttered the words, when two men rode up to me, one of whom I found to be the parson, whom I had never before seen in the parish, and the other his tithe valuator. After the latter had examined the crop, the parson asked me whether I would pay in kind or money?

"How much is it parson?" asked I.—"Only the tenth of the crop," replied he; "you must be very ignorant to ask such a question."

"But," said I, "if your reverence takes the tenth of the crop, it will be three-tenths of the produce of my laud; for I have been three years bringing the land into cultivation before it could grow any thing."—"I don't understand you," said the parson; "I must have my tithe."

"Why surely," said I, "your reverence will not rob my poor little children, by taking two-tenths more than you have a right to?"—"Rob them!" roared out the parson; "I see, my good fellow, you are a Radical, but I'll make you pay me my right; you shall not defraud the church of its lawful dues."

The parson went away, and the overseers came and demanded the poor-rates; the churchwardens called for an applotment, made to repair and beautify the church, and the landlord took his rent, and I was a ruined man. My whole three years' labour went amongst them, without leaving me one shilling for myself. I was now broken in purse and spirit, and could no longer bear up against the misfortunes that had fallen upon me. I gave up my land, and as I could procure no employment, I was obliged to apply to the parish. In order to lessen the poor-rates as much as possible, the overseers and farmers met each Sunday, and every able-bodied labourer was set up to auction, and the farmer who bid most for him had him to work for him during the ensuing week. One farmer bid three shillings a week for me, and I was ordered to work for him for that sum, and four shillings that the overseer gave me, making together seven shillings a week, to support my wife, five children, and myself. At the end of a week the farmer had no further occasion for my services, and I was on the following Monday, in company with some others, yoked to a cart, and made to draw gravel to the road. "Good God!" exclaimed I, when I found the harness upon me, "what is England reduced to, when, without any fault of my own, in the same parish that so many generations of my forefathers lived comfortable and happy, I am obliged to submit so be treated as a beast of burthen!" The work of drawing stones was so dreadfully severe, and so unlike what I had been accustomed to, that a few weeks' trial soon convinced me it would soon kill me; and I determined leaving my native parish, and seeking employment elsewhere; and with this intention I came into Kent. ✳ ✳ ✳

In Kent I found myself still worse off than at home, for I could procure no employment whatever, and as I had no claim on the poor-rates, I was in danger of starving, and felt myself compelled to return home; before, however, I could do so, my poor wife fell ill of fever, and in order to prevent her perishing from want, I was obliged to go and beg—downright hunger having conquered my reluctance to ask charity. I proceeded along the road in order to do so, and saw a fat man, dressed in black, approaching me, to whom I applied for something to prevent my wife and children dying of starvation.—"I cannot *afford* to give you any thing," replied he; "go to your parish." His manner was so repulsive, that I considered it useless to make a second application, and passed on: when I had walked a few yards, I began to think I had somewhere before seen the gentleman in black, and, after a few minutes recollection, remembered he was the Rev. Mr. Saint Paul, who had taken my cow in payment of his small tithes, and who afterwards took three-tenths of my crop for his tithe of my plot of ground: he was a pluralist; and, having five livings, seldom or never came to the parish I had lived in, except to receive his tithes, so that I did not at first recognise him. I walked on for some time longer, and not meeting any person, was obliged to return to the cottage that my wife was in, without any thing to give her; as I could not bring myself to enter the cottage and behold my wife dying for want, I sat down on the road, a little distance from the door, and soon beheld the parson returning from his walk. He had a cake in his hand, which, as he had no inclination to eat, he threw to a large pampered dog that walked beside him. The dog, having no better appetite than his master, took the cake in his mouth, played with it for a moment, then tossed it in the dirt and left it there, A little child of mine beheld the scene from the cottage door, and ran and picked the cake out of the gutter, when the parson demanded how dare she take it from his dog? "Oh, Sir!" said the little girl, "the dog will not eat it, and I wish to bring it to my poor mother, who is starving."—"Your mother and yourself ought to be in the workhouse," said the parson; "it is a shame for the parish officers to allow little naked vagabonds like you to be running about the roads."

"Can this man," thought I, "be a descendant of the Apostles, who carried nothing with them but scrip and staff, and who preached that we should consider every man as our brother, and relieve the necessities of our fellow-creatures?" Such an impression did his conduct make on me, that I got a piece of paper, and wrote a few lines, cautioning him against the consequences of his cruelty, and having signed it with my real name, "SWING," I left it at his hall-door during the night, and the following day the village rung with the report of the parson's having received a threatening notice, and that if the author could be detected, he would certainly be transported.

When writing the notice, I had not the most distant intention of making myself the instrument of punishment to the parson; it was an ebullition of the moment, called forth by my suffering, and I thought no more about it. In a few days after the serving of the notice my wife died, and I was obliged to procure a coffin from the parish to bury her; no person attended her remains to the grave but a man who helped me to carry the coffin, and my five motherless children; it was late in the afternoon when we reached the churchyard, and as the man was obliged to leave me before the grave was entirely covered in, it became quite dark ere I could finish it, and I was obliged to procure a lantern to enable me to do so. When I completed it, I beheld my five children starving and shivering with cold beside the grave of their poor mother, without the smallest prospect of obtaining any food for them before morning; and in this condition I returned towards the cottage from whence I had that day carried my wife to be buried; the idea of passing the night on the straw on which she had expired was so repugnant to me, that I determined not to do so, and as the parson's haggard was only a short distance from me, I brought my children to pass the night on some loose straw that was lying on the ground. I was too much overwhelmed with grief and misery to attend to any thing, and I forgot to extinguish the light in the lantern which was carried by one of my children; the child incautiously placed the candle close to a rick, which caught fire, and was in a few minutes in a blaze; frightened and confounded at the accident, I immediately left the place, and the next morning journeyed homewards, begging for subsistence along the road: every where I went I heard of fires and notices signed "SWING." "How happens this," thought I. "I am not the author of these burnings!—What can have caused them?" A few minutes' reflection on the history of my own life, which without any alteration may stand for that of thousands of others, enabled me to give myself a satisfactory answer. "Those fires," said I, "are caused by farmers having been turned out of their lands to make room for foxes—peaceable people assembled to petition Parliament, massacred by the military—peasants confined two years in prison for picking up a dead partridge, English labourers set up to auction like slaves, and treated as beasts of burthen,—and pluralist parsons taking a poor man's only cow for the tythe of his cabbage garden. These are the things that have caused the burnings, and not unfortunate 'SWING!'" I continued my route, reached home, and am again harnessed like a horse to a gravel cart. But I bear it with patience, under the conviction that, in a very short time, Reform or Revolution must release me from it.

REVIEW QUESTIONS

1. What change initially uprooted Swing from his prosperity, and what factors continued to cause him misfortune?
2. How had traditional authority changed in the countryside?
3. What are Swing's political sympathies at the story's beginning? How do they evolve?
4. How does this story blur the boundaries of criminality and social justice?

FRANCIS PLACE

The People's Charter and National Petition

As the first movement that explicitly advocated the political rights of unpropertied laborers, Chartism was a watershed in European political history. Following the Reform Act of 1832, which enfranchised the upper echelons of the bourgeoisie, radical democrats broke allegiance with liberals and sought ways to renew the call for political reform. With unions outlawed in 1834, reformers turned to the strategy of petitioning Parliament for reform. In 1838, Francis Place (1771–1854), a venerable figure in English radical politics, drew up a statement entitled the People's Charter, a set of demands presented in the National Petition submitted to Parliament in 1839. Committees throughout England and Wales circulated the charter as a petition, and collected millions of signatures. The charter was presented to Parliament in 1839 and 1842, and rejected. In 1848, with revolution rampant on the continent, Chartists organized 6 million signatures for a final petition; its submission to Parliament was demonstratively attended by 500,000 workers. England's political establishment did not bow to Chartism, but the dignity and discipline of most Chartist demonstrations commanded respect and paved the way for trade associations in 1855 and a second reform act in 1867.

From *The People's Charter and National Petition*, by Francis Place (Quigley, 1839).

Unto the Honourable the Commons of the United Kingdom of Great Britain and Ireland, in Parliament assembled, the Petition of the undersigned, their suffering Countrymen,

Humbly Sheweth,

That we, your Petitioners, dwell in a land whose merchants are noted for enterprise, whose manufacturers are very skilful, and whose workmen are proverbial for their industry.

The land itself is goodly, the soil rich, and the temperature wholesome; it is abundantly furnished with the materials of commerce and trade; it has numerous and convenient harbours; in facility of internal communication it exceeds all others.

For three-and-twenty years we have enjoyed a profound peace.

Yet, with all these elements of national prosperity, and with every disposition and capacity to take advantage of them, we find ourselves overwhelmed with public and private suffering.

We are bowed down under a load of taxes; which, notwithstanding, fall greatly short of the wants of our rulers; our traders are trembling on the verge of bankruptcy; our workmen are starving; capital brings no profit, and labour no remuneration; the home of the artificer is desolate, and the warehouse of the pawnbroker is full; the workhouse is crowded, and the manufactory is deserted.

We have looked on every side, we have searched diligently, in order to find out the causes of a distress so sore and so long continued.

We can discover none in nature, or in providence.

Heaven has dealt graciously by the people; but the foolishness of our rulers has made the goodness of God of none effect.

The energies of a mighty kingdom have been wasted in building up the power of selfish and ignorant men, and its resources squandered for their aggrandisement.

The good of a party has been advanced to the sacrifice of the good of the nation; the few have governed for the interest of the few, while the interest of the many has been neglected, or insolently and tyrannously trampled upon.

It was the fond expectation of the people that a remedy for the greater part, if not for the whole, of their grievances, would be found in the Reform Act of 1832.

They were taught to regard that Act as a wise means to a worthy end; as the machinery of an improved legislation, where the will of the masses would be at length potential.

They have been bitterly and basely deceived.

The fruit, which looked so fair to the eye, has turned to dust and ashes when gathered.

The Reform Act has effected a transfer of power from one domineering faction to another, and left the people as helpless as before.

Our slavery has been exchanged for an apprenticeship to liberty, which has aggravated the painful feeling of our social degradation, by adding to it the sickening of still deferred hope.

We come before your Honourable House to tell you, with all humility, that this state of things must not be permitted to continue, that it cannot long continue without very seriously endangering the stability of the throne, and the peace of the kingdom; that if, by God's help, and all lawful and constitutional appliances, an end can be put to it, we are fully resolved that it shall speedily come to an end.

We tell your Honourable House, that the capital of the master must no longer be deprived of its due profit; that the labour of the workman must no longer be deprived of its due reward; that the laws which make food dear, and those which, by making money scarce, make labour cheap, must be abolished; that taxation must be made to fall on property, not on industry; that the good of the many, as it is the only legitimate end, so must it be the sole study of the government.

As a preliminary essential to these and other requisite changes; as the means by which alone the interests of the people can be effectually vindicated and secured, we demand that those interests be confided to the keeping of the people.

When the State calls for defenders, when it calls for money, no consideration of poverty or ignorance can be pleaded in refusal or delay of the call.

Required as we are, universally, to support and to obey the laws, nature and reason entitle us to demand that, in the making of the laws, the universal voice shall be implicitly listened to.

We perform the duties of freemen: we must have the privileges.

We Demand Universal Suffrage.

The Suffrage, to be exempt from the corruption of the wealthy and the violence of the powerful, must be secret.

The assertion of our right necessarily involves the power of its uncontrolled exercise.

We ask for the reality of a good, not for its semblance.

We Demand the Ballot.

The connection between the representatives and the people, to be beneficial, must be intimate.

The legislative and constituent powers, for correction and for instruction, ought to be brought into frequent contact.

Errors, which are comparatively light when susceptible of a speedy popular remedy, may produce the most disastrous effect when permitted to grow inveterate through years of compulsory endurance.

To public safety, as well as public confidence, frequent elections are essential.

We Demand Annual Parliaments.

With power to choose, and freedom in choosing, the range of our choice must be unrestricted.

We are compelled by the existing law, to take for our representatives, men who are incapable of appreciating our difficulties, or who have little sympathy with them; merchants who have retired from trade, and no longer feel its harassings; proprietors of land, who are alike ignorant of its evils and their cures; lawyers, by whom the honours of the Senate are sought after only as a means of obtaining notice in the Courts.

The labours of a representative, who is sedulous in the discharge of his duty, are numerous and burdensome.

It is neither just, nor reasonable, nor safe, that they should continue to be gratuitously rendered.

We demand that, in the future election of Members of your Honourable House, the approbation of the constituency shall be the sole qualification; and that, to every representative so chosen, shall be assigned, out of the public taxes, a fair and adequate remuneration for the time which he is called upon to devote to the public service.

Finally, we would most earnestly impress on your Honourable House, that this petition has not been dictated by any idle love of change; that it springs out of no inconsiderate attachment to fanciful theories—but that it is the result of much and long deliberation, and of convictions, which the events of each succeeding year tend more and more to strengthen.

The management of this mighty kingdom has hitherto been a subject for contending factions, to try their selfish experiments upon.

We have felt the consequences, in our sorrowful experience—short glimmerings of uncertain enjoyment, swallowed up by long and dark seasons of suffering.

If the self-government of the people should not remove their distresses, it will at least remove their repinings.

Universal Suffrage will, and it alone can, bring true and lasting peace to the nation; we firmly believe that it will bring prosperity.

May it, therefore, please your Honourable House to take this our Petition into your most serious consideration; and to use your utmost endeavours, by all constitutional means, to have a law passed granting to every male of lawful age, sane mind, and unconvicted of crime, the right of voting for Members of Parliament; and directing all future elections of Members of Parliament to be in the way of secret ballot; and ordaining that the duration of Parliament so chosen shall in no case exceed one year; and abolishing all property qualifications in the Members: and providing for their due remuneration while in attendance on their Parliamentary duties.

And your Petitioners, &c.

REVIEW QUESTIONS

1. What were, according to the petition, the economic and political circumstances that occasioned this plea?
2. What are the specific points of the petition? What do these demands implicitly reveal about British political culture in the 1830s?
3. How radical were these demands? Why were they unacceptable to Parliament?

20 ❧ FROM RESTORATION TO REVOLUTION, 1815–1848

At the core of most discussions explaining change from the traditional to the modern world lies an evolving form of liberalism. After the Glorious Revolution of 1688 in England, elements of a liberal social contract emerged, many of which we have accented in earlier chapters: individual liberties guaranteed by constitutional law; the sanctity of private property; unrestricted movement of individuals, ideas, and goods; and, finally, social advancement based on merit. Such beliefs irreparably undermined the social foundations of the old regime.

The principles of the Enlightenment and liberalism largely overlap. Liberalism, for example, inherited the Enlightenment's emphasis on reason, social utility, pragmatic reform, and aversion to arbitrary rule. Above all, both embraced the indomitable belief in progress. The French Revolution, however, significantly affected liberalism's development. Scarred by the experiences of the Terror and Napoleonic demagoguery, liberals reasserted the Lockeian emphasis on the limits of power that public authority held over the individual. Governments based on popular will, they argued, could be as despotic as absolute monarchy, for both sacrificed individual liberties in the name of general welfare and collective happiness. For liberals, the whole could never be greater than the sum of its parts; the irreducible unit of a free civil society remained the individual, not the general will. Following classical economic theory, liberals averred that the "invisible hand" of individual self-interest best secured the greater good of society. Liberalism further distinguished itself from democracy by rejecting universal human suffrage, assigning those classes lacking property and education merely passive rights of citizenship. Consequently, liberalism evolved into a solidly bourgeois ideology.

For the traditional elite, liberalism remained a subversive threat. Its advocacy of constitutions, civil liberties, and centralized government challenged the post-Napoleonic restoration of dynastic legitimacy and aristocratic privilege. Be-

cause liberals in the Italian, German, and eastern European states coupled their ideals of constitutionalism with a unified nation-state, the doctrine was doubly alarming. In the first half of the nineteenth century, conservative statesmen and rulers vigorously strove to contain the spread of liberal national ideals.

The economic and cultural dimensions of liberalism are particularly important in understanding the doctrine's impact on European society. Economically, Europeans largely associated liberalism as the promoter of laissez-faire capitalism. Liberals believed that society and government were compelled to acquiesce in the natural laws of the market. Between 1840 and 1870 the doctrine of free trade assumed the status of a moral imperative for British and European liberals, who associated material wealth with the advance of civilization. If governments minimized their presence in the marketplace, liberals argued, industry and commerce could expand markets, lower the costs of food and goods, and thus lift the diligent out of privation. In this fashion, thrift, self-reliance, and industry were watchwords of the liberal's personal credo. Culturally, liberalism advocated a secular civil society in which religion played a diminished role in public affairs. Liberals viewed the Catholic Church as obscurantist, an outmoded institution that hindered the diffusion of rational, materialist knowledge. Education, the battle for children's minds, was a particularly divisive issue. Denying the church its traditional role as educator by instituting state-supervised school systems with national curricula and state-trained teachers became a central plank in the platform of many liberal parties. On another cultural front, bourgeois liberal society envisioned ideals of male and female activity. Just as men were cast as breadwinners and public leaders, so too were women expected to govern the domestic sphere with feminine probity, maternal virtue, and wifely subservience. Such prescribed and divided roles did not always correspond to practice.

In all its facets, liberalism was a critical agent of change in the first century of the modern era after 1789. By locating its role in such overarching themes as individualism, constitutional rights, capitalism, free trade, nationalism, and secular state building, we can see liberalism as a preponderant force in nineteenth-century civil society.

MARY WOLLSTONECRAFT

FROM *A Vindication of the Rights of Woman*

Mary Wollstonecraft (1759–1797), a teacher and writer, wrote this essay as a critical response to the French Revolution. An enthusiastic supporter of the revolution, she was nonetheless angered that the National Assembly did not extend the same liberties to women as to men. Her essay, appealing to reason, utility, and natural law, exhorted both men and women to reform education for women and enable them to participate in civil society as useful members. Although scorned as a radical Francophile by her contemporaries, Wollstonecraft convincingly applied liberal reasoning to the cause of women at a critical juncture in European history.

From *A Vindication of the Rights of Woman*, by Mary Wollstonecraft (New York: Norton, 1970).

After considering the historic page, and viewing the living world with anxious solicitude, the most melancholy emotions of sorrowful indignation have depressed my spirits, and I have sighed when obliged to confess that either Nature has made a great difference between man and man, or that the civilization which has hitherto taken place in the world has been very partial. I have turned over various books written on the subject of education, and patiently observed the conduct of parents and the management of schools; but what has been the result?—a profound conviction that the neglected education of my fellow-creatures is the grand source of the misery I deplore, and that women, in particular, are rendered weak and wretched by a variety of concurring causes, originating from one hasty conclusion. The conduct and manners of women, in fact, evidently prove that their minds are not in a healthy state; for, like the flowers which are planted in too rich a soil, strength and usefulness are sacrificed to beauty; and the flaunting leaves, after having pleased a fastidious eye, fade, disregarded on the stalk, long before the season when they ought to have arrived at maturity. One cause of this barren blooming I attribute to a false system of education, gathered from the books written on this subject by men who, considering females rather as women than human creatures, have been more anxious to make them alluring mistresses than affectionate wives and rational mothers; and the understanding of the sex has been so bubbled by this specious homage, that the civilized women of the present century, with a few exceptions, are only anxious to inspire love, when they ought to cherish a nobler ambition, and by their abilities and virtues exact respect.

In a treatise, therefore, on female rights and manners, the works which have been particularly written for their improvement must not be overlooked, especially when it is asserted, in direct terms, that the minds of women are enfeebled by false refinement; that the books of instruction, written by men of genius, have had the same tendency as more frivolous productions; and that, in the true style of Mahometanism, they are treated as a kind of subordinate beings, and not as a part of the human species, when improvable reason is allowed to be the dignified distinction which raises men above the brute creation, and puts a natural sceptre in a feeble hand.

Yet, because I am a woman, I would not lead my readers to suppose that I mean violently to agitate the contested question respecting the quality or inferiority of the sex; but as the subject lies in my way, and I cannot pass it over without subjecting the main tendency of my reasoning to misconstruction, I shall stop a moment to deliver, in a few words, my opinion. In the government of the physical world it is observable that the female in point of strength is, in general, inferior to the male. This is the law of Nature; and it does not appear to be suspended or abrogated in favour of woman. A degree of physical superiority cannot, therefore, be denied, and it is a noble prerogative! But not content with this natural pre-eminence, men endeavour to sink us still lower, merely to render us alluring objects for a moment; and women, intoxicated by the adoration which men, under the influence of their senses, pay them, do not seek to obtain a durable interest in their hearts, or to become the friends of the fellow-creatures who find amusement in their society.

I am aware of an obvious inference. From every quarter have I heard exclamations against masculine women, but where are they to be found? If by this appellation men mean to inveigh against their ardour in hunting, shooting, and gaming, I shall most cordially join in the cry; but if it be against the imitation of manly virtues, or, more properly speaking, the attainment of those talents and virtues, the exercise of which ennobles the human character, and which raises females in the scale of animal being, when they are comprehensively termed mankind, all those who view them with a philosophic eye must, I should think, wish with me, that they may every day grow more and more masculine.

This discussion naturally divides the subject. I shall first consider women in the grand light of human creatures, who, in common with men, are placed on this earth to unfold their faculties; and afterwards I shall more particularly point out their peculiar designation.

I wish also to steer clear of an error which many respectable writers have fallen into; for the instruction which has hitherto been addressed to women, has rather been applicable to *ladies,* if the little indirect advice that is scattered through "Sandford and Merton" be excepted; but, addressing my sex in a firmer tone, I pay particular attention to those in the middle class, because they appear to be in the most natural state. Perhaps the seeds of false refinement, immorality, and vanity, have ever been shed by the great. Weak, artificial beings, raised above the common wants and affections of their race, in a premature unnatural manner, undermine the very foundation of virtue, and spread corruption through the whole mass of society! As a class of mankind they have the strongest claim to pity; the education of the rich tends to render them vain and helpless, and the unfolding mind is not strengthened by the practice of those duties which dignify the human character. They only live to amuse themselves, and by the same law which in Nature invariably produces certain effects, they soon only afford barren amusement.

But as I purpose taking a separate view of the different ranks of society, and of the moral character of women in each, this hint is for the present sufficient; and I have only alluded to the subject because it appears to me to be the very essence of an introduction to give a cursory account of the contents of the work it introduces.

My own sex, I hope, will excuse me, if I treat them like rational creatures, instead of flattering their *fascinating* graces, and viewing them as if they were in a state of perpetual childhood, unable to stand alone. I earnestly wish to point out in what true dignity and human happiness consists. I wish to persuade women to endeavour to acquire strength, both of mind and body, and to convince them that the soft phrases, susceptibility of heart, delicacy of sentiment, and refinement of taste, are almost synonymous with epithets of weakness, and that those beings who are only the objects of pity, and that kind of love which has been termed its sister, will soon become objects of contempt.

Dismissing, then, those pretty feminine phrases, which the men condescendingly use to soften our slavish dependence, and despising that weak elegancy of mind, exquisite sensibility, and sweet docility of manners, supposed to be the sexual characteristics of the weaker vessel, I wish to show that elegance is inferior to virtue, that the first object of laudable ambition is to obtain a character as a human being, regardless of the distinction of sex, and that secondary views should be brought to this simple touchstone.

This is a rough sketch of my plan; and should I express my conviction with the energetic emotions that I feel whenever I think of the subject, the dictates of experience and reflection will be felt by some of my readers. Animated by this important object, I shall disdain to cull my phrases or polish my style. I aim at being useful, and sincerity will render me unaffected; for wishing rather to persuade by the force of my arguments than dazzle by the elegance of my language, I shall not waste my time in rounding periods, or in fabricating the turgid bombast of artificial feelings, which, coming from the head, never reach the heart. I shall be employed about things, not words! and, anxious to render my sex more respectable members of society, I shall try to avoid that flowery diction which has slided from essays into novels, and from novels into familiar letters and conversations.

These pretty superlatives, dropping glibly from the tongue, vitiate the taste, and create a kind of sickly delicacy that turns away from simple unadorned truth; and a deluge of false sentiments and overstretched feelings, stifling the natural emotions of the heart, render the domestic pleasures insipid, that ought to sweeten the exercise of those severe duties, which educate a rational and immortal being for a nobler field of action.

The education of women has of late been more attended to than formerly; yet they are still reckoned a frivolous sex, and ridiculed or pitied by the writers who endeavour by satire or instruction to improve them. It is acknowledged that they spend many of the first years of their lives in acquiring a smattering of accomplishments; meanwhile strength of body and mind are sacrificed to libertine notions of beauty, to the desire of establishing themselves—the only way women can rise in the world—by marriage. And this desire making mere animals of them, when they marry they act as such children may be expected to act—they dress, they paint, and nickname God's creatures. Surely these weak beings are only fit for a seraglio! Can they be expected to govern a family with judgement, or take care of the poor babes, whom they bring into the world?

If, then, it can be fairly deduced from the present conduct of the sex, from the prevalent fondness for pleasure which takes place of ambition and those nobler passions that open and enlarge the soul, that the instruction which women have hitherto received has only tended, with the constitution of civil society, to render them insignificant objects of desire—mere propagators of fools!—if it can be proved that in aiming to accomplish them, without cultivating their understandings, they are taken out of their sphere of duties, and made ridiculous and useless when the short-lived bloom of beauty is over, I presume that *rational* men will excuse me for endeavouring to persuade them to become more masculine and respectable.

Indeed the word masculine is only a bugbear; there is little reason to fear that women will acquire too much courage or fortitude, for their apparent inferiority with respect to bodily strength must render them in some degree dependent on men in the various relations of life; but why should it be increased by prejudices that give a sex to virtue, and confound simple truths with sensual reveries?

Women are, in fact, so much degraded by mistaken notions of female excellence, that I do not mean to add a paradox when I assert that this artificial weakness produces a propensity to tyrannize, and gives birth to cunning, the natural opponent of strength, which leads them to play off those contemptible infantine airs that undermine esteem even whilst they excite desire. Let men become more chaste and modest, and if women do not grow wiser in the same ratio it will be clear that they have weaker understandings. It seems scarcely necessary to say that I now speak of the sex in general. Many individuals have more sense than their male relatives; and, as nothing preponderates where there is a constant struggle for an equilibrium without it has naturally more gravity, some women govern their husbands without degrading themselves, because intellect will always govern.

REVIEW QUESTIONS

1. Why is Wollstonecraft's emphasis on education critical for her argument?
2. What are the similarities and differences between this essay and Olympe de Gouges's declaration (pp. 291–293)?
3. At which social classes was this essay aimed? What are Wollstonecraft's criticisms of the women from these classes?
4. What distinctions does Wollstonecraft make between men and women? What is her point in drawing such distinctions?

BENJAMIN CONSTANT

FROM *The Principles of Politics*

The political writings of Benjamin Constant de Rebecque (1767–1830) addressed critical issues of popular sovereignty and individual liberty in the immediate post-revolutionary period. An advocate of parliamentary monarchy, Constant sought in his many essays to check the abuses of the general will against individual rights. The following passage, written weeks before Napoleon's final defeat at Waterloo, constitutes a classic liberal argument, distinguishing between sovereignty, authority, and individual freedom.

From "On the Sovereignty of the People," by Benjamin Constant, translated by David Sidorsky, in *The Liberal Tradition in European Thought*, edited by David Sidorsky (New York: Putnam, 1970), pp. 211–15.

Of the Sovereignty of the People

The error of those who, sincere in their love of freedom, have attributed unlimited power to the sovereign people, comes of the manner in which their ideas about politics have been formed. They have seen in history a few men, or even one man alone, possessed of immense and very harmful power; and their anger has turned against the possessors of power and not against power itself. Instead of destroying it, they dreamt only of displacing it. It was a scourge, but they looked upon it as something to be conquered. They endowed society as a whole with it. And it passed perforce from the whole to the majority, and from the majority into the hands of a few men, and often of one man alone; and it has done as much harm as before. Manifold examples, objections, arguments and facts have been used to condemn all political institutions.

Certainly, in a society where the people's sovereignty is accepted as a basic principle, no man and no class may subject the others to his or their particular will; but it is not true that society as a whole possesses over its members an unlimited sovereignty.

The generality of citizens constitute the sovereign in the sense that no individual, no fraction, no partial association can assume the sovereignty unless it has been delegated to him or them. But it does not follow that the citizens generally, or those in whom they have vested the sovereignty, may dispose absolutely of the lives of individuals. On the contrary, there is a part of life which necessarily remains personal and independent, which of right is beyond the competence of society. Sovereignty can be only limited and relative. At the point where personal independence and life begin, the jurisdiction of the sovereign ceases. If society goes beyond this point, it is as guilty as the despot whose only title is the sword of the destroyer; society cannot pass beyond the sphere of its competence without usurpation, nor the majority without factiousness. The assent of the majority is not always enough to make its acts legitimate: there are some which nothing can justify. When authority commits such actions, it matters little from what source the authority is alleged to come, or whether it belongs to an individual or a nation; even when it is exercised by the whole nation, except for the citizen oppressed, it is not the more legitimate for that.

Rousseau failed to recognize this truth, and his error has made of his *Social Contract,* so often invoked in favour of liberty, the most terrible support of all kinds of despotism. He defines the contract made by society with its members as the complete and unreserved alienation of each individual with all his rights to the community. To reassure us about the consequences of so absolute a surrender of all aspects of our life to an abstract being, he tells us that the sovereign, that is to say the social body, cannot injure either its members in general or any one of them in particular; that, since each gives himself entire, the condition is the same for all, and none has an interest in making it burdensome to others; that each in giving himself to all gives himself to nobody, that each acquires over all his associates the rights which he grants to them, and gains the equivalent of all that he loses together with greater power to preserve what he has. But he forgets that all these preservative attributes which he confers on the abstract being he calls the sovereign derive from its including within it all individuals without exception. But, as soon as the sovereign has to make use of the power belonging to him—that is to say, as soon as authority has to be organized for practical purposes—the sovereign, since he cannot himself exercise it, must delegate it; and all these attributes disappear. Since the action taken in the name of all is willy nilly done by one person or by a few, it is not true that in giving oneself to all one gives oneself to no one; on the contrary, one gives oneself to those who act in the name of all. Whence it follows that, in giving oneself entire, one does not enter a condition which is equal for all, because there are some who alone benefit from the sacrifice of the others. It is not true that no one has an interest in making the condition a burden to others, since there are associates to whom the condition does not apply. It is not true that all the associates acquire over others the rights which they grant to them over themselves; they do not all gain the equivalent of what they lose, and what results from their sacrifice is, or may be, the establishment of a power which takes from them what they have.

Rousseau himself took fright at these consequences. Appalled by the immensity of the social power he had created, he did not know in what hands to place that monstrous power, and could find as a safeguard against the danger inseparable from sovereignty thus conceived only an expedient which made its exercise impossible. He declared that sovereignty could not be alienated or delegated or represented; which amounted to saying that it could not be exercised. This was to annihilate the principle he had just proclaimed. . . .

Where sovereignty is unlimited, there is no way of protecting the individual against the government. It is in vain that you claim to subject governments to the general will. It is they who give utterance to that will, and all precautions become illusory.

The people, says Rousseau, are sovereign in one respect, and subjects in another: but in practice these two respects merge into one another. Authority can easily oppress the people taken as subjects in order to compel them in their sovereign capacity to express a will prescribed to them by authority.

No political organization can remove this danger. It is in vain that you separate the powers: if the sum total of power is unlimited, the separate powers have only to make an alliance, and there is despotism without a remedy. What matters is not that our rights should be inviolable by one power without the approval of another, but that the violation be forbidden to all the powers. It is not enough that executive agents should have to invoke a grant of authority by the legislator; the legislator must be able to grant them authority to act only within a legitimate sphere. It is of little moment that the executive power should not have the right to act without the backing of the law, if limits are not set to that backing; if it is not laid down that there are matters about which the lawmaker may not make law—or, in other words, that sovereignty is limited, and there are decisions which neither the people nor their delegates have the right to make.

It is this that must be proclaimed; this, the important truth, the essential principle, to be established.

No authority on earth is unlimited; whether it

resides in the people, or in the men who claim to be their representatives, or in kings, whatever their title to rule, or in the law, which, being only the expression of the people's or the prince's will (depending on the form of government), must be confined within the same limits as that will.

Citizens possess rights independently of all social or political authority, and every authority which violates these rights becomes illegitimate. These rights are freedom of person, of religious worship, and of opinion (including its publication), the enjoyment of property, and security against arbitrary power. No one in authority can infringe these rights without destroying his own title to authority. . . .

We owe to public tranquillity many sacrifices; and we should be morally to blame if, by holding inflexibly to our rights, we resisted all laws which appeared to us to impair them; but no duty binds us to those pretended laws whose corrupting influence threatens the noblest aspects of life, to the laws which not only restrict our legitimate rights but require of us actions contrary to the eternal principles of justice and compassion which man cannot cease to observe without degrading and belying his nature.

So long as a law, though a bad one, does not tend to deprave us, so long as the encroachments of authority require only sacrifices which do not make us vile or cruel, we can submit. We then make compromises which affect only ourselves. But if the law should require us to tread underfoot our affections or our duties; if, on the pretext of an extraordinary and factitious sacrifice, in favour either of the monarchy or the republic (as the case may be), it should forbid loyalty to friends in misfortune; if it should require us to betray our allies, or even to persecute vanquished enemies, anathema upon the promotion of injustices and crimes thus covered with the name of law!

Whenever a law appears unjust, it is a positive, general unrestricted duty not to become an executor of it. This force of inertia entails neither upheavals, nor revolutions, nor disorders.

Nothing justifies the man who gives his support to a law which he believes is iniquitous. . . .

*   *   *

REVIEW QUESTIONS

1. What are Constant's reservations about sovereignty of the people? What are his criticisms of Rousseau?
2. According to Constant, on what individual liberties may no authority trespass?
3. What justifications does Constant cite for obeying and breaking laws?

ALEXIS DE TOCQUEVILLE

FROM *Democracy in America*

Alexis Charles Henri Clerel de Tocqueville (1805–1859) ranks as one of the brilliant political minds of the liberal era, a politician and writer who was among the first to compare and systematize the liberal political systems of the postrevolutionary era. Tocqueville balanced an active career as a magistrate and legislative deputy during the July Monarchy (1830–1848) with extensive trips to the United States and Britain. These trips allowed him to observe the customs and manners of two political systems that differed significantly from France's inherited tradition of centralized authority. His Democracy in America *(1835) and* The Old Regime and the French Revolution *(1856) are enduring works on the relationship of individual liberty and equality to central and federal political power. Both combine pragmatic political experience with a detached, analytical understanding of differing political systems and their respective benefits. His observations on the civic culture of democratic politics are evinced in the following sections on political associations and freedom of the press from* Democracy in America.

From *The World's Greatest Classics: Democracy in America,* by Alexis de Tocqueville, translated by Henry Reeve (New York: Colonial Press, 1989), pp. 182–85, 188, 191, 196–99.

*　　*　　*

Political Associations in the United States

In no country in the world has the principle of association been more successfully used, or more unsparingly applied to a multitude of different objects, than in America. Besides the permanent associations which are established by law under the names of townships, cities, and counties, a vast number of others are formed and maintained by the agency of private individuals. . . .

The most natural privilege of man, next to the right of acting for himself, is that of combining his exertions with those of his fellow-creatures, and of acting in common with them. I am therefore led to conclude that the right of association is almost as inalienable as the right of personal liberty. No legislator can attack it without impairing the very foundations of society. Nevertheless, if freedom of association is a fruitful source of advantages and prosperity to some nations, it may be perverted or carried to excess by others, and a source of vigor may be changed into one of destruction. A comparison of the different methods which associations pursue, in those countries in which they are managed with discretion, as well as in those where liberty degenerates into license, may perhaps be thought useful both to governments and to parties.

The greater part of Europeans look upon an association as a weapon which is to be hastily fashioned, and immediately tried in conflict. A society is formed for discussion, but the idea of impending action prevails in the minds of those who constitute it: it is, in fact, an army; and the time given to parley serves to reckon up the strength and to inspire the troops, after which they march against the enemy. Resources which lie within the bounds of the law may suggest themselves to the persons who compose it as means, but never as the only means, of success.

Such, however, is not the manner in which the right of association is understood in the United States. In America the citizens who form the minority associate, in order, in the first place, to show their numerical strength, and so to diminish the moral authority of the majority; and, in the second place, to stimulate competition, and to discover those arguments which are most fitted to act upon the majority: for they always entertain hopes of drawing over their opponents to their own side, and of afterwards disposing of the supreme power in their name. Political associations in the United States are therefore peaceable in their intentions, and strictly legal in the means which they employ; and they assert with perfect truth, that they only aim at success by lawful expedients.

The difference which exists between the Americans and ourselves depends on several causes. In Europe there are numerous parties so diametrically opposed to the majority, that they can never hope to acquire its support, and at the same time they think that they are sufficiently strong in themselves to struggle and to defend their cause. When a party of this kind forms an association, its object is, not to conquer, but to fight. In America, the individuals who hold opinions very much opposed to those of the majority are no sort of impediment to its power; and all other parties hope to win it over to their own principles in the end. The exercise of the right of association becomes dangerous in proportion to the impossibility which excludes great parties from acquiring the majority. In a country like the United States, in which the differences of opinion are mere differences of hue, the right of association may remain unrestrained without evil consequences. The inexperience of many of the European nations in the enjoyment of liberty, leads them only to look upon freedom of association as a right of attacking the Government. The first notion which presents itself to a party, as well as to an individual, when it has acquired a consciousness of its own strength, is that of violence: the notion of persuasion arises at a later period, and is only derived from experience. The English, who are divided into parties which differ most essentially from each other, rarely abuse the right of association, because they have long been accustomed to exercise it. In France, the passion for war is so intense that there is no undertaking so mad, or so injurious to the welfare of the State, that a man does not consider himself honoured in defending it, at the risk of his life.

But perhaps the most powerful of the causes which tend to mitigate the excesses of political association in the United States is universal suffrage. In countries in which universal suffrage exists, the majority is never doubtful, because neither party can pretend to represent that portion of the community which has not voted. The associations which are formed are aware, as well as the nation at large, that they do not represent the majority. This is, indeed, a condition inseparable from their existence, for if they did represent the preponderating power, they would change the law instead of soliciting its reform. The consequence of this is that the moral influence of the Government which they attack is very much increased, and their own power is very much enfeebled.

In Europe there are few associations which do not affect to represent the majority, or which do not believe that they represent it. This belief or pretence tends greatly to increase their power, and serves admirably to legitimate their actions. For what is more excusable than violence in a righteous cause against oppression? Thus it is, in the vast labyrinth of human laws, that extreme liberty sometimes corrects the abuses of license, and that extreme democracy obviates the dangers of democratic government. In Europe, associations consider themselves in some degree the legislative and executive councils of the people, which is unable to speak for itself. In America, where they only represent a minority of the nation, they argue and they petition.

The means which the associations of Europe employ are in accordance with the end which they propose to obtain. As the principal aim of these bodies is to act, and not to debate, to fight rather than to persuade, they are naturally led to adopt a form of organization which differs from the ordinary customs of civil bodies, and which assumes the habits and the maxims of military life. They centralize the direction of their resources as much as possible, and they entrust the power of the whole party to a very small number of leaders.

The members of these associations reply to a watchword, like soldiers on duty; they profess the doctrine of passive obedience, or rather in uniting together they at once abjure the exercise of their own judgment and free will. And the tyrannical control which these societies exercise, is often far more insupportable than the authority possessed over society by the Government which they attack. Their moral force is much diminished by these excesses. They lose the sacred quality which always characterises a struggle between oppressors and the oppressed. The man who in given cases consents to obey his fellows with servility, and who submits his actions and even his opinions to their control, can have no claim to rank as a free citizen.

The Americans have also established certain forms of government for their associations, but these are invariably borrowed from the forms of the civil administration. The independence of each individual is formally recognized. As in society at large, all the members work towards the same end, but they are not obliged to follow exactly the same track. No-one abjures the exercise of his reason and his free will; rather everyone exercises that reason and that will for the benefit of a common undertaking.

*   *   *

Freedom of the Press

There are certain nations which have peculiar reasons for cherishing the freedom of the press. For in certain countries which profess to enjoy the privileges of freedom, every individual agent of the Government may violate the laws with impunity, since those whom he oppresses cannot prosecute him before the courts of justice. In this case the freedom of the press is not merely a guarantee, but the *only* guarantee of their liberty and their security which the citizens possess. If the rulers of these nations proposed to abolish the independence of the press, the people would be justified in saying: Give us the right of prosecuting your offences before ordinary tribunals, and perhaps we may then waive our right of appeal to the tribunal of public opinion.

But in the countries in which the doctrine of the sovereignty of the people ostensibly prevails, the censorship of the press is not only dangerous, it is absurd. When the right of every citizen to cooperate in the government of society is acknowledged, every citizen must be presumed to possess the power of discriminating between the different opinions of his contemporaries, and of appreciating the different facts from which inferences may be drawn. The sovereignty of the people and the freedom of the press may therefore be looked upon as inseparable institutions; the censorship of the press and universal suffrage are two things which are irreconcileably opposed, and which cannot long be retained among the institutions of the same people. Not a single individual of the twelve millions who inhabit the territory of the United States has as yet dared to propose any restrictions to the liberty of the press. . . .

In France it is not uncommonly imagined that the virulence of the press originates in the uncertain social condition, in the political excitement, and the consequent sense of general malaise which prevail in that country; and it is therefore supposed that as soon as society has resumed a certain degree of composure, the press will abandon its present vehemence. I am inclined to think that these causes explain the extraordinary ascendency it has acquired over the nation, but that they do not exercise much influence upon the tone of its language. The periodical press appears to me to be actuated by passions and propensities independent of the circumstances in which it is placed; and the present position of America corroborates this opinion.

America is perhaps, at this moment, the country of the whole world which contains the fewest germs of revolution, but the press is no less destructive in its principles than in France, and it displays the same violence without the same reasons for indignation. In America, as in France, it constitutes a singular power, so strangely composed of mingled good and evil, that it is at the same time indispensable to the existence of freedom, and nearly incompatible with the maintenance of public order. Its power is certainly much greater in France than in the United States; though nothing is more rare in the latter country than to hear of a prosecution having been instituted against it. The reason for this is perfectly simple: the Americans having once accepted the doctrine of the sovereignty of the people, apply it with perfect consistency. They never intended to establish laws for all eternity on foundations which change from day to day. There is consequently nothing criminal in an attack upon the existing laws, provided it be not attended with a violent infraction of them. They are moreover of the opinion that Courts of Justice are unable to check the abuses of the press; and that as the subtlety of human language perpetually eludes the severity of judicial analysis, offences of this nature are apt to escape the hand which attempts to apprehend them. They hold that to act with efficacy upon the press, it would be necessary to find a tribunal not only devoted to the existing order of things, but capable of surmounting the influence of public opinion, a tribunal which should conduct its proceedings without publicity, which should pronounce its decrees without assigning its motives, and punish the intentions even more than the language of the author. Whoever had the power of creating and maintaining a tribunal of this kind would be wasting his time in prosecuting the liberty of the press, for he would be the supreme master of the whole community, and he would be as free to rid himself of the authors as of their writings. In this question, therefore, there is no middle way between servitude and extreme licence. In order to enjoy the inestimable benefits which the freedom of the press ensures, it is necessary to submit to the inevitable evils which it engenders. To expect to acquire the former, and to escape the latter, is to cherish one of those illusions which commonly mislead nations in their times of sickness, when, tired with faction and exhausted by effort, they attempt to combine hostile opinions and contrary opinions upon the same soil. . . .

The influence of the press upon America is immense. It is the power which impels the circulation of political life through all the districts of that vast territory. Its eye is constantly open to detect the secret springs of political designs, and to summon the leaders of all parties to the bar of public opinion. It rallies the interests of the community round certain principles, and it draws up the creed which factions adopt. It affords a means of intercourse between parties which hear, and which address each other, without ever having been in immediate contact. When a great number of the organs of the press adopt the same line of conduct, their influence becomes irresistible; and public opinion, when it is perpetually assailed from the same side, eventually yields to the attack. In the United States each separate journal exercises but little authority: but the power of the periodical press is only second to that of the people.

*   *   *

REVIEW QUESTIONS

1. Why does de Tocqueville find the right of association as important as rights of personal liberty?
2. According to de Tocqueville, what role do associations play for minority views?
3. How did French and American political associations differ?
4. Why is the press, for de Tocqueville, "indispensable to the existence of freedom"?
5. Why did de Tocqueville consider the power of the press greater in France than in the United States?

WILLIAM WILBERFORCE

FROM *An Appeal to the Religion, Justice, Humanity of the Inhabitants of the British Empire, in Behalf of the Negro Slaves in the West Indies*

William Wilberforce (1759–1833) was the principal herald of a sustained political campaign to abolish both the slave trade and slavery in the British Empire. An evangelical Christian whose advocacy of social reform was based on Christian ethics, Wilberforce embodied the progressive religious reform movement of the early nineteenth-century bourgeoisie. As a member of Parliament between 1780 and 1825, Wilberforce unrelentingly exposed the horror and tyranny of slavery. In 1823, the year of the tract printed below, he founded and became co-president of the Anti-Slavery Society, an association that agitated for public support of the Emancipation Bill, thus bringing together conservatives and liberals alike to espouse the universal right to personal liberty. A month after Wilberforce died, his bill became law.

From *An Appeal to the Religion, Justice, Humanity of the Inhabitants of the British Empire, in Behalf of the Negro Slaves in the West Indies*, by William Wilberforce (London: Printed for J. Hatchard, 1823), pp. 9–14.

*   *   *

But though the evils which have been already enumerated are of no small amount, in estimating the physical sufferings of human beings, especially of the lower rank, yet, to a Christian eye, they shrink almost into insignificance when compared with the moral evils that remain behind—with that, above all, which runs through the whole of the various cruel circumstances of the Negro Slave's condition, and is at once the effect of his wrongs and sufferings, their bitter aggravation, and the pretext for their continuance—his extreme degradation in the intellectual and moral scale of being, and in the estimation of his White oppressors.

The proofs of the extreme degradation of the slaves, in the latter sense, are innumerable; and indeed it must be confessed, that in the minds of Europeans in general, more especially in vulgar minds, whether vulgar from the want of education, or morally vulgar (a more inwrought and less curable vulgarity), the personal peculiarities of the Negro race could scarcely fail, by diminishing sympathy, to produce impressions, not merely of contempt, but even of disgust and aversion. But how strongly are these impressions sure to be confirmed and augmented, when to all the effects of bodily distinctions are superadded all those arising from the want of civilization and knowledge, and still more, all the hateful vices that slavery never fails to engender or to aggravate. Such, in truth, must naturally be the effect of these powerful causes, that even the most ingeniously constructed system which humanity and policy combined could have devised, would in vain have endeavoured to counteract them: how much more powerfully then must they operate, especially in low and uneducated minds, when the whole system abounds with institutious and practices which tend to confirm and strengthen their efficiency, and to give to a contemptuous aversion for the Negro race the sanction of manners and of law.

It were well if the consequences of these impressions were only to be discovered among the inferior ranks of the privileged class, or only to be found in the opinions and conduct of individuals. But in the earlier laws of our colonies they are expressed in the language of insult, and in characters of blood. And too many of these laws still remain unrepealed, to permit the belief that the same odious spirit of legislation no longer exists, or to relieve the injured objects of them from their degrading influence. The slaves were systematically depressed below the level of human beings. And though I confess, that it is of less concern to a slave, under what laws he lives, than what is the character of his master, yet if the laws had extended to them favour and protection instead of degradation, this would have tended to raise them in the social scale, and, operating insensibly on the public mind, might, by degrees, have softened the extreme rigour of their bondage. Such, however, had been the contrary effects of an opposite process, on the estimation of the Negro race, before the ever-to-be-honoured Granville Sharpe, and his followers, had begun to vindicate their claim to the character and privileges of human nature, that a writer of the highest authority on all West-India subjects, Mr. Long, in his celebrated History of Jamaica, though pointing out some of the particulars of their ill treatment, scrupled not to state it as his opinion, that in the gradations of being, Negroes were little elevated above the oran ou-tang, "that type of man." Nor was this an unguarded or a hastily thrown-out assertion. He institutes a laborious comparison of the Negro race with that species of baboon; and declares, that, "ludicrous as the opinion may seem, he does not think that an oran outang husband would be any dishonour to a Hottentot female." When we find such sentiments as these to have been unblushingly avowed by an author of the highest estimation among the West India colonists, we are prepared for what we find to have been, and, I grieve to say, still continues to be, the practical effects of these opinions.

The first particular of subsisting legal oppression that I shall notice, and which is at once a decisive proof of the degradation of the Negro race, in the eyes of the Whites, and a powerful cause of its continuance, is of a deeply rooted character, and often productive of the most cruel effects. In the contemplation of law they are not persons, but mere chattels; and as such are liable to be seized and sold by creditors and by executors, in payment of their owner's debts; and this separately from the estates on which they are settled. By the operation of this system, the most meritorious slave who may have accumulated a little peculium, and may be living with his family in some tolerable comfort, who by long and faithful services may have endeared himself to his proprietor or manager—who, in short, is in circumstances that mitigate greatly the evils of his condition—is liable at once to be torn for ever from his home, his family, and his friends, and to be sent to serve a new master, perhaps in another island, for the rest of his life.

Another particular of their degradation by law, which, in its effects, most perniciously affects their whole civil condition, and of which their inadequate legal protection is a sure and necessary con-

sequence, is their evidence being inadmissible against any free person. The effect of this cannot be stated more clearly or compendiously than in the memorable evidence of a gentleman eminently distinguished for the candour with which he gave to the Slave-Trade Committee the result of his long personal experience in the West Indies, the late Mr. Otley, Chief-justice of St. Vincent's, himself a planter: "As the evidence of Slaves is never admitted against White men, the difficulty of legally establishing the facts is so great, that White men are in a manner put beyond the reach of the law." It is due also to the late Sir William Young, long one of the most active opponents of the abolition, to state, that he likewise, when Governor of Tobago, acknowledged, as a radical defect in the administration of justice, that the law of evidence "covered the most guilty European with impunity."

The same concession was made by both houses of the legislature of Grenada, in the earliest inquiries of the Privy Council. The only difficulty, as they stated, that had been found in putting an effectual stop to gross and wanton cruelty towards slaves, was that of bringing home the proof of the fact against the delinquent by satisfactory evidence, those who were capable of the guilt, being in general artful enough to prevent any but slaves being witnesses of the fact. "As the matter stands," they add, "though we hope the instances in this island are at this day not frequent, yet it must be admitted with regret, that the persons prosecuted, and who certainly were guilty, have escaped for want of legal proof."

It is obvious that the same cause must produce the same effect in all our other slave colonies, although there has not been found the same candour in confessing it.

The next evil which I shall specify, for which the extreme degradation of these poor beings, in the eyes of their masters, can alone account, is the driving system. Not being supposed capable of being governed like other human beings, by the hope of reward, or the fear of punishment, they are subjected to the immediate impulse or present terror of the whip, and are driven at their work like brute animals. Lower than this it is scarcely possible for man to be depressed by man. If such treatment does not find him vile and despised, it must infallibly make him so. Let it not however be supposed, that the only evil of this truly odious system is its outraging the moral character of the human species, or its farther degrading the slaves in the eyes of all who are in authority over them, and thereby extinguishing that sympathy which would be their best protection. The whip is itself a dreadful instrument of punishment; and the mode of inflicting that punishment shockingly indecent and degrading. The drivers themselves, commonly, or rather always slaves, are usually the strongest and stoutest of the Negroes; and though they are forbidden to give more than a few lashes at a time, as the immediate chastisement of faults committed at their work, yet the power over the slaves which they thus possess unavoidably invests them with a truly formidable tyranny, the consequences of which, to the unfortunate subjects of it, are often in the highest degree oppressive and pernicious. No one who reflects on the subject can be at a loss to anticipate one odious use which is too commonly made of this despotism, in extorting, from the fears of the young females who are subject to it, compliances with the licentious desires of the drivers, which they might otherwise have refused from attachment to another, if not from moral feelings and restraints. It is idle and insulting to talk of improving the condition of these poor beings, as rational and moral agents, while they are treated in a manner which precludes self-government, and annihilates all human motives but such as we impose on a maniac, or on a hardened and incorrigible convict.

Another abuse, which shows, like the rest, the extreme degradation of the Negro race, and the apathy which it creates in their masters, is the cruel, and, at least in the case of the female sex, highly indecent punishments inflicted in public, and in the face of day, often in the presence of the gang, or of the whole assembled population of an estate. From their low and ignominious condition it doubtless proceeds, that they are in some degree regarded as below the necessity of observing towards others the proper decencies of life, or of having those decencies observed by others towards them.

It is no doubt also chiefly owing to their not being yet raised out of that extreme depth in which they are sunk, so much below the level of the human species, that no attempts have been made to introduce among them the Christian institution of marriage, that blessed union which the Almighty himself established as a fundamental law at the creation of man, to be as it were the well-spring of all the charities of life—the source of all domestic comfort and social improvement—the moral cement of civilized society.

*   *   *

REVIEW QUESTIONS

1. What are the "moral evils" of slavery that Wilberforce refers to?
2. How were slaves degraded? Why did Wilberforce find this so offensive?
3. Why is slavery incompatible with the political doctrine of liberalism?

SATIRE OF LIBERAL REFORMS (1833)

This anonymous cartoon satirically underscores one of the glaring contradictions of British life during the early years of the liberal era. Following the Reform Act of 1832, which enfranchised the propertied middle classes, Parliament abolished slavery in the British Empire in 1833, the year of this cartoon. The illustration juxtaposes the conditions of a common British worker and a Jamaican slave (whose condition is cruelly misrepresented), reversing the labels of slavery and freedom. The man in the middle, presumably a bourgeois politician, states: "Think of the poor suffering African called a Slave unpossess'd of any of the rights & privileges that you enjoy, while you sit under the vine of your Reform Bill and the fig-tree of your Magna Chart. He knows nothing of such blessings." How is this cartoon a parody of Britain's liberal reforms?

W. J. FOX

FROM *Speech on Corn Laws*

Following the enfranchisement of the British middle class in 1832, the greatest indicator of bourgeois political influence was the repeal of the Corn Laws in 1846. In 1815, parliamentary landed interests levied tariffs on cheap imported wheat (corn is a British term for grain, including wheat) to ensure that domestic grain would not be undersold, thus promoting the continued prosperity of Britain's landed elite. Businessmen, however, sharply criticized the tariff. They argued that it kept bread prices artificially high and, in turn, raised the cost level of a worker's sustenance, by which employers set wages. Claiming that the Corn Laws blunted the competitive edge of British manufactured exports, business interests formed the Anti–Corn Law League in 1839. This pressure group tirelessly promoted free trade as a policy benefiting the entire nation. Bad harvests and the specter of famine in the 1840s magnified the league's charge that cheap, plentiful bread was a moral necessity. The following anti–Corn Law speech from 1844 typifies the arguments of free traders.

From *Speech on Corn Laws*, by W. J. Fox (New York: Kelley, 1903).

*   *   *

Who that lives by eating bread has not an interest in the repeal of the bread tax? Who that is endeavouring to support himself and his family by commerce has not an interest in Free Trade? Who has not an interest in what advances the general prosperity of the country, even though his pursuits are artistical or intellectual, ministering to the spiritual rather than the material portions of our nature? For as one thrives will all thrive—they react the one upon the other—the starving do not encourage literature and art—they are bound together by the ties which Providence formed to uphold society; and it is because they and we have an interest in this matter that we are determined the question shall not drop until it is satisfactorily settled.

I say all classes have an interest in this matter; even they who are represented as the great opposing class—the landlord class. For what has made England the paradise of landowners but its being the workshop of the world? In the progress of manufacture, if machinery has enabled one man to do the work of two hundred, it has also employed two hundred, and two thousand, where one was employed; all bread eaters, coming to the landowner for his produce. And while the manufacturers of this country have been thus advancing in the last century, its growth of wheat has been tripled, and the rents of the farmers have been in many cases quadrupled. The landlords gain by railways enhancing the worth of their property; they gain by the rich and flourishing community arising around them; and if for a while they should have to make some slight sacrifice—if at first their rents should fall in the change—why, they will still be gaining that which gold could never buy. By the graceful concession they would be gaining the goodwill and gratitude of their fellow-countrymen; they would gain for themselves an exemption from the execration that pursues their class—from the infamy of their names in history—from the reprobation of their consciences, and the pollution of their souls.

*   *   *

Some affect to sneer at abstract principles; but abstract good is the real, practical good, after all; the exceptions made to it are some little, dirty contrivances of those who would have trade free for others, but would reserve the monopoly for themselves—would have free trade as to what they buy, but restrictions as to what they sell; and who tell us that those principles are sound and excellent things in reference to all other commodities whatever, but that there is some one exception left—the exception of that in which the exceptor deals; and each in turn will tell you that Free Trade is the noblest thing in the world, except for corn, except for sugar, except for coffee, and except for this, that, and the other, till once, even in the House of Commons, it came to an exception of second-hand glass bottles. I say this is a principle recognized by all—recognized even by the Government in its measures of last year, however paltry their nature and limited their operation; recognized in their Canada Corn Bill; recognized in the repeal of the laws against the exportation of machinery, the last rag of that form of monopoly; and the repeal of the duties on imports must follow that of restriction on exports. A principle thus practically recognized by foes, as well as by friends, is certain of success. Thus was it that the great principle of Negro liberty was recognized, and thus eventually carried. And did not the recognition of a principle emancipate the Roman Catholics of Ireland? Ask Sir Robert Peel and the Duke of Wellington whether this was not the secret of the success of that measure.

*   *   *

Why, the corn laws and the policy of our agricultural legislators hunt poverty and wretchedness from their own districts into ours. The landlord class call themselves feeders of the people. They speak of their ability, if properly encouraged and protected, to feed the nation. What feeds the people? Not the growing of corn, but the people being able to buy it. The people are no more fed, for all the wheat that is grown, than as if there were so many stones covering the rich valleys of the country. It is in the price required of the people who eat it; and if that is beyond the power of the multitude to give, the landlords become starvers instead of feeders of the people. Agriculture cannot support its own population; it is not in the course of nature that it should, for one man is vested with the ability to raise food for the many. Twenty-eight per cent of the population are amply sufficient to cultivate the ground so as to yield food for the remainder of the hundred. How are the rest to be fed? By opening markets for the products of their industry, that they may obtain the means.

*   *   *

Wisely has the Council appealed to the great towns, for there is the power. What can the poor farmer do? His money is in his landlord's ground, and the man who has money in another man's ground must needs be a slave. His freedom is buried there with it, not, like the grain, to germinate, but only to rot and dissolve in corruption. It is where great bodies are congregated that they can stand by one another; where not the importance of the individual, but the importance of the many, is the great thing for all. And how independent are such places, if they but knew their position, of all that aristocracy is, or can do! Landlords! They built not this magnificent metropolis; they covered not these forty square miles with the great mass of human dwellings that spread over them; they crowd not our ports with shipping; they filled not your city with its monuments of science and art, with its institutions of literature and its temples of religion; they poured not that stream of commercial prosperity into the country which during the last century has made the grandeur of London, quadrupling its population, and showing that it has one heart with the entire community.

*   *   *

The time is opportune for the appeal which has been made to the inhabitants of this metropolis, and for the appeal to those among you who enjoy the franchise of the city of London. There will, in a very short period, be an opportunity for you to show decidedly that the principle of Free Trade is consecrated in your hearts and guides your votes. I trust the contest will be by no means a personal one, but one wholly of principle, and that no ambiguous pretensions, no praise of Free Trade, with certain qualifications and accommodations necessary to the hustings, will be tolerated for an instant; but that the plain and simple test will be the complete, total, and immediate abolition of the monopoly of food.* * * Here, then, I hope, will one of the first great electoral experiments be tried, that not merely every member of the League, but every inhabitant of London, who can honourably influence the result of that election, should feel himself bound to do so, as amongst his earliest pledges of adherence to this great cause—the commencement of his answer to the appeal which has now been made to him for support. Other ways will soon open themselves; and I trust that its past backwardness will be amply redeemed by the metropolis in the readiness with which it will respond to the great call now made for its pecuniary liberality, and in the ardour which many will manifest in other modes of cooperating in this great work, showing that we look to yet higher principles and considerations than any that belong either to rural districts or to particular classes, and that we regard this as the common cause of humanity. And so it is; for Free-Trade principles are the dictates of Nature plainly written on the surface of land and ocean, so that the simplest may read them and imbibe their

spirit. For that Power which stretched abroad the land, poured forth the ocean, and piled up the mountains; that Power which gave Western America its broad prairies, and reared the gigantic and boundless forests of the north; that Power which covered with rich vineyards the smiling hills of France, which wafts sweet odours from the "spicy shores of Araby the blest," which has endowed this country with its minerals and its insular advantages, and its people with their indomitable Saxon energy, with their skill, their hardihood, their perseverance, their enterprise;—that Power which doth all this, evidently designed it for the common good, for the reciprocal advantage of all; it intended that all should enrich all by the freest interchange, thus making the world no longer the patrimony of a class, but the heritage and the paradise of humanity.

REVIEW QUESTIONS

1. What are the principal criticisms that Fox raises against the landlord class?
2. What are the chief differences between the commercial and agricultural interests?
3. Why does Fox believe that free trade is more than just an economic doctrine?
4. What attributes does Fox project onto this trade policy?
5. Why does Fox consider London so important for the repeal?

JOHN STUART MILL

FROM *On Liberty*

In 1859 John Stuart Mill (1806–1873) presented to Victorian society his now classic statement on individual freedom, On Liberty. *Mill, however, should not be mistaken for a typical liberal. He not only abandoned classical economic theory early in his career, advocating certain forms of government regulation, but also foresaw the moral necessity of extending the vote to workers and women. Yet he continued to harbor distrust of state authority and governments' ability to guarantee the rights of minorities. His statements on individual liberty, freedom of opinion, and limits of authority over the individual are critical to the canon of liberal political philosophy.*

From *On Liberty*, by John Stuart Mill, edited by David Spitz (New York: Norton, 1975).

Chapter I
Introductory

The subject of this Essay is not the so-called Liberty of the Will so unfortunately opposed to the misnamed doctrine of Philosophical Necessity; but Civil, or Social Liberty: the nature and limits of the power which can be legitimately exercised by society over the individual. A question seldom stated, and hardly ever discussed, in general terms, but which profoundly influences the practical controversies of the age by its latent presence, and is likely soon to make itself recognised as the vital question of the future. It is so far from being new, that, in a certain sense, it has divided mankind, almost from the remotest ages; but in the stage of progress into which the more civilised portions of the species have now entered, it presents itself under new conditions, and requires a different and more fundamental treatment.

The struggle between Liberty and Authority is the most conspicuous feature in the portions of history with which we are earliest familiar, particularly in that of Greece, Rome, and England. But in old times this contest was between subjects, or some classes of subjects, and the Government. By liberty, was meant protection against the tyranny of the political rulers. The rulers were conceived (except in some of the popular governments of Greece) as in a necessarily antagonistic position to the people whom they ruled. They consisted of a governing One, or a governing tribe or caste, who derived their authority from inheritance or conquest, who, at all events, did not hold it at the pleasure of the governed, and whose supremacy men did not venture, perhaps did not desire, to contest, whatever precautions might be taken

against its oppressive exercise. Their power was regarded as necessary, but also as highly dangerous; as a weapon which they would attempt to use against their subjects, no less than against external enemies. To prevent the weaker members of the community from being preyed upon by innumerable vultures, it was needful that there should be an animal of prey stronger than the rest, commissioned to keep them down. But as the king of the vultures would be no less bent upon preying on the flock than any of the minor harpies, it was indispensable to be in a perpetual attitude of defence against his beak and claws. The aim, therefore, of patriots was to set limits to the power which the ruler should be suffered to exercise over the community; and this limitation was what they meant by liberty. It was attempted in two ways. First, by obtaining a recognition of certain immunities, called political liberties or rights, which it was to be regarded as a breach of duty in the ruler to infringe, and which if he did infringe, specific resistance, or general rebellion, was held to be justifiable. A second, and generally a later expedient, was the establishment of constitutional checks, by which the consent of the community, or of a body of some sort, supposed to represent its interests, was made a necessary condition to some of the more important acts of the governing power. To the first of these modes of limitation, the ruling power, in most European countries, was compelled, more or less, to submit. It was not so with the second; and, to attain this, or when already in some degree possessed, to attain it more completely, became everywhere the principal object of the lovers of liberty. And so long as mankind were content to combat one enemy by another, and to be ruled by a master, on condition of being guaranteed more or less efficaciously against his tyranny, they did not carry their aspirations beyond this point.

A time, however, came, in the progress of human affairs, when men ceased to think it a necessity of nature that their governors should be an independent power, opposed in interest to themselves. It appeared to them much better that the various magistrates of the State should be their tenants or delegates, revocable at their pleasure. In that way alone, it seemed, could they have complete security that the powers of government would never be abused to their disadvantage. By degrees this new demand for elective and temporary rulers became the prominent object of the exertions of the popular party, wherever any such party existed; and superseded, to a considerable extent, the previous efforts to limit the power of rulers. As the struggle proceeded for making the ruling power emanate from the periodical choice of the ruled, some persons began to think that too much importance had been attached to the limitation of the power itself. *That* (it might seem) was a resource against rulers whose interests were habitually opposed to those of the people. What was now wanted was, that the rulers should be identified with the people; that their interest and will should be the interest and will of the nation. The nation did not need to be protected against its own will. There was no fear of its tyrannising over itself. Let the rulers be effectually responsible to it, promptly removable by it, and it could afford to trust them with power of which it could itself dictate the use to be made. Their power was but the nation's own power, concentrated, and in a form convenient for exercise. This mode of thought, or rather perhaps of feeling, was common among the last generation of European liberalism, in the Continental section of which it still apparently predominates. Those who admit any limit to what a government may do, except in the case of such governments as they think ought not to exist, stand out as brilliant exceptions among the political thinkers of the Continent. A similar tone of sentiment might by this time have been prevalent in our own country, if the circumstances which for a time encouraged it, had continued unaltered.

But, in political and philosophical theories, as well as in persons, success discloses faults and infirmities which failure might have concealed from observation. The notion, that the people have no need to limit their power over themselves, might seem axiomatic, when popular government was a thing only dreamed about, or read of as having existed at some distant period of the past. Neither was that notion necessarily disturbed by such temporary aberrations as those of the French Revolution, the worst of which were the work of a usurping few, and which, in any case, belonged, not to the permanent working of popular institutions, but to a sudden and convulsive outbreak against monarchical and aristocratic depotism. In time, however, a democratic republic came to occupy a large portion of the earth's surface, and made itself felt as one of the most powerful members of the community of nations; and elective and responsible government became subject to the observations and criticisms which wait upon a great existing fact. It was now perceived that such phrases as "self-government," and "the power of the people over themselves," do not express the true state of the case. The "people" who exercise the power are not always the same people with those over whom it is exercised; and the "self-government" spoken of is not the government of each by himself, but of each by all the rest. The will of the people, moreover, practically means the will of the most numerous or the most active *part* of the people; the majority, or those who succeed in making themselves accepted as the majority; the people, consequently, *may* desire to oppress a part of their number; and precautions are as much needed against this as against any other abuse of power. The limitation, therefore, of the power of government over individuals loses none of its importance when the holders of power are regularly accountable to the community, that is, to the strongest party therein. This view of things, recommending itself equally to the intelligence of thinkers and to the inclination of those important classes in European society to whose real or supposed interests democracy is adverse, has had no difficulty in establishing itself; and in political speculations "the tyranny of the majority" is now generally included among the evils against which society requires to be on its guard.

*   *   *

The object of this Essay is to assert one very simple principle, as entitled to govern absolutely the dealings of society with the individual in the way of compulsion and control, whether the means used be physical force in the form of legal penalties, or the moral coercion of public opinion. That principle is, that the sole end for which mankind are warranted, individually or collectively, in interfering with the liberty of action of any of their number, is self-protection. That the only purpose for which power can be rightfully exercised over any member of a civilised community, against his will, is to prevent harm to others. His own good, either physical or moral, is not a sufficient warrant. He cannot rightfully be compelled to do or forbear because it will be better for him to do so, because it will make him happier, because, in the opinions of others, to do so would be wise, or even right. These are good reasons for remonstrating with him, or reasoning with him, or persuading him, or entreating him, but not for compelling him, or visiting him with any evil in case he do otherwise. To justify that, the conduct from which it is desired to deter him must be calculated to produce evil to some one else. The only part of the conduct of any one, for which he is amenable to society, is that which concerns others. In the part which merely concerns himself, his independence is, of right, absolute. Over himself, over his own body and mind, the individual is sovereign.

*   *   *

We have now recognised the necessity to the mental well-being of mankind (on which all their other well-being depends) of freedom of opinion, and freedom of the expression of opinion, on four distinct grounds; which we will now briefly recapitulate.

First, if any opinion is compelled to silence, that opinion may, for aught we can certainly know,

be true. To deny this is to assume our own infallibility.

Secondly, though the silenced opinion be an error, it may, and very commonly does, contain a portion of truth; and since the general or prevailing opinion on any subject is rarely or never the whole truth, it is only by the collision of adverse opinions that the remainder of the truth has any chance of being supplied.

Thirdly, even if the received opinion be not only true, but the whole truth; unless it is suffered to be, and actually is, vigorously and earnestly contested, it will, by most of those who receive it, be held in the manner of a prejudice, with little comprehension or feeling of its rational grounds. And not only this, but, fourthly, the meaning of the doctrine itself will be in danger of being lost, or enfeebled, and deprived of its vital effect on the character and conduct; the dogma becoming a mere formal profession, inefficacious for good, but cumbering the ground, and preventing the growth of any real and heartfelt conviction, from reason or personal experience.

*   *   *

Chapter IV
Of the Limits to the Authority of Society over the Individual

What, then, is the rightful limit to the sovereignty of the individual over himself? Where does the authority of society begin? How much of human life should be assigned to individuality, and how much to society?

Each will receive its proper share, if each has that which more particularly concerns it. To individuality should belong the part of life in which it is chiefly the individual that is interested; to society, the part which chiefly interests society.

Though society is not founded on a contract, and though no good purpose is answered by inventing a contract in order to deduce social obligations from it, every one who receives the protection of society owes a return for the benefit, and the fact of living in society renders it indispensable that each should be bound to observe a certain line of conduct towards the rest. This conduct consists, first, in not injuring the interests of one another; or rather certain interests, which, either by express legal provision, or by tacit understanding, ought to be considered as rights; and secondly, in each person's bearing his share (to be fixed on some equitable principle) of the labours and sacrifices incurred for defending the society or its members from injury and molestation. These conditions society is justified in enforcing, at all costs to those who endeavour to withhold fulfilment. Nor is this all that society may do. The acts of an individual may be hurtful to others, or wanting in due consideration for their welfare, without going to the length of violating any of their constituted rights. The offender may then be justly punished by opinion, though not by law. As soon as any part of a person's conduct affects prejudicially the interests of others, society has jurisdiction over it, and the question whether the general welfare will or will not be promoted by interfering with it, becomes open to discussion. But there is no room for entertaining any such question when a person's conduct affects the interests of no persons besides himself, or needs not affect them unless they like (all the persons concerned being of full age, and the ordinary amount of understanding). In all such cases, there should be perfect freedom, legal and social, to do the action and stand the consequences.

It would be a great misunderstanding of this doctrine to suppose that it is one of selfish indifference, which pretends that human beings have no business with each other's conduct in life, and that they should not concern themselves about the well-doing or well-being of one another, unless their own interest is involved. Instead of any diminution, there is need of a great increase of disinterested exertion to promote the good of others. But disinterested benevolence can find other instruments to persuade people to their good than whips and scourges, either of the literal or the metaphorical sort. I am the last person to undervalue the self-regarding virtues; they are only second in importance, if even second, to the social. It is equally the business of education to cultivate both. But even education works by conviction and persuasion as well as by compulsion, and it is by the former only that, when the period of education is passed, the self-regarding virtues should be inculcated. Human beings owe to each other help to distinguish the better from the worse, and encouragement to choose the former and avoid the latter. They should be forever stimulating each other to increased exercise of their higher faculties, and increased direction of their feelings and aims towards wise instead of foolish, elevating instead of degrading, objects and contemplations. But neither one person, nor any number of persons, is warranted in saying to another human creature of ripe years, that he shall not do with his life for his own benefit what he chooses to do with it. He is the person most interested in his own well-being: the interest which any other person, except in cases of strong personal attachment, can have in it, is trifling, compared with that which he himself has; the interest which society has in him individually (except as to his conduct to others) is fractional, and altogether indirect; while with respect to his own feelings and circumstances, the most ordinary man or woman has means of knowledge immeasurably surpassing those that can be possessed by any one else. The interference of society to overrule his judgment and purposes in what only regards himself must be grounded on general presumptions; which may be altogether wrong, and even if right, are as likely as not to be misapplied to individual cases, by persons no better acquainted with the circumstances of such cases than those are who look at them merely from without. In this department, therefore, of human affairs, Individuality has its proper field of action. In the conduct of human beings towards one another it is necessary that general rules should for the most part be observed, in order that people may know what they have to expect: but in each person's own concerns his individual spontaneity is entitled to free exercise.

*   *   *

REVIEW QUESTIONS

1. According to Mill, what are the liberties of the individual? What is the relationship of these liberties to society?

2. What is the importance of freedom of opinion for society?

3. Why would Mill consider the "tyranny of the majority" one of the prominent ills of nineteenth-century society?

POPE LEO XIII

FROM *Rerum Novarum*

Throughout the modern era, the Catholic Church's position on modern science, secular civil society, and republican politics remained critical and oppositional. In 1864 Pope Pius IX issued the Syllabus of Errors, *an encyclical that reinforced the Church's irresolvable differences on progress, liberalism, and modern civilization. A subsequent declaration of papal infallibility in 1870 inflamed anew the tension between church and state. Pope Leo XIII (1878–1903), however, took a different tack. He accepted the principal features of the modern age but strove to offer moral leadership with constructive criticism of civil society's disregard for social justice and economic morals. His encyclical of 1896,* Rerum Novarum *(About New Things), critiqued both capitalism and socialism, and its influence unintentionally spawned a wave of Christian socialist movements throughout Europe.*

From *Rerum Novarum, Encyclical Letter of Pope Leo XIII on the Condition of Labor,* by Pope Leo XIII (Mahwah, N.J.: Paulist Press, 1939), pp. 3–6, 9–10, 12–13, 14–15, 29–31.

It is not surprising that the spirit of revolutionary change, which has long been predominant in the nations of the world, should have passed beyond politics and made its influence felt in the cognate field of practical economy. The elements of a conflict are unmistakable: the growth of industry, and the surprising discoveries of science; the changed relations of masters and workmen; the enormous fortunes of individuals and the poverty of the masses; the increased self-reliance and the closer mutual combination of the working population; and, finally, a general moral deterioration. The momentous seriousness of the present state of things just now fills every mind with painful apprehension; wise men discuss it; practical men propose schemes; popular meetings, legislatures, and sovereign princes, all are occupied with it—and there is nothing which has a deeper hold on public attention.

Therefore, Venerable Brethren, as on former occasions, when it seemed opportune to refute false teaching, We have addressed you in the interests of the Church and of the commonwealth, and have issued Letters on Political Power, on Human Liberty, on the Christian Constitution of the State, and on similar subjects, so now We have thought it useful to speak on

The Condition of Labor

It is a matter on which we have touched once or twice already. But in this Letter the responsibility of the Apostolic office urges Us to treat the question expressly and at length, in order that there may be no mistake as to the principles which truth and justice dictate for its settlement. The discussion is not easy, nor is it free from danger. It is not easy to define the relative rights and the mutual duties of the wealthy and of the poor, of capital and of labor. And the danger lies in this, that crafty agitators constantly make use of these disputes to pervert men's judgments and to stir up the people to sedition.

But all agree, and there can be no question whatever, that some remedy must be found, and quickly found, for the misery and wretchedness which press so heavily at this moment on the large majority of the very poor. The ancient workmen's Guilds were destroyed in the last century, and no other organization took their place. Public institutions and the laws have repudiated the ancient religion. Hence by degrees it has come to pass that Working Men have been given over, isolated and defenceless, to the callousness of employers and the greed of unrestrained competition. The evil has been increased by rapacious Usury, which, although more than once condemned by the Church, is nevertheless, under a different form but with the same guilt, still practiced by avaricious and grasping men. And to this must be added the custom of working by contract, and the concentration of so many branches of trade in the hands of a few individuals, so that a small number of very rich men have been able to lay upon the masses of the poor a yoke little better than slavery itself.

To remedy these evils the *Socialists,* working on the poor man's envy of the rich, endeavor to destroy private property, and maintain that individual possessions should become the common property of all, to be administered by the State or by municipal bodies. They hold that, by thus transferring property from private persons to the community, the present evil state of things will be set to rights, because each citizen will then have his equal share of whatever there is to enjoy. But their proposals are so clearly futile for all practical purposes, that if they were carried out the working man himself would be among the first to suffer. Moreover they are emphatically unjust, because they would rob the lawful possessor, bring the State into a sphere that is not its own, and cause complete confusion in the community.

Private Ownership

It is surely undeniable that, when a man engages in remunerative labor, the very reason and motive of his work is to obtain property, and to hold it as his own private possession. If one man hires out to another his strength or his industry, he does this for the purpose of receiving in return what is necessary for food and living; he thereby expressly proposes to acquire a full and real right, not only to the remuneration, but also to the disposal of that remuneration as he pleases. Thus, if he lives sparingly, saves money, and invests his savings, for greater security, in land, the land in such a case is only his wages in another form; and, consequently, a working man's little estate thus purchased should be as completely at his own disposal as the wages he receives for his labor. But it is precisely in this power of disposal that ownership consists, whether the property be land or movable goods. The *Socialists,* therefore, in endeavoring to transfer the possessions of individuals to the community, strike at the interests of every wage earner, for they deprive him of the liberty of disposing of his wages, and thus of all hope and possibility of increasing his stock and of bettering his condition in life.

What is of still greater importance, however, is that the remedy they propose is manifestly against justice. For every man has by nature the right to possess property as his own. This is one of the *chief points of distinction* between man and the animal creation. For the brute has no power of self-direction, but is governed by two chief instincts, which keep his powers alert, move him to use his strength, and determine him to action without the power of choice. These instincts are self-preservation and the propagation of the species. Both can attain their purpose by means of things which are close at hand; beyond their surroundings the brute creation cannot go, for they are moved to action by sensibility alone, and by the things which sense perceives. But with man it is different indeed. He possesses, on the one hand, the full perfection of animal nature, and therefore he enjoys, at least, as much as the rest of the animal race, the fruition of the things of the body. But animality, however perfect, is far from being the whole of humanity, and is indeed humanity's humble handmaid, made to serve and obey. It is the mind, or the reason, which is the chief thing in us who are human beings; it is this which makes a human being human, and distinguishes him essentially and completely from the brute. And on this account—viz., that man alone among animals possesses reason—it must be within his right to have things not merely for temporary and momentary use, as other living beings have them, but in stable and permanent possession; he must have not only things which perish in the using, but also those which, though used, remain for use in the future.

*   *   *

Socialism Rejected

The idea, then, that the civil government should, at its own discretion, penetrate and pervade the family and the household, is a great and pernicious mistake. True, if a family finds itself in great difficulty, utterly friendless, and without prospect of help, it is right that extreme necessity be met by public aid; for each family is a part of the commonwealth. In like manner, if within the walls of the household there occur grave disturbance of mutual rights, the public power must interfere to force each party to give the other what is due; for this is not to rob citizens of their rights, but justly and properly to safeguard and strengthen them. But the rulers of the State must go no further: nature bids them stop here. Paternal authority can neither be abolished by the State nor absorbed; for it has the same source as human life itself; "the child belongs to the father," and is, as it

were, the continuation of the father's personality; and, to speak with strictness, the child takes its place in civil society not in its own right, but in its quality as a member of the family in which it is begotten. And it is for the very reason that "the child belongs to the father," that, as St. Thomas of Aquin says, "before it attains the use of free-will, it is in the power and care of its parents." The Socialists, therefore, in setting aside the parent and introducing the providence of the State, act *against natural justice,* and threaten the very existence of family life.

And such interference is not only unjust, but is quite certain to harass and disturb all classes of citizens, and to subject them to odious and intolerable slavery. It would open the door to envy, to evil speaking, and to quarrelling; the sources of wealth would themselves run dry, for no one would have any interest in exerting his talents or his industry; and that ideal equality of which so much is said would, in reality, be the leveling down of all to the same condition of misery and dishonor.

Thus it is clear *that the main tenet of Socialism, the community of goods, must be utterly rejected;* for it would injure those whom it is intended to benefit, it would be contrary to the natural rights of mankind, and it would introduce confusion, and disorder into the commonwealth. Our first and most fundamental principle, therefore, when we undertake to alleviate the condition of the masses, must be the inviolability of private property. This laid down, We go on to show where we must find the remedy that we seek.

*   *   *

Employer and Employee

The great mistake that is made in the matter now under consideration, is to possess oneself of the idea that class is naturally hostile to class; that rich and poor are intended by nature to live at war with one another. So irrational and so false is this view, that the exact contrary is the truth. Just as the symmetry of the human body is the result of the disposition of the members of the body, so in a State it is ordained by nature that these two classes should exist in harmony and agreement, and should, as it were, fit into one another, so as to maintain the equilibrium of the body politic. Each requires the other; capital cannot do without labor, nor labor without capital. Mutual agreement results in pleasantness and good order; perpetual conflict necessarily produces confusion and outrage. Now, in preventing such strife as this, and in making it impossible, the efficacy of Christianity is marvelous and manifold. First of all, there is nothing more powerful than Religion (of which the Church is the interpreter and guardian) in drawing rich and poor together, by reminding each class of its duties to the other, and especially of the duties of justice. Thus Religion teaches the laboring man and the workman to carry out honestly and well all equitable agreements freely made, never to injure capital, nor to outrage the person of an employer; never to employ violence in representing his own cause, nor to engage in riot and disorder; and to have nothing to do with men of evil principles, who work upon the people with artful promises, and raise foolish hopes which usually end in disaster and in repentance when too late. Religion teaches the rich man and the employer that their work people are not their slaves; that they must respect in every man his dignity as a man and as a Christian; that labor is nothing to be ashamed of, if we listen to right reason and to Christian philosophy, but is an honorable employment, enabling a man to sustain his life in an upright and creditable way, and that it is shameful and inhuman to treat men like chattels to make money by, or to look upon them merely as so much muscle or physical power.

*　　*　　*

The Right Use of Money

Therefore, those whom fortune favors are warned that freedom from sorrow and abundance of earthly riches, are no guarantee of that beatitude that shall never end, but rather the contrary; that the rich should tremble at the threatenings of Jesus Christ—threatenings so strange in the mouth of our Lord; and that a most strict account must be given to the Supreme Judge for all that we possess. The chiefest and most excellent rule for the right use of money is one which the heathen philosophers indicated, but which the Church has traced out clearly, and has not only made known to men's minds, but has impressed upon their lives. It rests on the principle that it is one thing to have a right to the possession of money, and another to have a right to use money as one pleases. Private ownership, as we have seen, is the natural right of man; and to exercise that right, especially as members of society, is not only lawful but absolutely necessary. "It is lawful," says St. Thomas of Aquin, "for a man to hold private property; and it is also necessary for the carrying on of human life." But if the question be asked, How must one's possessions be used? the Church replies without hesitation in the words of the same holy Doctor: "Man should not consider his outward possessions as his own, but as common to all, so as to share them without difficulty when others are in need. Whence the Apostle saith, Command the rich of this world . . . to give with ease, to communicate." True, no one is commanded to distribute to others that which is required for his own necessities and those of his household; nor even to give away what is reasonably required to keep up becomingly his condition in life; "for no one ought to live unbecomingly." But when necessity has been supplied, and one's position fairly considered, it is a duty to give to the indigent out of that which is over. "That which remaineth give alms." It is a duty, not of justice (except in extreme cases), but of Christian Charity—a duty which is not enforced by human law.

*　　*　　*

Workmen's Associations

In the first place—employers and workmen may themselves effect much in the matter of which We treat, by means of those institutions and organizations which afford opportune assistance to those in need, and which draw the two orders more closely together. Among these may be enumerated:

societies for mutual help; various foundations established by private persons for providing for the workman, and for his widow or his orphans, in sudden calamity, in sickness, and in the event of death; and what are called "patronages," or institutions for the care of boys and girls, for young people, and also for those of more mature age.

The most important of all are Workmen's Associations; for these virtually include all the rest. History attests what excellent results were affected by the Artificer's Guilds of a former day. They were the means not only of many advantages to the workmen, but in no small degree of the advancement of art, as numerous monuments remain to prove. Such associations should be adapted to the requirements of the age in which we live—an age of greater instruction, of different customs, and of more numerous requirements in daily life. It is gratifying to know that there are actually in existence not a few societies of this nature, consisting either of workmen alone, or of workmen and employers together; but it were greatly to be desired that they should multiply and become more effective. We have spoken of them more than once; but it will be well to explain here how much they are needed, to show that they exist by their own right, and to enter into their organization and their work.

*   *   *

These lesser societies and the society which constitutes the State differ in many things, because their immediate purpose and end is different. Civil society exists for the common good, and, therefore, is concerned with the interests of all in general, and with the individual interests in their due place and proportion. Hence, it is called *public* society, because by its means, as St. Thomas of Aquin says, "Men communicate with one another in the setting up of a commonwealth." But the societies which are formed in the bosom of the State are called *private,* and justly so, because their immediate purpose is the private advantage of the associates. "Now, a private society," says St. Thomas again, "is one which is formed for the purpose of carrying out private business; as when two or three enter into partnership with the view

of trading in conjunction." Particular societies, then, although they exist within the State, and are each a part of the State, nevertheless cannot be prohibited by the State absolutely and as such. For to enter into a "society" of this kind is the natural right of man; and the State must protect natural rights, not destroy them; and if it forbids its citizens to form associations, it contradicts the very principle of its own existence; for both they and it exist in virtue of the same principle, viz., the natural propensity of man to live in society.

*   *   *

Conclusion

We have now laid before you, Venerable Brethren, who are the persons, and what are the means, by which this most difficult question must be solved. Every one must put his hand to work which falls to his share, and that at once and immediately, lest the evil which is already so great may by delay become absolutely beyond remedy. Those who rule the State must use the law and the institutions of the country; masters and rich men must remember their duty; the poor, whose interests are at stake, must make every lawful and proper effort; since Religion alone, as We said at the beginning, can destroy the evil at its root, all men must be persuaded that the primary thing needful is to return to real Christianity, in the absence of which all the plans and devices of the wisest will be of little avail.

*   *   *

REVIEW QUESTIONS

1. What was the position of the Catholic Church on the condition of labor?
2. What were Leo XIII's criticisms of capitalism and socialism?
3. How did the Catholic Church's view of civil society differ from the views of those two doctrines?
4. What reforms of market economy did the encyclical propose? How were these critical of liberalism?

SAMUEL SMILES

FROM *Thrift*

One of the most powerful ideological buttresses of the bourgeois social order was the doctrine of self-help. The Scottish author Samuel Smiles (1812–1904) achieved enormous success in a number of books that presented the virtues of self-reliance and self-education in an appealing and accessible manner. As a radical who believed in universal suffrage, Smiles hoped that working-class respectability would in turn bring political equality. His biography of George Stephenson, the self-made railroad engineer, was followed by Self-Help *(1859), a primer on individualism that was translated into seventeen languages. The book's success spawned similar works:* Character *(1871),* Thrift *(1875), and* Duty *(1880). The following section from* Thrift *is particularly characteristic of his avuncular style and his themes of sobriety and frugality.*

From *Thrift*, by Samuel Smiles (London: Murray, 1875).

Improvidence

*   *   *

England is one of the richest countries in the world. Our merchants are enterprizing, our manufacturers are industrious, our labourers are hardworking. There is an accumulation of wealth in the country to which past times can offer no parallel. The Bank is gorged with gold. There never was more food in the empire; there never was more money. There is no end to our manufacturing productions, for the steam-engine never tires. And yet, notwithstanding all this wealth, there is an enormous mass of poverty. Close alongside the Wealth of Nations, there gloomily stalks the Misery of Nations,—luxurious ease resting upon a dark background of wretchedness.

Parliamentary reports have again and again revealed to us the miseries endured by certain portions of our working population. They have described the people employed in factories, workshops, mines, and brick-fields, as well as in the pursuits of country life. We have tried to grapple with the evils of their condition by legislation, but it seems to mock us. Those who sink into poverty are fed, but they remain paupers. Those who feed them, feel no compassion; and those who are fed, return no gratitude. There is no bond of sympathy between the givers and the receivers. Thus the Haves and the Have-nots, the opulent and the indigent, stand at the two extremes of the social scale, and a wide gulf is fixed between them.

*   *   *

With respect to the poorer classes, * * *

They work, eat, drink, and sleep: that constitutes their life. They think nothing of providing for to-morrow, or for next week, or for next year. They abandon themselves to their sensual appetites; and make no provision whatever for the future. The thought of adversity, or of coming sorrow, or of the helplessness that comes with years and sickness, never crosses their minds. In these respects, they resemble the savage tribes, who know no better, and do no worse. Like the North American Indians, they debase themselves by the vices which accompany civilization, but make no use whatever of its benefits and advantages.

*   *   *

No one can reproach the English workman with want of industry. He works harder and more skilfully than the workman of any other country; and he might be more comfortable and independent in his circumstances, were he as prudent as he is laborious. But improvidence is unhappily the defect of the class. Even the best-paid English workmen, though earning more money than the average of professional men, still for the most part belong to the poorer classes because of their thoughtlessness. In prosperous times they are not accustomed to make provision for adverse times; and when a period of social pressure occurs, they are rarely found more than a few weeks ahead of positive want.

*   *   *

Though trade has invariably its cycles of good and bad years, like the lean and fat kine in Pharaoh's dream—its bursts of prosperity, followed by glut, panic, and distress—the thoughtless and spendthrift take no heed of experience, and make no better provision for the future. Improvidence seems to be one of the most incorrigible of faults. "There are whole neighbourhoods in the manufacturing districts," says Mr. Baker in a recent Report, "where not only are there no savings worth mentioning, but where, within a fortnight of being out of work, the workers themselves are starving for want of the merest necessaries." Not a strike takes place, but immediately the workmen are plunged in destitution; their furniture and watches are sent to the pawnshop, whilst deplorable appeals are made to the charitable, and numerous families are cast upon the poor-rates.

This habitual improvidence—though of course there are many admirable exceptions—is the real cause of the social degradation of the artizan. This too is the prolific source of social misery. But the misery is entirely the result of human ignorance and self-indulgence. For though the Creator has ordained poverty, the poor are not necessarily, nor as a matter of fact, the miserable. Misery is the result of moral causes, most commonly of individual vice and improvidence.

*   *   *

We have certainly had numerous "Reforms." We have had household suffrage, and vote by ballot. We have relieved the working classes of the taxes on corn, cattle, coffee, sugar, and provisions generally; and imposed a considerable proportion of the taxes from which they have been relieved on the middle and upper ranks. Yet these measures have produced but little improvement in the condition of the working people. They have not applied the principle of Reform to themselves. They have not begun at home. Yet the end of all Reform is the improvement of the individual. Everything that is wrong in Society results from that which is wrong in the Individual. When men are bad, society is bad.

*   *   *

Complaining that the laws are bad, and that the taxes are heavy, will not mend matters. Aristocratic government, and the tyranny of masters, are nothing like so injurious as the tyranny of vicious appetites. Men are easily led away by the parade of their miseries, which are for the most part voluntary and self-imposed, the results of idleness, thriftlessness, intemperance, and misconduct. To blame others for what we suffer, is always more agreeable to our self-pride, than to blame ourselves. But it is perfectly clear that people who live from day to day without plan, without rule, without forethought—who spend all their earnings, without saving anything for the future—are preparing beforehand for inevitable distress. To provide only for the present, is the sure means of sacrificing the future. What hope can there be for a people whose only maxim seems to be, "Let us eat and drink, for to-morrow we die"?

All this may seem very hopeless; yet it is not entirely so. The large earnings of the working classes is an important point to start with. The gradual diffusion of education will help them to use, and not abuse, their means of comfortable living. The more extended knowledge of the uses of economy, frugality, and thrift, will help them to spend their lives more soberly, virtuously, and religiously.

*   *   *

REVIEW QUESTIONS

1. To what does Smiles attribute most workers' impoverished condition?

2. What worth does Smiles ascribe to reform laws for the worker? What is for him the genuine source of improvement?

3. How does Smiles's argument compare with Engels's account of workers' improvidence?

ISABELLA BEETON

FROM *Mrs. Beeton's Book of Household Management*

First published in serial form in 1859–1861, Mrs. Beeton's Book of Household Management *remained in print for the remainder of the century, establishing itself as a self-evident necessity for bourgeois Victorian households. Today the book is an excellent example of prescriptive literature: a source documenting how proper bourgeois families ought to have led their social and domestic lives. The book provided a broad window on Victorian tastes in food, bourgeois attitudes toward other classes, and proper comportment in and outside the home. The following section is taken from the book's first chapter, which sets rules of conduct for the mistress of the household.*

From *Mrs. Beeton's Book of Household Management,* by Isabella Beeton (London: S. O. Beeton, 1861).

The Mistress

*   *   *

1. As with the Commander of an Army, or the leader of any enterprise, so is it with the mistress of a house. Her spirit will be seen through the whole establishment; and just in proportion as she performs her duties intelligently and thoroughly, so will her domestics follow in her path. Of all those acquirements, which more particularly belong to the feminine character, there are none which take a higher rank, in our estimation, than such as enter into a knowledge of household duties; for on these are perpetually dependent the happiness, comfort, and well-being of a family. In this opinion we are borne out by the author of "The Vicar of Wakefield," who says: "The modest virgin, the prudent wife, and the careful matron, are much more serviceable in life than petticoated philosophers, blustering heroines, or virago queens. She who makes her husband and her children happy, who reclaims the one from vice and trains up the other to virtue, is a much greater character than ladies described in romances, whose whole occupation is to murder mankind with shafts from their quiver, or their eyes."

2. Pursuing this Picture, we may add, that to be a good housewife does not necessarily imply an abandonment of proper pleasures or amusing recreation; and we think it the more necessary to express this, as the performance of the duties of a

mistress may, to some minds, perhaps seem to be incompatible with the enjoyment of life. Let us, however, now proceed to describe some of those home qualities and virtues which are necessary to the proper management of a Household, and then point out the plan which may be the most profitably pursued for the daily regulation of its affairs.

3. Early Rising is one of the most Essential Qualities which enter into good Household Management, as it is not only the parent of health, but of innumerable other advantages. Indeed, when a mistress is an early riser, it is almost certain that her house will be orderly and well-managed. On the contrary, if she remain in bed till a late hour, then the domestics, who, as we have before observed, invariably partake somewhat of their mistress's character, will surely become sluggards. To self-indulgence all are more or less disposed, and it is not to be expected that servants are freer from this fault than the heads of houses. The great Lord Chatham thus gave his advice in reference to this subject:—"I would have inscribed on the curtains of your bed, and the walls of your chamber, 'If you do not rise early, you can make progress in nothing.'"

4. Cleanliness is also indispensable to Health, and must be studied both in regard to the person and the house, and all that it contains. Cold or tepid baths should be employed every morning, unless, on account of illness or other circumstances, they should be deemed objectionable. The bathing of *children* will be treated of under the head of "MANAGEMENT OF CHILDREN."

5. Frugality and Economy are Home Virtues, without which no household can prosper. Dr. Johnson says: "Frugality may be termed the daughter of Prudence, the sister of Temperance, and the parent of Liberty. He that is extravagant will quickly become poor, and poverty will enforce dependence and invite corruption." The necessity of practising economy should be evident to every one, whether in the possession of an income no more than sufficient for a family's requirements, or of a large fortune, which puts financial adversity out of the question. We must always remember that it is a great merit in housekeeping to manage a little well. "He is a good waggoner," says

Bishop Hall, "that can turn in a little room. To live well in abundance is the praise of the estate, not of the person. I will study more how to give a good account of my little, than how to make it more." In this there is true wisdom, and it may be added, that those who can manage a little well, are most likely to succeed in their management of larger matters. Economy and frugality must never, however, be allowed to degenerate into parsimony and meanness.

*   *   *

13. The Dress of the Mistress should always be adapted to her circumstances, and be varied with different occasions. Thus, at breakfast she should be attired in a very neat and simple manner, wearing no ornaments. If this dress should decidedly pertain only to the breakfast-hour, and be specially suited for such domestic occupations as usually follow that meal, then it would be well to exchange it before the time for receiving visitors, if the mistress be in the habit of doing so. It is still to be remembered, however, that, in changing the dress, jewellery and ornaments are not to be worn until the full dress for dinner is assumed. Further information and hints on the subject of the toilet will appear under the department of the "LADY'S-MAID."

*   *   *

16. A Housekeeping Account-book should invariably be kept, and kept punctually and precisely. The plan for keeping household accounts, which we should recommend, would be to make an entry, that is, write down into a daily diary every amount paid on that particular day, be it ever so small; then, at the end of the month, let these various payments be ranged under their specific heads of Butcher, Baker, &c.; and thus will be seen the proportions paid to each tradesman, and any one month's expenses may be contrasted with another. The housekeeping accounts should be balanced not less than once a month; so that you may see that the money you have in hand tallies with your account of it in your diary. Judge Haliburton never wrote truer words than when he said,

No man is rich whose expenditure exceeds his means, and no one is poor whose incomings exceed his outgoings.

When, in a large establishment, a housekeeper is kept, it will be advisable for the mistress to examine her accounts regularly. Then any increase of expenditure which may be apparent, can easily be explained, and the housekeeper will have the satisfaction of knowing whether her efforts to manage her department well and economically, have been successful.

17. Engaging Domestics is one of those duties in which the judgment of the mistress must be keenly exercised. There are some respectable registry-offices, where good servants may sometimes be hired; but the plan rather to be recommended is, for the mistress to make inquiry amongst her circle of friends and acquaintances, and her tradespeople. The latter generally know those in their neighbourhood, who are wanting situations, and will communicate with them, when a personal interview with some of them will enable the mistress to form some idea of the characters of the applicants, and to suit herself accordingly.

We would here point out an error—and a grave one it is—into which some mistresses fall. They do not, when engaging a servant, expressly tell her all the duties which she will be expected to perform. This is an act of omission severely to be reprehended. Every portion of work which the maid will have to do, should be plainly stated by the mistress, and understood by the servant. If this plan is not carefully adhered to, domestic contention is almost certain to ensue, and this may not be easily settled; so that a change of servants, which is so much to be deprecated, is continually occurring.

18. In obtaining a Servant's Character, it is not well to be guided by a written one from some unknown quarter; but it is better to have an interview, if at all possible, with the former mistress. By this means you will be assisted in your decision of the suitableness of the servant for your place, from the appearance of the lady and the state of her house. Negligence and want of cleanliness in her and her household generally, will naturally lead you to the conclusion, that her servant has suffered from the influence of the bad example.

The proper course to pursue in order to obtain a personal interview with the lady is this:—The servant in search of the situation must be desired to see her former mistress, and ask her to be kind enough to appoint a time, convenient to herself, when you may call on her; this proper observance of courtesy being necessary to prevent any unseasonable intrusion on the part of a stranger. Your first questions should be relative to the honesty and general morality of her former servant; and if no objection is stated in that respect, her other qualifications are then to be ascertained. Inquiries should be very minute, so that you may avoid disappointment and trouble, by knowing the weak points of your domestic.

19. The Treatment of Servants is of the highest possible moment, as well to the mistress as to the domestics themselves. On the head of the house the latter will naturally fix their attention; and if they perceive that the mistress's conduct is regulated by high and correct principles, they will not fail to respect her. If, also, a benevolent desire is shown to promote their comfort, at the same time that a steady performance of their duty is exacted, then their respect will not be unmingled with affection, and they will be still more solicitous to continue to deserve her favour.

*   *   *

REVIEW QUESTIONS

1. According to Beeton, what are the duties and expectations of bourgeois women?
2. What virtues and attitudes are extolled?
3. What does Beeton reveal about the way bourgeois families lived?
4. What are the shortcomings of such prescriptive literature?

ELIZABETH POOLE SANFORD

FROM *Woman in Her Social and Domestic Character*

The widened separation of domestic and public spheres in the nineteenth century brought with it fundamental changes in the economic and social roles of bourgeois women. No longer expected to work in the productive sphere, middle-class married women took on domestic, motherly, and religious duties. Not surprisingly, character-ological assumptions accompanied this role of the "angel in the house." Alongside purity, delicacy, and virtue, subservience to husbands was foremost among the traits considered desirable for women. The following excerpt from Elizabeth Poole San-ford's book (1833) is an early example of the prescriptive literature aimed at middle-class women of the Victorian era.

From *Woman in Her Social and Domestic Character,* by Elizabeth Poole Sanford (Boston: Bowles, 1833).

*   *   *

Domestic comfort is the chief source of her influence, and the greatest debt society owes her; for happiness is almost an element of virtue, and nothing conduces more to improve the character of men than domestic peace. A woman may make a man's home delightful, and may thus increase his motives for virtuous exertion. She may refine and tranquillise his mind,—may turn away his anger or allay his grief. Her smile may be the happy influence to gladden his heart, and to disperse the cloud that gathers on his brow. And she will be loved in proportion as she makes those around her happy,—as she studies their tastes, and sympathises in their feelings. In social relations adaptation is therefore the true secret of her influence.

*   *   *

Domestic life is a woman's sphere, and it is there that she is most usefully as well as most appropriately employed. But society, too, feels her influence, and owes to her, in great measure, its balance and its tone. She may be here a corrective of what is wrong, a moderator of what is unruly, a restraint on what is indecorous. Her presence

may be a pledge against impropriety and excess, a check on vice, and a protection to virtue.

And it is her delicacy which will secure to her such an influence, and enable her to maintain it. It is the policy of licentiousness to undermine where it cannot openly attack, and to weaken by stratagem what it may not rudely assail. But a delicate woman will be as much upon her guard against the insidious as against the direct assault, and will no more tolerate the innuendo than the avowal. She will shrink from the licentiousness which is couched in ambiguous phrase or veiled in covert allusion, and from the immorality which, though it may not offend the ear, is meant to corrupt the heart. And though a depraved taste may relish the condiments of vice, or an unscrupulous palate receive them without detection, her virtue will be too sensitive not to reject the poison, and to recoil spontaneously from the touch.

Delicacy is, indeed, the point of honor in woman. And her purity of manner will ensure to her deference, and repress, more effectually than any other influence, impropriety of every kind. A delicate woman, too, will be more loved, as well as more respected, than any other; for affection can scarcely be excited, and certainly cannot long subsist, unless it is founded on esteem.

Yet such delicacy is neither prudish nor insipid. Conversation, for instance, is one great source of a woman's influence; and it is her province, and her peculiar talent, to give zest to it. She is, and ought to be, the enlivener of society: if she restrains impropriety, she may promote cheerfulness; and it is not because her conversation is innocent that it need therefore be dull. The sentiment of woman contributes much to social interest: her feeling imparts life, and her gentleness a polish.

*   *   *

Again, to be agreeable, a woman must avoid egotism. It is no matter how superior she is, she will never be liked, if she talks chiefly of herself. The impression of her own importance can convey no pleasure to others: on the contrary, as a desire for distinction is always mutual, a sense of inferiority must be depressing.

If we would converse pleasingly, we must endeavor to set others at ease: and it is not by flattery that we can succeed in doing so, but by a courteous and kind address, which delicately avoids all needless irritation, and endeavors to infuse that good humor of which it is itself the result.

In woman this is a Christian duty. How often should they suppress their own claims rather than interfere with those of others! How often should they employ their talent in developing that of their associates, and not for its own display! How invariably should they discard pretension, and shun even the appearance of conceit; and seek to imbibe the spirit of that lovely religion, of which sympathy is the characteristic feature, and humility the pre-eminent grace!

*   *   *

It is seldom, indeed, that women are great proficients. The *chefs-d'oeuvre* of the sculptress need the polish of the master chisel; and the female pencil has never yet limned the immortal forms of beauty. The mind of woman is, perhaps, incapable of the originality and strength requisite for the sublime. Even Saint Cecilia exists only in an elegant legend, and the poetry of music, if often felt and expressed, has seldom been conceived by a female adept. But the practical talents of women are far from contemptible; and they may be both the encouragers and the imitators of genius. They should not grasp at too much, nor be content with superficial attainment; they should not merely daub a few flowers, or hammer out a few tunes, or trifle away their time in inept efforts, which at best claim only indulgence; but they should do well what they do attempt, and do it without affectation or display.

*   *   *

REVIEW QUESTIONS

1. According to Sanford, what were the character traits assigned to women? For what goals should women strive?
2. What attributes constituted the domestic sphere of women?
3. What was the ideal relationship between husband and wife? How was this ideal justified?

21 ❧ WHAT IS A NATION? TERRITORIES, STATES, AND CITIZENS, 1848–1871

Nationalism is a modern phenomenon. Arising as a cultural doctrine in the late eighteenth century, the sentiment of nationalism quickly became a widespread political force, constantly evolving over time and adapting to particular needs. Its impact was registered at all levels of public life. As one of the chief solvents of the old regime, the principle of national unity not only realigned the European state system but also radically recast political culture with a new consciousness of citizenship. Political and economic change eroded older forms of local and regional loyalties, enabling the ideal of national citizenship to embed itself as a self-evident assumption for millions of Europeans.

The cultural dominance of the French Enlightenment, and its insistence on uniform standards, produced a wave of cultural resistance among European writers. In contrast to the Enlightenment's search for social and artistic norms applicable to all societies, select intellectuals celebrated instead the teeming heterogeneity of European language, customs, and culture. Each culture or people, they argued, embodied a national spirit: unique manifestations of geography, climate, and language that defied qualitative comparison. Humanitas, argued cultural nationalists, was not reducible to core characteristics but rather was the aggregate of humankind's cultural diversity. By honoring all cultures and nations and conferring on them the self-evident right to develop of their own accord, early forms of cultural nationalism perceived the nation within a tolerant, cosmopolitan worldview.

The French Revolution converted this cultural sentiment into political strength. By endowing the nation with political sovereignty and transforming subjects into citizens, the French Revolution evinced the enormous potential of nationalism to wield political and military power. Reaffirmed in flags, anthems, emblems, festivals, and dress, the words nation *and* fatherland *("la patrie") stirred the blood of patriots, enabling the revolutionary government to mobilize its citizenry to serve the nation-state with unprecedented engagement. Under the leadership of Napoleon, the massive revolutionary armies of citizen-soldiers* developed into a superior fighting force, compelling the great powers of Europe to adapt or perish.

Napoleonic occupation, in turn, awakened national consciousness in other European cultures. The traditional elite initially tapped patriotism to counter Napoleon's armies but unwittingly set in motion popular movements whose ideals of national sovereignty, unified nation-states, and constitutional liberties challenged kingdoms, multinational empires, and conservative principles of social hierarchy. Emancipating peoples from the injustice of imposed foreign rule gripped the imagination of artists, writers, and poets, who depicted nationalist movements as romantic quests for liberty and freedom. In the first half of the nineteenth century, liberals, democrats, and nationalists formed strong bonds, for they saw a constitutional nation-state as the vehicle of progress for all social groups. The struggle to unify a culture under modern principles of citizenship assumed a universal, humanitarian character that could also be applied to colonized peoples outside of Europe. Advocates of nationalism adopted rhetoric, imagery, and ceremonies once reserved exclusively for religions. The ideal of self-sacrifice further sanctified nationalist movements; bloodshed consecrated the nation as a higher purpose for which to die.

The principle of nationalism shaped the course of nineteenth-century state building but not in the manner envisioned by liberals. Statesmen reworked nationalism into a conservative mold, using patriotism and nationalist sentiment to support conservative monarchism and authoritarian government. Calculating that rural voters were inherently resistant to innovative change, conservative rulers shrewdly introduced constitutions and universal male suffrage to lend popular legitimacy to their conservative policies, thereby checking the reformist impulses of urban liberals. Yet nationalism did not remain the manipulative tool of conservative statesmen. Urbanization, improved communications, and the vote produced grassroots political movements that invoked nationalism to protect domestic industry, agitate for imperial expansion, and brand socialists, Jews, and foreigners as pernicious influences on the nation's political body. The numerous hybrid forms of nationalism circulating in Europe by the end of the nineteenth century contributed to the increasingly chauvinistic political culture that condoned aggressive militarism, xenophobia, and racial exclusion. In this atmosphere emerged Theodor Herzl's program to found a Jewish nation-state outside of Europe.

In the wake of the Industrial and French revolutions, political consciousness underwent radical change. Traditional authority was either modified or replaced by political communities whose legitimacy and power hinged on their representation of the nation. Yet the meaning of nationalism never became fixed; it remained a protean ideology serving a wide array of political interests and social classes over the long period from 1789 to 1914.

JOHANN GOTTFRIED HERDER

FROM *Reflections on the Philosophy of the History of Mankind*

Johann Gottfried Herder (1744–1803), a theologian by training and profession, greatly influenced German letters with his literary criticism and his philosophy of history. In his later years, Herder resided in the Duchy of Weimar and his presence, along with those of J. W. Goethe and F. Schiller, made Weimar the seat of German neohumanism. His analogy of national cultures as organic beings had an enormous impact on modern historical consciousness. Nations, he argued, possessed not only the phases of youth, maturity, and decline but also singular, incomparable worth. His mixture of anthropology and history, as illustrated in the passage below, is characteristic of the age.

From *Reflections on the Philosophy of the History of Mankind*, by Johann Gottfried Herder, edited by Frank E. Manuel (Chicago: University of Chicago Press, 1970).

Chapter 1
Notwithstanding the Varieties of the Human Form, There Is but One and the Same Species of Man throughout the Whole of Our Earth

No two leaves of any one tree in nature are to be found perfectly alike; and still less do two human faces, or human frames, resemble each other. Of what endless variety is our artful structure susceptible! Our solids are decomposable into such minute and multifariously interwoven fibres, as no eye can trace; and these are connected by a gluten of such a delicate composition, as the utmost skill is insufficient to analyse. Yet these constitute the least part of us: they are nothing more than the containing vessels and conduits of the variously compounded, highly animated fluid, existing in much greater quantity, by means of which we live and enjoy life. "No man," says Haller, "is exactly similar to another in his internal structure: the courses of the nerves and blood vessels differ in millions and millions of cases, so that amid the variations of these delicate parts, we are scarcely able to discover in what they agree." But if the eye of the anatomist can perceive this infinite variety, how much greater must that be, which dwells in the invisible powers of such an artful organization! So that every man is ultimately a world, in external appearance indeed similar to others, but internally an individual being, with whom no other coincides.

And since man is no independent substance, but is connected with all the elements of nature; living by inspiration of the air, and deriving nutriment from the most opposite productions of the Earth, in his meats and drinks; consuming fire, while he absorbs light, and contaminates the air he breathes; awake or asleep, in motion or at rest, contributing to the change of the universe; shall not he also be changed by it? It is far too little, to compare him to the absorbing sponge, the sparkling tinder: he is a multitudinous harmony, a living self, on whom the harmony of all the powers that surround him operates.

The whole course of a man's life is change: the different periods of his life are tales of transformation, and the whole species is one continued metamorphosis. Flowers drop and wither; others sprout out and bud: the vast tree bears at once all the seasons on its head. If, from a calculation of the insensible perspiration alone, a man of eighty have renovated his whole body at least four and twenty times; who can trace the variations of matter and its forms through all the race of mankind upon the Earth, amid all the causes of change; when not one point on our complicated Globe, not one wave in the current of time, resembles another? A few centuries only have elapsed since the inhabitants of Germany were Patagonians: but they are so no longer, and the inhabitants of its future climates will not equal us. If now we go back to those times, when every thing upon Earth was apparently so different; the times for instance, when elephants lived in Siberia and North America, and those large animals existed, the bones of which are to be found on the Ohio; if men then lived in those regions, how different must they have been from those, who now inhabit them! Thus the history of man is ultimately a theatre of transformations, which He alone can review, who animates all these figures, and feels and enjoys in them all. He builds up and destroys, improves and alters forms, while he changes the World around them. The wanderer upon Earth, the transient ephemeron, can only admire the wonders of this great spirit in a narrow circle, enjoy the form that belongs to him in the general choir, adore, and disappear with this form. "I too was in Arcadia": is the monumental inscription of all living beings in the ever-changing, ever-renewing creation.

As the human intellect, however, seeks unity in every kind of variety, and the divine mind, its prototype, has stamped the most innumerable multiplicity upon the Earth with unity, we may venture from the vast realm of change to revert to the simplest position: *all mankind are only one and the same species.*

*   *   *

For each genus Nature has done enough, and to each has given its proper progeny. The ape she has divided into as many species and varieties as possible, and extended these as far as she could: but thou, O man, honour thyself: neither the pongo nor the gibbon is thy brother: the American and the Negro are: these therefore thou shouldst not oppress, or murder, or steal; for they are men, like thee: with the ape thou canst not enter into fraternity.

Lastly, I could wish the distinctions between the human species, that have been made from a laudable zeal for discriminating science, not carried beyond due bounds. Some for instance have thought fit, to employ the term of *races* for four or five divisions, originally made in consequence of country or complexion: but I see no reason for this appellation. Race refers to a difference of origin, which in this case either does not exist, or in each of these countries, and under each of these complexions, comprises the most different races. For every nation is one people, having its own national form, as well as its own language: the climate, it is true, stamps on each its mark, or spreads over it a slight veil, but not sufficient to destroy the original national character. This originality of character extends even to families, and its transitions are as variable as imperceptible. In short, there are neither four or five races, nor exclusive varieties, on this Earth. Complexions run into each other: forms follow the genetic character: and upon the whole, all are at last but shades of the same great picture, extending through all ages, and over all parts of the Earth. They belong not, therefore, so properly to systematic natural history, as to the physico-geographical history of man.

*   *   *

Now as mankind, both taken as a whole, and in its particular individuals, societies, and nations, is a permanent natural system of the most multifarious living powers; let us examine, wherein its stability consists; in what point its highest beauty, truth, and goodness, unite; and what course it takes, in order to reapproach its permanent condition, on every aberration from it, of which many are exhibited to us by history and experience.

1. The human species is such a copious scheme of energies and capacities, that, as every thing in nature rests on the most determinate individuality, its great and numerous capacities could not appear on our planet otherwise than *divided among millions*. Every thing has been born, that could be born upon it; and every thing has maintained itself, that could acquire a state of permanence according to the laws of Nature. Thus every individual bears within himself that symmetry, for which he is made, and to which he must mould himself, both in his bodily figure, and mental capacities. Human existence appears in every shape and kind, from the most sickly deformity, that can scarcely support life, to the superhuman form of a Grecian demigod; from the passionate ardour of the Negro brain, to the capacity for consummate wisdom. Through faults and errrours, through education, necessity, and exercise, every mortal seeks the symmetry of his powers; as in this alone the most complete enjoyment of his existence lies: yet few are sufficiently fortunate, to attain it in the purest, happiest manner.

2. As an individual man can subsist of himself but very imperfectly, *a superiour maximum of cooperating powers* is formed with every society. These powers contend together in wild confusion, till, agreeably to the unfailing laws of nature, opposing regulations limit each other, and a kind of equilibrium and harmony of movement takes place. Thus nations modify themselves, according to time, place, and their internal character: each bears in itself the standard of its perfection, totally independent of all comparison with that of others. Now the more pure and fine the maximum on which a people hit, the more useful the objects to which it applied the exertions of its nobler powers, and, lastly, the more firm and exact the bond of union, which most intimately connected all the members of the state, and guided them to this good end; the more stable was the nation itself, and the more brilliant the figure it made in history. The course that we have hitherto taken through certain nations shows how different, according to place, time, and circumstances, was the object for which they strove. With the Chinese it was refined political morality; with the Hindoos, a kind of retired purity, quiet assiduity in labour, and endurance; with the Phoenicians, the spirit of navigation, and commercial industry. The culture of the Greeks, particularly at Athens, proceeded on the maximum of sensible beauty, both in arts and manners, in science and in political institutions. In Sparta, and in Rome, men emulated the virtues of the patriot and hero; in each, however, in a very different mode. Now as in all these most depended on time and place, the ancients will scarcely admit of being compared with each other in the most distinguished features of national fame.

3. In all, however, we see the operation of *one principle*, namely *human reason*, which endeavours to produce unity out of multiplicity, order out of disorder, and out of variety of powers and designs one symmetrical and durably beautiful whole. From the shapeless artificial rocks, with which the Chinese ornaments his garden, to the Egyptian pyramid, or the ideal beauty of Greece, the plan and design of a reflecting understanding is every where observable, though in very different degrees. The more refined the reflections of this understanding were, and the nearer it came to the point, which is the highest in its kind, and admits no deviation to the right or to the left; the more were its performances to be considered as models, for they contain eternal rules for the human understanding in all ages. Thus nothing of the kind can be conceived superior to an Egyptian pyramid, or to several Greek and Roman works of art. They are simple solutions of certain problems of the understanding, which admit no arbitrary supposition, that the problems are perhaps not yet solved, or might be solved in a better way, for in them the simple idea of what they ought to be is displayed in the easiest, fullest, and most beautiful manner. Every deviation from them would be a fault; and were they to be repeated and diversified in a thousand modes, we must still return to that single point, which is the highest of its kind.

4. Thus through all the polished nations, that we have hitherto considered, or shall hereafter consider,

a chain of cultivation may be drawn, flying off in extremely divergent curves. In each it designates increasing and decreasing greatness, and has maximums of every kind. Many of these exclude or limit one another, till at length a certain symmetry takes place in the whole; so that were we to reason from one perfection of any nation concerning another, we should form very treacherous conclusions. Thus, because Athens had exquisite orators, it does not follow, that its form of government must likewise have been the best possible; or that, because the Chinese moralize so excellently, their state must be a pattern for all others. Forms of government refer to a very different maximum, from that of beautiful morals, or a pathetic oration; notwithstanding, at bottom, all things in any nation have a certain connexion, if it be only that of exclusion and limitation. No other maximum, but that of the most perfect bond of union, produces the most happy states; even supposing the people are in consequence obliged to dispense with many shining qualities.

5. But in one and the same nation every maximum of its commendable endeavours ought not and cannot endure for ever; since it is but one point in the progress of time. This incessantly moves on; and the more numerous the circumstances, on which the beautiful effect depends, the sooner is it liable to pass away. Happy if its master pieces remain as rules for future ages.

*   *   *

REVIEW QUESTIONS

1. What is Herder's argument regarding difference and similarity in the human race?
2. What are the roles of time, place, and climate in Herder's view of civilizations?
3. How is Herder's presentation of cultural development different from that of the Enlightenment?

JOHANN GOTTLIEB FICHTE

FROM *Addresses to the German Nation*

One of the most important ramifications of the revolutionary era was the awakening of nationalist sentiment in Europe. The origin of German national consciousness provides a good example. Following the stunning victories of France over Germany between 1802 and 1807, Napoleon redrew the map of Germany, reducing the great power status of Prussia, erecting a federation of satellite states, and creating new kingdoms. Faced with this humiliation, German rulers, statesmen, and intellectuals realized that reform from above was necessary so that the untapped energies of German citizenry could be summoned to defeat the French foe. In the occupied Prussian capital of Berlin in the winter of 1807–8, the philosopher Johann Gottlieb Fichte gave a series of lectures that called for the spiritual renewal of Germany through a program of reformed education that stressed the German nation's character and strength. His program typified the idealism and romanticism of German patriotism in this era.

From *Addresses to the German Nation*, by Johann Gottlieb Fichte, translated by R. F. Jones and G. H. Turnbull (Ashland, Ohio: Open Court, 1922).

*　　*　　*

Fourteenth Address

*　　*　　*

CONCLUSION

In the addresses which I conclude today, I have spoken aloud to you first of all, but I have had in view the whole German nation, and my intention has been to gather round me, in the room in which you are bodily present, everyone in the domain of the German language who is able to understand me. If I have succeeded in throwing into any heart which has beaten here in front of me a spark which will continue to glow there and to influence its life, it is not my intention that these hearts should remain apart and lonely; I want to gather to them from over the whole of our common soil men of similar sentiments and resolutions, and to link them together, so that at this central point a single, continuous, and unceasing flame of patriotic disposition may be kindled, which will spread over the whole soil of the fatherland to its utmost boundaries. These addresses have not been meant for the entertainment of indolent ears and eyes in the present age; on the contrary, I want to know once for all, and everyone of like disposition shall know it with me, whether there is anyone besides ourselves whose way of thinking is akin to ours. Every German who still believes himself to be a member of a nation, who thinks highly and nobly of that nation, hopes for it, ventures, endures, and suffers for it, shall at last have the uncertainty of his belief

removed; he shall see clearly whether he is right or is only a fool and a dreamer; from now on he shall either pursue his way with the glad consciousness of certainty, or else firmly and vigorously renounce a fatherland here below, and find in the heavenly one his only consolation. To them, not as individuals in our everyday limited life, but as representatives of the nation, and so through their ears to the whole nation, these addresses make this appeal:

Centuries have come and gone since you were last convoked as you are to-day; in such numbers; in a cause so great, so urgent, and of such concern to all and everyone; so entirely as a nation and as Germans. Never again will the offer come to you in this way. If you now take no heed and withdraw into yourselves, if you again let these addresses go by you as if they were meant merely to tickle your ears, or if you regard them as something strange and fabulous, then no human being will ever take you into account again. Hearken now at last; reflect now at last. Go not from your place this time at least without first making a firm resolution; and let everyone who hears my voice make this resolution by himself and for himself, just as if he were alone and had to do everything alone. If very many individuals think in this way, there will soon be formed a large community which will be fused into a single close-connected force. But if, on the contrary, each one, leaving himself out, puts his hope in the rest and leaves the matter to others, then there will be no others, and all together will remain as they were before. Make it on the spot, this resolution.

*　　*　　*

To all you Germans, whatever position you may occupy in society, these addresses solemnly appeal; let every one of you, who can think, think first of all about the subject here suggested, and let each do for it what lies nearest to him individually in the position he occupies.

Your forefathers unite themselves with these addresses, and make a solemn appeal to you. Think that in my voice there are mingled the voices of your ancestors of the hoary past, who with their own bodies stemmed the onrush of Roman world-dominion, who with their blood won the independence of those mountains, plains, and rivers which under you have fallen a prey to the foreigner. They call to you: "Act for us; let the memory of us which you hand on to posterity be just as honourable and without reproach as it was when it came to you, when you took pride in it and in your descent from us. Until now, the resistance we made has been regarded as great and wise and noble; we seemed the consecrated and the inspired in the divine world-purpose. If our race dies out with you, our honour will be turned to shame and our wisdom to foolishness. For if, indeed, the German stock is to be swallowed up in Roman civilization, it were better that it had fallen before the Rome of old than before a Rome of today. The former we resisted and conquered; by the latter you have been ground to dust. Seeing that this is so, you shall now not conquer them with temporal weapons; your spirit alone shall rise up against them and stand erect. To you has fallen the greater destiny, to found the empire of the spirit and of reason, and completely to annihilate the rule of brute physical force in the world. If you do this, then you are worthy of your descent from us."

Then, too, there mingle with these voices the spirits of your more recent forefathers, those who fell in the holy war for the freedom of belief and of religion. "Save our honour too," they cry to you. "To us it was not entirely clear what we fought for; besides the lawful resolve not to let ourselves be dictated to by external force in matters of conscience, there was another and a higher spirit driving us, which never fully revealed itself to us. To you it is revealed, this spirit, if you have the power of vision in the spiritual world; it beholds you with eyes clear and sublime. The varied and confused mixture of sensuous and spiritual motives that has hitherto ruled the world shall be displaced, and spirit alone, pure and freed from all sensuous motives, shall take the helm of human affairs. It was in order that this spirit might have freedom to develop and grow to independent existence—it was for this that we poured forth our blood. It is for you to justify and give meaning to our sacrifice, by setting this spirit to fulfil its purpose and to rule the world. If this does not come about as the final goal to which the whole previous development of our nation has been tending, then the battles we fought will turn out to be a vain and fleeting farce, and the freedom of conscience and of spirit that we won is a vain word, if from now onwards spirit and conscience are to be no more."

*   *   *

All ages, all wise and good men who have ever breathed upon this earth, all their thoughts and intuitions of something loftier, mingle with these voices and surround you and lift up imploring hands to you; even, if one may say so, providence and the divine plan in creating a race of men, a plan which exists only to be thought out by men and to be brought by men into the actual world—the divine plan, I say, solemnly appeals to you to save its honour and its existence. Whether those were right who believed that mankind must always grow better, and that thoughts of a true order and worth of man were no idle dreams, but the prophecy and pledge of the real world that is to be—whether they are to be proved right, or those who continue to slumber in an animal and vegetable existence and mock at every flight into higher worlds—to give a final and decisive judgment on this point is a work for you. The old world with its glory and its greatness, as well as its defects, has fallen by its own unworthiness and by the violence of your fathers. If there is truth in what has been expounded in these addresses, then are you of all modern peoples the one in whom the seed of human perfection most unmistakably lies, and to whom the lead in its development is committed. If you perish in this your essential nature, then there perishes together with you every hope of the whole human race for salvation from the depths of its miseries. Do not console yourselves with an opinion based on thin air and depending on the mere recurrence of cases that have already happened; do not hope that when the old civilization has fallen a new one will arise once more out of a semi-barbarous nation on the ruins of the first. In ancient times there was such a people in existence, equipped with every requirement for such a destiny and quite well known to the civilized people, who have left us their description of it; and they themselves, if they had been able to imagine their own downfall, would have been able to discover in this people the means of reconstruction. To us the whole surface of the globe is also quite well known and all the peoples that dwell thereon. But do we know a people akin to the ancestral stock of the modern world, of whom we may have the same expectation? I think that everyone who does not merely base his hopes and beliefs on idle dreaming, but investigates thoroughly and thinks, will be bound to answer this question with a NO. There is, therefore, no way out; if you go under, all humanity goes under with you, without hope of any future restoration.

This it was, gentlemen, which at the end of these addresses I wanted and was bound to impress upon you, who to me are the representatives of the nation, and through you upon the whole nation.

Review Questions

1. How does Fichte define the nation? What is the significance of Fichte's stress on continuity between contemporary Germans and their forefathers?
2. What is the relationship of Fichte's nationalism to humanity?

Adam Mickiewicz

from *The Books of the Polish Nation*

The Polish uprising of 1830–31 against Russian imperial control produced an outpouring of sympathy in western Europe. Adam Mickiewicz (1798–1855), a Polish patriot living in Paris, wrote the following moral account of Polish nationhood in 1832. The heroic epic typifies the histrionic nature of patriotic Romantic verse, but the interpretation is especially significant in its attempt to breathe religious spirituality into the cause of Polish nationalism.

From *Konrad Wallenrod and Other Writings*, translated by Jewel Parish and others (Berkeley, CA: University of California Press, 1925), pp. 133–43.

In the beginning there was belief in one God, and there was freedom in the world. And there were no laws, only the will of God, and there were no lords and slaves, only patriarchs and their children.

But later the people denied the one God, and made for themselves idols, and bowed themselves down to them, and slew in their honor bloody offerings, and waged war for the honor of their idols.

Therefore God sent upon the idolaters the greatest punishment, which is slavery.

*   *   *

GREECE EXPIRING ON THE RUINS OF MISSOLONGHI (1826)   EUGÈNE DELACROIX

Many nationalist movements in Europe fashioned the Greek struggle for emancipation against the Ottoman Empire in the 1820s as a romantic, epic struggle for national freedom and statehood. And in a period of reaction and censorship in Europe, artists, authors, and poets used Greek emancipation and the pan-Hellenic movement as larger metaphors for the political aspirations of liberal nationalism throughout Europe. Eugène Delacroix painted a number of allegories of Greek enslavement in the 1820s; this painting was inspired by the fall of the Greek fortress to Missolonghi Turkish forces. In personifying Greece as the female figure in the foreground, what does Delacroix imply about the nature of nation-statehood?

Finally in idolatrous Europe there rose three rulers; the name of the first was *Frederick the Second* of Prussia, the name of the second was *Catherine the Second* of Russia, the name of the third was *Maria Theresa* of Austria.

And this was a Satanic trinity, contrary to the Divine Trinity, and was in the manner of a mock and a derision of all that is holy.

Frederick, whose name signifieth *friend of peace,* contrived wars and pillage throughout his whole life, and was like Satan eternally panting for war, who in derision should be called Christ, the God of peace.

*   *   *

Now *Catherine* signifieth in Greek pure, but she was the lewdest of women, and it was as though the shameless Venus had called herself a pure virgin.

And this Catherine assembled a council for the establishing of laws, that she might turn lawmaking into a mockery, for the rights of her neighbors she overthrew and destroyed.

And this Catherine proclaimed that she protected freedom of conscience or tolerance, that she might make a mock of freedom of conscience, for she forced millions of her neighbors to change their faith. And *Maria Theresa* bore the name of the most meek and immaculate Mother of the Savior, that she might make a mock of humility and holiness.

For she was a proud she-devil, and carried on war to make subject the lands of others.

*   *   *

Then this trinity, seeing that not yet were the people sufficiently foolish and corrupt, fashioned a new idol, the most abominable of all, and they called this idol *Interest,* and this idol was not known among the pagans of old.

*   *   *

But the Polish nation alone did not bow down to the new idol, and did not have in its language the expression for christening it in Polish, neither for christening its worshipers, whom it calls by the French word *egoists.*

The Polish nation worshiped God, knowing that he who honoreth God giveth honor to everything that is good.

The Polish nation then from the beginning to the end was true to the God of its ancestors.

Its kings and men of knightly rank never assaulted any believing nation, but defended Christendom from the pagans and barbarians who brought slavery.

And the Polish kings went to the defense of Christians in distant lands, King Wladislaw to Varna, and King Jan to Vienna, to the defense of the east and the west.

And never did their kings and men of knightly rank seize neighboring lands by force, but they received the nations into brotherhood, uniting them with themselves by the gracious gift of faith and freedom.

And God rewarded them, for a great nation, Lithuania, united itself with Poland, as husband with wife, two souls in one body. And there was never before this such a union of nations. But hereafter there shall be.

For that union and marriage of Lithuania and Poland is the symbol of the future union of all Christian peoples in the name of faith and freedom.

And God gave unto the Polish kings and knights freedom, that all might be called brothers, both the richest and the poorest. And such freedom never was before. But hereafter there shall be.

The king and the men of knightly rank received into their brotherhood still more people; they received whole armies and whole tribes. And the number of brothers became as great as a nation, and in no nation were there so many people free and calling each other brothers as in Poland.

And finally, on the Third of May, the king and the knightly body determined to make all Poles brothers, at first the burghers and later the peasants.

And they called the brothers the nobility, because they had become noble, that is, had become brothers with the Lachs, who were men free and equal.

And they wished to bring it about that every Christian in Poland should be ennobled and called a Nobleman, for a token that he should have a noble soul and always be ready to die for freedom.

Just as of old they called each man accepting the gospel a Christian, for a token that he was ready to shed his blood for Christ.

Nobility then was to be the baptism of freedom, and every one who was ready to die for freedom was to be baptized of the law and of the sword.

And finally Poland said: "Whosoever will come to me shall be free and equal, for I am FREEDOM."

But the kings when they heard of this were terrified in their hearts and said: "We banished freedom from the earth; but lo, it returneth in the person of a just nation, that doth not bow down to our idols! Come, let us slay this nation." And they plotted treachery among themselves.

And the King of Prussia came and kissed the Polish Nation and greeted it, saying: "My ally," but already he had sold it for thirty cities of Great Poland, even as Judas for thirty pieces of silver.

And the two other rulers fell upon and bound the Polish Nation. And Gaul was judge and said: "Verily I find no fault in this nation, and France my wife, a timid woman, is tormented with evil dreams; nevertheless, take for yourselves and martyr this nation." And he washed his hands.

And the ruler of France said: "We cannot ransom this innocent nation by our blood or by our money, for my blood and my money belong to me, but the blood and money of my nation belong to my nation."

And this ruler uttered the last blasphemy against Christ, for Christ taught that the blood of the Son of Man belongeth to all our brother men.

And when the ruler had uttered these words, then the crosses fell from the towers of the godless capital, for the sign of Christ could no longer shine upon a people worshiping the idol *Interest*.

And this ruler was called Casimir-Périer, a Slavic first name and a Roman last name. His first name signifieth corrupter or annihilator of peace, and his last name signifieth, from the word *perire* or *périr*, destroyer or son of destruction. And these two names are anti-Christian. And they shall be alike accursed among the Slavic race and among the Roman race.

And this man rent the league of peoples as that Jewish priest rent his clothes upon hearing the voice of Christ.

And they martyred the Polish Nation and laid it in the grave, and the kings cried out: "We have slain and we have buried Freedom."

But they cried out foolishly, for in committing the last sin they filled up the measure of their iniquities, and their power was coming to an end at the time when they exulted most.

For the Polish Nation did not die: its body lieth in the grave, but its spirit hath descended from the earth, that is, from public life, to the abyss, that is to the private life of people who suffer slavery in their country and outside of their country, that it may see their sufferings.

But on the third day the soul shall return to the body, and the Nation shall arise and free all the peoples of Europe from slavery.

And already two days have gone by. One day passed with the first capture of Warsaw, and the second day passed with the second capture of Warsaw, and the third day shall begin, but shall not pass.

And as after the resurrection of Christ bloody offerings ceased in all the world, so after the resurrection of the Polish Nation wars shall cease in all Christendom.

REVIEW QUESTIONS

1. Why is the text's biblical cadence significant?
2. According to Mickiewicz, how does Christianity serve the cause of Polish nationalism?
3. How does the author recount Poland's plight in the history of eastern Europe?

GIUSEPPE MAZZINI

FROM *Duties of Man*

Giuseppe Mazzini (1805–1872) was one of the best-known liberal national revolutionaries of the nineteenth century. Mazzini achieved international renown for his founding of Young Italy in 1831, an organization that strove for an Italian republic and that spawned the parallel associations Young Poland, Young Germany, and Young Ireland. In 1849 Mazzini assisted Garibaldi in defending the Roman republic, and after its defeat he was compelled to flee Italy. In exile he continued his efforts as a writer for a unified Italian republic. The eventual unification of Italy during the period 1859–71 brought him little satisfaction, because it was realized under the conservative political settlement of a constitutional monarchy. His Duties of Man, *first begun in weekly installments in 1840, best characterized Mazzini's liberal-democratic humanitarian spirit, which endowed the nationalism of this period with an ethical core.*

From "Duties of Man," by Giuseppe Mazzini, translated by Ella Noyes (1870), as reprinted in *The Liberal Tradition in European Thought*, edited by David Sidorsky (New York: Putnam, 1970).

To the Italian Working Class

To you, sons and daughters of the people, I dedicate this little book, wherein I have pointed out the principles in the name and strength of which you may, if you so will, accomplish your mission in Italy; a mission of republican progress for all and of emancipation for yourselves. Let those who are specially favoured by circumstances or in understanding, and able to comprehend these principles more easily, explain and comment on them to the others, and may that spirit of love inspire them with which, as I wrote, I thought on your griefs and on your virgin aspirations towards the new life which—once the unjust inequality now stifling your faculties is overcome—you will kindle in the Italian country.

I loved you from my first years. The republican instincts of my mother taught me to seek out among my fellows the Man, not the merely rich and powerful individual; and the simple unconscious virtue of my father accustomed me to admire, rather than conceited and pretentious

semi-knowledge, the silent and unnoticed virtue of self-sacrifice so often found in you. Later on I gathered from the history of our country that the true life of Italy is the life of the people, and that the slow work of the centuries has constantly tended, amid the shock of different races and the superficial transitory changes wrought by usurpations and conquests, to prepare the great democratic National Unity. . . .

DUTIES TO COUNTRY

Your first Duties—first, at least, in importance—are, as I have told you, to Humanity. You are *men* before you are *citizens* or *fathers*. If you do not embrace the whole human family in your love, if you do not confess your faith in its unity —consequent on the unity of God—and in the brotherhood of the Peoples who are appointed to reduce that unity for fact—if wherever one of your fellowmen groans, wherever the dignity of human nature is violated by falsehood or tyranny, you are not prompt, being able, to succour that wretched one, or do not feel yourself called, being able, to fight for the purpose of relieving the deceived or oppressed—you disobey your law of life, or do not comprehend the religion which will bless the future.

But what can *each* of you, with his isolated powers, *do* for the moral improvement, for the progress of Humanity? . . . God gave you this means when he gave you a Country, when, like a wise overseer of labour, who distributes the different parts of the work according to the capacity of the workmen, he divided Humanity into distinct groups upon the face of our globe, and thus planted the seeds of nations. Bad governments have disfigured the design of God, which you may see clearly marked out, as far, at least, as regards Europe, by the courses of the great rivers, by the lines of the lofty mountains, and by other geographical conditions; they have disfigured it by conquest, by greed, by jealousy of the just sovereignty of others; disfigured it so much that today there is perhaps no nation except England and France whose confines correspond to this design. They did not, and they do not, recognise any country except their own families and dynasties, the egoism of caste. But the divine design will infallibly be fulfilled. Natural divisions, the innate spontaneous tendencies of the people will replace the arbitrary divisions sanctioned by bad governments. The map of Europe will be remade. The Countries of the People will rise, defined by the voice of the free, upon the ruins of the Countries of Kings and privileged castes. Between these Countries there will be harmony and brotherhood. And then the work of Humanity for the general amelioration, for the discovery and application of the real law of life, carried on in association and distributed according to local capacities, will be accomplished by peaceful and progressive development; then each of you, strong in the affections and in the aid of many millions of men speaking the same language, endowed with the same tendencies, and educated by the same historic tradition, may hope by your personal effort to benefit the whole of Humanity.

To you, who have been born in Italy, God has allotted, as if favouring you specially, the best-defined country in Europe. In other lands, marked by more uncertain or more interrupted limits, questions may arise which the pacific vote of all will one day solve, but which have cost, and will yet perhaps cost, tears and blood; in yours, no. God has stretched round you sublime and indisputable boundaries; on one side the highest mountains of Europe, the Alps; on the other the sea, the immeasurable sea. Take a map of Europe and place one point of a pair of compasses in the north of Italy on Parma; point the other to the mouth of the Var, and describe a semicircle with it in the direction of the Alps; this point, which will fall, when the semicircle is completed, upon the mouth of the Isonzo, will have marked the frontier which God has given you. As far as this frontier your language is spoken and understood; beyond this you have no rights. Sicily, Sardinia, Corsica, and the smaller islands between them and the mainland of Italy belong undeniably to you. Brute force may for a little while contest these frontiers with you, but they have been recognised from of old by the tacit general consent of the peoples; and the day when, rising with one accord for the final trial, you plant your tricoloured flag upon that frontier, the whole of Europe will acclaim re-risen Italy, and receive her into the community of the nations. To this final trial all your efforts must be directed.

Without Country you have neither name, token, voice, nor rights, no admission as brothers into the fellowship of the Peoples. You are the bastards of Humanity. Soldiers without a banner, Israelites among the nations, you will find neither faith nor protection; none will be sureties for you. Do not beguile yourselves with the hope of emancipation from unjust social conditions if you do not first conquer a Country for yourselves; where there is no Country there is no common agreement to which you can appeal; the egoism of self-interest rules alone, and he who has the upper hand keeps it, since there is no common safeguard for the interests of all. Do not be led away by the idea of improving your material conditions without first solving the national question. You cannot do it. Your industrial associations and mutual help societies are useful as a means of educating and disciplining yourselves; as an economic fact they will remain barren until you have an Italy. The economic problem demands, first and foremost, an increase of capital and production; and while your Country is dismembered into separate fragments—while shut off by the barrier of customs and artificial difficulties of every sort, you have only restricted markets open to you—you cannot hope for this increase. Today—do not delude yourselves—you are not the working-class of Italy; you are only fractions of that class; powerless, unequal to the great task which you propose to yourselves. Your emancipation can have no practical beginning until a National Government, understanding the signs of the times, shall, seated in Rome, formulate a Declaration of Principles to be the guide for Italian progress, and shall insert into it these words, *Labour is sacred, and is the source of the wealth of Italy.*

Do not be led astray, then, by hopes of material progress which in your present conditions can only be illusions. Your Country alone, the vast and rich Italian Country, which stretches from the Alps to the farthest limit of Sicily, can fulfil these hopes. You cannot obtain your *rights* except by obeying the commands of *Duty*. Be worthy of them, and you will have them. O my Brothers! love your Country. Our Country is our home, the home which God has given us, placing therein a numerous family which we love and are loved by, and with which we have a more intimate and quicker communion of feeling and thought than with others; a family which by its concentration upon a given spot, and by the homogeneous nature of its elements, is destined for a special kind of activity. Our Country is our field of labour; the products of our activity must go forth from it for the benefit of the whole earth; but the instruments of labour which we can use best and most effectively exist in it, and we may not reject them without being unfaithful to God's purpose and diminishing our own strength. In labouring according to true principles for our Country we are labouring for Humanity; our Country is the fulcrum of the lever which we have to wield for the common good. If we give up this fulcrum we run the risk of becoming useless to our Country and to Humanity. Before *associating* ourselves with the Nations which compose Humanity we must exist as a Nation. There can be no association except among equals; and you have no recognised collective existence.

Humanity is a great army moving to the conquest of unknown lands, against powerful and wary enemies. The Peoples are the different corps and divisions of that army. Each has a post entrusted to it; each a special operation to perform; and the common victory depends on the exactness with which the different operations are carried out. Do not disturb the order of the battle. Do not abandon the banner which God has given you. Wherever you may be, into the midst of whatever people circumstances may have driven you, fight for the liberty of that people if the moment calls for it; but fight as Italians, so that the blood which you shed may win honour and love, not for you only, but for your Country. And may the constant thought of your soul be for Italy, may all the acts of your life be worthy of her, and may the standard beneath which you range yourselves to work for Humanity be Italy's. Do not say *I*; say *we*. Be every one of you an incarnation of your Country, and feel himself and make himself responsible for his fellow-countrymen; let each one of you learn to act in such a way that in him men shall respect and love his Country.

Your Country is one and indivisible. As the members of a family cannot rejoice at the common table if one of their number is far away, snatched from the affection of his brothers, so you should have no joy or repose as long as a portion of the territory upon which your language is spoken is separated from the Nation.

*   *   *

A Country is a fellowship of free and equal men bound together in a brotherly concord of labour towards a single end. You must make it and maintain it such. A Country is not an aggregation, it is an *association*. There is no true Country without a uniform right. There is no true Country where the uniformity of that right is violated by the existence of caste, privilege, and inequality—where the powers and faculties of a large number of individuals are suppressed or dormant—where there is no common principle accepted, recognised, and developed by all. In such a state of things there can be no Nation, no People, but only a multitude, a fortuitous agglomeration of men whom circumstances have brought together and different circumstances will separate. In the name of your love of your Country you must combat without truce the existence of every privilege, every inequality, upon the soil which has given you birth.

*   *   *

The laws made by one fraction of the citizens only can never by the nature of things and men do otherwise than reflect the thoughts and aspirations and desires of that fraction; they represent, not the whole country, but a third, a fourth part, a class, a zone of the country. The law must express the general aspiration, promote the good of all, respond to a beat of the nation's heart. The whole nation therefore should be, directly or indirectly, the legislator. By yielding this mission to a few men, you put the egoism of one class in the place of the Country, which is the union of *all* the classes.

A Country is not a mere territory; the particular territory is only its foundation. The Country is the idea which rises upon that foundation; it is the sentiment of love, the sense of fellowship which binds together all the sons of that territory. So long as a single one of your brothers is not represented by his own vote in the development of the national life—so long as a single one vegetates uneducated among the educated—so long as a single one able and willing to work languishes in poverty for want of work—you have not got a Country such as it ought to be, the Country of all and for all. *Votes, education, work* are the three main pillars of the nation; do not rest until your hands have solidly erected them.

*   *   *

REVIEW QUESTIONS

1. How is Mazzini's nationalism related to the larger issue of humanity?
2. For Mazzini what is necessary to achieve progress in humanity?
3. How does Mazzini define a country?
4. Why might Mazzini's nationalism be termed utopian?

OTTO VON BISMARCK

FROM *The Memoirs*

Otto von Bismarck (1815–1898), a Prussian noble, served the Prussian crown as its premier statesman from 1862 to 1890. Under his aegis, Prussia united Germany, creating in 1871 the German Empire, a nation-state whose power and size significantly altered the European state system. Prussia's bid to unite Germany brought armed conflict with Austria in 1866. Yet Prussia's military victory was only partly successful, for Prussia's role as unifier could become legitimate only with popular support. On the eve of war with Austria, Bismarck promulgated a constitution that included a bicameral legislation and universal male suffrage, a political move that sought to shift public opinion in favor of Prussia. The move achieved the intended effect, enabling Bismarck to sever the once-indivisible bond between nationalism and liberalism. The following passage, written at the end of his life, throws light on a conservative's views of popular politics and nationalism.

From *The Memoirs*, by Otto von Bismarck, translated by A. J. Butler (New York: Fertig, 1890).

*   *   *

Looking to the necessity, in a fight against an overwhelming foreign Power, of being able, in extreme need, to use even revolutionary means, I had had no hesitation whatever in throwing into the frying-pan, by means of the circular dispatch of June 10, 1866, the most powerful ingredient known at that time to liberty-mongers, namely, universal suffrage, so as to frighten off foreign monarchies from trying to stick a finger into our national omelette. I never doubted that the German people would be strong and clever enough to free themselves from the existing suffrage as soon as they realised that it was a harmful institution. If it cannot, then my saying that Germany can ride when once it has got into the saddle was erroneous. The acceptance of universal suffrage was a weapon in the war against Austria and other foreign countries, in the war for German Unity, as well as a threat to use the last weapons in a struggle against coalitions. In a war of this sort, when it becomes a matter of life and death, one does not look at the weapons that one seizes, nor the value of what one destroys in using them: one is guided at the moment by no other thought than the issue of the war, and the preservation of one's external independence; the settling of affairs and reparation of the damage has to take place after the peace. Moreover, I still hold that the principle of universal suffrage is a just one, not only in theory but also in practice, provided always that voting be not secret, for secrecy is a quality that is indeed incompatible with the best characteristics of German blood.

The influence and the dependence on others that the practical life of man brings in its train are God-given realities which we cannot and must not ignore. If we refuse to transfer them to political life, and base that life on a faith in the secret in sight of everybody, we fall into a contradiction between public law and the realities of human life which practically leads to constant frictions, and finally to an explosion, and to which there is no theoretical solution except by way of the insanities of social-democracy, the support given to which rests on the fact that the judgment of the masses is sufficiently stultified and undeveloped to allow them, with the assistance of their own greed, to be continually caught by the rhetoric of clever and ambitious leaders.

The counterpoise to this lies in the influence of the educated classes, which would be greatly strengthened if voting were public, as for the Prussian Diet. It may be that the greater discretion of the more intelligent classes rests on the material basis of the preservation of their possessions. The other motive, the struggle for gain, is equally justifiable; but a preponderance of those who represent property is more serviceable for the security and development of the state. A state, the control of which lies in the hands of the greedy, of the *novarum rerum cupidi*, and of orators who have in a higher degree than others the capacity for deceiving the unreasoning masses, will constantly be doomed to a restlessness of development, which so ponderous a mass as the commonwealth of the state cannot follow without injury to its organism. Ponderous masses, and among these the life and development of great nations must be reckoned, can only move with caution, since the road on which they travel to an unknown future has no smooth iron rails. Every great state-commonwealth that loses the prudent and restraining influence of

BATTLE OF NATIONS MONUMENT IN LEIPZIG (1913)

Modern nation-states require mass civic participation to claim the legitimacy of nations and the states that rule in their name. In this regard, national monuments became important components of nineteenth-century national movements, acting as physical markers and sacred spaces of collective national memory. The Battle of Nations Monument in Leipzig, Germany, illustrates well the function of national monuments in late nineteenth-century Europe. Designed by Bruno Schmitz and constructed between 1894 and 1913, this structure not only commemorates the important milestone for German nationhood—the defeat of Napoleon in 1813—but also is a pantheon of German heroes and nation builders. What characteristics do this monument and its surrounding space project about the German nation?

the propertied class, whether that influence rests on material or moral grounds, will always end by being rushed along at a speed which must shatter the coach of state, as happened in the development of the French Revolution. The element of greed has the preponderance arising from large masses which in the long run must make its way. It is in the interests of the great mass itself to wish decision to take place without dangerous acceleration of the speed of the coach of state, and without its destruction. If this should happen, however, the wheel of history will revolve again, and always in a proportionately shorter time, to dictatorship, to despotism, to absolutism, because in the end the masses yield to the need of order; if they do not recognise this need *a priori,* they always realise it eventually after manifold arguments *ad hominem;* and in order to purchase order from a dictatorship and Caesarism they cheerfully sacrifice that justifiable amount of freedom which ought to be maintained, and which the political society of Europe can endure without ill-health.

I should regard it as a serious misfortune, and as an essential weakening of our security in the future, if we in Germany are driven into the vortex of this French cycle. Absolutism would be the ideal form of government for an European political structure were not the King and his officials ever as other men are to whom it is not given to reign with superhuman wisdom, insight and justice. The most experienced and well-meaning absolute rulers are subject to human imperfections, such as overestimation of their own wisdom, the influence and eloquence of favourites, not to mention petticoat influence, legitimate and illegitimate. Monarchy and the most ideal monarch, if in his idealism he is not to be a common danger, stand in need of criticism; the thorns of criticism set him right when he runs the risk of losing his way. Joseph II is a warning example of this.

Criticism can only be exercised through the medium of a free press and parliaments in the modern sense of the term. Both correctives may easily weaken, and finally lose their efficacy if they abuse their powers. To avert this is one of the tasks of a conservative policy, which cannot be accomplished without a struggle with parliament and press. The measuring of the limits within which such a struggle must be confined, if the control of the government, which is indispensable to the country, is neither to be checked nor allowed to gain a complete power, is a question of political tact and judgment.

It is a piece of good fortune for his country if a monarch possess the judgment requisite for this—a good fortune that is temporary, it is true, like all human fortune. The possibility of establishing ministers in power who possess adequate qualifications must always be granted in the constitutional organism; but also the possibility of maintaining in office ministers who satisfy these requirements in face of occasional votes of an adverse majority and of the influence of courts and camarillas. This aim, so far as human imperfections in general allow its attainment, was approximately reached under the government of William I.

*　　*　　*

Review Questions

1. What was Bismarck's opinion of universal suffrage?
2. What political system and balance of social forces did Bismarck advocate?
3. Why is Bismarck often viewed as a conservative revolutionary?

ERNEST RENAN

What Is a Nation?

First delivered as a lecture in 1882 at the University of Paris, this essay by Ernest Renan (1823–1892), a prolific French author on philosophical and historical subjects, provided a remarkably detached critique of theories that defined and legitimized European nationalisms. By dismantling the dominant explanations of nationalism of his time, Renan led the way toward viewing nations as cultural entities willed into existence by the "daily plebiscite" of believing communities. For Renan, nations had less to do with authentic historical development than with the contemporary cultural needs of social groups seeking an idealistic collective identity. For this reason Renan's argument has greatly influenced contemporary theories on nationalism.

From *What Is a Nation?*, by Ernest Renan, edited by Homi K. Bhabba, translated by Martin Thom (London: Routledge, 1990), pp. 42, 46–54.

What I propose to do today is to analyse with you an idea which, though seemingly clear, lends itself to the most dangerous misunderstandings. * * *

*   *   *

If one were to believe some political theorists, a nation is above all a dynasty, representing an earlier conquest, one which was first of all accepted, and then forgotten by the mass of the people. According to the above-mentioned theorists, the grouping of provinces effected by a dynasty, by its wars, its marriages, and its treaties, ends with the dynasty which had established it. It is quite true that the majority of modern nations were made by a family of feudal origin, which had contracted a marriage with the soil and which was in some sense a nucleus of centralization. France's frontiers in 1789 had nothing either natural or necessary about them. The wide zone that the House of Capet had added to the narrow strip of land granted by the partition of Verdun was indeed the personal acquisition of this House. During the epoch when these acquisitions were made, there was no idea of natural frontiers, nor of the rights of nations, nor of the will of provinces. The union of England, Ireland, and Scotland was likewise a dynastic fact. Italy only tarried so long before becoming a nation because, among its numerous reigning houses, none, prior to the present century, constituted itself as the centre of [its] unity. Strangely enough, it was through the obscure island of Sardinia, a land that was scarcely Italian, that [the house of Savoy] assumed a royal title. Holland, which—through an act of heroic resolution—created itself, has nevertheless contracted an intimate marriage with the House of Orange, and it will run real dangers the day this union is compromised.

Is such a law, however, absolute? It undoubtedly is not. Switzerland and the United States, which have formed themselves, like conglomerates, by successive additions, have no dynastic basis. I shall not discuss this question in relation to France, for I would need to be able to read the secrets of the future in order to do so. Let me simply say that so loftily national had this great French royal principle been that, on the morrow of its fall, the nation was able to stand without her. Furthermore, the eighteenth century had changed everything. Man had returned, after centuries of abasement, to the spirit of antiquity, to [a sense of] respect for himself, to the idea of his own rights. The words *patrie* and citizen had recovered their former meanings. Thus it was that the boldest operation ever yet put into effect in history was brought to completion, an operation which one might compare with the attempt, in physiology, to restore to its original identity a body from which one had removed the brain and the heart.

It must therefore be admitted that a nation can exist without a dynastic principle, and even that nations which have been formed by dynasties can be separated from them without therefore ceasing to exist. The old principle, which only takes account of the right of princes, could no longer be maintained; apart from dynastic right, there is also national right. Upon what criterion, however, should one base this national right? By what sign should one know it? From what tangible fact can one derive it?

Several confidently assert that it is derived from race. The artificial divisions, resulting from feudalism, from princely marriages, from diplomatic congresses are, [these authors assert], in a state of decay. It is a population's race which remains firm and fixed. This is what constitutes a right, a legitimacy. The Germanic family, according to the theory I am expounding here, has the right to reassemble the scattered limbs of the Germanic order, even when these limbs are not asking to be joined together again. The right of the Germanic order over such-and-such a province is stronger than the right of the inhabitants of that province over themselves. There is thus created a kind of primordial right analogous to the divine right of kings: an ethnographic principle is substituted for a national one. This is a very great error, which, if it were to become dominant, would destroy European civilization. The primordial right of races is as narrow and as perilous for genuine progress as the national principle is just and legitimate.

*   *   *

The truth is that there is no pure race and that to make politics depend upon ethnographic analysis is to surrender it to a chimera. The noblest countries, England, France, and Italy, are those where the blood is the most mixed. Is Germany an exception in this respect? Is it a purely Germanic country? This is a complete illusion. The whole of the south was once Gallic; the whole of the east, from the river Elbe on, is Slav. Even those parts which are claimed to be really pure, are they in fact so? We touch here on one of those problems in regard to which it is of the utmost importance that we equip ourselves with clear ideas and ward off misconceptions.

*   *   *

The fact of race, which was originally crucial, thus becomes increasingly less important. Human history is essentially different from zoology, and race is not everything, as it is among the rodents or the felines, and one does not have the right to go through the world fingering people's skulls, and taking them by the throat saying: "You are of our blood; you belong to us!" Aside from anthropological characteristics, there are such things as reason, justice, the true, and the beautiful, which are the same for all. Be on your guard, for this ethnographic politics is in no way a stable thing and, if today you use it against others, tomorrow you may see it turned against yourselves. Can you be sure that the Germans, who have raised the banner of ethnography so high, will not see the Slavs in their turn analyse the names of villages in Saxony and Lusatia, search for any traces of the Wiltzes or of the Obotrites, and demand recompense for the massacres and the wholesale enslavements that the Ottoss inflicted upon their ancestors? It is good for everyone to know how to forget.

*   *   *

What we have just said of race applies to language too. Language invites people to unite, but it does not force them to do so. The United States and England, Latin America and Spain, speak the same languages yet do not form single nations. Conversely, Switzerland, so well made, since she was made with the consent of her different parts, numbers three or four languages. There is something in man which is superior to language, namely, the will. The will of Switzerland to be united, in spite of the diversity of her dialects, is a fact of far greater importance than a similitude often obtained by various vexatious measures.

* * *

Religion cannot supply an adequate basis for the constitution of a modern nationality either. Originally, religion had to do with the very existence of the social group, which was itself an extension of the family. Religion and the rites were family rites. * * *

* * * In our own time, the situation is perfectly clear. There are no longer masses that believe in a perfectly uniform manner. Each person believes and practises in his own fashion what he is able to and as he wishes. There is no longer a state religion; one can be French, English, or German, and be either Catholic, Protestant, or orthodox Jewish, or else practise no cult at all. Religion has become an individual matter; it concerns the conscience of each person. The division of nations into Catholics and Protestants no longer exists. Religion, which, fifty-two years ago, played so substantial a part in the formation of Belgium, preserves all of its [former] importance in the inner tribunal of each; but it has ceased almost entirely to be one of the elements which serve to define the frontiers of peoples.

A community of interest is assuredly a powerful bond between men. Do interests, however, suffice to make a nation? I do not think so. Community of interest brings about trade agreements, but nationality has a sentimental side to it; it is both soul and body at once; a *Zollverein* is not a *patrie*.

* * *

A nation is a soul, a spiritual principle. Two things, which in truth are but one, constitute this soul or spiritual principle. One lies in the past, one in the present. One is the possession in common of a rich legacy of memories; the other is present-day consent, the desire to live together, the will to perpetuate the value of the heritage that one has received in an undivided form. Man, Gentlemen, does not improvise. The nation, like the individual, is the culmination of a long past of endeavours, sacrifice, and devotion. Of all cults, that of the ancestors is the most legitimate, for the ancestors have made us what we are. A heroic past, great men, glory (by which I understand genuine glory), this is the social capital upon which one bases a national idea. To have common glories in the past and to have a common will in the present; to have performed great deeds together, to wish to perform still more—these are the essential conditions for being a people. One loves in proportion to the sacrifices to which one has consented, and in proportion to the ills that one has suffered. One loves the house that one has built and that one has handed down. The Spartan song—"We are what you were; we will be what you are"—is, in its simplicity, the abridged hymn of every *patrie*.

More valuable by far than common customs posts and frontiers conforming to strategic ideas is the fact of sharing, in the past, a glorious heritage and regrets, and of having, in the future, [a shared] programme to put into effect, or the fact of having suffered, enjoyed, and hoped together. These are the kinds of things that can be understood in spite of differences of race and language. I spoke just now of "having suffered together" and, indeed, suffering in common unifies more than joy does. Where national memories are concerned, griefs are of more value than triumphs, for they impose duties, and require a common effort.

A nation is therefore a large-scale solidarity, constituted by the feeling of the sacrifices that one has made in the past and of those that one is prepared to make in the future. It presupposes a past; it is summarized, however, in the present by a tangible fact, namely, consent, the clearly expressed desire to continue a common life. A nation's existence is, if you will pardon the metaphor, a daily plebiscite, just as an individual's existence is a perpetual affirmation of life. That, I know full well, is less metaphysical than divine right and less brutal than so-called historical rights. According to the ideas that I am outlining to you, a nation has no more right than a king does to say to a province: "You belong to me. I am seizing you." A province, as far as I am concerned, is its inhabitants; if anyone has the right to be consulted in such an affair, it is the inhabitant. A nation never has any real interest in annexing or holding on to a country against its will. The wish of nations is, all in all, the sole legitimate criterion, the one to which one must always return.

*   *   *

Let me sum up, Gentlemen. Man is a slave neither of his race nor his language, nor of his religion, nor of the course of rivers nor of the direction taken by mountain chains. A large aggregate of men, healthy in mind and warm of heart, creates the kind of moral conscience which we call a nation. So long as this moral consciousness gives proof of its strength by the sacrifices which demand the abdication of the individual to the advantage of the community, it is legitimate and has the right to exist. If doubts arise regarding its frontiers, consult the populations in the areas under dispute. They undoubtedly have the right

to a say in the matter. This recommendation will bring a smile to the lips of the transcendants of politics, these infallible beings who spend their lives deceiving themselves and who, from the height of their superior principles, take pity upon our mundane concerns. "Consult the populations, for heaven's sake! How naive! A fine example of those wretched French ideas which claim to replace diplomacy and war by childishly simple methods." Wait a while, Gentlemen; let the reign of the transcendants pass; bear the scorn of the powerful with patience. It may be that, after many fruitless gropings, people will revert to our more modest empirical solutions. The best way of being right in the future is, in certain periods, to know how to resign oneself to being out of fashion.

REVIEW QUESTIONS

1. Which explanations for nationalism does Renan reject? Why?
2. How does Renan finally view nationalism? Does he reject that doctrine?
3. What implications does Renan's argument have for the making and unmaking of nation-states?

22 ❧ IMPERIALISM AND COLONIALISM, 1870–1914

The striking escalation of Europe's formal political control over other lands and peoples during the last half of the nineteenth century is often called the new imperialism. *The term refers to the West's renewed enthusiasm and drive for colonial empires—a calculus of political power, economic exploitation, and "alleged" cultural superiority—that first began in the early modern era. The earlier practice of private trading companies holding monopolistic economic and military dominion over foreign territories is best exemplified by England's East India Company (1600–1873), an enterprise that conducted lucrative trade in spices, cotton, tea, and opium on the Indian subcontinent, as well as in Asian and African territories. The shift from informal economic advantages to direct political control began slowly after 1850 but gathered a frenetic momentum in the 1870s with widespread European competition for new colonies. Following the Indian Mutiny in 1857, Britain first changed its informal economic relationship with the subcontinent by introducing direct colonial rule. Between the years 1880 and 1914 European powers radically increased their dominion in Africa, expanding their formal control of the continent from 10 to 90 percent. Similarly, by 1900 nearly all of Asia had been divided among the British, French, Dutch, Germans, and Americans. The feverish pace of colonization during this period erected unstable structures within which twentieth-century global economies, politics, and cultural exchanges would operate. Modern world history is simply inexplicable without an understanding of nineteenth-century imperialism.*

Colonies assumed a new status in European culture: economically, colonies promised cheap raw materials, high yields on investments, and markets for finished goods; culturally, they provided the points of entry for the spread of Christianity and European civilization; and politically, they signified great-power status and offered a glorious, nation-uniting mission to European publics seeking solace from contentious domestic politics. Contemporaries, however, usually perceived the various justifications for imperialism as a totality: the civilizing effects of commerce and religion followed the glory of the flag. Thus proceeded the "friendly competition" among European nations to carve up Africa and penetrate the Far East.

Prior to the First World War, Europe almost exclusively viewed imperialism in terms of its own interests and needs, presuming that non-Western peoples benefited from the "civilizing mission" of the "white man's burden." Some contemporaries, however, criticized such arrogance, pointing out the crushing "black man's burden" that had accumulated from the imperialist legacy. Similarly, Near Eastern writers took note of the large discrepancy between the West's notions of the "exotic" Orient and the lived realities of the Near East, a dichotomy explained in part by Europe's desire to articulate cultural difference between Western "civilization" and Eastern "barbarism." Indeed, the Western imperial gaze saw the world as a vast space in need of transformation. In meeting that challenge to remake the world in its own image, the West redefined itself and its role in the world.

The legacies of colonial ruling classes, imperial plantation economies, and European mass consumer markets on non-Western manufactures forever changed indigenous societies. In creating a new set of economic, political, and social relationships between the West and the world, imperialism interpenetrated and irrevocably transformed European and non-Western cultures. Metropole and colony, once separate entities, became fused over time into an imperial alloy, rendering a return to precolonial conditions impossible. For this reason the multifaceted phenomenon of imperialism is a central element of modernity. It not only defined the national and cultural identities of European states but also shaped colonials' aspirations for independence and their visions of postcolonial society.

ANONYMOUS

FROM "An Inquiry into the Rights of the East India Company of Making War and Peace" (1772)

In 1600, the English crown granted the British East India Company a charter that gave this commercial enterprise a monopoly to exploit the spice trade in India, Southeast Asia, and the East, which until the defeat of the Spanish Armada in 1588 had been the preserve of Spain and Portugal. From its earliest days, the company combined its commercial ventures with military might. To penetrate India for its spices, cotton, silk, indigo, saltpeter, and other goods, the company defeated and evicted the Portuguese in 1612 and thereafter used military force to open up trade in India's interior. Controlled exclusively by shareholders between 1600 and 1773, the company produced enormous wealth for its owners and administrators. Following the brutal conquest of Bengal in the 1750s, the company came under greater public scrutiny, leading to two government acts in 1773 and 1784 that placed the company under the supervision of Parliament. In the nineteenth century, the company lost its trade monopoly and evolved into an administrative agency of the British government. Following the Indian Mutiny in 1857, the company lost even this bureaucratic function and eventually dissolved itself in 1873. The anonymous author below, most likely a company shareholder, published this preface and letter in pamphlet form as public criticism of the company. Printed a year prior to Parliament's Regulating Act in 1773, the tract throws light on the company's extensive powers.

From *An Inquiry into the Rights of the East India Company of Making War and Peace*, by Anonymous (London: Walter Shropshire and Samuel Bladon, 1772).

Preface

It is long since the nations, which have the misfortune to live near the East-India Company's settlements, have stretched out their industrious and helpless hands to our gracious Sovereign, imploring his protection from the oppressions they were sinking under; and it must give great pleasure to every one who knows how much the interests of Great Britain are connected with those of humanity, to learn, from his Majesty's speech, at the opening of this session, that he had turned his eye to an object so worthy of the royal attention. And, surely, if there is any situation in this life more deplorable than another, it is that of living under the dominion of men, who, wholly intent upon gain, have contrived to establish the most complete system ever known of fraud and violence, by uniting, in the same persons, the several functions of Merchant, Soldier, Financier and Judge; depriving, by that union, all those functions of their mutual checks, by which alone they can be made useful to society.

It is to be hoped that the time is not far off, when those functions, so improperly combined, will be again separated: when his Majesty will resume, from those Merchants, the sword, which, by our happy Constitution, cannot be placed, with energy or safety, in any hand but his own: and when those great territorial revenues in Bengal, which

have, of late, been so extravagantly accumulated in the coffers of private men, for trifling or destructive purposes, will be employed in reducing the national debt, as well as in protecting our trade and acquisitions in those distant parts of the world. We might then hope to see an impartial administration of justice in India, without its being subject to the controul of those who are most likely to be the greatest delinquents. We might then hope to see an end to those cruel monopolies, carried on by the Servants of the Company, in the necessaries of life, and to which the wretched natives are obliged to submit, with the bayonet at their throats: and we might then hope to see those Servants once more attentive to the commercial interests of their employers; without attempting to equal, in riches and splendor, the first nobility of the kingdom. But, what is still of greater importance to the free Constitution of this country, we might then hope to see some stop put to the rapid progress of corruption at home; which has been, for some years past, so much promoted by the immense sums lavished by those Servants of the Company, upon their return from India, in order to procure themselves admittance into the House of Commons; where none of them, from the nature of their education, can be supposed to have any thing to say; and where some of them seem to come, as if they were proud of the privilege they had acquired, of mocking the insufficiency of our laws, and of insulting that honourable Assembly, by their presence.

In objection to this salutary change, it has been often urged, "That in a free country like ours, the individuals have their legal rights as well as the state; and that it is always matter of just alarm when the supreme legislative power lays its heavy hand upon those rights, even where there is reason to believe that they have been abused." In this I entirely agree. But when they proceed to tell us, "That the East-India Company have a legal right of making War and Peace, and of possessing their territorial acquisitions, without the participation or inspection of the British Government," I find myself obliged to give my dissent. The grounds of that dissent are to be found in the following Letter, written above two years ago, when Sir JOHN LINDSAY was appointed to command his Majesty's ships in the East-Indies; and though the occasion which produces it now, is somewhat different from that which at first gave birth to it; yet I have suffered it to appear before the public in its original shape; and the rather, because in that shape it recalls the memory of a transaction, by which the true spirit of the Gentlemen who have the management of the Company's affairs in Leadenhall-street, had a fair opportunity of displaying itself.

London, Feb. 18, 1772.

A Letter

You may perceive, my fellow Proprietors, that in this long letter I have said very little with regard to the expediency or utility of the proposed measure. This is owing to my having observed, that the controversy, at our last meeting, did not turn upon that point, but barely upon the impropriety of suffering any encroachment to be made upon the Company's established Rights. Were any encroachment intended upon the just or legal Rights of the Company, there is no one would be seen more forward in their defence than myself, both as a friend to the Company, and as a friend to the state. The security of private property, and of private rights of every kind, is the root of commerce, of population, of riches, and of strength in every state; and the statesman, who takes any step by which those private Rights are rendered precarious, discovers himself to be but ill qualified for the place he fills. But here is no such invasion attempted; but, on the contrary, an attempt of private persons to invade the Rights of the public, by challenging to themselves a prerogative which belongs only to the heads of kingdoms and independent Republics. I have, therefore, endeavoured to show you what are in reality the Rights of the East-India Company with regard to making peace and war, by quoting what is to be found in our several charters concerning them, and shall now recapitulate and sum up the whole, by observing:

That whatever passages are to be found in those charters concerning peace and war, are merely emanations of the royal Will and Pleasure; no such being specified in the Act of Parliament, which only authorizes King WILLIAM and his successors to grant to the Company, from time to time, by their letters patent, such powers and privileges as to him or them shall seem fitting.

That in none of these letters patent, or charters, is it said, in express terms, that the Company is absolutely empowered to make war and peace; and that what is mentioned in those charters concerning acts of hostility, is strictly confined to such acts of hostility as are for the defence of the Company's property, retaliation of injuries, or other *just cause*, the judgment of which cannot, in common sense, rest with the Company; but falls to His Majesty, the supreme Arbiter, by the British constitution, of all matters of peace and war.

That, although King WILLIAM and the succeeding Kings of England, had not expressly reserved to themselves their sovereign Right and Authority over the East-Indian settlements, and had granted to the Company the most unlimited power of making war and peace; yet could they not, by any form of words, denude themselves of that sovereign power, and could only be supposed to have delegated it to the Company, as to their Attorney or Plenipotentiary, till such time as it should be their royal pleasure to resume or limit it.

That, as by the Charters of the 13th of King GEORGE the first, and of the 27th of King GEORGE the second, the Company is authorized *to invade and destroy upon Just Cause* only, and are particularly amenable to His Majesty for any breach of their Charter in this respect, it is perfectly regular and necessary that His Majesty should have complete knowledge, from his own Officer, of the rise and progress of all wars carried on in the East-Indies, in order to know what wars are carried on in compliance with the terms of the Charter, and what not.

And lastly, That when there is the greatest reason to believe, that the Company's Servants have made a greedy and dangerous use of those powers, we ought to admire His Majesty's goodness, who, instead of depriving us of them altogether, endeavours to interpose his fatherly care in preventing any farther abuse of them.

Before I conclude this paper, give me leave, my fellow Proprietors, to add one general Observation, which struck me on comparing together the several Charters of the East-India Company, which is, that in proportion as the *real* power of the Company increased, its *legal* power and authority have been diminished. How far it will be for the advantage of the Proprietors, that Government should still proceed in narrowing the bounds of the Company's authority, I will not now enquire: but those who think farther limitations disadvantageous, will, in my humble opinion, find that the most effectual method to prevent them, will be by using the power they still possess, with justice and humanity towards those they call their subjects in India; and with modesty and obedience to those whom they ought to consider as their Rulers in Great Britain, I am, with great respect,

> Gentlemen,
> Your most obedient,
> and most humble Servant,
> AN OLD PROPRIETOR.
> London, August 18, 1769.

*   *   *

REVIEW QUESTIONS

1. What kinds of authority did the East India Company possess?
2. How does the author characterize the manner in which company officials exercised their powers?
3. What political and military problems persist between the company and the British crown? Does the author offer solutions?
4. What does this source tell us about the era of informal imperialism?

DAVID LIVINGSTONE

FROM Cambridge Speech of 1857

David Livingstone (1813–1873), the Scottish missionary and explorer of Africa, personified for Britain the higher cause of imperialism. Between 1840 and 1873, Livingstone traversed nearly a third of Africa, missionizing Christianity, opposing the persistent slave trade, and recording the geography and ethnographic customs of its peoples. His achievement and his self-effacing devotion to opening up Africa to commerce and Christianity provided inspiration to a nineteenth-century British public in search of a moral center to its imperialist policies in Africa. Livingstone presented this irenic speech in the same year as the Indian Mutiny, a rebellion on the subcontinent that cost thousands of lives.

From *Dr. Livingstone's Cambridge Lectures*, edited by William Monk (Cambridge: Bell, 1858).

*   *   *

My object in going into the country south of the desert was to instruct the natives in a knowledge of Christianity, but many circumstances prevented my living amongst them more than seven years, amongst which were considerations arising out of the slave system carried on by the Dutch Boers. I resolved to go into the country beyond, and soon found that, for the purposes of commerce, it was necessary to have a path to the sea. I might have gone on instructing the natives in religion, but as civilization and Christianity must go on together, I was obliged to find a path to the sea, in order that I should not sink to the level of the natives. The chief was overjoyed at the suggestion, and furnished me with twenty-seven men, and canoes, and provisions, and presents for the tribes through whose country we had to pass.

*   *   *

In a commercial point of view communication with this country is desirable. Angola is wonderfully fertile, producing every kind of tropical plant in rank luxuriance. Passing on to the valley of Quango, the stalk of the grass was as thick as a quill, and towered above my head, although I was mounted on my ox; cotton is produced in great abundance, though merely woven into common cloth; bananas and pine-apples grow in great luxuriance; but the people having no maritime communication, these advantages are almost lost. The country on the other side is not quite so fertile, but in addition to indigo, cotton, and sugarcane, produces a fibrous substance, which I am assured is stronger than flax.

The Zambesi has not been thought much of as a river by Europeans, not appearing very large at its mouth; but on going up it for about seventy miles, it is enormous. The first three hundred miles might be navigated without obstacle: then there is a rapid, and near it a coal-field of large extent. The elevated sides of the basin, which form the most important feature of the country, are far different in climate to the country nearer the sea, or even the centre. Here the grass is short, and the Angola goat, which could not live in the centre, had been seen on the east highland by Mr Moffat.

My desire is to open a path to this district, that civilization, commerce, and Christianity might find their way there. I consider that we made a great mistake, when we carried commerce into India, in being ashamed of our Christianity; as a matter of common sense and good policy, it is always best to appear in one's true character. In travelling through Africa, I might have imitated certain Portuguese, and have passed for a chief; but I never attempted anything of the sort, although endeavouring always to keep to the lessons of cleanliness rigidly instilled by my mother long ago; the consequence was that the natives respected me for that quality, though remaining dirty themselves.

I had a pass from the Portuguese consul, and on arriving at their settlement, I was asked what I was. I said, "A missionary, and a doctor too." They asked, "Are you a doctor of medicine?"—"Yes."—"Are you not a doctor of mathematics too?"—"No."—"And yet you can take longitudes and latitudes."—Then they asked me about my moustache; and I simply said I wore it, because men had moustaches to wear, and ladies had not. They could not understand either, why a sacerdote should have a wife and four children; and many a joke took place upon that subject. I used to say, "Is it not better to have children with than without a wife?" Englishmen of education always command respect, without any adventitious aid. A

Portuguese governor left for Angola, giving out that he was going to keep a large establishment, and taking with him quantities of crockery, and about five hundred waistcoats; but when he arrived in Africa, he made a 'deal' of them. Educated Englishmen seldom descend to that sort of thing.

A prospect is now before us of opening Africa for commerce and the Gospel. Providence has been preparing the way, for even before I proceeded to the Central basin it had been conquered and rendered safe by a chief named Sebituane, and the language of the Bechuanas made the fashionable tongue, and that was one of the languages into which Mr Moffat had translated the Scriptures. Sebituane also discovered Lake Ngami some time previous to my explorations in that part. In going back to that country my object is to open up traffic along the banks of the Zambesi, and also to preach the Gospel. The natives of Central Africa are very desirous of trading, but their only traffic is at present in slaves, of which the poorer people have an unmitigated horror: it is therefore most desirable to encourage the former principle, and thus open a way for the consumption of free productions, and the introduction of Christianity and commerce. By encouraging the native propensity for trade, the advantages that might be derived in a commercial point of view are incalculable; nor should we lose sight of the inestimable blessings it is in our power to bestow upon the unenlightened African, by giving him the light of Christianity. Those two pioneers of civilization—Christianity and commerce—should ever be inseparable; and Englishmen should be warned by the fruits of neglecting that principle as exemplified in the result of the management of Indian affairs. By trading with Africa, also, we should at length be independent of slave-labour, and thus discountenance practices so obnoxious to every Englishman.

Though the natives are not absolutely anxious to receive the Gospel, they are open to Christian influences. Among the Bechuanas the Gospel was well received. These people think it a crime to shed a tear, but I have seen some of them weep at the recollection of their sins when God had opened their hearts to Christianity and repentance. It is true that missionaries have difficulties to encounter; but what great enterprise was ever accomplished without difficulty? It is deplorable to think that one of the noblest of our missionary societies, the Church Missionary Society, is compelled to send to Germany for missionaries, whilst other societies are amply supplied. Let this stain be wiped off. The sort of men who are wanted for missionaries are such as I see before me; men of education, standing, enterprise, zeal, and piety. It is a mistake to suppose that *any one*, as long as he is pious, will do for this office. Pioneers in every thing should be the ablest and best qualified men, not those of small ability and education. This remark especially applies to the first teachers of Christian truth in regions which may never have before been blest with the name and Gospel of Jesus Christ. In the early ages the monasteries were the schools of Europe, and the monks were not ashamed to hold the plough. The missionaries now take the place of those noble men, and we should not hesitate to give up the small luxuries of life in order to carry knowledge and truth to them that are in darkness. I hope that many of those whom I now address will embrace that honourable career. Education has been given us from above for the purpose of bringing to the benighted the knowledge of a Saviour. If you knew the satisfaction of performing such a duty, as well as the gratitude to God which the missionary must always feel, in being chosen for so noble, so sacred a calling, you would have no hesitation in embracing it.

For my own part, I have never ceased to rejoice that God has appointed me to such an office. People talk of the sacrifice I have made in spending so much of my life in Africa. Can that be called a sacrifice which is simply paid back as a small part of a great debt owing to our God, which we can never repay?—Is that a sacrifice which brings its own blest reward in healthful activity, the consciousness of doing good, peace of mind, and a bright hope of a glorious destiny hereafter?—Away with the word in such a view, and with such a thought! It is emphatically no sacrifice. Say rather it is a privilege. Anxiety, sickness, suffering, or danger, now and then, with a foregoing of the common conveniences and charities of this life, may make us pause, and cause the spirit to waver, and the soul to sink, but let this only be for a moment. All these are nothing when compared with the glory which shall hereafter be revealed in, and for, us. I never made a sacrifice. Of this we ought not to talk, when we remember the great sacrifice which HE made who left His Father's throne on high to give Himself for us.

* * *

REVIEW QUESTIONS

1. What was for Livingstone the relationship between commerce and missionary work?
2. What were Livingstone's perceptions of African culture?
3. Judging from this speech, how do you think Livingstone inspired a generation to enter into missionary work?

MUHAMMED AS-SAFFAR

FROM *Travels of a Moroccan Scholar in France in 1845–46*

Between 1841 and 1844, the French army, in its attempt to consolidate political control in Algeria, engaged in a border war with Morocco so that France could win wider Arab recognition of its sovereignty over Algeria. Following a naval bombardment of Tangiers in August 1844, the Moroccans confronted the decision of choosing either a holy war or a diplomatic conciliation with the French. The Moroccan sultan chose the latter and sent a mission to Paris to effect a diplomatic compromise. As the secretary to the sultan's ambassador to France, Muhammed As-Saffar traveled to Paris. A learned scholar in law, Hadith, and Arabic grammar, As-Saffar kept a precise diary of his journey to Paris in 1845–46. Through this invaluable source, we see a Moroccan scholar's perception of Europe as an alien civilization. Passages on Christianity and the press provide a glimpse into this foreigner's impressions, at once critical and admiring.

From *Disorienting Encounters: Travels of a Moroccan Scholar in France in 1845–46*, by Muhammed As-Saffar, translated by Susan Gilson Miller (Berkeley: University of California Press, 1992), pp. 108–10, 150–53.

* * *

In Aix we saw a huge cross made of wood standing on one side of the town square. At its top was a smaller bit of wood made into the likeness of a crucified man, naked except for a cloth covering his maleness. What a sight it was! We were terrified to see it and thought that he was a criminal they had hung there, for without a doubt, whoever saw it [would think it] was a crucified man. I asked about this and they told me that it was the deity and the crucifix which they worshipped. They claim he is Jesus, that is to say, a likeness of him crucified. And there is no doubt that they believe in his divinity just as the Koran tells us, and there is no doubt about the untruth of their claim and the falsity of their belief. "*For they have no knowledge of it, and only follow conjecture.*"[1] Those are the words of their mouths, which is [false] like the speech of those who become infidels just before they die. My God how they lie! This is the cross set up in their churches to worship and glorify, and which Jesus, may peace be unto him, will break upon his return, refuting the falsehood of their belief and the wrongheadedness of the Christian religion.

Al-Qaṣṭallānī in his commentary on the *Ṣaḥīḥ* mentions the tradition about breaking the cross as follows: It is said that its origin is that a group of Jews insulted Jesus and his mother, peace be unto them, and God called upon the [Jews] and changed them into pigs and monkeys. Then the Jews decided to kill [Jesus]. God warned him and said he would raise him to heaven. Then [Jesus] said to his companions, "Which of you wishes to take on my likeness, be killed and crucified, and so enter the Garden of Eden?" One of them got up and God cast upon him the likeness [of Jesus], so that it would be he who was killed and crucified. And then people said, perhaps this man is a dissembler, and tried to prove it by entering the house of Jesus, but Jesus had already left and his likeness was cast on the other. So that when the Jews entered, they killed [the dissembler], claiming he was Jesus. Then they disagreed and some said that he was God and could not be killed; and others said that a dissembler had been killed and crucified; and others said that if it was Jesus, then where was his companion; and if it was his companion, then where was Jesus? And some said he was raised to heaven, and others said his face is the face of Jesus, and his body the body of the companion. Then the Jews oppressed the companions of Jesus, peace be unto him, by killing and crucifying and jailing [them], until the matter came before the Master of Rome. He was told that the Jews were oppressing the companions of Jesus, because he said he was the Messenger of God, he was giving life to the dead, he was healing the dumb and the leprous, and working miracles, and that the Jews had killed him and crucified him.

And [the Master of Rome] sent for the crucified body, which was taken down from the wooden pieces. The pieces of wood on which he was crucified were brought to the Master of Rome, who began to worship them. From them they made many crosses and from that day on Christians have worshipped the cross. The end.

The cross of the crucifixion appears there in different guises, but always in the same form. Sometimes it is large, at other times it is small. It may be of wood, stone, metal, brass, or gold, or in a picture. Sometimes the form of the crucified Jesus is on it, sometimes it is the cross alone, as was mentioned by al-Qaṣṭallānī. Many are sold in the shops. The figure of Jesus is portrayed in various ways: as a grown man, or a small boy in the lap or arms of Mary. In the church they pray to them both. If you ask one of them about this likeness, he will explain to you that it is God, or His son, or His mother if Mary is there. May [God] preserve them from that, and may He be raised high above what the sinners say. The proof of our eyes only increased our insight into their unbelief, the falsity of their creed, and the stupidity of their reasoning. Thanks be to God who guided us to the true religion. We ask God, praise be unto Him, to keep us in the true faith until death. Amen. With the help of our faithful prophet, may prayers and the purest peace be upon him until the Day of Judgment.

*　　*　　*

The Gazettes

The people of Paris, like all the French—indeed, like all of Rūm—are eager to know the latest news and events that are taking place in other parts. For this purpose they have the gazette. These are papers in which they write all the news that has reached them that day about events in their own country and in other lands both near and far.

This is the way it is done. The owner of a newspaper dispatches his people to collect everything they see or hear in the way of important events or unusual happenings. Among the places where they collect the news are the two Chambers,

---

[1] Koran 4:157.

the Great and the Small, where they come together to make their laws. When the members of the Chamber meet to deliberate, the men of the gazette sit nearby and write down everything that is said, for all debating and ratifying of laws is matter for the gazette and is known to everyone. No one can prevent them from doing this. However, if their words are about a disgraceful subject, they must conceal them from the public, and are not allowed [to write them].

They also have correspondents and reporters in other lands, who know what is happening there. You will find that the newspaper people are advised about unusual events before anyone else. [They] spend their day collecting news, handing in at night what they have gathered during the day. The owner of the newspaper then prints it, making numerous sheets by means of the printing press, which will be explained later. Then it is distributed to everyone who takes it, each receiving a set. All the leaders of France, and especially in Paris, make a contract with the owner of the newspaper to receive a new gazette each day, in return for a fixed sum paid annually. Likewise, all the cafés receive numerous gazettes each day from many places. When someone enters a café, first the waiter brings him a newspaper so he may learn what is new, and then he serves him his coffee. The newspapers are handed back and kept there. Whoever wishes to know what has happened in the past can hunt around in the café for a gazette from that time, and read about it.

On the front of the gazette is written its price each year. Every day during our stay in Paris, a new gazette with the most correct news arrived at our house. Written at the top was its price—sixteen *riyals* per year. One makes a contract with the owner [of the newspaper] and receives it for a short or long period, but never less than a month. They say that about fifteen thousand copies are printed daily. Each [sheet] is a piece of paper about two cubits long, written on both sides. In it you will find the news from Paris and the rest of the land of the French; from all the lands of the Christians; from the lands of the East and the West; in fact, from everywhere. Some copies even travel to other countries. Whenever you enter another part of France you will find the gazette of Paris, just as in Paris you find gazettes from the provinces.

For this reason they are well acquainted with all the news, whether it is local or foreign. Nor is it all necessarily true; it may be that the lies in it are more numerous than the truths, because it includes news that human nature loves to hear. But there are benefits in it too, such as learning what is new. Moreover, if someone has an idea about a subject but he is not a member of the press, he may write about it in the gazette and make it known to others, so that the leaders of opinion learn about it. If the idea is worthy they may follow it, and if its author was out of favor it may bring him recognition. As the poet says:

> Don't reject an idea if it is suitable,
> Or Truth even if it comes from error.
> Pearls are precious to acquire,
> But it is not the diver who decides their worth.

Among the many laws which their Sultan Louis XVIII has made for them and they are obliged to follow is that no person in France is prohibited from expressing his opinion or from writing it and printing it, on condition that he does not violate the law. If he does, it is erased. One of the reasons they were so hostile to their King Charles X, who preceded the present king, and a cause for their overthrow of his rule, is that he proclaimed a ban on anyone expressing ideas, or writing them, or printing them in the newspapers, unless one of the men of state had read it [first]. Therefore nothing appeared except what he wanted to appear.

In the newspapers they write rejoinders to the men of the two Chambers about the laws they are making. If their Sultan demands gifts from the notables or goes against the law in any way, they write about that too, saying that he is a tyrant and in the wrong. He cannot confront them or cause them harm. Also, if someone behaves out of the ordinary, they write about that too, making it common knowledge among people of every rank. If his deeds were admirable, they praise and delight in him, lauding his example; but if he behaved badly, they revile him to discourage the like.

Moreover, if someone is being oppressed by another, they write about that too, so that everyone will know the story from both sides just as it happened, until it is decided in court. One can also read in it what their courts have decided. Whoever wishes to advertise his wares can write about them in the newspaper, praising them and mentioning their location and price in the hope of selling them; and whoever wishes to sell a house or property can publish it in the gazette to inform people. All in all, the gazette is of such importance that one of them would do without food or drink sooner than do without reading the newspaper.

*   *   *

REVIEW QUESTIONS

1. Why was As-Saffar so disturbed by the crucifix as a religious symbol?
2. What were his perceptions of Christianity?
3. How is the French press described? Was the author disturbed that the lies may be "more numerous than the truths"?
4. Why is an outsider's perspective on Western religion, manners, and customs instructive?

F. A. STEEL AND G. GARDINER

FROM *The Complete Indian Housekeeper & Cook*

Following the institution of formal political rule in India in 1857, British colonial life grew as generations of administrators, merchants, and missionaries pursued their careers in the colonies. British women, too, increasingly followed their husbands on their colonial tours, bringing with them British notions of cuisine and domestic order. The following primer on keeping a proper household in imperial India throws light on how Victorian perceptions of class intersected with imperial notions of foreign cultures.

From *The Complete Indian Housekeeper & Cook*, by F. A. Steel and G. Gardiner (London: Heinemann, 1898), pp. 1–4, 9.

This book, it is hoped, will meet the very generally felt want for a practical guide to young housekeepers in India. A large proportion of English ladies in this country come to it newly married, to begin a new life, and take up new responsibilities under absolutely new conditions.

Few, indeed, have had any practical experience of housekeeping of any sort or kind; whilst those who have find themselves almost as much at sea as their more ignorant sisters. How can it be otherwise, when the familiar landmarks are no longer visible, and, amid the crowd of idle, unintelligible servants, there seems not one to carry on the usual routine of household work, which in England follows as a matter of course?

The kitchen is a black hole, the pantry a sink. The only servant who will condescend to tidy up is a skulking savage with a reed broom; whilst pervading all things broods the stifling, enervating atmosphere of custom, against which energy beats itself unavailingly, as against a feather bed.

The authors themselves know what it is to look round on a large Indian household, seeing that all things are wrong, all things slovenly, yet feeling paralysed by sheer inexperience in the attempt to find a remedy.

* * *

Housekeeping in India, when once the first strangeness has worn off, is a far easier task in many ways than it is in England, though it none the less requires time, and, in this present transitional period, an almost phenomenal patience; for, while one mistress enforces cleanliness according to European methods, the next may belong to the opposite faction, who, so long as the dinner is nicely served, thinks nothing of it being cooked in a kitchen which is also used as a latrine; the result being that the servants who serve one and then the other stamp of mistress, look on the desire for decency as a mere personal and distinctly disagreeable attribute of their employer, which, like a bad temper or stinginess, may be resented or evaded.

And, first, it must be distinctly understood that it is not necessary, or in the least degree desirable, that an educated woman should waste the best years of her life in scolding and petty supervision. Life holds higher duties, and it is indubitable that friction and over-zeal is a sure sign of a bad housekeeper. But there is an appreciable difference between the careworn Martha vexed with many things, and the absolute indifference displayed by many Indian mistresses, who put up with a degree of slovenliness and dirt which would disgrace a den in St. Giles, on the principle that it is no use attempting to teach the natives.

They never go into their kitchens, for the simple reason that their appetite for breakfast might be marred by seeing the *khitmutgâr*[1] using his toes

as an efficient toast-rack (*fact*); or their desire for dinner weakened by seeing the soup strained through a greasy *pugri*.

* * *

Easy, however, as the actual housekeeping is in India, the personal attention of the mistress is quite as much needed here as at home. The Indian servant, it is true, learns more readily, and is guiltless of the sniffiness with which Mary Jane receives suggestions, but a few days of absence or neglect on the part of the mistress, results in the servants falling into their old habits with the inherited conservatism of dirt. This is, of course, disheartening, but it has to be faced as a necessary condition of life, until a few generations of training shall have started the Indian servant on a new inheritance of habit. It must never be forgotten that at present those mistresses who aim at anything beyond keeping a good table are in the minority, and that pioneering is always arduous work.

The first duty of a mistress is, of course, to be able to give intelligible orders to her servants; therefore it is necessary she should learn to speak Hindustani. No sane Englishwoman would dream of living, say, for twenty years, in Germany, Italy, or France, without making the *attempt*, at any rate, to learn the language. She would, in fact, feel that by neglecting to do so she would write herself down an ass. It would be well, therefore, if ladies in India were to ask themselves if a difference in longitude increases the latitude allowed in judging of a woman's intellect.

The next duty is obviously to insist on her orders being carried out. And here we come to the burning question, "How is this to be done?" Certainly, there is at present very little to which we can appeal in the average Indian servant, but then, until it is implanted by training, there is very little sense of duty in a child; yet in some well-regulated nurseries obedience is a foregone conclusion. The secret lies in making rules, and *keeping to them*. The Indian servant is a child in everything save age, and should be treated as a child; that is to say, kindly, but with the greatest firmness. The laws of the household should be those of the

---

[1] The object of this book being to enable a person who is absolutely unacquainted with India, its language and people, to begin housekeeping at once, the authors have decided on adhering throughout to purely phonetic spelling. The only accent used will be the circumflex.

Medes and Persians, and first faults should never go unpunished. By overlooking a first offence, we lose the only opportunity we have of preventing it becoming a habit.

But it will be asked, How are we to punish our servants when we have no hold either on their minds or bodies?—when cutting their pay is illegal, and few, if any, have any real sense of shame.

The answer is obvious. Make a hold.

In their own experience the authors have found a system of rewards and punishments perfectly easy of attainment. One of them has for years adopted the plan of engaging her servants at so much a month—the lowest rate at which such servant is obtainable—and so much extra as *buksheesh*, conditional on good service. For instance, a *khitmutgâr* is engaged permanently on Rs. 9 a month, but the additional rupee which makes the wage up to that usually demanded by good servants is a fluctuating assessment! From it small fines are levied, beginning with one pice for forgetfulness, and running up, through degrees of culpability, to one rupee for lying. The money thus returned to imperial coffers may very well be spent on giving small rewards; so that each servant knows that by good service he can get back his own fines. That plan has never been objected to, and such a thing as a servant giving up his place has never been known in the author's experience. On the contrary, the household quite enters into the spirit of the idea, infinitely preferring it to volcanic eruptions of fault-finding.

To show what absolute children Indian servants are, the same author has for years adopted castor oil as an ultimatum in all obstinate cases, on the ground that there must be some physical cause for inability to learn or to remember. This is considered a great joke, and exposes the offender to much ridicule from his fellow-servants; so much so, that the words, "*Mem Sahib tum ko zuroor kâster ile pila dena hoga*" (*The Mem Sahib will have to give you castor oil*), is often heard in the mouths of the upper servants when newcomers give trouble. In short, without kindly and reasonable devices of this kind, the usual complaint of a want of hold over servants *must* remain true until they are educated into some sense of duty. Of course, common-sense is required to adjust the balance of rewards and punishments, for here again Indian servants are like children, in that they have an acute sense of justice. A very good plan for securing a certain amount of truthfulness in a servant is to insist that any one who has been caught out in a distinct falsehood should invariably bring witnesses to prove the truth of the smallest detail. It is a great disgrace and worry, generally producing a request to be given another chance after a few days. These remarks, written ten years ago, are still applicable, though the Indian mistress has now to guard against the possibility of impertinence. It should never be overlooked for an instant.

*   *   *

We do not wish to advocate an unholy haughtiness; but an Indian household can no more be governed peacefully, without dignity and prestige, than an Indian Empire. * * *

*   *   *

REVIEW QUESTIONS

1. What differences do Steel and Gardiner see between Indian and British servants? Why?
2. What must an English lady have done with her servants to have kept a well-run household?
3. How would you characterize the authors' attitude toward Indian workers?
4. What differences and similarities do you see between this colonial household manual and Mrs. Beeton's manual for Britain (see pp. 367–369)?

ODALISQUE WITH SLAVE (1839)   JEAN AUGUST DOMINIQUE INGRES

Over the course of the eighteenth and nineteenth centuries, literary and visual representations of the Orient became bound up in a larger colonial project of defining cultural differences between East and West. French artists particularly developed the odalisque as a genre of the imperial exotic. Odalik is the Turkish word for the slave attendant to women of the harem, but it entered into the French language as a word signifying a harem temptress. Odalisque paintings typify the West's eroticized fantasies of the Orient, which mix the sensually delightful with the tyrannical. Jean August Dominique Ingres's Odalisque with Slave, *presented in 1839, is a classic example of the genre. How did this fantasy of Middle Eastern culture help define the West?*

FRIEDRICH FABRI

FROM *Does Germany Need Colonies?*

The small pamphlet Does Germany Need Colonies? *by Friedrich Fabri (1824–1891), a former inspector of the Rhenish Missionary Association, was published in 1879. It was one among many publications that generated a widespread public debate in Germany regarding its need for colonies. Fabri cited overpopulation as a motivating factor, and his emphasis on Germany's "cultural mission" infused imperialism with an idealism that the general public embraced. The domestic agitation for colonial expansion by pressure groups and grass-roots associations radically affected domestic politics. Germany's decision in the 1880s to enter the race for colonial territories in Africa and Asia had, moreover, a profound impact on the European balance of power.*

From *The Imperialism Reader*, edited by Louis L. Snyder (New York: Van Nostrand, 1962), pp. 116–17.

*   *   *

Should not the German nation, so seaworthy, so industrially and commercially minded, more than other peoples geared to agricultural colonization, and possessing a rich and available supply of labor, all these to a greater extent than other modern culture-peoples, should not this nation successfully hew a new path on the road of imperialism? We are convinced beyond doubt that the colonial question has become a matter of life or death for the development of Germany. Colonies will have a salutary effect on our economic situation as well as on our entire national progress.

Here is a solution for many of the problems that face us. In this new Reich of ours there is so much bitterness, so much unfruitful, sour, and poisoned political wrangling, that the opening of a new, promising road of national effort will act as a kind of liberating influence. Our national spirit will be renewed, a gratifying thing, a great asset. A people that have been led to a high level of power can maintain its historical position only as long as it understands and proves itself to be *the bearer of a cultural mission*. At the same time, this is the only way to stability and to the growth of national welfare, the necessary foundation for a lasting expansion of power.

At one time Germany contributed only intellectual and literary activity to the tasks of our century. That era is now over. As a people we have become politically minded and powerful. But if political power becomes the primary goal of a nation, it will lead to harshness, even to barbarism. We must be ready to serve for the ideal, moral, and economic culture-tasks of our time. The French national-economist, Leroy Beaulieu, closed his words on colonization with these words: "That nation is the greatest in the world which colonizes most; if she does not achieve that rank today, she will make it tomorrow."

No one can deny that in this direction England has by far surpassed all other countries. Much has been said, even in Germany, during the last few decades about the "disintegrating power of England." Indeed, there seems to be something to it when we consider the Palmerston era and Gladstonian politics. It has been customary in our age of military power to evaluate the strength of a state in terms of its combat-ready troops. But anyone who looks at the globe and notes the steadily increasing colonial possessions of Great Britain, how she extracts strength from them, the skill with which she governs them, how the Anglo-Saxon strain occupies a dominant position in the overseas territories, he will begin to see the military argument as the reasoning of a philistine.

The fact is that England tenaciously holds on to its world-wide possessions with scarcely one-fourth the manpower of our continental military state. That is not only a great economic advantage but also a striking proof of the solid power and cultural fiber of England. Great Britain, of course, isolates herself far from the mass warfare of the continent, or only goes into action with dependable allies; hence, the insular state has suffered and will suffer no real damage. In any case, it would be wise for us Germans to learn about colonial skills from our Anglo-Saxon cousins and to begin a friendly competition with them. When the German Reich centuries ago stood at the pinnacle of the states of Europe, it was the Number One

trade and sea power. If the New Germany wants to protect its newly won position of power for a long time, it must heed its *Kultur*-mission and, above all, delay no longer in the task of renewing the call for colonies.

*   *   *

REVIEW QUESTIONS

1. Why does Fabri consider the acquisition of colonies "a matter of life or death for the development of Germany"?
2. How does Fabri compare Germany's political status with that of Britain?
3. According to Fabri, what political, economic, and cultural uses will Germany derive from colonies?

RUDYARD KIPLING

"The White Man's Burden"

Rudyard Kipling (1865–1936), a prolific poet, novelist, and short-story author who won the Nobel Prize for literature in 1907, was born in Bombay to parents of high Anglo-Indian society. Schooled in England, Kipling returned to India and drew on its imperial atmosphere for his fiction and verse to great success. Alongside his literary feats, Kipling also championed the "civilizing mission" of empire throughout his life, devoutly believing in Britain's and the West's duty to educate and govern the "Sloth and heathen Folly" of the non-Western world. Composed as an exhortation to the United States to fulfill its imperial role in the Pacific, "The White Man's Burden" originally appeared in McClure's Magazine *in February 1899 during the Spanish-American War. The poem's title was immediately taken up as a slogan by imperialists.*

From *McClure's Magazine*, vol. 12 (Feb. 1899).

Take up the White Man's burden—
  Send forth the best ye breed—
Go bind your sons to exile
  To serve your captives' need;
To wait in heavy harness,
  On fluttered folk and wild—
Your new-caught, sullen peoples,
  Half-devil and half-child.

Take up the White Man's burden—
  In patience to abide,
To veil the threat of terror
  And check the show of pride;
By open speech and simple,
  An hundred times made plain,
To seek another's profit,
  And work another's gain.

Take up the White Man's burden—
  The savage wars of peace—
Fill full the mouth of Famine
  And bid the sickness cease;
And when your goal is nearest
  The end for others sought,
Watch Sloth and heathen Folly
  Bring all your hope to nought.

Take up the White Man's burden—
  No tawdry rule of kings,
But toil of serf and sweeper—
  The tale of common things.
The ports ye shall not enter,
  The roads ye shall not tread,
Go make them with your living,
  And mark them with your dead.

Take up the White Man's burden—
  And reap his old reward:

The blame of those ye better,
  The hate of those ye guard—
The cry of hosts ye humour
  (Ah, slowly!) toward the light:—
"Why brought ye us from bondage,
  "Our loved Egyptian night?"

Take up the White Man's burden—
  Ye dare not stoop to less—
Nor call too loud on Freedom
  To cloak your weariness;
By all ye cry or whisper,
  By all ye leave or do,
The silent, sullen peoples
  Shall weigh your Gods and you.

Take up the White Man's burden—
  Have done with childish days—
The lightly proffered laurel,
  The easy, ungrudged praise.
Comes now, to search your manhood
  Through all the thankless years,
Cold, edged with dear-bought wisdom,
  The judgment of your peers!

REVIEW QUESTIONS

1. What was the burden of the white man?
2. How does Kipling glorify the white man's role?
3. How are Kipling's imperial subjects characterized?
4. What were the civil and military aspects of the "white man's burden"?

The first step towards lightening

The White Man's Burden

is through teaching the virtues of cleanliness.

Pears' Soap

is a potent factor in brightening the dark corners of the earth as civilization advances, while amongst the cultured of all nations it holds the highest place—it is the ideal toilet soap.

"LIGHTENING THE WHITE MAN'S BURDEN" (1899)

Popular culture in the late nineteenth century articulated Western imperial themes in numerous ways. This 1899 soap advertisement, which plays on Kipling's "White Man's Burden," offers a clear illustration of the negative characterization of non-Western peoples in the high imperial era. Admiral George Dewey, a hero of the Spanish-American War, is featured washing with Pears' Soap; the corner illustrations and the text express the advertisement's sentiment. Alongside steamboats and commerce, soap and hygiene are characterized as new items that the West can introduce to the non-Western world. The word lighten *works, then, as a racist pun. How does this advertisement help us understand how the beliefs of imperial politics became a self-evident, everyday practice?*

EDMUND D. MOREL

FROM *The Black Man's Burden*

Alongside the dominant ideological assertion that moral responsibility obliged the West to build empires, critics of imperialism voiced their dissent. Although the most consistent denunciations came from socialists, liberals also criticized imperialism on a number of economical and political principles. Edmund D. Morel (1873–1924), a British journalist writing in the immediate aftermath of the First World War, offers here a stinging indictment of imperialism's fatal impact on Africa. Written in 1920, Morel's scathing criticism of Britain must be situated in the postwar debate concerning the future of the colonies and the question of African self-determination.

From *The Black Man's Burden*, by Edmund D. Morel (London: National Labour Press, 1920).

* * *

It is with the peoples of Africa, then, that our inquiry is concerned. It is they who carry the "Black man's" burden. They have not withered away before the white man's *occupation*. Indeed, if the scope of this volume permitted, there would be no difficulty in showing that Africa has ultimately absorbed within itself every Caucasian and, for that matter, every Semitic invader too. In hewing out for himself a fixed abode in Africa, the white man has massacred the African in heaps. The African has survived, and it is well for the white settlers that he has.

In the process of imposing his political dominion over the African, the white man has carved broad and bloody avenues from one end of Africa to the other. The African has resisted, and persisted.

For three centuries the white man seized and enslaved millions of Africans and transported them, with every circumstance of ferocious cruelty, across the seas. Still the African survived and, in his land of exile, multiplied exceedingly.

But what the partial occupation of his soil by the white man has failed to do; what the mapping out of European political "spheres of influence" has failed to do; what the maxim and the rifle, the slave gang, labour in the bowels of the earth and the lash, have failed to do; what imported measles, smallpox and syphilis have failed to do; what even the oversea slave trade failed to do, the power of modern capitalistic exploitation, assisted by modern engines of destruction, may yet succeed in accomplishing.

For from the evils of the latter, scientifically applied and enforced, there is no escape for the African. Its destructive effects are not spasmodic: they are permanent. In its permanence resides its fatal consequences. It kills not the body merely, but the soul. It breaks the spirit. It attacks the African at every turn, from every point of vantage. It wrecks his polity, uproots him from the land, invades his family life, destroys his natural pursuits and occupations, claims his whole time, enslaves him in his own home.

Economic bondage and wage slavery, the grinding pressure of a life of toil, the incessant demands of industrial capitalism—these things a landless European proletariat physically endures, though hardly. * * * The recuperative forces of a temperate climate are there to arrest the ravages, which alleviating influences in the shape of prophylactic and curative remedies will still further circumscribe. But in Africa, especially in tropical Africa, which a capitalistic imperialism threatens and has, in part, already devastated, man is incapable of reacting against unnatural conditions. In those regions man is engaged in a perpetual struggle against disease and an exhausting climate, which tells heavily upon child-bearing; and there is no scientific machinery for salving the weaker members of the community. The African of the tropics is capable of tremendous physical labours. But he cannot accommodate himself to the European system of monotonous, uninterrupted labour, with its long and regular hours, involving, moreover, as it frequently does, severance from natural surroundings and nostalgia, the condition of melancholy resulting from separation from home, a malady to which the African is specially prone. Climatic conditions forbid it. When the system is forced upon him, the tropical African droops and dies.

Nor is violent physical opposition to abuse and injustice henceforth possible for the African in any part of Africa. His chances of effective resistance have been steadily dwindling with the increasing perfectibility in the killing power of modern armament. Gunpowder broke the effectiveness of his resistance to the slave trade, although he continued to struggle. He has forced and, on rare occasions and in exceptional circumstances beaten, in turn the old-fashioned musket, the elephant gun, the seven-pounder, and even the repeating rifle and the gatling gun. He has been known to charge right down repeatedly, foot and horse, upon the square, swept on all sides with the pitiless and continuous hail of maxims.[1] But against the latest inventions, physical bravery, though associated with a perfect knowledge of the country, can do nothing. The African cannot face the high-explosive shell and the bomb-dropping aeroplane. He has inflicted sanguinary reverses upon picked European troops, hampered by the climate and by commissariat difficulties. He cannot successfully oppose members of his own race free from these impediments, employed by his white adversaries, and trained in all

the diabolical devices of scientific massacre. And although the conscripting of African armies for use in Europe or in Africa as agencies for the liquidation of the white man's quarrels must bring in its train evils from which the white man will be the first to suffer, both in Africa and in Europe; the African himself must eventually disappear in the process. Winter in Europe, or even in Northern Africa, is fatal to the tropical or sub-tropical African, while in the very nature of the case anything approaching real European control in Africa, of hordes of African soldiery armed with weapons of precision is not a feasible proposition. The Black man converted by the European into a scientifically-equipped machine for the slaughter of his kind, is certainly not more merciful than the white man similarly equipped for like purposes in dealing with unarmed communities. And the experiences of the civilian population of Belgium, East Prussia, Galicia and Poland is indicative of the sort of visitation involved for peaceable and powerless African communities if the white man determines to add to his appalling catalogue of past misdeeds towards the African, the crowning wickedness of once again, as in the day of the slave trade, supplying him with the means of encompassing his own destruction.

Thus the African is really helpless against the material gods of the white man, as embodied in the trinity of imperialism, capitalistic-exploitation, and militarism. If the white man retains these gods and if he insists upon making the African worship them as assiduously as he has done himself, the African will go the way of the Red Indian, the Amerindian, the Carib, the Guanche, the aboriginal Australian, and many more. And this would be at once a crime of enormous magnitude, and a world disaster.

*   *   *

An endeavour will now be made to describe the nature, and the changing form, which the burden inflicted by the white man in modern times upon the black has assumed. It can only be sketched here in the broadest outline, but in such a way as will, it is hoped, explain the differing causes and motives which have inspired white activities in Africa and

[1] The Maxim gun was a self-powered machine gun first used in the 1880s.

illustrate, by specific and notable examples, their resultant effects upon African peoples. It is important that these differing causes and motives should be understood, and that we should distinguish between them in order that we may hew our way later on through the jungle of error which impedes the pathway to reform. Diffused generalities and sweeping judgments generate confusion of thought and hamper the evolution of a constructive policy based upon clear apprehension of the problem to be solved.

The history of contact between the white and black peoples in modern times is divisible into two distinct and separate periods: the period of the slave trade and the period of invasion, political control, capitalistic exploitation, and, the latest development, militarism. Following the slave trade period and preceding the period of invasion, occurs the trade interlude which, indeed, had priority of both periods, as when the Carthagenians bartered salt and iron implements for gold dust on the West Coast. But this interlude concerns our investigations only when we pass from destructive exposure to constructive demonstration.

The first period needs recalling, in order to impress once more upon our memories the full extent of the African's claim upon us, the white imperial peoples, for tardy justice, for considerate and honest conduct.

Our examination of the second period will call for sectional treatment. The history of contact and its consequences during this period may be roughly sub-divided thus:

a. The struggle for supremacy between European invading *Settlers* and resident African peoples in those portions of Africa where the climate and other circumstances permit of Europeans rearing families of white children.

b. *Political action* by European Governments aiming at the assertion of sovereign rights over particular areas of African territory.

c. *Administrative policy,* sanctioned by European Governments, and applied by their local representatives in particular areas, subsequent to the successful assertion of sovereign rights.

These sub-divisions are, perhaps, somewhat arbitrary. The distinctiveness here given to them cannot be absolutely preserved. There is, for instance, a natural tendency for both *a* and *b* to merge into *c* as, through efflux of time, the originating cause and motive of contact is obscured by developments to which contact has given rise.

Thus racial contention for actual possession of the soil, and political action often resulting in so-called treaties of Protectorate thoroughly unintelligible to the African signees, are both landmarks upon the road leading to eventual administrative policy: *i.e.,* to direct government of the black man by the white.

*   *   *

It is often argued that the agricultural and arboricultural methods of the African are capable of improvement. The statement is undoubtedly true. It applies with equal force to the land of Britain. There is no difference of opinion among British agricultural experts as to the capacities for improvement in the methods of British agriculture. As for British arboriculture it is still an almost entirely neglected field of British home enterprise. We can afford to be patient with the African if he has not yet attained perfection. Why, it is only since the beginning of the 18th century that the rotation of crops has been practised in England! But the Kano farmers in Northern Nigeria have understood rotation of crops and grass manuring for at least five hundred years.

To advance such truisms as an excuse for robbing the native communities of their land, degrading farmers in their own right to the level of hired labourers urged on by the lash, and conferring monopolistic rights over the land and its fruits to private corporations, is to make truth the stalking horse of oppression and injustice. The statement of fact may be accurate. The claim put forward on the strength of it is purely predatory.

Those who urge this and kindred arguments only do so to assist the realisation of their purpose. That purpose is clear. It is to make of Africans all over Africa a servile race; to exploit African labour, and through African labour, the soil of Africa for their own exclusive benefit. They are blind to the cost in human suffering. They are indifferent to the fact that in the long run their policy must defeat its own ends. They care only for the moment, and for the objects of the moment they are prepared to sacrifice the future. But since their purpose is selfish, short-sighted and immoral it must be striven against without pause or relaxation. There can be no honest or safe compromise with these people and their policy. A great moral issue is involved. But although that issue comes first, and must come first, it is not the only issue.

For a time it may be possible for the white man to maintain a white civilisation in the colonisable, or partly colonisable, areas of the African Continent based on servile or semi-servile labour: to build up a servile State. But even there the attempt can be no more than fleeting. The days of Roman imperialism are done with for ever. Education sooner or later breaks all chains, and knowledge cannot be kept from the African. The attempt will be defeated in the north by Islam, which confers power of combination in the political sphere, and a spiritual unity which Europe has long lost in the mounting tides of her materialism. It will fail in the south through the prolificness of the African, through the practical impossibility of arresting his intellectual advance and through race admixture, which is proceeding at a much more rapid rate than most people realise. In the great tropical regions the attempt must fail in the very nature of things, if for no other reason, because it can only be enforced by employing the black man, trained in the art of modern warfare as the medium through which to coerce his unarmed brother. The former will be well content to play that part for a period more or less prolonged, but when he becomes alive to his power the whole fabric of European domination will fall to pieces in shame and ruin. From these failures the people of Europe will suffer moral and material damage of a far-reaching kind.

And the criminal folly of it! The white imperial peoples have it in their power, if their rulers will cultivate vision and statesmanship enough to thrust aside the prompting of narrow, ephemeral interests—anti-national in the truest sense—to make of Africa the home of highly-trained and prosperous peoples enriching the universe as their prosperity waxes, dwelling in plains and valleys, in forests and on plateaux made fruitful by their labours, assisted by science; a country whose inhabitants will be enterprising and intelligent, loving their land, looking to it for inspiration, co-operating faithfully in the work of the world, developing their own culture, independent, free, self-respecting, attaining to higher mental growth as the outcome of internal evolutionary processes. Why cannot the white imperial peoples, acknowledging in some measure the injuries they have inflicted upon the African, turn a new leaf in their treatment of him? For nearly two thousand years they have professed to be governed by the teachings of Christ. Can they not begin in the closing century of that era, to practise what they profess—and what their missionaries of religion teach the African? Can they not cease to regard the African as a producer of dividends for a selected few among their number, and begin to regard him as a human being with human rights? Have they made such a success of their own civilisation that they can contemplate with equanimity the forcing of all its social failures upon Africa—its hideous and devastating inequalities, its pauperisms, its senseless and destructive egoisms, its vulgar and soulless materialism? It is in their power to work such good to Africa—and such incalculable harm! Can they not make up their minds that their strength shall be used for noble ends? Africa demands at their hands, justice, and understanding sympathy—not ill-informed sentiment. And when these are dealt out to her she repays a thousandfold.

*   *   *

REVIEW QUESTIONS

1. How does Morel outline the history of gradual European domination over indigenous Africans?
2. What is the extent of blame that Morel lays at Europe's door?
3. List the range of abuse and exploitation that Morel ascribes to the Western imperial powers.
4. What does Morel's criticism of Europe's exportation of industrial work habits to Africa suggest about European attitudes toward colonies?
5. Why does Morel call the preservation of colonies in Africa a criminal folly?

VLADIMIR LENIN

FROM *Imperialism, the Highest Stage of Capitalism*

Imperialists' justification for formal control of colonies in the last half of the nineteenth century often carried the economic rationale of securing monopoly outlets for domestic-made goods and capital investment. Hence, although Marx never integrated imperialism into his critique of capitalism, second-generation socialists perceived capitalism in the imperial era as having entered a new phase, which witnessed the anxious attempts of banking consortiums and large-scale industrial enterprises to stake out high-yielding investments, new markets, and cheaper raw materials. In the highly influential pamphlet Imperialism, the Highest Stage of Capitalism, *first written in 1917 (and posthumously revised in the 1920s and 1930s), Lenin (1870–1924) argued that imperialism must be viewed as "parasitic or decaying capitalism." The apparent success of combining empire and capitalism, he argued, hid profound structural contradictions that brought on not only the First World War but also the imminent revolt of the colonial world from capitalist exploitation. The following passage, drawn from the pamphlet's final chapter, summarizes his principal arguments for viewing imperialism as the highest—that is, the final—stage of capitalism.*

From *Imperialism, the Highest Stage of Capitalism*, by V. I. Lenin (New York: International, 1939), pp. 123–27.

*   *   *

We have seen that the economic quintessence of imperialism is monopoly capitalism. This very fact determines its place in history, for monopoly that grew up on the basis of free competition, and precisely out of free competition, is the transition from the capitalist system to a higher social-economic order. We must take special note of the four principal forms of monopoly, or the four principal manifestations of monopoly capitalism, which are characteristic of the epoch under review.

Firstly, monopoly arose out of the concentration of production at a very advanced stage of development. This refers to the monopolist capitalist combines, cartels, syndicates and trusts. We have seen the important part that these play in modern economic life. At the beginning of the twentieth century, monopolies acquired complete supremacy in the advanced countries. And although the first steps towards the formation of the cartels were first taken by countries enjoying the protection of high tariffs (Germany, America), Great Britain, with her system of free trade, was not far behind in revealing the same basic phenomenon, namely, the birth of monopoly out of the concentration of production.

Secondly, monopolies have accelerated the capture of the most important sources of raw materials, especially for the coal and iron industries, which are the basic and most highly cartelised industries in capitalist society. The monopoly of the most important sources of raw materials has enormously increased the power of big capital, and has sharpened the antagonism between cartelised and non-cartelised industry.

Thirdly, monopoly has sprung from the banks. The banks have developed from modest intermediary enterprises into the monopolists of finance capital. Some three or five of the biggest banks in each of the foremost capitalist countries have achieved the "personal union" of industrial and bank capital, and have concentrated in their hands the disposal of thousands upon thousands of millions which form the greater part of the capital and income of entire countries. A financial oligarchy, which throws a close net of relations of dependence over all the economic and political institutions of contemporary bourgeois society without exception—such is the most striking manifestation of this monopoly.

Fourthly, monopoly has grown out of colonial policy. To the numerous "old" motives of colonial policy, finance capital has added the struggle for the sources of raw materials, for the export of capital, for "spheres of influence," *i.e.,* for spheres for profitable deals, concessions, monopolist profits and so on; in fine, for economic territory in general. When the colonies of the European powers in Africa, for instance, comprised only one-tenth of that territory (as was the case in 1876) colonial policy was able to develop by methods other than

those of monopoly—by the "free grabbing" of territories, so to speak. But when nine-tenths of Africa had been seized (approximately by 1900), when the whole world had been divided up, there was inevitably ushered in a period of colonial monopoly and, consequently, a period of particularly intense struggle for the division and the redivision of the world.

The extent to which monopolist capital has intensified all the contradictions of capitalism is generally known. It is sufficient to mention the high cost of living and the oppression of the cartels. This intensification of contradictions constitutes the most powerful driving force of the transitional period of history, which began from the time of the definite victory of world finance capital.

Monopolies, oligarchy, the striving for domination instead of the striving for liberty, the exploitation of an increasing number of small or weak nations by an extremely small group of the richest or most powerful nations—all these have given birth to those distinctive characteristics of imperialism which compel us to define it as parasitic or decaying capitalism. More and more prominently there emerges, as one of the tendencies of imperialism, the creation of the "bond-holding" (rentier) state, the usurer state, in which the bourgeoisie lives on the proceeds of capital exports and by "clipping coupons." It would be a mistake to believe that this tendency to decay precludes the possibility of the rapid growth of capitalism. It does not. In the epoch of imperialism, certain branches of industry, certain strata of the bourgeoisie and certain countries betray, to a more or less degree, one or other of these tendencies. On the whole, capitalism is growing far more rapidly than before. But this growth is not only becoming more and more uneven in general; its unevenness also manifests itself, in particular, in the decay of the countries which are richest in capital (such as England).

In regard to the rapidity of Germany's economic development, Riesser, the author of the book on the big German banks, states:

The progress of the preceding period (1848–70), which had not been exactly slow, stood in about the same ratio to the rapidity with which the whole of Germany's national economy, and with it German banking, progressed during this period (1870–1905) as the mail coach of the Holy Roman Empire of the German nation stood to the speed of the present-day automobile . . . which in whizzing past, it must be said, often endangers not only innocent pedestrians in its path, but also the occupants of the car.

In its turn, this finance capital which has grown so rapidly is not unwilling (precisely because it has grown so quickly) to pass on to a more "tranquil" possession of colonies which have to be seized— and not only by peaceful methods—from richer nations. In the United States, economic development in the last decades has been even more rapid than in Germany, and *for this very reason* the parasitic character of modern American capitalism has stood out with particular prominence. On the other hand, a comparison of, say, the republican American bourgeoisie with the monarchist Japanese or German bourgeoisie shows that the most pronounced political distinctions diminish to an extreme degree in the epoch of imperialism—not because they are unimportant in general, but because in all these cases we are discussing a bourgeoisie which has definite features of parasitism.

The receipt of high monopoly profits by the capitalists in one of the numerous branches of industry, in one of numerous countries, etc., makes it economically possible for them to corrupt certain sections of the working class, and for a time a fairly considerable minority, and win them to the side of the bourgeoisie of a given industry or nation against all the others. The intensification of antagonisms between imperialist nations for the division of the world increases this striving. And so there is created that bond between imperialism and opportunism, which revealed itself first and most clearly in England, owing to the fact that certain features of imperialist development were observable there much earlier than in other countries.

Some writers, L. Martov, for example, try to evade the fact that there is a connection between imperialism and opportunism in the labour movement—which is particularly striking at the present time—by resorting to "official optimistic" arguments (*à la* Kautsky and Huysmans) like the following: the cause of the opponents of capitalism would be hopeless if it were precisely progressive capitalism that led to the increase of opportunism, or, if it were precisely the best paid workers who were inclined towards opportunism, etc. We must have no illusion regarding "optimism" of this kind. It is optimism in regard to opportunism; it is optimism which serves to conceal opportunism. As a matter of fact the extraordinary rapidity and the particularly revolting character of the development of opportunism is by no means a guarantee that its victory will be durable: the rapid growth of a malignant abscess on a healthy body only causes it to burst more quickly and thus to relieve the body of it. The most dangerous people of all in this respect are those who do not wish to understand that the fight against imperialism is a sham and humbug unless it is inseparably bound up with the fight against opportunism.

From all that has been said in this book on the economic nature of imperialism, it follows that we must define it as capitalism in transition, or, more precisely, as moribund capitalism. It is very instructive in this respect to note that the bourgeois economists, in describing modern capitalism, frequently employ terms like "interlocking," "absence of isolation," etc.; "in conformity with their functions and course of development," banks are "not purely private business enterprises; they are more and more outgrowing the sphere of purely private business regulation." And this very Riesser, who uttered the words just quoted, declares with all seriousness that the "prophecy" of the Marxists concerning "socialisation" has "not come true"!

What then does this word "interlocking" express? It merely expresses the most striking feature of the process going on before our eyes. It shows that the observer counts the separate trees, but cannot see the wood. It slavishly copies the superficial, the fortuitous, the chaotic. It reveals the observer as one who is overwhelmed by the mass of raw material and is utterly incapable of appreciating its meaning and importance. Ownership of shares and relations between owners of private property "interlock in a haphazard way." But the underlying factor of this interlocking, its very base, is the changing social relations of production. When a big enterprise assumes gigantic proportions, and, on the basis of exact computation of mass data, organises according to plan the supply of primary raw materials to the extent of two-thirds, or three-fourths of all that is necessary for tens of millions of people; when the raw materials are transported to the most suitable place of production, sometimes hundreds or thousands of miles away, in a systematic and organised manner; when a single centre directs all the successive stages of work right up to the manufacture of numerous varieties of finished articles; when these products are distributed according to a single plan among tens and hundreds of millions of consumers (as in the case of the distribution of oil in America and Germany by the American "oil trust")—then it becomes evident that we have socialisation of production, and not mere "interlocking"; that private economic relations and private property relations constitute a shell which is no longer suitable for its contents, a shell which must inevitably begin to decay if its destruction be delayed by artificial means; a shell which may continue in a state of decay for a fairly long period (particularly if the cure of the opportunist abscess is protracted), but which will inevitably be removed.

REVIEW QUESTIONS

1. According to Lenin, why are monopolies a contradiction and a problem for capitalism?
2. Why does Lenin emphasize finance (as opposed to industrial) capital in his interpretation of imperialism?
3. How would imperial monopolies spur the collapse of capitalism?

23 ∽ MODERN INDUSTRY AND MASS POLITICS, 1870–1914

In the period 1870–1914, the West's prosperity as an industrial powerhouse and its maturity as a modern civil society produced an array of economic, political, and cultural challenges. Although Europe stood at the zenith of its power, its political turmoil and intellectual developments nonetheless questioned and mitigated the bourgeoisie's triumphant belief in progress and civilization.

Industrialization entered a second, more mature stage, which produced innovative technologies and greater scales of economy. Department stores marked the arrival of mass consumer culture, with its breadth of goods and its new sales techniques. Newly invented machinery, which sewed, cut, pressed, and molded with labor-saving efficiency, allowed entrepreneurs to meet increased demands at lower prices. Employers furthermore maximized profit margins with "scientific" time-work studies, producing more efficient, rationalized regimens of work. Although hardly proportional to employers' gains, the living standards of workers rose, demonstrating capitalism's innovative abilities to adapt and prosper. But the new economic growth also brought keener competition for markets and national wealth, which sharpened political rivalries. Although Britain remained the undisputed leader of the first Industrial Revolution, the emergence of such new leading sectors as steel, chemicals, and electrical engineering enabled German companies to achieve explosive economic expansion and thus vie with England and France for a greater share of world markets. After 1890 Britain felt the sting of its free-trade policy when other countries, especially Germany, competed in Britain's colonies and in Britain itself. The ubiquitous label "made in Germany" vexed British industrialists, reminding them of their relative decline. Economic nationalism became an increasingly important component of political discussions.

The widespread introduction of universal male suffrage after 1870 launched the era of mass politics. The enfranchisement of unpropertied laborers significantly broadened the political landscape, producing a range of political views that shook the delicate equilibrium of bourgeois and aristocratic governance. Syndicalists, anarchists, socialists, communists, and democratic labor parties now competed for workers' political loyalty. In this period Marxism also ceased to be a monolithic tenet. Although such socialists as Eduard Bernstein argued that socialism should revise its belief in the imminent collapse of capitalism and start to participate in parliamentary politics for incremental reform, Vladimir Lenin and other radical socialists continued to embrace Marx's tenet of class struggle for new revolutionary programs.

Women also emerged as a new political constituency. No longer content with the "natural" roles of reproduction and domesticity, women contested the right arrogated by men to deny them political citizenship and control over their property and legal affairs. Awakening to new identities, women demanded the vote, the right to higher education, and overall respect for their intelligence and ability to serve society. The failure of the political establishment to initiate change for women abetted the rise of women's associations to agitate for the vote. And when peaceful petitioning failed to produce parliamentary debates, British women resorted to civil disobedience and militancy. Hunger strikes, destruction of property, and contentious demonstrations by women scandalized Europeans and disturbed ideals of peaceful, evolutionary change. Rejecting bourgeois movements, socialist feminists advocated the economic and political mobilization of women as an important weapon for the working-class movement.

In the last third of the nineteenth century, Europe's leading intellectuals, artists, and scientists also shook the foundations of the bourgeois world, questioning the fundamental premises by which bourgeois values and norms organized society and politics. Scientific discussion of Charles Darwin's theory of natural selection threw doubt on the ordered harmony of a divine, moral universe and furthermore became susceptible to false analogies to social behavior (Social Darwinism) and to pseudoscientific doctrines of hereditary health (eugenics). Philosophers attacked Judeo-Christian values of social justice as spiritually enervating and culturally debilitating. The fledgling science of psychoanalysis further challenged the bourgeoisie's belief in rational, purposive action by demonstrating that behavior was largely determined by the inner mechanisms of the unconscious. Although the richness of European letters defies simple generalization, many of the enduring voices from this period felt increasingly detached from normative bourgeois assumptions, especially those grounded in rationality and progress.

EDUARD BERNSTEIN

FROM *Evolutionary Socialism*

At the turn of the century, Eduard Bernstein (1850–1932) was a leading member of the Social Democratic Party of Germany (SPD), Europe's largest, best-organized Marxist party. In 1899 Bernstein published The Premises of Socialism and the Tasks of Social Democracy, *which called attention to the evolutionary changes in capitalism that rendered orthodox Marxist doctrine obsolete. In the book Bernstein argued for the need to revise tactics and goals for working-class constituencies. Bernstein's treatise, which sparked an important debate among socialists, is a useful document, for it throws light not only on the revisionist political strategies of socialists but also on the changing nature of late-nineteenth-century capitalist political economy.*

From *Evolutionary Socialism: A Criticism and Affirmation,* by Eduard Bernstein, translated by Edith C. Harvey (New York: B. W. Huebsch, 1911).

*   *   *

It has been maintained in a certain quarter that the practical deductions from my treatises would be the abandonment of the conquest of political power by the proletariat organised politically and economically. That is quite an arbitrary deduction, the accuracy of which I altogether deny.

I set myself against the notion that we have to expect shortly a collapse of the bourgeois economy, and that social democracy should be induced by the prospect of such an imminent, great, social catastrophe to adapt its tactics to that assumption. That I maintain most emphatically.

The adherents of this theory of a catastrophe, base it especially on the conclusions of the *Communist Manifesto.* This is a mistake in every respect.

The theory which the *Communist Manifesto* sets forth of the evolution of modern society was correct as far as it characterised the general tendencies of that evolution. But it was mistaken in several special deductions, above all in the estimate of the *time* the evolution would take. The last has been unreservedly acknowledged by Friedrich Engels, the joint author with Marx of the *Manifesto,* in his preface to the *Class War in France.* But it is evident that if social evolution takes a much greater period of time than was assumed, it must also take upon itself *forms* and lead to forms that were not foreseen and could not be foreseen then.

Social conditions have not developed to such an acute opposition of things and classes as is depicted in the *Manifesto.* It is not only useless, it is the greatest folly to attempt to conceal this from ourselves. The number of members of the possessing classes is today not smaller but larger. The enormous increase of social wealth is not accompanied by a decreasing number of large capitalists but by an increasing number of capitalists of all degrees. The middle classes change their character but they do not disappear from the social scale.

The concentration in productive industry is not being accomplished even today in all its departments with equal thoroughness and at an equal rate. In a great many branches of production it certainly justifies the forecasts of the socialist critic of society; but in other branches it lags even today behind them. The process of concentration in agriculture proceeds still more slowly. Trade statistics show an extraordinarily elaborated graduation of enterprises in regard to size. No rung of the ladder is disappearing from it. The significant changes in the inner structure of these enterprises and their inter-relationship cannot do away with this fact.

In all advanced countries we see the privileges of the capitalist bourgeoisie yielding step by step to democratic organisations. Under the influence of this, and driven by the movement of the working classes which is daily becoming stronger, a social reaction has set in against the exploiting tendencies of capital, a counteraction which, although it still proceeds timidly and feebly, yet does exist, and is always drawing more departments of economic life under its influence. Factory legislation, the democratising of local government, and the extension of its area of work, the freeing of trade unions and systems of co-operative trading from legal restrictions, the consideration of standard conditions of labour in the work undertaken by public authorities—all these characterise this phase of the evolution.

But the more the political organisations of modern nations are democratised the more the needs and opportunities of great political catastrophes are diminished. He who holds firmly to the catastrophic theory of evolution must, with all his power, withstand and hinder the evolution described above, which, indeed, the logical defenders of that theory formerly did. But is the conquest of political power by the proletariat simply to be by a political catastrophe? Is it to be the appropriation and utilisation of the power of the State by the proletariat exclusively against the whole non-proletarian world?

He who replies in the affirmative must be reminded of two things. In 1872 Marx and Engels announced in the preface to the new edition of the *Communist Manifesto* that the Paris Commune had exhibited a proof that "the working classes cannot simply take possession of the ready-made State machine and set it in motion for their own aims." And in 1895 Friedrich Engels stated in detail in the preface to *War of the Classes* that the time of political surprises, of the "revolutions of small conscious minorities at the head of uncon-

scious masses" was today at an end, that a collision on a large scale with the military would be the means of checking the steady growth of social democracy and of even throwing it back for a time—in short, that social democracy would flourish far better by lawful than by unlawful means and by violent revolution. And he points out in conformity with this opinion that the next task of the party should be "to work for an uninterrupted increase of its votes" or to carry on a slow *propaganda of parliamentary activity.*

Thus Engels, who, nevertheless, as his numerical examples show, still somewhat overestimated the rate of process of the evolution! Shall we be told that he abandoned the conquest of political power by the working classes, because he wished to avoid the steady growth of social democracy secured by lawful means being interrupted by a political revolution?

If not, and if one subscribes to his conclusions, one cannot reasonably take any offence if it is declared that for a long time yet the task of social democracy is, instead of speculating on a great economic crash, "to organise the working classes politically and develop them as a democracy and to fight for all reforms in the State which are adapted to raise the working classes and transform the State in the direction of democracy."

That is what I have said in my impugned article and what I still maintain in its full import. As far as concerns the question propounded above it is equivalent to Engel's dictum, for democracy is, at any given time, as much government by the working classes as these are capable of practising according to their intellectual ripeness and the degree of social development they have attained. Engels, indeed, refers at the place just mentioned to the fact that the *Communist Manifesto* has "proclaimed the conquest of the democracy as one of the first and important tasks of the fighting proletariat."

In short, Engels is so thoroughly convinced that the tactics based on the presumption of a catastrophe have had their day, that he even considers a revision of them necessary in the Latin countries where tradition is much more favourable to them than in Germany. "If the conditions of war between nations have altered," he writes, "no less have those for the war between classes." Has this already been forgotten?

No one has questioned the necessity for the working classes to gain the control of government. The point at issue is between the theory of a social cataclysm and the question whether with the given social development in Germany and the present advanced state of its working classes in the towns and the country, a sudden catastrophe would be desirable in the interest of the social democracy. I have denied it and deny it again, because in my judgment a greater security for lasting success lies in a steady advance than in the possibilities offered by a catastrophic crash.

And as I am firmly convinced that important periods in the development of nations cannot be leapt over, I lay the greatest value on the next tasks of social democracy, on the struggle for the political rights of the working man, on the political activity of working men in town and country for the interests of their class, as well as on the work of the industrial organisation of the workers.

In this sense I wrote the sentence that the movement means everything for me and that what is *usually* called "the final aim of socialism" is nothing; and in this sense I write it down again today. Even if the word "usually" had not shown that the proposition was only to be understood conditionally, it was obvious that it *could* not express indifference concerning the final carrying out of socialist principles, but only indifference— or, as it would be better expressed, carelessness— as to the form of the final arrangement of things. I have at no time had an excessive interest in the future, beyond general principles; I have not been able to read to the end any picture of the future.

My thoughts and efforts are concerned with the duties of the present and the nearest future, and I only busy myself with the perspectives beyond so far as they give me a line of conduct for suitable action now.

The conquest of political power by the working classes, the expropriation of capitalists, are no ends in themselves but only means for the accomplishment of certain aims and endeavours. As such they are demands in the programme of social democracy and are not attacked by me. Nothing can be said beforehand as to the circumstances of their accomplishment; we can only fight for their realisation. But the conquest of political power necessitates the possession of political *rights*; and the most important problem of tactics which German social democracy has at the present time to solve, appears to me to be to devise the best ways for the extension of the political and economic rights of the German working classes.

*   *   *

That which concerns me, that which forms the chief aim of this work, is, by opposing what is left of the utopian mode of thought in the socialist theory, to strengthen equally the realistic and the idealistic element in the socialist movement.

REVIEW QUESTIONS

1. According to Bernstein, in what ways was the *Communist Manifesto* incorrect?
2. What aspects of political and economic life had alleviated class conflict?
3. What is Bernstein's solution? How does it differ from orthodox Marxism?

VLADIMIR LENIN

FROM *Our Programme*

The extreme conservatism of tsarist government officials found its answer in the revolutionary aspirations of late-nineteenth-century Russian political activists. Whereas populists—the narodniki—*sought to mobilize the Russian peasantry as a revolutionary force, the emergence of an industrial working class convinced Marxist socialists that the urban proletariat would spearhead a revolution against the capitalist development being fostered by the tsarist state itself.*

Vladimir Ilich Ulyanov, better known as Lenin (1870–1924), was drawn into the Russian opposition movement after his brother was executed in 1887 for conspiring to assassinate Tsar Alexander III. In subsequent years, Lenin became one of the leading theorists of the Russian Social Democratic Workers' Party. In 1899, at the end of a period of exile in Siberia, he wrote the following statement of revolutionary principles, affirming his adherence to revolutionary Marxism and rejecting "reformist" tendencies within the international socialist movement. Four years prior to the historic schism between the Social Democratic Party's revolutionary Bolsheviks and the reformist Mensheviks, it was clear that Lenin had already begun to reject worker cooperation with the liberal bourgeoisie and that he was becoming committed to the idea that a "vanguard" of professional revolutionaries must lead the workers' revolution.

From *Our Programme*, by Vladimir Lenin (1899), Internet Modern History Sourcebook, www.fordham.edu/halsall/mod/1899lenin-program.html [accessed 5/17/11].

International social democracy is at present going through a period of theoretical vacillations. Up to the present the doctrines of Marx and Engels were regarded as a firm foundation of revolutionary theory—nowadays voices are raised everywhere declaring these doctrines to be inadequate and antiquated. Anyone calling himself a social-democrat and having the intention to publish a social-democratic organ, must take up a definite attitude as regards this question, which by no means concerns German social-democrats alone.

We base our faith entirely on Marx's theory; it was the first to transform socialism from a Utopia into a science, to give this science a firm foundation and to indicate the path which must be trodden in order further to develop this science and to elaborate it in all its details. It discovered the nature of present-day capitalist economy and explained the way in which the employment of workers—the purchase of labour power—the enslavement of millions of those possessing no property by a handful of capitalists, by the owners of the land, the factories, the mines, etc., is concealed. It has shown how the whole development of modern capitalism is advancing towards the large producer ousting the small one, and is creating the prerequisites which make a socialist order of society possible and necessary. It has taught us to see, under the disguise of ossified habits, political intrigues, intricate laws, cunning theories, the class struggle, the struggle between, on the one hand, the various species of the possessing classes, and, on the other hand, the mass possessing no property, the proletariat, which leads all those who possess nothing. It has made clear what is the real task of a revolutionary socialist party—not to set up projects for the transformation of society, not to preach sermons to the capitalists and their admirers about improving the position of the workers, not the instigation of conspiracies, but the organisation of the class struggle of the proletariat and the carrying on of this struggle, the final aim of which is the seizure of political power by the proletariat and the organisation of a socialist society.

We now ask: What new elements have the touting "renovators" introduced into this theory, they who have attracted so much notice in our day and have grouped themselves round the German socialist Bernstein? Nothing, nothing at all; they have not advanced by a single step the science which Marx and Engels adjured us to develop; they have not taught the proletariat any new methods of fighting; they are only marching backwards in that they adopt the fragments of antiquated theories and are preaching to the proletariat not the theory of struggle but the theory of submissiveness— submissiveness to the bitterest enemies of the proletariat, to the governments and bourgeois parties who never tire of finding new methods of persecuting socialists. Plekhanov, one of the founders and leaders of Russian social-democracy, was perfectly right when he subjected to merciless criticism the latest "Criticism" of Bernstein, whose views have now been rejected even by the representatives of the German workers at the Party Congress in Hanover [1899].

We know that on account of these words we shall be drenched with a flood of accusations; they will cry out that we want to turn the Socialist Party into a holy order of the "orthodox," who persecute the "heretics" for their aberrations from the "true dogma," for any independent opinion, etc. We know all these nonsensical phrases which have become the fashion nowadays. Yet there is no shadow of truth in them, no iota of sense. There can be no strong socialist party without a revolutionary theory which unites all socialists, from which the socialists draw their whole conviction, which they apply in their methods of fighting and working. To defend a theory of this kind, of the truth of which one is completely convinced, against unfounded attacks and against attempts to debase it, does not mean being an enemy of criticism in general. We by no means regard the theory of Marx as perfect and inviolable; on the contrary, we are convinced that this theory has only laid the foundation stones of that science on which the socialists must continue to build in every direction, unless they wish to be left behind by life. We believe that it is particularly necessary for Russian socialists to work out the Marxist theory independently, for this theory only gives general precepts, the details of which must be applied in England otherwise than in France, in France otherwise than in Germany, and in Germany otherwise than in Russia. * * *

What are the main questions which arise in applying the common programme of all social-democrats to Russia?

We have already said that the essence of this programme consists in the organisation of the class struggle of the proletariat and in carrying on this struggle, the final aim of which is the seizure of political power by the proletariat and the construction of a socialist society. The class struggle of the proletariat is divided into: the economic fight (the fight against [the] individual capitalist, or against the individual groups of capitalists by the improvement of the position of the workers) and the political fight (the fight against the Government for the extension of the rights of the people, i.e., for democracy, and for the expansion of the political power of the proletariat). Some Russian social-democrats * * * regard the economic fight as incomparably more important and almost go so far as to postpone the political fight to a more or less distant future. This standpoint is quite wrong. All social-democrats are unanimous in believing that it is necessary to carry on an agitation among the workers on this basis, i.e., to help the workers in their daily fight against the employers, to direct their attention to all kinds and all cases of chicanery, and in this way to make clear to them the necessity of unity. To forget the political for the economic fight would, however, mean a digression from the most important principle of international social-democracy; it would mean forgetting what the whole history of the Labour movement has taught us. Fanatical adherents of the bourgeoisie and of the government which serves it, have indeed repeatedly tried to organise purely economic unions of workers and thus to deflect them from the "politics" of socialism. It is quite possible that the Russian Government will also be clever enough to do something of the kind, as it has always endeavored to throw some largesse or other sham presents to the people in order to prevent them becoming conscious that they are oppressed and are without rights.

No economic fight can give the workers a permanent improvement of their situation, it cannot, indeed, be carried on a large scale unless the workers have the free right to call meetings, to join in unions, to have their own newspapers and to send their representatives to the National Assembly as do the workers in Germany and all European countries (with the exception of Turkey and Russia). In order, however, to obtain these rights, a political fight must be carried on. In Russia, not only the workers but all the citizens are deprived of political rights. Russia is an absolute monarchy. The Tsar alone promulgates laws, nominates officials and controls them. For this reason it seems as though in Russia the Tsar and the Tsarist Government were dependent on no class and cared for all equally. In reality, however, all the officials are chosen exclusively from the possessing class, and all are subject to the influence of the large capitalists who obtain whatever they want—the Ministers dance to the tune the large capitalists play. The Russian worker is bowed under a double yoke; he is robbed and plundered by the capitalists and the landowners, and, lest he should fight against them, he is bound hand and foot by the police, his mouth is gagged and any attempt to defend the rights of the people is followed by persecution. Any strike against a capitalist results in the military and police being let loose on the workers. Every economic fight of necessity turns into a political fight, and social-democracy must indissolubly combine the economic with the political fight into a united class struggle of the proletariat.

The first and chief aim of such a fight must be the conquest of political rights, the conquest of political freedom. Since the workers of St. Petersburg alone have succeeded, in spite of the inadequate support given them by the socialists, in obtaining concessions from the Government within a short time—the passing of a law for shortening the hours of work—the whole working class, led by a united "Russian Social-Democratic Labour Party," will be able, through obstinate fighting, to obtain incomparably more important concessions.

The Russian working class will see its way to carrying on an economic and political fight alone, even if no other class comes to its help. The workers are not alone, however, in the political fight. The fact that the people is absolutely without rights and the unbridled arbitrary rule of the officials rouses the indignation of all who have any pretensions to honesty and educations, who cannot reconcile themselves with the persecution of all free speech and all free thought; it rouses the indignation of the persecuted Poles, Finns, Jews, Russian sects, it rouses the indignation of small traders, of the industrialists, the peasants, of all who can nowhere find protection against the chicanery of the officials and the police. All these groups of the population are incapable of carrying on an obstinate political fight alone; if, however, the working class raises the banner of a fight of this kind it will be supported on all sides. Russian social-democracy will place itself at the head of all fights for the rights of the people, of all fights for democracy, and then it will be invincible.

*   *   *

REVIEW QUESTIONS

1. What tendencies within the socialist movement does Lenin reject here? Why?
2. Why, according to Lenin, must workers combine the fight for economic rights with the fight for political rights?

CLARA ZETKIN

FROM "Women's Work and the Organization of Trade Unions"

The German socialist Clara Zetkin (1857–1933) was well known throughout Europe for her ardent support of working women. Unlike the many left-wing activists who rejected feminism in the belief that the workers' revolution would inevitably bring gender equality in its wake, Zetkin argued that an active commitment to women's rights must go hand in hand with the socialist struggle against capitalism. Although Zetkin was a strong supporter of women's right to vote, as a socialist she rejected the liberal feminism of middle-class suffragettes such as those represented by Emmeline Pankhurst (see selection in this chapter) and instead focused her efforts on seeking solutions to the specific forms of economic oppression suffered by women as workers.

The following article appeared in Gleichheit *("Equality"), the highly successful German socialist women's newspaper that Zetkin edited between 1892 and 1917. Responding to male labor organizers who saw low-paid women workers as competitors and who wished to exclude women from the industrial workforce, Zetkin argues here that the socialist movement would benefit more if male workers sought to bring working women into trade union organizations.*

From *Clara Zetkin: Selected Writings*, edited by Phillip S. Foner, translated by Kai Schoenhals (New York: International, 1984), pp. 51–59.

*   *   *

In all capitalist countries, women's work in industry plays an ever larger role. The number of industrial branches in which women nowadays toil and drudge from morning till night increases with every year. Factories which have traditionally employed women, employ more and more women workers. It is not only that the number of all industrially employed women is constantly growing, but their number in relation to the men who are working in industry and trade is also on the increase.

Some branches of industry (one has only to think of clothing) are virtually dominated by women's labor which constantly reduces and replaces men's labor.

For understandable reasons, particularly during periods of recession (like the one we are experiencing right now), the number of women workers has increased in both relative and absolute terms whereas the number of employed male laborers has decreased.

*   *   *

The reasons for the constantly growing use of female laborers have been repeatedly pointed out: their cheapness and the improvement of the mechanical means and methods of production. The automatic machine, which in many cases does not even stand in need of having to be regulated, works with the powers of a giant, possesses unbelievable skill, speed and exactness and renders muscle power and acquired skills superfluous. The capitalist entrepreneur can employ only female labor at those places where he previously had to use male employees. And he just loves to hire women because female labor is cheap, much cheaper than male labor.

Even though the productive capacity of female workers does not lag behind that of male workers, the difference between men's and women's wages is very significant. The latter is often only half of the former and often only a third.

*   *   *

* * * [T]he living conditions of these female workers correspond to their miserable earnings. It is easily understandable that these customary starvation wages for female laborers push thousands of them from the proletariat into the lumpenproletariat.[1] Their dire straits force some of them to take up part-time or temporary prostitution so that by selling their bodies, they may earn the piece of bread that they cannot secure by the sale of their labor.

But it is not just the women workers who suffer because of the miserable payment of their labor. The male workers, too, suffer because of it. As a consequence of their low wages, the women are transformed from mere competitors into unfair competitors who push down the wages of men. Cheap women's labor eliminates the work of men and if the men want to continue to earn their daily bread, they must put up with low wages. Thus women's work is not only a cheap form of labor, it also cheapens the work of men and for that reason it is doubly appreciated by the capitalist, who craves profits.

*   *   *

The transfer of hundreds of thousands of female laborers to the modernized means of production that increase productivity ten or even a

hundredfold should have resulted (and did result in some cases) in a higher standard of living for the proletariat, given a rationally organized society. But as far as the proletariat is concerned, capitalism has changed blessing into curse and wealth into bitter poverty. The economic advantages of the industrial activity of proletarian women only aid the tiny minority of the sacrosanct guild of coupon clippers and extortionists of profit.

Frightened by the economic consequences of women's work and the abuses connected with it, organized labor demanded for a while the prohibition of female labor. It was viewing this question merely from the narrow viewpoint of the wage question. Thanks to Socialist propaganda, the class-conscious proletariat has learned to view this question from another angle, from the angle of its historical importance for the liberation of women and the liberation of the proletariat. It understands now how impossible it is to abolish the industrial labor of women. Thus it has dropped its former demand and it attempts to lessen the bad economic consequences of women's work within capitalist society (and only within it!) by two other means; by the legal protection of female workers and by their inclusion in trade union organizations. We have already mentioned above the necessity and the advantageous effects of the legal protection of women workers. * * *

Given the fact that many thousands of female workers are active in industry, it is vital for the trade unions to incorporate them into their movement. In individual industries where female labor plays an important role, any movement advocating better wages, shorter working hours, etc., would be doomed from the start because of the attitude of those women workers who are not organized. Battles which began propitiously enough, ended up in failure because the employers were able to play off non-union female workers against those that are organized in unions. These non-union workers continued to work (or took up work) under any conditions, which transformed them from competitors in dirty work to scabs.

It is not only because of the successful economic battles of trade unions that women should

---

[1] In Marxist terminology, the *lumpenproletariat* consists of the lowest ranks of the working class. It verges on being a criminal underclass and is disinclined to join with honest workers in the struggle against capitalism.

be included in them. The improvement of the starvation wages of female workers and the limitation of competition among them requires their organization into unions.

The fact that the pay for female labor is so much lower than that of male labor has a variety of causes. Certainly one of the reasons for these poor wages for women is the circumstance that female workers are practically unorganized. They lack the strength which comes with unity. They lack the courage, the feeling of power, the spirit of resistance and the ability to resist which is produced by the strength of an organization in which the individual fights for everybody and everybody fights for the individual. Furthermore, they lack the enlightenment and the training which an organization provides. Without an understanding of modern economic life in whose machinery they are inextricably caught up, they will neither be able to take advantage of periods of boom through conscious, calculating and unified conduct nor will they be able to protect themselves against the disadvantages occurring during periods of economic recession. If, under the pressure of unbearable conditions they finally fight back, they usually do so at an inopportune moment and in a disorganized fashion.

This situation exercises a great influence upon the miserable state of women's work and is further reflected by the bitterness that male workers feel about women's competition. Thus in the interest of both men and women workers, it is urgently recommended that the latter be included in the trade unions. The larger the number of organized female workers who fight shoulder to shoulder with their comrades from the factory or workshop for better working conditions, the sooner and the greater will women's wages rise so that soon there may be the realization of the principle: Equal pay for equal work regardless of the difference in sex. The organized female worker who has become the equal of the male worker ceases to be his scab competitor.

The unionized male workers realize more and more just how important it is that the female workers are accepted into the ranks of their organization. During these past few years, there was no lack of effort on the part of the unions in regard to this endeavor. And yet how little has been accomplished and how incredibly much remains to be done in this respect.

*   *   *

Even in those industrial branches in which the trade union organization of women began, these organizations are still in their infancy.

*   *   *

As far as the percentage of female membership is concerned, the Tobacco Workers rank first, and yet these women workers do not even constitute a fourth of its entire membership. In 1882, 43.1% of all tobacco industry workers were women. In the other four trade unions which come next, as far as the percentage of women that work in the industries they represent are concerned, women workers do not even constitute 10% of the membership. The Organization of Gold and Silver Workers does not have a female membership of even 5% even though there are large numbers of women workers who are employed by the gold and silver industry. In 1882, 60% of all laborers in spinning mills and 30% of all laborers in weaving mills happened to be women, yet the percentage of them who were unionized amounted to only 9½%. These numbers, in conjunction with the slave wages which generally prevail in the textile industry, speak whole volumes about the necessity of unionizing women.

In recognition of this necessity, the trade unions should use all of their energies to work for the inclusion of women in their organizations.

We certainly do not fail to recognize the difficulties raised by women workers which are detrimental to the solution of this problem. Stupid resignation, lack of a feeling of solidarity, shyness, prejudices of all kinds and fear of the factory tyrant keep many women from joining unions. Even more than the just mentioned factors, the lack of time on the part of female workers represents a major obstacle against their mass organization because women are house as well as factory slaves and are forced to bear a double workload. The economic developments, however, as well as the increasing acuteness of the class struggle, educate both male and female laborers and force them to overcome the above-mentioned difficulties. ✶ ✶ ✶

Theoretically, most male union members admit that the common unionization of both male and female workers of the same trade has become an unavoidable necessity. In practice, however, many of them do not make the effort that they could be making. Rather there are only a few unions and within them only certain individuals who pursue with energy and perseverance the organization of female workers. The majority of trade union members give them precious little support. They treat such endeavors as a hobby which should be tolerated but not supported "as long as there are still so many indifferent non-union male workers." This point of view is totally wrong.

The unionization of women workers will make significant progress only when it is no longer merely aided by the few, but by every single union member making every effort to enlist their female colleagues from factory and workshop. In order to fulfill this task, two things are necessary. The male workers must stop viewing the female worker primarily as a woman to be courted if she is young, beautiful, pleasant and cheerful (or not). They must stop (depending on their degree of culture or lack of it) molesting them with crude and fresh sexual advances. The workers must rather get accustomed to treat female laborers primarily as

female proletarians, as working-class comrades fighting class slavery and as equal and indispensable co-fighters in the class struggle. The unions make such a big thing out of having all of the members and followers of the political party become members of the unions. It seems to us that it would be much more important to put the emphasis on enrolling the broad, amorphous masses in the labor movement. In our opinion, the main task of the unions is the enlightenment, disciplining and education of all workers for the class struggle. In view of the increasing use of female labor and the subsequent results, the labor movement will surely commit suicide if, in its effort to enroll the broad masses of the proletariat, it does not pay the same amount of attention to female workers as it does to male ones.

REVIEW QUESTIONS

1. To what extent does Zetkin's discussion of women's work reflect the changes in industrial work conditions brought about by the second industrial revolution?
2. According to Zetkin, what factors cause divisions between male and female workers?
3. How does Zetkin suggest that socialist workers build solidarity within their ranks?
4. What sort of socialist is Zetkin? What sort of feminist is she?

PETER KROPOTKIN

FROM "Anarchism: Its Philosophy and Ideal"

Written by a leading theoretician of anarchism, this pamphlet of 1896 concisely outlined the movement's rejection of the state. In place of the "dominating minorities" of governments and ruling classes, Peter Kropotkin (1842–1921) proposed organizing society through networks of voluntary associations. Anarchism, a libertarian socialism, envisioned free individuals satisfying their needs through mutual-aid societies, which promised to render superfluous all governments, armies, religions, and capitalist economies. Although anarchism focused on the positive side of unfettered individuality, it did not reject violence as a means to realize a free society. For this reason, nineteenth-century anarchists defended assassinations as moral acts benefiting humanity. Kropotkin, the son of a Russian prince, was a soldier, geographer, and government official before he left Russia to join socialist organizations in Switzerland, France, and Britain. After embracing the anarchist creed in the 1870s, he took a leading role in disseminating its ideals through numerous publications.

From "Anarchism: Its Philosophy and Ideal," by Peter Kropotkin (San Francisco: Free Society, 1898), pp. 15–17.

*   *   *

In proportion as the human mind frees itself from ideas inculcated by minorities of priests, military chiefs and judges, all striving to establish their domination, and of scientists paid to perpetuate it, a conception of society arises in which there is no longer room for those dominating minorities. A society entering into possession of the social capital accumulated by the labour of preceding generations, organizing itself so as to make use of this capital in the interests of all, and constituting itself without reconstituting the power of the ruling minorities. It comprises in its midst an infinite variety of capacities, temperaments and individual energies: it excludes none. It even calls for struggles and contentions; because we know that periods of contests, so long as they were freely fought out without the weight of constituted authority being thrown on one side of the balance, were periods when human genius took its mightiest flights and achieved the greatest aims. Acknowledging, as a fact, the equal rights of its members to the treasures accumulated in the past, it no longer recognizes a division between exploited and exploiters, governed and governors, dominated and dominators, and it seeks to establish a certain harmonious compatibility in its midst—not by subjecting all its members to an authority that is fictitiously supposed to represent society, not by crying to establish uniformity, but by urging all men to develop free initiative, free action, free association.

It seeks the most complete development of individuality combined with the highest development of voluntary association in all its aspects, in all possible degrees, for all imaginable aims; ever changing, ever modified associations which carry in themselves the elements of their durability and constantly assume new forms which answer best to the multiple aspirations of all.

A society to which pre-established forms, crystallized by law, are repugnant; which looks for harmony in an ever-changing and fugitive equilibrium between a multitude of varied forces and influences of every kind, following their own course,—these forces themselves promoting the energies which are favourable to their march towards progress, towards the liberty of developing in broad daylight and counterbalancing one another.

. . . [I]f man, since his origin, has always lived in societies, the State is but one of the forms of social life, quite recent as far as regards European societies. Men lived thousands of years before the first States were constituted; Greece and Rome existed for centuries before the Macedonian and Roman Empires were built up, and for us modern Europeans the centralized States date but from the sixteenth century. It was only then, after the defeat of the free medieval communes had been completed that the mutual insurance company between military, judicial, landlord, and capitalist authority, which we call the "State," could be fully established. . . .

We know well the means by which this association of lord, priest, merchant, judge, soldier, and king founded its domination. It was by the annihilation of all free unions: of village communities, guilds, trades unions, fraternities, and medieval cities. It was by confiscating the land of the communes and the riches of the guilds. It was by the absolute and ferocious prohibition of all kinds of free agreement between men. It was by massacre, the wheel, the gibbet, the sword, and fire that church and State established their domination, and that they succeeded henceforth to reign over an incoherent agglomeration of "subjects" who had no more direct union among themselves.

It is only recently that we began to reconquer, by struggle, by revolt, the first steps of the right of association that was freely practiced by the artisans and the tillers of the soil through the whole of the middle ages.

And, already now, Europe is covered by thousands of voluntary associations for study and teaching, for industry, commerce, science, art, literature, exploitation, resistance to exploitation, amusement, serious work, gratification and self-denial, for all that makes up the life of an active and thinking being. We see these societies rising in all nooks and corners of all domains: political, economic, artistic, intellectual. Some are as short lived as roses, some hold their own for several decades, and all strive—while maintaining the independence of each group, circle, branch, or section—to federate, to unite, across frontiers as well as among each nation; to cover all the life of civilized men with a net, meshes of which are intersected and interwoven. Their numbers can already be reckoned by tens of thousands, they comprise millions of adherents—although less than fifty years have elapsed since church and State began to tolerate a few of them—very few, indeed.

These societies already begin to encroach everywhere on the functions of the State, and strive to substitute free action of volunteers for that of a centralized State. In England we see insurance companies arise against theft; societies for coast defence, volunteer societies for land defence, which the State endeavours to get under its thumb, thereby making them instruments of domination, although their original aim was to do without the State. Were it not for church and State, free societies would have already conquered the whole of the immense domain of education. And, in spite of all difficulties, they begin to invade this domain as well, and make their influence already felt.

And when we mark the progress already accomplished in that direction, in spite of and against the State, which tries by all means to maintain its supremacy of recent origin; when we see how voluntary societies invade everything and are only impeded in their development by the State, we are forced to recognize a powerful *tendency*, a latent force in modern society. And we ask ourselves this question: If five, ten, or twenty years hence—it matters little—the workers succeed by revolt in destroying the said mutual insurance societies of landlords, bankers, priests, judges, and soldiers; if the people become masters of their destiny for a few months, and lay hands on the riches they have created, and which belong to them by right—will they really begin to reconstitute that blood-sucker, the State? Or will they not rather try to organize from the simple to the complex according to mutual agreement and to the infinitely varied, ever-changing needs of each locality, in order to secure the possession of those riches for themselves, to mutually guarantee one another's life, and to produce what will be found necessary for life?

. . . It is often said that anarchists live in a world of dreams to come, and do not see the things which happen today. We see them only too well, and in their true colours, and that is what makes us carry the hatchet into the forest of prejudices that besets us.

Far from living in a world of visions and imagining men better than they are, we see them as they are; and that is why we affirm that the best of men is made essentially bad by the exercise of authority, and that the theory of the "balancing of powers" and "control of authorities" is a hypocritical formula, invented by those who have seized power, to make the "sovereign people," whom they despise, believe that the people themselves are governing. It is because we know men that we say to those who imagine that men would devour one another without those governors: "You reason like the king, who, being sent across the frontier, called out, 'What will become of my poor subjects without me?'"

Ah, if men were those superior beings that the utopians of authority like to speak to us of, if we could close our eyes to reality and live like them in a world of dreams and illusions as to the superiority of those who think themselves called to power, perhaps we also should do like them; perhaps we also should believe in the virtues of those who govern.

If the gentlemen in power were really so intelligent and so devoted to the public cause, as panegyrists of authority love to represent, what a pretty government and paternal utopia we should be able to construct! The employer would never be the tyrant of the worker; he would be the father! The factory would be a palace of delight, and never would masses of workers be doomed to physical deterioration. A judge would not have the ferocity to condemn the wife and children of the one whom he sends to prison to suffer years of hunger and misery and to die some day of anemia; never would a public prosecutor ask for the head of the accused for the unique pleasure of showing off his oratorical talent; and nowhere would we find a jailer or an executioner to do the bidding of judges who have not the courage to carry out their sentences themselves.

*   *   *

All the science of government, imagined by those who govern, is imbued with these utopias. But we know men too well to dream such dreams. We have not two measures for the virtues of the governed and those of the governors; we know that we ourselves are not without faults and that the best of us would soon be corrupted by the exercise of power. We take men for what they are worth—and that is why we hate the government of man by man, and why we work with all our might—perhaps not strong enough—to put an end to it.

But it is not enough to destroy. We must also know how to build, and it is owing to not having thought about it that the masses have always been led astray in all their revolutions. After having demolished they abandoned the care of reconstruction to the middle-class people who possessed a more or less precise conception of what they wished to realize, and who consequently reconstituted authority to their own advantage.

That is why anarchism, when it works to destroy authority in all its aspects, when it demands the abrogation of laws and the abolition of the mechanism that serves to impose them, when it refuses all hierarchical organization and preaches free agreement, at the same time strives to maintain and enlarge the precious kernel of social customs without which no human or animal society can exist. Only instead of demanding that those social customs should be maintained through the authority of a few, it demands it from the continued action of all.

*   *   *

REVIEW QUESTIONS

1. In what ways does anarchism object to the principle and practice of the state?
2. Is Kropotkin optimistic about the development of anarchism in his time?
3. How does Kropotkin respond to the charge that anarchists are dreamers?
4. How does anarchism differ from socialism?

GEORGES SOREL

FROM *Reflections on Violence*

Although Marxist socialism was the dominant political ideology of workers, syndicalism was widely preferred in areas of France, Spain, and Italy. Syndicalism grew out of trade union associations that espoused the utopian vision of one day controlling their industries and, eventually, the political state. The strike became the central weapon of syndicalism, but it was the general strike that made syndicalism revolutionary. The thousands of strikes in Europe at the end of the nineteenth century offered the potential of one mighty, total work stoppage that would ruin capitalism and dismantle the state. Georges Sorel (1847–1922) wrote his treatise on syndicalism in 1908. The following excerpt includes Sorel's important notion of the general strike as a mythic belief, the widespread acceptance of which would prompt collective action by workers as well as soften employers' resolve against concessions.

From *Reflections on Violence*, by Georges Sorel, edited by T. E. Hulme (New York: Huebsch, 1914).

* * *

Against this noisy, garrulous, and lying Socialism, which is exploited by ambitious people of every description, which amuses a few buffoons, and which is admired by decadents—revolutionary Syndicalism takes its stand, and endeavours, on the contrary, to leave nothing in a state of indecision; its ideas are honestly expressed, without trickery and without mental reservations; no attempt is made to dilute doctrines by a stream of confused commentaries. Syndicalism endeavours to employ methods of expression which throw a full light on things, which put them exactly in the place assigned to them by their nature, and which bring out the whole value of the forces in play. Oppositions, instead of being glazed over, must be thrown into sharp relief if we desire to obtain a clear idea of the Syndicalist movement; the groups which are struggling one against the other must be shown as separate and as compact as possible; in short, the movements of the revolted masses must be represented in such a way that the soul of the revolutionaries may receive a deep and lasting impression.

These results could not be produced in any very certain manner by the use of ordinary language; use must be made of a body of images which, *by intuition alone*, and before any considered analyses are made, is capable of evoking as an undivided whole the mass of sentiments which corresponds to the different manifestations of the war undertaken by Socialism against modern society. The Syndicalists solve this problem perfectly, by concentrating the whole of Socialism in the drama of the general strike; there is thus no longer any place for the reconciliation of contraries in the equivocations of the professors; everything is clearly mapped out, so that only one interpretation of Socialism is possible. This method has all the advantages which "integral" knowledge has over analysis, according to the doctrine of Bergson; and perhaps it would not be possible to cite another example which would so perfectly demonstrate the value of the famous professor's doctrines.

The possibility of the actual realisation of the general strike has been much discussed; it has been stated that the Socialist war could not be decided in one single battle. To the people who think themselves cautious, practical, and scientific the difficulty of setting great masses of the proletariat in motion at the same moment seems prodigious; they have analysed the difficulties of detail which such an enormous struggle would present. It is the opinion of the Socialist-sociologists, as also of the politicians, that the general strike is a popular dream, characteristic of the beginnings of a working-class movement; we have had quoted against us the authority of Sidney Webb, who has decreed that the general strike is an illusion of youth, of which the English workers—whom the monopolists of sociology have so often presented to us as the depositaries of the true conception of the working-class movement—soon rid themselves.

*   *   *

And yet without leaving the present, without reasoning about this future, which seems for ever condemned to escape our reason, we should be unable to act at all. Experience shows that the *framing of a future, in some indeterminate time,* may, when it is done in a certain way, be very effective, and have very few inconveniences; this happens when the anticipations of the future take the form of those myths, which enclose with them all the strongest inclinations of a people, of a party or of a class, inclinations which recur to the mind with the insistence of instincts in all the circumstances of life; and which give an aspect of complete reality to the hopes of immediate action by which, more easily than by any other method, men can reform their desires, passions, and mental activity. We know, moreover, that these social myths in no way prevent a man profiting by the observations which he makes in the course of his life, and form no obstacle to the pursuit of his normal occupations.

The truth of this may be shown by numerous examples.

The first Christians expected the return of Christ and the total ruin of the pagan world, with the inauguration of the kingdom of the saints, at the end of the first generation. The catastrophe did not come to pass, but Christian thought profited so greatly from the apocalyptic myth that certain contemporary scholars maintain that the whole preaching of Christ referred solely to this one point. The hopes which Luther and Calvin had formed of the religious exaltation of Europe were by no means realised; these fathers of the Reformation very soon seemed men of a past era; for present-day Protestants they belong rather to the Middle Ages than to modern times, and the problems which troubled them most occupy very little place in contemporary Protestantism. Must we for that reason deny the immense result which came from their dreams of Christian renovation?

*   *   *

In our own times Mazzini pursued what the wiseacres of his time called a mad chimera; but it can no longer be denied that, without Mazzini, Italy would never have become a great power, and that he did more for Italian unity than Cavour and all the politicians of his school.

*   *   *

The myth must be judged as a means of acting on the present; any attempt to discuss how far it can be taken literally as future history is devoid of sense. *It is the myth in its entirety which is alone important:* its parts are only of interest in so far as they bring out the main idea. No useful purpose is served, therefore, in arguing about the incidents which may occur in the course of a social war, and about the decisive conflicts which may give victory to the proletariat; even supposing the revolutionaries to have been wholly and entirely deluded in setting up this imaginary picture of the general strike, this picture may yet have been, in the course of the preparation for the Revolution, a great element of strength, if it has embraced all the aspirations of Socialism, and if it has given to the whole body of Revolutionary thought a precision and a rigidity which no other method of thought could have given.

To estimate, then, the significance of the idea of the general strike, all the methods of discussion which are current among politicians, sociologists, or people with pretensions to political science, must be abandoned. Everything which its opponents endeavour to establish may be conceded to them, without reducing in any way the value of the theory which they think they have refuted. The question whether the general strike is a partial reality, or only a product of popular imagination, is of little importance. All that it is necessary to know is, whether the general strike contains everything that the Socialist doctrine expects of the revolutionary proletariat.

To solve this question we are no longer compelled to argue learnedly about the future; we are not obliged to indulge in lofty reflections about philosophy, history, or economics; we are not on the plane of theories, and we can remain on the level of observable facts. We have to question men who take a very active part in the real revolutionary movement amidst the proletariat, men who do not aspire to climb into the middle class and whose mind is not dominated by corporative prejudices. These men may be deceived about an infinite number of political, economical, or moral questions; but their testimony is decisive, sovereign, and irrefutable when it is a question of knowing what are the ideas which most powerfully move them and their comrades, which most appeal to them as being identical with their socialistic conceptions, and thanks to which their reason, their hopes, and their way of looking at particular facts seem to make but one indivisible unity.

Thanks to these men, we know that the general strike is indeed what I have said: the *myth* in which Socialism is wholly comprised, *i.e.* a body of images capable of evoking instinctively all the sentiments which correspond to the different manifestations of the war undertaken by Socialism against modern society. Strikes have engendered in the proletariat the noblest, deepest, and most moving sentiments that they possess; the general strike groups them all in a co-ordinated picture, and, by bringing them together, gives to each one of them its maximum of intensity; appealing to their painful memories of particular conflicts, it colours with an intense life all the details of the composition presented to consciousness. We thus obtain that intuition of Socialism which language cannot give us with perfect clearness—and we obtain it as a whole, perceived instantaneously.

We may urge yet another piece of evidence to prove the power of the idea of the general strike. If that idea were a pure chimera, as is so frequently said, Parliamentary Socialists would not attack it with such heat; I do not remember that they ever attacked the senseless hopes which the Utopists have always held up before the dazzled eyes of the people.

*　　*　　*

They struggle against the conception of the general strike, because they recognise, in the course of their propagandist rounds, that this conception is so admirably adapted to the working-class mind that there is a possibility of its dominating the latter in the most absolute manner, thus leaving no place for the desires which the Parliamentarians are able to satisfy. They perceive that this idea is so effective as a motive force that once it has entered the minds of the people they can no longer be controlled by leaders, and that thus the power of the deputies would be reduced to nothing. In short, they feel in a vague way that the whole Socialist movement might easily be absorbed by the general strike, which would render useless all those compromises between political groups in view of which the Parliamentary régime has been built up.

The opposition it meets with from official Socialists, therefore, furnishes a confirmation of our first inquiry into the scope of the general strike.

*　　*　　*

REVIEW QUESTIONS

1. How does Sorel differentiate between socialism and syndicalism?
2. For Sorel, what is the real significance of the general strike?
3. How does Sorel compare syndicalism with Christianity and nationalism?
4. What, for Sorel, is the importance of myth in political struggle?

ÉDOUARD DRUMONT

FROM *Jewish France*

During the first half of the nineteenth century, European Jews won many new guarantees of legal and political equality, largely as a result of political liberalism and the growing secularization of European society. In western Europe especially, it almost seemed that centuries of anti-Semitism would be brought to an end through the quiet assimilation of Jews into mainstream national cultures. However, in the final quarter of the century, a new and virulent form of anti-Semitism emerged, threatening Jewish communities' fragile political and social gains.

In France as elsewhere, Jews became scapegoats for deep-seated cultural anxieties stimulated by the political instability of the Third Republic, as well as the massive social and economic changes generated by French industrialization. During the Dreyfus affair, French anti-Semites were rallied to the cause by Édouard Drumont (1844–1917), the editor of La Libre parole *("The Free Word"), a conservative anti-Semitic journal, and the founder of the French Anti-Semitic League. Drumont's* Jewish France, *published in 1885, enjoyed immense popularity: at least 150,000 copies were sold within two years of its first appearance, and it remained in print long into the twentieth century. As the following excerpt from his work demonstrates, Drumont's anti-Semitism took the form of an argument that "old France" was being "conquered" by an alien and parasitic Jewish culture.*

From *La France juive: Essai d'histoire contemporaine*, by Édouard Drumont (Paris: Marpon and Flammarion, 1997), translated by Cat Nilan for the present edition.

The only one who has benefitted from the Revolution [of 1789] is the Jew. Everything comes from the Jew; everything returns to the Jew.

We have here a veritable conquest, an entire nation returned to serfdom by a minute but cohesive minority, just as the Saxons were forced into serfdom by William the Conqueror's 60,000 Normans.

The methods are different, the result is the same. One can recognize all the characteristics of a conquest: an entire population working for another population, which appropriates, through a vast system of financial exploitation, all of the profits of the other. Immense Jewish fortunes, castles, Jewish townhouses, are not the fruit of any actual labor, of any production: they are the booty taken from an enslaved race by a dominant race.

It is certain, for example, that the Rothschild family, whose French branch alone possesses a declared fortune of three billion [francs], did not have that money when it arrived in France; it has invented nothing, it has discovered no mine, it has tilled no ground. It has therefore appropriated these three billion francs from the French without giving them anything in exchange.

*   *   *

All Jewish fortunes have been built up in the same manner, through an appropriation of the work of others.

*   *   *

Today, thanks to the Jew, money—to which the Christian world attached only a secondary importance and assigned only a subordinate role—has become all powerful. Capitalist power concentrated in a tiny number of hands governs at will the entire economic life of the people, enslaves their labor, and feasts on iniquitous profits acquired without labor.

These problems, familiar to all thinking Europeans, are all but unknown in France. The reason is simple. The Jew Lassalle himself has noted how slender are the intellectual foundations of the bourgeoisie, whose opinions are fabricated by the newspapers. * * *

Now, since almost all newspapers and all organs of publicity in France are in the hands of Jews or belong to them indirectly, it is not surprising that the significance and the scope of the immense anti-Semitic movement that has begun to organize itself everywhere is being carefully hidden from us.

* * *

In any case, it seems to me interesting and useful to describe the successive phases of this *Jewish Conquest,* to indicate how, little by little, as a result of Jewish activities, old France has been dissolved, broken up, how its unselfish, happy, loving people has been replaced by a hateful people, hungry for gold and soon to be dying of hunger.

* * *

Thanks to the Jews' cunning exploitation of the principles of '89, France was collapsing into dissolution. Jews had monopolized all of the public wealth, had invaded everything, except the army. The representatives of the old [French] families, whether noble or bourgeois, had divided themselves into two camps. Some gave themselves up to pleasure, and were corrupted by the Jewish prostitutes they had taken as mistresses or were ruined by the horse-sellers and money-lenders, also Jews, who aided the prostitutes. The others obeyed the attraction exercised over the Aryan race by the infinite, the Hindu Nirvana, Odin's paradise. They became almost uninterested in contemporary life, they lost themselves in ecstasy, they barely had one foot still planted in the real world.

If the Semites could have been patient for a few years they would have achieved their goal. Jules Simon, one of the few truly wise men they count among their ranks * * * , told them exactly what they needed to do: quietly take over the earth and let the Aryans migrate up to heaven.

The Jews never wanted to listen to this message: they preferred the Semite Gambetta to the Semite Simon. * * * they believed that [Gambetta] was going to help them get rid of Christ, whom they still hated just as much as they had on the day they crucified him. Freemasonry made its contribution, Jewish journals stirred up public opinion, gold was freely distributed, police superintendents were richly paid off, although they refused to make themselves guilty of a crime up to the last minute.

What happened? * * * The Aryan—provoked, troubled, wounded in his innate feelings of nobility and generosity—felt his blood rise to his face when he saw unfortunate old [monks] dragged from their cells by the dregs of the police. He took a while to deliberate, to gather his thoughts, to reflect.

"In the name of what principle are you acting?" he asked.

"In the name of the principle of liberty," replied in unison the newspapers of Porgès, Reinach, Dreyfus, Eugène Mayer, Camille Sée, Naquet.

"And what does this principle consist of?"

"Of this: some Jew or another leaves Hamburg, Frankfurt, Vilna, or anyplace else, and he amasses a certain number of millions at the expense of the *goyim* [gentiles]. He can take his carriage out for a ride, his domicile is inviolable, unless a warrant is issued, and naturally it never is. On the other hand, a native Frenchman, a *natural Frenchman,* to use the words of Saint-Simon, gives away everything he owns to help the poor; he goes barefoot, he lives in a narrow, whitewashed cell that the servant of Rothschild's servant wouldn't want. He is the outlaw. He can be thrown out in the street like a dog."

The Aryan, roused from his slumbers, decides, not without reason, that once this so precious tolerance—talked about so much for the last hundred years—is interpreted in this way, it is better to strike back than be struck. He decides that it is more than time to wrest the country from such impatient masters. "Since the monk's rough robe is so annoying to your frock-coat, we'll give you back the yellow rag, my old Shem." Such was the upshot of [the Aryan's] meditations. It is from that moment that one can date the establishment of the first anti-Semitic—or, to be more precise, anti-Jewish—committee.

* * *

* * * The fatherland, in the sense that we attach to that word, has no meaning for the Semite. The Jew, to use the energetic expression of the *Israelite Alliance,* is characterized by an *inexorable universalism.*

I can see no reason for reproaching the Jews for thinking this way. What does the word "Fatherland" mean? Land of the fathers. One's feelings for the Fatherland are engraved in one's heart in the same way that a name carved in a tree is driven deeper into the bark with each passing year, so that the tree and the name eventually become one. You can't become a patriot through improvization; you are a patriot in your blood, in your marrow.

Can the Semite, a perpetual nomad, ever experience such enduring impressions?

* * * The first requirement for adopting a new fatherland, is to renounce the old one. Now, the Jew has a fatherland he never renounces: Jerusalem, the holy and mysterious city Jerusalem. In triumph or persecution, joyous or sad, it serves as a link uniting all of those children who say every year at Rosh Hashanah: "next year in Jerusalem!"

Aside from Jerusalem, every other country, whether France, or Germany, or England, is only a residence for the Jew, any old place, a social agglomeration, in the midst of which he may find himself at home, whose interests he may even find it profitable to serve for the moment, but which he joins only as a free agent, as a temporary member.

* * *

To succeed in their attack against Christian civilization, the Jews of France had to use deceit, to lie, to disguise themselves as freethinkers. If they had said frankly: "We want to destroy that France of old, so glorious, so beautiful, and replace it with domination by a fistful of Hebrews from many lands," our fathers, less soft than ourselves, would not have let this happen. For a long time [the Jews] kept things vague, working with Freemasonry, hiding behind sonorous words: emancipation, enfranchisement, the struggle against superstition and the prejudices of another age.

* * *

* * * Among the Jews, religious persecution takes on a particularly bitter character. For them, nothing has changed: they hate Christ as much in 1885 as they hated him at the time of Tiberius Augustus, and they heap the same outrages upon him. Whipping the crucifix on Good Friday, profaning the host, besmirching sacred images: such was the great joy of the medieval Jew, and such is his great joy today. Then, he attacked the bodies of children; today, he tries to get at their souls through atheist education. Then, he bled them; today, he poisons their minds: which is worse?

* * *

Despite everything, it is difficult to escape the influence of what one hears from morning to night, from the impression of the artificial intellectual climate created by the Jewish press, and even the best sometimes are subject, despite themselves, to what we have already named the *prejudices of modernism.*

* * *

As for myself, I repeat that I claim to have done nothing more than to attempt a work of good will, to demonstrate by what an underhanded and crafty enemy France has been invaded, corrupted, and brutalized, to such a point that she has broken with her proper hands everything that once made her powerful, respected, and happy. Have I written our last will and testament? Have I laid the foundations for our rebirth? I do not know. I have done my duty, in any case, by responding with insults to the numberless insults that the Jewish press directs at Christians. In proclaiming the Truth, I have obeyed the imperious command of my conscience: *liberavi animam meam* [I have freed my soul]. ✶ ✶ ✶

✶   ✶   ✶

REVIEW QUESTIONS

1. Of what "crimes" were the Jews of France guilty, according to Drumont?
2. How did they get away with these crimes?
3. What does Drumont mean by "tolerance"? Why does he reject it?
4. What, for Drumont, are the "prejudices of modernism"?
5. Why does Drumont associate Jews with modernism?
6. After reading this excerpt, why do you think Drumont hated Jews?
7. Why do you think his arguments might have appealed to many late-nineteenth-century Europeans?

EMMELINE PANKHURST

FROM *Why We Are Militant*

In 1903, Emmeline Pankhurst (1858–1928) founded the Women's Social and Political Union, an organization that advocated militancy and direct action to promote the cause of female suffrage, which had become an international movement since the 1890s. Angered by the insouciance of the British political establishment, which remained unfazed by the massive petitions and peaceful demonstrations of suffragistes, Pankhurst's association organized hunger strikes and assaults on private property to signify the gravity of the matter. In the following speech of October 21, 1913, delivered in New York, Pankhurst justified the tactics of the Women's Social and Political Union.

From *Why We Are Militant: A Speech Delivered by Mrs. Pankhurst in New York, October 21, 1913* (London: Women's Press, 1914).

I know that in your minds there are questions like these; you are saying, "Woman Suffrage is sure to come; the emancipation of humanity is an evolutionary process, and how is it that some women, instead of trusting to that evolution, instead of educating the masses of people of their country, instead of educating their own sex to prepare them for citizenship, how is it that these militant women are using violence and upsetting the business arrangements of the country in their undue impatience to attain their end?"

Let me try to explain to you the situation.

Although we have a so-called democracy, and so called representative government there, England is the most conservative country on earth. Why, your forefathers found that out a great many years ago! If you had passed your life in England as I have, you would know that there are certain words which certainly, during the last two generations, certainly till about ten years ago, aroused a feeling of horror and fear in the minds of the mass of the people. The word revolution, for instance, was identified in England with all kind of horrible ideas. The idea of change, the idea of unsettling the established order of things was repugnant.

*   *   *

The extensions of the franchise to the men of my country have been preceded by very great violence, by something like a revolution, by something like civil war. In 1832, you know we were on the edge of a civil war and on the edge of revolution, and it was at the point of the sword —no, not at the point of the sword—it was after the practice of arson on so large a scale that half the city of Bristol was burned down in a single night, it was because more and greater violence and arson were feared that the Reform Bill of 1832 was allowed to pass into law. In 1867, John Bright urged the people of London to crowd the approaches to the Houses of Parliament in order to show their determination, and he said that if they did that no Parliament, however obdurate, could resist their just demands. Rioting went on all over the country, and as the result of that rioting, as the result of that unrest, which resulted in the pulling down of the Hyde Park railings, as a result of the fear of more rioting and violence the Reform Act of 1867 was put upon the statute books.

In 1884 came the turn of the agricultural labourer. Joseph Chamberlain, who afterwards became a very conservative person, threatened that, unless the vote was given to the agricultural labourer, he would march 100,000 men from Birmingham to know the reason why. Rioting was threatened and feared, and so the agricultural labourers got the vote.

Meanwhile, during the '80's, women, like men, were asking for the franchise. Appeals, larger and more numerous than for any other reform, were presented in support of Woman's Suffrage. Meetings of the great corporations, great town councils, and city councils, passed resolutions asking that women should have the vote. More meetings were held, and larger, for Woman Suffrage than were held for votes for men, and yet the women did not get it. Men got the vote because they were and would be violent. The women did not get it because they were constitutional and law-abiding. Why, is it not evident to everyone that people who are patient where mis-government is concerned may go on being patient! Why should anyone trouble to help them? I take to myself some shame that through all those years, at any rate from the early '80's, when I first came into the Suffrage movement, I did not learn my political lessons.

I believed, as many women still in England believe, that women could get their way in some mysterious manner, by purely peaceful methods. We have been so accustomed, we women, to accept one standard for men and another standard for women, that we have even applied that variation of standard to the injury of our political welfare.

Having had better opportunities of education, and having had some training in politics, having in political life come so near to the "superior" being as to see that he was not altogether such a fount of wisdom as they had supposed, that he had his human weaknesses as we had, the twentieth century women began to say to themselves. "Is it not time, since our methods have failed and the men's have succeeded, that we should take a leaf out of their political book?"

We were led to that conclusion, we older women, by the advice of the young—you know there is a French proverb which says, "If youth knew; if age could," but I think that when you can bring together youth and age, as we have done, and get them to adopt the same methods and take the same point of view, then you are on the high road to success.

Well, we in Great Britain, on the eve of the General Election of 1905, a mere handful of us—

why, you could almost count us on the fingers of both hands—set out on the wonderful adventure of forcing the strongest Government of modern times to give the women the vote. Only a few in number; we were not strong in influence, and we had hardly any money, and yet we quite gaily made our little banners with the words "Votes for Women" upon them, and we set out to win the enfranchisement of the women of our country.

The Suffrage movement was almost dead. The women had lost heart. You could not get a Suffrage meeting that was attended by members of the general public. We used to have about 24 adherents in the front row. We carried our resolutions and heard no more about them.

Two women changed that in a twinkling of an eye at a great Liberal demonstration in Manchester, where a Liberal leader, Sir Edward Grey, was explaining the programme to be carried out during the Liberals' next turn of office. The two women put the fateful question, "When are you going to give votes to women?" and refused to sit down until they had been answered. These two women were sent to gaol, and from that day to this the women's movement, both militant and constitutional, has never looked back. We had little more than one moribund society for Woman Suffrage in those days. Now we have nearly 50 societies for Woman Suffrage, and they are large in membership, they are rich in money, and their ranks are swelling every day that passes. That is how militancy has put back the clock of Woman Suffrage in Great Britain.

Now, some of you have said how wicked it is (the immigration commissioners told me that on Saturday afternoon), how wicked it is to attack the property of private individuals who have done us no harm. Well, you know there is a proverb which says that you cannot make omelettes without breaking eggs. I wish we could.

I want to say here and now that the only justification for violence, the only justification for damage to property, the only justification for risk to the comfort of other human beings is the fact that you have tried all other available means and have failed to secure justice, and as a law-abiding

person—and I am by nature a law-abiding person, as one hating violence, hating disorder—I want to say that from the moment we began our militant agitation to this day I have felt absolutely guiltless in this matter.

I tell you that in Great Britain there is no other way. We can show intolerable grievances. The Chancellor of the Exchequer, Mr Lloyd George, who is no friend of the woman's movement, although a professed one, said a very true thing when speaking of the grievances of his own country, of Wales. He said that there comes a time in the life of human beings suffering from intolerable grievances when the only way to maintain their self respect is to revolt against that injustice.

Well, I say the time is long past when it became necessary for women to revolt in order to maintain their self respect in Great Britain. The women who are waging this war are women who would fight, if it were only for the idea of liberty—if it were only that they might be free citizens of a free country—I myself would fight for that idea alone. But we have, in addition to this love of freedom, intolerable grievances to redress.

*　　*　　*

All my life I have tried to understand why it is that men who value their citizenship as their dearest possession seem to think citizenship ridiculous when it is to be applied to the women of their race. And I find an explanation, and it is the only one I can think of. It came to me when I was in a prison cell, remembering how I had seen men laugh at the idea of women going to prison. Why they would confess they could not bear a cell door to be shut upon themselves for a single hour without asking to be let out. A thought came to me in my prison cell, and it was this: that to men women are not human beings like themselves. Some men think we are superhuman; they put us on pedestals; they revere us; they think we are too fine and too delicate to come down into the hurly-burly of life. Other men think us sub-human; they think we are a strange species unfortunately having to exist for the perpetuation of the race. They think that we are fit for drudgery, but that in some

THE PREVENTION OF HUNGER STRIKES

In the decade prior to the First World War, the political campaign for women's suffrage reached a feverish pitch in Great Britain. Emmeline Pankhurst and followers of the Women's Social and Political Union (WSPU) embarked on a course of militant action that included damaging private property, disrupting meetings, and attempting entry into Parliament. When imprisoned and denied the status of political prisoners, WSPU women organized hunger strikes to press their case. In response, the government ordered force feedings of the prisoners, a role that cast the Liberal government of England as a cruel political hypocrite. The cartoon captures the horrific dimensions of English political life on the eve of the war. How did this cartoon criticize both the British government and the suffragist movement?

strange way our minds are not like theirs, our love for great things is not like theirs, and so we are a sort of sub-human species.

We are neither superhuman nor are we sub-human. We are just human beings like yourselves.

*   *   *

When we were patient, when we believed in argument and persuasion, they said, "You don't really want it because, if you did, you would do something unmistakable to show you were deter-mined to have it." And then when we did some-thing unmistakable they said, "You are behaving so badly that you show you are not fit for it."

Now, gentlemen, in your heart of hearts you do not believe that. You know perfectly well that there never was a thing worth having that was not worth fighting for. You know perfectly well that if the situation were reversed, if you had no consti-tutional rights and we had all of them, if you had the duty of paying and obeying and trying to look as pleasant, and we were the proud citizens who could decide our fate and yours, because we knew what was good for you better than you knew your-selves, you know perfectly well that you wouldn't stand it for a single day, and you would be per-fectly justified in rebelling against such intolerable conditions.

Well, in Great Britain, we have tried persua-sion, we have tried the plan of showing (by going upon public bodies, where they allowed us to do work they hadn't much time to do themselves) that we are capable people. We did it in the hope that we should convince them and persuade them to do the right and proper thing. But we had all our labour for our pains, and now we are fighting for our rights, and we are growing stronger and better women in the process. We are getting more fit to use our rights because we have such difficulty in getting them.

*   *   *

People have said that women could never vote, never share in the government, because govern-

ment rests upon force. We have proved that is not true. Government rests not upon force; gov-ernment rests upon the consent of the governed; and the weakest woman, the very poorest wo-man, if she withholds her consent cannot be gov-erned.

They sent me to prison, to penal servitude for three years. I came out of prison at the end of nine days. I broke my prison bars. Four times they took me back again; four times I burst the prison door open again. And I left England openly to come and visit America, with only three or four weeks of the three years' sentence of penal servi-tude served. Have we not proved, then, that they cannot govern human beings who withhold their consent?

And so we are glad we have had the fighting experience, and we are glad to do all the fighting for all the women all over the world. All that we ask of you is to back us up. We ask you to show that although, perhaps, you may not mean to fight as we do, yet you understand the meaning of our fight; that you realise we are women fighting for a great idea; that we wish the betterment of the human race, and that we believe this betterment is coming through the emancipation and uplifting of women.

REVIEW QUESTIONS

1. What precedents in history does Pankhurst cite to justify her cause and tactics?
2. According to Pankhurst, what is the catalyst of political reform?
3. Why were contemporaries outraged by the idea of women's undertaking militant civil disobe-dience and going to prison for political beliefs?
4. Compare the positions and pleas of Wollstone-craft (Chapter 20) and Pankhurst.
5. What had changed over the course of the century?

CHARLES DARWIN

FROM *The Origin of Species*

The impact of the work of Charles Darwin (1809–1882) cannot be overestimated. The theory of natural selection not only framed the modern view of evolution but also diminished the authority of the Bible in modern thinking. Darwin's theory of how species adapted and evolved over time grew out of his five-year voyage aboard HMS Beagle *(1831–1836) as the ship's naturalist. Published in 1859,* The Origin of Species *was followed by* The Descent of Man *in 1871, which applied the theory of evolution to humans. Darwin's argument that humans descended from apes shocked a Victorian society teethed on Genesis, the biblical creation myth. The following selection comes from the conclusion of* The Origin of Species.

From *The Origin of Species*, by Charles Darwin (New York: Penguin, 1859).

*   *   *

Chapter XIV
Recapitulation and Conclusion

*   *   *

As this whole volume is one long argument, it may be convenient to the reader to have the leading facts and inferences briefly recapitulated.

That many and grave objections may be advanced against the theory of descent with modification through natural selection, I do not deny. I have endeavoured to give to them their full force. Nothing at first can appear more difficult to believe than that the more complex organs and instincts should have been perfected, not by means superior to, though analogous with, human reason, but by the accumulation of innumerable slight variations, each good for the individual possessor. Nevertheless, this difficulty, though appearing to our imagination insuperably great, cannot be considered real if we admit the following propositions, namely, that gradations in the perfection of any organ or instinct, which we may consider, either do now exist or could have existed, each good of its kind, that all organs and instincts are, in ever so slight a degree, variable, and, lastly, that there is a struggle for existence leading to the preservation of each profitable deviation of structure or instinct. The truth of these propositions cannot, I think, be disputed.

It is, no doubt, extremely difficult even to conjecture by what gradations many structures have been perfected, more especially amongst broken and failing groups of organic beings; but we see so many strange gradations in nature, as is proclaimed by the canon, 'Natura non facit saltum,' [nature does not make a leap] that we ought to be extremely cautious in saying that any organ or instinct, or any whole being, could not have arrived at its present state by many graduated steps. There are, it must be admitted, cases of special difficulty on the theory of natural selection; and one of the most curious of these is the existence of two or three defined castes of workers or sterile females in the same community of ants; but I have attempted to show how this difficulty can be mastered.

*   *   *

As on the theory of natural selection an interminable number of intermediate forms must have

MAN · IS · BVT · A · WORM ·

MAN IS BUT A WORM (1881)

Charles Darwin's pathbreaking Origin of Species (1859) was followed by his Descent of Man in 1871, which applied his theory of natural selection to the evolution of the human species. The implication that man descended from apes was by far the most controversial aspect of his larger argument on natural selection. Illustrating the cultural disquiet about the reconfigured relationship of humankind to the animal world, this cartoon from Punch, a British satirical magazine, parodied Darwin with its version of evolution, from worm to gentleman. What beliefs and social structures might Darwin's theories have threatened to undermine?

448

existed, linking together all the species in each group by gradations as fine as our present varieties, it may be asked, Why do we not see these linking forms all around us? Why are not all organic beings blended together in an inextricable chaos? With respect to existing forms, we should remember that we have no right to expect (excepting in rare cases) to discover *directly* connecting links between them, but only between each and some extinct and supplanted form. Even on a wide area, which has during a long period remained continuous, and of which the climate and other conditions of life change insensibly in going from a district occupied by one species into another district occupied by a closely allied species, we have no just right to expect often to find intermediate varieties in the intermediate zone. For we have reason to believe that only a few species are undergoing change at any one period; and all changes are slowly effected. I have also shown that the intermediate varieties which will at first probably exist in the intermediate zones, will be liable to be supplanted by the allied forms on either hand; and the latter, from existing in greater numbers, will generally be modified and improved at a quicker rate than the intermediate varieties, which exist in lesser numbers; so that the intermediate varieties will, in the long run, be supplanted and exterminated.

*   *   *

As each species tends by its geometrical ratio of reproduction to increase inordinately in number; and as the modified descendants of each species will be enabled to increase by so much the more as they become more diversified in habits and structure, so as to be enabled to seize on many and widely different places in the economy of nature, there will be a constant tendency in natural selection to preserve the most divergent offspring of any one species. Hence during a long-continued course of modification, the slight differences, characteristic of varieties of the same species, tend to be augmented into the greater differences characteristic of species of the same genus. New and improved varieties will inevitably supplant and ex-

terminate the older, less improved and intermediate varieties; and thus species are rendered to a large extent defined and distinct objects. Dominant species belonging to the larger groups tend to give birth to new and dominant forms; so that each large group tends to become still larger, and at the same time more divergent in character. But as all groups cannot thus succeed in increasing in size, for the world would not hold them, the more dominant groups beat the less dominant. This tendency in the large groups to go on increasing in size and diverging in character, together with the almost inevitable contingency of much extinction, explains the arrangement of all the forms of life, in groups subordinate to groups, all within a few great classes, which we now see everywhere around us, and which has prevailed throughout all time. This grand fact of the grouping of all organic beings seems to me utterly inexplicable on the theory of creation.

As natural selection acts solely by accumulating slight, successive, favourable variations, it can produce no great or sudden modification; it can act only by very short and slow steps. Hence the canon of 'Natura non facit saltum,' which every fresh addition to our knowledge tends to make more strictly correct, is on this theory simply intelligible. We can plainly see why nature is prodigal in variety, though niggard in innovation. But why this should be a law of nature if each species has been independently created, no man can explain.

Many other facts are, as it seems to me, explicable on this theory. How strange it is that a bird, under the form of woodpecker, should have been created to prey on insects on the ground; that upland geese, which never or rarely swim, should have been created with webbed feet; that a thrush should have been created to dive and feed on sub-aquatic insects; and that a petrel should have been created with habits and structure fitting it for the life of an auk or grebe! and so on in endless other cases. But on the view of each species constantly trying to increase in number, with natural selection always ready to adapt the slowly varying descendants of each to any unoccupied or ill-occupied place in nature, these facts cease to be strange, or perhaps might even have been anticipated.

As natural selection acts by competition, it adapts the inhabitants of each country only in relation to the degree of perfection of their associates; so that we need feel no surprise at the inhabitants of any one country, although on the ordinary view supposed to have been specially created and adapted for that country, being beaten and supplanted by the naturalised productions from another land. Nor ought we to marvel if all the contrivances in nature be not, as far as we can judge, absolutely perfect; and if some of them be abhorrent to our ideas of fitness. We need not marvel at the sting of the bee causing the bee's own death; at drones being produced in such vast numbers for one single act, and being then slaughtered by their sterile sisters; at the astonishing waste of pollen by our fir-trees; at the instinctive hatred of the queen bee for her own fertile daughters; at ichneumonidae feeding within the live bodies of caterpillars; and at other such cases. The wonder indeed is, on the theory of natural selection, that more cases of the want of absolute perfection have not been observed.

*   *   *

The fact, as we have seen, that all past and present organic beings constitute one grand natural system, with group subordinate to group, and with extinct groups often falling in between recent groups, is intelligible on the theory of natural selection with its contingencies of extinction and divergence of character. On these same principles we see how it is, that the mutual affinities of the species and genera within each class are so complex and circuitous. We see why certain characters are far more serviceable than others for classification; why adaptive characters, though of paramount importance to the being, are of hardly any importance in classification; why characters derived from rudimentary parts, though of no service to the being, are often of high classificatory value; and why embryological characters are the most valuable of all. The real affinities of all organic

beings are due to inheritance or community of descent. The natural system is a genealogical arrangement, in which we have to discover the lines of descent by the most permanent characters, however slight their vital importance may be.

The framework of bones being the same in the hand of a man, wing of a bat, fin of the porpoise, and leg of the horse—the same number of vertebrae forming the neck of the giraffe and of the elephant—and innumerable other such facts, at once explain themselves on the theory of descent with slow and slight successive modifications. The similarity of pattern in the wing and leg of a bat, though used for such different purposes, in the jaws and legs of a crab, in the petals, stamens, and pistils of a flower, is likewise intelligible on the view of the gradual modification of parts or organs, which were alike in the early progenitor of each class. On the principle of successive variations not always supervening at an early age, and being inherited at a corresponding not early period of life, we can clearly see why the embryos of mammals, birds, reptiles, and fishes should be so closely alike, and should be so unlike the adult forms. We may cease marvelling at the embryo of an air-breathing mammal or bird having branchial slits and arteries running in loops, like those in a fish which has to breathe the air dissolved in water, by the aid of well-developed branchiae.

*   *   *

In the distant future I see open fields for far more important researches. Psychology will be based on a new foundation, that of the necessary acquirement of each mental power and capacity by gradation. Light will be thrown on the origin of man and his history.

Authors of the highest eminence seem to be fully satisfied with the view that each species has been independently created. To my mind it accords better with what we know of the laws impressed on matter by the Creator, that the production and extinction of the past and present inhabitants of the world should have been due to secondary causes, like those determining the birth and death of the individual. When I view all beings not as special creations, but as the lineal descendants of some few beings which lived long before the first bed of the Silurian system was deposited, they seem to me to become ennobled. Judging from the past, we may safely infer that not one living species will transmit its unaltered likeness to a distant futurity. And of the species now living very few will transmit progeny of any kind to a far distant futurity; for the manner in which all organic beings are grouped, shows that the greater number of species of each genus, and all the species of many genera, have left no descendants, but have become utterly extinct. We can so far take a prophetic glance into futurity as to fortell that it will be the common and widely-spread species, belonging to the larger and dominant groups, which will ultimately prevail and procreate new and dominant species. As all the living forms of life are the lineal descendants of those which lived long before the Silurian epoch, we may feel certain that the ordinary succession by generation has never once been broken, and that no cataclysm has desolated the whole world. Hence we may look with some confidence to a secure future of equally inappreciable length. And as natural selection works solely by and for the good of each being, all corporeal and mental endowments will tend to progress towards perfection.

It is interesting to contemplate an entangled bank, clothed with many plants of many kinds, with birds singing on the bushes, with various insects flitting about, and with worms crawling through the damp earth, and to reflect that these elaborately constructed forms, so different from each other, and dependent on each other in so complex a manner, have all been produced by laws acting around us. These laws, taken in the largest sense, being Growth with Reproduction; Inheritance which is almost implied by reproduction; Variability from the indirect and direct action of the external conditions of life, and from use and disuse; a Ratio of Increase so high as to lead to a Struggle for Life, and as a consequence to Natural Selection, entailing Divergence of Character and the Extinction of less-improved forms. Thus, from the war of nature, from famine and death, the most exalted object which we are capable of conceiving, namely, the production of the higher animals, directly follows. There is grandeur in this view of life, with its several powers, having been originally breathed into a few forms or into one; and that, whilst this planet has gone cycling on according to the fixed law of gravity, from so simple a beginning endless forms most beautiful and most wonderful have been, and are being, evolved.

REVIEW QUESTIONS

1. According to Darwin, what are the driving forces of natural selection?
2. What, according to Darwin, is the relationship between heredity and environment?
3. Why is the last paragraph so successful in conveying the gist of Darwin's argument?
4. Why was the theory of natural selection so threatening to Christianity?

FRANCIS GALTON

"Eugenics: Its Definition, Scope, and Aims"

Sir Francis Galton (1822–1911), a cousin of Charles Darwin, was a British explorer, an anthropologist, and a leading figure on intelligence studies. In 1883, he coined the term eugenics, *the study of human change through genetic means, and advocated improving the human species through selective parenthood. Building on Darwin's argument of natural selection, Galton believed that mental abilities were equally inheritable and further averred that rigorous statistical investigation could demonstrate genius as an inherited trait. In so doing, he encouraged "healthy parents" to marry and reproduce often. Galton's writings spurred early twentieth-century scientists to pursue eugenics. Although conceived as a scientific doctrine of biological health to improve humankind, eugenics soon manifested racist and class prejudices. In the United States, eugenics offered a pseudo-scientific basis to posit the superiority of whites over African Americans; and it further spurred state legislatures to sanction the involuntary sterilization of insane, epileptic, and mentally handicapped citizens. The worst abuse came with National Socialism, which used eugenics to mask an entirely different program of "racial hygiene." Nazis institutionalized the sterilization and killing of "asocial" cases as well as the physically and mentally handicapped into its larger genocidal policies toward Jews, Roma, and others deemed "racially inferior." The following speech was delivered to a learned society in London in 1909.*

From "Eugenics: Its Definition, Scope, and Aims," by Francis Galton, in *The American Journal of Sociology*, vol. 10, no. 1 (July 1904), pp. 1–25.

Eugenics is the science which deals with all influences that improve the inborn qualities of a race; also with those that develop them to the utmost advantage. The improvement of the inborn qualities, or stock, of some one human population, will alone be discussed here.

What is meant by improvement? What by the syllable *Eu* in Eugenics, whose English equivalent is *good*? There is considerable difference between goodness in the several qualities and in that of the character as a whole. The character depends largely on the *proportion* between qualities whose balance may be much influenced by education. We must therefore leave morals as far as possible out of the discussion, not entangling ourselves with the almost hopeless difficulties they raise as to whether a character as a whole is good or bad. Moreover, the goodness or badness of character is not absolute, but relative to the current form of civilisation. A fable will best explain what is meant. Let the scene be the Zoological Gardens in the quiet hours of the night, and suppose that, as in old fables, the animals are able to converse, and that some very wise creature who had easy access to all the cages, say a philosophic sparrow or rat, was engaged in collecting the opinions of all sorts of animals with a view of elaborating a system of absolute morality. It is needless to enlarge on the contrariety of ideals between the beasts that prey and those they prey upon, between those of the animals that have to work hard for their food and the sedentary parasites that cling to their bodies and suck their blood, and so forth. A large number of suffrages in favour of maternal affection would be obtained, but most species of fish would repudiate it, while among the voices of birds would be heard the musical protest of the cuckoo. Though no agreement could be reached as to absolute morality, the essentials of Eugenics may be easily defined. All creatures would agree that it was better to be healthy than sick, vigorous than weak, well fitted than ill-fitted for their part in life. In short that it was better to be good rather than bad specimens of their kind, whatever that kind might be. So with men. There are a vast number of conflicting ideals of alternative characters, of incompatible civilisations; but all are wanted to give fulness and interest to life. Society would be very dull if every man resembled the highly estimable Marcus Aurelius or Adam Bede. The aim of Eugenics is to represent each class or sect by its best specimens; that done, to leave them to work out their common civilisation in their own way.

A considerable list of qualities can be easily compiled that nearly every one except "cranks" would take into account when picking out the best specimens of his class. It would include health, energy, ability, manliness and courteous disposition. Recollect that the natural differences between dogs are highly marked in all these respects, and that men are quite as variable by nature as other animals in their respective species. Special aptitudes would be assessed highly by those who possessed them, as the artistic faculties by artists, fearlessness of inquiry and veracity by scientists, religious absorption by mystics, and so on. There would be self-sacrificers, self-tormentors and other exceptional idealists, but the representatives of these would be better members of a community than the body of their electors. They would have more of those qualities that are needed in a State, more vigour, more ability, and more consistency of purpose. The community might be trusted to refuse representatives of criminals, and of others whom it rates as undesirable.

Let us for a moment suppose that the practice of Eugenics should hereafter raise the average quality of our nation to that of its better moiety at the present day and consider the gain. The general tone of domestic, social and political life would be higher. The race as a whole would be less foolish, less frivolous, less excitable and politically more provident than now. Its demagogues who "played to the gallery" would play to a more sensible gallery than at present. We should be better fitted to fulfil our vast imperial opportunities. Lastly, men of an order of ability which is now very rare, would become more frequent, because the level out of which they rose would itself have risen.

The aim of Eugenics is to bring as many influences as can be reasonably employed, to cause the useful classes in the community to contribute *more* than their proportion to the next generation.

The course of procedure that lies within the functions of a learned and active Society such as the Sociological may become, would be somewhat as follows:—

1. Dissemination of a knowledge of the laws of heredity so far as they are surely known, and promotion of their farther study. Few seem to be aware how greatly the knowledge of what may be termed the *actuarial* side of heredity has advanced in recent years. The *average* closeness of kinship in each degree now admits of exact definition and of being treated mathematically, like birth- and death-rates, and the other topics with which actuaries are concerned.

2. Historical inquiry into the rates with which the various classes of society (classified according to civic usefulness) have contributed to the population at various times, in ancient and modern nations. There is strong reason for believing that national rise and decline is closely connected with this influence. It seems to be the tendency of high civilisation to check fertility in the upper classes, through numerous causes, some of which are well known, others are inferred, and others again are wholly obscure. The latter class are apparently analogous to those which bar the fertility of most species of wild animals in zoological gardens. Out of the hundreds and thousands of species that have been tamed, very few indeed are fertile when their liberty is restricted and their struggles for livelihood are abolished; those which are so and are otherwise useful to man becoming domesticated. There is perhaps some connection between this obscure action and the disappearance of most savage races when brought into contact with high civilization, though there are other and well-known concomitant causes. But while most barbarous races disappear, some, like the negro, do not. It may therefore be expected that types of our race will be found to exist which can be highly civilised without losing fertility; nay, they may become

more fertile under artificial conditions, as is the case with many domestic animals.

3. Systematic collection of facts showing the circumstances under which large and thriving families have most frequently originated; in other words, the *conditions* of Eugenics. The names of the thriving families in England have yet to be learnt, and the conditions under which they have arisen. We cannot hope to make much advance in the science of Eugenics without a careful study of facts that are now accessible with difficulty, if at all. The definition of a thriving family, such as will pass muster for the moment at least is one in which the children have gained distinctly superior positions to those who were their class-mates in early life. Families may be considered "large" that contain not less than three adult male children. It would be no great burden to a Society including many members who had Eugenics at heart, to initiate and to preserve a large collection of such records for the use of statistical students. The committee charged with the task would have to consider very carefully the form of their circular and the persons entrusted to distribute it. The circular should be simple, and as brief as possible, consistent with asking all questions that are likely to be answered truly, and which would be important to the inquiry. They should ask, at least in the first instance, only for as much information as could be easily, and would be readily, supplied by any member of the family appealed to. The point to be ascertained is the *status* of the two parents at the time of their marriage, whence its more or less eugenic character might have been predicted, if the larger knowledge that we now hope to obtain had then existed. Some account would, of course, be wanted of their race, profession, and residence; also of their own respective parentages, and of their brothers and sisters. Finally, the reasons would be required

why the children deserved to be entitled a "thriving" family, to distinguish worthy from unworthy success. This manuscript collection might hereafter develop into a "golden book" of thriving families. The Chinese, whose customs have often much sound sense, make their honours retrospective. We might learn from them to show that respect to the parents of noteworthy children, which the contributors of such valuable assets to the national wealth richly deserve. The act of systematically collecting records of thriving families would have the further advantage of familiarising the public with the fact that Eugenics had at length become a subject of serious scientific study by an energetic Society.

4. Influences affecting marriage. The remarks of Lord Bacon in his essay on Death may appropriately be quoted here. He says with the view of minimising its terrors:

"There is no passion in the mind of men so weak but it mates and masters the fear of death. Revenge triumphs over death; love slights it; honour aspireth to it; grief flyeth to it; fear pre-occupateth it."

Exactly the same kind of considerations apply to marriage. The passion of love seems so overpowering that it may be thought folly to try to direct its course. But plain facts do not confirm this view. Social influences of all kinds have immense power in the end, and they are very various. If unsuitable marriages from the Eugenic point of view were banned socially, or even regarded with the unreasonable disfavour which some attach to cousin-marriages, very few would be made. The multitude of marriage restrictions that have proved prohibitive among uncivilised people would require a volume to describe.

5. Persistence in setting forth the national importance of Eugenics. There are three stages to be passed through. *Firstly* it must be made familiar as an academic question, until its

exact importance has been understood and accepted as a fact; *Secondly* it must be recognised as a subject whose practical development deserves serious consideration; and *Thirdly* it must be introduced into the national conscience, like a new religion. It has, indeed, strong claims to become an orthodox religious tenet of the future, for Eugenics cooperates with the workings of Nature by securing that humanity shall be represented by the fittest races. What Nature does blindly, slowly, and ruthlessly, man may do providently, quickly, and kindly. As it lies within his power, so it becomes his duty to work in that direction; just as it is his duty to succour neighbours who suffer misfortune. The improvement of our stock seems to me one of the highest objects that we can reasonably attempt. We are ignorant of the ultimate destinies of humanity, but feel perfectly sure that it is as noble a work to raise its level in the sense already explained, as it would be disgraceful to abase it. I see no impossibility in Eugenics becoming a religious dogma among mankind, but its details must first be worked out sedulously in the study. Overzeal leading to hasty action would do harm, by holding our expectations of a near golden age, which will certainly be falsified and cause the science to be discredited. The first and main point is to secure the general intellectual acceptance of Eugenics as a hopeful and most important study. Then let its principles work into the heart of the nation, who will gradually give practical effect to them in ways that we may not wholly foresee.

REVIEW QUESTIONS

1. In what kinds of traits is Galton interested?
2. What are the proposed goals of eugenics?
3. How developed was eugenics as a scientific body of knowledge?
4. Can morality be separated from science? Why or why not?

THEODOR HERZL

FROM *The Jewish State*

Against the backdrop of Europe's rising tide of physical violence and political mobilization against Jews, Theodor Herzl (1860–1904) penned The Jewish State *in 1896. This landmark pamphlet redefined Zionism, the movement for a Jewish homeland, as a political question. An Austrian Jewish journalist who covered the Dreyfus affair in Paris for a Viennese newspaper, Herzl apparently became convinced that not even assimilated Jews could find a place in the nation-states of western Europe. Although not the first to propose a Jewish state in modern times, Herzl is credited with reconceptualizing Zionism as a political program of secular nationhood to be achieved through international cooperation. In 1897, after organizing the first congress of Zionists in Basel, Switzerland, he became the president of the World Zionist Organization and thereafter acted as a diplomat to convince world leaders, public opinion, and Jewish communities of Zionism's legitimacy and pragmatism. Toward this end, he also published the Zionist weekly* Die Welt. *Herzl's efforts raised Zionism to worldwide significance, generating a political impulse that contributed to Israeli national statehood in 1948.*

From *The Jewish State*, by Theodor Herzl, translated by Sylvie d'Avigdor (London: D. Nutt, 1896).

The Jewish Question

No one can deny the gravity of the situation of the Jews. Wherever they live in perceptible numbers, they are more or less persecuted. Their equality before the law, granted by statute, has become practically a dead letter. They are debarred from filling even moderately high positions, either in the army, or in any public or private capacity. And attempts are made to thrust them out of business also: "Don't buy from Jews!"

Attacks in Parliaments, in assemblies, in the press, in the pulpit, in the street, on journeys—for example, their exclusion from certain hotels—even in places of recreation, become daily more numerous. The forms of persecutions varying according to the countries and social circles in which they occur. In Russia, imposts are levied on Jewish villages; in Rumania, a few persons are put to death; in Germany, they get a good beating occasionally; in Austria, Anti-Semites exercise terrorism over all public life; in Algeria, there are travelling agitators; in Paris, the Jews are shut out of the so-called best social circles and excluded from clubs. Shades of anti-Jewish feeling are innumerable. But this is not to be an attempt to make out a doleful category of Jewish hardships.

I do not intend to arouse sympathetic emotions on our behalf. That would be a foolish, futile, and undignified proceeding. I shall content myself with putting the following questions to the Jews: Is it not true that, in countries where we live in perceptible numbers, the position of Jewish lawyers, doctors, technicians, teachers, and employees of all descriptions becomes daily more intolerable? Is it not true, that the Jewish middle classes are seriously threatened? Is it not true, that the passions of

the mob are incited against our wealthy people? Is it not true, that our poor endure greater sufferings than any other proletariat? I think that this external pressure makes itself felt everywhere. In our economically upper classes it causes discomfort, in our middle classes continual and grave anxieties, in our lower classes absolute despair.

Everything tends, in fact, to one and the same conclusion, which is clearly enunciated in that classic Berlin phrase: *"Juden Raus!"* (Out with the Jews!)

I shall now put the Question in the briefest possible form: Are we to "get out" now and where to?

Or, may we yet remain? And, how long?

Let us first settle the point of staying where we are. Can we hope for better days, can we possess our souls in patience, can we wait in pious resignation till the princes and peoples of this earth are more mercifully disposed towards us? I say that we cannot hope for a change in the current of feeling. And why not? Even if we were as near to the hearts of princes as are their other subjects, they could not protect us. They would only feel popular hatred by showing us too much favor. By "too much," I really mean less than is claimed as a right by every ordinary citizen, or by every race. The nations in whose midst Jews live are all either covertly or openly Anti-Semitic.

The common people have not, and indeed cannot have, any historic comprehension. They do not know that the sins of the Middle Ages are now being visited on the nations of Europe. We are what the Ghetto made us. We have attained pre-eminence in finance, because mediaeval conditions drove us to it. The same process is now being repeated. We are again being forced into finance, now it is the stock exchange, by being kept out of other branches of economic activity. Being on the stock exchange, we are consequently exposed afresh to contempt. At the same time we continue to produce an abundance of mediocre intellects who find no outlet, and this endangers our social position as much as does our increasing wealth. Educated Jews without means are now rapidly becoming Socialists. Hence we are certain to suffer very severely in the struggle between classes, because we stand in the most exposed position in the camps of both Socialists and capitalists.

* * *

Causes of Anti-Semitism

We shall not again touch on those causes which are a result of temperament, prejudice and narrow views, but shall here restrict ourselves to political and economical causes alone. Modern Anti-Semitism is not to be confounded with the religious persecution of the Jews of former times. It does occasionally take a religious bias in some countries, but the main current of the aggressive movement has now changed. In the principal countries where Anti-Semitism prevails, it does so as a result of the emancipation of the Jews. When civilized nations awoke to the inhumanity of discriminatory legislation and enfranchised us, our enfranchisement came too late. It was no longer possible to remove our disabilities in our old homes. For we had, curiously enough, developed while in the Ghetto into a bourgeois people, and we stepped out of it only to enter into fierce competition with the middle classes. Hence, our emancipation set us suddenly within this middle-class circle, where we have a double pressure to sustain, from within and from without. The Christian bourgeoisie would not be unwilling to cast us as a sacrifice to Socialism, though that would not greatly improve matters.

At the same time, the equal rights of Jews before the law cannot be withdrawn where they have once been conceded. Not only because their withdrawal would be opposed to the spirit of our age, but also because it would immediately drive all Jews, rich and poor alike, into the ranks of subversive parties. Nothing effectual can really be done to our injury. In olden days our jewels were seized. How is our movable property to be got hold of now? It consists of printed papers which are locked up somewhere or other in the world, perhaps in the coffers of Christians. It is, of course, possible to get at shares and debentures in railways, banks and industrial undertakings of all descriptions by taxation, and where the progressive income-tax is in force all our movable property can eventually be laid hold of. But all these efforts cannot be directed against Jews alone, and wherever they might nevertheless be made, severe economic crises would be their immediate consequences, which would be by no means confined to the Jews who would be the first affected. The very impossibility of getting at the Jews nourishes and embitters hatred of them. Anti-Semitism increases day by day and hour by hour among the nations; indeed, it is bound to increase, because the causes of its growth continue to exist and cannot be removed. Its remote cause is our loss of the power of assimilation during the Middle Ages; its immediate cause is our excessive production of mediocre intellects, who cannot find an outlet downwards or upwards—that is to say, no wholesome outlet in either direction. When we sink, we become a revolutionary proletariat, the subordinate officers of all revolutionary parties; and at the same time, when we rise, there rises also our terrible power of the purse.

Effects of Anti-Semitism

The oppression we endure does not improve us, for we are not a whit better than ordinary people. It is true that we do not love our enemies; but he alone who can conquer himself dare reproach us with that fault. Oppression naturally creates hostility against oppressors, and our hostility aggravates the pressure. It is impossible to escape from this eternal circle.

"No!" Some soft-hearted visionaries will say: "No, it is possible! Possible by means of the ultimate perfection of humanity."

Is it necessary to point to the sentimental folly of this view? He who would found his hope for improved conditions on the ultimate perfection of humanity would indeed by relying upon a Utopia!

I referred previously to our "assimilation." I do not for a moment wish to imply that I desire such an end. Our national character is too historically famous, and, in spite of every degradation, too fine to make its annihilation desirable. We might perhaps be able to merge ourselves entirely into surrounding races, if these were to leave us in peace for a period of two generations. But they will not leave us in peace. For a little period they manage to tolerate us, and then their hostility breaks out again and again. The world is provoked somehow by our prosperity, because it has for many centuries been accustomed to consider us as the most contemptible among the poverty-stricken. In its ignorance and narrowness of heart, it fails to observe that prosperity weakens our Judaism and extinguishes our peculiarities. It is only pressure that forces us back to the parent stem; it is only hatred encompassing us that makes us strangers once more.

Thus, whether we like it or not, we are now, and shall henceforth remain, a historic group with unmistakable characteristics common to us all.

We are one people—our enemies have made us one without our consent, as repeatedly happens in history. Distress binds us together, and, thus united, we suddenly discover our strength. Yes, we are strong enough to form a State, and, indeed, a model State. We possess all human and material resources necessary for the purpose.

This is therefore the appropriate place to give an account of what has been somewhat roughly termed our "human material." But it would not be appreciated till the broad lines of the plan, on which everything depends, has first been marked out.

The Plan

The whole plan is in its essence perfectly simple, as it must necessarily be if it is to come within the comprehension of all.

Let the sovereignty be granted us over a portion of the globe large enough to satisfy the rightful requirements of a nation; the rest we shall manage for ourselves.

The creation of a new State is neither ridiculous nor impossible. We have in our day witnessed the process in connection with nations which were not largely members of the middle class, but poorer, less educated, and consequently weaker than ourselves. The Governments of all countries scourged by Anti-Semitism will be keenly interested in assisting us to obtain the sovereignty we want.

The plan, simple in design, but complicated in execution, will be carried out by two agencies: The Society of Jews and the Jewish Company.

The Society of Jews will do the preparatory work in the domains of science and politics, which the Jewish Company will afterwards apply practically.

The Jewish Company will be the liquidating agent of the business interests of departing Jews, and will organize commerce and trade in the new country.

We must not imagine the departure of the Jews to be a sudden one. It will be gradual, continuous, and will cover many decades. The poorest will go first to cultivate the soil. In accordance with a preconceived plan, they will construct roads, bridges, railways and telegraph installations; regulate rivers; and build their own dwellings; their labor will create trade, trade will create markets and markets will attract new settlers, for every man will go voluntarily, at his own expense and his own risk. The labor expended on the land will enhance its value, and the Jews will soon perceive that a new and permanent sphere of operation is opening here for that spirit of enterprise which has heretofore met only with hatred and obloquy.

If we wish to found a State today, we shall not do it in the way which would have been the only possible one a thousand years ago. It is foolish to revert to old stages of civilization, as many Zionists would like to do. Supposing, for example, we were obliged to clear a country of wild beasts, we should not set about the task in the fashion of Europeans of the fifth century. We should not take spear and lance and go out singly in pursuit of bears; we would organize a large and active hunting party, drive the animals together, and throw a melinite bomb into their midst.

If we wish to conduct building operations, we shall not plant a mass of stakes and piles on the shore of a lake, but we shall build as men build now. Indeed, we shall build in a bolder and more stately style than was ever adopted before, for we now possess means which men never yet possessed.

The emigrants standing lowest in the economic scale will be slowly followed by those of a higher grade. Those who at this moment are living in despair will go first. They will be led by the mediocre intellects which we produce so superabundantly and which are persecuted everywhere.

This pamphlet will open a general discussion on the Jewish Question, but that does not mean that there will be any voting on it. Such a result would ruin the cause from the outset, and dissidents must remember that allegiance or opposition is entirely voluntary. He who will not come with us should remain behind.

Let all who are willing to join us, fall in behind our banner and fight for our cause with voice and pen and deed.

Those Jews who agree with our idea of a State will attach themselves to the Society, which will thereby be authorized to confer and treat with Governments in the name of our people. The Society will thus be acknowledged in its relations with Governments as a State-creating power. This acknowledgment will practically create the State.

Should the Powers declare themselves willing to admit our sovereignty over a neutral piece of land, then the Society will enter into negotiations for the possession of this land. Here two territories come under consideration, Palestine and Argentine. In both countries important experiments in colonization have been made, though on the mistaken principle of a gradual infiltration of Jews. An infiltration is bound to end badly. It continues till the inevitable moment when the native population feels itself threatened, and forces the Government to stop a further influx of Jews. Immigration is consequently futile unless we have the sovereign right to continue such immigration.

The Society of Jews will treat with the present masters of the land, putting itself under the protectorate of the European Powers, if they prove friendly to the plan. We could offer the present possessors of the land enormous advantages, assume part of the public debt, build new roads for traffic, which our presence in the country would render necessary, and do many other things. The creation of our State would be beneficial to adjacent countries, because the cultivation of a strip of land increases the value of its surrounding districts in innumerable ways.

*   *   *

REVIEW QUESTIONS

1. For Herzl, what is the "Jewish Question"?
2. What is modern anti-Semitism? What does Herzl believe to be its causes and effects?
3. How does Herzl envision achieving statehood for the Jewish people?

FRIEDRICH NIETZSCHE

FROM *The Genealogy of Morals*

Over the course of his numerous writings, the German philosopher Friedrich Nietzsche (1844–1900) leveled an impressively sustained attack on Western values. Although his philosophical inquiries ranged over a wide area, his devastating criticisms of Judeo-Christian values of individual worth and social justice are probably the most disturbing of his literary corpus. Nietzsche countered his scorn for the "slave mentality" of Judeo-Christian ethics with a wholly different set of ethics that dismissed guilt and a moral conscience as corrosive to life-affirming creativity, which he called the will to power. Written in a vivid aphoristic prose and organized loosely in detached paragraphs, Nietzsche's writings were frequently misunderstood and often abused in the twentieth century. He remains among the most influential writers of the modern era.

From *The Genealogy of Morals*, by Friedrich Nietzsche, translated by Horace B. Samuel (New York: Modern Library, 1918).

*   *   *

9.

"But why do you talk of nobler ideals? Let us submit to the facts; that the people have triumphed—or the slaves, or the populace, or the herd, or whatever name you care to give them—if this has happened through the Jews, so be it! In that case no nation ever had a greater mission in the world's history. The 'masters' have been done away with; the morality of the vulgar man has triumphed. This triumph may also be called a blood-poisoning (it has mutually fused the races)—I do not dispute it; but there is no doubt but that this intoxication has succeeded. The 'redemption' of the human race (that is, from the masters) is progressing swimmingly; everything is obviously becoming Judaised, or Christianised, or vulgarised (what is there in these words?). It seems impossible to stop the course of the poisoning through the whole body politic of mankind—but its *tempo* and pace may from the present time be slower, more delicate, quieter, more discreet—there is time enough. *   *   *

10.

The revolt of the slaves in morals begins in the very principle of *resentment* becoming creative and giving birth to values—a resentment experienced by creatures who, deprived as they are of the proper outlet of action, are forced to find their compensation in an imaginary revenge. While every aristocratic morality springs from its triumphant affirmation of its own demands, the slave morality says "no" from the very outset to what is "outside itself," "different from itself," and "not itself": and this "no" is its creative deed. This volte-face of the valuing standpoint—this *inevitable* gravitation to the objective instead of back to the subjective—is typical of resentment": the slave-morality requires as the condition of its existence an external and objective world, to employ physiological terminology, it requires objective stimuli to be capable of action at all—its action is fundamentally a reaction. The contrary is the case when we come to the aristocrat's system of values: it acts and grows spontaneously, it merely seeks its antithesis in order to pronounce a more grateful and exultant "yes" to its own self;—its negative conception, "low," "vulgar," "bad," is merely a pale late-born foil in comparison with its positive and fundamental conception (saturated as it is with life and passion), of "we aristocrats, we good ones, we beautiful ones, we happy ones."

When the aristocratic morality goes astray and commits sacrilege on reality, this is limited to that particular sphere with which it is *not* sufficiently acquainted—a sphere, in fact, from the real knowledge of which it disdainfully defends itself. It misjudges, in some cases, the sphere which it despises, the sphere of the common vulgar man and the low people: on the other hand, due weight should be given to the consideration that in any case the mood of contempt, of disdain, of superciliousness, even on the supposition that it *falsely* portrays the abject of its contempt, will always be far removed from that degree of falsity which will always characterise the attacks—in effigy, of course—of the vindictive hatred and revengefulness of the weak in onslaughts on their enemies. In point of fact, there is in contempt too strong an admixture of nonchalance, of casualness, of boredom, of impatience, even of personal exultation, for it to be capable of distorting its victim into a real caricature or a real monstrosity. Attention again should be paid to the almost benevolent *nuances* which, for instance, the Greek nobility imports into all the words by which it distinguishes the common people from itself; note how continuously a kind of pity, care, and consideration imparts its honeyed *flavour*, until at last almost all the words which are applied to the vulgar man survive finally as expressions for "unhappy," "worthy of pity" * * *—and how, conversely, "bad," "low," "unhappy" have never ceased to ring in the Greek ear with a tone in which "unhappy" is the predominant note: * * * The "wellborn" simply *felt* themselves the "happy"; they did not have to manufacture their happiness artificially through looking at their enemies, or in cases to talk and lie themselves into happiness (as is the custom with all resentful men); and similarly, complete men as they were, exuberant with strength, and consequently *necessarily* energetic, they were too wise to dissociate happiness from action—activity

becomes in their minds necessarily counted as happiness * * *—all in sharp contrast to the "happiness" of the weak and the oppressed, with their festering venom and malignity, among whom happiness appears essentially as a narcotic, a deadening, a quietude, a peace, a "Sabbath," an enervation of the mind and relaxation of the limbs,—in short, a purely *passive* phenomenon. While the aristocratic man lived in confidence and openness with himself * * * the resentful man, on the other hand, is neither sincere nor naïf, nor honest and candid with himself. His soul *squints;* his mind loves hidden crannies, tortuous paths and backdoors, everything secret appeals to him as *his* world, *his* safety, *his* balm; he is past master in silence, in not forgetting, in waiting, in provisional self-depreciation and self-abasement. A race of such *resentful* men will of necessity eventually prove more *prudent* than any aristocratic race, it will honour prudence on quite a distinct scale, as, in fact, a paramount condition of existence, while prudence among aristocratic men is apt to be tinged with a delicate flavour of luxury and refinement; so among them it plays nothing like so integral a part as that complete certainty of function of the governing *unconscious* instincts, or as indeed a certain lack of prudence, such as a vehement and valiant charge, whether against danger or the enemy, or as those ecstatic bursts of rage, love, reverence, gratitude, by which at all times noble souls have recognized each other. When the resentment of the aristocratic man manifests itself, it fulfils and exhausts itself in an immediate reaction, and consequently instills no *venom:* on the other hand, it never manifests itself at all in countless instances, when in the case of the feeble and weak it would be inevitable. An inability to take seriously for any length of time their enemies, their disasters, their *misdeeds*—that is the sign of the full strong natures who possess a superfluity of moulding plastic force, that heals completely and produces forgetfulness: * * * Such a man indeed shakes off with a shrug many a worm which would have buried itself in another; it is only in characters like these that we see the possibility (supposing, of course, that there is such a possibility in the world) of the real "*love* of one's enemies." What respect for his enemies is found, forsooth, in an aristocratic man—and such a reverence is already a bridge to love! He insists on having his enemy to himself as his distinction. He tolerates no other enemy but a man in whose character there is nothing to despise and *much* to honour! On the other hand, imagine the "enemy" as the resentful man conceives him—and it is here exactly that we see his work, his creativeness; he has conceived "the evil enemy," the "evil one," and indeed that is the root idea from which he now evolves as a contrasting and corresponding figure a "good one," himself—his very self!

*   *   *

12.

I cannot refrain at this juncture from uttering a sigh and one last hope. What is it precisely which I find intolerable? That which I alone cannot get rid of, which makes me choke and faint? Bad air! Bad air! That something misbegotten comes near me; that I must inhale the odour of the entrails of a misbegotten soul!—That excepted, what can one not endure in the way of need, privation, bad weather, sickness, toil, solitude? In point of fact, one manages to get over everything, born as one is to a burrowing and battling existence; one always returns once again to the light, one always lives again one's golden hour of victory—and then one stands as one was born, unbreakable, tense, ready for something more difficult, for something more distant, like a bow stretched but the tauter by every strain. But from time to time do ye grant me—assuming that "beyond good and evil" there are goddesses who can grant—one glimpse, grant me but one glimpse only, of something perfect, fully realised, happy, mighty, triumphant, of something that still gives cause for fear! A glimpse of a man that justifies the existence of man, a glimpse of an incarnate human happiness that realises and redeems, for the sake of which one may hold fast to *the belief in man!* For the position is this: in the dwarfing and levelling of the European man lurks *our* greatest peril, for it is this outlook which fatigues—we see today nothing which wishes to be

greater, we surmise that the process is always still backwards, still backwards towards something more attentuated, more inoffensive, more cunning, more comfortable, more mediocre, more indifferent, more Chinese, more Christian—man, there is no doubt about it, grows always "better"—the destiny of Europe lies even in this—that in losing the fear of man, we have also lost the hope in man, yea, the will to be man. The sight of man now fatigues.—What is present-day Nihilism if it is not *that?*—We are tired of *man.* * * *

16.

Let us come to a conclusion. The two *opposing values,* "good and bad," "good and evil," have fought a dreadful, thousand-year fight in the world, and though indubitably the second value has been for a long time in the preponderance, there are not wanting places where the fortune of the fight is still undecisive. It can almost be said that in the meanwhile the fight reaches a higher and higher level, and that in the meanwhile it has become more and more intense, and always more and more psychological; so that nowadays there is perhaps no more decisive mark of the *higher nature,* of the more psychological nature, than to be in that sense self-contradictory, and to be actually still a battleground for those two opposites. The symbol of this fight, written in a writing which has remained worthy of perusal throughout the course of history up to the present time, is called "Rome against Judæa, Judæa against Rome." Hitherto there has been no greater event *than* that fight, the putting of *that* question, *that* deadly antagonism. Rome found in the Jew the incarnation of the unnatural, as though it were its diametrically opposed monstrosity, and in Rome the Jew was held to be *convicted of hatred* of the whole human race: and rightly so, in so far as it is right to link the well-being and the future of the human race to the unconditional mastery of the aristocratic values, of the Roman values. What, conversely, did the Jews feel against Rome? One can surmise it from a thousand symptoms, but it is sufficient to carry one's mind back to the Johannian Apocalypse, that most obscene of all the written outbursts, which has revenge on its conscience. (One should also appraise at its full value the profound logic of the Christian instinct, when over this very book of hate it wrote the name of the Disciple of Love, that self-same discile to whom it attributed that impassioned and ecstatic Gospel—therein lurks a portion of truth, however much literary forging may have been necessary for this purpose.) The Romans were the strong and aristocratic; a nation stronger and more aristocratic has never existed in the world, has never even been dreamed of; every relic of them, every inscription enraptures, granted that one can divine *what* it is that writes the inscription. The Jews, conversely, were that priestly nation of resentment *par excellence*, possessed by a unique genius for popular morals: just compare with the Jews the nations with analogous gifts, such as the Chinese or the Germans, so as to realise afterwards what is first rate, and what is fifth rate.

Which of them has been provisionally victorious, Rome or Judæa? but there is not a shadow of doubt; just consider to whom in Rome itself nowadays you bow down, as though before the quintessence of all the highest values—and not only in Rome, but almost over half the world, everywhere where man has been tamed or is about to be tamed—to *three Jews*, as we know, and *one Jewess* (to Jesus of Nazareth, to Peter the fisher, to Paul the tentmaker, and to the mother of the aforesaid Jesus, named Mary). This is very remarkable: Rome is undoubtedly defeated. At any rate there took place in the Renaissance a brilliantly sinister revival of the classical ideal, of the aristocratic valuation of all things: Rome herself, like a man waking up from a trance, stirred beneath the burden of the new Judaised Rome that had been built over her, which presented the appearance of an œcumenical synagogue and was called the "Church": but immediately Judæa triumphed again, thanks to that fundamentally popular (German and English) movement of revenge, which is called the Reformation, and taking also into account its inevitable corollary, the restoration of the Church—the restoration also of the ancient graveyard peace of classical Rome. Judæa proved yet once more victorious over the classical ideal in the French Revolution, and in a sense which was even more crucial and even more profound: the last political aristocracy that existed in Europe, that of the *French* seventeenth and eighteenth centuries, broke into pieces beneath the instincts of a resentful populace—never had the world heard a greater jubilation, a more uproarious enthusiasm: indeed, there took place in the midst of it the most monstrous and unexpected phenomenon; the ancient ideal *itself* swept before the eyes and conscience of humanity with all its life and with unheard-of splendour, and in opposition to resentment's lying war-cry of *the prerogative of the most*, in opposition to the will to lowliness, abasement, and equalisation, the will to a retrogression and twilight of humanity, there rang out once again, stronger, simpler, more penetrating than ever, the terrible and enchanting counter-war-cry of *the prerogative of the few!* Like a final sign-post to other ways, there appeared Napoleon, the most unique and violent anachronism that ever existed, and in him the incarnate problem *of the aristocratic ideal in itself*—consider well what a problem it is:—Napoleon, that synthesis of Monster and Superman.

*   *   *

REVIEW QUESTIONS

1. What are "slave morals"? Why is Nietzsche so critical of them?
2. In contrast, what does Nietzsche construe as "noble" values?
3. Is Nietzsche criticizing or endorsing the spirit of the Enlightenment?
4. What is Nietzsche's relationship with European society?
5. What does he not like about modern times?
6. Where is there room for abuse in such an argument?

SIGMUND FREUD

FROM *Five Lectures on Psychoanalysis*

Sigmund Freud (1856–1939), an Austrian doctor, is largely credited as the first scientist of psychoanalysis, a discipline that seeks to understand the mechanisms of the unconscious and to explain the role of repressed desire in determining people's actions and dysfunctions. In doing so, Freud fundamentally changed the way humankind perceived itself, thus affecting numerous disciplines of knowledge and a wide range of literary and art movements. Perhaps it is impossible to interpret twentieth-century culture without first weighing Freud's impact. Psychoanalysis arose in 1895 when Freud and Josef Breuer, a physician friend, published a case study that posited the link between hysteria and sexual malfunctions, and the need to uncover repressed memory for recovery. Freud outlined the early development of his understanding of resistance and repression in five lectures, excerpted below, presented at Clark University, Worcester, Massachusetts, in 1912.

From *Five Lectures on Psychoanalysis*, by Sigmund Freud, translated by James Strachey (London: Hogarth Press, 1976).

*   *   *

When, later on, I set about continuing on my own account the investigations that had been begun by Breuer, I soon arrived at another view of the origin of hysterical dissociation (the splitting of consciousness). A divergence of this kind, which was to be decisive for everything that followed, was inevitable, since I did not start out, like Janet, from laboratory experiments, but with therapeutic aims in mind.

I was driven forward above all by practical necessity. The cathartic procedure, as carried out by Breuer, presupposed putting the patient into a state of deep hypnosis; for it was only in a state of hypnosis that he attained a knowledge of the pathogenic connections which escaped him in his normal state. But I soon came to dislike hypnosis, for it was a temperamental and, one might almost say, a mystical ally. When I found that, in spite of all my efforts, I could not succeed in bringing more than a fraction of my patients into a hypnotic state, I determined to give up hypnosis and to make the cathartic procedure independent of it. Since I was not able at will to alter the mental state of the majority of my patients, I set about working with them in their *normal* state. At first, I must confess, this seemed a senseless and hopeless undertaking. I was set the task of learning from the patient something that I did not know and that he did not know himself. How could one hope to elicit it? But there came to my help a recollection of a most remarkable and instructive experiment which I had witnessed when I was with Bernheim at Nancy. Bernheim showed us that people whom he had put into a state of hypnotic somnambulism, and who had had all kinds of experiences while they were in that state, only *appeared* to have lost the memory of what they had experienced during somnambulism; it was possible to revive these memories in their normal state. It is true that, when he questioned them about their somnambulistic experiences, they began by maintaining that they knew nothing about them; but if he refused to give way, and insisted, and assured them that they *did* know about them, the forgotten experiences always reappeared.

So I did the same thing with my patients. When I reached a point with them at which they maintained that they knew nothing more, I assured them that they *did* know it all the same, and that they had only to say it; and I ventured to declare that the right memory would occur to them at the moment at which I laid my hand on their forehead. In that way I succeeded, without using hypnosis, in obtaining from the patients whatever was required for establishing the connection between the pathogenic scenes they had forgotten and the symptoms left over from those scenes. But it was a laborious procedure, and in the long run an exhausting one; and it was unsuited to serve as a permanent technique.

I did not abandon it, however, before the observations I made during my use of it afforded me decisive evidence. I found confirmation of the fact that the forgotten memories were not lost. They were in the patient's possession and were ready to emerge in association to what was still known by him; but there was some force that prevented them from becoming conscious and compelled them to remain unconscious. The existence of this force could be assumed with certainty, since one became aware of an effort corresponding to it if, in opposition to it, one tried to introduce the unconscious memories into the patient's consciousness. The force which was maintaining the pathological condition became apparent in the form of *resistance* on the part of the patient.

It was on this idea of resistance, then, that I based my view of the course of psychical events in hysteria. In order to effect a recovery, it had proved necessary to remove these resistances. Starting out from the mechanism of cure, it now became possible to construct quite definite ideas of the origin of the illness. The same forces which, in the form of resistance, were now offering opposition to the forgotten material's being made conscious, must formerly have brought about the forgetting and must have pushed the pathogenic experiences in question out of consciousness. I gave the name of "*repression*" to this hypothetical process, and I considered that it was proved by the undeniable existence of resistance.

The further question could then be raised as to what these forces were and what the determinants were of the repression in which we now recognized the pathogenic mechanism of hysteria. A comparative study of the pathogenic situations which we had come to know through the cathartic procedure made it possible to answer this question. All these experiences had involved the emergence of a wishful impulse which was in sharp contrast to the subject's other wishes and which proved incompatible with the ethical and aesthetic standards of his personality. There had been a short conflict, and the end of this internal struggle was that the idea which had appeared before consciousness as the vehicle of this irreconcilable wish fell a victim to repression, was pushed out of consciousness with all its attached memories, and was forgotten. Thus the incompatibility of the wish in question with the patient's ego was the motive for the repression; the subject's ethical and other standards were the repressing forces. An acceptance of the incompatible wishful impulse or a prolongation of the conflict would have produced a high degree of unpleasure; this unpleasure was avoided by means of repression, which was thus revealed as one of the devices serving to protect the mental personality.

To take the place of a number of instances, I will relate a single one of my cases, in which the determinants and advantages of repression are sufficiently evident. For my present purpose I shall have once again to abridge the case history and omit some important underlying material. The patient was a girl, who had lost her beloved father after she had taken a share in nursing him—a situation analogous to that of Breuer's patient. Soon afterwards her elder sister married, and her new brother-in-law aroused in her a peculiar feeling of sympathy which was easily masked under a disguise of family affection. Not long afterwards her sister fell ill and died, in the absence of the patient and her mother. They were summoned in all haste without being given any definite information of the tragic event. When the girl reached the bedside of her dead sister, there came to her for a brief moment an idea that might be expressed in these words: 'Now he is free and can marry me.' We may assume with certainty that this idea, which betrayed to her consciousness the intense love for her brother-in-law of which she had not herself been conscious, was surrendered to repression a moment later, owing to the revolt of her feelings. The girl fell ill with severe hysterical symptoms; and while she was under my treatment it turned out that she had completely forgotten the scene by her sister's bedside and the odious egoistic impulse that had emerged in her. She remembered it during the treatment and reproduced the pathogenic moment with signs of the most violent emotion, and, as a result of the treatment, she became healthy once more.

Perhaps I may give you a more vivid picture of repression and of its necessary relation to resistance, by a rough analogy derived from our actual situation at the present moment. Let us suppose that in this lecture-room and among this audience, whose exemplary quiet and attentiveness I cannot sufficiently commend, there is nevertheless someone who is causing a disturbance and whose ill-mannered laughter, chattering and shuffling with his feet are distracting my attention from my task. I have to announce that I cannot proceed with my lecture; and thereupon three or four of you who are strong men stand up and, after a short struggle, put the interrupter outside the door. So now he is "repressed," and I can continue my lecture. But in order that the interruption shall not be repeated, in case the individual who has been expelled should try to enter the room once more, the gentlemen who have put my will into effect place their chairs up against the door and thus establish a "resistance" after the repression has been accomplished. If you will now translate the two localities concerned into psychical terms as the "conscious" and the "unconscious," you will have before you a fairly good picture of the process of repression.

You will now see in what it is that the difference lies between our view and Janet's. We do not derive the psychical splitting from an innate incapacity for synthesis on the part of the mental apparatus; we explain it dynamically, from the conflict of opposing mental forces and recognize it as the outcome of an active struggling on the part of the two psychical groupings against each other. But our view gives rise to a large number of fresh problems. Situations of mental conflict are, of course, exceedingly common; efforts by the ego to ward off painful memories are quite regularly to be observed without their producing the result of a mental split. The reflection cannot be escaped that further determinants must be present if the conflict is to lead to dissociation. I will also readily grant you that the hypothesis of repression leaves us not at the end but at the beginning of a psychological theory. We can only go forward step by step however, and complete knowledge must await the results of further and deeper researches.

*   *   *

To put the matter more directly. The investigation of hysterical patients and of other neurotics leads us to the conclusion that their repression of the idea to which the intolerable wish is attached has been a *failure*. It is true that they have driven it out of consciousness and out of memory and have apparently saved themselves a large amount of unpleasure. *But the repressed wishful impulse continues to exist in the unconscious.* It is on the look-out for an opportunity of being activated, and when that happens it succeeds in sending into consciousness a disguised and unrecognizable *substitute* for what had been repressed, and to this there soon become attached the same feelings of unpleasure which it was hoped had been saved by the repression. This substitute for the repressed idea—the *symptom*—is proof against further attacks from the defensive ego; and in place of the short conflict an ailment now appears which is not brought to an end by the passage of time. Alongside the indication of distortion in the symptom, we can trace in it the remains of some kind of indirect resemblance to the idea that was originally repressed. The paths along which the substitution was effected can be traced in the course of the patient's psychoanalytic treatment; and in order to bring about recovery, the symptom must be led back along the same paths and once more turned into the repressed idea. If what was repressed is brought back again into conscious mental activity—a process which presupposes the overcoming of considerable resistances—the resulting psychical conflict, which the patient had tried to avoid, can, under the physician's guidance, reach a better outcome than was offered by repression. There are a number of such opportune solutions, which may bring the conflict and the neurosis to a happy end, and which may in certain instances be combined. The patient's personality may be convinced that it has been wrong in rejecting the pathogenic wish and may be led into accepting it wholly or in part; or the wish itself may be directed to a higher and consequently unobjectionable aim (this is what we call its "sublimation"); or the rejection of the wish may be recognized as a justifiable one, but the automatic and therefore inefficient mechanism of repression may be replaced by a condemning judgement with the help of the highest human mental functions—conscious control of the wish is attained.

*   *   *

REVIEW QUESTIONS

1. How does Freud view the pathology of hysteria and its solution?
2. What does Freud's theory of repression imply for individuals' identities and actions?
3. What were the implications of Freud's theory of the unconscious for bourgeois culture?

24 ❧ THE FIRST WORLD WAR

The assassination of Archduke Franz Ferdinand in Sarajevo in August 1914 unleashed a cataclysm of unparalleled magnitude. For four years the European combatants and their allies confronted each other in a war of global dimensions. By 1918 millions of soldiers had been killed on the battlefront, and the lives of civilians living behind the lines on the home front had been unalterably disrupted.

Europeans initially responded to the outbreak of war with jubilation and enthusiasm. Young men rushed to enlist, worried that the war—which everyone expected to be over by Christmas—would end before they could reach the front lines. But soldiers who had yearned for high drama and the chance to prove what one poet-soldier called their "untested manhood" soon discovered the sullen face of modern warfare. The new technologies of war, especially the machine gun and heavy artillery, reduced the individual soldier to insignificance, making a mockery of his bravery and leading him to fear not only the clean death brought by bullets but also the utter annihilation of being blown to bits or the long, drawn out agony of gas poisoning. For those who survived this ordeal, the Great War was a fundamental experience, forever separating them from the prewar world—and from noncombatants—and leaving deep physical and psychological scars.

Although civilians were protected from the worst horrors of the trenches, they too were deeply affected by the war. The lines between the home front and the battlefront blurred as production of armaments and munitions made civilian workers crucial to the military effort and as government-sponsored propaganda campaigns encouraged noncombatants to do their part for the war effort. Although the war brought hardships to civilians, it also brought new opportunities and even adventure, especially to young women who were suddenly freed from the restraints of prewar society.

When the war ended, Europeans were eager to believe that they had, in fact, fought "the war to end all wars." But the end of hostilities did not bring an end to the trauma and dislocation occasioned by the war. The peace settlement itself, promoted by its framers as a new, more hopeful beginning, was widely condemned as an inadequate guarantee of international security and stability.

The Trench Poets of the First World War

The outbreak of the First World War inspired a spate of poetry; one historian estimates that more than one million poems were written in 1914 alone. Like Rupert Brooke (1887–1915), many poets initially greeted the war as a release from the dreariness of civilian life. Educated at Cambridge, Brooke composed finely crafted idealistic wartime poems, especially the sonnet series "1914," which earned him lasting fame. However, as the war dragged on, soldier-poets' initial enthusiasm gave way to resignation. The British poet Wilfred Owen (1893–1918), a graduate of the University of London, condemned the older generation that had allowed the war to happen and that was now refusing to end the slaughter of "half the seed of Europe, one by one." Owen's "Dulce et decorum est," perhaps the most famous of all the First World War poems, is noteworthy not only for its antiwar sentiments but also for its stylistic innovation. Brooke died in 1915 on a hospital ship off the island of Skyros, Greece. Owen was killed in action in France one week before Armistice Day in November 1918.

Rupert Brooke*

FROM **"1914"**

I. PEACE

Now, God be thanked Who has matched us with
    His hour,
  And caught our youth, and wakened us from
    sleeping,
With hand made sure, clear eye, and sharpened
    power,
  To turn, as swimmers into cleanness leaping,

* From *The Collected Poems*, by Rupert Brooke, edited by George E. Woodbury (New York: Lane, 1916).

Glad from a world grown old and cold and weary,
  Leave the sick hearts that honour could not
    move,
And half-men, and their dirty songs and dreary,
  And all the little emptiness of love!

Oh! we, who have known shame, we have found
    release there,
  Where there's no ill, no grief, but sleep has
    mending,
    Naught broken save this body, lost but breath;
Nothing to shake the laughing heart's long peace
    there
  But only agony, and that has ending;
    And the worst friend and enemy is but
    Death.

*   *   *

V. THE SOLDIER

If I should die, think only this of me:
   That there's some corner of a foreign field
That is for ever England. There shall be
   In that rich earth a richer dust concealed;
A dust whom England bore, shaped, made
      aware,
   Gave, once, her flowers to love, her ways to
      roam,
A body of England's, breathing English air,
   Washed by the rivers, blest by suns of home.

And think, this heart, all evil shed away,
   A pulse in the eternal mind, no less
      Gives somewhere back the thoughts by
      England given;
Her sights and sounds; dreams happy as her day;
   And laughter, learnt of friends; and gentleness,
      In hearts at peace, under an English heaven.

*   *   *

Wilfred Owen*

"Dulce et decorum est"

Bent double, like old beggars under sacks,
Knock-kneed, coughing like hags, we cursed
      through sludge,
Till on the haunting flares we turned our backs
And towards our distant rest began to trudge.
Men marched asleep. Many had lost their boots
But limped on, blood-shod. All went lame; all
      blind;
Drunk with fatigue; deaf even to the hoots

---

*From *Poems*, by Wilfred Owen (Huebsch, 1921).

Of tired, outstripped Five-Nines that dropped
      behind.

Gas! GAS! Quick, boys!

An ecstasy of fumbling,
Fitting the clumsy helmets just in time;
But someone still was yelling out and stumbling,
And flound'ring like a man in fire or lime . . .
Dim, through the misty panes and thick green
      light,
As under a green sea, I saw him drowning.
In all my dreams, before my helpless sight,
He plunges at me, guttering, choking, drowning.
If in some smothering dreams you too could
      pace
Behind the wagon that we flung him in,
And watch the white eyes writhing in his face,
His hanging face, like a devil's sick of sin;
If you could hear, at every jolt, the blood
Come gargling from the froth-corrupted lungs,
Obscene as cancer, bitter as the cud
Of vile, incurable sores on innocent tongues,
My friend, you would not tell with such high
      zest
To children ardent for some desperate glory,
The old Lie: *Dulce et decorum est*
Pro patria mori.[1]

REVIEW QUESTIONS

1. Why does Rupert Brooke welcome war?
2. What virtues does he find in death on the battlefield?
3. How does Wilfred Owen's perception of warfare differ from Brooke's?
4. How do Owen's and Brooke's attitudes toward patriotism differ?

---

[1] "It is sweet and fitting to die for one's country." A line taken from the *Odes* of Horace (65–8 B.C.E.).

BATTLE OF VERDUN (1916)

On February 21, 1916, the German army laid siege to the fortress town of Verdun, France. The attack, although initially successful, degenerated into a long-term battle, claiming over four hundred thousand French casualties and approximately as many German. The town was never taken, and the German high command ended the campaign in July. For contemporaries and subsequent generations, the massive expense of life at the battle of Verdun, which included the use of gas and flamethrowers, epitomized the cruelty and futility of modern war. This frame is taken from front-line film footage of a French officer leading his men in a charge across No Man's Land and confronting the deadly efficiency of machine guns. How did this image of the Western Front undermine Western idealism for war and military valor?

Press Reports from the Front

In every belligerent nation, the government attempted to control the news of the war that was available to civilians. Censorship of news and correspondence home was the rule from the very beginning of the war, and as a result, families of soldiers often had only the vaguest notion of events at the front. In addition, many journalists and newspapers censored themselves, choosing to emphasize the positive, even at moments of terrible loss. The history of the war that one could read in newspapers thus often diverged remarkably from the grimmer stories that made their way back to civilians from their relatives and neighbors serving in the trenches. The following selections from French newspapers between 1914 and 1918 were collected and published in 1931 by a French magazine entitled Evolution, *under the title "Wartime Bombast (1914–1918)."*

Reprinted in *The Great War and the French People,* by Jean-Jacques Becker (Dover, N.H.: Berg, 1986), pp. 30–39.

Mobilisation, Troop Concentration and Initial Skirmishes (2–20 August 1914)

Rue des Martyrs . . . a sergeant, uncertain how to react to the ovations raised his rifle and kissed it passionately. (*Le Matin,* 7 August 1914).

My wound? It doesn't matter. . . . But make sure you tell them that all Germans are cowards and that the only problem is how to get at them. In the skirmish where I got hit, we had to shout insults at them to make them come out and fight. (*Echo de Paris,* "Story of a wounded soldier," Franc-Nohain, 15 August 1914).

I think what is happening is a very good thing. . . . I've been waiting for it these last forty years. . . . France is pulling herself together and it's my opinion she couldn't have done that without being purged by war. . . (*Petit Parisien,* statement by Monseigneur Baudrillart, 16 August 1914).

Antwerp, by contrast, is believed to be virtually impregnable. (*Le Matin,* 20 August 1914).

Morhange, Charleroi, the Retreat on the Marne (20 August–15 September 1914)

As far as our slight retreat in Lorraine is concerned, it is of no consequence. Just a minor incident. . . . I would add . . . that the enormous quantity of material we captured from the Germans bears witness to a remarkable weakening on their side. (*Petit Parisien,* Lieutenant-Colonel Rousset, 22 August 1914).

It is impossible for this great battle [of Charleroi] to end in anything but success for us. And even if it should not give us the decisive victory that we still have every right to expect, the enemy will have been winded, crushed, a prisoner of his own losses and supply problems. (*Echo de Paris,* General Cherfils, 29 August 1914).

The wing-beat [of victory] shall carry our armies to the Rhine. . . . That will spell their complete collapse. (*Echo de Paris,* General Cherfils, 15 September 1914).

Play on, then, you blind fools, play the game of your Kaiser and of his vile brood. Play on, but at least while you do so, think about what you are doing and weep with rage. And may they think of it too, our dear soldiers, and may they double up with laughter, our good lads, as they merrily split your hides, you miserable fools. (*Petit Journal*, Jean Richepin, 25 September 1914).

My impression is that the great German army is about to retreat . . . it is only a question of days. . . . The German objective is to beat a retreat on as wide a front as possible. (*Le Matin*, dispatch from the war correspondent of *The Times*, 16 October 1914).

Like a wasp trapped in a clear crystal carafe, the vile and brutish [German] army is beating against the walls of its prison. . . . It struggles, damaging itself a little more with every vain attempt. It is wearing itself out. (*Le Matin*, 22 October 1914).

The 1915 Offensives

They all go into battle as to a fête. (*Petit Parisien*, Lieutenant-Colonel Rousset, 15 May 1915).

A sudden delirium seizes each of the men. At last we are going to emerge from our torpor! A storm of steel passes over our heads but leaves us unmoved. . . . Magic nights. (*Petit Parisien*, "Letter from the front," 17 May 1915).

Apart from about five minutes a month, the danger is minimal, even in critical situations. I don't know how I'll be able to do without this sort of life when the war is over. Casualties and death . . . that's the exception. (*Petit Parisien*, "Letter from a soldier," 22 May 1915).

Verdun (February–December 1916)

The very fact that he [the enemy] is not advancing is an outstanding success and raises immense hopes. (*Echo de Paris*, Marcel Hutin, 24 February 1916).

At the gates of Beaumont, our soldiers, who had pretended to retreat, were tremendously amused. (*Journal*, reporting the remarks of an evacuee from Verdun, 28 February 1916).

However, our losses have been great. (*Petit Parisien*, 1 March 1916).

That fact is that they [the cellars of Verdun] were relatively comfortable—central heating and electricity, if you please—and that we were not too bored in them. (*Petit Journal*, 1 March 1916).

The Russian Front (1914–1917)

He [the Cossack] has no trouble in running several Hungarians through at one go, as many as will fit on the shaft of his lance, then he flings the whole skewer away. (*Le Matin*, Halberine-Kaminsky, 5 October 1914)

The "decisive defeat" at Warsaw with which the Russian armies have this time opened up unlimited prospects to the West must seem disastrous to the Hohenzollern Empire. Let us watch now as hour by hour our allies continue their great thrust towards the Oder, towards Breslau, towards Berlin. (*Petit Parisien*, 26 October 1914).

The Russian army is admirably equipped with everything it needs for modern battle. (*Le Matin*, 8 February 1915).

The distress of our men was moving. They fell to their knees before their officers and implored them: "Let us fight with stones, with sticks, if need be with our fists." (*Le Matin*, statement by Madame Motelev, a Russian nurse, 14 May 1916).

Russia will fight to the death. . . . There will be no quitters among the Allies. (*Echo de Paris*, statement by Lloyd George, 30 September 1916).

If there is an upsurge in Russia, it is an upsurge in favour of total war. (*Echo de Paris*, J. Herbette, 11 January 1917).

The Russian Revolution (1917–1918)

Russia has been liberated. . . . If her people are in revolt . . . it is not to shirk the harsh duties of war, but on the contrary to acquit themselves with even more nobility and self-sacrifice. . . . Long live liberated Russia, which tomorrow will be Russia the liberator. (*Journal*, C. Humbert, 17 March 1917).

"How did the men at the front receive the theories of those few socialists who preached a separate peace?"

"Nobody worried about them, because no one

took that poisonous propaganda seriously." (*Journal*, statement by General Filatier, Paul Erio, 2 May 1917).

Russia will never agree to a separate peace. (*Le Matin*, declaration by Milyukov to the Soviet of Workers and Soldiers, 5 May 1917).

The [U.S.] State Department does not believe that Lenin and Trotsky can stay in power for long and is ready for their fall. Those who know Trotsky consider him a lightweight, without personal worth and quite incapable of taking on the job of an organiser. (*Petit Journal*, 27 November 1917).

The reign of Lenin and Trotsky seems to be reaching its end. . . . Lenin no longer dares to leave Smolny. . . . Lenin . . . trembles for his miserable person. . . . Their dream will not be realized. . . . The hours of Lenin and Trotsky's reign are numbered. (*Journal*, Paul Erio, 26 December 1917).

Poison Gas (1915–1918)

There is no need to be inordinately alarmed about the deadly effects of poison-gas bombs. Rest assured, they are not as bad as all that. . . . They [the bombs] are quite harmless. . . . If . . . we were to tot up all the victims of poison gas and compare their numbers with all the others, we should not pay them any further attention. (*Le Matin*, André Lefebvre, 27 April 1915)

Our soldiers don't give a b— for poison gases. (*Echo de Paris*, 16 December 1916).

The German Artillery

The Germans aim low and poorly; as for their shells, 80 per cent of them do not burst. (*Journal*, 19 August 1914).

Like them, their heavy artillery is nothing but bluff. Their shells have very little effect . . . and all the noise . . . just comes from firing into the blue. (*Le Matin*, "Letter from the front," 15 September 1914).

Anyway, our troops laugh at machine-guns now. . . . Nobody pays the slightest attention to them. (*Petit Parisien*, L. Montel, 11 October 1914).

Combatants and Casualties

Our brave young lads [though injured] are far from beaten. They laugh, joke and beg to be allowed back to the firing line. (*Le Matin*, 19 August 1914).

Not at all, they said to me, we're not all that bothered, the danger is not nearly as great as you think. (*Petit Journal*, 26 October 1914).

The longer the war goes on, the less dreadful I find it. (*Echo de Paris*, "Letter from the front," 31 October 1914).

It's nothing to speak of, I'll be disabled, that's all. (*Le Matin*, remark attributed to a badly wounded soldier, 19 April 1915).

But at least they [those killed by bayoneting] will have died a beautiful death, in noble battle. . . . With cold steel, we shall rediscover poetry . . . epic and chivalrous jousting. (*Echo de Paris*, Hébrard de Villeneuve, 10 July 1915).

REVIEW QUESTIONS

1. What sentiments were expressed at the beginning of the war?
2. How do you think the public reacted when their initial hopes for a quick victory were disappointed?
3. How might the relentless optimism of such press reports have been received by the troops themselves, after the hundreds of thousands of casualties at Verdun or the Somme?
4. How did the French press portray their enemies, or their allies on the Eastern Front?
5. How might the news-reading public have reacted to this kind of nationalist enthusiasm in 1918, at the end of the war?

ERNST JÜNGER

FROM *The Storm of Steel: From the Diary of a German Storm-Troop Officer on the Western Front*

The German author Ernst Jünger (1895–1998) was so eager for adventure that he ran away from home and joined the French Foreign Legion at the age of eighteen. Still only nineteen when the First World War broke out, Jünger volunteered immediately and served with considerable distinction as an officer. The Storm of Steel, *Jünger's autobiographical account of his life in the trenches, was published in 1920 and is still recognized as one of the great wartime memoirs.*

The following excerpt from The Storm of Steel *provides a description of the German soldier's experience during the futile but extremely deadly First Battle of the Somme in 1916. In an attempt to relieve the French line during the German assault on Verdun, British and French troops first bombarded the German line north of the Somme River with heavy artillery and then launched an all-out assault. In the course of this battle 650,000 Germans were killed or wounded; French and British casualties totaled 195,000 and 420,000, respectively.*

From *The Storm of Steel: From the Diary of a German Storm-Troop Officer on the Western Front*, by Ernst Jünger, translated by Basil Creighton (London: Chatto and Windus, 1929).

*   *   *

In the evening we sat up a long while drinking coffee that two Frenchwomen made for us in a neighboring house. It was the strongest drink we could procure. We knew that we were on the verge this time of a battle such as the world had never seen. Soon our excited talk rose to a pitch that would have rejoiced the hearts of any freebooters, or of Frederick's Grenadiers. A few days later there were very few of that party still alive.

Guillemont

On the 23d of August we were transported in lorries to Le Mesnil. Our spirits were excellent, though we knew we were going to be put in where the battle of the Somme was at its worst. Chaff and laughter went from lorry to lorry. We marched from Le Mesnil at dusk to Sailly-Saillisel,

and here the battalion dumped packs in a large meadow and paraded in battle order.

Artillery fire of a hitherto unimagined intensity rolled and thundered on our front. Thousands of twitching flashes turned the western horizon into a sea of flowers. All the while the wounded came trailing back with white, dejected faces, huddled into the ditches by the gun and ammunition columns that rattled past.

A man in a steel helmet reported to me as guide to conduct my platoon to the renowned Combles, where for the time we were to be in reserve. Sitting with him at the side of the road, I asked him, naturally enough, what it was like in the line. In reply I heard a monotonous tale of crouching all day in shell holes with no one on either flank and no trenches communicating with the rear, of unceasing attacks, of dead bodies littering the ground, of maddening thirst, of wounded and dying, and of a lot besides. The face half-framed by the steel rim of the helmet was unmoved; the voice accompanied by the sound of battle droned on, and the impression they made on me was one of unearthly solemnity. One could see that the man had been through horror to the limit of despair and there had learned to despise it. Nothing was left but supreme and superhuman indifference.

"Where you fall, there you lie. No one can help you. No one knows whether he will come back alive. They attack every day, but they can't get through. Everybody knows it is life and death."

One can fight such with fellows. We marched on along a broad paved road that showed up in the moonlight as a white band on the dark fields. In front of us the artillery fire rose to a higher and higher pitch. *Lasciate ogni speranza!*[1]

Soon we had the first shells on one side of the road and the other. Talk died down and at last ceased. Everyone listened—with that peculiar intentness that concentrates all thought and sensation in the ear—for the long-drawn howl of the approaching shell. Our nerves had a particularly severe test passing Frégicourt, a little hamlet near Combles cemetery, under continuous fire.

As far as we could see in the darkness, Combles was utterly shot to bits. The damage seemed to be recent, judging from the amount of timber among the ruins and the contents of the houses slung over the road. We climbed over numerous heaps of débris—rather hurriedly, owing to a few shrapnel shells—and reached our quarters. They were in a large, shot-riddled house. Here I established myself with three sections. The other two occupied the cellar of a ruin opposite.

At 4 A.M. we were aroused from our rest on the fragments of bed we had collected, in order to receive steel helmets. It was also the occasion of discovering a sack of coffee beans in a corner of the cellar; whereupon there followed a great brewing of coffee.

After breakfast I went out to have a look round. Heavy artillery had turned a peaceful little

billeting town into a scene of desolation in the course of a day or two. Whole houses had been flattened by single direct hits or blown up so that the interiors of the rooms hung over the chaos like the scenes on a stage. A sickly scent of dead bodies rose from many of the ruins, for many civilians had been caught in the bombardment and buried beneath the wreckage of their homes. A little girl lay dead in a pool of blood on the threshold of one of the doorways.

*   *   *

In the course of the afternoon the firing increased to such a degree that single explosions were no longer audible. There was nothing but one terrific tornado of noise. From seven onward the square and the houses round were shelled at intervals of half a minute with fifteen-centimeter shells. There were many duds among them, which all the same made the houses rock. We sat all this while in our cellar, round a table, on armchairs covered in silk, with our heads propped on our hands, and counted the seconds between the explosions. Our jests became less frequent, till at last the foolhardiest of us fell silent, and at eight o'clock two direct hits brought down the next house.

From nine to ten the shelling was frantic. The earth rocked and the sky boiled like a gigantic cauldron.

Hundreds of heavy batteries were concentrated on and round Combles. Innumerable shells came howling and hurtling over us. Thick smoke, ominously lit up by Very lights, veiled everything. Head and ears ached violently, and we could only make ourselves understood by shouting a word at a time. The power of logical thought and the force of gravity seemed alike to be suspended. One had the sense of something as unescapable and as unconditionally fated as a catastrophe of nature. An N. C. O. of No. 3 platoon went mad.

At ten this carnival of hell gradually calmed down and passed into a steady drum fire. It was still certainly impossible to distinguish one shell from another.

---

[1] "Abandon all hope!" These words are written on the gate of Hell in Dante Alighieri's *Inferno*.

*   *   *

At last we reached the front line. It was held by men cowering close in the shell holes, and their dead voices trembled with joy when they heard that we were the relief. A Bavarian sergeant major briefly handed over the sector and the Very-light pistol.

My platoon front formed the right wing of the position held by the regiment. It consisted of a shallow sunken road which had been pounded by shells. It was a few hundred meters left of Guillemont and a rather shorter distance right of Bois-de-Trônes. We were parted from the troops on our right, the Seventy-sixth Regiment of Infantry, by a space about five hundred meters wide. This space was shelled so violently that no troops could maintain themselves there.

The Bavarian sergeant major had vanished of a sudden, and I stood alone, the Very-light pistol in my hand, in the midst of an uncanny sea of shell holes over which lay a white mist whose swaths gave it an even more oppressive and mysterious appearance. A persistent, unpleasant smell came from behind. I was left in no doubt that it came from a gigantic corpse far gone in decay. * * *

When day dawned we were astonished to see, by degrees, what a sight surrounded us.

The sunken road now appeared as nothing but a series of enormous shell holes filled with pieces of uniform, weapons, and dead bodies. The ground all round, as far as the eye could see, was plowed by shells. You could search in vain for one wretched blade of grass. This churned-up battlefield was ghastly. Among the living lay the dead. As we dug ourselves in we found them in layers stacked one upon the top of another. One company after another had been shoved into the drum fire and steadily annihilated. The corpses were covered with the masses of soil turned up by the shells, and the next company advanced in the place of the fallen.

The sunken road and the ground behind were full of German dead; the ground in front, of English. Arms, legs, and heads stuck out stark above the lips of the craters. In front of our miserable defenses there were torn-off limbs and corpses over many of which cloaks and ground sheets had been thrown to hide the fixed stare of their distorted features. In spite of the heat no one thought for a moment of covering them with soil.

The village of Guillemont was distinguished from the landscape around it only because the shell holes there were of a whiter color by reason of the houses which had been ground to powder. Guillemont railway station lay in front of us. It was smashed to bits like a child's plaything. Delville Wood, reduced to matchwood, was farther behind.

*   *   *

It was the days at Guillemont that first made me aware of the overwhelming effects on the war of material. We had to adapt ourselves to an entirely new phase of war. The communications between the troops and the staff, between the artillery and the liaison officers, were utterly crippled by the terrific fire. Dispatch carriers failed to get through the hail of metal, and telephone wires were no sooner laid than they were shot into pieces. Even light-signaling was put out of action by the clouds of smoke and dust that hung over the field of battle. There was a zone of a kilometer behind the front line where explosives held absolute sway.

Even the regimental staff only knew exactly where we had been and how the line ran when we came back after three days and told them. Under such circumstances accuracy of artillery fire was out of the question. We were also entirely in the dark about the English line, though often, without our knowing it, it was only a few meters from us. Sometimes a Tommy, feeling his way from one shell hole to another like an ant along a track in the sand, landed in one that we occupied, and *vice versa,* for our front line consisted merely of isolated and unconnected bits that were easily mistaken.

Once seen, the landscape is an unforgettable one. In this neighborhood of villages, meadows, woods, and fields there was literally not a bush or a tiniest blade of grass to be seen. Every hand's-breadth of ground had been churned up again and again; trees had been uprooted, smashed, and ground to touchwood, the houses blown to bits and turned to dust; hills had been leveled and the arable land made a desert.

And yet the strangest thing of all was not the horror of the landscape in itself, but the fact that these scenes, such as the world had never known before, were fashioned by men who intended them to be a decisive end to the war. Thus all the frightfulness that the mind of man could devise was brought into the field; and there, where lately had been the idyllic picture of rural peace, there was as faithful a picture of the soul of scientific war. In earlier wars, certainly, towns and villages had been burned, but what was that compared with this sea of craters dug out by machines? For even in this fantastic desert there was the sameness of the machine-made article. A shell hole strewn with bully tins, broken weapons, fragments of uniform, and dud shells, with one or two dead bodies on its edge—this was the never-changing scene that surrounded each one of all these hundreds of thousands of men. And it seemed that man, on this landscape he had himself created, became different, more mysterious and hardy and callous than in any previous battle. The spirit and the tempo of the fighting altered, and after the battle of the Somme the war had its own peculiar impress that distinguished it from all other wars. After this battle the German soldier wore the steel helmet, and in his features there were chiseled the lines of an energy stretched to the utmost pitch, lines that future generations will perhaps find as fascinating and imposing as those of many heads of classical or Renaissance times.

For I cannot too often repeat, a battle was no longer an episode that spent itself in blood and fire; it was a condition of things that dug itself in remorselessly week after week and even month after month. What was a man's life in this wilderness whose vapor was laden with the stench of thousands upon thousands of decaying bodies? Death lay in ambush for each one in every shell hole, merciless, and making one merciless in turn. Chivalry here took a final farewell. It had to yield to the heightened intensity of war, just as all fine and personal feeling has to yield when machinery gets the upper hand. The Europe of today appeared here for the first time on the field of battle. . . .

*   *   *

REVIEW QUESTIONS

1. What impact did the British bombardment have on the battle zone that Jünger describes?
2. What effect does the bombardment seem to have had on the psyches of individual soldiers?
3. How does the kind of warfare described here differ from that of the past?
4. In what sense is this warfare a product of "the Europe of today"?

VERA BRITTAIN

FROM *Testament of Youth*

Despite an eminently respectable "provincial young ladyhood," the British author Vera Brittain (1893–1970) rebelled early against the constraints imposed by age, class, and sex. Brittain insisted on pursuing her education, despite her parents' protests, and attended Sommerville, a college for women affiliated with Oxford. She experienced the outbreak of the First World War as "an infuriating personal interruption rather than a world-wide catastrophe," but this attitude changed dramatically after her fiancé, her brother, and her best male friends enlisted and then died, one by one. Frustrated by her inability to become a soldier and share the hardships of her male peers, she chose the nearest thing: service as a Voluntary Aid Detachment nurse. After a period of training in England, she attended wounded soldiers on the island of Malta and on the Western Front. The following excerpts from Brittain's widely read memoir, Testament of Youth, *demonstrate the various ways in which the lives of ordinary individuals were disrupted and transformed during the course of the war.*

From *Testament of Youth: An Autobiographical Study of the Years 1900–1925,* by Vera Brittain (London: V. Gollancz, 1933).

*   *   *

Nurse's Training

On Sunday morning, June 27th, 1915, I began my nursing at the Devonshire Hospital. * * *

From our house above the town I ran eagerly downhill to my first morning's work, not knowing, fortunately for myself, that my servitude would last for nearly four years. The hospital had originally been used as a riding-school, but a certain Duke of Devonshire, with exemplary concern for the welfare of the sick but none whatever for the feet of the nursing staff, had caused it to be converted to its present charitable purpose. The main part of the building consisted of a huge dome, with two stone corridors running one above the other round its quarter-mile circumference. The nurses were not allowed to cross its diameter, which contained an inner circle reserved for convalescent patients, so that everything forgotten or newly required meant a run round the circumference. * * *

My hours there ran from 7.45 a.m. until 1 p.m., and again from 5.0 p.m. until 9.15 p.m.—a longer day, as I afterwards discovered, than that normally required in many Army hospitals. No doubt the staff was not unwilling to make the utmost use of so enthusiastic and unsophisticated a probationer. Meals, for all of which I was expected

to go home, were not included in these hours. As our house was nearly half a mile from the hospital on the slope of a steep hill, I never completely overcame the aching of my back and the soreness of my feet throughout the time that I worked there, and felt perpetually as if I had just returned from a series of long route marches.

I never minded these aches and pains, which appeared to me solely as satisfactory tributes to my love for Roland. What did profoundly trouble and humiliate me was my colossal ignorance of the simplest domestic operations. Among other "facts of life," my expensive education had omitted to teach me the prosaic but important essentials of egg-boiling, and the Oxford cookery classes had triumphantly failed to repair the omission. I imagined that I had to bring the saucepan to the boil, then turn off the gas and allow the egg to lie for three minutes in the cooling water. The remarks of a lance-corporal to whom I presented an egg "boiled" in this fashion led me to make shamefaced inquiries of my superiors, from whom I learnt, in those first few days, how numerous and devastating were the errors that it was possible to commit in carrying out the most ordinary functions of everyday life. To me, for whom meals had hitherto appeared as though by clockwork and the routine of a house had seemed to be worked by some invisible mechanism, the complications of sheer existence were nothing short of a revelation.

Despite my culinary shortcomings, the men appeared to like me; none of them were very ill, and no doubt my youth, my naïve eagerness and the clean freshness of my new uniform meant more to them than any amount of common sense and efficiency. Perhaps, too, the warm and profoundly surprising comfort that I derived from their presence produced a tenderness which was able to communicate back to them, in turn, something of their own rich consolation.

Throughout my two decades of life, I had never looked upon the nude body of an adult male; I had never even seen a naked boy-child since the nursery days when, at the age of four or five, I used to share my evening baths with Edward. I had therefore expected, when I first started nursing, to be overcome with nervousness and embarrassment, but, to my infinite relief, I was conscious of neither. Towards the men I came to feel an almost adoring gratitude for their simple and natural acceptance of my ministrations. Short of actually going to bed with them, there was hardly an intimate service that I did not perform for one or another in the course of four years, and I still have reason to be thankful for the knowledge of masculine functioning which the care of them gave me, and for my early release from the sex-inhibitions that even to-day—thanks to the Victorian tradition which up to 1914 dictated that a young woman should know nothing of men but their faces and their clothes until marriage pitchforked her into an incompletely visualised and highly disconcerting intimacy—beset many of my female contemporaries, both married and single.

In the early days of the War the majority of soldier patients belonged to a first-rate physical type which neither wounds nor sickness, unless mortal, could permanently impair, and from the constant handling of their lean, muscular bodies, I came to understand the essential cleanliness, the innate nobility, of sexual love on its physical side. Although there was much to shock in Army hospital service, much to terrify, much, even, to disgust, this day-by-day contact with male anatomy was never part of the shame. Since it was always

Roland whom I was nursing by proxy, my attitude towards him imperceptibly changed; it became less romantic and more realistic, and thus a new depth was added to my love.

In addition to the patients, I managed to extract approval from most of the nurses—no doubt because, my one desire being to emulate Roland's endurance, I seized with avidity upon all the unpleasant tasks of which they were only too glad to be relieved, and took a masochistic delight in emptying bed-pans, washing greasy cups and spoons, and disposing of odoriferous dressings in the sink-room. The Matron described as "a slave-driver" by one of the elegant lady V.A.D.s who intermittently trotted in to "help" in the evenings after the bulk of the work was done—treated me with especial kindness, and often let me out through her private gate in order to save me a few yards of the interminable miles upon my feet.

My particular brand of enthusiasm, the nurses told me later, was rare among the local V.A.D.s, most of whom came to the hospital expecting to hold the patients' hands and smooth their pillows while the regular nurses fetched and carried everything that looked or smelt disagreeable. Probably this was true, for my diary records of one Buxton girl a month later: "Nancy thinks she would like to take up Red Cross work but does not want to go where she would have to dust wards and clean up as she does not think she would like that."

*   *   *

At the Western Front

Only a day or two afterwards I was leaving quarters to go back to my ward, when I had to wait to let a large contingent of troops march past me along the main road that ran through our camp. They were swinging rapidly towards Camiers, and though the sight of soldiers marching was now too familiar to arouse curiosity, an unusual quality of bold vigour in their swift stride caused me to stare at them with puzzled interest.

They looked larger than ordinary men; their tall, straight figures were in vivid contrast to the under-sized armies of pale recruits to which we had grown accustomed. At first I thought their spruce, clean uniforms were those of officers, yet obviously they could not be officers, for there were too many of them; they seemed, as it were, Tommies in heaven. Had yet another regiment been conjured out of our depleted Dominions? I wondered, watching them move with such rhythm, such dignity, such serene consciousness of self-respect. But I knew the colonial troops so well, and these were different; they were assured where the Australians were aggressive, self-possessed where the New Zealanders were turbulent.

Then I heard an excited exclamation from a group of Sisters behind me.

"Look! Look! Here are the Americans!"

I pressed forward with the others to watch the United States physically entering the War, so god-like, so magnificent, so splendidly unimpaired in comparison with the tired, nerve-racked men of the British Army. So these were our deliverers at last, marching up the road to Camiers in the spring sunshine! There seemed to be hundreds of them, and in the fearless swagger of their proud strength they looked a formidable bulwark against the peril looming from Amiens.

Somehow the necessity of packing up in a hurry, the ignominious flight to the coast so long imagined, seemed to move further away. An uncontrollable emotion seized me—as such emotions often seized us in those days of insufficient sleep; my eyeballs pricked, my throat ached, and a mist swam over the confident Americans going to the front. The coming of relief made me realise all at once how long and how intolerable had been the tension, and with the knowledge that we were not, after all, defeated, I found myself beginning to cry.

*   *   *

War's End

When the sound of victorious guns burst over London at 11 a.m. on November 11th, 1918, the men and women who looked incredulously into each other's faces did not cry jubilantly: "We've won the War!" They only said "The War is over."

From Millbank I heard the maroons crash with terrifying clearness, and, like a sleeper who is determined to go on dreaming after being told to wake up, I went on automatically washing the dressing bowls in the annex outside my hut. Deeply buried beneath my consciousness there stirred the vague memory of a letter that I had written Roland in those legendary days when I was still at Oxford and could spend my Sundays in thinking of him while the organ echoed grandly through New College Chapel. It had been a warm May evening, when all the city was sweet with the scent of wallflowers and lilac, and I had walked back to Micklem Hall after hearing an Occasional Oratorio by Handel, which described the mustering of troops for battle, the lament for the fallen and the triumphant return of the victors.

"As I listened," I told him, "to the organ swelling forth into a final triumphant burst in the song of victory, after the solemn and mournful dirge over the dead, I thought with what mockery and irony the jubilant celebrations which we hail the coming of peace will fall upon the ears of those to whom their best will never return, upon whose sorrow victory is built, who have paid with their mourning for the others' joy. I wonder if I shall be one of those who take happy part in the triumph—or if I shall listen to the merriment with a heart that breaks and ears that try to keep out the mirthful sounds."

And as I dried the bowls, I thought: "It's come too late for me. Somehow I knew, even at Oxford, that it would. Why couldn't it have ended rationally, as it might have ended, in 1916, instead of all that trumpet-blowing against a negotiated peace, and the ferocious talk of secure civilians about marching to Berlin? It's come five months too late—or is it three years? It might have ended last June, and let Edward, at least, be saved! Only five months—it's such a little time, when Roland died nearly three years ago."

But on Armistice Day not even a lonely survivor drowning in black waves of memory could be left alone with her thoughts. A moment after the guns had subsided into sudden, palpitating silence, the other V.A.D. from my ward dashed excitedly into the annex.

"Brittain! Brittain! Did you hear the maroons? It's over—it's all over! Do let's come out and see what's happening!" Mechanically, I followed her into the road, as I stood there, stupidly rigid, long after the triumphant explosions from Westminster had turned into a distant crescendo of shouting, I saw a taxicab turn swiftly in from the Embankment toward the hospital. The next moment there was a cry for doctors and nurses from passers-by, for in rounding the corner the taxi had knocked down a small elderly woman who in listening, like myself, to the wild noise of a world released from nightmare, had failed to observe its approach.

As I hurried to her side I realised that she was all but dead and already past speech. Like Victor in the mortuary chapel, she seemed to have shrunk to the dimensions of a child with the sharp features of age, but on the tiny chalk-white face an expression of shocked surprise still lingered, and she stared hard at me as Geoffrey had stared at his orderly in those last moments of conscious silence beside the Scarpe. Had she been thinking, I wondered, when the taxi struck her, of her sons at the front, now safe? The next moment a medical officer and some orderlies came up, and I went back to my ward.

But I remembered her at intervals throughout that afternoon, during which, with a half-masochistic notion of "seeing the sights," I made a circular tour to Kensington by way of the intoxicated West End. With aching persistence my thoughts went back to the dead and the strange irony of their fates—to Roland, gifted, ardent, ambitious, who had died without glory in the conscientious performance of a routine job; to Victor and Geoffrey, gentle and diffident, who, conquering nature by resolution, had each gone down bravely in a big "show"; and finally to Edward, musical, serene, a lover of peace, who had fought courageously through so many battles and at last had been killed while leading a vital counter-attack in one of the few decisive

actions of the War. As I struggled through the waving, shrieking crowds in Piccadilly and Regent Street on the overloaded top of a 'bus, some witty enthusiast for contemporary history symbolically turned upside down the sign-board "Seven Kings."

Late that evening, when supper was over, a group of elated V.A.D.s who were anxious to walk through Westminster and Whitehall to Buckingham Palace prevailed upon me to join them. Outside the Admiralty a crazy group of convalescent Tommies were collecting specimens of different uniforms and bundling their wearers into flag-strewn taxis; with a shout they seized two of my companions and disappeared into the clamorous crowd, waving flags and shaking rattles. Wherever we went a burst of enthusiastic cheering greeted our Red Cross uniform, and complete strangers adorned with wound stripes rushed up and shook me warmly by the hand. After the long, long blackness, it seemed like a fairy-tale to see the street lamps shining through the chill November gloom.

I detached myself from the others and walked slowly up Whitehall, with my heart sinking in a sudden cold dismay. Already this was a different world from the one that I had known during four life-long years, a world in which people would be light-hearted and forgetful, in which themselves and their careers and their amusements would blot out political ideals and great national issues. And in that brightly lit, alien world I should have no part. All those with whom I had really been intimate were gone; not one remained to share with me the heights and the depths of my memories. As the years went by and youth departed and remembrance grew dim, a deeper and ever deeper darkness would cover the young men who were once my contemporaries.

For the first time I realised, with all that full realisation meant, how completely everything that had hitherto made up my life had vanished with Edward and Roland, with Victor and Geoffrey. The War was over; a new age was beginning; but the dead were dead and would never return.

REVIEW QUESTIONS

1. How did Brittain's experiences as a nurse change her attitude toward human sexuality?
2. Why did she so willingly accept the hard and sometimes unpleasant work nursing entailed?
3. How does Brittain describe the newly arrived American troops?
4. In a letter to her fiancé, Brittain expressed the fear that the war would put "a barrier of indescribable experience between men and the women whom they loved." Do you think this concern was valid?

FROM **The Versailles Treaty**

Toward the end of the war, the American president Woodrow Wilson began to lobby for a "peace without victory" and proposed a set of Fourteen Points as the basis for eventual peace negotiations. Wilson envisioned a just settlement that would permanently eradicate recourse to armed conflict by striking at the root causes of all wars and not simply at the incidental factors that had precipitated this particular war. He called for an end to the arms races and secret diplomacy of the prewar era, and he proposed that the new international order be based on the principles of democracy, international free trade, and the right of ethnic minorities to self-determination, all of which would be guaranteed by a league of nations. When the new German government sued for peace in late 1918, it did so in the hope that the peace settlement would be negotiated on the basis of Wilson's proposals. However, Germany was not allowed to send representatives to the Versailles Conference, and the representatives of the European Allies—Georges Clemenceau for France, David Lloyd George for Britain, and Vittorio Orlando for Italy—produced a rather different treaty from that suggested by the Fourteen Points. Despite Wilson's very active role in the framing of the settlement, the Versailles Treaty of 1919 was not ratified by the U.S. Congress, and the United States never joined Wilson's cherished League of Nations.

From The Versailles Treaty, World War I Document Archive Web page, http://wwi .lib.byu.edu/index.php/Peace_Treaty_of_Versailles [accessed 5/19/11].

*   *   *

The Covenant of the League of Nations

The HIGH CONTRACTING PARTIES, In order to promote international cooperation and to achieve international peace and security

by the acceptance of obligations not to resort to war by the prescription of open, just and honourable relations between nations

by the firm establishment of the understandings of international law as the actual rule of conduct among Governments, and

by the maintenance of justice and a scrupulous respect for all treaty obligations in the dealings of organised peoples with one another

Agree to this Covenant of the League of Nations.

*   *   *

ARTICLE 8

The Members of the League recognise that the maintenance of peace requires the reduction of national armaments to the lowest point consistent with national safety and the enforcement by common action of international obligations. The Council, taking account of the geographical situation and circumstances of each State, shall formulate plans for such reduction for the consideration and action of the several Governments. Such plans shall be subject to reconsideration and revision at least every ten years.

*   *   *

ARTICLE 10

The Members of the League undertake to respect and preserve as against external aggression the territorial integrity and existing political independence of all Members of the League. * * *

ARTICLE 11

Any war or threat of war, whether immediately affecting any of the Members of the League or not, is hereby declared a matter of concern to the whole League, and the League shall take any action that may be deemed wise and effectual to safeguard the peace of nations. * * *

ARTICLE 12

The Members of the League agree that if there should arise between them any dispute likely to lead to a rupture, they will submit the matter either to arbitration or to inquiry by the Council, and they agree in no case to resort to war until three months after the award by the arbitrators or the report by the Council.

*   *   *

ARTICLE 16

Should any Member of the League resort to war in disregard of its covenants * * *, it shall ipso facto be deemed to have committed an act of war against all other Members of the League, which hereby undertake immediately to subject it to the severance of all trade or financial relations, the prohibition of all intercourse between their nations and the nationals of the covenant-breaking State, and the prevention of all financial, commercial, or personal intercourse between the nationals of the covenant-breaking State and the nationals of any other State, whether a Member of the League or not. * * * Any Member of the League which has violated any covenant of the League may be declared to be no longer a Member of the League by a vote of the Council concurred in by the Representatives of all the other Members of the League represented thereon.

*   *   *

ARTICLE 18

Every treaty or international engagement entered into hereafter by any Member of the League shall be forthwith registered with the Secretariat and shall as soon as possible be published by it. No such treaty or international engagement shall be binding until so registered.

*   *   *

ARTICLE 22

To those colonies and territories which as a consequence of the late war have ceased to be under the sovereignty of the States which formerly governed them and which are inhabited by peoples not yet able to stand by themselves under the strenuous conditions of the modern world, there should be applied the principle that the well-being and development of such peoples form a sacred trust of civilisation and that securities for the performance of this trust should be embodied in this Covenant. The best method of giving practical effect to this principle is that the tutelage of such peoples should be entrusted to advanced nations who by reason of their resources, their experience or their geographical position can best undertake this responsibility, and who are willing to accept it, and that this tutelage should be exercised by them as Mandatories on behalf of the League. The character of the mandate must differ according to the stage of the development of the people, the geographical situation of the territory, its economic conditions, and other similar circumstances. Certain communities formerly belonging to the Turkish Empire have reached a stage of development where their existence as independent nations can be provisionally recognised subject to the rendering of administrative advice and assistance by a Mandatory until such time as they are able to stand alone. The wishes of these communities must be a principal consideration in the selection of the Mandatory. Other peoples, especially those of Central Africa, are at such a stage that the Mandatory must be responsible for the administration of the territory under conditions which will guarantee freedom of conscience and religion, subject only to the maintenance of public order and morals, the prohibition of abuses such as the slave trade, the arms traffic, and the liquor traffic, and the prevention of the establishment of fortifications or military and naval bases and of military training of the natives for other than police purposes and the defence of territory, and will also secure equal opportunities for the trade and commerce of other Members of the League. There are territories, such as South-West Africa and certain of the South Pacific Islands, which, owing to the sparseness of their population, or their small size, or their remoteness from the centres of civilisation, or their geographical contiguity to the territory of the Mandatory, and other circumstances, can be best administered under the laws of the Mandatory as integral portions of its territory, subject to the safeguards above mentioned in the interests of the indigenous population. In every case of mandate, the Mandatory shall render to the Council an annual report in reference to the territory committed to its charge. * * *

ARTICLE 23

* * * The Members of the League: (a) will endeavour to secure and maintain fair and humane conditions of labour for men, women, and children, both in their own countries and in all countries to which their commercial and industrial relations extend, and for that purpose will establish and maintain the necessary international organisations; (b) undertake to secure just treatment of the native inhabitants of territories under their control; (c) will entrust the League with the general supervision over the execution of agreements with regard to the traffic in women and children, and the traffic in opium and other dangerous drugs; (d) will entrust the League with the general supervision of the trade in arms and ammunition with the countries in which the control of this traffic is necessary in the common interest; (e) will make provision to secure and maintain freedom of communications and of transit and equitable treatment for the commerce of all Members of the League. In this connection, the special necessities of the regions devastated during the war of 1914–1918 shall be borne in mind; (f) will endeavour to take steps in matters of international concern for the prevention and control of disease.

* * *

ARTICLE 42

Germany is forbidden to maintain or construct any fortifications either on the left bank of the Rhine or on the right bank to the west of a line drawn 50 kilometres to the East of the Rhine.

ARTICLE 43

In the area defined above the maintenance and the assembly of armed forces, either permanently or temporarily, and military maneuvers of any kind, as well as the upkeep of all permanent works for mobilization, are in the same way forbidden.

ARTICLE 44

In case Germany violates in any manner whatever the provisions of Articles 42 and 43, she shall be regarded as committing a hostile act against the Powers signatory of the present Treaty and as calculated to disturb the peace of the world.

ARTICLE 45

As compensation for the destruction of the coal-mines in the north of France and as part payment towards the total reparation due from Germany for the damage resulting from the war, Germany cedes to France in full and absolute possession, with exclusive rights of exploitation, unencumbered and free from all debts and charges of any kind, the coal-mines situated in the Saar Basin. * * *

*   *   *

ARTICLE 49

* * * At the end of fifteen years from the coming into force of the present Treaty the inhabitants of the [Saar Basin] shall be called upon to indicate the sovereignty under which they desire to be placed.

*   *   *

ARTICLE 51

The territories [of Alsace and Lorraine] which were ceded to Germany in accordance with the Preliminaries of Peace signed at Versailles on February 26, 1871, and the Treaty of Frankfort of May 10, 1871, are restored to French sovereignty as from the date of the Armistice of November 11, 1918. * * *

*   *   *

ARTICLE 80

Germany acknowledges and will respect strictly the independence of Austria * * * ; she agrees that this independence shall be inalienable, except with the consent of the Council of the League of Nations.

ARTICLE 81

Germany * * * recognises the complete independence of the Czecho-Slovak State. * * *

*   *   *

ARTICLE 84

German nationals habitually resident in any of the territories recognised as forming part of the Czecho-Slovak State will obtain Czecho-Slovak nationality ipso facto and lose their German nationality.

*   *   *

ARTICLE 87

Germany, in conformity with the action already taken by the Allied and Associated Powers, recognises the complete independence of Poland. * * *

*   *   *

ARTICLE 102

The Principal Allied and Associated Powers undertake to establish the town of Danzig, together with the rest of the territory described in Article 100, as a Free City. It will be placed under the protection of the League of Nations.

*   *   *

ARTICLE 116

Germany acknowledges and agrees to respect as permanent and inalienable the independence of all the territories which were part of the former Russian Empire on August 1, 1914.

✻ ✻ ✻ Germany accepts definitely the abrogation of the Brest-Litovsk Treaties and of all other treaties, conventions, and agreements entered into by her with the Maximalist Government in Russia.

✻   ✻   ✻

ARTICLE 119

Germany renounces in favour of the Principal Allied and Associated Powers all her rights and titles over her oversea possessions.

✻   ✻   ✻

ARTICLE 160

✻ ✻ ✻ The total number of effectives in the Army of the States constituting Germany must not exceed one hundred thousand men, including officers and establishments of depots. The Army shall be devoted exclusively to the maintenance of order within the territory and to the control of the frontiers.

The total effective strength of officers, including the personnel of staffs, whatever their composition, must not exceed four thousand. ✻ ✻ ✻

✻   ✻   ✻

ARTICLE 168

The manufacture of arms, munitions, or any war material, shall only be carried out in factories or works the location of which shall be communicated to and approved by the Governments of the Principal Allied and Associated Powers, and the number of which they retain the right to restrict. ✻ ✻ ✻

✻   ✻   ✻

ARTICLE 173

Universal compulsory military service shall be abolished in Germany.

The German Army may only be constituted and recruited by means of voluntary enlistment.

✻   ✻   ✻

ARTICLE 181

✻ ✻ ✻ The German naval forces in commission must not exceed:

6 battleships of the Deutschland or Lothringen type, 6 light cruisers, 12 destroyers, 12 torpedo boats. ✻ ✻ ✻

No submarines are to be included.

All other warships, except where there is provision to the contrary in the present Treaty, must be placed in reserve or devoted to commercial purposes.

✻   ✻   ✻

ARTICLE 198

The armed forces of Germany must not include any military or naval air forces. ✻ ✻ ✻

✻   ✻   ✻

ARTICLE 227

The Allied and Associated Powers publicly arraign William II of Hohenzollern, formerly German Emperor, for a supreme offence against international morality and the sanctity of treaties. ✻ ✻ ✻

✻   ✻   ✻

ARTICLE 231

The Allied and Associated Governments affirm and Germany accepts the responsibility of Germany and her allies for causing all the loss and damage to which the Allied and Associated Governments and their nationals have been subjected as a consequence of the war imposed upon them by the aggression of Germany and her allies. ✻ ✻ ✻

ARTICLE **232**

The Allied and Associated Governments recognise that the resources of Germany are not adequate, after taking into account permanent diminutions of such resources which will result from other provisions of the present Treaty, to make complete reparation for all such loss and damage.

The Allied and Associated Governments, however, require, and Germany undertakes, that she will make compensation for all damage done to the civilian population of the Allied and Associated Powers and to their property during the period of the belligerency of each as an Allied or Associated Power against Germany. ✶ ✶ ✶

ARTICLE **233**

The amount of the above damage for which compensation is to be made by Germany shall be determined by an Inter-Allied Commission. ✶ ✶ ✶

✶   ✶   ✶

Organisation of Labour

Whereas the League of Nations has for its object the establishment of universal peace, and such a peace can be established only if it is based upon social justice;

And whereas conditions of labour exist involving such injustice, hardship, and privation to large numbers of people as to produce unrest so great that the peace and harmony of the world are imperilled; and an improvement of those conditions is urgently required; ✶ ✶ ✶

Whereas also the failure of any nation to adopt humane conditions of labour is an obstacle in the way of other nations which desire to improve the conditions in their own countries;

The HIGH CONTRACTING PARTIES, moved by sentiments of justice and humanity as well as by the desire to secure the permanent peace of the world, agree to the following:

ARTICLE **387**

A permanent organisation is hereby established for the promotion of the objects set forth in the Preamble. ✶ ✶ ✶

✶   ✶   ✶

ARTICLE **427**

[The HIGH CONTRACTING PARTIES] recognise that differences of climate, habits, and customs, of economic opportunity and industrial tradition, make strict uniformity in the conditions of labour difficult of immediate attainment. But, holding as they do, that labour should not be regarded merely as an article of commerce, they think that there are methods and principles for regulating labour conditions which all industrial communities should endeavour to apply, so far as their special circumstances will permit.

Among these methods and principles, the following seem to the High Contracting Parties to be of special and urgent importance:

First. The guiding principle above enunciated that labour should not be regarded merely as a commodity or article of commerce.

Second. The right of association for all lawful purposes by the employed as well as by the employers.

Third. The payment to the employed of a wage adequate to maintain a reasonable standard of life as this is understood in their time and country.

Fourth. The adoption of an eight hours day or a forty-eight hours week as the standard to be aimed at where it has not already been attained.

Fifth. The adoption of a weekly rest of at least twenty-four hours, which should include Sunday wherever practicable.

Sixth. The abolition of child labour and the imposition of such limitations on the labour of young persons as shall permit the continuation of their education and assure their proper physical development.

Seventh. The principle that men and women should receive equal remuneration for work of equal value.

Eighth. The standard set by law in each country with respect to the conditions of labour should have due regard to the equitable economic treatment of all workers lawfully resident therein.

Ninth. Each State should make provision for a system of inspection in which women should take part, in order to ensure the enforcement of the laws and regulations for the protection of the employed. * * *

ARTICLE 428

As a guarantee for the execution of the present Treaty by Germany, the German territory situated to the west of the Rhine, together with the bridgeheads, will be occupied by Allied and Associated troops for a period of fifteen years from the coming into force of the present Treaty.

*   *   *

ARTICLE 430

In case either during the occupation or after the expiration of the fifteen years referred to above the Reparation Commission finds that Germany refuses to observe the whole or part of her obligations under the present Treaty with regard to reparation, the whole or part of the areas specified in Article 429 will be reoccupied immediately by the Allied and Associated forces.

ARTICLE 431

If before the expiration of the period of fifteen years Germany complies with all the undertakings resulting from the present Treaty, the occupying forces will be withdrawn immediately.

*   *   *

ARTICLE 434

Germany undertakes to recognise the full force of the Treaties of Peace and Additional Conventions which may be concluded by the Allied and Associated Powers with the Powers who fought on the side of Germany and to recognise whatever dispositions may be made concerning the territories of the former Austro-Hungarian Monarchy, of the Kingdom of Bulgaria and of the Ottoman Empire, and to recognise the new States within their frontiers as there laid down.

REVIEW QUESTIONS

1. What guarantees of permanent international peace are incorporated into this treaty?
2. Assuming that all of the clauses in this treaty were to be enforced, does it provide the basis for a lasting peace?
3. Is this a "peace without victory"?
4. How do you think Germans responded to this treaty?
5. To what extent are the rights and liberties of disenfranchised minorities—whether ethnic minorities in eastern Europe, colonial subjects, or the world's laborers—guaranteed by this treaty?

War Propaganda

Poster art was a leading form of propaganda used by all belligerents in the First World War to enlist men, sell war bonds, and sustain morale on the home front. Posters also demonized the enemy and glorified the sacrifices of soldiers the better to rationalize the unprecedented loss of life and national wealth. The following posters, from a wide range of combatant nations during the war, share a common desire to link the war effort to a highly gendered set of obligations and allegiances. Why would nationalism resort to such gendered images in a time of crisis? What does this tell us about the way that myths of national belonging are created and sustained in times of urgency?

E. V. KEALY, 1915
Britain

ARTIST UNKNOWN, C. 1914
Russia

HOWARD CHANDLER CHRISTY, 1917
Britain

CHARLES STAFFORD DUNCAN, 1918
United States

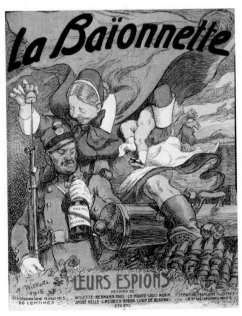

ADOLPHE LEON WILLETTE, 1915
France

25 ❧ TURMOIL BETWEEN THE WARS

The Great War was not only physically devastating but it also did considerable psychological and spiritual damage. During the war, the trauma of trench warfare sometimes pushed soldiers over the edge of sanity into madness, a condition euphemistically known as shell shock. In the aftermath of the war, it almost seemed as if European society as a whole was suffering from a nervous breakdown of monumental proportions. Peace, so long desired, did not bring the security and prosperity for which so many yearned. Instead, the European nations lurched from one crisis to the next during the 1920s and 1930s, and another episode of international warfare erupted at the end of these two short decades of uneasy peace.

The crisis of "total" war produced conditions conducive to the rise of totalitarianism, a distinctively modern form of authoritarian government. In Russia, the initial stages of the Soviet revolution generated hopes for the creation of a modern communist utopia, hopes shared both by Russian revolutionaries and by many progressives outside of Russia. However, Stalin's rise to power and his imposition of a Communist Party dictatorship put an end to this dream. Stalin's authoritarianism of the left was paralleled by fascist movements in eastern and central Europe. Mussolini's fascism and Hitler's Nazism shared many elements of traditional right-wing ideology, but they also sought to incorporate elements of left-wing theory and practice, producing a revolutionism of the right. Many Europeans, disillusioned with liberalism and democracy, greeted charismatic dictatorship as a new and attractive political option.

The tendency to look to extremist political movements for solutions to social problems was greatly reinforced by the economic crisis brought on by the Great Depression of the 1930s. Throughout Europe, the Depression caused a dramatic polarization of the political spectrum and a realignment of political allegiances. The greatest losers were the centrist parties still committed to liberalism and parliamentary democracy.

In response to the dislocations of the era, many intellectuals subjected traditional orthodoxies to ruthless scrutiny. Philosophers, scientists, and artists all puzzled over the purpose of human existence in a cosmos that seemed bereft of transcendent meaning, and many wondered whether God was dead, or at least unwilling to intervene in human affairs. The pointless carnage of the war had crushed the optimism of Belle Époque culture. That Europeans had allowed such a cataclysm to occur at all suggested that irrational impulses played an important role in human behavior and that progress was not so inevitable as nineteenth-century positivists had thought. Technological and scientific advances, though impressive, brought new dangers—including devastating increases in the destructiveness of military weapons—and they did not provide answers to human beings' deepest yearnings for spiritual knowledge and sustenance.

N. N. SUKHANOV

FROM *The Russian Revolution 1917*

Nikolai Nikolayevich Himmer (1882–1940), known more widely as Sukhanov, was a well-known journalist who commented frequently on political and economic affairs in St. Petersburg (Petrograd). A firsthand observer of the outbreak of revolution in the Russian capital in 1917, he was not affiliated with any political party at the time. By temperament, however, his allegiances were on the left—he was well connected throughout the socialist movement, he had worked closely with Maxim Gorky before the revolution, and he counted Alexander Kerensky among his friends.

Sukhanov's account of the first meeting of the reconstituted Petrograd Soviet on February 27, 1917 captures something of the euphoria of these first days of revolution. The first meeting of the Soviet took place in the Tauride Palace, the seat of the Russian Duma. It was attended by fifty deputies—mostly intellectuals from the various socialist party organizations in the capital and a few unaffiliated militants—and approximately two hundred onlookers. Few workers attended this meeting, and none were elected to serve on the executive committee. In spite of this, however, the deputies showed their enthusiasm for the popular resistance in the capital to the forces of the tsar's police force and unanimously resolved to call themselves the Petrograd Soviet of Workers' and Soldiers' Deputies.

The Petrograd Soviet had first convened during the failed revolution of 1905, and its reappearance in 1917 was a marker of the new movement's radical potential. Not yet controlled by the Bolsheviks, the Soviet was seen by many at the time as the only legitimate voice of the Russian people and a necessary complement to the more elite and liberal center of power being created simultaneously by Kerensky and his partners in the provisional government. Ultimately, this "dual" power structure—an elite movement instigated by former Duma politicians and a popular movement that brought together radicals, socialists, and elements from the military's rank and file— would prove unworkable. Threatened both from the right—in the Kornilov affair— and eventually also from the left by the Bolsheviks, the provisional government's power-sharing experiment with the Petrograd Soviet lasted only until October, when the Bolshevik coup brought to power a new group led by Lenin and Trotsky.

From *The Russian Revolution 1917, a Personal Record*, by N. N. Sukhanov, edited, abridged, and translated by Joel Carmichael (Princeton, N.J.: Princeton University Press, 1984), pp. 58–64.

*   *   *

I elbowed my way through the crowd from the Catherine Hall to the rooms occupied by the Soviet.

The hall was filling up. Sokolov was running around giving orders and seating the deputies. In an authoritative way, without, however, any discernible justification, he was explaining to those present what sort of vote they had, whether consulting or deciding,[1] and who had no voice at all. In particular he explained to me that I had a vote— I don't remember now what kind. But of course these judicial decisions of the future senator had not the slightest practical significance.

I ran into Tikhonov, and we took places at the table at a respectful distance from its head, which was occupied by official personages, the deputies Chkheidze and Skobelev, members of the self-appointed Ex. Com., Gvozdev, Kapelinsky of the Cooperative movement,[2] and Grinevich, one of the leaders of the Petersburg Mensheviks.

B. O. Bogdanov, the most active member of the Ex. Com., was missing for some reason; I think he only turned up a day later. Nearby at the table towered the massive figure of Steklov,[3] more reminiscent of a bearded central-Russian smallholder than an Odessa Jew.

Also there at the head of the table, pestering all and sundry with something or other, was Khrustalev-Nosar, the former chairman and leader (together with Trotsky) of the Soviet in 1905. Sokolov was bustling about there too; at 9 o'clock precisely he opened the session of the Soviet with a resolution to elect the Praesidium . . . Kerensky turned up for a short time.

I no longer felt any longing for the centres of the movement; I had no feeling of being cut off from the living process. I was in the very crucible of great events, the laboratory of the revolution.

*   *   *

At the moment the meeting opened around 250 deputies were there. But new groups kept pouring into the hall, God knows with what mandates or intentions.

What ought to be the agenda for this plenipotentiary assembly of the representatives of

---

[1] A 'consulting' vote or voice merely gave one the right to express his opinion without participating in the voting. [Editor.]

[2] A broad democratic movement completely independent of the Government, created to organize the so-called consumers' unions in an attempt to dispense with middlemen in retail commerce, thus substantially lowering prices of consumer commodities. Started in Russia in the [1860s], and developed vigorously after 1905. It also had cultural aims, and was strongly supported by workers, peasants, and liberals. Before the First World War it comprised more than two million members. [Editor.]

[3] Steklov (Nakhamkes), Yurii Mikhailovich (1873–1937): active revolutionary from the beginning of the nineties in Odessa. Outside all factions for a long time. Joined the Bolsheviks after the October insurrection and for a long time was the editor of the official *Izvestiya* (News). [Editor.]

the democracy in the decisive hour of the revolution? Under any circumstances it was plainly impossible to make the *political* problem the first item, and force the task of forming the revolutionary Government. What with the general vagueness of the situation and the above-mentioned temper of the right wing of the Tauride Palace, this problem could only be put on the agenda with one object—to decide it out of hand by proclaiming the Soviet the supreme state power. Under these conditions it was up to others to place the question of power on the agenda—to the advocates of an immediate dictatorship of the Soviet, who might have been the Bolsheviks headed by Shlyapnikov, or the SRs led by Alexandrovich.

In any case both these groups were weak and unprepared, without initiative and incapable of taking their bearings in the situation. Neither introduced the question. Meanwhile circumstances themselves introduced some absolutely unpostponable business concerning the technique of revolution itself.

The people I talked to incidentally about the agenda were of course right: the movement would be crushed without emergency *economic* measures—organizing the provisioning of the capital, taking immediate steps to defend the city and stop anarchy, and mobilizing the forces of the local garrison and the working-class population to repel a possible attack on Petersburg—that is, without the strategic defence of the revolution. Whatever the ultimate form of government, only the Soviet could achieve this "technique" of the revolution.

As for the strategic measures, defensive and offensive, they were being handled by the Military Commission, the kernel and majority of which in those hours was composed of Soviet elements. To carry strategy into the general meeting of the Soviet was absurd. But it was vital to do something else—place under Soviet control the activities of the Military Commission, which was established—topographically—in the right wing of the Palace.

Naturally, the Duma deputies Chkheidze, Kerensky, and Skobelev were nominated to the Praesidium and elected immediately without opposition. Besides the chairman and his two col-

leagues four secretaries were elected—Gvozdev, Sokolov, Grinevich, and the worker Pankov, a Left Menshevik. If I'm not mistaken Kerensky declaimed a few meaningless phrases that were supposed to be a hymn to the people's revolution, and immediately vanished into the right wing, not to appear again in the Soviet.

I don't remember what happened to the future permanent chairman of the Soviet, Chkheidze. Skobelev was left to take the chair; in the midst of the hurly-burly and the general excitement he had neither a general plan of action nor control of the meeting itself, which proceeded noisily and quite chaotically. But this by no means prevented the Soviet from performing at this very first session its basic task, vital to the revolution—that of concentrating into one centre all the ideological and organizational strength of the Petersburg democracy, with undisputed authority and a capacity for rapid and decisive action.

Immediately after the formation of the Praesidium the customary demands for "order" rang out from various sides. The chairman, wishing to end formalities, put forward for confirmation the already functioning Credentials Committee, headed by Gvozdev, but it was not in the least surprising that business was interrupted at this point by the soldiers, who demanded the floor to make their reports. The demand was enthusiastically supported, and the scene that followed was worthy of enthusiasm.

Standing on stools, their rifles in their hands, agitated and stuttering, straining all their powers to give a connected account of the messages entrusted to them, with their thoughts concentrated on the narrative itself, in unaccustomed and half-fantastic surroundings, without thinking and perhaps quite unaware of the whole significance of the facts they were reporting, in simple, rugged language that infinitely strengthened the effect of the absence of emphasis—one after another the soldiers' delegates told of what had been happening in their companies. Their stories were artless, and repeated each other almost word for word. The audience listened as children listen to a wonderful, enthralling fairy-tale they know by heart, holding their breaths, with craning necks and unseeing eyes.

'We're from the Volhynian Regiment . . . the Pavlovsky . . . the Lithuanian . . . the Keksholm . . . the Sappers . . . the Chasseurs . . . the Finnish . . . the Grenadiers . . .'

The name of each of the magnificent regiments that had launched the revolution was met with a storm of applause.

'We had a meeting . . .' 'We've been told to say . . .' 'The officers hid . . .' 'To join the Soviet of Workers' Deputies . . .' 'They told us to say that we refuse to serve against the people any more, we're going to join with our brother workers, all united, to defend the people's cause . . . We would lay down our lives for that.' 'Our general meeting told us to greet you . . .' 'Long live the revolution!' the delegate would add in a voice already completely extinguished by the throbbing roar of the meeting.

Dreadful rifles, hateful greatcoats, strange words! Theoretically all this had been known, well known, known since that morning. But in practice no one had understood or digested the events that had turned everything topsy-turvy . . .

It was then and there proposed, and approved with storms of applause, to fuse together the revolutionary army and the proletariat of the capital and create a united organization to be called from then on the 'Soviet of Workers' and Soldiers' Deputies . . .'

But a great many regiments were still not with us. Were they hesitating, consciously neutral, or ready to fight the 'enemy within'?

The situation was still critical. There was the possibility of bloody skirmishes between the organized regiments and their officers. The revolution might still be captured with bare hands.

*　　*　　*

Frankorussky, the 'Supply Man,' finally got the floor, and having given a short sketch of the supply position in Petersburg and all the possible consequences of hunger amongst the masses, proposed that a Supply Commission be elected, ordered to set to work at once, and given adequate powers. There was of course no debate on this. The Commission was elected at once from the Socialist sup-

ply specialists headed by V. G. Grohman. Having waited for this moment, all those elected immediately withdrew in order to work.

Meanwhile M. A. Braunstein, who had apparently been elected to the Supply Commission, came up to me and urged me to take the floor at once with a resolution on the defence of the city. I didn't see the slightest advantage in coming forward and suggested that I merely second his motion. He got the floor and very successfully, with the full attention and sympathy of the meeting, described the state of affairs.

Braunstein proposed that directives be given the city districts through the delegates present for every factory to appoint a militia (100 men out of every thousand), for district committees to be formed, and for plenipotentiary Commissars to be appointed in each district to restore order and direct the struggle against anarchy and pogroms.[4] I spoke in support of his resolution, after informing the meeting of the activities of the Military Commission and warning them of the danger of confusing functions and powers. The resolution was accepted in principle, but there was still no machinery to put it into practice; there were neither boundaries between the districts (were they to be the future Soviet and municipal wards or the old police divisions?) nor assembly points, nor volunteer Commissars . . .

In connexion with the defence of the city there naturally cropped up a proposal for a proclamation to the populace in the name of the Soviet. In general, supplying the capital, and as far as possible the provinces, with information and elementary directives to the populace was the most pressing task of the moment, even though it was relatively simple and required no special attention from the meeting. One of my neighbours proposed the election of a Literary Commission to be entrusted with the immediate composition of an appeal to be presented to the Soviet later for confirmation.

---

[4] Braunstein, by the way, was the first of us to use this word Commissar, which was later so needlessly misused.

But this organizational work, which had already taken up about an hour, was interrupted again. A young soldier burst through the flimsy barrier at the doors and rushed to the centre of the hall. Without asking for the floor or waiting for permission to speak he raised his rifle above his head and shook it, choking and gasping as he shouted the joyful news:

'Comrades and brothers, I bring you brotherly greetings from all the lower ranks of the entire Semyonovsky regiment of Life Guards. All of us to the last man are determined to join the people against the accursed autocracy, and we swear to serve the people's cause to the last drop of our blood!'

In his emotion, bordering on frenzy, the youthful delegate of the mutinous Semyonovskys, who had plainly attended a school of party propaganda, was really, in these banal phrases and stereotyped terminology, pouring out his soul, overflowing with the majestic impressions of the day and consciousness that the longed-for victory had been achieved. In the meeting, disturbed in the midst of current business, there gushed forth once again a torrent of romantic enthusiasm. No one stopped the Semyonovsky from finishing his lengthy speech, accompanied by thunderous applause. The importance of this news was obvious to everyone: the Semyonovsky Regiment had been one of the most trustworthy pillars of Tsarism. There was not a man in the room who was not familiar with the 'glorious' traditions of the 'Semyonovsky boys' and in particular did not remember their Moscow exploits in 1905.[5] All that was over. In a flash the stinking fog was dispersed by the light of this new and blinding sun.

It appeared that there were delegates from the newly insurgent regiments in the hall. They had not ventured to ask for the floor but now came forward after the Semyonovsky had opened the way for them. Once again the assembly heard tales of a whole series of army units—one of the Cossack regiments, I think an armoured division, an electro-technical battalion, a machine-gun regiment—the terrible enemies of the people just a short while before and from now on a firmly united band of friends of the revolution. The revolution was growing and increasing in strength with every moment.

Elections continued for the Literary Commission. Sokolov, Peshekhonov, Steklov, Grinevich, and I were elected. No objections were raised: there were no factional struggles or party candidates. Moreover, no directives at all were given to the Commission, and it was clear to everyone that the proclamation would be published in the form in which they submitted it. Thus was accomplished the Soviet's first act of any political significance.

*　　*　　*

REVIEW QUESTIONS

1. What does Sukhanov's account reveal about the intentions and priorities of those who participated in the formation of the Petrograd Soviet?
2. Whom did the Soviet claim to speak for?
3. What was the significance of the support the Soviet's deputies received from soldiers?
4. Why was one of the first acts of the Soviet the election of a Literary Commission?
5. Was the Petrograd Soviet taking the initiative in the February Revolution? Or was it responding to events that were not fully within its control?

---

[5] The Semyonovskys were notorious for their part in the brutal suppression of the Moscow uprising in 1905. [Editor.]

PETROGRAD SOVIET OF WORKERS' AND SOLDIERS' DEPUTIES

Order Number One, 1 March 1917

Once the provisional government and the Petrograd Soviet were created—and operating from the left and right wings of the Tauride Palace—the primary goal of the new revolutionary authority in St. Petersburg was to reestablish order in the streets and to convince the soldiers who had mutinied against their officers to return to their barracks. The violence at the end of February had taken everybody by surprise, and it was imperative for the new government to establish itself as a legitimate authority. Many of the soldiers were afraid that they would be punished for their acts of disobedience, however, and they would not comply without guarantees of immunity. Suspicious of the provisional government, which they feared would take the side of their officers, the soldiers turned to the Petrograd Soviet. The Soviet readily complied with their demands, issuing Order Number One, which replaced the authority of the army's officer corps with a system of soldiers' committees that would operate on a democratic principle.

The historian William Henry Chamberlin described the creation of this order in the following terms: "On the night of the 14th, in one of the rooms of the crowded, noisy, smoke-filled Tauride Palace the radical lawyer, N. D. Sokolov, suddenly elevated by the Revolution to the post of a Soviet leader, sat at a writing desk, surrounded by a throng of soldiers. First one soldier, then another threw out suggestions, all of which Sokolov obediently wrote down. When the suggestions were exhausted the paper received the heading: 'Order Number One.' When the monarchist Shulgin read the contents of this extraordinary document he exclaimed to himself, 'This is the end of the army'; and this view was widely shared in conservative military circles."[1] Another historian, Orlando Figes, has written, "This crucial document . . . did more than anything else to destroy the discipline of the army, and thus in a sense brought the Bolsheviks to power."[2]

From *The Russian Revolution, 1917–1921*, by William Henry Chamberlin (Princeton, N.J.: Princeton University Press, 1987, first published in 1935 by Macmillan), vol. 1, pp. 429–30.

March 1, 1917

To the garrison of the Petrograd District. To all the soldiers of the Guard, army, artillery and fleet

for immediate and precise execution, and to the workers of Petrograd for information.

The Soviet of Workers' and Soldiers' Deputies has decided:

1. In all companies, battalions, regiments, depots, batteries, squadrons and separate branches of military service of every kind and on warships immediately choose committees

---

[1] William Henry Chamberlin, *The Russian Revolution, 1917–1921* (Princeton, N.J.: Princeton University Press, 1987), vol. 1, p. 86.

[2] Orlando Figes, *A People's Tragedy: The Russian Revolution, 1891–1924* (New York: Penguin, 1996), pp. 330–31.

from the elected representatives of the soldiers and sailors of the above mentioned military units.

2. In all military units which have still not elected their representatives in the Soviet of Workers' Deputies elect one representative to a company, who should appear with written credentials in the building of the State Duma at ten o'clock on the morning of March 2.

3. In all its political demonstrations a military unit is subordinated to the Soviet of Workers' and Soldiers' Deputies and its committees.

4. The orders of the military commission of the State Duma are to be fulfilled only in those cases which do not contradict the orders and decisions of the Soviet of Workers' and Soldiers' Deputies.

5. Arms of all kinds, as rifles, machine-guns, armored automobiles and others must be at the disposition and under the control of the company and battalion committees and are not in any case to be given out to officers, even upon their demand.

6. In the ranks and in fulfilling service duties soldiers must observe the strictest military discipline; but outside of service, in their political, civil, and private life soldiers cannot be discriminated against as regards those rights which all citizens enjoy. Standing at attention and compulsory saluting outside of service are especially abolished.

7. In the same way the addressing of officers with titles: Your Excellency, Your Honor, etc. is abolished and is replaced by the forms of address: Mr. General, Mr. Colonel, etc.

Rude treatment of soldiers of all ranks, and especially addressing them as "thou" is forbidden; and soldiers are bound to bring to the attention of the company committees any violation of this rule and any misunderstandings between officers and soldiers.

This order is to be read in all companies, battalions, regiments, marine units, batteries and other front and rear military units.

REVIEW QUESTIONS

1. What authority did Order Number One require all military units to recognize?
2. In what way was the Duma's power over the military curtailed by Order Number One?
3. In what way did this document recognize the rights of citizenship possessed by the rank and file in the military?
4. How did these rights of citizenship challenge the conventional definition of military discipline?
5. What kinds of difficulties might officers at the front have faced in the aftermath of Order Number One?

OCTOBER (1927)

SERGEI EISENSTEIN

The reconstruction of history through film often treads the fine line between art and political persuasion. Created in 1927 for the tenth anniversary of the Bolshevik Revolution, Sergei Eisenstein's October *depicted the Bolshevik storming of the Winter Palace on October 25, 1917 as a spectacular expression of popular will and revolutionary valor. In reality, the event had little dramatic flair; the Winter Palace, the seat of Aleksandr Kerensky's provisional government, was guarded by only a handful of cadets who offered little or no resistance. How might this film have influenced Soviet citizens' perception and memory of the October Revolution?*

ALEXANDRA KOLLONTAI

FROM *The Autobiography of a Sexually Emancipated Communist Woman*

Alexandra Kollontai (1872–1952) grew up in an educated, affluent, and fairly liberal Russian family. She married young, but left her husband and son to study political economy in Switzerland, where she became actively involved in socialist organizing. Originally a Menshevik, Kollontai became a Bolshevik in 1915, largely because of the Bolshevik opposition to the war, and entered into a friendly correspondence with Lenin.

After the October Revolution, Kollontai was named People's Commissar of Social Welfare, becoming the only woman to hold a cabinet post in the new Bolshevik government. As director of the Women's Bureau (Zhenotdel), she agitated in favor of economic liberty for working women and state welfare benefits for mothers. Her advocacy of women's rights and free love was not universally popular, and in the years following the revolution she found herself increasingly at odds with the Communist Party leadership. In 1922, Kollontai was assigned a diplomatic post in Norway—a gentle form of exile—and she spent much of the rest of her life outside of Russia. In memoirs written in 1926, she recounted the heady early days of the revolution, when a total transformation of Russian society still seemed possible.

From *The Autobiography of a Sexually Emancipated Communist Woman*, by Alexandra Kollontai, translated by Salvator Attanasio (New York: Herder and Herder, 1971).

*   *   *

When one recalls the first months of the Workers' Government, months which were so rich in *magnificent illusions,*[1] plans, ardent initiatives to improve life, to organize the world anew, months of the real romanticism of the Revolution, one would in fact like to write about all else save about one's self. I occupied the post of Minister of Social Welfare from October of 1917 *to March of 1918.* It was not without opposition that I was received by the former officials of the Ministry. Most of them sabotaged us openly and simply did not show up for work. But precisely this office could not interrupt its work, come what may, since in itself it was an extraordinarily complicated operation. It included the whole welfare program for the war-disabled, hence for hundreds of thousands of crippled soldiers and officers, the pension system in general, foundling homes, homes for the aged, orphanages, hospitals for the needy, the work-shops making artificial limbs, the administration of playing-card factories (the manufacture of playing cards was a State monopoly), *the educational system,* clinical hospitals for women. In addition a whole series of educational institutes for

---

[1] By 1926, it was already necessary to be cautious about how one described one's involvement in the revolution, and Kollontai censored her own writing. Italics indicate passages in the original manuscript that were not included in the published version of her memoirs.

young girls were also under the direction of this Ministry. One can easily imagine the enormous demands these tasks made upon a small group of people who, at the same time, were novices in State administration. In a clear awareness of these difficulties *I formed,* immediately, an auxiliary council in which experts such as physicians, jurists, pedagogues were represented alongside the workers and the minor officials of the Ministry. The sacrifice, the energy with which the minor employees bore the burden of this difficult task was truly exemplary. It was not only a matter of keeping the work of the Ministry going, but also of initiating reforms and improvements. New, fresh forces replaced the sabotaging officers of the old regime. A new life stirred in the offices of the formerly highly conservative Ministry. Days of grueling work! And at night the sessions of the councils of the People's Commissar (of the cabinet) under Lenin's chairmanship. A small, modest room and only one secretary who recorded the resolutions which changed Russia's life to its bottommost foundations.

*   *   *

My main work as People's Commissar consisted in the following: by decree to improve the situation of the war-disabled, to abolish religious instruction in the schools for young girls which were under the Ministry (this was still before the general separation of Church and State), and to transfer priests to the civil service, to introduce the right of self-administration for pupils in the schools for girls, to reorganize the former orphanages into government Children's Homes (*no distinction was to be made between orphaned children and those who still had fathers and mothers*), to set up the first hostels for the needy and street-urchins, to convene a committee, composed *only* of doctors, which was to be commissioned *to elaborate* the free public health system for the whole country. In my opinion the most important accomplishment of the People's Commissariat, however, was the legal foundation of a Central Office for Maternity and Infant Welfare. The draft of the bill relating to this Central Office was signed by me in January of 1918. A second decree followed in which *I* changed all maternity hospitals into free Homes for Maternity and Infant Care, in order thereby to set the groundwork for a comprehensive government system of pre-natal care. I was greatly assisted in coping with these tasks by Dr. Korolef. We also planned a "Pre-Natal Care Palace," a model home with an exhibition room in which courses for mothers would be held *and, among many other things,* model day nurseries were also to be established. We were just about completing preparations for such a facility in the building of a girls' boarding school at which formerly young girls of the nobility had been educated and which was still under the direction of a countess, when a fire destroyed our work, which had barely begun! Had the fire been set deliberately? . . . I was dragged out of bed in the middle of the night. I rushed to the scene of the fire; the beautiful exhibition room was totally ruined, as were all the other rooms. Only the huge name-plate "Pre-Natal Care Palace" still hung over the entrance door.

My efforts to nationalize maternity and infant care set off a new wave of insane attacks against me. All kinds of lies were related about the "nationalization of women," *about my legislative proposals which assertedly ordained that little girls of 12 were to become mothers.* A special fury gripped the religious followers of the old regime when, *on my own authority (the cabinet later criticized me for this action),* I transformed the famous Alexander Nevsky monastery into a home for war-invalids. The monks resisted and a shooting fray ensued. The press again raised a loud hue and cry against me. The Church organized street demonstrations *against my action* and also pronounced "anathema" against me. . . .

I received countless threatening letters, but I never requested military protection. I always went out alone, unarmed and without any kind of a bodyguard. In fact I never gave a thought to any kind of danger, being all too engrossed in matters of an utterly different character. In February of 1918 a first State delegation of the Soviets was sent to Sweden in order to clarify different economic and political questions. As Peoples' Commissar I headed this delegation. But our vessel was shipwrecked; we were saved by landing on the Aland Islands which belonged to Finland. At this very time the struggle between the Whites and the Reds in the country had reached its most crucial moment and the German Army was also making ready to wage war against Finland.

*   *   *

Now began a *dark time* of my life which I cannot treat of here since the events are still too fresh in my mind. *But the day will also come when I will give an account of them.*

There were differences of opinion in the Party. I resigned from my post as People's Commissar *on the ground of total disagreement with the current policy. Little by little I was also relieved of all my other tasks. I again gave lectures and espoused my ideas on "the new woman" and "the new morality."* The Revolution was in full swing. The struggle was becoming increasingly irreconcilable and bloodier, *much of what was happening did not fit in with my outlook.* But after all there was still the unfinished task, women's liberation. Women, of course, had received all rights but in practice, of course, they still lived under the old yoke: without authority in family life, enslaved by a thousand menial household chores, bearing the whole burden of maternity, even the material cares, because many women now found life alone as a result of the war and other circumstances.

*   *   *

A flood of new work was waiting for me. The question now was one of drawing women into the people's kitchens and of educating them to devote their energies to children's homes and day-care centers, the school system, household reforms, and still many other pressing matters. The main thrust of all this activity was to implement, in fact, equal rights for women as a labor unit in the national economy and as a citizen in the political sphere and, of course, with the special proviso: maternity was to be appraised as a social function and therefore protected and provided for by the State.

*   *   *

A serious illness tore me away from the exciting work for months. Hardly having recovered— at that time I was in Moscow—I took over the direction of the Coordinating Office for Work among Women and again a new period of intensive, grueling work began. A communist women's *newspaper* was founded, conferences and congresses of women workers were convoked. The foundation was laid for work with the women of the East (Mohammedans). Two world conferences of communist women took place in Moscow. The law liberalizing abortion was put through and a number of regulations of benefit to women were introduced by our Coordinating Office and legally confirmed. *At this time I had to do more writing and speaking than ever before. . . .* Our work received wholehearted support from Lenin. And Trotsky, although he was overburdened with military tasks, unfailingly and gladly appeared at our conferences. Energetic, gifted women, two of whom are no longer alive, sacrificially devoted all their energies to the work of the Coordinating Office.

At the eighth Soviet Congress, as a member of the Soviet executive (*now there were already several women on this body*), I proposed a motion that the Soviets in all areas contribute to the creation of a consciousness of the struggle for equal rights for women and, accordingly, to involve them in State and communal work. I managed to push the motion through and to get it accepted but not without resistance. It was a great, an enduring victory.

A heated debate flared up when I published my thesis on the new morality. *For our Soviet marriage law, separated from the Church to be sure, is not essentially more progressive than the same laws that after all exist in other progressive democratic countries.* * * * [A]lthough the illegitimate child *was* placed on a legal par with the legitimate child, in practice a great deal of hypocrisy and injustice still exists in this area. When one speaks of the "immorality" which the Bolsheviks purportedly propagated, it suffices to submit our marriage laws to a close scrutiny to note that in the divorce question we are on a par with North America whereas in the question of the illegitimate child we have *not yet even* progressed as far as the Norwegians.

The most radical wing of the Party was formed around this question. My theses, my *sexual and moral* views, were bitterly fought *by many Party comrades of both sexes: as were still other differences of opinion in the Party regarding political guiding principles.* Personal and family cares were added thereto and thus months in 1922 went by without fruitful work. Then in the autumn of 1922 came my official appointment to the legation of the Russian Soviet representation in Norway. I really believed that this appointment would be purely formal and that therefore in Norway I would find time to devote to myself, to my literary activity. Things turned out quite differently. With the day

of my entry into office in Norway I also entered upon a wholly new course of work in my life which drew upon all my energies to the highest degree.

*　　*　　*

REVIEW QUESTIONS

1. What kind of work did Kollontai do as People's Commissar of Social Welfare?
2. What does her work tell you about the social welfare policies of the revolutionary government?
3. Who opposed Kollontai's efforts in favor of women's liberation? Why?

Daily Life under Stalin

Josef Stalin ruled the Soviet Union unchallenged from 1928 until his death in 1953. It was during this period that the institutions of Soviet rule that would last until the 1990s were largely created. From Lenin, Stalin had inherited the one-party state, and his goal was to use this state to build a socialist nation in Russia. Socialism, in theory, meant the abolition of private property and the establishment of an economy in which the state would replace the market as the primary mechanism for the distribution of goods and resources. In practice, Stalinism meant an abrupt and brutal transformation of a largely peasant society into a modern industrial nation, unified by a common Soviet culture. The early years of his rule, 1928–1931, were years of extraordinary change, as the first Five-Year Plan of industrial development was announced, and private property in agriculture was abolished. Millions of rural Russians were forced to adapt to a new kind of collective agricultural production organized by local kolkhoz, *or cooperatives. In order to feed the urban populations that were conscripted into the building of the Soviet Union's industrial infrastructure, the state simply confiscated the grain produced in the countryside, leaving very little for those who had actually grown the crops. Historians estimate that as many as 5 million people died in the ensuing famines in Ukraine in 1931–32.*

In recent decades, the history of Stalin's revolution has been rewritten as historians have found new documentation on the effects of Stalinism on ordinary people in the Soviet Union. The following three documents show the effects of Stalin's revolution in the countryside: the first two give a glimpse of the opinions of industrial workers and rural farmers during the first Five-Year Plan, and the third indicates the efforts—not always successful—of Stalin's officials to remake Russian culture by controlling the sources of information and its circulation.

From *Stalinism as a Way of Life: A Narrative in Documents,* edited by Lewis Siegelbaum and Andrei Sokolov (New Haven: Yale University Press, 2000), pp. 44–46, 52–53, 64–65.

Letter to Stalin and Kalinin [ostensibly] from Workers at Red Putilovets Factory, Leningrad, March 1930. ✳ ✳ ✳ Typed Copy.

[*Translator's note:* Much of the spelling, punctuation, capitalization, usage, and syntax in this letter is that of a person with little education. To convey the meaning of the text fully, these characteristics are reflected only minimally here.]

To the Secretary and to the Head of the VTsIK (Vsesoiuznyi Tsentral'nyi Ispolnitel'nyi Komitet [All-Union central executive committee] Stalin and Kalinin.

We, the workers of the Red Putilovets Plant, fifty in number, have discussed and have decided that we once and for all protest against the terors [*sic*] and persecutions of the peasants and the one who you deprive of the vote and consider them kulaks. We all as one, members of the VKPb [Vsesoiuznaia Kommunisticheskaia Partitia (bol'shevikov), All-Union Communist Party of the Soviet Union] have a tie with the countryside, to us write our fathers and brothers how they're deprived of the vote and are not asked if they are agreed to be on the kolkhoz or not, but right off the bat their property is taken away by the careerists, and they're driven into prisons the shame of Soviet power, as capitalists do not do as you do in a free country, you throw into prison those who worked from morning till late night, the toilers who've put their whole life into their home and into their farm. You've called them kulaks only because they slept on their fist [the literal meaning of *kulak*] not having a pillow to themselves in their home, [*sic*] You regard those as kulaks who made their farm prosper and gave income to the state. You drove them

into cellars and want them to rot alive, these fathers and brothers of ours, and posted their grandson with a rifle to guard them like wild animals. We're indignant against this, for what have we fought, for what have we shed blood when we did not expect this, that our worker-peasant reign would torment our fathers and brothers so. Why then do we need the VKP since it makes life impossible for all of us?

They kill, throw people into prison, and take all that we have gained with hands hardened by toil. We demand an order be given immediately to the local organizations and stop the teror [*sic*] in our free country, pay attention what they're saying, all the Leningrad workers they're leaving the party only because nowadays everyone's being persecuted. No one has a liking for Soviet authority, but consider you torturers of the Russian people. Why do we have to do the five-year plan so thoroughly when we've become poor after such wealth as we have in Russia even if you take only sugar that they used to feed the pigs with, and now you can't buy it even if you have the money, and also our children are starving and we have absolutely nothing to feed them with. We want Comrade Trotsky to be right and Comrade Bukharin and other comrades, but you squeeze everyone tighter and tighter, you want to complete the five-year plan in four years. You like it that the Komsomol members shout, but they are really dumbbells and sheep who don't understand anything, and you must pay attention to all of the proletariat and peasantry now this is why they send you a thousand curses and consider you violators and not rulers of the Russian people. You've robbed all the capitalists and you have your hands on small-time property owners and on the peasants. You're sending millions of toilers before their time to the next world at the same time you are writing that we are a nation of free laborers. We didn't know that poor peasants would be shown so much respect. It seems like it would be better if everyone was a poor peasant and beggars. You can't get nothing from a poor peasant, a poor peasant is a loafer and that's just why he's poor he is used to getting everything from others for nothing. You are now collecting scrap metal and rags. Doesn't that mean that you're begging alms from workers? But what you ought to do is give to him. Where is the wealth that we inherited from the capitalists? Even the poor peasants, they are gasping, specially in the country they don't look a lump of sugar in the eye, why the hell a five-year plan when they don't let you live here and now, who have we built the damn five-year plan for. You are destroying millions of people. It's become ridiculous you forced registering of old men workers for the Party, and who doesn't join up you threaten to fire. ∗ ∗ ∗

One day I was talking with an elderly worker he openly declared how we now have a time of persecution of everybody they don't let you live out your days peacefully. There's a fact no one can deny. ∗ ∗ ∗

Letter to *Pravda* on Collectivization in Lower Volga Krai, 1930. ∗ ∗ ∗ Typed Copy.

In one village I went to an exhibition. Before looking at the exhibits we had to go to a big meeting. Speeches are given: a spokesman for the RIK [Raionnyi Ispolnitel'nyi Komitet, district executive committee], the agronomist, the supervisor of the reading room [*izbach*], the chairman of the ural soviet [*sel'sovet*] and its secretary. The RIK spokesman and the agronomist talk about successes of the state together with lavish praise of collective kolkhoz cultivation of the land and its advantages over private cultivation and so on. The members of the rural soviet speak about the achievements of that village. After finishing his speech while others were speaking, the RIK spokesman started composing a resolution about the desirability of organizing a land society. Having finished composing, he reads that

the land society is going to promote the idea of contributing to a loan for industrialization in each peasant household; during the current year he wants to organize two large-scale collectives, etc. He finishes reading. Then he asks the peasants to speak from the floor, those in favor and those against. Everyone remains silent, no one says a word. The supervisor of the reading room gets up, repeats the question, again there is silence. The RIK spokesman says, "So, everyone's agreed?" Laughter in the crowd. Here you have an irrefutable picture of the self-inspired kolkhoz movement. Precisely this type of information is given to the press about the kolkhoz movement and the party acts upon it, a great amount of it is fake documentation invented and composed by those party members who pursue the personal goal of advancing themselves, and the peasant's silence results from unwillingness and fears of being accused of espionage, of exile, of being put in prison, fines, having to suffer confiscation, and having to pay various burdensome taxes.

Then a look at the exhibits. An example of the judging process: representing horticulture are apple trees two or three years old, some belonging to a private peasant and others from a kolkhoz. The chairman, an agronomist, having looked over the kolkhoz apple trees along with the judging committee, goes up to the peasant and says, "Although these apple trees both in the roots and in the crown are better than the kolkhoz ones, we should give precedence to the kolkhoz because of our class distinctions." Laughter again in the crowd. As a result the first prize goes to the kolkhoz, and the peasant gets a certificate of merit. Peasant experts understood this fake judging and how the local authorities, using agronomists, aim to show agricultural achievement in their village and to show that such achievements supposedly occur not because of peasant experts but because of the activities of the local authorities. In point of fact no one made even the slightest effort to look into any aspect of the middle-sized peasant farm economy, nor was anyone willing to do more than compile official charts, and therefore exhibitions in many villages did not take place. The sentence dished out by the agronomist judging the apple trees is nothing more than subtle mockery of the party's class line. So this is what all educated people working in the Soviet Union survive on, and their slogan, like that of the peasants, is to own something. On account of this peasants say that former landowners sit in our central offices and hold power, taking vengeance on us for land and estates taken from them. * * *

Letter from W. M. Kovalchuk on Flight from Collective Farms in North Caucausus Krai, 1932. * * * Typed Copy.

I write not as one who gives in to difficulties, not as an enemy of Soviet power, but as a man who fought for it.

In Chamlyk Raion there is one kolkhoz, second in size in the krai, that fulfills a three hundred thousand-pood state grain procurement, but the trouble is this socialist farm is melting like the spring snow, people are fleeing the kolkhoz for who knows where. At the kolkhoz they took all the grain away and left a little field corn for the people to live on. All this is the result of the kolkhoz's unavoidable disintegration, and what disgrace that is!

The kolkhoz plants wheat and lives on corn. Everyone's mood is almost anti-Soviet. Dear comrades, now you go and take any one of us, set in front us only field corn without any grease, dress us in rags, shoes without soles, and force us to work on the steppe when the temperature is twenty-five degrees below zero; wouldn't any of you become a deviant and curse all and everything?

Here is one example. At the stanitsa, we have some thirteen thousand hectares of land; before the revolution there were twelve thousand people, and now there are eight thousand. There has been a decrease in people, the rest don't have the strength to do the harvesting; as a result thousands of hectares of various crops are rotting on the steppe, overgrown with weeds.

The people have become pretty malicious, they look disapprovingly at the Communists, the Communist cell has lost its authority. Members of the party also. Now we have to meet contract require-ments for delivery of hens, this also intensifies anger among the peasants. Out of people fighting for Soviet power they are now making people who are against Soviet power because every last kernel of grain has been taken from them and they have nothing to chew on. Every night seven to ten households abandon the stanitsa. This on account of the good life. I've permitted myself to express my opinion as one comrade to another, to the masses I speak differently, the way Soviet authority talks.

Memorandum of N. Malstev to Ya. Rudzutak and Ye. Yaroslavsky on Purge of Libraries, 16 October 1932. * * * Typed Original.

Libraries have been purged of pernicious and outdated literature by NKPros [Narodnyi Komissariat Provescheniia, People's Commissariat of Education] without adequate instructions and control. The only instructions from Glavpol[it]prosvet [Glavnoe upravlenie politicheskogo proveshchevniia, chief directorate of political education], dated 29 March 1930, present no defined order for book inspection and removal and are filled with ambiguities and obviously incorrect and harmful directives that could not serve as a practical guide for conducting a purge. Therefore in some oblasts (Moscow and Leningrad) instructions solely for those oblasts appeared; more often than not, in view of the difficulty of this undertaking and the risks involved the matter was allowed to take its own course, whatever happened would happen, and responsibility could be placed on those who actually carried out the work.

And what happened was very bad. At a meeting of those who conducted the purges, it came to light that more than 60 percent of all book holdings have been withdrawn. There are libraries in which the portion of books withdrawn reached 80 or 90 percent. Correspondance from very different corners of the USSR indicates that the classics of philosophy, science, belles-lettres, and even revolutionary Marxism have been removed: Marx,

Engels, Lenin, Stalin, Tolstoy, Turgenev, Goncharov, Dickens, Hugo, resolutions of party congresses, reports of congresses of soviets, Sechenov, Timirazev, Khvolson, Ivan Pavlov. The names of these "withdrawn" authors alone indicate criminal activity in the way the purge was conducted.

It is difficult to explain all this by lack of sophistication and stupidity in those carrying out the purge. It is one thing that in certain instances Lenin's books were withdrawn, for instance, because they were listed under the last name Il'in, or Marx's "Communist Manifesto" with Riazanov's foreword, but in many other instances this explanation breaks down.

Lists of works recommended for removal produced by purging committees in Moscow and Leningrad drawn up by "authoritative" and "educated" people give directions that in the provinces could lead to nothing else. Under "Philosophy" the Leningrad instructions propose that "idealistic philosophy should be removed entirely from circulation" (leaving only Kant's and Hegel's works). The works of bourgeois sociologists Spencer, Tarde, M. Kovalevsky, and Simmel are being withdrawn, as are Bukharin's *Istmat* [*Istoricheskii materializm,* historical materialism], Deborin, Kornilov, from the section of antireligious literature Kautsky's *Foundations of Christianity* and the titles of ninety books that I personally am unacquainted with but which include many surnames of Communists. From the "Social and Political" section Kautsky's *The Economic Doctrines of Karl Marx,* Luxemburg's *Accumulation of Capital,* Rosenberg's *Commentaries on Das Kapital,* Sabsovich, Borian's *State Control in the Soviet Union and in Western Europe,* Yaroslavsky, volumes 2 and 4, Nevsky, Kerzhentsev, Bogdanov's *Lessons in Political Economy,* Hilferding, Tugan-Baranovsky.

＊ ＊ ＊ The lists for belles-lettres was drawn up in a completely arbitrary way. Why withdraw Hamsun, Dickens, Hauptmann, Zlatovratsky, Potapenko, Rostand, Oscar Wilde, Fet, Hugo, Sudermann, even Lunacharsky, Balmont, A. K. Tolstoy, and many, many others who by the humblest and most general assessment are on a higher level and

less pernicious than the hundreds of junky kinds of belles-lettres that Gosizdat [Gosudarstvennoe izdatel'stvo, state publishing firm] puts out even now?

A kind of sadistic guardianship of the reader results from all this. The main instructions of Glavpolitprosvet are more restrained and balanced. But even according to them, "all prerevolutionary literature" concerned with upbringing and education, all prerevolutionary mathematics textbooks, all anthologies of Russian literature, collections of pieces for recitation, oral public reading and narration "should be removed from local public libraries and transferred to central and pedagogical libraries." ＊ ＊ ＊

This is a really terrible peril to all this because of the quite unacceptable and unregulated way in which the books were removed. What is the "central" library that is supposed to make the final decision about the fate of a book withdrawn, whether to throw it out or sell it? ＊ ＊ ＊ This decision has been left to the discretion of the local authorities. The Moscow Oblast Library created such centers in twenty-three spots. Glavpolitprosvet instructions propose that "all books deemed properly withdrawn—once two copies have been deposited in the archives and a selection made of those having potential value for research and specialized libraries—are to be sold unbound to factories for recycling into paper."

According to the Glavpolitprosvet instructions, two copies of a huge number of books of great value are supposed to be kept in the "archives" of a library. ＊ ＊ ＊ Except for books "worthy of being actively promoted to the reading masses," all other books not subject to the purge and removal process are to be put into these repositories. These books should be "kept separate from the main core [of books] in a special room or on separate shelves or in separate cabinets. Free access to them should not occur, catalogue cards for them are to be removed from the general catalogue and maintained separately for reference purposes." The only possible meaning is that, after the official purge, readers can only use permitted books made available to them by a librarian at the latter's discretion, for there is no way for them even to know what else the library has (the catalogue cards having been withdrawn).

All the instructions put great emphasis on the urgency of this work and the need to speed it up. Books were hauled to the Moscow Oblast Library by the truckload during the night; any organized receiving of them was out of the question. To tell what is what in such a mass of books is utterly impossible. An easy solution was sought and found: sell the books. The Oblast Library got itself a pretty good source of income out of the purge. The result? Secondhand book dealers all had books with uncanceled library identification stamps. This bacchanalia of stupidity was followed by a bacchanalia of stealing, for you couldn't have created a more irresponsible atmosphere for the bad element among library workers than by letting books with library identification stamps appear on the secondhand book market legally. ⋆ ⋆ ⋆

Therefore I propose:

1. To put forward a proposal ⋆ ⋆ ⋆ to stop immediately the purging, transportation, and reselling of books from all libraries.

2. To create ⋆ ⋆ ⋆ a commission to unmask the real culprits of criminal purging activity and to develop measures to liquidate the harmful consequences of this activity.

REVIEW QUESTIONS

1. Are the criticisms of Stalinist policies that are evident in these documents aimed at the goals of the revolution itself or at the ways the representatives of the Soviet state are going about achieving these revolutionary goals? What is the significance of this distinction for the authors of these critiques?

2. What is the attitude of the Leningrad workers in the first document toward the rural peasantry? What does this tell you about the relationship between urban workers and rural peasants in the first decade of the Soviet Union's history?

3. What does the second document reveal about attitudes in the countryside toward the Soviet policy of favoring collective farms?

4. What does the third document reveal about the effects of the collectivization program on agricultural production and the condition of the peasantry?

5. What does the fourth document, on the purging of libraries, reveal about the wider cultural goals of the Stalinist revolution?

BENITO MUSSOLINI

FROM "Born of a Need for Action"

Fascism emerged during the 1920s as a response to the unsettled political, economic, and social climate of the postwar period. Although it was a global phenomenon, it enjoyed its greatest successes in Germany and Italy.

As the first fascist head of state, Benito Mussolini (1883–1945) was an inspiration to other would-be dictators throughout the 1920s. Mussolini began his political career as a socialist journalist, but his ardent support for Italian participation in the First World War caused him to be expelled from the Socialist Party. In the chaos of the immediate postwar years in Italy, Mussolini created his own Fascist Party, encouraging his followers to silence political opponents through the use of violence. The

Italian ruling elite, confronted with widespread strike activity and the threat of a communist takeover, handed over the reins of government to Mussolini in 1922, after he demonstrated the strength of the fascist movement with a march on Rome. Many Italians welcomed this development, seeing Mussolini as a great leader— Duce—whose forceful rule would bring order, prosperity, and a renewal of national strength and pride. In 1932, ten years after his seizure of power, Mussolini wrote an article on fascism for an Italian encyclopedia, setting down in writing for the first time the ideological premises of the movement.

From *The Estate of Benito Mussolini*, translated by Jane Soames (London: Hogarth Press, 1933).

*　　*　　*

Fascism was not the nursling of a doctrine worked out beforehand with detailed elaboration; it was born of the need for action and it was itself from the beginning practical rather than theoretical; it was not merely another political party but, even in the first two years, in opposition to all political parties as such, and itself a living movement.

*　　*　　*

The years which preceded the march to Rome were years of great difficulty, during which the necessity for action did not permit of research or any complete elaboration of doctrine. The battle had to be fought in the towns and villages. There was much discussion, but—what was more important and more sacred—men died. They knew how to die. Doctrine, beautifully defined and carefully elucidated, with headlines and paragraphs, might be lacking; but there was to take its place something more decisive—Faith.

*　　*　　*

Fascism is now a completely individual thing, not only as a regime but as a doctrine. And this means that to-day Fascism, exercising its critical sense upon itself and upon others, has formed its own distinct and peculiar point of view, to which it can refer and upon which, therefore, it can act in the face of all problems, practical or intellectual, which confront the world.

And above all, Fascism, the more it considers and observes the future and the development of humanity quite apart from political considerations of the moment, believes neither in the possibility nor the utility of perpetual peace. It thus repudiates the doctrine of Pacifism—born of a renunciation of the struggle and an act of cowardice in the face of sacrifice. War alone brings up to its highest tension all human energy and puts the stamp of nobility upon the peoples who have the courage to meet it. All other trials are substitutes, which never really put men into the position where they have to make the great decision—the alternative of life or death. Thus a doctrine which is founded upon this harmful postulate of peace is hostile to Fascism.

*　　*　　*

* * * Fascism [is] the complete opposite of * * * so-called scientific and Marxian Socialism, the materialist conception of history; according to which the history of human civilization can be explained simply through the conflict of interests among the various social groups and by the change and development in the means and instruments of production. That the changes in the economic field—new discoveries of raw materials, new methods of working them, and the inventions of science—have their importance no one can deny; but that these factors are sufficient to explain the history of humanity excluding all others is an absurd delusion. Fascism, now and always, believes in holiness and in heroism; that is to say, in actions influenced by no economic motive, direct or indirect.

*   *   *

* * * Fascism repudiates the conception of "economic" happiness, to be realized by Socialism and, as it were, at a given moment in economic evolution to assure to everyone the maximum of well-being. Fascism denies the materialist conception of happiness as a possibility, * * * : that is to say, Fascism denies the validity of the equation, well-being = happiness, which would reduce men to the level of animals, caring for one thing only— to be fat and well-fed—and would thus degrade humanity to a purely physical existence.

After Socialism, Fascism combats the whole complex system of democratic ideology, and repudiates it, whether in its theoretical premises or in its practical application. Fascism denies that the majority, by the simple fact that it is a majority, can direct human society; it denies that numbers alone can govern by means of a periodical consultation, and it affirms the immutable, beneficial and fruitful inequality of mankind, which can never be permanently levelled through the mere operation of a mechanical process such as universal suffrage.

*   *   *

* * * Fascism denies, in democracy, the absurd conventional untruth of political equality dressed out in the garb of collective irresponsibility, and the myth of "happiness" and indefinite progress. But, if democracy may be conceived in diverse forms—that is to say, taking democracy to mean a state of society in which the populace are not reduced to impotence in the State—Fascism may write itself down as "an organized, centralized and authoritative democracy."

*   *   *

A party which entirely governs a nation is a fact entirely new to history, there are no possible references or parallels. Fascism uses in its construction whatever elements in the Liberal,

Social or Democratic doctrines still have a living value * * *

*   *   *

* * * If the nineteenth century was a century of individualism (Liberalism always signifying individualism) it may be expected that this will be the century of collectivism, and hence the century of the State.

*   *   *

The foundation of Fascism is the conception of the State, its character, its duty, and its aim. Fascism conceives of the State as an absolute, in comparison with which all individuals or groups are relative, only to be conceived of in their relation to the State. * * * In 1929, at the first five-yearly assembly of the Fascist regime, I said:

"For us Fascists, the State is not merely a guardian, preoccupied solely with the duty of assuring the personal safety of the citizens; nor is it an organization with purely material aims, such as to guarantee a certain level of well-being and peaceful conditions of life; for a mere council of administration would be sufficient to realize such objects. Nor is it a purely political creation, divorced from all contact with the complex material reality which makes up the life of the individual and the life of the people as a whole. The State, as conceived of and as created by Fascism, is a spiritual and moral fact in itself, since its political, juridical and economic organization of the nation is a concrete thing: and such an organization must be in its origins and development a manifestation of the spirit. The State is the guarantor of security both internal and external, but it is also the custodian and transmitter of the spirit of the people, as it has grown up through the centuries in language, in customs and in faith. And the State is not only a living reality of the present, it is also linked with the past and above all with the future, and thus transcending the brief limits of individual life, it represents the immanent spirit of the nation. The forms in which States express themselves may change, but the necessity for such forms is eternal. It is the State which educates its citizens in civic virtue, gives them a consciousness of their mission and welds them into unity; harmonizing their various interests through justice, and transmitting to future generations the mental conquests of science, of art, of law and the solidarity of humanity. It leads men from primitive tribal life to that highest expression of human power which is Empire: it links up through the centuries the names of those of its members who have died for its existence and in obedience to its laws, it holds up the memory of the leaders who have increased its territory and the geniuses who have illumined it with glory as an example to be followed by future generations. When the conception of the State declines, and disunifying and centrifugal tendencies prevail, whether of individuals or of particular groups, the nations where such phenomena appear are in their decline."

*   *   *

* * * The Fascist State is unique, and an original creation. It is not reactionary, but revolutionary, in that it anticipates the solution of the universal political problems which elsewhere have to be settled in the political field by the rivalry of parties, the excessive power of the Parliamentary regime and the irresponsibility of political assemblies; while it meets the problems of the economic field by a system of syndicalism which is continually increasing in importance, as much in the sphere of labour as of industry: and in the moral field enforces order, discipline, and obedience to that which is the determined moral code of the country. Fascism desires the State to be a strong and organic body, at the same time reposing upon broad and popular support. The Fascist State has drawn into itself even the economic activities of the nation, and, through the corporative social and educational institutions created by it, its influence reaches every aspect of the national life and includes, framed in their respective organizations, all the political, economic and spiritual forces of the nation. A State which reposes upon the support of millions of individuals who recognize its authority, are continually conscious of its power and are ready at once to serve it, is not the old tyrannical State of the medieval lord nor has it anything in common with the absolute governments either before or after 1789. The individual in the Fascist State is not annulled but rather multiplied, just in the same way that a soldier in a regiment is not diminished but rather increased by the number of his comrades. The Fascist State organizes the nation, but leaves a sufficient margin of liberty to the individual; the latter is deprived of all useless and possibly harmful freedom, but retains what is essential; the deciding power in this question cannot be the individual, but the State alone.

*   *   *

REVIEW QUESTIONS

1. Why did Mussolini reject pacifism?
2. What implications do his comments about war have for the policies of the fascist state?
3. Which aspects of socialism and democracy does Mussolini reject? Which does he retain?
4. What exactly does Mussolini mean when he defines the fascist state as "an organized, centralized and authoritative democracy"?
5. What role does the individual play in this state?

ADOLF HITLER

FROM *Mein Kampf*

German Nazism shared many of the tenets of Italian fascism. Like Mussolini, Adolf Hitler (1889–1945) rejected democracy as bankrupt and promoted an authoritarian politics based on the "leadership principle." Hitler was also an ardent militarist who believed that war was a crucial test of a nation's vigor. Germany's defeat in 1918 was not the result of military failure, he insisted, but rather the product of the diseased condition of German society in general. This corruption and weakness was caused by the diabolical machinations of the Jewish people, whom Hitler portrayed as a degenerate "race" engaged in an international conspiracy designed to destroy the "national principle" binding the German people together as a "master race." In response to this threat, Hitler offered himself as the leader—Führer—of a revitalized, militantly nationalist Germany purged of all those who would weaken or diminish the racial purity of the German people.

Hitler was jailed for nine months after a failed coup d'état, the Beer Hall Putsch of 1923. During his imprisonment, he wrote Mein Kampf *("My Struggle"), a massive, rambling political memoir detailing the political agenda of the Nazi Party. Many of the political arguments presented in* Mein Kampf *parallel those underpinning Italian fascism. What distinguishes Hitler's thought is his obsessive preoccupation with racial "hygiene" as the basis of national strength.*

From *Mein Kampf*, by Adolf Hitler, translated by Alvin Johnson (New York: Reynal and Hitchcock, 1940).

*   *   *

What we have to fight for is the security of the existence and the increase of our race and our people, the nourishment of its children and the preservation of the purity of the blood, the freedom and independence of the fatherland in order to enable our people to mature for the fulfillment of the mission which the Creator of the universe has allotted also to them.

*   *   *

A further example for the half-heartedness and the weakness of the leading authority in pre-War Germany in the most important vital questions of the nation can be the following: Parallel with the political and moral infection of the people went a no less terrible poisoning of the health of the national body. Syphilis began to spread more and more, especially in the great cities. * * *

*   *   *

The cause * * * lies primarily in our prostitution of love. Even if the result of this were not this terrible disease, yet it would still be of deepest danger for the people, for the moral devastation which this depravity brings with it are sufficient to destroy a people slowly but surely. The Judaization of our spiritual life and the mammonization of our mating impulse sooner or later befouls our entire new generation, for instead of vigorous children of natural feeling, only the miserable specimens of financial expedience come forth. For this becomes more and more the basis and the only prerequisite for our marriages. Love, however, finds an outlet somewhere else.

Naturally, one can also here mock Nature for a certain time, but the revenge will not fail to appear, it only will appear later, or rather, it is often recognized too late by the people.

*   *   *

The sin against the blood and the degradation of the race are the hereditary sin of this world and the end of a mankind surrendering to them.

*   *   *

Prostitution is a disgrace to mankind, but one cannot abolish it by moral lectures, pious intentions, etc., but its limitation and its final elimination warrant the abolition of quite a number of preliminary conditions. But the first is and remains the creation of the possibility of early marriage, according to human nature, above all for the man; because the woman is here only the passive part, anyhow.

*   *   *

Marriage also cannot be an end in itself, but has to serve the one greater aim, the propagation and preservation of the species and the race. Only this is its meaning and its task.

*   *   *

* * * Education and training have to eliminate quite a series of evils about which one hardly cares at all today. Above all, in our present-day education a balance between intellectual instruction and physical training has to take place. What today calls itself a *gymnasium* is an insult to the Greek example. With our education one has entirely forgotten that in the long run a healthy mind is able to dwell only in a healthy body. Especially when, with a few exceptions, one looks at the great masses of the people, this principle receives absolute validity.

In pre-War Germany there was a time when one no longer cared for this truth. One simply went on sinning against the body, and one thought that in the one-sided training of the 'mind' one possessed a safe guaranty for the greatness of the nation. A mistake which began to avenge itself much sooner than one thought. It is no accident that the bolshevistic wave found nowhere a better ground than in those places where a population, degenerated by hunger and constant undernourishment, lives: in Central Germany, Saxony, and the Ruhr district. In all these districts, however, a serious resistance on the part of the so-called "intelligentsia" to this Jewish disease hardly takes place any longer for the simple reason that the intelligentsia itself is physically completely degenerated, though less by reasons of distress than by reasons of education. The exclusively intellectual attitude of our education of the higher classes makes them unable—in a time where not the mind but the fist decides—even to preserve themselves, let alone to hold their ground. In physical deficiencies there lies not infrequently the first cause of personal cowardice.

The exceeding stress on a purely intellectual training and the neglect of physical training favor also in much too early youth the formation of sexual conceptions. The boy who, by sports and gymnastics, is brought to an ironlike inurement succumbs less to the need of sensual gratification than the stay-at-home who is fed exclusively on intellectual food. A reasonable education, however, must take this into consideration. Further, it must not forget that on the part of the healthy young man the expectations of the woman will be different than on the part of a prematurely corrupted weakling.

Thus the entire education has to be directed towards employing the free time of the boy for the useful training of his body. He has no right to loaf about idly in these years, to make streets and movie theaters insecure, but after his daily work he has to steel and harden his young body so that life will not find him too soft some day. To get this under way and also to carry it out, to guide and to lead is the task of the education of youth, and not the exclusive infiltration of so-called wisdom. It has also to do away with the conception that the treatment of the body were the concern of each individual. There is no liberty to sin at the expense of posterity and, with it, of the race.

*   *   *

It is a half measure to allow incurably ill people the permanent possibility of contaminating the other healthy ones. But this corresponds entirely to a humaneness which, in order not to hurt one individual, lets hundreds of others perish. The demand that for defective people the propagation of an equally defective offspring be made impossible is a demand of clearest reason and in its planful execution it means the most humane act of mankind. It will spare undeserved suffering to millions of unfortunates, but in the future it will lead to an increasing improvement of health on the whole. The determination to proceed in this direction will also put up a dam against the further spreading of venereal diseases. For here, if necessary, one will have to proceed to the pitiless isolation of incurably diseased people; a barbaric measure for one who was unfortunate enough to be stricken with it, but a blessing for the contemporaries and for posterity. The temporary pain of a century may and will redeem millenniums from suffering.

*   *   *

Any crossing between two beings of not quite the same high standard produces a medium between the standards of the parents. That means: the young one will probably be on a higher level than the racially lower parent, but not as high as the higher one. Consequently, it will succumb later on in the fight against the higher level. But such a mating contradicts Nature's will to breed life as a whole towards a higher level.

*   *   *

Just as little as Nature desires a mating between weaker individuals and stronger ones, far less she desires the mixing of a higher race with a lower one, as in this case her entire work of higher breeding, which has perhaps taken hundreds of thousands of years, would tumble at one blow.

Historical experience offers countless proofs of this. It shows with terrible clarity that with any mixing of the blood of the Aryan with lower races the result was the end of the culture-bearer. North America, the population of which consists for the greatest part of Germanic elements—which mix only very little with the lower, colored races—displays a humanity and a culture different from those of Central and South America, where chiefly the Romanic immigrants have sometimes mixed with the aborigines on a large scale. By this example alone one may clearly and distinctly recognize the influence of the race mixture. The Germanic of the North American continent, who has remained pure and less intermixed, has become the master of that continent, he will remain so until he, too, falls victim to the shame of blood-mixing.

*   *   *

Everything that today we admire on this earth—science and art, technique and inventions—is only the creative product of a few peoples and perhaps originally of *one* race. On them now depends also the existence of this entire culture. If they perish, then the beauty of this earth sinks into the grave with them.

*   *   *

All great cultures of the past perished only because the originally creative race died off through blood-poisoning.

*   *   *

He who wants to live should fight, therefore, and he who does not want to battle in this world of eternal struggle does not deserve to be alive.

*   *   *

What we see before us of human culture today, the results of art, science, and techniques, is almost exclusively the creative product of the Aryan.

*   *   *

If one were to divide mankind into three groups: culture-founders, culture-bearers, and culture-destroyers, then, as representative of the first kind, only the Aryan would come in question. It is from him that the foundation and the walls of all human creations originate, and only the external form and color depend on the characteristics of the various peoples involved. He furnishes the gigantic building-stones and also the plans for all human progress, and only the execution corresponds to the character of the people and races in the various instances.

*   *   *

But if it is ascertained that a people receives, takes in, and works over the essential basic elements of its culture from other races, and if then, when a further external influence is lacking, it stiffens again and again, then one can perhaps call such a race a *"culture-bearing"* one but never a *"culture-creating"* one.

*   *   *

The Jew forms the strongest contrast to the Aryan. Hardly in any people of the world is the instinct of self-preservation more strongly developed than in the so-called "chosen people." The fact of the existence of this race alone may be looked upon as the best proof of this. Where is the people that in the past two thousand years has been exposed to so small changes of the inner disposition, of character, etc., as the Jewish people? Which people finally has experienced greater changes than this one—and yet has always come forth the same from the most colossal catastrophes of mankind? What an infinitely persistent will for life, for preserving the race do these facts disclose!

Also the intellectual abilities were schooled in the course of centuries. Today the Jew is looked upon as "clever," and in a certain sense he has been so at all times. But his reason is not the result of his own development, but that of object lessons from without.

*   *   *

As now the Jew (for reasons which will immediately become evident from the following) was never in the possession of a culture of his own, the bases for his spiritual activity have always been furnished by others. At all times his intellect has developed through the culture that surrounds him.

*   *   *

In the Jewish people, the will to sacrifice oneself does not go beyond the bare instinct of self-preservation of the individual. The seemingly great feeling of belonging together is rooted in a very primitive herd instinct, as it shows itself in a similar way in many other living beings in this world. Thereby the fact is remarkable that in all these cases a common herd instinct leads to mutual support only as long as a common danger makes this seem useful or unavoidable. The same pack of wolves that jointly falls upon its booty dissolves when its hunger abates.

*   *   *

The Jew remains united only if forced by a common danger or is attracted by a common booty; if both reasons are no longer evident, then the qualities of the crassest egoism come into their own, and, in a moment, the united people becomes a horde of rats, fighting bloodily among themselves.

If the Jews were alone in this world, they would suffocate as much in dirt and filth, as they would carry on a detestable struggle to cheat and to ruin each other, although the complete lack of the will to sacrifice, expressed in their cowardice, would also in this instance make the fight a comedy.

Thus it is fundamentally wrong to conclude, merely from the fact of their standing together in a fight, or, more rightly expressed, in their exploiting their fellow human beings, that the Jews have a certain idealistic will to sacrifice themselves.

*   *   *

✳ ✳ ✳ The Jewish people, with all its apparent intellectual qualities, is nevertheless without any true culture, especially without a culture of its own. For the sham culture which the Jew possesses today is the property of other peoples, and is mostly spoiled in his hands.

✳   ✳   ✳

No, the Jew possesses no culture-creating energy whatsoever, as the idealism, without which there can never exist a genuine development of man towards a higher level, does not and never did exist in him. His intellect, therefore, will never have a constructive effect, but only a destructive one. ✳ ✳ ✳

✳   ✳   ✳

The Jews were always a people with definite racial qualities and never a religion, only their progress made them probably look very early for a means which could divert disagreeable attention from their person. But what would have been more useful and at the same time more harmless than the "purloining" of the appearance of being a religious community? For here, too, everything is purloined, or rather, stolen. But resulting from his own original nature the Jew cannot possess a religious institution for the very reason that he lacks all idealism in any form and that he also does not recognize any belief in the hereafter.

✳   ✳   ✳

The State is a means to an end. Its end is the preservation and the promotion of a community of physically and psychically equal living beings. This very preservation comprises first the racial stock and thereby it permits the free development of all the forces slumbering in this race. Again and again a part of them will primarily serve the preservation of the physical life and only another part will serve the promotion of a further mental development. But actually the one always creates the presumption for the other.

States that do not serve this purpose are faulty specimens, even miscarriages.

✳   ✳   ✳

Thus the highest purpose of the folkish State is the care for the preservation of those racial primal elements which, supplying culture, create the beauty and dignity of a higher humanity. We, as Aryans, are therefore able to imagine a State only to be the living organism of a nationality which not only safeguards the preservation of that nationality, but which, by a further training of its spiritual and ideal abilities, leads it to the highest freedom.

✳   ✳   ✳

REVIEW QUESTIONS

1. What were the greatest threats to the racial purity of Germans, according to Hitler?
2. What solutions did he propose?
3. What were the fundamental goals of education in the Nazi state?
4. In what sense did Jews pose a threat to Aryans?
5. On what evidence did Hitler base his arguments?

VICTOR KLEMPERER

FROM *I Will Bear Witness, 1933–1941: A Diary of the Nazi Years*

Victor Klemperer (1881–1960), a German professor of French literature who taught at the Technical University of Dresden until 1935, was born into a Jewish family and educated in Berlin and Munich. In spite of his Jewish origins (he was nonpracticing as an adult), he survived the Nazi period's persecution and murder of German Jews through a combination of circumstance and luck. After Hitler came to power in 1933, Klemperer's status as a combat veteran of the First World War afforded him limited protection against the petty economic persecutions that preceded the more serious threats to German Jews under Nazi rule. Later, a certain degree of relative privilege was accorded to him because of his marriage to a non-Jewish German woman, Eva Schlemmer, a pianist and musicologist. Because of his marriage, Klemperer was able to avoid being deported during the first years of the war. In February 1945, when Jewish spouses of non-Jews were systematically being arrested and sent to extermination camps, only 198 registered Jews remained in Dresden, including Klemperer himself. He was "saved," however, by the Allied firebombing of the city on February 13, the very day that all the remaining Jews were ordered to report for deportation. In the chaos that followed the devastation of the city, Victor Klemperer was able to remove from all his clothing the yellow star that identified him as a Jew in Nazi Germany, and he and his wife fled the city along with thousands of other refugees. For three months the Klemperers continued on foot through southern Germany, until they were liberated by American forces in a Bavarian village. After the war, Klemperer's professorship at the Technical University in Dresden was restored, and he finished his career with an appointment at the University of Halle. Also in 1945, Klemperer joined the German Communist Party because he found in this group the strongest condemnation of German fascism. He continued to live in and support the German Democratic Republic (East Germany) until his death in 1960.

Klemperer was a compulsive and thoughtful diarist who recorded the events of his days in a journal that now constitutes one of our most valuable sources about daily life in Nazi Germany. Rather than focusing on high politics or the major events of these years, Klemperer's journal emphasizes the everyday struggle to maintain one's sense of dignity and composure while living in the midst of those who had enthusiastically embraced an ideology of hatred. The following excerpt records the events in the Klemperers' household in the weeks after Kristallnacht (November 9, 1938), a night of organized violence by Nazis and their supporters against German Jews. In an assault that was coordinated at the highest level of the Nazi hierarchy, thousands of Jewish-owned business establishments and homes were attacked across Germany, and nearly all the synagogues and Jewish cemeteries in the country were damaged in some way, many temples being destroyed completely. Officially, ninety-one Jews were murdered in attacks between November 9 and November 11, 1938, but an estimated thirty thousand German Jews were arrested and held in concentration camps, most at Buchenwald (near Weimar), Dachau (near Munich), and Sachsenhausen (in the suburbs of Berlin). Historians believe that as many as two thousand of those arrested were killed in the camps over the weeks that followed. The remaining prisoners were released within three months, many under the condition that they leave Germany. In the previous entry to his diary, Klemperer noted the events of Kristallnacht briefly and wrote simply: "I do not need to describe the historic events of the following days, the acts of violence, our depression. Only the immediately personal and what concretely affected us." For the Klemperers, this meant reconsidering their previous strategy for coping. Since he had lost his job in 1935, they had invested all their savings in an attempt to build a small house in the country that would remove them from the scrutiny of their neighbors and allow them to live out the Nazi regime in obscurity. Now, for the first time, they contemplated emigration.

Klemperer's journal of the Nazi years, I Will Bear Witness, *was published in Germany in 1995 and translated into English in 1998.*

From *I Will Bear Witness, 1933–1941: A Diary of the Nazi Years,* by Victor Klemperer, translated by Martin Chalmers (New York: Modern Library, 1998), pp. 275–83.

November 27 [1938]

On the morning of the eleventh two policemen accompanied by a "resident of Dölzschen." Did I have any weapons?—Certainly my saber, perhaps even my bayonet as a war memento, but I wouldn't know where.—We have to help you find it.—The house was searched for hours. At the beginning Eva made the mistake of quite innocently telling one of the policemen he should not go through the clean linen cupboard without washing his hands. The man, considerably affronted, could hardly be calmed down. A second, younger policeman was more friendly, the civilian was the worst. Pigsty, etc. We said we had been without domestic help for months, many things were dusty and still unpacked. They rummaged through everything, chests and wooden constructions Eva had made were broken open with an ax. The saber was found in a suitcase in the attic, the bayonet was not found. Among the books they found a copy of the *Sozialistische Monatshefte* (Socialist Monthly Magazine— an SPD theoretical journal) * * * this was also confiscated. At one point when Eva wanted to fetch one of her tools, the young policeman ran after

her; the older one called out: You are making us suspicious, you are making your situation worse. At about one o'clock the civilian and the older policeman left the house, the young one remained and took a statement. He was good-natured and courteous, I had the feeling he himself found the thing embarrassing. In addition he complained about an upset stomach and we offered him a schnapps, which he declined. Then the three of them appeared to hold a conference in the garden. The young policeman returned: You must dress and come to the court building at Münchner Platz with me. There's nothing to fear, you will probably (!) be back by evening. I asked whether I was now under arrest. His reply was good-natured and noncommittal, it was only a war memento after all, I would probably be released right away. I was allowed to shave (with the door half open), I slipped Eva some money, and we made our way down to the tram. I was allowed to walk through the park alone while the policeman wheeled his bicycle at a distance behind me. We got onto the platform of the number 16 and got off at Münchner Platz; the policeman kindly covered up the fact that I was being taken into custody. A wing in the court building: Public Prosecutor. A room with clerks and policeman. Sit down. The policeman had to copy the statement. He took me to a room with a typewriter. He led me back to the first room. I sat there apathetically. The policeman said: Perhaps you'll even be home in time for afternoon coffee. A clerk said: The Public Prosecutor's Office makes the decision. The policeman disappeared, I continued to sit there apathetically. Then someone called: Take the man to relieve himself, and someone took me to the lavatory. Then: To Room X. There: This is the new committals room! More waiting. After a while a young man with a Party badge appeared, evidently the examining magistrate. You are Professor Klemperer? You can go. But first of all a certificate of discharge has to be made out, otherwise the police in Freital will think you have escaped and arrest you again. He returned immediately, he had telephoned, I could go. At the exit of the wing, by the first room into which I had been led, a clerk rushed toward me: Where do you think you're going? I said: Home, and calmly stood there. They telephoned, to verify that I had been released. The examining magistrate had also replied to my inquiry, that the matter was not being passed on to the Public Prosecutor. At four o'clock I was on the street again with the curious feeling, free—but for how long? Since then we have both been unceasingly tormented by the question, go or stay? To go too early, to stay too late? To go where we have nothing, to remain in this corruption? We are constantly trying to shed all subjective feelings of disgust, of injured pride, of frame of mind and only weigh up the concrete facts of the situation. In the end we shall literally be able to throw dice for pro and contra. Our first response to events was to think it absolutely necessary to leave and we started making preparations and inquiries. On Sunday, November 12, the day after my arrest, I wrote urgent SOS letters to Frau Schaps and Georg. The short letter to Georg began: With a heavy heart, in a quite altered situation, pushed right to the edge, no details. Can you stand surety for my wife and myself, can you help the two of us over there for a couple of months? By my own efforts I would surely find some post as a teacher or in an office.—

I telephoned the Arons—the husband had spoken to me on Bismarckplatz on the day of the Munich Agreement. Herr Aron was not at home, Frau Aron would receive me at eight in the evening. I drove there: a weathy villa in Bernhardstrasse. I learned that he and very many others with him had been arrested and taken away; at present we still don't know whether they are in the camp at Weimar [Buchenwald] or are working on the fortifications in the West as convicts and hostages.

November 28

Frau Aron advised us in the strongest terms to take immediate steps to emigrate and to sell the house; everything here is lost, German money is almost valueless abroad, the mark is worth sixpence half-penny sterling. The next day, on Frau Aron's advice, went to the Public Information Office for Emigrants (the man in charge, a Major Stübel, is a very decent gentleman). In the waiting room a voluptuous, blond Eastern Jewess to a girl: At police headquarters they sent us away, they didn't know where the men had been taken. . . . The old major said to me: Within these four walls you can speak your mind. In recent days I have heard a great deal that is very distressing, in my free moments I walk in the Great Garden in order to calm myself down.—I set out my situation. I said, a regime that espouses banditry with such openness, must be in a desperate plight.—He: That is what every decent German thinks.—What did he advise me to do?—He could not advise me.—Were the situation to change tomorrow (which I do not believe), then you would be sorry to have gone.—From his explanations it emerged that they really would let us out stripped and naked and with seven and a half percent of the proceeds of the house.

December 2

On Sunday, November 13, we drove to Leipzig to see Trude Öhlmann. Would she be able to take Mujel [the Klemperer's cat]?—No, he would hardly be able to adapt, it would be more humane to have him put down. She told us how the SA had mounted the attack in Leipzig, poured gasoline into the synagogue and into a Jewish department store, how the fire brigade was allowed to protect only the surrounding buildings but not fight the fire itself, how the owner of the department store was then arrested for arson and insurance fraud. In Leipzig we also learned about the billion-mark fine the German nation had imposed on the Jews. ✳ ✳ ✳ Trude pointed out an open bay window on the other side of the street. It has been open for days; the people have been taken away. She wept as we drove off. On the way Eva's nerves gave way; supper in Meissen did little to help, at home she had a screaming fit.

Then letters came from London, from Frau Schaps and from Friedrich Salzburg, who, driven out of Italy, is now applying to the USA from England. One would so much like to help but cannot. They approach Demuth again and again, who has failed to be of any help to me for three years. Salzburg wrote, only my brother in the USA could help me.

✳   ✳   ✳

December 15, Thursday

We continue in this simultaneously crushing and stupefying chaos, this empty and breathless busyness, this absolute uncertainty.

My letter to Georg sets out the facts of the USA–Havana possibility. The visit to the American consul very amusing. Large, elegantly furnished offices in Schlosstrasse. After some back and forth received by a younger black-haired gentleman. Handshake, courtesy. He could not speak a word of German, called a blond Dr. Dietrich (introduction, handshake) as interpreter; then it turned out that the consul spoke Italian—(Maltese, says Natscheff, whose wife is American)—so there was a curious mixture of languages. Result: no hope, it is not even possible to register me as a professor because for that I would have to have been dismissed for two years at most, but not as long ago as 1935. I told the story of my saber, etc. Finally Dr. Dietrich

said: Go to Haessel's Travel Agency with a recommendation from the American consulate and ask to see Herr Haessel in person; he can probably tell you more than we can! Afterward I realized that they were suggesting an unofficial way. As soon as I entered the agency on the Altmarkt, I had the definite impression from the physiognomy of a customer and from a fragment of conversation I caught (You must not lose heart. You must wait in Hamburg . . .) that I was in the right place. Two young people, brothers. As soon as I opened my mouth: The American consul ✳ ✳ ✳ I was interrupted: You have the affidavit and can't do anything with it. ✳ ✳ ✳ All you get in Berlin is trouble and cold feet! And then I was advised to take the Cuba route. I asked myself and still ask myself. Just business, or really good advice?—To day I received a letter from the agency: Please call; I shall hear more then.

Toward Evening

The Havana possibility is virtually settled. I now have to decide by January 1 at latest whether to book two berths for June, everything before that is sold out, even though the number of sailings has been doubled; after that there are no more places to be had until 1940.

Rush on Haessel by fleeing Jews. The recent impression considerably strengthened. Meanwhile another mysterious possibility has turned up. Without any explanation a Sydney newspaper arrived from London, in all probability from Demuth. First riddle: Has an application on my behalf been made in London, or should I take steps myself? Second riddle: What is Sydney (New England)? The Sydney in Australia or one in USA, or a Sydney in Canada? No one can answer these questions. After long, passionate discussions, I sent an application in German by airmail to Australia. I thought the counter clerk in our little post office would be astonished and not know exactly what to do. Instead he was in the picture immediately and said disapprovingly, the letter would take some time to arrive, perhaps a whole week. Piccolo mondo moderno.

I went to see Edith Aulhorn, in order to have the Sydney riddle interpreted. She too was uncertain. She had been about to write to me, to give me the address of an English woman who is working as inconspicuously and secretly as possible for the Quakers to help those non-Aryans whom the Jewish aid organizations turn away. I wrote to Miss Livingstone in Berlin-Charlottenburg. ✶ ✶ ✶ The desire to go to the colonies is Eva's favorite idea. Plans repeatedly surface, according to which some colonies are supposed to be earmarked for mass emigration. First they said Alaska, now Rhodesia. Eva thinks a schoolteacher will always be needed, and she can be an organist, draw building plans, perform agricultural work. Her latest plan is a mineral water factory in Rhodesia. The times are so crazy that no plan is too fantastic. And in any case these plans sustain her. I assume that what is most probable is that we shall be forced to stay here. Sometimes we think we could never be happy here again or feel at home, even if things were to change; but sometimes we also cling to this place.

In April, when, in wise anticipation of the Grünspan murder and its atonement, Jewish assets had to be declared, I innocently gave the rebuild value of the house and the value of the Iduna policies on which money had been borrowed. As a consequence I was called on to pay a property assessment of 1,600M. Enlightened meanwhile, I inquired as to the repurchase value of the policies and had the current sale value of the house estimated (which all in all has cost us 26,000 M). Result: Idnua surrender value 240M, house estimated at 16,500, of which 12,000 mortgage. I do not therefore have 5,000 assets, the level at which the assessment begins. I went to the Tax Office in Sidonienstrasse. They were not unfriendly. I had to submit an appeal immediately, and the first 40M installment due today is in abeyance until it is dealt with. We did and do feel quite indifferent to this business: because one way or another all our property will be lost anyway. The house will certainly be expropriated in the next few months; they have also begun to encroach on pensions, for the time being of those dismissed on full salary (of whom I should have really been one). In my case it has been

calculated that I have mistakenly been paid 6M a month too much, so that I owe the state about 280, which will be deducted in monthly installments of 20M. (That is precisely the amount of my now superfluous car tax.) We responded just as apathetically to the fact that one thousand marks were transferred to us from Georg's blocked account as we did to the business of the property assessment. What am I supposed to do with it? I cannot take anything out of the country, and here—what is certain here, and what pleasant things can one do? We can no longer go for drives, we can no longer make purchases for house and garden. Still, for the moment the 1,000M saves me from petty miseries. But what pleasure it would have given us only a few weeks ago. District Judge Moral, whose acquaintance we made at Frau Schaps', visited us. The man looks very old, but is only sixty. We hatched Rhodesia plans together, half jokingly, half in earnest; we puzzled over the future together.

Beresin recommended a Frau Bonheim to us for housework (since Eva's eyes continue to be affected, both eyes now). Latvian Jew, young divorced woman, her husband, German and Aryan, wanted to be free of her, gymnastics teacher, grammar school education, real lady. A pretty, obligingly hardworking person. We treat her as a friend, she has coffee with us and does the heavy work of scrubbing well and without squeamishness for 50 pfennigs an hour. I told her about Rhodesia and Sydney. Piccolo mondo moderno. Curious: At the very moment modern technology annuls all frontiers and distances (flying, radio, television, economic interdependence), the most extreme nationalism is raging. Perhaps a last convulsive uprising of what is already a thing of the past. And another oddity: The National Socialists have always talked about World Jewry; it was idée fixe and a phantom. They have gone on talking about this phantom for so long until it has become a reality.

I now take learning English more seriously, much more seriously. Sometimes a chapter in *Little Yankee* and sometimes a section of grammar. And from half past three till five I have just had my first arduous and not quite unsuccessful lesson with Mrs. Meyer. Natscheff recommended her to me. His wife is American and a friend of hers. Fifty-seven years of age and actually a musician and organist at the American Church. But the church is a German charity, and Meyer is of Jewish descent and has therefore lost her post and is not allowed to teach Aryans. She is English, her husband an unbelievably vigorous eighty-two-year-old, looks sixty-five at most; German, retired opera chorus singer. I went to see them on the fourth floor of a good house on Feldherrenstrasse, was cordially received in the kitchen-parlor; a large birdcage and the little budgerigars treated tenderly, taken out and kissed, at the same time tears because of the situation and thoughts of emigration and fear for the pension and fear of giving lessons at home. So today she came out here. One and a half hours for three marks with 30 pfennigs tram fare on top of that. I intend to carry it on assiduously. Shattering letters—more exactly and honestly: letters, which would be shattering without the present deadening and the fact that our fate is identical—from Sussmann and the Jelskis. Both letters in part the same word for word: We go as beggars, dependent on the support of our children, Sussmann to Stockholm, to his youngest daughter who has married there, Jelskis to Lilly in Montevideo. The Reform Community has been wound up, the pension has stopped, a lump sum will be paid as compensation, out of which the passage can be paid. A little while ago Constable Radke was here from the local council. I should come up to the council office because of the identity card. We had a friendly conversation, the man shook my hand, told me to keep my spirits up. We know from before that he is certainly no Nazi, that his sister is in difficulties, because her husband, a gardener, has a grandmother who is not Aryan. But then the next day, when I was up there, he happened to come through the room; he stared ahead as he went past, as much a stranger as possible. In his behavior the man probably represents 79 million Germans, perhaps half a million more than that, rather than less.

REVIEW QUESTIONS

1. What does the attitude of the police who are searching for weapons in the Klemperer household reveal about the way the regime treated German Jews and war veterans such as Victor Klemperer?

2. What options for emigration from Germany did the Klemperers have? Where did they consider going? What difficulties did they face in organizing their departure?

3. In their legal and economic isolation from other Germans, what connections did the Klemperers maintain with friends and acquaintances during this period of persecution? How did they relate to the non-Jewish Germans whom they encountered in their daily lives?

GEORGE ORWELL

FROM *The Road to Wigan Pier*

Europeans had hoped that the end of the First World War would signal a renewed prosperity: instead they experienced one economic crisis after another in the 1920s and 1930s. A feverish period of economic revival began in 1925, but it was brought to a precipitous halt by the crash of the U.S. stock market in 1929. Although the global economy was gradually stabilized during the middle to late 1930s, the Depression did not truly come to an end until a new world war—and a tremendous increase in the production of armaments—kicked the economies of the industrialized nations back into high gear.

The United States and Germany endured the greatest hardships during the Depression, but all of the industrialized nations of western Europe suffered from high rates of unemployment and the demoralization caused by economic collapse. In the mid-1930s, George Orwell (pseudonym of Eric Arthur Blair, 1903–1950), was asked by the Left Book Club to travel through northern England and write a report on workers' conditions for the book club's members. Already known to progressive readers as the author of Down and Out in Paris and London *(1933), a sympathetic account of life among the transient poor, Orwell was an unorthodox socialist whose perceptions of workers were strongly shaped by his rejection of the prejudices of the "shabby-genteel" lower middle class into which he had been born. In* The Road to Wigan Pier *(1937), Orwell describes the lives of unemployed workers living "on the dole," the welfare benefits provided by the British government.*

From *The Road to Wigan Pier*, by George Orwell (New York: Harcourt, Brace, 1958), pp. 76–77, 79–82, 85–90.

*   *   *

When you see the unemployment figures quoted at two millions, it is fatally easy to take this as meaning that two million people are out of work and the rest of the population is comparatively comfortable. I admit that till recently I was in the habit of doing so myself. I used to calculate that if you put the registered unemployed at round about two millions and threw in the destitute and those who for one reason and another were not registered, you might take the number of underfed people in England (for *everyone* on the dole or thereabouts is underfed) as being, at the very most, five millions.

This is an enormous under-estimate, because, in the first place, the only people shown on unemployment figures are those actually drawing the dole—that is, in general, heads of families. An unemployed man's dependants do not figure on the list unless they too are drawing a separate allowance. A Labour Exchange officer told me that to get at the real number of people *living on* (not drawing) the dole, you have got to multiply the

official figures by something over three. This alone brings the number of unemployed to round about six millions. But in addition there are great numbers of people who are in work but who, from a financial point of view, might equally well be unemployed, because they are not drawing anything that can be described as a living wage. Allow for these and their dependants, throw in as before the old-age pensioners, the destitute and other nondescripts, and you get an *underfed* population of well over ten millions. * * *

Take the figures for Wigan, which is typical enough of the industrial and mining districts. The number of insured workers is round about 36,000 (26,000 men and 10,000 women). Of these, the number unemployed at the beginning of 1936 was about 10,000. But this was in winter when the mines are working full time; in summer it would probably be 12,000. Multiply by three, as above, and you get 30,000 or 36,000. The total population of Wigan is a little under 87,000; so that at any moment more than one person in three out of the whole population—not merely the registered workers—is either drawing or living on the dole.

Those ten or twelve thousand unemployed contain a steady core of from four to five thousand miners who have been continuously unemployed for the past seven years. And Wigan is not especially badly off as industrial towns go. Even in Sheffield, which has been doing well for the last year or so because of wars and rumours of war, the proportion of unemployment is about the same—one in three of registered workers unemployed.

* * *

Nevertheless, in spite of the frightful extent of unemployment, it is a fact that poverty—extreme poverty—is less in evidence in the industrial North than it is in London. Everything is poorer and shabbier, there are fewer motor-cars and fewer well-dressed people; but also there are fewer people who are obviously destitute. Even in a town the size of Liverpool or Manchester you are struck by the fewness of the beggars. London is a sort of whirlpool which draws derelict people towards it, and it is so vast that life there is solitary and anonymous. Until you break the law nobody will take any notice of you, and you can go to pieces as you could not possibly do in a place where you had neighbours who knew you. But in the industrial towns the old communal way of life has not yet broken up, tradition is still strong and almost everyone has a family—potentially, therefore, a home. In a town of 50,000 or 100,000 inhabitants there is no casual and as it were unaccounted-for population; nobody sleeping in the streets, for instance. Moreover, there is just this to be said for the unemployment regulations, that they do not discourage people from marrying. A man and wife on twenty-three shillings a week are not far from the starvation line, but they can make a home of sorts; they are vastly better off than a single man on fifteen shillings.

* * *

But there is no doubt about the deadening, debilitating effect of unemployment upon everybody, married or single, and upon men more than upon women.

* * *

Take a miner, for instance, who has worked in the pit since childhood and has been trained to be a miner and nothing else. How the devil is he to fill up the empty days? It is absurd to say that he ought to be looking for work. There is no work to look for, and everybody knows it. You can't go on looking for work every day for seven years.

* * *

I first became aware of the unemployment problem in 1928. * * * At that time nobody cared to admit that unemployment was inevitable, because this meant admitting that it would probably continue. The middle classes were still talking about "lazy idle loafers on the dole" and saying that "these men could all find work if they wanted to," and naturally these opinions percolated to the working class themselves. I remember the shock of astonishment it gave me, when I first mingled with tramps and beggars, to find that a fair proportion, perhaps a quarter, of these beings whom I had been taught to regard as cynical parasites, were decent young miners and cotton-workers gazing at their destiny with the same sort of dumb amazement as an animal in a trap. They simply could not understand what was happening to them. They had been brought up to work, and behold! it seemed as if they were never going to have the chance of working again. In their circumstances it was inevitable, at first, that they should be haunted by a feeling of personal degradation. That was the attitude towards unemployment in those days: it was a disaster which happened to *you* as an individual and for which *you* were to blame.

When a quarter of a million miners are unemployed, it is part of the order of things that Alf Smith, a miner living in the back streets of Newcastle, should be out of work. Alf Smith is merely one of the quarter million, a statistical unit.

* * *

When people live on the dole for years at a time they grow used to it, and drawing the dole, though it remains unpleasant, ceases to be shameful. * * * The people have at any rate grasped that unemployment is a thing they cannot help. It is not only Alf Smith who is out of work now; Bert Jones is out of work as well, and both of them have been "out" for years. It makes a great deal of difference when things are the same for everybody.

*   *   *

But they don't necessarily lower their standards by cutting out luxuries and concentrating on necessities; more often it is the other way about—the more natural way, if you come to think of it. Hence the fact that in a decade of unparalleled depression, the consumption of all cheap luxuries has increased. The two things that have probably made the greatest difference of all are the movies and the mass-production of cheap smart clothes since the war. The youth who leaves school at fourteen and gets a blind-alley job is out of work at twenty, probably for life; but for two pounds ten on the hire-purchase system he can buy himself a suit which, for a little while and at a little distance, looks as though it had been tailored in Savile Row. The girl can look like a fashion plate at an even lower price. You may have three halfpence in your pocket and not a prospect in the world, and only the corner of a leaky bedroom to go home to; but in your new clothes you can stand on the street corner, indulging in a private daydream of yourself as Clark Gable or Greta Garbo, which compensates you for a great deal. And even at home there is generally a cup of tea going—a "nice cup of tea"—and Father, who has been out of work since 1929, is temporarily happy because he has a sure tip for the Cesarewitch.

Trade since the war has had to adjust itself to meet the demands of underpaid, underfed people, with the result that a luxury is nowadays almost always cheaper than a necessity. One pair of plain solid shoes costs as much as two ultra-smart

pairs. For the price of one square meal you can get two pounds of cheap sweets. You can't get much meat for threepence, but you can get a lot of fish-and-chips. Milk costs threepence a pint and even "mild" beer costs fourpence, but aspirins are seven a penny and you can wring forty cups of tea out of a quarter-pound packet. And above all there is gambling, the cheapest of all luxuries. Even people on the verge of starvation can buy a few days' hope ("Something to live for," as they call it) by having a penny on a sweepstake.

*   *   *

Of course the post-war development of cheap luxuries has been a very fortunate thing for our rulers. It is quite likely that fish and chips, art-silk stockings, tinned salmon, cut-price chocolate (five two-ounce bars for sixpence), the movies, the radio, strong tea and the Football Pools have between them averted revolution. Therefore we are sometimes told that the whole thing is an astute manœuvre by the governing class—a sort of "bread and circuses" business—to hold the unemployed down. What I have seen of our governing class does not convince me that they have that much intelligence. The thing has happened, but by an unconscious process—the quite natural interaction between the manufacturer's need for a market and the need of half-starved people for cheap palliatives.

*   *   *

REVIEW QUESTIONS

1. Why, according to Orwell, was extreme poverty less common in the north of England than in the south?
2. What impact did long-term unemployment have on workers in northern England?
3. Why were the poor addicted to cheap luxuries?

SIGMUND FREUD

FROM *Civilization and Its Discontents*

The interwar years witnessed a generalized collapse of confidence in the values and practices promoted by nineteenth-century liberalism. Many Europeans rejected the principles of parliamentary democracy, individualism, and reason in favor of authoritarianism, collectivism, and the reign of instinct. Writing in the late 1920s, Sigmund Freud asked himself, "How has it happened that so many people have come to take up this strange attitude of hostility to civilization?" Freud was puzzled and disturbed by the rise of irrationalist political movements, and he sought psychological explanations for the seething discontent with civilized society expressed by so many Europeans during this period. While Freud's earlier writings had focused on the expression—and repression—of the sexual instinct, Civilization and Its Discontents *(1930) dealt with what Freud identified as a countervailing aggressive instinct.*

Freud's own perspective on civilization revealed a deep pessimism about human nature. Although he conceived of modern European society as marking a high point in human cultural development, he argued that Western "civilization" could only be realized and maintained through the painful repression of the individual's instinctual sexual and aggressive drives. When instinct was successfully sublimated— redirected into socially beneficial ends—it produced art, literature, science, industry, and stable government. On the other hand, no amount of human progress could ever compensate the individual for the loss of the spontaneous expression of these primordial impulses.

From *Civilization and Its Discontents*, by Sigmund Freud, translated by James Strachey (New York: Norton, 1961), pp. 55–59.

*   *   *

* * * Sexual love is a relationship between two individuals in which a third can only be superfluous or disturbing, whereas civilization depends on relationships between a considerable number of individuals. When a love-relationship is at its height there is no room left for any interest in the environment; a pair of lovers are sufficient to themselves, and do not even need the child they have in common to make them happy. * * *

So far, we can quite well imagine a cultural community consisting of double individuals like this, who, libidinally satisfied in themselves, are connected with one another through the bonds of common work and common interests. If this were so, civilization would not have to withdraw any energy from sexuality. But this desirable state of things does not, and never did, exist. Reality shows us that civilization is not content with the ties we have so far allowed it. It aims at binding the members of the community together in a libidinal way as well and employs every means to that end. It favours every path by which strong identifications can be established between the members of the community, and it summons up aim-inhibited libido on the largest scale so as to strengthen the communal bond by relations of friendship. In order for these aims to be fulfilled, a restriction upon sexual life is unavoidable. But we are unable to understand what the necessity is which forces civilization along this path and which causes its antagonism to sexuality. There must be some disturbing factor which we have not yet discovered.

The clue may be supplied by one of the ideal demands, as we have called them, of civilized society. It runs: "Thou shalt love thy neighbour as thyself." It is known throughout the world and is undoubtedly older than Christianity, which puts it forward as its proudest claim. Yet it is certainly not very old; even in historical times it was still strange to mankind. Let us adopt a naïve attitude towards it, as though we were hearing it for the first time; we shall be unable then to suppress a feeling of surprise and bewilderment. Why should we do it? What good will it do us? But, above all, how shall we achieve it? How can it be possible? My love is something valuable to me which I ought not to throw away without reflection. It imposes duties on me for whose fulfilment I must be ready to make sacrifices. If I love someone, he must deserve it in some way. (I leave out of account the use he may be to me, and also his possible significance for me as a sexual object, for neither of these two kinds of relationship comes into question where the precept to love my neighbour is concerned.) He deserves it if he is so like me in important ways that I can love myself in him; and he deserves it if he is so much more perfect than myself that I can love my ideal of my own self in him. Again, I have to love him if he is my friend's son, since the pain my friend would feel if any harm came to him would be my pain too—I should have to share it. But if he is a stranger to me and if he cannot attract me by any worth of his own or any significance that he may already have acquired for my emotional life, it will be hard for me to love him. Indeed, I should be wrong to do so, for my love is valued by all my own people as a sign of my preferring them, and it is an injustice to them if I put a stranger on a par with them. But if I am to love him (with this universal love) merely because he, too, is

an inhabitant of this earth, like an insect, an earthworm or a grass-snake, then I fear that only a small modicum of my love will fall to his share—not by any possibility as much as, by the judgement of my reason, I am entitled to retain for myself. What is the point of a precept enunciated with so much solemnity if its fulfilment cannot be recommended as reasonable?

On closer inspection, I find still further difficulties. Not merely is this stranger in general unworthy of my love; I must honestly confess that he has more claim to my hostility and even my hatred. He seems not to have the least trace of love for me and shows me not the slightest consideration. If it will do him any good he has no hesitation in injuring me, nor does he ask himself whether the amount of advantage he gains bears any proportion to the extent of the harm he does to me. Indeed, he need not even obtain an advantage; if he can satisfy any sort of desire by it, he thinks nothing of jeering at me, insulting me, slandering me and showing his superior power; and the more secure he feels and the more helpless I am, the more certainly I can expect him to behave like this to me. If he behaves differently, if he shows me consideration and forbearance as a stranger, I am ready to treat him in the same way, in any case and quite apart from any precept. Indeed, if this grandiose commandment had run "Love thy neighbour as thy neighbour loves thee," I should not take exception to it. And there is a second commandment, which seems to me even more incomprehensible and arouses still stronger opposition in me. It is "Love thine enemies." If I think it over, however, I see that I am wrong in treating it as a greater imposition. At bottom it is the same thing.

I think I can now hear a dignified voice admonishing me: "It is precisely because your neighbour is not worthy of love, and is on the contrary your enemy, that you should love him as yourself." * * *

Now it is very probable that my neighbour, when he is enjoined to love me as himself, will answer exactly as I have done and will repel me for the same reasons. I hope he will not have the same objective grounds for doing so, but he will have the same idea as I have.

*   *   *

The element of truth behind all this, which people are so ready to disavow, is that men are not gentle creatures who want to be loved, and who at the most can defend themselves if they are attacked; they are, on the contrary, creatures among whose instinctual endowments is to be reckoned a powerful share of aggressiveness. As a result, their neighbour is for them not only a potential helper or sexual object, but also someone who tempts them to satisfy their aggressiveness on him, to exploit his capacity for work without compensation, to use him sexually without his consent, to seize his possessions, to humiliate him, to cause him pain, to torture and to kill him. *Homo homini lupus.*[1] Who, in the face of all his experience of life and of history, will have the courage to dispute this assertion? As a rule this cruel aggressiveness waits for some provocation or puts itself at the service of some other purpose, whose goal might also have been reached by milder measures. In circumstances that are favourable to it, when the mental counter-forces which ordinarily inhibit it are out of action, it also manifests itself spontaneously and reveals man as a savage beast to whom consideration towards his own kind is something alien. Anyone who calls to mind the atrocities committed during the racial migrations or the invasions of the Huns, or by the people known as Mongols under Jenghiz Khan and Tamerlane, or at the capture of Jerusalem by the pious Crusaders, or even, indeed, the horrors of the recent World War—anyone who calls these things to mind will have to bow humbly before the truth of this view.

The existence of this inclination to aggression, which we can detect in ourselves and justly assume to be present in others, is the factor which disturbs our relations with our neighbour and which forces civilization into such a high expenditure [of energy]. In consequence of this primary mutual hostility of human beings, civilized society is perpetually threatened with disintegration. The interest of work in common would not hold it together; instinctual passions are stronger than reasonable interests. Civilization has to use its utmost efforts in order to set limits to man's aggressive instincts and to hold the manifestations of them in check by psychical reaction-formations. Hence, therefore, the use of methods intended to incite people into identifications and aim-inhibited relationships of love, hence the restriction upon sexual life, and hence too the ideal's commandment to love one's neighbour as oneself—a commandment which is really justified by the fact that nothing else runs so strongly counter to the original nature of man. In spite of every effort, these endeavours of civilization have not so far achieved very much. It hopes to prevent the crudest excesses of brutal violence by itself assuming the right to use violence against criminals, but the law is not able to lay hold of the more cautious and refined manifestations of human aggressiveness. The time comes when each one of us has to give up as illusions the expectations which, in his youth, he pinned upon his fellow-men, and when he may learn how much difficulty and pain has been added to his life by their ill-will.

*   *   *

REVIEW QUESTIONS

1. Why is it so difficult to love one's neighbor as oneself?
2. Why is this commandment a necessary requirement of civilized society?
3. What is human nature like, according to Freud?
4. What specific historical events and developments might be explained by Freud's theory of aggression?

---

[1] "Man is a wolf to man."

26   THE SECOND WORLD WAR

The Great War had been disastrous, but its outbreak could be blamed on the errors of political leaders and military planners who had allowed diplomatic arrangements and mobilization timetables to take on a life of their own. That a second world war could occur so soon after the first suggested that periodic outbreaks of global warfare were perhaps essential elements in the functioning of modern industrial societies. Similarly, this second failure of the nations of the world to avoid armed conflict suggested that human beings were incapable of controlling their innate aggressiveness and learning from their past mistakes. The Second World War was a total war whose worst horrors—the Holocaust and the bombing of major urban areas—resulted in the slaughter of civilians on a scale hitherto unimagined. Once again, the war made painfully clear the astounding degree of devastation that might occur when humans directed the technologies of industry toward destructive ends.

Yet if the Second World War was dishearteningly destructive it was not so absurd as the First World War had been. In 1914, the outbreak of war seemed almost arbitrary, and even the War Guilt Clause of the Versailles Treaty could not dispel the postwar conviction that the war had been the fault of no one and everyone. In 1939, on the other hand, the outbreak of war took the form of an overt act of aggression by Germany. Many attempts had been made to appease Hitler, but all diplomatic negotiations had failed in the face of his determination to go to war. During the Great War, the military leadership's adoption of a strategy of attrition had stripped the individual soldier's death of meaning, depriving military service of all heroism. During the Second World War, the German army's lightning-war strategy returned the elements of speed and mobility to warfare. Military engagements once again reached decisive conclusions, producing clear winners and losers.

However, from the start, the Second World War was most clearly distinguished from the First World War by its ideological component. To both soldiers and civilians, this new conflict presented itself as a struggle not merely between competing nations but between two fundamentally opposed political and social philosophies, between fascism and antifascism. On the personal level this meant that the war presented clear choices, even if these choices often took the form of extremely difficult ethical decisions. On both sides, government propaganda fanned the flames of political passions, producing a strong sense of conviction among fascists and antifascists alike. At the same time, the increasingly manifest viciousness and brutality of the fascist regimes generated intense opposition both within Germany and Italy and in the territories the two states occupied. Participants in resistance movements experienced an acute sense of human agency: having committed themselves to the antifascist cause, they engaged in actions that exposed them to the risk of imprisonment, torture, and execution.

The defeat of the Axis powers—Germany, Italy, and Japan—seemed like a triumph for the principles of democracy, tolerance, and individual liberty. After the war, the world's nations renewed their commitment to international governance through the creation of the United Nations, but many people continued to fear that the twentieth century was doomed to experience yet another global cataclysm, especially as growing tensions between the Soviet Union and the United States developed into an ominously tense Cold War. At the same time, peoples who lived under European colonial regimes in Africa and Asia were ultimately disappointed in their hopes that a postwar settlement would bring reform or national independence for their societies. Any optimism generated by the return of peace was quickly overshadowed by the emergence of a bipolar system of international relations: The world's two superpowers, armed to the teeth with devastating weapons of destruction, insisted that the rest of the world choose sides.

The Atlantic Charter and Third World Nationalism

The Atlantic Charter was the product of a meeting between Winston Churchill and Franklin D. Roosevelt in August 1941. Churchill, the prime minister of Britain, had already been at war with Hitler's armies for almost two years. Meanwhile, Hitler had just invaded the Soviet Union in the east, and the Japanese were preparing their surprise attack on Pearl Harbor, which would bring the United States into the war four months later. In this tense atmosphere, Churchill and Roosevelt met in secret in Placentia Bay, Newfoundland, to issue the Atlantic Charter. Subsequently adopted by the Declaration by the United Nations (January 1, 1942), the charter was a declaration of common aims between Britain and the United States. The two nations avowed their commitment to the principles of national self-determination, freedom of trade and commerce, international cooperation to improve standards of living and economic justice throughout the world, and a pledge to work toward international peace and disarmament. During the postwar period, U.S. support for the United Nations and the rebuilding of Europe reflected the continued power of these goals.

Many people living under European colonial regimes in Asia and Africa assumed that the Atlantic Charter would lead to the end of colonialism and national independence for their countries after the defeat of Germany and Japan. At a minimum they expected that colonial governments that denied basic citizenship rights to colonial subjects would be reformed. This was especially true in French colonies such as Algeria and Indochina, because the Vichy government in France had collaborated extensively with the Nazis during the war. In Indochina, for example, nationalists were disappointed when the United States did not support their cause of independence from the French, and angry that the new French government in 1944 did not promise to reform the colonial system. Ho Chi Minh (1890–1969), who became a communist and an anticolonial militant in the years after World War I while working as a laborer in France and Britain, led the Vietnamese nationalist movement for almost thirty years. In the speech reproduced here, he tried to portray those who supported French colonialism as being on the side of the Axis powers—Japan, Italy, and Germany—and he placed the struggle of Vietnamese nationalism on the same side as the United States, Britain, China, and Russia, allied during the war years.

The Atlantic Charter*

On 14 August 1941, President Roosevelt and Prime Minister Churchill, at the conclusion of their midocean conference made the following joint declaration of "certain common principles in the national policies of their respective countries on which they base their hopes for a better future of the world."

FIRST, their countries seek no aggrandizement, territorial or other;

SECOND, they desire to see no territorial changes that do not accord with the freely expressed wishes of the people concerned;

THIRD, they respect the right of all peoples to choose the form of government under which they live; and the wish to see sovereign rights and self government restored to those who have been forcibly deprived of them;

FOURTH, they will endeavor, with due respect for their existing obligations to further the enjoyment by all States, great or small, victor or vanquished, of access, on equal terms, to the trade and to the raw materials of the world which are needed for their economic prosperity;

FIFTH, they desire to bring about the fullest collaboration between all nations in the economic field with the object of securing, for all, improved labor standards, economic advancement and social security;

SIXTH, after the final destruction of the Nazi tyranny, they hope to see established a peace which will afford to all nations the means of dwelling in safety within their own boundaries, and which will afford assurance that all the men in all the lands may live out their lives in freedom from fear and want;

---

* From *The Atlantic Charter*, edited by Douglas Brinkley and David R. Facey-Crowther (New York: St. Martin's Press, 1994), pp. xvii–xviii.

SEVENTH, such a peace should enable all men to traverse the high seas and oceans without hindrance;

EIGHTH, they believe that all of the nations of the world, for realistic as well as spiritual reasons, must come to the abandonment of the use of force. Since no future peace can be maintained if land, sea or air armaments continue to be employed by nations which threaten, or may threaten, aggression outside of their frontiers, they believe, pending the establishment of a wider and permanent system of general security, that the disarmament of such nations is essential. They will likewise aid and encourage all other practicable measures which will lighten for peace-loving peoples the crushing burden of armaments.

By *Franklin D. Roosevelt*
Winston Churchill

Ho Chi Minh's Speech Delivered in the First Days of the Resistance War in South Viet-Nam (November 1945)*

Compatriots!

During the Second World War, the French colonialists twice sold out our country to the Japanese. Thus they betrayed the allied nations, and helped the Japanese to cause the latter many losses.

Meanwhile they also betrayed our people, exposing us to the destruction of bombs and bullets. In this way, the French colonialists withdrew of their own accord from the Allied ranks and tore up the treaties they had earlier compelled us to sign.

Notwithstanding the French colonialists' treachery, our people as a whole are determined to side with the allies and oppose the invaders. When the Japanese surrendered, our entire people single-mindedly changed our country into a Democratic

Republic and elected a provisional Government which is to prepare for a national congress and draw up our draft Constitution. Not only is our act in line with the Atlantic and San Francisco Charters, etc., solemnly proclaimed by the Allies, but it entirely conforms with the glorious principles upheld by the French people: Liberty, Equality, and Fraternity.

It is thus clear that in the past the colonialists betrayed the Allies and our country, and surrendered to the Japanese. At present, in the shadow of the British and Indian troops, and behind the Japanese soldiers, they are attacking the South of our country.

They have sabotaged the peace that China, the United States, Britain, and Russia won at the cost of scores of millions of lives. They have run counter to the promises concerning democracy and liberty that the allied powers have proclaimed. They have of their own accord sabotaged their fathers' principles of liberty and equality. In consequence, it is for a just cause, for justice of the world, and for Viet Nam's land and people that our compatriots throughout the country have risen to struggle, and are firmly determined to maintain their independence. We do not hate the French people and France. We are energetically fighting slavery, and the ruthless policy of the French colonialists. We only safeguard our own against the French invaders. Hence we are not alone. The countries which love peace and democracy, and the weaker nations all over the world, all sympathize with us. With the unity of the whole people within the country, and having many sympathizers abroad, we are sure of total victory.

The French colonialists have behaved lawlessly in the South for almost one-and-a-half months. Our southern compatriots have sacrificed their lives in a most valiant struggle. Public opinion in the great countries—China, the United States, Russia, and Britain—has supported our just cause.

Compatriots throughout the country! Those in the South will do their utmost to resist the enemy. Those in the Center and the North will endeavor to help their southern compatriots and be on the alert.

---

* Reprinted from *On Revolution: Selected Writings*, by Ho Chi Minh, edited by Bernard B. Fall (New York: Frederick A. Praeger, 1967), pp. 158–59.

The French colonialists should know that the Vietnamese people do not want bloodshed, that they love peace. But we are determined to sacrifice even millions of combatants and fight a long-term war of resistance in order to safeguard Viet-Nam's independence and free her children from slavery. We are sure that our war of resistance will be victorious.

Let the whole country be determined in the war of resistance!

Long live independent Viet-Nam!

REVIEW QUESTIONS

1. Why did Churchill and Roosevelt choose this moment to reaffirm their commitment to na-tional self-determination and international cooperation to ensure economic development?
2. Do you think they both intended that this commitment would extend to people in Asia and Africa living under the colonial authority of European powers?
3. Why would Ho Chi Minh choose to express his support for the Allied powers in 1945?
4. What is Ho Chi Minh's opinion of France's revolutionary republican tradition?
5. Why does Ho Chi Minh emphasize the nationalist side of his political program, rather than his commitment to socialism? Is there a tension between these two allegiances?

PRIMO LEVI

Survival in Auschwitz

In December 1943, Primo Levi (1919–1987) was a twenty-four-year-old former chemistry student attempting to connect with a partisan group in the mountains north of Turin. Captured by the Facist Militia, Levi admitted he was Jewish. The Italians handed him over to the Germans and he was deported to Auschwitz in Poland, the largest of the Nazi concentration camps. Auschwitz was in reality a complex of three different camps—an extermination camp at Birkenau, a slave-labor camp called Buna, and a prison camp for political prisoners. Almost 1.5 million people were killed at Auschwitz by the Nazis; 90 percent of this number were Jews.

Levi noted in the preface of his book that it was his "good fortune to be deported to Auschwitz only in 1944, that is after the German Government had decided, owing to the growing scarcity of labour, to lengthen the average life-span of the prisoners destined for elimination; it conceded noticeable improvements in the camp routine and temporarily suspended killings at the whim of individuals." Levi was held in Auschwitz for over a year, much of it working for the rubber factory in Buna run by the German company IG Farben. He managed to stay behind when the camp was abandoned in the face of advances by the Russian army in the spring of 1945. Forced to go east to escape the continuing war, he spent an additional year struggling to return home as a refugee. His two-volume memoir of these experiences has been translated into English as Survival in Auschwitz *(first published in*

MAP OF *EINSATZGRUPPEN* MASSACRES (1941–1942)

Barbed wire, disease-ridden barracks, malnourished prisoners, gas chambers, and crematoria are the principal images of the Holocaust inflicted on Jews and other Europeans by the racial genocide of Nazi Germany. Yet before such death camps as Auschwitz and Treblinka were put into full operation, approximately 1.2 million Jews were killed with rifles by mobile killing units in 1941–42. Four select groups, composed of approximately one thousand SS and auxiliary police units, swept behind the advancing German army in its invasion of the Soviet Union in August 1941 to carry out the first massive wave of racial and political murder, primarily of Russian Jews and Soviet partisans. Typically, victims were rounded up, forced to dig a mass grave, and then executed with rifles at the gravesite. This map of eastern central Europe, which constituted the cultural center of European Jewry, locates the principal sites of massacres by the mobile killing units. What does this map convey about the geographic breadth of Nazi genocide before the death camps were put into operation?

Italy in 1947 as Se questo è un uomo*) and* The Reawakening *(*La tregua, *1963).
After returning to Italy, Levi worked as a manager in a Turin chemical factory,
simultaneously pursuing a career as a writer. He died in 1987, an apparent suicide.*

*Levi's autobiographical writings are remarkable for their ability to document the
inverted moral universe of camp life, the irrational rules that all prisoners had to master to ensure their survival for another day. Throughout his experience he never lost
his powers of observation—this was perhaps a vestige of his scientific training. Some
might be horrified at his suggestion that we look at the* Lager *(the German word for
camps) as an enormous biological and social experiment, but Levi manages to suggest
that we can learn from even the most unfathomable of horrors. The first section begins
with the arrival of the deportees' train at Auschwitz after several days' journey in winter without heat, food, water, or sanitary facilities. Levi notes that there were forty-five
people in his wagon when they arrived at the camp, and only four returned to their
homes after the war. His, he says, was "by far the most fortunate wagon."*

From *Survival in Auschwitz: The Nazi Assault on Humanity,* by Primo Levi, translated by Stuart Woolf (New York: Collier, 1993), pp. 19–20, 27–28, 33–35, 42–43, 87–89.

The door opened with a crash, and the dark echoed with outlandish orders in that curt, barbaric barking of Germans in command which seems to give vent to millennial anger. A vast platform appeared before us, lit up by reflectors. A little beyond it, a row of lorries. Then everything was silent again. Someone translated: we had to climb down with our luggage and deposit it alongside the train. In a moment the platform was swarming with shadows. But we were afraid to break that silence: everyone busied himself with his luggage, searched for someone else, called to some-body, but timidly, in a whisper.

A dozen SS men stood around, legs akimbo, with an indifferent air. At a certain moment they moved among us, and in a subdued tone of voice, with faces of stone, began to interrogate us rapidly, one by one, in bad Italian. They did not interrogate everybody, only a few: "How old? Healthy or ill?" And on the basis of the reply they pointed in two different directions.

Everything was silent as an aquarium, or as in certain dream sequences. We had expected some-thing more apocalyptic: they seemed simple police agents. It was disconcerting and disarming. Some-one dared ask for his luggage: they replied, "lug-gage afterwards." Someone else did not want to leave his wife: they said, "together again after-wards." Many mothers did not want to be sepa-rated with their children: they said "good, good, stay with child." They behaved with the calm as-surance of people doing their normal duty of every day. But Renzo stayed an instant too long to say good-bye to Francesca, his fiancée, and with a sin-gle blow they knocked him to the ground. It was their everyday duty.

In less than ten minutes all the fit men had been collected together in a group. What happened to the others, to the women, to the children, to the old men, we could establish neither then nor later: the night swallowed them up, purely and simply. Today, however, we know that in that rapid and summary choice each one of us had been judged capable or not of working usefully for the Reich; we know that of our convoy no more than ninety-six men and twenty-nine women entered the respective camps of Monowitz-Buna and Birkenau, and that of all the others, more than five hundred in number, not one was living two days later. We also know that not even this tenuous principle of discrimination be-tween fit and unfit was always followed, and that later the simpler method was often adopted of merely opening both the doors of the wagon with-out warning or instructions to the new arrivals.

Those who by chance climbed down on one side of the convoy entered the camp; the others went to the gas chamber.

On the Bottom

Häftling[1]: I have learnt that I am Häftling. My number is 174517; we have been baptized, we will carry the tattoo on our left arm until we die.

The operation was slightly painful and extraordinarily rapid: they placed us all in a row, and one by one, according to the alphabetical order of our names, we filed past a skilful official, armed with a sort of pointed tool with a very short needle. It seems that this is the real, true initiation: only by "showing one's number" can one get bread and soup. Several days passed, and not a few cuffs and punches, before we became used to showing our number promptly enough not to disorder the daily operation of food-distribution: weeks and months were needed to learn its sound in the German language. And for many days, while the habits of freedom still led me to look for the time on my wristwatch, my new name ironically appeared instead, a number tattooed in bluish characters under the skin.

Only much later, and slowly, a few of us learnt something of the funereal science of the numbers of Auschwitz, which epitomize the stages of destruction of European Judaism. To the old hands of the camp, the numbers told everything: the period of entry into the camp, the convoy of which formed a part, and consequently the nationality. Everyone will treat with respect the numbers from 30,000 to 80,000: there are only a few hundred left and they represented the few survivals from the Polish ghettos. It is as well to watch out in commercial dealings with a 116,000 or a 117,000: they now number only about forty, but they represent the Greeks of Salonica, so take care that they do not pull the wool over your eyes. As for the high numbers they carry an essentially comic air about them, like the words "freshman" or "conscript" in ordinary life. The typical high number is a corpulent, docile and stupid

fellow: he can be convinced that leather shoes are distributed at the infirmary to all those with delicate feet, and can be persuaded to run there and leave his bowl of soup "in your custody."

* * *

We had soon learned that the guests of the Lager are divided into three categories: the criminals, the politicals and the Jews. All are clothed in stripes, all are Häftlinge, but the criminals wear a green triangle next to the number sewn on the jacket; the politicals wear a red triangle; and the Jews, who form the large majority, wear the Jewish star, red and yellow. SS men exist but are few and outside the camp, and are seen relatively infrequently. Our effective masters in practice are the green triangles, who have a free hand over us, as well as those of the other two categories who are ready to help them—and they are not few.

And we have learnt other things, more or less quickly, according to our intelligence: to reply "*Jawohl*," never to ask questions, always to pretend to understand. We have learnt the value of food; now we also diligently scrape the bottom of the bowl after the ration and we hold it under our chins when we eat bread so as not to lose the crumbs. We, too, know that it is not the same thing to be given a ladleful of soup from the top or from the bottom of the vat, and we are already able to judge, according to the capacity of the various vats, what is the most suitable place to try and reach in the queue when we line up.

We have learnt that everything is useful; the wire to tie up our shoes, the rags to wrap around our feet, waste paper to (illegally) pad out our jacket against the cold. We have learnt, on the other hand, that everything can be stolen, in fact is automatically stolen as soon as attention is relaxed; and to avoid this, we had to learn the art of sleeping with our head on a bundle made up of our jacket and containing all our belongings, from the bowl to the shoes.

* * *

In addition, there are innumerable circumstances, normally irrelevant, which here become

---

[1] Prisoner.

problems. When one's nails grow long, they have to be shortened, which can only be done with one's teeth (for the toenails, the friction of the shoes is sufficient); if a button comes off, one has to tie it on with a piece of wire; if one goes to the latrine or the washroom, everything has to be carried along, always and everywhere, and while one washes one's face, the bundle of clothes has to be held tightly between one's knees: in any other manner it will be stolen in that second. If a shoe hurts, one has to go in the evening to the ceremony of the changing of the shoes: this tests the skill of the individual who, in the middle of the incredible crowd, has to be able to choose at an eye's glance one (not a pair, one) shoe, which fits. Because once the choice is made, there can be no second change.

And do not think that shoes form a factor of secondary importance in the life of the Lager. Death begins with the shoes; for most of us, they show themselves to be instruments of torture, which after a few hours of marching cause painful sores which become fatally infected. Whoever has them is forced to walk as if he was dragging a convict's chain (this explains the strange gait of the army which returns every evening on parade); he arrives last everywhere, and everywhere he receives blows. He cannot escape if they run after him; his feet swell and the more they swell, the more the friction with the wood and the cloth of the shoes becomes insupportable. Then only the hospital is left: but to enter the hospital with a diagnosis of "*dicke Füsse*" (swollen feet) is extremely dangerous, because it is well known to all, and especially to the SS, that here there is no cure for that complaint.

[Null Achtzehn]

He is Null Achtzehn. He is not called anything except that, Zero Eighteen, the last three figures of his entry number; as if everyone was aware that only a man is worthy of a name, and that Null Achtzehn is no longer a man. I think that even he has forgotten his name, certainly he acts as if this was so. When he speaks, when he looks around, he gives the impression of being empty inside, nothing

more than an involucre, like the slough of certain insects which one finds on the banks of swamps, held by a thread to the stones and shaken by the wind.

Null Achtzehn is very young, which is a grave danger. Not only because boys support exhaustion and fasting worse than adults, but even more because a long training is needed to survive here in the struggle of each one against all, a training that young people rarely have. Null Achtzehn is not even particularly weak, but all avoid working with him. He is indifferent to the point of not even troubling to avoid tiredness and blows or to search for food. He carries out all the orders that he is given, and it is foreseeable that when they send him to his death he will go with the same total indifference.

He has not even the rudimentary astuteness of a draughthorse, which stops pulling a little before it reaches exhaustion: he pulls or carries or pushes as long as his strength allows him, then he gives way at once, without a word of warning, without lifting his sad, opaque eyes from the ground. He made me think of the sledge-dogs in London's books, who slave until the last breath and die on the track.

But as all the rest of us try by every possible means to avoid work, Null Achtzehn is the one who works more than all. It is because of this, and because he is a dangerous companion, that no one wants to work with him; and as, on the other hand, no one wants to work with me, because I am weak and clumsy, it often happens that we find ourselves paired together.

The Drowned and the Saved

*   *   *

We can perhaps ask ourselves if is necessary or good to retain any memory of this exceptional human state. To this question we feel that we have to reply in the affirmative. We are in fact convinced that no human experience is without meaning or unworthy of analysis, and that fundamental values, even if they are not positive, can be deduced from this particular world which we are describing. We would also like to consider that the Lager was pre-eminently a gigantic biological and social experiment.

Thousands of individuals, differing in age, condition, origin, language, culture and customs, are enclosed within barbed wire: there they live a regular, controlled life which is identical for all and inadequate to all needs, and which is more rigorous than any experimenter could have set up to establish what is essential and what adventitious to the conduct of the human animal in the struggle for life.

We do not believe in the most obvious and facile deduction: that man is fundamentally brutal, egoistic and stupid in his conduct once every civilized institution is taken away, and that the Häftling is consequently nothing but a man without inhibitions. We believe, rather, that the only conclusion to be drawn is that in the face of driving necessity and physical disability many social habits and instincts are reduced to silence.

But another fact seems to us worthy of attention: there comes to light the existence of two particularly well differentiated categories among men—the saved and the drowned. Other pairs of opposites (the good and the bad, the wise and the foolish, the cowards and the courageous, the unlucky and the fortunate) are considerably less distinct, they seem less essential, and above all they allow for more numerous and complex intermediary gradations.

This division is much less evident in ordinary life; for there it rarely happens that a man loses himself. A man is normally not alone, and in his rise or fall is tied the destinies of his neighbours; so that it is exceptional for anyone to acquire unlimited power, or to fall by a succession of defeats into utter ruin. Moreover, everyone is normally in possession of such spiritual, physical and even financial resources that the probabilities of shipwreck, of total inadequacy in the face of life, are relatively small. And one must take into account a definite cushioning effect exercised both by the law, and by the moral sense which constitutes a self-imposed law; for a country is considered the more civilized the more the wisdom and efficiency of its laws hin-

der a weak man from becoming too weak or a powerful man too powerful.

But in the Lager things are different: here the struggle to survive is without respite, because everyone is desperately and ferociously alone. If some [prisoner] vacillates, he will find no one to extend a helping hand; on the contrary, someone will knock him aside, because it is in no one's interest that there will be one more "muselman"[2] dragging himself to work every day; and if someone, by a miracle of savage patience and cunning, finds a new method of avoiding the hardest work, a new art which yields him an ounce of bread, he will try to keep his method secret, and he will be esteemed and respected for this, and will derive from it an exclusive, personal benefit; he will become stronger and so will be feared, and who is feared is ipso facto, a candidate for survival.

In history and in life one sometimes seems to glimpse a ferocious law which states: "to he that has will be given; from he that has not, will be taken away." In the Lager, where man is alone and where the struggle for life is reduced to its primordial mechanism, this unjust law is openly in force, is recognized by all. With the adaptable, the strong and astute individuals, even the leaders willingly keep contact, sometimes even friendly contact, because they hope later to perhaps derive some benefit. But with the muselmans, the men in decay, it is not even worth speaking, because one knows already that they will complain and will speak about what they used to eat at home. Even less worthwhile is it to make friends with them, because they have no distinguished acquaintances in the camp, they do not gain any extra rations, they do not work in profitable Kommandos, and they know no secret method of organizing. And in any case, one knows that they are only here on a visit, that in a few weeks nothing will remain of them but a handful of ashes in some near-by field and a crossed-out number on a register. Although engulfed and swept along without rest by the innumerable crowd of

---

[2] This word "*Muselmann*," I do not know why, was used by the old ones of the camp to describe the weak, the inept, those doomed to selection.

those similar to them, they suffer and drag themselves along in an opaque intimate solitude, and in solitude they die or disappear, without leaving a trace in anyone's memory.

REVIEW QUESTIONS

1. Levi notes the cursory or even arbitrary nature of the selection process that decided whether new arrivals at the camp would be killed or put to work, and elsewhere he notes that the rubber factory at Buna never produced a single piece of rubber. Why did the camp authorities insist on rules and procedures to select laborers, when they obviously didn't care if these procedures were followed carefully, or if the prisoners were actually fit enough to do productive labor?

2. What was the purpose of the camp practice of numbering prisoners?

3. What was the significance of the various hierarchies that Levi identifies within camp society?

4. Why does Levi describe the camp as a "struggle of each one against all"?

5. Who are the "drowned" and the "saved"?

FROM *Trials of War Criminals before the Nuremberg Military Tribunals*

Although many postwar philosophers emphasized the moral ambiguities of human action and the relativism of all moral and ethical systems, these postmodern approaches were counterbalanced by a desire to reaffirm the existence of clear lines between good and evil, right and wrong. Survivors sought to ensure that all of humanity would know about the murder of millions of concentration camp inmates, and they called for a judgment on those who had committed crimes against humanity.

Beginning in 1945, many surviving members of the Nazi leadership were put on trial in the city of Nuremberg. The "doctors' trial," which began in December 1946, involved the prosecution of twenty-three German doctors and administrators who had used concentration camp inmates as unwilling subjects in a variety of gruesome and often pointless experiments, including intentional infection with contagious diseases such as malaria and spotted fever, experimental surgery, and exposure to extreme cold, mustard gas, and various poisons. On December 6, 1946, Brigadier General Telford Taylor presented the opening statement for the prosecution, detailing both the specific crimes committed by the defendants and the broader significance of their trial.

From *Trials of War Criminals before the Nuremberg Military Tribunals under Control Council Law No. 10. Nuremberg, October 1946–April 1949* (Washington, D.C.: U.S. Government Printing Office, 1949–53).

Opening Statement of the Prosecution by Brigadier General Telford Taylor, 9 December 1946

The defendants in this case are charged with murders, tortures, and other atrocities committed in the name of medical science. The victims of these crimes are numbered in the hundreds of thousands. A handful only are still alive; a few of the survivors will appear in this courtroom. But most of these miserable victims were slaughtered outright or died in the course of the tortures to which they were subjected.

For the most part they are nameless dead. To their murderers, these wretched people were not individuals at all. They came in wholesale lots and were treated worse than animals. They were 200 Jews in good physical condition, 50 gypsies, 500 tubercular Poles, or 1,000 Russians. The victims of these crimes are numbered among the anonymous millions who met death at the hands of the Nazis and whose fate is a hideous blot on the page of modern history.

*   *   *

The mere punishment of the defendants, or even of thousands of others equally guilty, can never redress the terrible injuries which the Nazis visited on these unfortunate peoples. For them it is far more important that these incredible events be established by clear and public proof, so that no one can ever doubt that they were fact and not fable; and that this Court, as the agent of the United States and as the voice of humanity, stamp these acts, and the ideas which engendered them, as barbarous and criminal.

We have still other responsibilities here. The defendants in the dock are charged with murder, but this is no mere murder trial. We cannot rest content when we have shown that crimes were committed and that certain persons committed them. To kill, to maim, and to torture is criminal under all modern systems of law. These defendants did not kill in hot blood, nor for personal enrichment. Some of them may be sadists who

killed and tortured for sport, but they are not all perverts. They are not ignorant men. Most of them are trained physicians and some of them are distinguished scientists. Yet these defendants, all of whom were fully able to comprehend the nature of their acts, and most of whom were exceptionally qualified to form a moral and professional judgment in this respect, are responsible for wholesale murder and unspeakably cruel tortures. It is our deep obligation to all peoples of the world to show why and how these things happened. It is incumbent upon us to set forth with conspicuous clarity the ideas and motives which moved these defendants to treat their fellow men as less than beasts.

*   *   *

To the German people we owe a special responsibility in these proceedings. Under the leadership of the Nazis and their war lords, the German nation spread death and devastation throughout Europe. This the Germans now know. So, too, do they know the consequences to Germany: defeat, ruin, prostration, and utter demoralization. Most German children will never, as long as they live, see an undamaged German city.

*   *   *

This case, and others which will be tried in this building, offer a signal opportunity to lay before the German people the true cause of their present misery. The walls and towers and churches of Nuremberg were, indeed, reduced to rubble by Allied bombs, but in a deeper sense Nuremberg had been destroyed a decade earlier, when it became the seat of the annual Nazi Party rallies, a focal point for the moral disintegration in Germany. * * *

*   *   *

That murder should be punished goes without the saying, but the full performance of our task requires more than the just sentencing of these defendants. Their crimes were the inevitable result of the sinister doctrines which they espoused, and these same doctrines sealed the fate of Germany, shattered Europe, and left the world in ferment.

Wherever those doctrines may emerge and prevail, the same terrible consequences will follow. That is why a bold and lucid consummation of these proceedings is of vital importance to all nations. That is why the United States has constituted this Tribunal.

*   *   *

Before taking up these experiments one by one, let us look at them as a whole. Are they a heterogeneous list of horrors, or is there a common denominator for the whole group?

A sort of rough pattern is apparent on the face of the indictment. Experiments concerning high altitude, the effect of cold, and the potability of processed sea water have an obvious relation to aeronautical and naval combat and rescue problems. The mustard gas and phosphorous burn experiments, as well as those relating to the healing value of sulfanilamide for wounds, can be related to air raid and battlefield medical problems. It is well known that malaria, epidemic jaundice, and typhus were among the principal diseases which had to be combated by the German Armed Forces and by German authorities in occupied territories.

To some degree, the therapeutic pattern outlined above is undoubtedly a valid one, and explains why the Wehrmacht, and especially the German Air Force, participated in these experiments. Fanatically bent upon conquest, utterly ruthless as to the means or instruments to be used in achieving victory, and callous to the sufferings of people whom they regarded as inferior, the German militarists were willing to gather whatever scientific fruit these experiments might yield.

But our proof will show that a quite different and even more sinister objective runs like a red thread through these hideous researches. We will show that in some instances the true object of these experiments was not how to rescue or to cure, but how to destroy and kill. The sterilization experiments were, it is clear, purely destructive in purpose. The prisoners at Buchenwald who were shot with poisoned bullets were not guinea pigs to test an antidote for the poison; their murderers really wanted to know how quickly the poison would kill.

*   *   *

The 20 physicians in the dock range from leaders of German scientific medicine, with excellent international reputations, down to the dregs of the German medical profession. All of them have in common a callous lack of consideration and human regard for, and an unprincipled willingness to abuse their power over the poor, unfortunate, defenseless creatures who had been deprived of their rights by a ruthless and criminal government. All of them violated the Hippocratic commandments which they had solemnly sworn to uphold and abide by, including the fundamental principles never to do harm. * * *

*   *   *

I intend to pass very briefly over matters of medical ethics, such as the conditions under which a physician may lawfully perform a medical experiment upon a person who has voluntarily subjected himself to it, or whether experiments may lawfully be performed upon criminals who have been condemned to death. This case does not present such problems. No refined questions confront us here.

None of the victims of the atrocities perpetrated by these defendants were volunteers, and this is true regardless of what these unfortunate people may have said or signed before their tortures began. Most of the victims had not been condemned to death, and those who had been were not criminals, unless it be a crime to be a Jew, or a Pole, or a gypsy, or a Russian prisoner of war.

Whatever book or treatise on medical ethics we may examine, and whatever expert on forensic medicine we may question, will say that it is a fundamental and inescapable obligation of every physician under any known system of law not to perform a dangerous experiment without the subject's consent. In the tyranny that was Nazi Germany, no one could give such a consent to the medical agents of the State; everyone lived in fear and acted under duress. I fervently hope that none of us here in the courtroom will have to suffer in silence while it is said on the part of these defendants that the wretched and helpless people whom they froze and drowned and burned and poisoned were volunteers.

*   *   *

This case is one of the simplest and clearest of those that will be tried in this building. It is also one of the most important. It is true that the defendants in the box were not among the highest leaders of the Third Reich. They are not the war lords who assembled and drove the German military machine, nor the industrial barons who made the parts, nor the Nazi politicians who debased and brutalized the minds of the German people. But this case, perhaps more than any other we will try, epitomizes Nazi thought and the Nazi way of life, because these defendants pursue the savage promises of Nazi thought so far. The things that these defendants did, like so many other things that happened under the Third Reich, were the result of the noxious merger of German militarism and Nazi racial objectives.

*   *   *

Germany surrendered herself to this foul conjunction of evil forces. The nation fell victim to the Nazi scourge because its leaders lacked the wisdom to foresee the consequences and the courage to stand firm in the face of threats. Their failure was the inevitable outcome of that sinister undercurrent of German philosophy which preaches the supreme importance of the state and the complete subordination of the individual. A nation in which the individual means nothing will find few leaders courageous and able enough to serve its best interests.

*   *   *

The Nazis have, to a certain extent, succeeded in convincing the peoples of the world that the Nazi system, although ruthless, was absolutely efficient; that although savage, it was completely scientific; that although entirely devoid of humanity, it was highly systematic—that "it got things done." The evidence which this Tribunal will hear will explode this myth. The Nazi methods of investigation were inefficient and unscientific, and their techniques of research were unsystematic.

These experiments revealed nothing which civilized medicine can use. It was, indeed, ascertained that phenol or gasoline injected intravenously will kill a man inexpensively and within 60 seconds. * * * There is no doubt that a number of these new methods may be useful to criminals everywhere and there is no doubt that they may be useful to a criminal state.

*   *   *

Apart from these deadly fruits, the experiments were not only criminal but a scientific failure. * * * The moral shortcomings of the defendants and the precipitous ease with which they decided to commit murder in quest of "scientific results," dulled also that scientific hesitancy, that thorough thinking-through, that responsible weighing of every single step which alone can insure scientifically valid results. Even if they had merely been forced to pay as little as two dollars for human experimental subjects, such as American investigators may have to pay for a cat, they might have thought twice before wasting unnecessary numbers, and thought of simpler and better ways to solve their problems. The fact that these investigators had free and unrestricted access to human beings to be experimented upon misled them to the dangerous and fallacious conclusion that the results would thus be better and more quickly obtainable than if they had gone through the labor of preparation, thinking, and meticulous preinvestigation.

*   *   *

In short, this conspiracy was a ghastly failure as well as a hideous crime. The creeping paralysis of Nazi superstition spread through the German medical profession and, just as it destroyed character and morals, it dulled the mind.

Guilt for the oppressions and crimes of the Third Reich is widespread, but it is the guilt of the leaders that is deepest and most culpable. Who could German medicine look to to keep the profession true to its traditions and protect it from the ravaging inroads of Nazi pseudo-science? This was the supreme responsibility of the leaders of German medicine. ✳ ✳ ✳ That is why their guilt is greater than that of any of the other defendants in the dock. They are the men who utterly failed their country and their profession, who showed neither courage nor wisdom nor the vestiges of moral character. It is their failure, together with the failure of the leaders of Germany in other walks of life, that debauched Germany and led to her defeat. It is because of them and others like them that we all live in a stricken world.

REVIEW QUESTIONS

1. Why, according to General Taylor, was it so important that the defendants be tried for their crimes?
2. Other than punishing specific guilty individuals, what purpose was being served by these trials?
3. To what extent is Taylor's statement an indictment of Nazi science in general?
4. How does Taylor's indictment of Nazi medical experiments on human subjects differ from Primo Levi's suggestion that the Lager be seen as a "gigantic biological and social experiment"?
5. Do you agree with Taylor's suggestion that it is necessary to distinguish between the "guilt of leaders" and the guilt of others, and that the former are more culpable? What potential problems might such an idea have caused in the postwar period?

TADATAKA KURIBAYASHI

FROM *A Child's Experience: My Experience of the Atomic Bomb*

On August 6, 1945, an atomic bomb was dropped on the Japanese city of Hiroshima, killing 66,000 people outright. On August 9, another bomb was dropped on Nagasaki, killing 39,000. In the following weeks and months, many more died as a result of radiation exposure and of injuries sustained at the time of the explosions.

The decision to drop the newly developed atomic bomb on Japan continues to generate heated debate among philosophers, historians, and the general public. Those who defend this particular deployment of nuclear weapons argue that it brought a more rapid end to the war, thereby saving the lives of countless American soldiers and Japanese civilians. Others counter that the Japanese government was already on the verge of surrender and that the targeting of civilian populations for military ends is, in any case, indefensible. Evaluation of this event is further complicated by the fact that the decision to use the atomic bomb was made in the context of emerging Cold War hostilities. Truman was eager to end the war with Japan and keep the Soviet Union out of the Asian theater, and he may also have wished to provide Stalin with a graphic demonstration of the enhanced military might of the United States.

During the war years, Allied propaganda supplied Americans and Europeans with highly stereotyped and racist caricatures of the Japanese. In the postwar period, this dehumanized image was challenged by movies and books documenting the tragic consequences of the use of nuclear weapons. In the 1960s, Tadataka Kuribayashi recounted his own experience of the bombing of Hiroshima. In early 1945, Kuribayashi had been attending school in Hiroshima. In April of that year, he was evacuated to the nearby peasant village of Tsutsuga, along with eighteen other children.

From *A Child's Experience: My Experience of the Atomic Bomb*, by Tadataka Kuribayashi, www.cooper.edu/humanities/core/hss3/t_kuribayashi.html [accessed 5/20/11].

The Fatal Day (6 August)

The weather was fine in the village on the morning of the 6 August, which was more than one month after the parents-visiting day. In the precincts of a shrine adjacent to the school, we boys in the 6th grade were undergoing training in the Morse signals. Cool breeze blew under ginkgo trees, and the cicadas seemed to be singing the joys of summer. Suddenly I felt something warm on my left cheek and turned back. It seemed like a strong reflection from a mirror. Then a roaring sound shook the whole village. While I was wondering what had happened, a column of clouds appeared above the mountains in the south. That was not an ordinary cloud but of a superb pink color. Gradually it assumed the shape of a mushroom and rose to the sky.

When I returned to the temple, the matron said she had felt a strong tremor even in the temple. As time passed, the fine sky gradually became dark, and in the late afternoon, a lot of cinders of paper and other things fell down from the sky. First a rumor said that an arsenal had exploded, but I later heard that a fire engine from an adjacent village had gone to Hiroshima City for rescue, but because of the strong fire, could not go beyond Yokogawa and returned. Thus, though I was small, I felt something unusual had happened. However, I didn't even imagine that the big city of Hiroshima had instantaneously become a sheet of fire.

Soon I heard that many people with severe burns had returned to the village. All of these people were from the village and were working in Hiroshima. Since then, there was no communication from the parents. After more than a week, a teacher told us that there had been an important announcement and that Japan had lost the war, but now I cannot remember sorrow or anxiety at that time. We might have been too young to have any direct emotion about the big change for the nation. Even though the war ended, we couldn't do anything. No one came to fetch us, and everyone lived anxiously from day to day.

At the beginning of September, I received a wrinkled-up postcard. Though my mother's name was mentioned, the handwriting with a pencil, some parts of which were blurred, was not my mother's. The card simply said, "I am in the reception center in Miyajima. Come here immediately." and a simple map of the place was shown. I wondered why my mother had not written it herself, but was glad to know where she was. However, the date on the card showed that many days had passed since it had been written. Next day, I, accompanied by Mr. Yamakawa, left for Miyajima. That was the 2 September.

I looked at the town of Hiroshima while I proceeded from Yokogawa to Koi. It was a field of charred ruins. The city streetcar which just began to run between Koami-cho and Koi had numerous flies on the ceiling. It was a strange sight. We took a boat from Miyajima-guchi. I saw the old big torii (Shinto shrine archway) and the beautiful Itsukushima Shrine, but they just looked a faded landscape painting to me. I wanted to go to the reception center and see the face of my mother as soon as possible. I was so eager to see her that I felt the boat was extremely slow. Soon we arrived at the center, which was a big building to the north of the shrine. When I stood at the entrance, I felt some kind of anxiety, which was an emotion difficult to express.

Attending on Mother

I looked for Mother with my teacher. It was a big room with tens of tatami mats, and the spaces between A-bomb survivors lying on futon (bedclothes) produced a forlorn atmosphere. We took one round, but couldn't find her. While I took the second round, looking into the face of each person, I was astonished to find Mother, lying on her face and exhausted. She was a small person, but she looked even smaller. Suppressing the tremor of my voice, I called her quietly. There was no answer. I called her again. Then she noticed and slightly raised her head. She saw the teacher behind me, and took out some bills to give to him. He refused to receive them, and left there after a short while saying that he had business at the school.

When Mother told me about the death of Father, I was not so surprised. I might have been somewhat ready to hear the news. Deprived of a flush of hope, I imagined my father being burnt to death in agony. My heart was wrung. We didn't know if my elder brother, who had gone abroad to war was dead or alive. I naturally had a dark prospect about our future, but resolved firmly to continue to live with my mother no matter how poor we would be. Mother told me to take the cloth off her back. I found brown burns all over her back. Because of the burns, she couldn't lie on her back. Why does my mother, as innocent as a person could be, have to be tortured like this? I could not suppress the anger I felt. From that day, I took care of her for 2 nights and 3 days. However, the only medicine provided was mercurochrome. We were even short of cresol. When Mother arrived at the center, she was fine and even washed other people's clothes, but when I got there she couldn't even move her body.

She was engaged in building-demolition work near the Tsurumi Bridge when she was exposed to the flash. She couldn't do anything for Mrs. Takai, who was immediately burned to death in front of her, and climbed the Hijiyama Hill in a hurry with her back burned. From the hill, she looked at the city, which was a hell on earth. With other people, she was first accommodated in the reception center in Ninoshima, and moved to Miyajima. The terrible gas which entered to the depth of her body gradually damaged her bones and organs. She had completely lost her appetite.

Remorse

No one had disposed of my mother's urine, so her lower body gave out a stench. Her stool was not like that of a human being. Its color and smell were like those of internal organs that had been melted and had become a sticky liquid. I felt that the only way to give humaneness back to her was to clean the chamber pot often. Though I was eager to care for her, I became negligent once. On the second night at the center, I heard Mother's small voice calling me, but I was so sleepy that I pretended as though I didn't hear her. She called me twice, but didn't say anything more. Whenever I remember this, there is a sharp pain in my heart.

At the camp, simple food such as salty soup with one dumpling was served three times. No boiled rice was served. We were allowed to drink as many cups of soup as we liked, and I had three or four more cups of soup. My mother smiled wryly. At that time, she was too weak to speak. I saw the front of a big torii, gateway to a Shinto shrine, from the window of the lavatory. Looking at the B-29 bomber which sometimes came flying, I shouted to myself "Idiot!" It was all the resistance I, as a boy, could offer. And I sometimes cried secretly in the lavatory.

Death of Mother

At lunch-time on 4 September, the third day, Mother started to writhe in pain. Her unusual action completely upset me. All I could do was to absentmindedly look at my suffering Mother. After suffering for 30 minutes, she regained her calmness. However, it was the last calmness, the sign of the end of life. I continued calling her name, clinging to her body. Tears welled up in the eyes of my speechless mother and tears rolled down her cheek. I wondered if the tears were from the sorrow of eternal parting between mother and child or from an anxiety about my future. I shall never forget the tears of my Mother I saw on that day.

I continued crying even after a white cloth was placed over Mother's face. Some irritated people reproached me, saying "Be quiet!" Shouldn't I feel sorry for the death of my most precious mother? My tears seemed to have forgotten to stop until evening.

Return to Tsutsuga Village

There was a middle-aged man who happened to come to the camp as an attendant. He was kind enough to offer to take charge of me, probably in pity of me who had been left an orphan. I answered I would decide after consulting with my teacher at the Saihoji Temple where I had been evacuated. He decided to take me there. Wrapping my mother's personal belongings, I had rice ball made for lunch. The man and I left Miyajima Island, leaving what had to be done including the burial of my dead mother to the officials at the camp.

Arriving at the Miyajima-guchi streetcar station, I found a streetcar already there. The streetcar was about to leave the station. I had a return ticket but the man did not have one and bought his own ticket. He hurried to the platform after he had his ticket punched. I tried to follow him, but a man at the gate told me that the ticket I had was for a train, not for a streetcar and showed me the way to the railway station. I started walking toward the station at once, never thinking of anything. There is no way of knowing if the man left for Hiroshima by streetcar or returned to Miyajima. The fact that the one ticket I had served as the turning point of my fate still makes me think of the mysteriousness of fate.

The train I got on took me close to Tsutsuga Village; from Miyajima-guchi to Yokogawa and from Yokogawa to Kabe to Aki-imuro. I felt relieved when I was picked up by a truck driver at Aki-imuro who took me to Kake. An old man who shared the ride had a water bottle and gave me some water. The water tasted so good and I felt the water coursing down through my bowels. The old man was returning to Tsutsuga Village and I asked him to take me there.

It was very far from Kake to Tsutsuga. The road along a river seemed to be endless. I tottered after several persons while half sleeping late at night. When I reached Tsutsuga Village, I noticed there were no other people except the old man who had given me water. We walked for another 40 minutes and finally reached the front of the Saihoji Temple at dawn. At that time I felt undescribably happy. I expressed my thanks and said farewell to the old man. I entered the main hall of the temple. I thought I had to report to my teacher that I had returned, but I decided to do so later in the morning because I did not want to wake him up. I stole into a mosquito net, under which some children were sleeping, carrying my bedclothes and lay down. In the morning, my teacher was very surprised to learn that I had returned. I had never experienced such a long trip.

Left Alone

I resumed my life at the temple. An increasing number of children were leaving the temple together with their parent or sibling or relative who came there to take them home. However, traffic was completely paralyzed due to a heavy flood caused by an unprecedented typhoon which hit the prefecture. So, there was no choice but to walk all the way to Hiroshima.

Children who had homes to return to were happy. Most of the children had lost either a parent or other family members. It was only I that had lost both parents and had no relatives. I had nowhere to go except an orphanage where I was taken care of. In spite of sheer unhappiness, I, as a child, did not think so seriously of it.

In the end, only three children including myself stayed behind at the temple. The temple was too big for the three of us. I heard that the relatives of Yoshihiro Inoue and Yoko Minematsu would come to the temple later for some reason. Then, it was decided that children including those living in neighboring villages who had no home to return would be accommodated in a temple at Togouchi adjacent to Tsutsuga. I was hurriedly crossing a mountain pass when it began to get dark on 3 October. There was no one to be seen and everything was ominously still and silent.

I, an 11-year-old boy, only thought of running out of the weird trees, not being afraid of my future life which would bring me loneliness and starvation. Frequently frightened at the sound of my footsteps, I kept running, only wishing I could reach the village as soon as possible.

*   *   *

REVIEW QUESTIONS

1. What does this account tell you about the Japanese experience in the Second World War?
2. To what extent might the testimony of survivors like Kuribayashi influence historical interpretations of the use of atomic weapons?
3. How should historians approach the analysis of events heavily charged with moral significance, such as the Holocaust and the deployment of nuclear weapons?
4. How do the bombings of Hiroshima and Nagasaki differ from the Holocaust?

FROM Charter of the United Nations

Before the atomic bomb brought the war in the Pacific to a dramatic close, a new international peacekeeping organization was already being organized to replace the League of Nations. On June 26, 1945, the United Nations was established by a formal charter drawn up at an international congress held in San Francisco. Vested with the authority to maintain and deploy peacekeeping forces, the United Nations was intended to be a more effective agency for world peace than its predecessor had been. And, although the United Nations was not able to solve the many problems generated by the Cold War, it nevertheless served as an important arena for the negotiation of conflicts between member nations. The preamble and first chapter of the United Nations Charter set out the primary goals of the organization.

From Charter of the United Nations, United Nations Web page, www.un.org/ [accessed 5/20/11].

Preamble

WE THE PEOPLES OF THE UNITED NATIONS DETERMINED

to save succeeding generations from the scourge of war, which twice in our lifetime has brought untold sorrow to mankind, and

to reaffirm faith in fundamental human rights, in the dignity and worth of the human person, in the equal rights of men and women and of nations large and small, and

to establish conditions under which justice and respect for the obligations arising from treaties and other sources of international law can be maintained, and

to promote social progress and better standards of life in larger freedom,

AND FOR THESE ENDS

to practice tolerance and live together in peace with one another as good neighbours, and

to unite our strength to maintain international peace and security, and

to ensure, by the acceptance of principles and the institution of methods, that armed force shall not be used, save in the common interest, and

to employ international machinery for the promotion of the economic and social advancement of all peoples,

HAVE RESOLVED TO COMBINE OUR EFFORTS TO ACCOMPLISH THESE AIMS

Accordingly, our respective Governments, through representatives assembled in the city of San Francisco, who have exhibited their full powers found to be in good and due form, have agreed to the present Charter of the United Nations and do hereby establish an international organization to be known as the United Nations.

ARTICLE 1

The Purposes of the United Nations are:

1. To maintain international peace and security, and to that end: to take effective collective measures for the prevention and removal of threats to the peace, and for the suppression of acts of aggression or other breaches of the peace, and to bring about by peaceful means, and in conformity with the principles of justice and international law, adjustment or settlement of international disputes or situations which might lead to a breach of the peace;

2. To develop friendly relations among nations based on respect for the principle of equal rights and self-determination of peoples, and to take other appropriate measures to strengthen universal peace;

3. To achieve international co-operation in solving international problems of an economic, social, cultural, or humanitarian character, and in promoting and encouraging respect for human rights and for fundamental freedoms for all without distinction as to race, sex, language, or religion; and

4. To be a centre for harmonizing the actions of nations in the attainment of these common ends.

ARTICLE 2

The Organization and its Members, in pursuit of the Purposes stated in Article 1, shall act in accordance with the following Principles.

1. The Organization is based on the principle of the sovereign equality of all its Members.

2. All Members, in order to ensure to all of them the rights and benefits resulting from membership, shall fulfill in good faith the obligations assumed by them in accordance with the present Charter.

3. All Members shall settle their international disputes by peaceful means in such a manner that international peace and security, and justice, are not endangered.

4. All Members shall refrain in their international relations from the threat or use of force against the territorial integrity or political independence of any state, or in any other manner inconsistent with the Purposes of the United Nations.

*　　*　　*

REVIEW QUESTIONS

1. How does this preamble compare with the Covenant of the League of Nations from the Versailles Treaty (pp. 483–489)?

2. To what extent was the United Nations statement of goals formulated as a response to the Second World War experience?

Aerial Bombardment

Aerial bombardment of cities and their civilian populations began in the First World War, but in the Second World War it became a routine strategy of every belligerent power. Beginning with the massive bombings of Polish towns and cities in 1939 and the destruction of Rotterdam and Coventry in 1940 during the German invasion of the Netherlands and the Battle of Britain, the practice soon became general. In May 1942, the British Royal Air Force launched a raid on Cologne that employed over 1,000 aircraft, dropping more than 2,000 tons of explosives on the city. Before the war ended similar attacks were carried out in Essen, Bremen, Hamburg, Kassel, Darmstadt, Pforzheim, Swinemunde, and Dresden. In many of these attacks the casualties were counted in the tens of thousands. The most extreme example in Europe may have been the July 1943 bombing of Hamburg, which had already been a frequent target of Allied bombing since 1940. During eight days and seven nights of repeated bombing raids a firestorm was created that generated winds of up to 150 mph and temperatures reaching 1,500 degrees Fahrenheit. Some estimates put the number of casualties as high as 45,000, most of whom died from lack of oxygen as the air was sucked out of their underground shelters. Eight square miles of the city were completely incinerated. Even this event was overshadowed by the destruction of central Tokyo by U.S. planes dropping conventional incendiary bombs in February 1945, when over 100,000 people were killed. The war in the Pacific ended with Japan's surrender soon after U.S. president Harry Truman ordered nuclear bombs dropped on Hiroshima and Nagasaki on August 6 and 9, 1945. Over 100,000 were killed outright by the blasts at Hiroshima and Nagasaki, with tens of thousands more dying in subsequent months of burns and radiation exposure. The targeting of civilian populations on such a massive scale was the culmination of the doctrine of total war, *in which the entire capacities of a nation were mobilized at times of conflict, a mobilization that effectively dismantled older distinctions between the front line and nonmilitarized zones.*

WARSAW, 1939

ST. PAUL'S CATHEDRAL, LONDON, January 23, 1941

THE BOMBING OF DRESDEN (1945)   WALTER HAHN

COLOGNE, GERMANY March 7, 1945

HAMBURG, GERMANY, August 1943

ROUEN, FRANCE, c. May 30, 1945

552

NAGASAKI, JAPAN, August 1945

HIROSHIMA, JAPAN, 1945

27 ❧ THE COLD WAR WORLD: GLOBAL POLITICS, ECONOMIC RECOVERY, AND CULTURAL CHANGE

At the beginning of the twentieth century, the European great powers dominated the world, both materially and—at least in the opinion of Europeans—culturally. Even after the First World War, European power seemed only slightly diminished, especially when the newest contender for world power status, the United States, chose to retreat again into isolationism after the war.

After the Second World War, the world was a dramatically different place. A second great cataclysm had left much of Europe in ruins, and the former great powers found themselves confronted with the enormous task of reconstructing what they themselves had destroyed. The new bipolar balance of world power, pitting the United States against the Soviet Union, decreased the global power and prestige of individual European nations, drawing them into the orbits of the two competing superpowers. Europe was divided in two by an "Iron Curtain," and the cultures, economies, and political systems of the two Europes were deeply marked by the new realities of the Cold War.

European dominance had ended, but the Western European nations soon rallied, achieving general levels of prosperity, technological sophistication, and democratic participation never before experienced in their histories. American economic aid reinvigorated Western European economies, greatly increasing the material well-being of ordinary people. Cradle-to-grave social welfare programs provided education, medical care, and guarantees that no citizen would be deprived of the minimum necessities of life. The appurtenances of consumer culture—radios, cars, televisions, dishwashers, seaside vacations—became available to the majority of Western Europeans.

The economic "miracle" did not come to Eastern Europe, always underdeveloped by Western standards. Eastern Europe's poverty and technological backwardness were only reinforced by the domination of the powerful Soviet Union. Communist regimes throughout Eastern Europe retained their hold on

*power not through popular support but through the threat of Soviet invasion.
Communist heads of state were forced to follow the dictates of economic and
military planners in Moscow, often to the detriment of their own citizens. The
death of Stalin in 1953 brought some easing of repression, and standards of living did improve, if more gradually and less opulently than in the West. But
Stalin's successors continued to rule Eastern Europe with a firm hand, stifling
dissent and emphasizing heavy industrial and military production at the expense
of consumer goods. When the Soviet bloc collapsed in the late 1980s, bringing a
surprisingly sudden end to the Cold War, Eastern Europe remained burdened
with the bitter legacy of economic underdevelopment and political immaturity.*

*In both the East and the West, postwar culture was unsettled and complex.
The war had demonstrated the moral bankruptcy of fascism (even if nostalgia
for militarism, nationalism, and racial cleansing lingered in the hearts of many),
but no other alternative ideologies won unqualified support. For many, the simple joys of life were enough. After the hardships of the war, consumerism and
leisure culture offered a welcome respite from ideology. On the other hand, intellectuals struggled to come to terms with the implications of wartime genocide,
economic and political globalization, and the Americanization of European culture. Although the Cold War left many feeling powerless in the face of impersonal
forces such as superpower politics and the threat of nuclear annihilation, others
drew renewed hope from the anticolonial struggles of Third World peoples and
the protests of civil rights activists around the world.*

WINSTON CHURCHILL

FROM **"The Sinews of Peace"**

*During the Second World War, long-standing tensions between the Soviet Union
and the other Allied states were set aside in favor of a unified war effort. However,
even before the war had ended, mutual suspicions were revived, especially as Allied
leaders began to negotiate postwar territorial settlements. The United States and
Great Britain promoted the creation of capitalist democracies throughout Europe,
whereas Stalin sought to establish communist satellite states in the East.*

*One of the defining moments of the emerging Cold War came on March 5,
1946, when Winston Churchill (1874–1965), who had been voted out of office as
prime minister by war-weary Britons that year, gave a speech at Westminster College in Fulton, Missouri, attended by the U.S. president Harry S Truman. In this*

speech, entitled "The Sinews of Peace," Churchill called on Americans and Western Europeans to maintain a unified front against the Soviet threat.

From *The Sinews of Peace,* vol. 7, edited by R. R. James (New York: Chelsea House, 1946).

*   *   *

A shadow has fallen upon the scenes so lately lighted by the Allied victory. Nobody knows what Soviet Russia and its Communist international organisation intends to do in the immediate future, or what are the limits, if any, to their expansive and proselytising tendencies. I have a strong admiration and regard for the valiant Russian people and for my wartime comrade, Marshal Stalin. There is deep sympathy and goodwill in Britain—and I doubt not here also—towards the peoples of all the Russias and a resolve to persevere through many differences and rebuffs in establishing lasting friendships. We understand the Russian need to be secure on her western frontiers by the removal of all possibility of German aggression. We welcome Russia to her rightful place among the leading nations of the world. We welcome her flag upon the seas. Above all, we welcome constant, frequent and growing contacts between the Russian people and our own people on both sides of the Atlantic. It is my duty however, for I am sure you would wish me to state the facts as I see them to you, to place before you certain facts about the present position in Europe.

From Stettin in the Baltic to Trieste in the Adriatic, an iron curtain has descended across the Continent. Behind that line lie all the capitals of the ancient states of Central and Eastern Europe. Warsaw, Berlin, Prague, Vienna, Budapest, Belgrade, Bucharest and Sofia, all these famous cities and the populations around them lie in what I must call the Soviet sphere, and all are subject in one form or another, not only to Soviet influence but to a very high and, in many cases, increasing measure of control from Moscow. Athens alone—Greece with its immortal glories—is free to decide its future at an election under British, American

and French observation. The Russian-dominated Polish Government has been encouraged to make enormous and wrongful inroads upon Germany, and mass expulsions of millions of Germans on a scale grievous and undreamed-of are now taking place. The Communist parties, which were very small in all these Eastern States of Europe, have been raised to pre-eminence and power far beyond their numbers and are seeking everywhere to obtain totalitarian control. Police governments are prevailing in nearly every case, and so far, except in Czechoslovakia, there is no true democracy.

*   *   *

The safety of the world requires a new unity in Europe, from which no nation should be permanently outcast. It is from the quarrels of the strong parent races in Europe that the world wars we have witnessed, or which occurred in former times, have sprung. Twice in our own lifetime we have seen the United States, against their wishes and their traditions, against arguments, the force of which it is impossible not to comprehend, drawn by irresistible forces, into these wars in time to secure the victory of the good cause, but only after frightful slaughter and devastation had occurred. Twice the United States has had to send several millions of its young men across the Atlantic to find the war; but now war can find any nation, wherever it may dwell between dusk and dawn. Surely we should work with conscious purpose for a grand pacification of Europe, within the structure of the United Nations and in accordance with its Charter. That I feel is an open cause of policy of very great importance.

*   *   *

From what I have seen of our Russian friends and Allies during the war, I am convinced that there is nothing they admire so much as strength, and there is nothing for which they have less respect than for weakness, especially military weakness. For that reason the old doctrine of a balance of power is unsound. We cannot afford, if we can help it, to work on narrow margins, offering temptations to a trial of strength. If the Western Democracies stand together in strict adherence to the principles of the United Nations Charter, their influence for furthering those principles will be immense and no one is likely to molest them. If however they become divided or falter in their duty and if these all-important years are allowed to slip away then indeed catastrophe may overwhelm us all.

*   *   *

REVIEW QUESTIONS

1. What was the Iron Curtain? Where was it?
2. What policies was Churchill promoting in this speech?
3. What specific response do you think he hoped to elicit from his U.S. audience?
4. To what extent were his remarks shaped by the existence of nuclear weapons? By the U.S. tradition of isolationism?

NIKITA KHRUSHCHEV

FROM "On the Cult of Personality and Its Consequences"

Stalin's death in 1953 was followed by an intense struggle for power within the Soviet leadership. At midnight on the night of February 25, 1956, the victor of this contest, first secretary Nikita Khrushchev (1894–1971), gave a "secret speech" to the twentieth congress of the Communist Party. In blunt language, Khrushchev denounced Stalin's authoritarianism as a deviation from the Marxist-Leninist principles of the Bolshevik revolution. Later that year, Khrushchev reestablished friendly relations with Yugoslavia's independent communist leader, Josip Broz Tito, demonstrating a new willingness on the part of the Soviet state to tolerate "different roads to Socialism." When he became premier in 1958, Khrushchev rejected the inevitability of war with noncommunist states, cultivating a foreign policy based on "peaceful coexistence."

As a loyal communist, Khrushchev remained committed to single-party rule, the planned economy, and state censorship, but his de-Stalinization campaign produced a notable thaw within the Soviet Union. Many political prisoners were released, and many of those who had died or been imprisoned during Stalin's reign of terror were exonerated of any crimes. Greater intellectual freedom was granted to artists, while ordinary Soviet citizens, who had long suffered as a result of Stalin's single-minded focus on the development of heavy industry, benefited from a redirection of the economy toward greater production of consumer goods.

From *The Stalin Dictatorship: Khrushchev's "Secret Speech" and Other Documents*, edited by T. H. Rigby (Sydney: Sydney University Press, 1968), pp. 23–25, 29–32, 36–37, 52–53, 58–62, 65, 84.

Comrades! In the report of the Central Committee of the party at the 20th Congress, in a number of speeches by delegates to the Congress, as well as before this during plenary sessions of the CPSU Central Committee, quite a lot has been said about the cult of the individual and about its harmful consequences.

After Stalin's death the Central Committee of the party began to implement a policy of explaining concisely and consistently that it is impermissible and foreign to the spirit of Marxism-Leninism to elevate one person, to transform him into a superman possessing supernatural characteristics akin to those of a god. Such a man supposedly knows everything, sees everything, thinks for everyone, can do anything, and is infallible in his behaviour.

This kind of belief about a man, namely about Stalin, was cultivated among us for many years.

* * *

The great modesty of the genius of the revolution, Vladimir Ilyich Lenin, is known. Lenin always stressed the role of the people as the creator of history, the directing and organizational role of the party as a living and creative organism, and also the role of the Central Committee.

Marxism does not negate the role of the leaders of the workers' class in directing the revolutionary liberation movement.

While ascribing great importance to the role of the leaders and organizers of the masses, Lenin at the same time mercilessly stigmatized every manifestation of the cult of the individual, inexorably combated views which are foreign to Marxism, about the "hero" and the "crowd," and countered all efforts to oppose the "hero" to the masses and to the people.

* * *

In addition to the great accomplishments of V. I. Lenin for the victory of the working class and of the working peasants, for the victory of our party and for the application of the ideas of scientific communism to life, his acute mind expressed itself also, in the fact that he detected in Stalin in time those negative characteristics which resulted later in grave consequences.

* * *

Stalin acted not through persuasion, explanation, and patient co-operation with people, but by imposing his concepts and demanding absolute submission to his opinion. Whoever opposed this concept or tried to prove his viewpoint, and the correctness of his position, was doomed to removal from the leading collective and to subsequent moral and physical annihilation. This was especially true during the period following the 17th Party Congress [in 1934], when many prominent party leaders and rank-and-file party workers, honest and dedicated to the cause of communism, fell victim to Stalin's despotism.

* * *

It was precisely during this period (1935–1937–1938) that the practice of mass repression through the government apparatus was born, first against the enemies of Leninism—Trotskyites, Zinovievites, Bukharinites, long since politically defeated by the party, and subsequently also against many honest communists, against those party cadres who had borne the heavy load of the Civil War and the first and most difficult years of industrialization and collectivization, who actively fought against the Trotskyites and the rightists for the Leninist party line.

Stalin originated the concept "enemy of the people." This term automatically rendered it unnecessary that the ideological errors of a man or men engaged in a controversy be proven; this term made possible the employment of the most cruel repression, violating all norms of revolutionary legality, against anyone who in any way disagreed with Stalin, against those who were only suspected of hostile intent, against those who had bad reputations. This concept, "enemy of the people," actually eliminated the possibility of any kind of ideological struggle or the making of one's views known on this or that issue, even those of a practical character. In the main, and in actuality, the only proof of guilt used, against all norms of current legal science, was the "confession" of the accused himself; and, as subsequent probing proved, "confessions" were acquired through physical pressures against the accused.

*   *   *

[Stalin] discarded the Leninist method of convincing and educating; he abandoned the method of ideological struggle for that of administrative violence, mass repressions, and terror. He acted on an increasingly larger scale and more stubbornly through punitive organs, at the same time often violating all existing norms of morality and of Soviet laws.

Arbitrary behavior by one person encouraged and permitted arbitrariness in others. Mass arrests and deportations of many thousands of people, execution without trial and without normal investigation created conditions of insecurity, fear and even desperation.

This, of course, did not contribute toward unity of the party ranks and of all strata of working people, but on the contrary brought about the annihilation and expulsion from the party of workers who were loyal but inconvenient to Stalin.

*   *   *

Were our party's sacred Leninist principles observed after the death of Vladimir Ilyich?

Whereas during the first few years after Lenin's death party congresses and Central Committee plenums took place more or less regularly, later, when Stalin began increasingly to abuse his power, these principles were crudely violated. This was especially evident during the last 15 years of his life. Was it a normal situation when over 13 years elapsed between the 18th and 19th Party Congresses, years during which our party and our country experienced so many important events? These events demanded categorically that the party pass resolutions pertaining to the country's defense during the Patriotic War and to peacetime construction after the war. Even after the end of the war a congress was not convened for over 7 years.

*   *   *

In practice Stalin ignored the norms of party life and trampled on the Leninist principle of collective party leadership.

Stalin's arbitrariness *vis-à-vis* the party and its Central Committee became fully evident after the 17th Party Congress which took place in 1934.

*   *   *

It has been established that of the 139 members and candidates of the Party's Central Committee who were elected at the 17th Congress, 98 persons, i.e. 70 percent, were arrested and shot (mostly in 1937–1938). (*Indignation in the hall.*)

*   *   *

The power accumulated in the hands of one person, Stalin, led to serious consequences during the Great Patriotic War.

When we look at many of our novels, films and historical "scientific studies," the role of Stalin in the Patriotic War appears to be entirely improbable. Stalin had foreseen everything. The Soviet Army, on the basis of a strategic plan prepared by Stalin long before, used the tactics of so-called "active defense," i.e., tactics which, as we know, allowed the Germans to come up to Moscow and Stalingrad. Using such tactics the Soviet Army, supposedly thanks only to Stalin's genius, turned to the offensive and subdued the enemy. The epic victory gained through the armed might of the Land of the Soviets, through our heroic people is ascribed in this type of novel, film and "scientific study" as being completely due to the strategic genius of Stalin.

* * *

During the war and after the war Stalin put forward the thesis that the tragedy which our nation experienced in the first part of the war was the result of the "unexpected" attack of the Germans against the Soviet Union. But, Comrades, this is completely untrue. As soon as Hitler came to power in Germany he assigned himself the task of liquidating communism. The fascists were saying this openly; they did not hide their plans. In order to attain this aggressive end all sorts of pacts and blocs were created, such as the famous Berlin-Rome-Tokyo axis. Many facts from the pre-war period clearly showed that Hitler was going all out to begin a war against the Soviet state and that he had concentrated large armed units, together with armored units, near the Soviet borders.

Documents which have now been published show that by April 3, 1941, Churchill, through his ambassador to the U.S.S.R., Cripps, personally warned Stalin that the Germans had begun regrouping their armed units with the intent of attacking the Soviet Union. It is self-evident that Churchill did not do this at all because of his friendly feeling toward the Soviet nation. He had in this his own imperialistic goals—to bring Germany and the U.S.S.R. into a bloody war and thereby to strengthen the position of the British Empire. Just the same, Churchill affirmed in his writings that he sought to "warn Stalin and call his attention to the danger which threatened him." Churchill stressed this repeatedly in his dispatches of April 18 and in the following days. However, Stalin took no heed of these warnings. What is more, Stalin ordered that no credence be given to information of this sort, in order not to provoke the initiation of military operations.

* * *

When there developed an exceptionally serious situation for our army in 1942 in the Kharkov region, we correctly decided to drop an operation whose objective had been to encircle Kharkov, be-

cause the real situation at that time would have threatened our army with fatal consequences if this operation had been proceeded with.

We communicated this to Stalin, stating that the situation demanded changes in operational plans in order to prevent the enemy from liquidating a sizable concentration of our army.

Contrary to common sense, Stalin rejected our suggestion and issued the order to continue the operation aimed at the encirclement of Kharkov, despite the fact that at this time many army concentrations were themselves actually threatened with encirclement and liquidation.

* * *

And what was the result of this? The worst that we had expected. The Germans surrounded our army concentrations and consequently we lost hundreds of thousands of our soldiers. This is Stalin's military "genius"; this what it cost us. (*Movement in the hall.*)

* * *

In the same vein, let us take, for instance, our historical and military films and some works of literature; they make us feel sick. Their true objective is the propagation of the theme of praising Stalin as a military genius. Let us recall the film, "The Fall of Berlin." Here only Stalin acts; he issues orders in the hall in which there are many empty chairs and only one man approaches him and reports something to him—that is Poskrebyshev, his loyal shieldbearer. (*Laughter in the hall.*)

And where is the military command? Where is the Political Bureau? Where is the Government? What are they doing and with what are they engaged? There is nothing about them in the film. Stalin acts for everybody; he does not reckon with anyone, he asks no one for advice. Everything is shown to the nation in this false light. Why? In order to surround Stalin with glory, contrary to the facts and contrary to historical truth.

* * *

Not Stalin, but the party as a whole, the Soviet Government, our heroic army, its talented leaders and brave soldiers, the whole Soviet nation—these are the ones who assured the victory in the Great Patriotic War. (*Tempestuous and prolonged applause.*)

* * *

Comrades, let us reach for some other facts. The Soviet Union is justly considered as a model of a multi-national state because we have in practice assured the equality and friendship of all nations which live in our great fatherland.

All the more monstrous are the acts whose initiator was Stalin and which represent crude violations of the basic Leninist principles of the nationality policy of the Soviet state. We refer to the mass deportations from their native places of whole nations, together with all communists and komsomol members without any exception; this deportation action was not dictated by any military considerations.

Thus, as early as the end of 1943, when there occurred a permanent breakthrough at the fronts of the Great Patriotic War benefiting the Soviet Union, a decision was taken and carried out concerning the deportation of all the Karachai from the lands on which they lived. In the same period, at the end of December 1943, the same lot befell the whole population of the Kalmyk Autonomous Republic. In March 1944 all the Chechen and Ingush peoples were deported and the Chechen-Ingush Autonomous Republic was liquidated. In April 1944, all Balkars were deported to faraway places from the territory of the Kabardino-Balkar Autonomous Republic and the Republic itself was renamed the Karbardin Autonomous Republic. The Ukrainians avoided meeting this fate only because there were too many of them and there was no place to which to deport them. Otherwise, he would have deported them also. (*Laughter and animation in the hall.*)

* * *

The willfulness of Stalin showed itself not only in decisions concerning the internal life of the country but also in the international relations of the Soviet Union.

The July plenary session of the Central Committee studied in detail the reasons for the development of conflict with Yugoslavia. It was a shameful role which Stalin played here. The "Yu-goslav affair" contained no problems which could not have been solved through party discussions among comrades. There was no significant basis for the development of this "affair"; it was completely possible to have prevented the rupture of relations with that country. This does not mean, however, that the Yugoslav leaders did not make mistakes or did not have shortcomings. But these mistakes and shortcomings were magnified in a monstrous manner by Stalin, which resulted in a break of relations with a friendly country.

* * *

Comrades! The 20th Congress of the Communist Party of the Soviet Union has manifested with a new strength the unshakable unity of our party, its cohesiveness around the Central Committee, its resolute will to accomplish the great task of building communism. (*Tumultuous applause.*) And the fact that we present in all their ramifications the basic problems of overcoming the cult of the individual which is alien to Marxism-Leninism, as well as the problem of liquidating its burdensome consequences, is evidence of the great moral and political strength of our party. (*Prolonged applause.*)

We are absolutely certain that our party, armed with the historical resolutions of the 20th Congress, will lead the Soviet people along the Leninist path to new successes, to new victories. (*Tumultuous, prolonged applause.*)

Long live the victorious banner of our party—Leninism! (*Tumultuous, prolonged applause ending in ovation. All rise.*)

REVIEW QUESTIONS

1. What was the cult of personality?
2. In what sense was Stalin's style of rule a violation of Marxist-Leninist theory, according to Khrushchev?
3. What specific errors is Stalin accused of in this speech?
4. What do these accusations tell you about Khrushchev's intentions as the new leader of the Soviet Union?

French Students and Workers Unite in Protest

In the Soviet bloc, the brief easing in state repression initiated by Khrushchev came to an end with his abrupt fall from power in 1964. Under Leonid Brezhnev, the Soviet political leadership returned to more traditional policies, although Stalinism was not revived. When the Czechoslovakian leadership sought to loosen its ties to the Soviet Union in 1968, tanks and Soviet troops soon put an end to the Prague spring.

During this same period, the centrist governments and white-collar bureaucrats of Western Europe cooperated to produce unprecedentedly prosperous economies. Yet affluence and political stability generated their own frustrations: young people, especially, rejected the stodgy conformity of their elders, calling for a radical recasting of social, political, and economic relations. De-Stalinization in the East had stimulated the revival of Socialist and Communist parties in the West, and this inspired a new generation of radical activists operating outside of the established left-wing parties. In 1968, French students in Paris followed the lead of their Czechoslovakian counterparts, engaging in violent protests against the stifling traditionalism of the universities and against the conservatism of Charles de Gaulle's government. They were eventually joined by as many as 10 million striking workers, bringing France to a virtual standstill in mid-1968.

From *Writing on the Wall, France 1968: A Documentary Anthology*, by Vladimir Fisera (New York: St. Martin's Press, 1978), pp. 133–34, 138–39.

Your Struggle Is Our Struggle!

We are occupying the faculties, you are occupying the factories. Aren't we fighting for the same thing? Higher education only contains 10 per cent workers' children. Are we fighting so that there will be more of them, for a democratic university reform? That would be a good thing, but it's not the most important. These workers' children would just become like other students. We are not aiming for a worker's son to be a manager. We want to wipe out segregation between workers and management.

There are students who are unable to find jobs on leaving university. Are we fighting so that they'll find jobs, for a decent graduate employment policy? It would be a good thing, but it is not vital. Psychology or sociology graduates will become the selectors, the planners and psychotechnicians who will try to organise your working conditions; mathematics graduates will become engineers, perfecting maximum-productivity machines to make your life even more unbearable. Why are we, students who are products of a middle-class life, criticising capitalist society? The son of a worker who becomes a student leaves his own class. For the son of a middle-class family, it could be his opportunity to see his class in its true light, to question the role he is destined for in society and the organisation of our society. We refuse to become scholars who are out of touch with real life. We refuse to be used for the benefit of the ruling class. We want to destroy the separation that exists between those who organise and think and those who execute their decisions. We want to form a classless society; your cause is the same as ours.

You are asking for a minimum wage of 1,000 francs in the Paris area, retirement at sixty, a 40-hour week for 48 hours' pay.

STUDENT UPRISING IN PARIS (MAY 1968)

In May 1968, sparked by the government's announcement that it was closing a French university in Nanterre, students at the Sorbonne University in Paris protested with street demonstrations, which quickly broadened into political protests against the French state. The protests escalated into a national crisis after thousands of workers went on strike to support the students' grievances. Although government officials sought to deny the magnitude and significance of the May protests, such photos as this one were instrumental in eliciting popular support by communicating the revolutionary mood of Paris to a national audience. With the student protests following revolts in communist Europe and colonial Africa in the 1950s and 1960s, why did this image of Paris shock the French nation in 1968?

These are long-standing and just demands: nevertheless, they seem to be out of context with our aims. Yet you have gone on to occupy factories, take your managers as hostages, strike without warning. These forms of struggle have been made possible by perseverance and lengthy action in various enterprises, and because of the recent student battles.

These struggles are even more radical than our official aims, because they go further than simply seeking improvements for the worker within the capitalist system, they imply the destruction of the system. They are political in the true sense of the word: you are fighting not to change the Prime Minister, but so that your boss no longer retains his power in business or society. The form that your struggle has taken offers us students the model for true socialist activity: the appropriation of the means of production and of the decision-making power by the workers.

Our struggles converge. We must destroy everything that seeks to alienate us (everyday habits, the press, etc.). We must combine our occupations in the faculties and factories.

Long live the unification of our struggles!

The Workers' Red Flag Is Flying over Renault: Down with the Anti-Popular Gaullist Régime

For ten years the working class has gradually fought to gain unity in each factory; to defend in each company its working conditions, which are systematically attacked by the big capitalists. Workers' fights have succeeded in containing the bosses' offensive, but the division of the workers' forces and the policy of class collaboration which has become the rule *even at the level of the confederate leadership of the CGT*[1] have prevented the mass struggles from bringing about the downfall of the anti-popular régime of unemployment and poverty.

For a month now the progressive students who reject the bourgeois university, who want to be on the side of the people struggling against the bosses' régime, have put their full strength into the battle.

By their tenacity, their resolution, their desire to link their struggle with that of the working class, which is the main force in the struggle against the big capitalist bosses and the government, the mass of progressive students has been able to strike a resounding blow against Gaullism. The workers have understood this: the progressive current in the student movement reflects the desire of the people to fight, its desire to get rid of Gaullism. The progressive students' determination has reminded the workers that only forceful action pays off. The class-collaborating unions which have encouraged the workers to demonstrate peacefully and with dignity only in order to receive alms, the unions which have sabotaged the mass struggles at Caen, at La Rhodia in Lyon, at Schwarz-Haumont, at Alluvac, at Alès in the ceramics industry, at Dassault, at Renault, *can today no longer resist the drive of the working masses.*

The battle flag has passed into the hands of the proletariat. The leaders of the CGT have first of all attacked the students' progressive movement in a disgusting way, using the same phrases as the government is using. Then, when the workers demonstrated their desire to intervene in force to take the lead in the battle against capitalism and its régime, the CGT and PCF[2] leaderships called for a strike with petty-bourgeois, academic slogans. But the workers understood, and put all their strength into the battle.

The government wishes to quell the revolt; Pompidou has just said so. The government is panic-stricken. The repression of the workers and the progressive students, the repression of the real communists who are fighting for popular victory, will change nothing. People's hatred of the class enemy will increase tenfold. A tremendous force is rising today. *The people will win!*

---

[1] *Confédération Générale du Travail* (General Confederation of Labor), a communist labor union.

[2] *Parti Communiste Français* ("French Communist Party").

Against unemployment, starvation wages, fiendish work rates. Against police and bosses' repression. Freedom for the people!

REVIEW QUESTIONS

1. In what sense was the workers' struggle also the students' struggle?

2. What specific reforms were students and workers seeking?
3. What were their broader goals?
4. Why did radical workers at Renault reject the leadership of the General Confederation of Labor and the French Communist Party?
5. Why did they seek to ally their movement with that of the student protesters?

VÁCLAV HAVEL

FROM *The Power of the Powerless*

Václav Havel (born 1936), a playwright and poet, was one of the participants in a political dissident movement in Czechoslovakia that became known as Charter 77. The Charter, issued in Prague on New Year's Day in 1977, was a declaration and defense of human and civil rights in Czechoslovakia, and a challenge to the Czech government to lift its censorship and persecution of those who disagreed with the regime. For his Charter activities, Havel was jailed for four months in 1977 and again from 1979 to 1983, when he was released because of very poor health. He remained under close surveillance by the Czech security police until the fall of communism in Eastern Europe. In November 1989, Havel emerged as a leader of a new group that had organized to push for democratic reforms, the Civic Forum. When this group succeeded in brokering the transfer of power from the discredited communist regime in Czechoslovakia's "Velvet Revolution," Havel was named interim president in December 1989. In July 1990 he was reelected president in a democratic election. He resigned from the presidency in protest when the Czechoslovakian union was dissolved in 1992, but in 1993, Havel was reelected president of the Czech Republic, an office he held until February 2003.

Along with fellow Charter activists Rudolf Battek, Václav Benda, and Václav Cerny, Havel succeeded in giving a theoretical foundation to movements of dissent in Eastern Europe in the 1970s and 1980s. Central to the Charter's work of dissent was its defense of a free arena for public expression and political association. Their success can be gauged by the important echoes of Charter 77 that can be found, for example, in the work of Solidarity activists in Poland, who readily acknowledged the influence of the Czech dissidents. In his famous essay "The Power of the Powerless," Havel explores the function of ideology in daily life in Czechoslovakia and looks for ways to challenge its embrace.

From *The Power of the Powerless*, by Václav Havel et al. (Armonk, N.Y.: Palach Press, 1985), pp. 27–29, 35–37, 39, 78–79.

The manager of a fruit and vegetable shop places in his window, among the onions and carrots, the slogan: "Workers of the World, Unite!" Why does he do it? What is he trying to communicate to the world? Is his enthusiasm so great that he feels an irrepressible impulse to acquaint the public with his ideals? Has he really given more than a moment's thought to how such a unification might occur and what it would mean?

I think it can safely be assumed that the overwhelming majority of shopkeepers never think about the slogans they put in their windows, nor do they use them to express their real opinions. That poster was delivered to our greengrocer from the enterprise headquarters along with the onions and carrots. He put them all into the window simply because it has been done that way for years, because everyone does it, and because that is the way it has to be. If he were to refuse, there could be trouble. He could be reproached for not having the proper "decoration" in his window; someone might even accuse him of disloyalty. He does it because these things must be done if one is to get along in life. It is one of the thousands of details that guarantee him a relatively tranquil life "in harmony with society," as they say.

Obviously the greengrocer is indifferent to the semantic content of the slogan on exhibit; he does not put the slogan in his window from any personal desire to acquaint the public with the ideal it expresses. This, of course, does not mean that his action has no motive or significance at all, or that the slogan communicates a subliminal but very definite message. Verbally, it might be expressed this way: "I, the greengrocer XY, live here and I know what I must do. I behave in the manner expected of me. I can be depended upon and am beyond reproach. I am obedient and therefore I have the right to be left in peace." This message, of course, has an addressee: it is directed above, to the greengrocer's superior, and at the same time it is a shield that protects the greengrocer from potential informers. The slogan's real meaning, therefore, is rooted firmly in the greengrocer's existence. It reflects his vital interests. But what are those vital interests?

Let us take note: if the greengrocer had been instructed to display the slogan, "I am afraid and therefore unquestioningly obedient," he would not be nearly as indifferent to its semantics, even though the statement would reflect the truth. The greengrocer would be embarrassed and ashamed to put such an unequivocal statement of his own degradation in the shop window, and quite naturally so, for he is a human being and thus has a sense of his own dignity. To overcome this complication, his expression of loyalty must take the form of a sign which, at least on its textual surface, indicates a level of disinterested conviction. It must allow the greengrocer to say "What's wrong with the workers of the world uniting?" Thus the sign helps the greengrocer to conceal from himself the low foundations of his obedience, at the same time concealing the low foundations of power. It hides them behind the façade of something high. And that something is *ideology.*

Ideology is a specious way of relating to the world. It offers human beings the illusion of an identity, of dignity, and of morality while making it easier for them to *part* with them. As the repository of something "supra-personal" and objective, it enables people to deceive their conscience and conceal their true position and their inglorious *modus vivendi,* both from the world and from themselves. It is a very pragmatic, but at the same time an apparently dignified, way of legitimizing what is above, below, and on either side. It is directed towards people and towards God. It is a veil behind which human beings can hide their own "fallen existence," their trivialization, and their adaptation to the status quo. It is an excuse that everyone can use, from the greengrocer, who conceals his fear of losing his job behind an alleged interest in the unification of the workers of the world, to the highest functionary, whose interest in staying in power can be cloaked in phrases about service to the working class. The primary excusatory function of ideology, therefore, is to provide people, both as victims and pillars of the post-totalitarian system, with the illusion that the system is in harmony with the human order and the order of the universe.

*   *   *

Why in fact did our greengrocer have to put his loyalty on display in the shop window? Had he not already displayed it sufficiently in various internal or semi-public ways? At trade-union meetings, after all, he had always voted as he should. He had always taken part in various competitions. He voted in elections like a good citizen. He had even signed the "anti-Charter." Why on top of all that, should he have to declare his loyalty publicly? After all, the people who walk past his window will certainly not stop to read that, in the greengrocer's opinion, the workers of the world ought to unite. The fact of the matter is, they don't read the slogan at all, and it can be fairly assumed they don't even see it. If you were to ask a woman who had stopped in front of his shop what she saw in the window, she could certainly tell you whether or not they had tomatoes today, but it is highly unlikely that she noticed the slogan at all, let alone what it said.

It seems senseless to require the greengrocer to declare his loyalty publicly. But it makes sense nevertheless. People ignore his slogan, but they do so because such slogans are also found in other shop windows, on lamp posts, bulletin boards, in apartment windows, and on buildings; they are everywhere, in fact. They form part of the panorama of everyday life. Of course, while they ignore the details, people are very aware of that panorama as a whole. And what else is the greengrocer's slogan but a small component in that huge backdrop to daily life?

The greengrocer had to put the slogan in his window, therefore, not in the hope that someone might read it or be persuaded by it, but to contribute, along with thousands of other slogans, to the panorama that everyone is very much aware of. This panorama, of course, has a subliminal meaning as well: it reminds people where they are living and what is expected of them. It tells them what everybody else is doing, and indicates to them what they must do as well, if they don't want to be excluded, to fall into isolation, alienate themselves from society, break the rules of the game, and risk the loss of their peace and tranquility and security.

If an entire district town is plastered with slogans that no one reads, it is on the one hand a message from the district secretary to the regional secretary, but it is also something more: a small example of the principle of social *auto-totality* at work. Part of the essence of the post-totalitarian system is that it draws everyone into its sphere of power, not so they may realize themselves as human beings, but so they may surrender their human identity in favour of the identity of the system, that is, so they may become agents of the system's general automatism and servants of its self-determined goals, so they may participate in the common responsibility for it, so they may be pulled into and ensnared by it, like Faust with Mephistopheles. More than this: so they may create through their involvement a general norm and, thus, bring pressure to bear on their fellow citizens. And further: so they may learn to be comfortable with their involvement, to identify with it as though it were something natural and inevitable and ultimately, so they may—with no external urging—come to treat any non-involvement as an abnormality, as arrogance, as an attack on themselves, as a form of dropping out of society. By pulling everyone into its power structure, the post-totalitarian system makes everyone instruments of a mutual totality, the auto-totality of society.

*   *   *

Let us now imagine that one day something in our greengrocer snaps and he stops putting up the slogans merely to ingratiate himself. He stops voting in elections he knows are a farce. He begins to say what he really thinks at political meetings. And he even finds the strength in himself to express solidarity with those for whom his conscience commands him to support. In this revolt the greengrocer steps out of living within the lie. He rejects the ritual and breaks the rules of the game. He discovers once more his suppressed identity and dignity. He gives his freedom a concrete significance. His revolt is an attempt to *live within the truth.*

The bill is not long in coming. He will be relieved of his post as manager of the shop and transferred to the warehouse. His pay will be reduced. His hopes for a holiday in Bulgaria will evaporate. His children's access to higher education will be threatened. His superiors will harass him and his fellow workers will wonder about him. Most of those who apply these sanctions, however, will not do so from any authentic inner conviction but simply under pressure from conditions, the same conditions that once pressured the greengrocer to display the official slogans. They will persecute the greengrocer either because it is expected of them, or to demonstrate their loyalty, or simply as part of the general panorama, to which belongs an awareness that this is how situations of this sort are dealt with, that this, in fact, is how things are always done, particularly if one is not to become suspect oneself. The executors, therefore, behave essentially like everyone else, to a greater or lesser degree: as components of the post-totalitarian system, as agents of its automatism, as petty instruments of the social auto-totality.

*　　*　　*

If the basic job of the "dissident movements" is to serve truth, that is to serve the real aims of life, and if that necessarily develops into a defense of the individual and his or her right to a free and truthful life (that is, a defence of human rights and a struggle to see the laws respected) then another stage of this approach, perhaps the most mature stage so far, is what Václav Benda has called the development of parallel structures.

*　　*　　*

What are these structures? Ivan Jirous was the first in Czechoslovakia to formulate and apply in practice the concept of a "second culture." Although at first he was thinking chiefly of non-conformist rock music and only certain literary, artistic or performance events close to the sensibilities of those non-conformist musical groups, the term "second culture" very rapidly came to be used for the whole area of independent and repressed culture, that is, not only for art and its various currents but also for the humanities, the social sciences and philosophical thought. This "second

culture," quite naturally, has created elementary organizational forms: *samizdat* editions of books and magazines, private performances and concerts, seminars, exhibitions and so on. (In Poland all of this is vastly more developed: there are independent publishing houses and many more periodicals, even political periodicals; they have means of proliferation other than carbon copies, and so on. In the Soviet Union, *samizdat* has a longer tradition and clearly its forms are quite different.) Culture, therefore, is a sphere in which the "parallel structures" can be observed in their most highly developed form. Benda, of course, gives thought to potential or embryonic forms of such structures in other spheres as well: from a parallel information network to parallel forms of education (private universities), parallel trade unions, parallel foreign contacts, to a kind of hypothesis on a parallel economy. On the basis of these parallel structures, he then develops the notion of a "parallel *polis*" or state or, rather, he sees the rudiments of such a *polis* in these structures.

*　　*　　*

These parallel structures, it may be said, represent the most articulated expressions so far of "living within the truth." One of the most important tasks the "dissident movements" have set themselves is to support and develop them. Once again, it confirms the fact that all attempts by society to resist the pressure of the system have their essential beginnings in the pre-political area. For what else are parallel structures than an area where a different life can be lived, a life that is in harmony with its own aims and which in turn structures itself in harmony with those aims? What else are those initial attempts at social self-organization than the efforts of a certain part of society to live—as a society—within the truth, to rid itself of the self-sustaining aspects of totalitarianism and, thus, to extricate itself radically from its involvement in the post-totalitarian system. What else is it but a non-violent attempt by people to negate the system within themselves and to establish their lives on a new basis, that of their own proper identity?

REVIEW QUESTIONS

1. Why does Havel begin his analysis of what he calls the "post-totalitarian system" with the example of the political slogan in the greengrocer's shop, rather than, say, with a discussion of the power of state institutions in communist Czechoslovakia?

2. How does Havel define ideology? What is the function of ideology in the society he describes?

3. What does he mean by "auto-totality"? How is it different from the more overt forms of coercion used by the Soviet state during the Stalinist period?

4. In what way did what Havel calls "living within the truth" constitute a challenge to the status quo in Czechoslovakia in the 1970s and 1980s?

5. Is there any way in which Havel's argument about the constraints of ideology and social conformity can be applied to other forms of society besides the late-twentieth-century Eastern European socialist states that are his focus here?

MIKHAIL GORBACHEV

FROM "On Restructuring the Party's Personnel Policy"

The Polish reform movement's eventual triumph in the late 1980s would have been unimaginable if it had not been for the dramatic changes taking place in the Soviet Union. After the ouster of Khrushchev in 1964, the aging Soviet political bureaucracy had returned to business as usual, under the leadership of Leonid Brezhnev. This ended when Mikhail Gorbachev (born 1931), the youngest member of the Politburo, was elected general secretary of the Communist Party in 1985, a position he held until the collapse of the Soviet Union in 1991. Beginning in 1987, Gorbachev initiated an extensive reform campaign, intended to revitalize the Soviet economy through increased democracy, greater "openness" (glasnost) and a substantial "restructuring" (perestroika) of the political and economic institutions of the Soviet state. At the same time, he encouraged reform movements within other Eastern European states, allowing organizations such as Solidarity in Poland and Civic Forum in Czechoslovakia to emerge as powerful and influential forces for change.

Although Gorbachev embraced democratization and economic modernization, he was not ready to relinquish state control over the Soviet economy. Restructuring introduced limited free-market mechanisms, but it also upheld the fundamental premise of the state-planned economy. In an important speech to the Communist Party Central Committee in January 1987, Gorbachev laid out his critiques of the existing Soviet system and his plans for reforming that system.

From *Speeches and Writings*, by Mikhail Gorbachev (New York: Pergamon Press, 1986).

Restructuring Is an Objective Necessity

Our Plenary Meeting is taking place in the year of the 70th anniversary of the Great October Socialist Revolution. Almost seven decades ago the Leninist Party raised over the country the victorious banner of Socialist revolution, of struggle for Socialism, freedom, equality, social justice and progress and against oppression and exploitation, poverty and the subjugation of minority nationalities.

For the first time in world history, the working man and his interests and needs were made the focal point of state policy. The Soviet Union achieved truly epoch-making successes in political, economic, social, cultural and intellectual development as it built Socialist society. Under the leadership of the Party, the Soviet people built Socialism, won the victory over Nazism in the Great Patriotic War, rehabilitated and strengthened the national economy and made their homeland a mighty power.

Our achievements are immense and indubitable and the Soviet people rightfully take pride in their successes. They constitute a firm base for the fulfilment of our current programmes and our plans for the future. But the Party must see life in its entirety and complexity. No accomplishments, not even the most impressive, should obscure either contradictions in societal development or our mistakes and failings.

*   *   *

A need for change was coming to a head in the economy and other fields—but it was not realized through the political and practical work of the Party and the State.

What was the reason for that complex and controversial situation?

The main cause—and the Politburo considers it necessary to say so with utmost frankness at the Plenary Meeting—was that the CPSU Central Committee and the leadership of the country failed, primarily for subjective reasons, to see in time and in full the need for change and the danger of the intensification of crisis phenomena in

society, and to formulate a clear policy for overcoming them and making better use of the opportunities intrinsic to the Socialist system.

*   *   *

In fact, a whole system of weakening the economic tools of government emerged and a mechanism of retarding socio-economic development and hindering progressive change developed, which made it possible to tap and use the advantages of Socialism. That retarding process was rooted in serious shortcomings in the functioning of the institutions of Socialist democracy, outdated political and theoretical concepts, that often did not correspond to reality, and conservative managerial machinery.

All this adversely affected development in many spheres in the life of society. Take material production: the growth rates of the national income in the past three five-year plan periods dropped by more than half. Most plan targets have not been met since the early 1970s. The economy as a whole became cumbersome and relatively unreceptive to innovation. The quality of a considerable part of the output no longer met current requirements, and imbalances in production became aggravated.

*   *   *

Having successfully resolved the question of employment and provided basic social guarantees, at the same time we failed to realize in full the potential of Socialism to improve housing conditions, food supply, transport, health care and education, and to solve a number of other vital problems.

There were violations of the most important principle of Socialism—distribution according to work. Efforts to control unearned income were indecisive. The policy of material and moral incentive to work efficiently was inconsistent. Large, unjustified bonuses and various additional incentives were paid and figure-padding for profit was allowed to take place. Parasitic sentiments grew stronger and the mentality of "wage levelling" began to take hold, and that hit workers who could work better and wanted to work better, while making life easier for the idle.

The violation of the organic relationship between the measure of work and measure of consumption not only perverts the attitude to work, holding back the growth of productivity, but leads to distortion of the principle of social justice—and that is a question of great political importance.

Elements of social corrosion that emerged in the past few years had a negative effect on society's morale and inconspicuously eroded the lofty moral values which have always been characteristic of our people and of which we are proud—ideological dedication, labour enthusiasm and Soviet patriotism.

As an inevitable consequence of all this, interest in the affairs of society slackened, manifestations of callousness and scepticism appeared and the role of moral incentive to work declined. The stratum of people, some of them young people, whose ultimate goal in life was material wellbeing and gain by any means, grew wider. Their cynical stand acquired more and more aggressive forms, poisoning the mentality of those around them and triggering a wave of consumerism. The spread of alcohol and drug abuse and a rise in crime became indicators of the decline of social mores.

Disregard for laws, report-padding, bribe-taking and the encouragement of toadyism and sycophancy had a deleterious influence on the moral atmosphere in society.

Real care for people, for the conditions of their life and work and for social wellbeing were often replaced with political flirtation—the mass distribution of awards, titles and prizes. An atmosphere of permissiveness was taking shape, and exactingness, discipline and responsibility were declining.

Serious shortcomings in ideological and political education were in many cases disguised with ostentatious activities and campaigns and celebrations of numerous jubilees at the centre and in the provinces. The world of day-to-day realities and that of make-believe wellbeing were increasingly parting ways.

The ideology and mentality of stagnation had their effect on culture, literature and the arts. Criteria in appraising artistic creative work were debased. As a consequence, quite a few mediocre, faceless works appeared, which did not give anything to the mind or the heart, along with works which raised serious social and moral problems and reflected true to life conflicts. Stereotypes from capitalist mass culture, with its propagation of vulgarity, primitive tastes and spiritual callousness, began to infiltrate Soviet society to a larger extent.

*   *   *

The situation in the Party was also influenced by the fact that in a number of cases the Party bodies did not attach proper attention to strict compliance with the Leninist principles and norms of Party life. This made itself especially manifest, perhaps, in breaches of the principle of collective leadership. What I mean is the weakening of the role of Party meetings and elective bodies, which denied Communists the opportunity to contribute energetically to the discussion of vital issues and, in the analysis, actually to influence the atmosphere in work collectives and in society as a whole.

The principle of equality between Communists was often violated. Many Party members in senior executive positions were beyond control or criticism, which resulted in failures in work and serious breaches of Party ethics.

We cannot overlook the just indignation of working people at the conduct of senior officials in whom trust and authority had been vested and who were called upon to stand guard over the interests of the state and its citizens, and who themselves abused their authority, suppressed criticism and sought personal gain, some even becoming accomplices in—if not organizers of—criminal activities.

*   *   *

It was in this situation that the question of accelerating the socio-economic development of the country—the question of restructuring—was raised. The case in point is actually a radical turn, comprising measures of a revolutionary character. When we talk about restructuring and associated processes of profound democratization, we mean truly revolutionary and comprehensive transformations in society.

We need to make this decisive turn because we simply do not have the choice of any other way. We must not retreat and do not have anywhere to retreat to.

*　　*　　*

The main purport of our strategy is to combine the achievements of the scientific and technological revolution with a plan-based economy and set the entire potential of Socialism going again.

Restructuring is reliance on the creative endeavour of the masses, all-round extension of democracy and Socialist self-government, encouragement of initiative and self-organized activities, better discipline and order, greater openness, criticism and self-criticism in all fields of public life, and high respect for the value and dignity of the individual.

Restructuring means the ever greater role of intensive growth factors in Soviet economic development, reinstatement and enhancement of Leninist principles of democratic centralism in the management of the national economy, employment of cost benefit methods of management everywhere, renunciation of the domineering style of management and administration by decree, conversion of all units of the economy to the principles of full-scale economic accountability and new forms of organizing labour and production, and every kind of incentive for innovation and Socialist enterprise.

Restructuring means a decisive turn to science, the businesslike partnership of science and practice for the sake of the highest possible end-results, the ability to ground any undertaking on sound scientific basis, readiness and keen desire on the part of scientists to assist the Party's policy of revitalizing society, and concern for the development of science and research personnel and for their active engagement in the process of change.

Restructuring means the priority development of the social sphere, increasingly satisfying the Soviet people's requirements for adequate working and living conditions, recreational facilities, education and medical services. It means unfailing concern for raising the intellectual and cultural standards of every person and of society as a whole: it is the ability to combine decision making on the major, cardinal problems of public life with that on the current issues of immediate interest to the people.

Restructuring means vigorously ridding society of any deviations from Socialist morals, consistently enforcing the principles of social justice, harmony between words and deeds, indivisibility of rights and duties, promotion of conscientious, high quality work, and overcoming pay-levelling and consumerism.

The final aim of the restructuring effort is, I believe, clear: it is to effect a thorough going change in all aspects of public life, to give Socialism the most advanced forms of social organization, and to bring out the humane nature of our system in all decisive aspects—economic, social, political and moral—to the fullest possible degree.

This is, comrades, the task we have in motion. The restructuring effort is unfolding along the entire front. It is acquiring a new quality, not only gaining in scope but also penetrating the deepest fibres of life.

*　　*　　*

To Deepen Socialist Democratism and Develop Self-government by the People

We now understand better than ever before the profundity of Lenin's thought about the vital, inner link between Socialism and democracy.

The entire historical experience of our country has convincingly demonstrated that the Socialist System has in practice ensured citizens' political and socio-economic rights and personal freedoms, demonstrated the advantages of Soviet democracy and given each person confidence in the morrow.

But in conditions of restructuring, when the task of intensifying the human factor has become so urgent, we must return once again to Lenin's approach to the question of the maximum democratism of the Socialist system under which people feel that they are their own masters and creators.

"We must be guided by experience, we must allow complete freedom to the creative faculties of the masses," Vladimir Lenin said.

Indeed, democracy, the essence of which is the power of the man of labour, is the form of realizing his extensive political and civil rights, his interest in transformations and practical participation in their implementation.

A simple and lucid thought is becoming increasingly entrenched in social consciousness: a house can be put in order only by a person who feels that he owns this house. This truth is correct not only in the wordly sense but also in the sociopolitical one.

This truth must be undeviatingly applied in practice. I repeat, in practice. Otherwise the human factor will be ineffectual.

It is only through the consistent development of the democratic forms inherent in Socialism, through a broadening of self-government, that our advancement in production, science and technology, literature, culture and the arts, in all areas of social life, is possible. It is only this way that ensures conscientious discipline. The restructuring itself is possible only through democracy and due to democracy. It is only this way that it is possible to give scope to Socialism's most powerful creative force—free labour and free thought in a free country.

Therefore the further democratization of Soviet society is becoming the Party's urgent task. Herein, properly speaking, lies the essence of the course of the April Plenum, of the 27th Congress of the CPSU for deepening Socialist self-government by the people. The point at issue is, certainly, not any break up of our political system. We should make use of all its potentialities with maximum effectiveness, fill the work of the Party, the Soviets and the government bodies, public organizations and work collectives with deep democratic contents, breathe new life into all cells of the social organism.

This process is already under way in the country. The life of the Party organizations is becoming more full-blooded. Criticism and self-criticism are broadening. The mass media have begun working more actively. The Soviet people can sense the salutary effect of openness, which is becoming a norm of society's life.

The congresses of the creative unions proceeded in an atmosphere of principledness and criticism. New public organizations are being set up. The All-Union Organization of War and Labour Veterans has come into being. The Soviet Cultural Fund has been set up. Work is under way to set up women's councils. All these facts indicate the growing participation of the working people in social affairs and in the administration of the country.

*   *   *

We wish to turn our country into a model of a highly developed state, into a society with the most advanced economy, the broadest democracy, the most humane and lofty ethics, where the working man will feel that he is master, will enjoy all the benefits of material and spiritual culture, where the future of his children will be secure, where he will have everything that is necessary for a full and interesting life. And even sceptics would be forced to say: yes, the Bolsheviks can accomplish anything. Yes, truth is on their side. Yes, Socialism is a system serving man, working for his benefit, in his social and economic interests, for his spiritual elevation.

REVIEW QUESTIONS

1. Why, according to Gorbachev, was restructuring an objective necessity?
2. What social, political, and economic forms would this restructuring take?

3. Why was it crucial that social, political, and economic reform go hand in hand?

4. What elements of free-market capitalism were included in Gorbachev's economic restructuring?

5. In what ways did Gorbachev remain a traditional communist in his economic thinking?

SIMONE DE BEAUVOIR

FROM *The Second Sex*

During the twentieth century, the traditional divisions between the experiences of men and women started to blur. New technologies decreased the premium once placed on men's greater physical strength, making it possible for women to do jobs once reserved only for men. At the same time, female fertility decreased substantially: as improved health conditions allowed more children to survive to adulthood, couples increasingly sought to have fewer children. New birth-control technologies made this increasingly easy. Whereas reproductive and child-rearing duties had once played a predominant role in most women's adult lives, motherhood now became only one aspect of a more varied lifetime experience.

However, if the material conditions of women's lives had changed significantly, attitudes toward women had not. If anything, the immediate postwar period saw a resurrection of traditional models of femininity and masculinity. On the other hand, the popularization of existentialist philosophy, which argued that every individual has the responsibility to be an active agent, to create the self through "engagement" with other human beings, helped to fuel a growing resistance to "objectification"— entrapment in the limiting conceptual categories of outside society—whether on the basis of race, gender, or class. In 1949 the French novelist and existential philosopher Simone de Beauvoir (1908–1986) published The Second Sex, *an extended philosophical essay that called on women to reject socially imposed models of appropriate feminine identity and to become authentic individuals in their own right.* The Second Sex *was initially greeted with outrage and howls of derision, but the revival of feminism in the 1960s brought de Beauvoir a new, more sympathetic audience, and her arguments exercised a strong influence over the U.S. and European women's movements.*

From *The Second Sex*, by Simone de Beauvoir (Paris: Gallimard, 1997), translated by Cat Nilan for the current edition.

I f being female is not a sufficient definition of woman, if we also refuse to explain her through "the eternal feminine," and if we nevertheless admit (if only provisionally), that there are women on this planet, then we are forced to ask ourselves the question: what is a woman?

Simply stating the problem suggests one immediate response. It is significant that I ask this question. A man would never think of writing a book about the peculiar position that males occupy in the ranks of humanity. If I want to define myself, I am first obligated to declare: "I am a woman." That truth constitutes the foundation upon which all other affirmations will be based. A man never begins by declaring himself an individual of a certain sex: that he is a man goes without saying. It is only as a formality that "male" and "female" appear as symmetrical terms in town hall records and identification papers. The relationship between the sexes is not that of two electrical poles: the man represents both the positive and the neutral to such an extent that in French one says "*les hommes*" ("men") to designate all human beings. * * * Woman is so strongly associated with the negative that her every trait is imputed to her as a limitation, without reciprocity. It annoys me when, during the course of an abstract discussion, a man says: "You think such and such a thing because you are a woman." I know that my only defense is to reply: "I believe it because it is true," eliminating in that manner my own subjectivity. It's out of the question to answer: "And you think the contrary because you are a man," because it is understood that the fact of being a man is not a peculiarity. A man is in the right in being a man; it is the woman who is in the wrong. In practice, just as the ancients identified an absolute vertical against which the oblique was defined, there is an absolute human type that is masculine. Woman has ovaries, a uterus; these are the peculiarities that enclose her in her subjectivity. It is often said that she thinks with her glands. Man arrogantly forgets that his own anatomy also includes hormones, testicles. He experiences his body as being in a direct and normal relationship with the world, which he believes he apprehends objectively, whereas he considers the body of a woman to be weighted down by all of its specificities: an obstacle, a prison. * * * Humanity is male and man defines woman not in and of herself but relative to him; she is not considered an autonomous being. * * * And she is nothing other than what man

decides; thus she is called "the sex," meaning that she appears to the male, in essence, as a sexuated being. For him, she is sex, and therefore she is so absolutely. She is defined and differentiated in relation to man and not he in relation to her; she is the inessential as compared with the essential. He is the Subject, he is the Absolute: she is the Other.

The category of the *Other* is as old as consciousness itself. * * * No collectivity ever defines itself as the One without immediately positing an Other in opposition to it. If three travelers happen to be gathered together by chance in the same cabin, that is enough to make all other travelers vaguely hostile "others." For the villager, all of the people who do not belong to his village are suspect "others"; for the native of one country, the inhabitants of other countries are "foreigners." Jews are "others" to the antisemite; Blacks are "others" to American racists; indigenous peoples are "others" to the colonizers; proletarians are "others" to the propertied classes. * * *

But the other consciousness opposes to this claim a reciprocal claim: when he travels, the native is shocked to discover that the natives of neighboring countries regard him in his turn as a foreigner. Between villages, clans, nations, and classes there are wars, potlatches, markets, treaties, and conflicts that deprive the idea of the Other of its absolute sense and reveal its relativity. Willingly or not, individuals and groups are forced to recognize the reciprocity of their relations. How then has it happened that between the sexes that reciprocity has not been admitted, that one of the terms has affirmed itself as the only essential one, denying all relativity in relation to its corollary, defining it as pure otherness? Why don't women contest male sovereignty? No subject spontaneously admits, from the first, that it is the inessential. It is not the Other who by defining himself as Other defines the One: he is posited as Other by the One posing himself as One. But in order for the return from Other to One not to happen, it is necessary that he submit to this foreign point of view. Where does woman's submission come from?

*   *   *

* * * The parallel established by Bebel between women and the proletariat is the most apt: like women, proletarians are not a minority and they have never constituted a separate collectivity. Nevertheless, in the absence of a *single* event, it is a historical development that explains their existence as a class and which accounts for the distribution of *these* individuals in that class. There have not always been proletarians; there have always been women. Women are women through their physiology. However far one goes back into history, women have always been subordinated to man. Their dependency is not the consequence of an event or a development; it did not *happen*. It is in part because otherness escapes the accidental character of a historical fact in this case that it appears here as an absolute. Something that happened over time can be undone at another time. The Blacks of Haiti, among others, have proved this. On the other hand, it would appear that a natural condition defies change. In truth, nature is no more an immutable given than historical reality. If woman reveals herself as the inessential that never returns to the essential, it is because she herself does not set that reversal into motion. Proletarians say "We." Blacks too. Positing themselves as subjects they change the bourgeoisie and Whites into "others." * * * Women do not say "we." Men say "women" and women use this word to designate themselves, but they do not posit themselves authentically as Subject. Proletarians made a revolution in Russia, the Blacks in Haiti, the Indochinese are fighting in Indochina. Women's action has never been anything more than a symbolic disturbance. They have won only what men were willing to concede to them. They have taken nothing: they have merely received.

*   *   *

There are deep analogies between the situation of women and that of Blacks. Today both are emancipating themselves from the same paternalism and the former master class wishes to keep them in "their place," that is to say, the place it has chosen for them. In both cases, that master class lavishes more or less sincere praise on the virtues of the "good Black," childish, happy-go-lucky, his soul slumbering, and on "the real woman," who is frivolous, puerile, irresponsible, submissive to man. In both cases, it derives its argument from the situation it has in fact created. George Bernard Shaw's witticism is well known: "The white American," he said, in essence, "relegates the Black to the rank of shoeshine boy and he concludes from this that the Black is good for nothing but shining shoes." This vicious circle is found in all analogous circumstances; when an individual, or a group of individuals, is held in a situation of inferiority, the fact is that he *is* inferior. But we must be clear about what we mean by *to be*. It is in bad faith to give it a substantial meaning, when it should be read in the dynamic, Hegelian sense: *to be* is to have become, it is to have been made that which one appears to be. Yes, as a whole women today *are* inferior to men, which is to say that their situation is offered them fewer opportunities. The problem is determining whether or not this state of affairs should continue.

Many men hope that it will; not all of them have disarmed themselves yet. The conservative bourgeoisie continues to see women's emancipation as a menace to its morality and its interests. Certain males fear feminine competition. Just the other day, a male student declared in the *Hebdo-Latin:* "Every female student who takes a position as a doctor or a lawyer *steals* a place from us." He certainly doesn't have any questions about his rights over this world. But it is not only economic concerns that are at play here. One of the benefits that oppression guarantees to the oppressors is that the humblest among them feels himself *superior:* a "poor White" in the Southern United States consoles himself by saying that he is not a "dirty Negro," and more affluent Whites skillfully exploit this pride. In the same way, the most mediocre of males believes himself a demigod compared with women.

REVIEW QUESTIONS

1. What *is* a woman, according to de Beauvoir?
2. How has woman become an "Other"?
3. How can she become a "Self"?

4. In what ways are the conditions of blacks, Jews, workers, and women similar? In what ways are they different?
5. Why do you think de Beauvoir chose to make these particular comparisons?

28 ✎ A WORLD WITHOUT WALLS: GLOBALIZATION AND THE WEST

At the beginning of recorded human history, the entire population of the world probably consisted of fewer than 10 million people. Ten thousand years later, the world population is rapidly approaching 7 billion. Human ingenuity has made possible the production of enough food and material goods to sustain this enormous population, but this achievement puts serious strains on the environment and creates intense competition for limited resources.

Innovations in transportation and communication have made it possible for people around the world to have far more intimate and informed relations with each other than ever before. Earth's surface remains subdivided by national boundaries, but the problems confronting humanity are, increasingly, international problems that can be solved only through global cooperation. From a historical perspective, it is already clear that human history has become world history and that even the most isolated regions are no longer insulated from the general trend toward global integration.

One of the most important factors in the emerging history of the contemporary world is the deep divide separating developed and developing nations. Most of the inhabitants of affluent and technologically advanced regions such as Japan, the United States, and Western Europe enjoy extremely high standards of living and can expect to live long and healthy lives. The four-fifths of Earth's people who live in developing regions (sometimes called the Third World) regularly suffer from a lack of basic necessities, including adequate food, clean drinking water, and a bare minimum of health care.

The reasons for this dramatic disparity in the distribution of wealth are complex, but they are closely linked to the historical processes of colonization and decolonization. During the late nineteenth century, imperialist powers acquired colonies in the hopes of procuring raw materials, cheap labor, and na-

tional grandeur. The builders of empire were largely uninterested in modernizing the economies or political systems of their colonies, and they often destroyed indigenous industries and governments at the same time that they crushed expressions of cultural resistance. After the Second World War, most of these colonies regained their independence, as a result of either more or less voluntary withdrawal on the part of the colonizers or violent conflict.

The newly independent states of Africa and Asia faced substantial challenges, not the least of which were the international tensions generated by the Cold War. When the Soviet Union and the United States sought allies in the Third World, both superpowers tended to support dictators friendly to their strategic aims, thereby discouraging the emergence of independent democracies. In addition, most former colonies were strongly disadvantaged in the economic arena by technological backwardness, a legacy of colonial rule. The developed nations have been slow to come to the aid of struggling Third World nations, and the political instability produced by desperate poverty and often violent competition for land and resources continues to threaten global peace and prosperity.

In the 1990s, all of these historical tensions converged as the world entered a new phase of instability. The collapse of communism in Eastern Europe and the Soviet Union brought greater political freedoms to many millions of people, but this sudden transformation also produced prolonged political crisis in many areas, leading to the violent breakup of Yugoslavia, the splitting of Czechoslovakia into two ethnically distinct nations, the war in Chechnya, and the ever-present threat of renewed ethnic violence throughout the former communist world. In this uncertain context, the international bodies that had their origins in the Cold War—NATO, the United Nations, the European Union—struggled to redefine their roles, often with only marginal success. In the former Yugoslavia and in Rwanda, over a million people were killed in genocidal conflicts, as the rest of the "civilized" world watched. The major powers in Europe and the United States were helpless to coordinate a coherent response or to stop the killing, in spite of fifty years of international treaties and legal decisions designed to prevent a recurrence of the Holocaust in the aftermath of World War II.

Al Qaeda's September 11, 2001 attacks on New York and Washington thus came at a moment when Europeans and Americans were less sure than ever about how best to confront the problems facing the world at the dawn of the twenty-first century. The Bush administration's response—a doctrine of preemptive war—was a major revision of decades of American policy that committed the United States to unilateral action in the face of perceived threats. In the buildup to the second Iraq war in 2003, it was difficult for many in the United States to avoid thinking in terms of a global clash of civilizations—East versus West. However, such simplistic formulations obscure the complex past that underlies the history of terrorism in the Middle East, its relationship to Islamic traditions, and more recent events in the region.

These immediate crises, as serious as they are, might only be a part of a larger set of problems facing the world today. As developing regions struggle to come to terms with the legacies of colonialism and superpower conflict, they are also called on to participate in forging global solutions to global problems. Uncontrolled population growth, the exploitation and mismanagement of natural resources, and unregulated industrial and commercial development pose serious dangers to the survival of all humanity. Similarly, the transfer of people, capital, and consumer goods and land, air, and water pollution can no longer be contained within national boundaries. While individual identity remains deeply rooted in local cultural traditions, the future history of humanity may hinge on our ability to develop a model of global citizenship that balances the rights of the individual with the responsibilities of all human beings to both the local and the global communities.

MAHATMA GANDHI

FROM *The Essential Writings*

The Indian struggle for independence from Great Britain can be traced back to the early nineteenth century, but it first became a mass movement after the First World War. Indian nationalists supported India's participation in the war on the Allied side, but they were angered by Britain's failure to reward this service with a greater degree of self-government. Under the charismatic leadership of Mahatma ("Great Soul") Gandhi (1869–1948), the Indian independence movement became a model for other colonial independence struggles.

Having trained as a lawyer in Britain, the young Mohandas Gandhi worked for many years among the East Indian community of South Africa, where he experienced the effects of racial discrimination in the acute form of apartheid. As he struggled to maintain his human dignity in a system that looked on him as nothing more than a common laborer, he drew sustenance from the Hindu religious traditions of India, building his "soul force" through a commitment to truth, love, and ascetic practices (such as vegetarianism, sexual abstinence, and manual labor). When he returned to India in 1913, Gandhi became active in the Indian National Congress and directed the fledgling independence movement toward adopting a strategy of peaceful noncooperation. At the same time, he also lobbied for economic self-sufficiency. Taking as his symbol the spinning wheel, he argued that the spiritual and material poverty of the Indian masses could be alleviated through the revival of indigenous traditions of small-scale, low-tech textile production.

From *The Essential Writings of Mahatma Gandhi*, edited by Raghavan Iyer (Oxford: Oxford University Press, 1991).

FROM **The Doctrine of the Sword**

In this age of the rule of brute force, it is almost impossible for anyone to believe that anyone else could possibly reject the law of the final supremacy of brute force. And so I receive anonymous letters advising me that I must not interfere with the progress of non-co-operation even though popular violence may break out. Others come to me and assuming that secretly I must be plotting violence, inquire when the happy moment for declaring open violence will arrive. They assure me that the English will never yield to anything but violence secret or open. Yet others, I am informed, believe that I am the most rascally person living in India because I never give out my real intention and that they have not a shadow of a doubt that I believe in violence just as much as most people do.

Such being the hold that the doctrine of the sword has on the majority of mankind, and as success of non-co-operation depends principally on absence of violence during its pendency and as my views in this matter affect the conduct of a large number of people, I am anxious to state them as clearly as possible.

I do believe that where there is only a choice between cowardice and violence I would advise violence. Thus when my eldest son asked me what he should have done, had he been present when I was almost fatally assaulted in 1908, whether he should have run away and seen me killed or whether he should have used his physical force which he could and wanted to use, and defended me, I told him that it was his duty to defend me even by using violence. Hence it was that I took part in the Boer War, the so-called Zulu rebellion and the late War. Hence also do I advocate training in arms for those who believe in the method of violence. I would rather have India resort to arms in order to defend her honour than that she should in a cowardly manner become or remain a helpless witness to her own dishonour.

But I believe that non-violence is infinitely superior to violence, forgiveness is more manly than punishment. *Kshama virasya bhushanam.* "For-giveness adorns a soldier." But abstinence is forgiveness only when there is the power to punish; it is meaningless when it pretends to proceed from a helpless creature. A mouse hardly forgives a cat when it allows itself to be torn to pieces by her. I, therefore, appreciate the sentiment of those who cry out for the condign punishment of General Dyer and his ilk. They would tear him to pieces if they could. But I do not believe India to be helpless. I do not believe myself to be a helpless creature. Only I want to use India's and my strength for a better purpose.

Let me not be misunderstood. Strength does not come from physical capacity. It comes from an indomitable will. An average Zulu is any way more than a match for an average Englishman in bodily capacity. But he flees from an English boy, because he fears the boy's revolver or those who will use it for him. He fears death and is nerveless in spite of his burly figure. We in India may in a moment realize that one hundred thousand Englishmen need not frighten three hundred million human beings. A definite forgiveness would therefore mean a definite recognition of our strength. With enlightened forgiveness must come a mighty wave of strength in us, which would make it impossible for a Dyer and a Frank Johnson to heap affront upon India's devoted head. It matters little to me that for the moment I do not drive my point home. We feel too downtrodden not to be angry and revengeful. But I must not refrain from saying that India can gain more by waiving the right of punishment. We have better work to do, a better mission to deliver to the world.

I am not a visionary. I claim to be a practical idealist. The religion of non-violence is not meant merely for the * * * saints. It is meant for the common people as well. Non-violence is the law of our species as violence is the law of the brute. The spirit lies dormant in the brute and he knows no law but that of physical might. The dignity of man requires obedience to a higher law—to the strength of the spirit.

I have therefore ventured to place before India the ancient law of self-sacrifice. * * *

Non-violence in its dynamic condition means

conscious suffering. It does not mean meek submission to the will of the evil-doer, but it means the putting of one's whole soul against the will of the tyrant. Working under this law of our being, it is possible for a single individual to defy the whole might of an unjust empire to save his honour, his religion, his soul and lay the foundation for that empire's fall or its regeneration.

And so I am not pleading for India to practise non-violence because it is weak. I want her to practise non-violence being conscious of her strength and power. No training in arms is required for realization of her strength. We seem to need it because we seem to think that we are but a lump of flesh. I want India to recognize that she has a soul that cannot perish and that can rise triumphant above every physical weakness and defy the physical combination of a whole world. What is the meaning of Rama, a mere human being, with his host of monkeys, pitting himself against the insolent strength of ten-headed Ravana surrounded in supposed safety by the raging waters on all sides of Lanka? Does it not mean the conquest of physical might by spiritual strength? However, being a practical man, I do not wait till India recognizes the practicability of the spiritual life in the political world. India considers herself to be powerless and paralysed before the machine-guns, the tanks and the aeroplanes of the English. And she takes up non-co-operation out of her weakness. It must still serve the same purpose, namely, bring her delivery from the crushing weight of British injustice if a sufficient number of people practise it.

* * * I invite even the school of violence to give this peaceful non-co-operation a trial. It will not fail through its inherent weakness. It may fail because of poverty of response. Then will be the time for real danger. The high-souled men, who are unable to suffer national humiliation any longer, will want to vent their wrath. They will take to violence. So far as I know, they must perish without delivering themselves or their country from the wrong. If India takes up the doctrine of the sword, she may gain momentary victory. Then India will cease to be the pride of my heart. I am wedded to India because I owe my all to her. I believe absolutely that she has a mission for the world. She is not to copy Europe blindly. India's acceptance of the doctrine of the sword will be the hour of my trial. I hope I shall not be found wanting. My religion has no geographical limits. If I have a living faith in it, it will transcend my love for India herself. My life is dedicated to service of India through the religion of non-violence which I believe to be the root of Hinduism.

Meanwhile I urge those who distrust me, not to disturb the even working of the struggle that has just commenced, by inciting to violence in the belief that I want violence. I detest secrecy as a sin. Let them give non-violent non-co-operation a trial and they will find that I had no mental reservation whatsoever.

FROM Non-Violence— The Greatest Force

* * *

The cry for peace will be a cry in the wilderness, so long as the spirit of non-violence does not dominate millions of men and women.

An armed conflict between nations horrifies us. But the economic war is no better than an armed conflict. This is like a surgical operation. An economic war is prolonged torture. And its ravages are no less terrible than those depicted in the literature on war properly so called. We think nothing of the other because we are used to its deadly effects.

Many of us in India shudder to see blood spilled. Many of us resent cow-slaughter, but we think nothing of the slow torture through which by our greed we put our people and cattle. But because we are used to this lingering death, we think no more about it.

The movement against war is sound. I pray for its success. But I cannot help the gnawing fear that the movement will fail, if it does not touch the root of all evil—man's greed.

Will America, England and the other great

GANDHI AT SPINNING WHEEL   MARGARET BOURKE-WHITE

Mahatma Gandhi's strategy of achieving independence for India through boycotts and nonparticipation in civil institutions marks a high point in nonviolent political struggles in the twentieth century. A cornerstone of Gandhi's political program was his assertion that when Indians could break their economic dependence on British manufacturers (of textiles, for example), Indian political independence could be achieved. How does this photograph of Gandhi capture the philosophy and program of his politics?

nations of the West continue to exploit the so-called weaker or uncivilized races and hope to attain peace that the whole world is pining for? Or will Americans continue to prey upon one another, have commercial rivalries and yet expect to dictate peace to the world?

Not till the spirit is changed can the form be altered. The form is merely an expression of the spirit within. We may succeed in seemingly altering the form but the alteration will be a mere make-believe if the spirit within remains unalterable. A whited sepulchre still conceals beneath it the rotting flesh and bone.

Far be it from me to discount or under-rate the great effort that is being made in the West to kill the war-spirit. Mine is merely a word of caution as from a fellow-seeker who has been striving in his own humble manner after the same thing, maybe in a different way, no doubt on a much smaller scale. But if the experiment demonstrably succeeds on the smaller field and, if those who are working on the larger field have not overtaken me, it will at least pave the way for a similar experiment on a large field.

I observe in the limited field in which I find myself, that unless I can reach the hearts of men and women, I am able to do nothing. I observe further that so long as the spirit of hate persists in some shape or other, it is impossible to establish peace or to gain our freedom by peaceful effort. We cannot love one another, if we hate Englishmen. We cannot love the Japanese and hate Englishmen. We must either let the Law of Love rule us through and through or not at all. Love among ourselves based on hatred of others breaks down under the slightest pressure. The fact is such love is never real love. It is an armed peace. And so it will be in this great movement in the West against war. War will only be stopped when the conscience of mankind has become sufficiently elevated to recognize the undisputed supremacy of the Law of Love in all the walks of life. Some say this will never come to pass. I shall retain the faith till the end of my earthly existence that it shall come to pass.

REVIEW QUESTIONS

1. Why must the strategy of nonviolence proceed from a position of strength, according to Gandhi?
2. In what ways were Indians strong, according to Gandhi?
3. What does Gandhi mean by "economic war"?
4. How can human beings bring an end to *all* wars?
5. Why do you think the strategy of passive resistance to oppression was so popular among many participants in the independence and civil rights movements of the mid–twentieth century?

FRANTZ FANON

FROM *The Wretched of the Earth*

Gandhi's strategy of peaceful resistance had a profound impact on other twentieth-century movements for social change. Yet many independence activists rejected this approach, arguing that the imperial powers would never relinquish their control over colonial holdings without violence. Instead, these activists looked for inspiration to the armed struggles led by Ho Chi Minh in Vietnam and Fidel Castro in Cuba.

Militant anti-imperialists recognized that resistance movements could never outgun the colonizers, but they were convinced that sustained guerilla warfare would eventually convince the imperial powers that the costs of maintaining control over a colony were simply too high.

For Frantz Fanon (1925–1961), violence was not simply a tactic in anti-imperial conflicts: it also served an important role in the psychological decolonization of subject peoples. Born in the French colony of Martinique, Fanon trained as a psychiatrist in Martinique and France before becoming an active participant in the Algerian independence movement of the 1950s. Fanon argued that the physical and psychological violence of the colonial system had traumatized colonized peoples, generating individual and communal mental illness. Violent resistance to imperialism would permit subject peoples to purge this trauma and to build a new and independent community based on their shared experience of retaliation. In The Wretched of the Earth, *published in 1961 shortly before his untimely death from cancer, Fanon analyzed anti-imperial violence as a pathological response to a pathological system and as a necessary therapy for the social maladies generated by colonialism.*

From *The Wretched of the Earth*, by Frantz Fanon, translated by Constance Farrington (New York: Grove/Atlantic, 1963), pp. 83–84, 88–90, 96–98, 102.

*   *   *

The existence of an armed struggle shows that the people are decided to trust to violent methods only. He of whom *they* have never stopped saying that the only language he understands is that of force, decides to give utterance by force. In fact, as always, the settler has shown him the way he should take if he is to become free. The argument the native chooses has been furnished by the settler, and by an ironic turning of the tables it is the native who now affirms that the colonialist understands nothing but force. The colonial regime owes its legitimacy to force and at no time tries to hide this aspect of things. Every statue, whether of Faidherbe or of Lyautey, of Bugeaud or of Sergeant Blandan—all these conquistadors perched on colonial soil do not cease from proclaiming one and the same thing: "We are here by the force of bayonets. . . ."

*   *   *

The violence of the colonial regime and the counter-violence of the native balance each other and respond to each other in an extraordinary reciprocal homogeneity. This reign of violence will be the more terrible in proportion to the size of the implantation from the mother country. The development of violence among the colonized people will be proportionate to the violence exercised by the threatened colonial regime. In the first phase of this insurrectional period, the home governments are the slaves of the settlers, and these settlers seek to intimidate the natives and their home governments at one and the same time. They use the same methods against both of them. The assassination of the Mayor of Evian, in its method and motivation, is identifiable with the assassination of Ali Boumendjel. For the settlers, the alternative is not between *Algérie algérienne* and *Algérie française* but between an independent Algeria and a colonial Algeria, and anything else is mere talk or attempts at treason. The settler's logic is implacable and one is only staggered by the counter-logic visible in the behavior of the native insofar as one has not clearly understood beforehand the mechanisms of the settler's ideas. From the moment that the native has chosen the methods of counter-violence, police reprisals automatically call forth reprisals on the side of the nationalists. However, the results are not equivalent, for machine-gunning from airplanes and bombardments from the fleet go far beyond in horror and magnitude any answer the natives can make. This recurring terror de-mystifies once and for all the most estranged members of the colonized race. They find out on the spot that all the piles of speeches on the equality of human beings do not hide the commonplace fact that the seven Frenchmen killed or wounded at the Col de Sakamody kindles the indignation of all civilized consciences, whereas the sack of the douars of Guergour and of the dechras of Djerah and the massacre of whole populations—which had merely called forth the Sakamody ambush as a reprisal—all this is of not the slightest importance. Terror, counter-terror, violence, counter-violence: that is what observers bitterly record when they describe the circle of hate, which is so tenacious and so evident in Algeria.

In all armed struggles, there exists what we might call the point of no return. Almost always it is marked off by a huge and all-inclusive repression which engulfs all sectors of the colonized people. This point was reached in Algeria in 1955 with the 12,000 victims of Phillippeville. * * *

*   *   *

Then it became clear to everybody, including even the settlers, that "things couldn't go on as before." Yet the colonized people do not chalk up the reckoning. They record the huge gaps made in their ranks as a sort of necessary evil. Since they have decided to reply by violence, they therefore are ready to take all its consequences. They only insist in return that no reckoning should be kept, either, for the others. To the saying "All natives are the same" the colonized person replies, "All settlers are the same."

*   *   *

The appearance of the settler has meant in the terms of syncretism the death of the aboriginal society, cultural lethargy, and the petrification of individuals. For the native, life can only spring up again out of the rotting corpse of the settler. This then is the correspondence, term by term, between the two trains of reasoning.

But it so happens that for the colonized people this violence, because it constitutes their only work, invests their characters with positive and creative qualities. The practice of violence binds them together as a whole, since each individual forms a violent link in the great chain, a part of the great organism of violence which has surged upward in reaction to the settler's violence in the beginning. The groups recognize each other and the future nation is already indivisible. The armed struggle mobilizes the people; that is to say, it throws them in one way and in one direction.

The mobilization of the masses, when it arises out of the war of liberation, introduces into each man's consciousness the ideas of a common cause, of a national destiny, and of a collective history. In the same way the second phase, that of the building-up of the nation, is helped on by the existence of this cement which has been mixed with blood and anger. Thus we come to a fuller appreciation of the originality of the words used in these underdeveloped countries. During the colonial period the people are called upon to fight against oppression; after national liberation, they are called upon to fight against poverty, illiteracy, and underdevelopment. The struggle, they say, goes on. The people realize that life is an unending contest.

We have said that the native's violence unifies the people. By its very structure, colonialism is separatist and regionalist. Colonialism does not simply state the existence of tribes; it also reinforces it and separates them. The colonial system encourages chieftaincies and keeps alive the old Marabout confraternities. Violence is in action all-inclusive and national. It follows that it is closely involved in the liquidation of regionalism and of tribalism. Thus the national parties show no pity at all toward the caids and the customary chiefs. Their destruction is the preliminary to the unification of the people.

At the level of individuals, violence is a

cleansing force. It frees the native from his inferiority complex and from his despair and inaction; it makes him fearless and restores his self-respect. Even if the armed struggle has been symbolic and the nation is demobilized through a rapid movement of decolonization, the people have the time to see that the liberation has been the business of each and all and that the leader has no special merit.

*   *   *

Today, national independence and the growth of national feeling in underdeveloped regions take on totally new aspects. In these regions, with the exception of certain spectacular advances, the different countries show the same absence of infrastructure. The mass of the people struggle against the same poverty, flounder about making the same gestures and with their shrunken bellies outline what has been called the geography of hunger. It is an underdeveloped world, a world inhuman in its poverty; but also it is a world without doctors, without engineers, and without administrators. Confronting this world, the European nations sprawl, ostentatiously opulent. This European opulence is literally scandalous, for it has been founded on slavery, it has been nourished with the blood of slaves and it comes directly from the soil and from the subsoil of that underdeveloped world. The well-being and the progress of Europe have been built up with the sweat and the dead bodies of Negroes, Arabs, Indians, and the yellow races. We have decided not to overlook this any longer. When a colonialist country, embarrassed by the claims for independence made by a colony, proclaims to the nationalist leaders: "If you wish for independence, take it, and go back to the Middle Ages," the newly independent people tend to acquiesce and to accept the challenge; in fact you may see colonialism withdrawing its capital and its technicians and setting up around the young State the apparatus of economic pressure. The apotheosis of independence is transformed into the curse of independence, and the colonial power through its immense resources of coercion condemns the young nation to regression. In plain words, the colonial power says: "Since you want independence, take it and starve." The na-

tionalist leaders have no other choice but to turn to their people and ask from them a gigantic effort. A regime of austerity is imposed on these starving men; a disproportionate amount of work is required from their atrophied muscles. An autarkic regime is set up and each state, with the miserable resources it has in hand, tries to find an answer to the nation's great hunger and poverty. We see the mobilization of a people which toils to exhaustion in front of a suspicious and bloated Europe.

*   *   *

* * * The imperialist states would make a great mistake and commit an unspeakable injustice if they contented themselves with withdrawing from our soil the military cohorts, and the administrative and managerial services whose function it was to discover the wealth of the country, to extract it and to send it off to the mother countries. We are not blinded by the moral reparation of national independence; nor are we fed by it. The wealth of the imperial countries is our wealth too. On the universal plane this affirmation, you may be sure, should on no account be taken to signify that we feel ourselves affected by the creations of Western arts or techniques. For in a very concrete way Europe has stuffed herself inordinately with the gold and raw materials of the colonial countries: Latin America, China, and Africa. From all these continents, under whose eyes Europe today raises up her tower of opulence, there has flowed out for centuries toward that same Europe diamonds and oil, silk and cotton, wood and exotic products. Europe is literally the creation of the Third World. The wealth which smothers her is that which was stolen from the underdeveloped peoples. The ports of Holland, the docks of Bordeaux and Liverpool were specialized in the Negro slave trade, and owe their renown to millions of deported slaves. So when we hear the head of a European state declare with his hand on his heart that he must come to the aid of the poor underdeveloped peoples, we do not tremble with gratitude. Quite the contrary; we say to ourselves: "It's a just reparation which will be paid to us."

*   *   *

REVIEW QUESTIONS

1. In what ways did colonial regimes breed violence?
2. What did Fanon believe were the positive benefits of anti-imperial violence for the community? For the individual?

3. According to Fanon, how did Europe compare with its former colonies?
4. In what sense is the wealth of Europe the "creation of the Third World"?

MARK MAZOWER

FROM *Dark Continent: Europe's Twentieth Century*

Mark Mazower was born in Britain in 1958 and is a professor of history at Columbia University. He has written widely on European history in the twentieth century and is a specialist in Greek and Balkan history. This excerpt is from his 1998 book Dark Continent: Europe's Twentieth Century, *in which he argued that the survival of democratic regimes in twentieth-century Europe may have been due more to chance and contingent circumstances than to any intrinsic association between democratic values and European identities.*

From "Epilogue: Making Europe," from *Dark Continent: Europe's Twentieth Century*, by Mark Mazower (New York: Random House, 2000), pp. 395–98.

"Democracy has won," wrote Zbigniew Brzezinski in 1990. "The free market has won. But what in the wake of this great ideological victory is today the substance of our beliefs?" As the euphoria which greeted the end of the Cold War gave way to gloomy misgivings, Francis Fukuyama saw communism's collapse ushering in the end of history and the dawning of a more prosaic and less heroic era. Others foresaw instead the rebirth of history's demons—nationalism, fascism and racial and religious struggle. They talked about "the return of history" and drew grim parallels—as Sarajevo hit the headlines—between 1992 and the eve of the First World War.

In fact, history had neither left Europe nor returned to it. But with the end of the Cold War, Europe's place in history changed. Europe is once again undivided, but it no longer occupies the central role in world affairs which it held before the Cold War began. Understanding where we stand today thus requires not only seeing how the present resembles the past, but how it differs from it as well. Sometimes it is easier to dream the old dreams—even when they are nightmares—than to wake up to unfamiliar realities.

"With the passing of the centuries," two French historians concluded in 1992, "Europe discovers that beyond the differences of its tongues and customs, its people partake of a common culture . . . Europe is becoming conscious of the existence of a European identity." Made with unfortunate timing in the year civil war broke out in Yugoslavia, this bold claim has a respectable pedigree. In 1936, another year of civil war, the British historian H. A. L. Fisher asserted that Europe was unified by a civilization which was "distinct . . . all pervading and preponderant," resting upon "an inheritance of thought and achievement and religious aspiration." And a few years later, in *The Limits and Divisions of European History*, the émigré Polish scholar Oskar Hàlecki pleaded for the fundamental unity of the continent at the very moment his country formed part of the Communist bloc.

It is as though one response to the bloody struggles of this century has been to deny their internecine character: one side is made to stand for the true Europe—*l'Europe européenne* in the striking phrase of Gonzague de Reynold—while the others are written off as usurpers or barbarians. The intellectual tradition which identifies Europe with the cause of liberty and freedom goes back many centuries. But if we face the fact that liberal democracy failed between the wars, and if we admit that communism and fascism also formed part of the continent's political heritage, then it is hard to deny that what has shaped Europe in this century is not a gradual convergence of thought and feeling, but on the contrary a series of violent clashes between antagonistic New Orders. If we search for Europe not as a geographical expression, but as what Federico Chabod called "an historic and moral individuality," we find that for much of the century it did not exist.

What was new in Europe's history was not the existence of conflict, but rather its scale. Compared with the great dynastic empires of the past— the long centuries of Byzantine, Habsburg and Ottoman rule—the utopian experiments of twentieth-century ideologies came and went with striking speed: yet their struggle brought new levels of violence into European life, militarizing society, strengthening the state and killing millions of people with the help of modern bureaucracies and technologies. In the 1870–71 Franco-Prussian War the death-toll was 184,000; in the First World War it was above eight million, and more than forty million Europeans—half of them civilians—died in the Second World War. The depth of these wounds was directly proportionate to the grandeur of the ambitions held by the various protagonists, each of whom aspired to remake Europe—inside

and out—more thoroughly than ever before. It is not surprising if today Europe is suffering from ideological exhaustion, and if politics has become a distinctly unvisionary activity. As Austria's former chancellor Franz Vranitsky once supposedly remarked: "Anyone with visions needs to see a doctor."

This disillusionment colours the strange post-1989 triumph of democracy in Europe. Seventy years earlier, the consolidation of democracy across the continent after the First World War fitted liberal dreams of a new world order: Europe seemed destined to become the model for mankind. Through the League of Nations the new states of eastern Europe would learn the habits of democracy from the more advanced and mature states of the West, while through colonies and mandates, the great imperial powers would spread democracy more widely. The defeat of communism in Europe in 1989 carried no such global implications, and no such evangelical dreams. Democracy suits Europeans today partly because it is associated with the triumph of capitalism and partly because it involves less commitment or intrusion into their lives than any of the alternatives. Europeans accept democracy because they no longer believe in politics. It is for this reason that we find both high levels of support for democracy in cross-national opinion polls and high rates of political apathy. In contemporary Europe, democracy allows racist parties of the Right to coexist with more active protection of human rights than ever before. It encompasses both the grass-roots politics of Switzerland and near-dictatorship in post-communist Croatia.

The real victor in 1989 was not democracy but capitalism, and Europe as a whole now faces the task which western Europe has confronted since the 1930s, of establishing a workable relationship between the two. The inter-war depression revealed that democracy might not survive a major crisis of capitalism, and in fact democracy's eventual triumph over communism would have been unimaginable without the reworked social contract which followed the Second World War. The ending of full employment and the onset of welfare retrenchment make this achievement harder than ever to sustain, especially in societies characterized by age-ing populations. The globalization of financial markets makes it increasingly difficult for nation-states to preserve autonomy of action, yet markets—as a series of panics and crashes demonstrates—generate their own irrationalities and social tensions. The globalization of labour, too, challenges prevailing definitions of national citizenship, culture and tradition. Whether Europe can chart a course between the individualism of American capitalism and the authoritarianism of East Asia, preserving its own blend of social solidarity and political freedom, remains to be seen. But the end of the Cold War means that there is no longer an opponent against whom democrats can define what they stand for in pursuit of this goal. The old political signposts have been uprooted, leaving most people without a clear sense of direction.

This sense of *fin de siècle* disorientation is largely a European problem which reflects the specific historical experience of Europe this century, and the carnage that followed its once-fervent faith in utopias. A self-belief rooted in Christianity, capitalism, the Enlightenment and massive technological superiority encouraged Europeans to see themselves over a long period as a civilizational model for the globe. Their trust in Europe's world mission was already evident in the seventeenth and eighteenth centuries and reached its apogee in the era of imperialism. Hitler was in many ways its culminating figure and through the Nazi New Order came closer to its realization than anyone else. Now that the Cold War has ended, Europe is once more undivided, and this makes its loss of belief in the pre-eminence of its civilization and values all the more obvious. Many of the newly freed states of the former Soviet Empire cannot wait to join "Europe." Yet what that "Europe" is, and where it stands in the world, seem less and less clear.

REVIEW QUESTIONS

1. What leads Mazower to question the relationship between Europe and "the cause of liberty and freedom"?
2. What does the history of Europe in the twentieth century tell us about the relationship between democracy and capitalism, according to Mazower?
3. Why does Mazower question the need for Europeans to claim a common identity at the dawn of the twenty-first century, in the wake of decolonization and the end of the Cold War?

NICOLAS SARKOZY

FROM Speech at the University of Cheikh Anta Diop, Senegal, July 26, 2007

Nicolas Sarkozy (b. 1955), a politician and leader within the French Gaullist party (the conservative political movement founded by the late president Charles de Gaulle), was elected president of France in May 2007. He has been an outspoken supporter of a more assertive and muscular foreign policy for France, while also supporting more restrictive laws against immigration from other countries. In July 2007, in his first visit to sub-Saharan Africa after being elected president, Sarkozy gave a controversial speech on the colonial past in which he seemed to imply that Africans had not embraced progress.

From The Unofficial Translation of Sarkozy's Speech, October 13, 2007, available at www.africaresource.com [accessed 5/23/11].

I have not come to erase the past because the past cannot be erased.

I have not come to deny mistakes or crimes—mistakes were made and crimes committed.

There was the black slave trade, there was slavery, men, women and children bought and sold as so much merchandise. And this crime was not only a crime against the Africans, it was a crime against man, it was a crime against all of humanity. . . .

This suffering of the black man, and I don't speak here in the sense of gender, I speak of man in the sense of a human being and of course of women and of man in its general use. This suffering of the black man is the suffering of all men. This open wound in the soul of the black man is an open wound in the soul of all men.

But no one can ask of the generations of today to expiate this crime perpetrated by past generations. No one can ask of the sons to repent for the mistakes of their fathers.

Youth of Africa, I have not come to talk to you about repentance. I have come to tell you that I consider the slave trade and slavery as crimes against humanity. I have come to tell you that your pain and your suffering are ours and therefore are mine.

I have come to propose to you to look together, as Africans and as French, beyond this pain and this suffering.

I have come to propose to you, youth of Africa[,] not to forget this pain and this suffering that cannot be forgotten, but to move beyond it.

I have come to propose to you, youth of Africa, not to dwell on the past, but for us to draw together lessons from it in order to face the future together.

I have come, youth of Africa, to face with you our common history.

Africa is partly responsible for its own misfortune. People have killed each other in Africa at least as much in Europe. But it is true that a long time ago the Europeans came to Africa as conquerors. They took the land of your ancestors. They banished their gods, their languages, their beliefs, the customs of your forefathers. They told your forefathers what they had to think, what they had to believe, what they had to do. They have cut your forefathers from their past, they have torn their souls from their roots. . . .

They were wrong.

They did not see the depth and the wealth of the African soul. They believed that they were superior, that they were more advanced, that they were progress, that they were civilisation.

They were wrong.

They wanted to convert the African[s], they wanted to make them in their image. They believed that they had all the rights and that they were all powerful, more powerful than the gods of Africa, more powerful than the African soul, more powerful than the sacred ties that men have woven patiently during thousands of years with the sky and earth of Africa, more powerful than the mysteries that came from the depths of time.

They were wrong. . . .

I therefore want to say, to the youth of Africa, that the tragedy of Africa does not come from the idea that the African soul would be impervious to logic and to reason. Because, the African is as logic[a]l and as reasonable as the European.

It is by drawing from the African imaginary world that your ancestors have left you, it is by drawing from their stories, their proverbs, their mythologies, their rites, by drawing from all these forms that, since the dawn of time were transmitted to and enriched generation after generation, that you will find the imagination and the power to invent a future for you. A unique future that does not resemble any other, where you will at last feel free, free youth of Africa to be yourselves, free to decide for yourselves.

I have come to tell you that you don't have to be ashamed of the values of African civilization, that they do not drag you down but elevate you, that they are an antidote to the materialism and the individualism that enslave modern man, that they are the most precious of legacies against the dehumanization and the "uniformisation" of the world of today.

I have come to tell you that modern man, who experiences the need to reconcile himself with nature, has much to learn from the African that has lived in a symbiotic relationship with nature for thousands of years.

I came to tell you that this divide between two parts of yourselves is your greatest force, or your greatest weakness, according to the extent to which you bring yourself to unite them in a synthesis, or not.

But I also came to tell you that there are in you, youth of Africa, two legacies, two wisdoms, two traditions that have struggled with each other for a long time: that of Africa and that of Europe.

I came to tell you that this African part and European part of yourselves form your torn identity.

I did not come, youth of Africa, to lecture you.

I did not come to preach, but I came to tell you that the part of Europe that is in you is the fruit of a great sin of pride of the West, but that this part of Europe in you is not unworthy.

Because it is the call of freedom, of emancipation and of justice and of equality between women and men.

Because it is the call to reason and to the universal conscience.

The tragedy of Africa is that the African has not fully entered into history. The African peasant, who for thousands of years [has] lived according to the seasons, whose life ideal was to be in harmony with nature, only knew the eternal renewal of time, whose rhythm came from the endless repetition of the same gestures and the same words.

In this imaginary world where everything starts over and over again there is no place for human adventure or for the idea of progress.

In this universe where nature commands all, man escapes from the anguish of history that torments modern man, but he rests immobile in the centre of a static order where everything seems to have been written beforehand.

This man (the traditional African) never launched himself towards the future. The idea never came to him to get out of this repetition and to invent his own destiny.

The problem of Africa, and allow a friend of Africa to say it, is to be found here. Africa's challenge is to enter to a greater extent into history. To take from it the energy, the force, the desire, the willingness to listen and to espouse its own history.

Africa's problem is to stop always repeating, always mulling over, to liberate itself from the myth of the eternal return. It is to realise that the golden age that Africa is forever recalling will not return because it has never existed.

Africa's problem is that it lives the present too much in nostalgia for a lost childhood paradise.

Africa's problem is that too often it judges the present in terms of a purity of origin that is totally imaginary and that no one can hope to achieve.

Africa's problem is not to invent for itself a more or less mythical past to help it to support the present, but to invent the future with suitable means.

Africa's problem is not to prepare itself for the return of misfortune, as if that is supposed to repeat itself indefinitely, but to want to give itself the means to combat misfortune, because Africa has the right to happiness like all the other continents of the world.

Africa's problem is to remain true to itself without remaining immobile.

Africa's challenge is to learn to view its accession to the universal not as a denial of what it is but as an accomplishment.

Africa's challenge is to learn to feel itself to be heir to all that which is universal in all human civilizations.

It is to appropriate for itself human rights,

democracy, liberty, equality and justice as the common legacy of all civilizations and of all people.

It is to appropriate for itself modern science and technology as the product of all human intelligence.

Africa's challenge is that of all civilizations, of all cultures, of all peoples that want to protect their identity without isolating themselves because they know that isolation is deadly.

Civilizations are great to the extent that they participate in the great mix of the human spirit.

The weakness of Africa, which has known so many brilliant civilizations on its soil, was for a long time not being able to participate fully in this great engagement. Africa has paid dearly for its disengagement from the world and that has rendered it so vulnerable. But from its misfortunes Africa has drawn new strength by re-engaging with itself. This re-engagement, regardless of the painful conditions of its origin, is the real force and the real chance for Africa at the moment when the first global civilization is emerging.

The Muslim civilization, Christianity and colonization, beyond the crimes and mistakes that were committed in their name and that are not excusable, have opened the African heart and mentality to the universal and to history.

Youth of Africa, don't let your future be stolen by those who only know how to combat intolerance with intolerance and racism with racism.

Youth of Africa, don't let your future be stolen by those who want to deprive you of a history that also belong[s] to you because it was the painful history of your parents, of your grandparents and those who went before.

Youth of Africa, don't listen to those who want to remove Africa from its history in the name of tradition because an Africa where nothing changes anymore will again be condemned to servitude.

REVIEW QUESTIONS

1. How does Sarkozy characterize the history of European colonialism and its effect on Africans?
2. How does Sarkozy characterize African cultures and societies?
3. What does Sarkozy mean by "history" when he says "the African has not fully entered into history"?
4. Who is Sarkozy's intended audience for this speech? Is he speaking only to the students at the University of Cheikh Anta Diop?

ACHILLE MBEMBE

FROM "Nicolas Sarkozy's Africa"

Achille Mbembe (b. 1957) is a philosopher and political scientist from Cameroon who divides his time between appointments at the Wits Institute for Social and Economic Research in South Africa and at Duke University in the United States. He is the author of On the Postcolony *(originally published in French in 2000 and in translation in 2001). His response to Nicholas Sarkozy's 2007 speech in Senegal was widely circulated in the African press and among students and specialists in African history.*

From "A Critique of Nicolas Sarkozy," by Achille Mbembe, *Le Messager* (Douala, Cameroun), August 18, 2007, translated by Melissa Thackway, available at www.africaresource.com [accessed 5/23/11].

In all his "candour" and his "sincerity," Nicolas Sarkozy openly revealed what, until now, went unspoken: that is that, both in terms of form and content, the intellectual framework underlying France's policy to Africa literally dates back to the end of the 19th century. It is thus a policy whose coherence depends, despite a few new touches here and there, on an obsolete intellectual heritage that is over a century old.

The new French president's speech shows how, trapped in a frivolous and exotic vision of the continent, the new French ruling elites claim to shed light on realities that they consider their worst fears or their fantasies (race) but which, in reality, they know nothing about. To address "the elite of African youth," then, [Sarkozy's speechwriter] contented himself to lifting, almost word for word, passages from the chapter Hegel devotes to Africa in his work *Reason in History*. . . .

According to Hegel, Africa is a land of unchanging substance and dazzling disorder, the joyful and tragic country in Creation. Black people, as we see them today, are as they have always been. In the immense energy of the natural arbitrariness that dominates them, neither the moral moment, nor ideas of freedom, justice and progress have any place or particular status. Whoever wants to discover the most appalling manifestations of human nature can find them in Africa. Strictly speaking, this part of the world has no history. What we understand, in short, going by the name of Africa, is an ahistoric, undeveloped world, entirely prisoner of its natural spirit and whose place remains on the threshold of universal history.

The new French elites do not believe anything different. They share this Hegelian prejudice. Unlike the generation of the "Papa-Commanders" (de Gaulle, Pompidou, Giscard d'Estaing, Mitterrand, or Chirac), who tacitly espoused the same prejudice whilst avoiding openly offending their interlocutors, France's "new elites" now consider that one can only address societies so deeply plunged into the night of childhood by speaking unguardedly, with a sort of virgin energy. And that is indeed what they have in mind when they now openly defend the idea of a nation no longer "hung up" about its colonial past. . . .

How then, can one be surprised that his definition of the continent and its people is ultimately purely negative? Indeed, our ethno-philosopher president's "African man" is above all characterized either by *what he hasn't got, what he isn't or by what he has never managed to achieve* (the dialectic of lack and incompletion), or by his opposition to "modern man" (read "white man"), an opposition which apparently results from his irrational attachment to the kingdom of childhood, the world of night, to simple pleasures and a golden age that never existed.

For the rest, the new French ruling elite's Africa is essentially a rural, magical, phantom Africa, partly bucolic, partly nightmarish, inhabited by peasant folk, composed of a community of sufferers who have nothing in common other than their common position on the margins of history, prostrate as they are in a outer world—that of sorcerers and griots, of magical beings who keep fountains, sing in rivers and hide in the trees, of the village dead and ancestors whose voices can be heard, of masks and forests full of symbols, of the clichés that are so-called "African solidarity," "community spirit," "warmth" and respect for elders and chiefs.

The Policy of Ignorance

The speech thus continues in a beatific will for ignorance of its object, as if, during the second half of the 20th century, we hadn't witnessed a spectacular development in the knowledge of the long-term changes in the African world.

I'm not referring just to the African researchers' own inestimable contribution to the understanding of their societies and to the internal critical analysis of their cultures—criticism to which some of us have widely contributed, sometimes with severity, but always with humanity. I'm talking about the billions of its public funds that the French government has devoted to this grand oeuvre and which hardly explain to me how, after such an investment, people can still, today, articulate such unintelligible arguments about the continent.

What is behind this policy of voluntary and assumed ignorance?

How is it possible to come to Cheikh Anta Diop University in Dakar at the start of the 21st century to address the intellectual elite as if Africa didn't have its own critical traditions and as if Senghor and Camara Laye, respective champions of black emotion and the kingdom of childhood, hadn't been the object of vigorous internal refutations?

What credibility can we afford such gloomy words that portray Africans as fundamentally traumatized beings incapable of acting on their own behalf and in their own recognized interests? What is this so-called historicity of the continent which totally silences the long tradition of resistance, including that against French colonialism, along with today's struggles for democracy, none of which receive the clear support of a country which, for many years, has actively backed the local satrapies? How is it possible to come to promise us a fanciful Eurafrica without even mentioning the internal efforts to build a unitary African economic framework? . . .

Denial of Responsibility

As for the same old tune about colonization and the refusal to "repent," . . . [W]ho's going to believe that there's no moral responsibility for acts perpetrated by a State in the course of its history? Who's going to swallow that to create a humane world, you must throw morals and ethics to the wind because in this world, there's no justice for complaints or justice for causes?

In order to exonerate an iniquitous system, there is a temptation today to rewrite the history of France and its empire, portraying it as a history of "pacification," of "the valorization of empty, leaderless territories," of "the spreading of education," of "the founding of modern medicine" and of the cre-

ation of road and rail infrastructures. This argument is based on the old lie that portrays colonization as a humanitarian enterprise that contributed to the modernization of old primitive, dying societies which, left to their own devices, would have probably ended up committing suicide.

In portraying colonization this way, such people authorize themselves, as in the Dakar speech, an intimate sincerity, an underlying authenticity so as better to find excuses—in which they alone believe—for a particularly cruel, abject and vile enterprise. They claim that the wars of conquest, the massacres, the deportations, the bloody incursions, the forced labour, the institutionalized racial discrimination, all that was simply "the corruption of a grand ideal" or, as Alexis de Tocqueville explained it, "an unfortunate necessity."

Asking France to recognize, as the very same de Tocqueville put it, that the colonial government was a "harsh, violent, arbitrary, crude government," or to ask it to stop supporting Africa's corrupt dictators amounts neither to denigrating nor hating it. It's simply asking it to assume its responsibilities and to practice what it claims to be its universal vocation. This request is absolutely necessary in today's context. And with regard to France's colonial past in particular, the policy of unlimited irresponsibility must be the object of firm, intelligent and unrelenting criticism. . . .

Conclusion

Today, the cultural and intellectual prism through which the new French ruling elites consider Africa, judge it, or [dole] it out lessons isn't just obsolete. It leaves no place for the amicable relationships that would be a sign of freedom because coextensive with relationships of justice and respect. For the time being, when it comes to Africa, France simply lacks the moral credit that would allow it to speak with certitude and authority.

That is why Nicolas Sarkozy's Dakar speech will not be heard, and even less taken seriously by those he was supposed to be addressing.

REVIEW QUESTIONS

1. What aspects of Sarkozy's speech lead Mbembe to assert that France's policy toward Africa has not changed substantially since the colonial period?

2. What does Mbembe criticize in Sarkozy's evocation of African traditions and cultures? How is this criticism related to Sarkozy's use of an opposition between "nature" and "history"?

3. What vision of African history does Mbembe refer to as a counter to Sarkozy's speech?

OLIVIER ROY

FROM *Globalized Islam: The Search for a New Ummah*

Olivier Roy is a professor at EHESS, the School of Advanced Studies in Social Sciences in Paris, France. He specializes in the study of Islamic political movements, especially in Afghanistan and Iran. His books include The Failure of Political Islam *and (with Mariam Abou Zahab)* Islamist Networks: The Afghan-Pakistan Connection. *This excerpt comes from his book* Globalized Islam *(2004), which focuses on the ways that globalization, westernization, and the experience of living as a minority has shaped the relationship between Muslims and Islam in the contemporary world. In this passage, he asks the question "What is Bin Laden's strategy?"*

From *Globalized Islam: The Search for a New Ummah*, by Olivier Roy (New York: Columbia University Press, 2004), pp. 55–57.

Osama Bin Laden has no strategy in the true sense of the word. Nothing was organised for the day after 9/11: no other attacks or assassinations, no upheavals in Egypt, Saudi Arabia or Algeria. Some elements suggest coherence in Osama Bin Laden's long-term outlook. The assassination of Commander Ahmed Shah Massoud, an anti-Taliban Afghan leader, on 9 September 2001 was planned months before (the two killers had been waiting for weeks to meet him). Taliban and Al Qaeda troops had been massed on the northern front since June 2001; for the first time fighters from the Islamic Movement of Uzbekistan (IMU) joined an anti-Massoud mobilisation, a sign that this was seen as the final battle. But no real battle happened, as if the troops had been waiting for something: the collapse of the United Front of Afghanistan in the wake of its leader's death. Massoud's assassination nevertheless came too late—just days before the first US military officers entered the Panjshir Valley. Obviously, however, Osama Bin Laden had wanted to clean up Afghanistan before an unavoidable US attack. He knew the United States would retaliate on Afghan territory and he was expecting the offensive. For Bin Laden the references were Vietnam, the Soviet defeat in Afghanistan, and the US withdrawals from Lebanon in 1984 and Somalia ten years later. He was convinced that the United States would not stand a long war and that in any case a protracted war would stir up plenty of turmoil and even uprisings in Pakistan, Saudi Arabia and Egypt—with no need to organise them. The US position would be unsustainable. In short, he was banking on a war of attrition that would destabilise the power of the United States and its allies in the region (the Saudis first, although I do not think that the Saudi regime was the primary target). In this sense, his aim has been inadvertently achieved in Iraq.

Bin Laden made two critical mistakes. First, he did not realise that the Afghan population was fed up with the Taliban and that the Pashtun tribesmen who have been supporting the Taliban (principally over issues of law and order, conservative Islam and Pashtun supremacy) were not willing to lose their lives and property for an uncertain worldwide *jihad* against the US hyperpower. The international agenda of Osama Bin Laden simply had no appeal in Afghanistan. He probably did not expect the sudden collapse of his Taliban allies or the thirst for revenge of the non-Pashtuns (ethnic issues were always logically downplayed by Bin Laden, who renounced his ethnic and national backgrounds to fight for a universal cause). Second, he overestimated the reaction of the 'Arab in the street'. Osama Bin Laden did not grasp that the genuine anti-Americanism of the 'average' Arab had never led to a sustainable political mobilisation, and that if such mobilisation ever did happen it would be over Palestine and Iraq—that is, over Arab and not Islamic issues.

In this sense Al Qaeda terrorism is totally different from that of the 'usual' terrorists in the Middle East and elsewhere. Iran-sponsored terrorism in the 1980s, as well as attacks by the Irish Republican Army (IRA) or Tamil Tigers, fitted into a political strategy: Iran wanted to bring about the end of Western support for Iraq and the departure of Western forces from Lebanon, while the IRA and Tamil Tigers wanted to achieve independence (which was also the aim of the Jewish underground movement Irgun Zvai Leumi in Palestine in the 1940s). Palestinian suicide bombers want an end to the Israeli occupation of Gaza and the West Bank

(although some would also like to see the end of Israel, which is another issue). Whatever the means, there is room for negotiation. The IRA, the PLO, the Tamil Tigers and even the Basque separatist group ETA are seen as legitimate political actors to the extent they will potentially cease terrorist actions. But with Bin Laden there is no room for negotiation. His aim is simply to destroy Babylon.

In this sense the historical continuity of which Osama Bin Laden is part has nothing to do with the Islamic tradition of *jihad*. Notwithstanding the debate on what the word really means, it is clear that *jihad*, as an armed struggle, has always been instrumentalised for political and strategic purposes, by state actors or would-be state actors. Bin Laden's *jihad* has more to do with the ethos of a modern Western terrorist, as we have seen above. For the sake and pleasure of Allah (*reza*), for the sake of self-achievement (in death), for escaping a corrupt world . . . There is a strange mix of deep personal pessimism and collective millenarianist optimism among this type of terrorists: they do not trust the people they are fighting for (they are also indifferent to killing Muslims), they are sure to die, and as political scientist Farhad Khosrokhavar pointed out in the case of the Iranian martyrs of the Iran–Iraq War, they know that, even if they succeed, in the future society will not match the ideals for which they are fighting.[1] It is reminiscent of the Russian socialist revolutionaries of the end of the nineteenth century, and the idea that a spectacular attack at the heart of the power will suddenly show the alienated masses that their time has come and they will rise up. As Lenin put it, this is a childish view. Osama Bin Laden has lived in a pre-Leninist world.

But what are the repercussions of these facts? First, there is no basis for negotiation with Osama Bin Laden: his fight, as we have seen, is not directly linked to the various conflicts in the Middle East. These conflicts will certainly provide Al Qaeda with new volunteers, and solving them will not

---

[1] Farhad Khosrokhavar, *L'islamisme et la mort. Le martyre révolutionnaire en Iran*, Paris: Harmattan, 1995.

necessarily dry up the pool from which Al Qaeda recruits, because this pool has more to do with the West than with the Middle East. The second consequence is that Al Qaeda is not a strategic threat but a security problem. The war on terrorism is a metaphor, not a real policy.

REVIEW QUESTIONS

1. Why does Roy suggest that Osama Bin Laden "has no strategy"?
2. According to Roy, what makes Bin Laden's terrorism different from the terrorism of what he refers to as the "usual terrorists in the Middle East and elsewhere"?
3. What conclusions does Roy draw from his analysis of Bin Laden's goals?

Credits

Photo Credits

Chapter 11: p. 386 University of Utah Press; Chapter 12: p. 396 Milan, Ambrosiana—Anatomical Notebooks; p. 402 Scala/Art Resource; Chapter 13: p. 426 BPK BERLIN/Kupferstichkabinett, SMB/J´rg P. Anders/Art Resource, NY; p. 431 AISA/Everett Collection; Chapter 14: p. 466(top) Josie Piller and Debra Doty, University Art Gallery, University of Pittsburgh, (middle) Bettmann/Corbis, (bottom) Josie Piller and Debra Doty, University Art Gallery, University of Pittsburgh; p. 478 The Gallery Collection/ Corbis; Chapter 15: p. 500 PHGCOM/WIKIMEDIA COMMONS; p. 505 Giraudon/Art Resource Chapter 16: p. 546 (top) Bettmann/Corbis; (bottom) Corbis; p. 566 The Granger Collection, New York; Chapter 17: p. 577 The Granger Collection, New York; p. 610 The Gallery Collection/Corbis; Chapter 18: p. 673 Reuion des Musees Nationaux/Art Resource; Chapter 19: p. 695 Manchester City Council, Dept. of Libraries and Theatres; p. 702 The Royal Collection 2001. Copyright HM Queen Elizabeth II; Chapter 20: p. 739 The Looking Glass, 1832; Chapter 21: p. 771 Erich Lessing/Art Resources; p. 780 Foto Marburg/Art Resources; Chapter 22: p. 799 Fogg Art Museum, Harvard University Art Museums, bequest of Grenville L. Winthrop; p. 803 North Wind Pictures; Chapter 23: p. 836 From the book Spectacle of Women by Lisa Tickner; p. 839 Punch Limited; Chapter 24: p. 861 Hulton-Deutsch Collection/Corbis; p. 880 (left) Corbis; (right) Corbis; p. 881 (top) Corbis; (bottom left) Corbis; (bottom right) Corbis; p. 25: PAGE 890 Ullstein Bild, Berlin; Chapter 26: p. 944 (left) Public Domain/Wikimedia Commons; (right) Corbis; p. 945 (top) Sachsische Landesbibliothek—Staats—und Universitatsbibliothek Dresden; (bottom) Corbis; p. 946 (top) The Granger Collection; (bottom) Corbis; p. 947 (top) Corbis; (bottom) Corbis; Chapter 27: p. 957 Hulton-Deutsch Collection/Corbis; Chapter 28: p. 977 Keystone Pressedienst, Hamburg

Text Selections

Leon B. Alberti: Reprinted by permission of Waveland Press, Inc. from Alberti, *The Family in Renaissance Florence, Book Three: I Libri Della Famiglia*, translated by Renee Neu Watkins. (Long Grove, IL: Waveland Press, Inc., 1994). All rights reserved.

Mohammed as-Saffar: From *Disorienting Encounters: Travels of a Moroccan Scholar in France in 1845–1846*, by Mohammed as-Saffar, trans./ed. Susan Miller, pp. 108–110, 150–153. © 1992 Regents of the University of California. Published by the University of California Press. Reprinted by permission of the publisher.

Jean Bodin: From *On Sovereignty*, pp. 46–50. Copyright © Cambridge University Press 1992. Reprinted with the permission of Cambridge University Press.

John Calvin: *Theological Treatises* From *John Calvin* by G. R. Potter and M. Greengrass London: Edward Arnold, 1983.

Catherine the Great: "Proposals for a New Code of Law" From *Documents of Catherine the Great: The Correspondence with Voltaire and the Instruction of 1767 in the English Text of 1768*, translated by W. F. Reddaway. Copyright © 1931 Cambridge University Press. Reprinted with permission from Cambridge University Press.

Benjamin Constant: "The Principals of Politics" From *On the Sovereignty of the People* by Benjamin Constant, translated by David Sidorsky, in *The Liberal Tradition in European Thought*, edited by David Sidorsky, pp. 211–215. New York: Putnam, 1970.

Marquis de Condorcet: From *Sketch for a Historical Picture on the Progress of the Human Mind*, translated by June Barraclough. Reprinted by permission of the publisher, Weidenfeld and Nicolson, an imprint of The Orion Publishing Group.

Olympe de Gouges: "Declaration of the Rights of Woman" from *Women, The Family and Freedom: The Debate in Documents, Volume 1, 1750–1880* by Susan Groag Bell and Karen M. Offen, eds. Copyright © 1983 by the Board of Trustees of the Leland Stanford Junior University. All rights reserved. Used with permission of Stanford University Press, www.sup.org.

Michel de Montaigne: pp. 132–135 and 150–159 from *The Complete Essays of Montaigne* by Donald Frame. Copyright © 1958 by the Board of Trustees of the Leland Stanford Junior University. All rights reserved. Used with the permission of Stanford University Press, www.sup.org.

Alvise da Mosto: "The Voyage of Alvise da Mosto," *The Voyages of Cadamosto and Other Documents on Western Africa*, edited and translated by G.R. Crone, The Hakluyt Society, 1937, pp. 20–33. Reprinted by permission of David Higham Associates, Ltd.

Comte de Saint-Simon: From "Rules of a Factory in Berlin," *Documents of Economic European History, Volume 1: The Process of Industrialization, 1750–1870*, edited by Sidney Pollard and C. Holmes. Copyright © 1968 Edward Arnold and Company Ltd. Reproduced with permission of Palgrave Macmillan.

Frantz Fanon: From *The Wretched of the Earth*, translated by Constance Farrington, pp. 83–84, 88–90, 92–94, 96–98, 102. Copyright © 1963 by *Présence Africaine*. Used by permission of Grove/Atlantic, Inc.

Vladimir Fisera: From *Writing on the Wall, France 1968: A Documentary Anthology* by Vladimir Fisera. Copyright © 1978 Vladimir Fisera. Reproduced with permission of Palgrave Macmillan.

Sigmund Freud: From *Civilization and Its Discontents* by Sigmund Freud, translated by James Strachey, pp. 55–59. Copyright © 1961 by James Strachey, renewed 1989 by Alix Strachey. Used by permission of W.W. Norton & Company, Inc. © Copyrights, The Institute of Psycho-Analysis and The Hogarth Press for permission to quote from *The Standard Edition of The Complete Psychological Works of Sigmund Freud*, translated and edited by James Strachey. Reprinted by permission of The Random House Group Ltd. "Five Lectures on Psychoanalysis" from Sigmund Freud © Copyrights, The Institute of Psycho-Analysis and The Hogarth Press for permission to quote from *The Standard Edition of The Complete Psychological Works of Sigmund Freud*, translated and edited by James Strachey. Reprinted by permission of The Random House Group Ltd.

Galileo Galilei: From *Discoveries and Opinions of Galileo* by Galileo Galilei, translated by Stillman Drake, copyright © 1957 by Stillman Drake. Used by permission of Doubleday, a division of Random House, Inc.